SOME NEW WORLD

In his famous argument against miracles, David Hume gets to the heart of the modern problem of supernatural belief. 'We are apt', says Hume, 'to imagine ourselves transported into some new world; where the whole form of nature is disjointed, and every element performs its operation in a different manner, from what it does at present'. This encapsulates, observes Peter Harrison, the disjuncture between contemporary Western culture and medieval societies. In the Middle Ages, people saw the hand of God at work everywhere. Indeed, many suppose that 'belief in the supernatural' is likewise fundamental nowadays to religious commitment. But dichotomising between 'naturalism' and 'supernaturalism' is actually a relatively recent phenomenon, just as the notion of 'belief' emerged historically late. In this masterful contribution to intellectual history, the author overturns crucial misconceptions – 'myths' – about secular modernity, challenging common misunderstandings of the past even as he reinvigorates religious thinking in the present.

Peter Harrison is a former Andreas Idreos Professor of Science and Religion in the University of Oxford, and Emeritus Professor of the History of Science at the University of Queensland, where he was also an Australian Laureate fellow and Founding Director of the Institute for Advanced Studies in the Humanities (IASH). His many celebrated books include *'Religion' and the Religions in the English Enlightenment* (Cambridge University Press, 1990), *The Fall of Man and the Foundations of Science* (Cambridge University Press, 2007), *The Cambridge Companion to Science and Religion* (Cambridge University Press, 2010), *The Territories of Science and Religion* (University of Chicago Press, 2015), and – co-edited with John Milbank – *After Science and Religion* (Cambridge University Press, 2022). In 2019, he delivered in the University Church of St Mary the Virgin the prestigious University of Oxford Bampton Lectures, which constitute the basis of the present work.

'This is a superb book that takes on big questions and offers satisfying answers. Harrison's very careful examination of the development of the concepts of "supernaturalism" and "belief" is full of brilliant, new insights. The book is also extremely well written. The author has a knack for expressing complex ideas succinctly, clearly, and in a provocative way. Harrison is an eminent scholar who has already written several very important books. This major new work will only add to his reputation as one of the leading figures in the humanities.'

—Bernard Lightman, Professor of Humanities, York University, Toronto, author of *Victorian Popularizers of Science: Designing Nature for New Audiences* (2007) and *The Origins of Agnosticism: Victorian Unbelief and the Limits of Knowledge* (1987)

'How, in the West, have our understandings of "the secular" and "religion" been built on entirely modern notions of belief and disbelief, natural and supernatural? This is the question at the core of Peter Harrison's brilliant and fascinating exploration of religion and science as they have come to be conceptualised, usually in opposition to each other, in the modern West. *Some New World* is a really important work, drawing on a wide range of thinkers and ideas, that will significantly shape future scholarly discussions.'

—Jane Shaw, Principal of Harris Manchester College, Professor of the History of Religion, and Pro-Vice-Chancellor, University of Oxford, and author of *Miracles in Enlightenment England* (2006)

'*Some New World* is an epochal piece of scholarly work. It forces us to question the foundational categories we use for thinking about science, religion, and their intersection. Peter Harrison challenges the reader to confront the reality that what is credible in one time and place is not so in another – and to turn that realisation back on modern science. Specifically, he wants us to examine the foundations of "scientific naturalism", a position that many see as the *sine qua non* of modern science. Naturalism claims that science requires us to take certain perspectives on belief in the supernatural. Here, Harrison argues that "belief" and "supernatural" are themselves complicated, problematic categories that require interrogation. The book concludes that scientific naturalism is the product of highly contingent historical developments and is very much not a universal, necessary part of science. This speaks to absolutely crucial issues in scholarly investigations of science and religion, philosophy of science, religious studies, and science education. It feels as though *Some New World* is the culmination of the trajectory of the work the author has been doing for decades. This outstanding book will surely be the focus of scholarly discussion for a generation to come.'

—Matthew Stanley, Professor of the History of Science, Gallatin School of Individualized Study, New York University, author of *Einstein's War: How Relativity Conquered Nationalism and Shook the World* (2019) and *Huxley's Church and Maxwell's Demon: From Theistic Science to Naturalistic Science* (2014)

SOME NEW WORLD

Myths of Supernatural Belief in a Secular Age

PETER HARRISON
University of Queensland

Shaftesbury Road, Cambridge CB2 8EA, United Kingdom

One Liberty Plaza, 20th Floor, New York, NY 10006, USA

477 Williamstown Road, Port Melbourne, VIC 3207, Australia

314–321, 3rd Floor, Plot 3, Splendor Forum, Jasola District Centre,
New Delhi – 110025, India

103 Penang Road, #05–06/07, Visioncrest Commercial, Singapore 238467

Cambridge University Press is part of Cambridge University Press & Assessment,
a department of the University of Cambridge.

We share the University's mission to contribute to society through the pursuit of
education, learning and research at the highest international levels of excellence.

www.cambridge.org
Information on this title: www.cambridge.org/9781009477222

DOI: 10.1017/9781009477215

© Peter Harrison 2024

This publication is in copyright. Subject to statutory exception and to the provisions
of relevant collective licensing agreements, no reproduction of any part may take
place without the written permission of Cambridge University Press & Assessment.

When citing this work, please include a reference to the DOI 10.1017/9781009477215

First published 2024

A catalogue record for this publication is available from the British Library

A Cataloging-in-Publication data record for this book is available from the Library of Congress

ISBN 978-1-009-47722-2 Hardback

Cambridge University Press & Assessment has no responsibility for the persistence
or accuracy of URLs for external or third-party internet websites referred to in this
publication and does not guarantee that any content on such websites is, or will
remain, accurate or appropriate.

CONTENTS

Acknowledgements	*page* vii
List of Abbreviations	xi
Introduction	1
1 **Hume's Dilemma**	13
2 **Languages of Belief**	24
2.1 Lost in Translation	24
2.2 Faith as Trust	32
2.3 Creedal Commitments	42
2.4 Belief without Knowledge?	50
3 **Inventing Epistemology**	68
3.1 Making Europe Christian	68
3.2 Implicit Faith and the Ethics of Belief	76
3.3 God and the Light of Nature	85
3.4 Reason Secularised	100
3.5 The Eclipse of Trust	110
3.6 Slogans of Modernity	116
4 **The Age of Evidences**	130
4.1 Arguments for Atheists?	131
4.2 The Forgotten Proof	139
4.3 Subterranean Homesick Blues	167
4.4 Divine Designs and First Causes	187
4.5 A New Natural Theology	202
4.6 The Consent of Nations Revisited	210

Contents

5	**The Birth of the Supernatural**	218
	5.1 Ionian Disenchantment?	220
	5.2 The Supernatural and the Scientific Revolution	233
	5.3 Law and Order in the Nineteenth Century	242
	5.4 The History of the Supernatural	253
	5.5 '-isms'	265
6	**The Shape of History**	283
	6.1 History Wars	283
	6.2 From Reform to Progress	301
	6.3 The Science of Society	306
	6.4 Providence Naturalised	319
	6.5 Genealogies of Naturalism	331
	6.6 The Perfume of an Empty Vase	342
7	**What the Greeks Saw**	353
	7.1 The Wine-Dark Sea and the Invisible Gorilla	355
	7.2 Language and the Limits of Thought	359
	7.3 Lost in Translation	364
	7.4 Contemporary Myths and Techno-Liturgies	367
	7.5 Modernity Stories	373
Bibliography		381
Index		457

ACKNOWLEDGEMENTS

This book has been longer in the making than I would have wished. I recall a dinner conversation that took place more than a decade ago when I was asked the question: at what period in Western history did people begin to speak about 'the supernatural'? I hazarded a guess that was tolerably close to the mark but resolved at the time to look into it further. An opportunity for a serious investigation of the question came with the invitation to the deliver the 2019 Bampton Lectures. Since 1780, these lectures have been delivered in Oxford's University Church, St Mary's which, by coincidence, is situated opposite the venue in which the question of the idea of the supernatural was first put to me. My plan in the lectures was to attempt to map out the evolution of conception of 'the supernatural' in the West, along with its implications for modern understandings of religion. This turned out not to be as straightforward as I had hoped. Lifting the lid on changing conceptions of the supernatural opened up connections with a range of related conceptual developments that were intimately connected to the appearance of the idea of the supernatural. It became clear that, at the very least, the history of the other term in the standard definition of religion – 'belief' – needed to be revisited if the full story was to be told. The same is true for 'religion', a term that is similarly absent from the historical self-understandings of most religions. Fortunately, much of the groundwork for both of these conceptions had already been done. But this necessary expansion of the scope of the project also led to delays in the production of this final version.

While all this was going on I was already engaged in a related project on science and secularisation, funded by a generous grant from the Australian Research Council in the form of a Laureate Fellowship. This was a five-year project, hosted by the University of Queensland's Institute for Advanced Studies in the Humanities (IASH), and involving a number of postdoctoral researchers. In the end I decided to incorporate some aspects of that project into the present book, mostly by way of a focus on naturalism which I take to be one of the key markers of secular modernity.

In some respects, this present volume builds on the approach adopted in previous books. Going all the way back to 1990, my first monograph dealt with the idea of 'religion' and the impact of that modern concept on how we presently conceptualise religious phenomena.[1] More recently *The Territories of Science and Religion* developed that thesis further, setting out the historically contingent nature of the categories 'science' and 'religion' and showing how the deployment of these ideas constrains, in ways that are not always helpful, how we think about present science–religion relations.[2] The present book expands the scope of these earlier works by adding new conceptions to the equation – 'belief' and 'the supernatural'. The goal is to better understand secular modernity, challenging some common misunderstandings of the past, and ask questions about the legitimacy and rationality of the dominant mode of naturalistic thinking that characterises much of our present academic discourse. A paragraph or two in this book comes from a previously published paper on 'Normativity and the Critical Functions of Genealogy: The Case of Modern Science' in *Modern Theology*. An abridged section of Chapter 4 on the *consensus gentium* argument has appeared in *Journal of Religion*.[3]

Along the way I have accumulated numerous intellectual debts. I am grateful to Michael Murray for having posed the original question about the origins of the idea of the supernatural. I must also express my gratitude to the electors of the Bampton Lectureship and their previous chairman, Sir Ralph Waller who, over a number of years, was a great source of support. The Vicar of the University Church of St Mary's, Will Lamb, was a most obliging host, and I am also grateful to Martyn Percy, then Dean of Christ Church, Oxford, who generously gave of his time and chaired the lecture series. Attendees at the lectures also helped shape the final version the lectures, not least on account of a new format that allowed for greater audience interaction. Harris Manchester College, as always, provided my home away from home in Oxford, and I am appreciative of their hospitality. Thanks to the staff there, and especially the Principal, Prof. Jane Shaw. I have had a number of helpful discussions with Bernie Lightman, who knows more

---

[1] Peter Harrison, *'Religion' and the Religions in the English Enlightenment* (Cambridge: Cambridge University Press, 1990).

[2] Peter Harrison, *The Territories of Science and Religion* (Chicago: University of Chicago Press, 2015).

[3] Peter Harrison, 'Normativity and the Critical Functions of Genealogy: The Case of Modern Science', *Modern Theology* 39 (2023), 682–707; 'The Forgotten Proof: The Existence of God and Universal Consent', *The Journal of Religion* 104 (2024), 1–34.

about nineteenth-century scientific naturalism than anyone and who, among other things, first alerted me to the significance of Henry Mansel (who happened to be the Bampton Lecturer for 1858) and offered helpful comments on some of the chapters. In Brisbane, IASH has provided a wonderfully stimulating environment for writing and research and it has been a privilege to have served as its director. Members of the Institute were subjected to drafts of various chapters and provided characteristically robust feedback. I am especially indebted to friends and colleagues Phil Almond, Ian Hunter, Peter Cryle, Anna Johnston, Nicholas Heron, Henry-James Miering, Ian Hesketh, Daniel Midena, Pete Jordan, Adam Bowles, Tom Aechtner, along with Samuel Loncar and Paul Tyson for stimulating conversations and debate about the subject matter of the book. Fred D'Agostino went above and beyond the call of duty by reading all of the chapters in draft, and the final version is much the better for his intelligent and insightful commentary. Matt Stanley also read the manuscript and offered many helpful comments. Andrew Moore has been a long-time and sympathetic correspondent on a number of the core themes of the book, and I am very thankful for our conversations and shared interests. I must also thank John Stenhouse, who generously hosted me for a semester at the University of Otago in 2022 during the writing process, not least for his almost weekly home-cooked meals and congenial conversations. I am similarly indebted to the Divinity School of the University of Chicago, who nominated me for the Sara H. Schaffner visiting professorship for 2023, affording me the opportunity to complete the final write-up. Special thanks to Willemien Otten who was a wonderful host and interlocutor, and who offered helpful advice on the medieval material. At the Max Planck Institute for the History of Science in Berlin I also had helpful and enlightening conversations and exchanges with Katja Krause on matters medieval (though, no doubt, many gaps remain). Alex Wright, Head of Humanities at Cambridge University Press, has been an ongoing source of encouragement and support. Alex saw my very first book to publication at CUP back in 1990 and it's been a special pleasure to be working back with him again. It was he who proposed the wonderful jacket art for the present book. Finally, through all of this, the unstinting love and support of Carol has kept me going. My deepest debt of gratitude is to her.

Epigraph permissions. Epigraphs have mostly been drawn from out-of-copyright sources, or my translations from such sources. In the case of the exceptions, I am grateful to Princeton University Press for permission to cite Marshall Sahlins (Introduction); the British Library for the David Hume entry from the old Catalogue of Printed Books (Ch. 1); Yale University Press for the David Hart reference (Ch. 2); and the Belknap Press of Harvard University Press for the Charles Taylor quotation (Ch. 5).

ABBREVIATIONS

ACW	*Ancient Christian Writers*, ed. Johannes Quaesten et al. (New York: Newman Press, 1946–).
ANF	*Ante-Nicene Fathers*, 10 vols., ed. Alexander Roberts and James Donaldson (Edinburgh: T&T Clark, 1867–85).
Aquinas, SCG	Thomas Aquinas, *Summa contra gentiles*, trans. Laurence Shapcote, Latin/English Edition of the Works of Thomas Aquinas, vols. 11–12 (Green Bay, WI: Aquinas Institute, 2018).
Aquinas, ST	Thomas Aquinas, *Summa theologiae*, trans. Laurence Shapcote, Latin/English Edition of the Works of Thomas Aquinas, vols. 13–20 (Lander, WY: Aquinas Institute, 2012).
Aristotle, *Complete Works*	*The Complete Works of Aristotle*, 2 vols., ed. Jonathan Barnes (Princeton: Princeton University Press, 1984).
Augustine, *Works*	*The Works of Saint Augustine*, 20 vols., ed. John Rotelle (New York, 1991–).
Bacon, *Works*	*The Works of Francis Bacon*, 14 vols., ed. James Spedding, Robert Ellis, and Douglas Heath (London: Longman, 1857–74).
Boyle, *Works*	*The Works of Robert Boyle*, 14 vols., ed. Michael Hunter and Edward B. Davis (London: Routledge, 2016).
Calvin, *Institutes*	John Calvin, *Institutes of the Christian Religion*, 2 vols., trans. Henry Beveridge (Edinburgh: Calvin Translation Society, 1845).

Descartes, AT	*Oeuvres de Descartes*, 12 vols., ed. Charles Adam and Paul Tannery (Paris: Cerf, 1897–1913).
Descartes, CSM	*The Philosophical Writings of Descartes*, 2 vols., trans. J. Cottingham, R. Stoothoff, and D. Murdoch (Cambridge: Cambridge University Press, 1985).
Descartes, CSMK	*The Philosophical Writings of Descartes* (vol. 3, *The Correspondence*), trans. J. Cottingham, R. Stoothoff, D. Murdoch, and Anthony Kenny (Cambridge: Cambridge University Press, 1991).
FC	*Fathers of the Church* (Washington, DC: Catholic University of America Press, 1947–).
Hobbes, *Leviathan*	Thomas Hobbes, *Leviathan*, 3 vols., ed. Noel Malcolm (Oxford: Clarendon Press, 2012).
Hume, *Enquiries*	David Hume, *Enquiries Concerning Human Understanding and Concerning the Principles of Morals*, 3rd ed., ed. L. A. Selby-Bigge and P. H. Nidditch (Oxford: Oxford University Press, 1975).
Huxley, *CE*	Thomas Henry Huxley, *Collected Essays of Thomas Henry Huxley*, 9 vols. (Bristol: Thoemmes Press, 2001).
LCL	Loeb Classical Library
Locke, *Essay*	John Locke, *An Essay Concerning Human Understanding*, ed. P. H. Nidditch (Oxford: Clarendon Press, 1975).
Luther, *LW*	*Luther's Works*, 55 vols., ed. J. Pelikan and H. Lehman (St Louis: Concordia, 1955–75).
Luther, WA	*D. Martin Luthers Werke: kritische Gesammtausgabe*, 72 vols. (Weimar, 1883–2009).
NPNF I	*Nicene and Post-Nicene Fathers, First Series*, ed. Philip Schaff (New York, 1886–9).
NPNF II	*Nicene and Post-Nicene Fathers, Second Series*, ed. Philip Schaff (New York, 1890–8).
OED	*The Oxford English Dictionary*, www.oed.com/.
PG	*Patrologia cursus completus, series Graeca*, 161 vols., ed. J.-P. Migne (Paris, 1857–66).
PL	*Patrologia cursus completus, series Latina*, 221 vols., ed. J.-P. Migne (Paris, 1844–64).

Plato, *Collected Dialogues*	*The Collected Dialogues*, ed. Edith Hamilton and Huntington Cairns (Princeton: Princeton University Press, 1961).
SEP	*The Stanford Encyclopedia of Philosophy*, Edward N. Zalta and Uri Nodelman (eds.). https://plato.stanford.edu/.
Spinoza, *CW*	*Spinoza: Complete Works*, ed. Michael L. Morgan, trans. Samuel Shirley (Indianapolis: Hackett, 2002).

INTRODUCTION

When we peruse the first Histories of all Nations, we are apt to imagine ourselves transported into some new World, where the whole Frame of Nature is disjointed, and every Element performs its Operations in a different Manner, from what it does at present.

    David Hume, *Philosophical Essays: concerning human understanding*

Each nation has its own objects of the imagination, be it gods, angels, devils or saints .... Christianity has emptied Valhalla, felled the sacred groves, uprooted the shameful superstitions of the people.

    G. W. F. Hegel, *The Positivity of the Christian Religion*

For the greater part of human history and the greater number of societies, human existence, as culturally constituted, has been heteronymous, subject to the governance of metaperson sources of life and livelihood. People are lesser, dependent beings of an enchanted universe.

    Marshall Sahlins, *The New Science of the Enchanted Universe*[1]

THE BOUNDS OF CREDIBILITY CHANGE ACROSS TIME AND PLACE. What was believable in one historical period is no longer in another; what one culture finds utterly incredible is an article of faith in another. There is perhaps no more conspicuous instance of this principle than the process of secularisation – the decline in religious beliefs and practices in the modern West. In the context of world history this development has been both momentous and anomalous. Almost all cultures, in almost all historical

---

[1] Epigraphs: David Hume, *Philosophical Essays: concerning human understanding* (London, 1748), p. 187; G. W. F. Hegel, *Die Positivität der christlichen Religion*, in *Hegels theologische Jugendschriften*, ed. Herman Nohl (Tübingen, 1907), pp. 214f.; Marshall Sahlins, *The New Science of the Enchanted Universe: An Anthropology of Most of Humanity* (Princeton: Princeton University Press, 2022), p. 175, used with permission of Princeton University Press, permission conveyed through Copyright Clearance Center, Inc.

epochs, have been religious, in the sense of assuming the existence of some extra-mundane reality. Not surprisingly, then, the phenomenon of secularisation has attracted a considerable amount of scholarly attention. Theorists have grappled with its multiple causes, passed judgement on whether or not it has been a good thing, and pondered whether it is an inevitable process that represents the ultimate destiny of all societies. This book offers a new perspective on secularisation that focuses on one of its central aspects – the phenomenon of modern naturalism, understood as denial of, or disbelief in, the existence of supernatural entities and powers. It proceeds by way of a history of the core categories in terms of which this denial is typically expressed, 'belief' and 'supernatural', and considers how and when these notions became embedded in Western self-understandings.

It is commonly assumed that 'belief in the supernatural' is constitutive of religious commitment. However, as this book seeks to establish, the two conceptions that appear in this definition were not available to most of the subjects to whom they are now routinely applied. As we shall see, in the West the expression 'supernatural' first came into use in the thirteenth century. Even then, the initial medieval usages are rather different from our present understandings. Only in the nineteenth century do we get the settled idea of a disjunction between natural and supernatural, accompanied by the respective '-isms' of 'naturalism' and 'supernaturalism'. The historically late arrival of a formal notion of the supernatural prompts the question of what adherents of pre-modern religions imagined themselves committed to. Christianity, for example, seemed to have managed quite well for a least a millennium without possessing a conception that is supposedly fundamental to its identity as a religion. Much the same seems to be true for other religious cultures. Paradoxically, then, it looks as though the concept of the supernatural is more important for the self-image of modern naturalism than it had been for those with traditional religious commitments.

The puzzle is deeper than this because the other key notion in the definition of religion – 'belief' – turns out to be characteristically Western and historically late as well. Unlike the case of 'supernatural', the belated appearance of a modern idea of belief is disguised by the existence of an older terminology of faith/belief that seems to map reasonably well on to modern understandings.[2] Yet, as we will see, these modern understandings of belief locate it within a new epistemological framework that is discontinuous with

---

[2] Use of this 'faith/belief' conjunction, while slightly awkward, signals the fact that the English (and Latin equivalents) for 'faith' and 'belief' are renditions of a single Greek word – *pistis*. See discussion in Chapter 2, n. 28, below.

its past in crucial ways. This is especially true when it comes to the question of whether faith commitments were voluntary and what kinds of justification were called for in order to hold beliefs. As Charles Taylor has noted, a distinctive feature of secular modernity is that belief in the supernatural has become 'one option among others'.[3] The historical possibility of *dis*belief was accompanied by a change in what belief itself was thought to consist in.

In short, the concepts of 'belief' and 'supernatural' as we presently understand them were not prominent in pre-modern Christianity nor, indeed, in other cultures. To recount the circumstances that led to the emergence of these conceptions is to tell the story of how Christianity came to assume a form that made its denial possible. As it turns out, these circumstances relate to neither philosophical critique of the rationality of theistic commitment, nor scientific assaults on the plausibility of religious beliefs, but mostly concern the downstream effects of historical developments internal to Christianity itself. This points to an ironic pattern of modern naturalism's indebtedness to a particular version of monotheism. Modern religion, understood as belief in the supernatural, and modern naturalism, understood as its denial, are two sides of the same historical trajectory.

A related theme of the book addresses the fact that, viewed in the light of our own history and considered in relation to that of other cultures, the dawn of a secular age and the rise of a naturalistic outlook is something of a historical aberration. When, in the eighteenth century, the Scottish philosopher David Hume wrote his sceptical account of miracles he declared that reading the records of ancient nations was akin to encountering 'some new world'. For Hume, the miraculous relations of these times and places suggested an alien nature that operated on entirely different principles to those with which he and his readers were familiar. But from a more dispassionate perspective it is the naturalistic world of secular modernity that is new and strange. Sustaining the intellectual foundations of naturalism thus requires not only an assumption of the universality of what are contingent and culturally unique historical categories – 'belief' and the 'supernatural' – it also needs a normative theory of history, tacit or otherwise, that lends legitimacy to the unique historical turn that the secular West has taken. That will usually be some theory of historical progress that places the West in the vanguard of civilisational advance. As will become apparent, eighteenth- and nineteenth-century theories of social evolution that

---

[3] Charles Taylor, *A Secular Age* (Cambridge, MA: Harvard University Press, 2007), p. 3. See also Ethan H. Shagan, *The Birth of Modern Belief: Faith and Judgment from the Middle Ages to the Enlightenment* (Princeton: Princeton University Press, 2018), pp. 29f.

purported to show how societies inexorably progress from some magical, mythical, religious stage of development to a more enlightened scientific one, continue to undergird contemporary naturalism despite this dependence rarely being acknowledged. The more overt assumption seems to be that the singular naturalism of the modern West is licensed by the success of the natural sciences. But in a sense, this is just a doubling down on the older stories of progress, but with an apparently larger and more defensible evidence base. The modern sciences, it can hardly be denied, *do* represent something unique and special, and for the most part in a good way. The achievements of science serve double duty in this discussion because they are argued to be the very embodiment of naturalism. Close examination of the relevant history reveals something different, however. As in the case of naturalism's conceptual indebtedness to theology, narratives of the uniquely progressive direction of Western history can be understood as repackaged theological notions of providence or eschatology presenting themselves in a secular guise. Moreover, the marriage of science and naturalism is a late nineteenth-century invention, advanced to counter the then standard assumption that the regularities of nature upon which science was premised were to be explained in terms of divinely instituted laws of nature. Viewed in the light of this history, naturalism looks like a simple redescription of a long-standing theistic account of nature's regularities. This points again to a curious dependence of naturalism on certain theological understandings of history and of nature.

Before setting out the structure of the book in relation to these historical contentions it is worth briefly clarifying exactly what 'naturalism' is taken to be for the purposes of the argument. One reason for focusing on naturalism is to avoid some of the misunderstandings and controversies that characterise discussions of the related themes of secularisation and disenchantment. Challenges to these latter conceptions have pointed to instances of desecularisation and re-enchantment, and it has been plausibly argued that enchantment never fully went away.[4] The case of naturalism is a little clearer, provided that we understand the term in a relatively straightforward

---

[4] For these issues see Peter Harrison (ed.), *Narratives of Secularization* (London: Routledge, 2017), pp. 1–6, and *passim*; Robert A. Yelle and Lorenz Trein (eds.), *Narratives of Disenchantment and Secularization: Critiquing Max Weber's Idea of Modernity* (London: Bloomsbury, 2021); Jonathan Sheehan, 'When Was Disenchantment? History and the Secular Age', in *Varieties of Secularism in a Secular Age*, ed. Jonathan VanAntwerpen, Craig Calhoun, and Michael Warner (Cambridge, MA: Harvard University Press, 2010), pp. 217–42; Jason Josephson Storm, *The Myth of Disenchantment* (Chicago: University of Chicago Press, 2017); Peter L. Berger (ed.), *The Desecularization of the World: Resurgent Religion and World Politics* (Grand Rapids: Eerdmans, 1999).

way. For our main purposes, naturalism is simply the view that there are no supernatural entities or spiritual powers. Caltech theoretical physicist Sean Carroll describes it this way:

> There is only one world, the natural world, exhibiting patterns of what we call the 'laws of nature', and which is discoverable by the methods of the sciences and empirical investigation. There is no separate realm of the supernatural, spiritual, or divine; nor is there any cosmic teleology or transcendent purpose inherent in the nature of the universe or in human life.[5]

It is common to distinguish methodological naturalism from metaphysical naturalism. Most straightforwardly, in the sciences, naturalism is a *methodological* commitment that rules out making explanatory reference to supernatural entities. This is relatively uncontroversial even among theistic scientists.[6] However, this methodological stance often shades into the stronger position of a *metaphysical* naturalism which holds that the sciences, in reality, are incompatible with the proposition that there any supernatural entities. In practice, the methodological stance (pursue science *as if* supernatural entities did not exist) is often assumed to entail the truth of some metaphysical commitment (supernatural entities do not *in fact* exist) – this, typically because the explanatory success of the natural sciences is thought to vindicate the view that nothing exists except the material realities that science is capable of investigating.[7]

Naturalism in this stronger metaphysical sense also reigns in the social sciences and humanities – and especially philosophy.[8] A century ago the American philosopher Roy Wood Sellars declared that 'we are all naturalists now'.[9] This announcement may have been premature, but there is

---

[5] Sean M. Carroll, *The Big Picture: On the Origins of Life, Meaning, and the Universe Itself* (Harmondsworth: Penguin, 2017), p. 11. For an almost identical characterisation of naturalism see Richard Dawkins, *The God Delusion* (London: Transworld, 2016), pp. 34f., contrasted with 'primitive, superstitious supernaturalism', p. 12.

[6] 'Methodological naturalism' was coined by Christian philosopher Edgar S. Brightman in 1937. 'An Empirical Approach to God', *The Philosophical Review* 46 (1937), 157–8. For the origin and development of the concept see the introduction to Peter Harrison and Jon H. Roberts (eds.), *Science without God? Historical Perspectives on Scientific Naturalism* (Oxford: Oxford University Press, 2019), pp. 1–18.

[7] Peter Harrison, 'Naturalism and the Success of Science', *Religious Studies* 56 (2020), 274–91.

[8] Brad S. Gregory, 'No Room for God: History, Science, Metaphysics and the Study of Religion', *History and Theory* 47 (2008), 495–519; David Gary Shaw, 'Modernity between Us and Them: The Place of Religion within History', *History and Theory* 45 (2006), 1–9 and other articles in this special issue that deal with the question of methodological naturalism in History.

[9] Roy Wood Sellars, *Evolutionary Naturalism* (Chicago: Open Court, 1922), p. i.

little doubt that most contemporary philosophers now identify themselves as naturalists in the sense of affirming that there are no supernatural entities. This is reflected in both the discipline of philosophy and the personal beliefs of its practitioners. The non-existence of God seems to be one of the very few things philosophers are able to agree on.[10] Related to this naturalistic orientation is a deference to the natural sciences and their methods. These are often held up as a model for philosophy and as the approach that offers the most secure path to reliable knowledge.[11] Wilfrid Sellars, following in his father's footsteps, put it concisely: 'science is the measure of all things'.[12] Philosopher Willard Quine, a strong advocate of naturalism, similarly recommended that philosophers accept 'the fundamental conceptual scheme of science and common sense'. For Quine, it was the natural

[10] Survey data suggest that only 14 per cent of philosophers are theists and that these are concentrated in the subfield of philosophy of religion. Atheism (or agnosticism) is thus one of three things upon which there is some degree of philosophical consensus, the other two being rather more banal: the existence of the external world and scientific realism. D. Bourget and D. J. Chalmers, 'What Do Philosophers Believe?', *Philosophical Studies* 170 (2014), 465–500 (476, 482). But cf. Quentin Smith, 'The Metaphilosophy of Naturalism', *Philo* 4 (2001), 195–215. Atheists are a significant minority in the global population at 7 per cent, although there are important national variations. Ariela Keyser and Juhem Navarro-Rivera, 'A World of Atheism: Global Demographics', in *The Oxford Handbook of Atheism*, ed. Stephen Bullivant and Michael Ruse (Oxford: Oxford University Press, 2013), pp. 553–86. Steve Bruce offers data showing that in the USA, religious commitment is even lower among social scientists than natural scientists. *God Is Dead: Secularization in the West* (Oxford: Blackwell, 2002), p. 110. But cf. Elaine Howard Ecklund and Christopher P. Scheitle, 'Religion among Academic Scientists: Distinctions, Disciplines, and Demographics', *Social Problems* 54 (2007), 289–307; and Neil Gross and Solon Simmons, 'The Religiosity of American College and University Professors', *Sociology of Religion* 70 (2009), 101–29.

[11] Hence David Papineau: 'The great majority of contemporary philosophers would happily accept naturalism as just characterized – that is, they would both reject "supernatural" entities, and allow that science is a possible route (if not necessarily the only one) to important truths about the "human spirit".' 'Naturalism', *SEP*, https://plato.stanford.edu/archives/sum2020/entries/naturalism/. 'Succinctly, *naturalism* seeks to apply the methods of the empirical sciences to explain natural events without reference to supernatural causes …. Naturalism is still widely regarded today as the dominant philosophical outlook in the West.' John R. Shook and Paul Kurtz, 'Introduction', in *The Future of Naturalism*, ed. Shook and Kurtz (Buffalo: Prometheus Books, 2009), p. 1. Barry Stroud, similarly, 'Naturalism on any reading is opposed to supernaturalism …. By supernaturalism I mean the invocation of an agent or force which somehow stands outside the natural world and so whose doings cannot be understood as part of it.' Stroud suggests that virtually all respectable contemporary philosophers are naturalists in this sense. 'The Charm of Naturalism', *Proceedings and Addresses of the American Philosophical Association* 70 (1996), 43–55 (44).

[12] Wilfrid Sellars, *Empiricism and the Philosophy of Mind* (Cambridge, MA: Harvard University Press, 1997), p. 83.

sciences, and not metaphysics, that most directly grappled with reality.[13] The deference to science that characterises analytic philosophy is not unrelated to the fact that for many philosophers theism was no longer an intellectually defensible position.

There are, however, different versions of philosophical naturalism that are important to distinguish from the straightforward denial of the existence of the supernatural. Another kind of philosophical naturalism focuses on the fact that human beings are natural creatures inhabiting a natural world. Things can get confusing here, because this recognition has spawned two rather different approaches which, following philosopher Huw Price, we can label 'objective' and 'subjective' naturalism.[14] Briefly, *objective naturalists*, in keeping with a privileging of scientific discourse, concern themselves with how phenomena such as consciousness might be related to neurons, or how human activities like making choices, having beliefs, and holding moral values might be understood in a world that on a standard scientific description consists only of fundamental particles interacting in space.

Subjective naturalists consider this a rather unpromising enterprise. They understand the problems identified by objective naturalists as essentially *linguistic*, arising out of the different ways in which the relevant terminologies are being deployed. The solution to philosophical problems, on this latter understanding is not, as in the project of objective naturalism, a matter of reconciling two different languages, or of reducing everyday language to scientific language, or indeed eliminating it if need be. Rather it is a matter of seeing how different vocabularies have come into existence and understanding the purposes they were originally intended to serve. In the first case, problems are *solved* by finding the best language with which to represent reality and by dispensing with imprecise expressions deemed to be inconsistent that (scientific) reality. In the second, problems are *dissolved*

---

[13] W. V. Quine, *Word and Object* (Cambridge, MA: MIT Press, 1960), p. 276; *Theories and Things* (Cambridge, MA: Harvard University Press, 1981), p. 21. On Quine's naturalism see Sander Verhaegh, *The Nature and Development of Quine's Naturalism* (Oxford: Oxford University Press, 2010). See also John Searle, 'Contemporary Philosophy in the United States', in *The Blackwell Companion to Philosophy*, ed. N. Bunnin and E. P. Tsui-James (Oxford: Blackwell, 1996), pp. 1–24; Stephen Gaukroger, *The Failures of Philosophy: A Historical Essay* (Princeton: Princeton University Press, 2020), pp. 261–82.

[14] Huw Price, 'Naturalism without Representationalism', in *Naturalism in Question*, ed. Mario De Caro and David Macarthur (Cambridge, MA: Harvard University Press, 2004), pp. 71–88. Brian Leiter makes a similar distinction between naturalists and 'Wittgensteinian quietists', in *The Future for Philosophy* (New York: Oxford University Press, 2004), pp. 2–3. For a succinct account of these different approaches see Richard Rorty, 'Naturalism and Quietism', in *Naturalism and Normativity*, ed. Mario De Caro and David Macarthur (New York: Columbia University Press, 2010), pp. 55–68.

by showing how they emerge out of the misapplication of vocabularies that have been forced to migrate out of their original social or historical context. These two positions give rise to different conceptions of the task of philosophy. For objective naturalists the goal is a reductive, ahistorical conceptual analysis; for subjective naturalists it consists in something closer to anthropological, historical, and social analysis.[15] The difference partly turns on what counts as the 'natural' in naturalism. For objective naturalists, 'nature' is understood as the reality depicted by scientific language. For subjective naturalists, 'nature' is the biological and social matrix in which human activities including the sciences themselves are embedded. The approach of subjective naturalism, with its focus on linguistic communities, thus offers an explanation for why there is this difference in the first place.

While this book problematises aspects of contemporary naturalism understood as a rejection of supernaturalism, the approach adopted nonetheless has affinities with subjective naturalism as described above. To some degree, the historical considerations offered here are akin to the 'therapeutic' approach of the subjective naturalists. But to return to the definitional question, 'naturalism' as used throughout the book bears the straightforward sense of denial of supernatural and spiritual powers or entities.

The structure of this volume closely follows the logic of the case outlined above. Following a brief prologue (on which more below) the second chapter traces the fortunes of our modern understanding of 'belief' which is deeply informed by its original uses in a religious context. It begins with an account of faith/belief in early Christianity, showing how the primary meanings of the relevant expression related to trust rather than intellectual assent. In the medieval period, this social component of faith/belief was formalised in the conception of 'implicit faith', which enabled lay believers to affirm abstruse theological doctrines without the requirement of a full intellectual comprehension of what was being affirmed.

The third chapter describes how, during the sixteenth century, implicit faith became one of the chief targets of the Protestant reformers, who insisted that individuals take full responsibility for what they believed. True belief was thought to entail explicit knowledge of what was being assented to, along with some capacity to justify that belief in a way that did not simply defer to authority. Critiques of implicit faith represent the first articulation of what is now referred to as the 'ethics of belief' – the principle

---

[15] Robert Brandom suggests that Hegel, Wittgenstein, and some of the pragmatists are to be understood as naturalists in this sense. *A Spirit of Trust: A Reading of Hegel's Phenomenology* (Cambridge, MA: Harvard University Press, 2019), pp. 9–12.

that we have an ethical duty to have evidence for the beliefs we hold. As a consequence of these critiques, belief came to be thought of more in terms of intellectual assent than affective trust. These early modern changes to the sociology and philosophy of religious belief contributed to the subsequent epistemological preoccupations of modern philosophy.

The chapter that follows reflects upon the implications of the new status of belief by reconsidering the history of traditional arguments for the existence of God. If disbelief in the supernatural had not been a genuinely live option before the appearance of modern secularity, and if there was little demand that beliefs be entertained only if supported by certain kinds of evidence, what was the point of articulating formal proofs of God's existence? The thrust of this chapter is that the so-called classical proofs for God's existence performed a very different function to the one that they were later to assume. They were more akin to spiritual exercises than logical arguments constructed from putatively neutral premises. Crucially, moreover, one of the central 'proofs' – that based on universal consensus – involved a simple appeal to the ubiquity and universality of religious belief. The demise of this argument in the early modern period signalled a major change in how belief in the supernatural came to be understood, indicating that the burden of proof was shifting from unbelievers to believers. At the same time there arose a new conception of natural theology, understood as an enterprise that could provide support for religious belief on rational grounds alone. The changing status of natural theology and proofs for God's existence thus correlated directly with the appearance of a new notion of belief and the requirements for its justification.

Chapter 5 turns to the origins of our present understanding of the natural/supernatural divide, showing how the terminology of 'the supernatural' first emerged in the Middle Ages and gradually assumed its modern form between the seventeenth and nineteenth centuries. The attendant '-isms' – naturalism and supernaturalism – arrive at the end of this period, during the 1800s. The original context for the naturalism/supernaturalism distinction was neither science nor philosophy, but the sphere of biblical criticism. From there it was imported into a scientific context. The nineteenth century also witnessed attempts to reconstruct the history of science with a view to arguing for a long-standing alliance between naturalism and science. A more accurate portrayal of the relevant history shows, to the contrary, that 'science' had been consistently aligned with theistic assumptions about the regularities of nature. These regularities were formalised as laws of nature in the seventeenth century, at which time they were understood as divinely authored imperatives to which nature necessarily conformed.

In the nineteenth century, what had originally been understood as expressions of the divine will were simply redescribed in purely naturalistic terms as laws of *nature* by advocates of naturalism. Ironically, in this redescribed form, they were now claimed to represent evidence against theistic readings of nature.

The sixth chapter considers how the exceptionalism of Western naturalism was given legitimacy through an appeal to narratives of progress. The basic form of these narratives was derived from an original Protestant model that had divided history into two periods – one in which miracles had genuinely taken place followed by a second that was characterised by the absence of genuine miracle-workers. From the principle of the historical cessation of miracles it followed that medieval and contemporary Catholic miracles were fraudulent. Protestants also understood the Reformation as having ushered in an age of light after a period of medieval darkness. Subsequent eighteenth-century thinkers simply generalised and extended this argument, contending that the miracle reports from *all* historical periods were fraudulent. History could now be divided into an earlier period characterised by a naïve credulity in relation to miracle reports, followed by a more mature phase of history during which there was increasing recognition of the falsity of miracle reports. These same eighteenth-century thinkers also arrogated to themselves the mantle of enlightenment. The progressivist histories characteristic of the early social sciences and endorsed by advocates of scientific naturalism were doubly indebted to religious models since they also drew upon providential or eschatological notions of historical directionality. This raises the question of whether their progressivist philosophy of history is problematically dependent upon covert theistic assumptions.

The concluding chapter briefly considers questions about the possibility of religious experience in a secular age and offers some concise theoretical conclusions. These address how the theses outlined in the book relate to other 'modernity stories', including those of Charles Taylor, Brad Gregory, John Milbank, and Alasdair MacIntyre.

Immediately following this introduction is a prologue that offers a brief consideration of David Hume's celebrated argument against believing miracle reports. The intention is not to add further to the oversupply of philosophical commentary on this argument, but rather to show how Hume's stance nicely exemplifies several key issues relating to the emergence of modern naturalism as discussed in the book. Hume assumes the universal and unproblematic nature of such core conceptions as 'supernatural' and 'laws of nature'. Lurking in the background of his logical argument, moreover, is a good deal of cultural condescension which is nonetheless central to making the argument work. Overstating the case somewhat, we might say his case against miracles can be read as a set of cultural prejudices and question-begging premises dressed up as a piece of philosophical reasoning. The prologue also makes reference to what I have called 'Hume's dilemma'. Hume relies upon the weight of the testimony to establish his case against believing miracle reports, but must also contend with the weight of testimony, across different times and cultures, to the existence of the supernatural. The dilemma is resolved by an appeal to historical progress (and arguably a dubious racial theory) that enables him to discount testimonies emanating from the past and/or other cultures. The real weight of the argument is thus borne by a set of historical assumptions that appear in the guise of non-essential afterthoughts. Hume's 'dilemma' has not gone away and, if anything, is even more acute, since the traditions and beliefs of non-Western cultures are now more difficult to dismiss on the basis of dubious historical accounts of Western exceptionalism. To advert to philosophical terminology, there is a tension between the traditional ethics of belief on the one hand and the demands of epistemic justice on the other. The former is to do with an ethical imperative to have good reasons for what we believe; the latter with a responsibility not to dismiss the reported experiences of others, based upon their status.

A brief comment about the approach taken and the notes, which are extensive, is in order. The argument set out in this book covers a rather wide historical range and calls upon a number of disciplines – mostly history, but also philosophy, theology, and anthropology. The historical range is necessary, partly because it enables us to see just how peculiar naturalism is when viewed in historical perspective, and partly because during the nineteenth century naturalism was provided with its own foundation myths which encompass a similar historical span. The disciplinary mix simply reflects what answering the core questions requires, along with the fact that our disciplines do not map onto the division of knowledge as understood in the historical periods under discussion. This approach is admittedly fraught, especially given the high degree of scholarly specialisation that characterises modern academia. I though it worth the risk since the project seems important and demands an ambitious scope of enquiry. Even so, I am acutely conscious of having omitted significant historical episodes and compressed others (especially the medieval period) while not including disciplinary knowledge that would have been relevant. My optimistic assumption has been that these omissions would have been supportive of the argument anyway. Reviewers will doubtless correct me if I am wrong. Ideally, I would also like to have devoted more space to the contemporary implications of this analysis, especially for cross-cultural understanding. But my first priority was to articulate the argument and so this important discussion must be taken up by others or await a future publication project. This brings me to the notes, which may seem excessive. Following on from the observations above, they are there to signal my indebtedness to the scholarly labours of others who work in times and disciplines in which I am not an expert. The notes also provide additional evidence for claims summarily made in the main text. Finally, the broad scope of the text provided challenges not only for the author but will do so for the reader as well. Some of the notes, accordingly, will add nuance and, on occasion, provide guidance to some of the more detailed discussions best kept out of the text. Leaving these details to the notes makes for a more readable book, but I also hope that there will be those who enjoy the notes, too.

I

HUME'S DILEMMA

'HUME (David) *the Historian*'
British Library Catalogue

They say miracles are past; and we have our philosophical persons to make modern and familiar, things supernatural and causeless. Hence it is that we make trifles of terrors, ensconcing ourselves into seeming knowledge, when we should submit ourselves to an unknown fear.

Shakespeare, *All's Well That Ends Well*, 2.3

BEFORE ITS 1997 RELOCATION TO ST PANCRAS, THE MAIN READING room of the British Library sat under a soaring Victorian dome in the heart of the British Museum in Bloomsbury. Researchers in possession of a coveted reader's ticket could work in one of the most atmospheric reading rooms in the world, inspired by the knowledge that such luminaries as Karl Marx, Virginia Woolf, George Bernard Shaw, and Mohandas Gandhi had laboured there before them. There were, it must be admitted, minor inconveniences. Ordering books was a time-consuming process that required the completion of call slips on triplicate carbon paper. These would be conveyed to the bookstacks in Perspex capsules, propelled by compressed air through a labyrinthine system of tubes. This process was preceded by perusal of the printed catalogue, which consisted of hundreds of large, blue, hard-bound volumes arranged in circular cases at the centre of the room. Individual entries gave the appearance of having almost been pasted in, giving the whole catalogue the appearance of massive multi-volume scrapbook. The system had its compensations, however. The arrangement of entries often revealed relationships between sources that might otherwise have gone undiscovered. The way in which authors were characterised was also revealing. The catalogue entry for David Hume, for example, reads: 'HUME (David) *the Historian*'.[1]

---

[1] See the introduction to Mark G. Spencer (ed.), *David Hume: Historical Thinker, Historical Writer* (University Park, PA: Pennsylvania State University Press, 2013), pp. 1–12. The entry

Twenty-first-century readers may find this categorisation puzzling. We now think of Hume as primarily a philosopher and, indeed, one of the progenitors of philosophical naturalism.[2] Hume is also something of a role model for many contemporary analytic philosophers, although few share his enthusiasm for history. Survey data reveal that more philosophers identify with Hume than with any other non-living philosopher and by a significant margin. (For those interested in the rankings, Aristotle comes a distant second, followed by Immanuel Kant.)[3] But in his day, and for a considerable period after, Hume was known as a historian. The subsequent change in the disciplinary identification of Hume is noteworthy, for at least some of his celebrated philosophical positions turn out to rely upon covert historical commitments. This is especially so for one of Hume's most admired arguments: his case against believing reports of supernatural activity in the form of miracles.

Hume's famous treatment of miracles is set out in section 10 of the *Essay concerning Human Understanding* (1748). The section has two parts. In the first, Hume outlines his logical case against lending credence to miracle reports. The second part seems to consist in ancillary historical and anthropological considerations that lend support in various ways to the core philosophical argument that precedes them. Most scholarly attention has accordingly focused on the argument of the first part, which a good number of present-day philosophers still regard as having dealt a telling blow against the rationality of believing in reports of supernatural occurrences. My suggestion will be that a key premise of Hume's argument lurks among the historical claims made in the second part of the chapter and that it is here that the real force of the argument is to be found. This goes to a more general thesis that the true foundations of modern naturalism lie not in philosophy or the logic of the natural sciences, but in tacit assumptions about historical progress and an accompanying hierarchy of cultures.

---

survives in the General Catalogue of Printed Books, now reprinted and located in the reference area of the new Humanities and Social Sciences Reading Room at St Pancras.

[2] 'Today, philosophers recognize Hume as a thoroughgoing exponent of philosophical naturalism' and 'as a precursor of contemporary cognitive science'. William Edward Morris and Charlotte R. Brown, 'David Hume', *SEP*, https://plato.stanford.edu/archives/spr2021/entries/hume/. Naturalism is understood here both in opposition to supernatural and in the sense of offering naturalising accounts of human thought and culture. See, e.g., Jennifer A. Herdt, 'Artificial Lives, Providential History, and the Apparent Limits of Sympathetic Understanding', in *David Hume*, ed. Spencer, pp. 37–59; John P. Wright, 'Kemp Smith and the Two Kinds of Naturalism in David Hume's Philosophy', *Rivista di Storia della Filosofia* 62/3, Supplemento (2007), 17–36. The relative importance of Hume's naturalism as opposed to his scepticism has been a matter of some debate. See Paul Russell, *The Riddle of Hume's Treatise: Scepticism, Naturalism, and Irreligion* (Oxford: Oxford University Press, 2008), pp. 3–11.

[3] Bourget and Chalmers, 'What Do Philosophers Believe?'

Hume recognises at the outset that the business of taking on reports of supernatural interventions is likely to be an endless task if each case has to be evaluated on its own merits. As he puts it: 'Does a man of sense run after every silly tale of witches or hobgoblins or fairies, and canvass particularly the evidence?'[4] The situation called for an approach that could in principle cover all instances. Hume believed that he had discovered just such an argument, one that could serve, for the wise and learned, as '*an everlasting check to all kinds of superstitious delusion*'.[5] His goal was thus to fashion a 'silver bullet' that would establish a presumption of guilt for all miracle reports.[6] In setting up his argument, Hume articulates three considerations. First, 'A wise man proportions his belief to the evidence.' Second is his definition of the miraculous: '*a transgression of a law of nature by a particular volition of the Deity, or by the interposition of some invisible agent*'. Third, laws of nature are said to be established by the weight of unvarying testimony to some uniformity in the natural world. What Hume thinks necessarily follows from this is that 'as a firm and unalterable experience has established these laws, the proof against a miracle, from the very nature of the fact, is as entire as any argument from experience can possibly be imagined'. This is because, by definition, testimony to the breach of a law of nature will always be outweighed by testimony to the law of nature which is supposedly being breached. Hence, the wise man, who weighs up competing testimonies, will always land on the side of the inviolability of laws of nature. For Hume, two further things follow: 'a miracle can never be proved, so as to be the foundation of a system of religion' and, because the various religions are incompatible with each other, the putative miracles of one religion necessarily cancel out those of another.

Allocating a key role to weight of testimony leaves Hume with a dilemma, however, although not one that he explicitly acknowledges. The framing of laws of nature might well rest upon cumulative testimony. But there was also cumulative testimony to the reality of miracles and wonders – and this from a variety of cultures past and present. Indeed, this was the very problem that Hume sought to address. Weight of testimony alone, therefore, was insufficient to settle the question. The resolution of this dilemma lay in the appeal to history and anthropology that is quietly introduced in the second part of the chapter. In essence, Hume needed to move from the issue

---

[4] Hume to Hugh Blair, in *Early Responses to Hume's Writings on Religion*, 2 vols., ed. James Fieser (London: Bloomsbury, 2005), vol. 2, p. 16.

[5] Hume, *Enquiries*, p. 110 (my emphasis).

[6] The descriptor 'silver bullet' comes from John Earman, *Hume's Abject Failure: The Argument against Miracles* (Oxford: Oxford University Press, 2000), p. 3.

of the quantity of testimony to its quality.[7] Apparently some testimonies are more equal than others:

> It forms a strong presumption against all supernatural and miraculous relations, that they are observed chiefly to abound among ignorant and barbarous nations; or if a civilized people has ever given admission to any of them, that people will be found to have received them from ignorant and barbarous ancestors.[8]

It turns out, then, that it is this 'strong presumption' that relieves the investigator of the obligation to pursue any serious enquiry into the veracity of particular relations of supernatural events. Typical purveyors of tales of the supernatural include, for Hume, 'monkish historians', 'the vulgar', 'ignorant people', 'barbarous Arabians', 'the ignorant and stupid', and so on.[9] The main thrust of Hume's argument, then, actually turns on a historical thesis about the process of civilisation, in which some cultures and races (civilised ones) are more advanced and trustworthy than the rest (ignorant, barbarous, and so on). It is this presumption that enables the testimony of certain groups to be discounted without further investigation. Stated in this uncompromising way and extracted from the matrix of philosophical argumentation in which Hume had embedded it, this stark assertion looks very much like an unsupported prejudice, couched in terms likely to be at least mildly offensive to present-day sensibilities.

Unhappily, in his essay 'Of National Characters' Hume would go still further and remark, albeit in a footnote, on the intellectual inferiority of non-white peoples. Only among civilised white nations, Hume remarked,

---

[7] Some contemporary critics maintained that even the quantitative aspect of Hume's argument was problematic, since he failed to consider the relevant probabilities as they relate to multiple independent testimonies to a miraculous event. George Campbell, *A Dissertation on Miracles* (Edinburgh, 1762); Earman, *Hume's Abject Failure*, pp. 54–6. Leibniz had already pointed out that 'Everyone agrees that appearances are against Mysteries, and that they are by no means probable when regarded only from the standpoint of reason.' *Theodicy* [1710] §28, trans. E. M. Huggard (London: Routledge & Kegan Paul, 1952), p. 91.

[8] Hume, *Enquiries*, p. 119. The second section offers four arguments: first, miracle testimony comes from unreliable witnesses; second, humans have a natural tendency to sensationalise; third, miracle reports abound in barbarous nations; fourth, miracles of different religions cancel each other out.

[9] Hume, *Enquiries*, pp. 120–4. Hume also found it convenient to ignore the testimonies of those who clearly did not fit these dismissive descriptions. In the previous century, for example, thinkers such as Henry More and Joseph Glanvill (both Fellows of the Royal Society) had sought to counter religious scepticism by collecting accounts of what they considered to be well-attested miraculous and preternatural events. Their idea was to provide incontrovertible empirical evidence for the existence of a non-material realm. See Joseph Glanvill, *Saducismus triumphatus* (London, 1681).

do we encounter excellence in action and speculation.[10] It is this superiority in speculative ability that enables judgement to be passed by the white and civilised on the beliefs and practices of the non-white and barbarous. My interest here is not in a posthumous prosecution of Hume on this issue, nor in mounting a guilt-by-association case against his modern admirers. Rather it is to wonder about the possibility of a lingering, covert influence of some of Hume's more dubious anthropological assumptions on our present naturalistic outlook. It is safe to say that few today would stand by the questionable cultural rankings expressed in 'Of Miracles' and we have long dispensed with the descriptor 'barbarous nations' to characterise peoples given to supernatural beliefs. Yet we might still enquire whether, protestations to the contrary, some implicit commitment to these sentiments sits beneath the surface of at least some of our modern, naturalistic forms of intellectual enquiry. To be sure, the prejudicial condescension of this stance will be less explicit, and the ostensible justifications for disbelief are far more likely be expressed in terms of references to science, or laws of nature, or, for philosophers, an adoption of the scepticism about the supernatural of the kind that Hume elaborates. There is little talk of barbarians or backward savages in the Western academy: on the contrary, and all to the good, there is an increasing effort to acknowledge the value of indigenous perspectives, notwithstanding their prima facie incompatibility with the ruling naturalistic assumptions of the modern natural and social sciences.[11] It is worth reflecting in more detail, then, on the ways in which unspoken historical assumptions might continue to inform contemporary disciplinary commitments and whether these might conflict with other values that are increasingly regarded as important.

---

[10] 'I am apt to suspect the negroes to be naturally inferior to the whites. There scarcely ever was a civilized nation of that complexion …. On the other hand, the most rude and barbarous of the whites … have still something eminent about them.' 'Of National Characters', in *Essays, Moral, Political, and Literary* [1758] (London, 1777), p. 208. Hume's stance was already contested at the time. See, e.g., James Beattie, *An Essay on the Nature and Immutability of Truth* [1770] (London, 1778), pp. 463–8. Beattie linked Hume's racism to his animus against Christianity. Other contemporaries already raised questions about Hume's definition of barbarous, contending the first-century Jews were not, in fact, 'barbarous'. See Fieser, *Early Responses to Hume*, vol. 1, pp. xxi, 66, 82, 209, 355.

[11] From a wide range of literature see Fikret Berkes, *Sacred Ecology*, 4th ed. (Abingdon: Routledge, 2018); J. Mistry, 'Indigenous Knowledges', in *International Encyclopedia of Human Geography*, ed. Rob Kitchin and Nigel Thrift (Amsterdam: Elsevier, 2009), pp. 371–6; Tyler D. Jessen, Natalie C. Ban, Nicholas XEMŦOLTW Claxton, and Chris T. Darimont, 'Contributions of Indigenous Knowledge to Ecological and Evolutionary Understanding', *Frontiers in Ecology and the Environment* 20 (2022), 93–101; N. C. Ban, A. Frid, M. Reid, B. Edgar, D. Shaw, and P. Siwallace, 'Incorporate Indigenous Perspectives

In Chapter 6 we will consider how the ideas of historical progress that Hume casually adverts to were formalised and written into the foundational narratives of the modern social sciences. Naturalism would play a prominent role in these progress stories as a marker of civilisational advance. For now, though, I want to shift the focus of attention to the conceptual framing of Hume's argument, which is equally revealing about some of the assumptions that underpin modern naturalism. These relate to the fact that certain concepts – 'belief', 'laws of nature', 'supernatural', 'religion' – are often treated as if they were unproblematic, self-evident, transhistorical, and universal.

As already noted, contemporary philosophers have focused most of their attention on the first part of Hume's 'Of Miracles', seeing in it Hume's most original contribution to the discussion.[12] These elements of the argument are among the most overworked of all in the philosophical literature, but one reason for revisiting them here is that the assumptions and concepts that underlie virtually every step in this chain of reasoning are illustrative of some general feature of our modern approach to the question of belief in the supernatural. These turn out to be problematic, to varying degrees, when viewed in historical perspective.

First is Hume's contention that a 'wise man' should proportion his belief to the evidence. Taken at face value, this seems an eminently sensible recommendation. On closer examination, however, the idea that our beliefs should be determined solely on the weight of evidence encounters some difficulties. There is a long-standing discussion among philosophers on 'the ethics of belief' – whether we have a moral obligation to believe only those things for which we have convincing evidence. A number of acute thinkers – Blaise Pascal, Immanuel Kant, Søren Kierkegaard, and William James among them – have argued that there are occasions on which for prudential, moral, or religious reasons we actually have an obligation to believe things without sufficient evidence. Indeed, it has been proposed that the

---

for Impactful Research and Effective Management', *Nature Ecology & Evolution* 2 (2018), 1680–3; Sandra Harding, *Objectivity and Diversity* (Chicago: University of Chicago Press, 2015), pp. 80–104, 127–49; O. Jiri, P. L. Mafongoya, and P. Chivenge, 'Indigenous Knowledge Systems, Seasonal "Quality" and Climate Change Adaptation in Zimbabwe', *Climate Research* 66 (2015), 103–11; Raelee Lancaster, 'Decolonisation to Indigenisation: How Can Institutions Centre Indigenous Knowledge?', *Times Higher Education Supplement*, 20 June 2023, www.timeshighereducation.com/campus/decolonisation-indigenisation-how-can-institutions-centre-indigenous-knowledge, accessed 18 July 2023.

[12] Much of Hume's purported originality on this issue turns out to be an artefact of the neglect of contemporary and preceding literature written by figures now less celebrated. See Robert M. Burns, *The Great Debate on Miracles from Joseph Glanvill to David Hume* (Lewisburg: Bucknell University Press, 1981).

most important things in life require conviction in the absence of adequate evidence. Added to this, most would allow that there are certain 'first principles' that we need to accept, without proof, if we are to know anything at all. As will become apparent in Chapter 4, it was long held that theistic belief was one such principle. Indeed, contra Hume, Cicero had maintained that *lack* of religious belief was a mark of barbarity.[13] My concern at this point is not to come down on one side or the other of these discussions, but to indicate that the issue is not quite as straightforward as Hume implies. More importantly, and looking ahead to Chapter 3, the emergence of an ethics of belief in the early modern period signals a major shift in Western understandings of what it is that faith and belief consist in. These early modern discussions, initially occurring in a religious context, established the conditions for the subsequent epistemological preoccupations of modern philosophy. They also point us in the direction of a potentially different way of assessing the merits of cultures that seem prone to the advocacy of supernatural beliefs.

Second, is Hume's definition of a miracle: '*a transgression of a law of nature by a particular volition of the Deity*'. Again, this may seem relatively straightforward and uncontroversial. But it is important to note that the formal conception of a 'law of nature', at least in the sense that Hume and early modern natural philosophers used it, did not come into existence until the seventeenth century.[14] It follows that earlier historical actors who either observed 'miracles' or gave credence to miracle accounts, could not have been operating with the same conception of miracle that Hume is urging upon us, since the idea of a law of nature was not available to them. Hume is thus engaging here in a kind of 'bait-and-switch' strategy – not uncommon in philosophy of religion – offering a stipulative definition of some notion or doctrine, and then proceeding to a critical analysis of it without being overly scrupulous about whether this version of the notion corresponds to the way in which it operates in the wild. In this case, there is a significant mismatch between the philosophical conception, cleaned up and abstracted for the purposes of philosophical argumentation, and the variety of ways in which native users had spoken about the miraculous.

---

[13] '… there is no nation so barbarous, no race so brutish, as not to be imbued with the conviction that there is a God'. Cicero, *Tusculan Disputations* 1.13 (LCL 141, p. 37).

[14] Hume's own view of laws was, admittedly, at odds with the then standard view according to which laws of nature *govern* events – a view that originally rested on the assumption that laws were divine edicts. The question would then be what, if anything, Humean laws *explain*. For some of these issues, see Harjit Bhogal, 'Humeanism about Laws of Nature', *Philosophy Compass* 15 (2020), 1–10. In any event, the point about anachronism holds.

Of course, it could be argued that it is precisely the lack of a conception of laws of nature that is the problem. This lack would become the mark of the intellectual immaturity or 'barbarism' of the cultures in question. But a retreat to this line of reasoning must contend with the fact that the early modern conception of laws of nature was strongly underpinned by theological considerations. From the seventeenth to the nineteenth century, laws formulated within the sciences were consistently aligned with theological readings of nature and offered as evidence for the divine superintendence of the natural world. The prominence of this view and its decline in the nineteenth century will be discussed in more detail in Chapter 5. For now, we can say that few of the theological champions of laws of nature understood them in ways that generated major difficulties for miracles. More generally, this historical grounding of laws of nature in the divine will is illustrative of one of the central themes of this book – a persistent pattern of the indebtedness of naturalism to covert theological premises. There might seem to be an irresolvable tension between conceiving of God as the source of both the regularities of nature and miraculous 'interventions'. But, leading on to the next point, this tension was largely the creature of a particular view of the natural/supernatural divide.

If the notion of 'laws' operating in Hume's argument cannot be accepted uncritically, this is even more so with respect to ideas of 'nature', 'supernatural', and 'transgression'. Hume's conception of the miraculous requires something like a natural/supernatural distinction as, more generally, does modern naturalism. But a two-tiered natural/supernatural understanding of reality was a relatively late historical development, as will become apparent in Chapter 5. Suffice it to say for now that earlier thinkers did not subscribe to a notion of divine transgressions, interpositions, or interventions into some relatively independent natural order. For Augustine, to take a single pre-modern example, miracles were not contrary to nature but contrary to our knowledge of nature.[15] Again, the suggestion might be that Hume is working with a more sophisticated conception of nature than his medieval predecessors – one based on the sciences, for example. But this is not something he argues for directly, and neither was this reading one that was shared by the scientific practitioners of the period. It might also be the case that Hume's argument works in the terms in which it is expressed. However, if it fails to match the historical instances it was intended to target, we are just back to the 'bait-and-switch' move. Admittedly, matters are complicated

---

[15] Augustine, *City of God* 21.8; *Against Faustus* 26.3. See Peter Harrison, 'Newtonian Science, Miracles, and the Laws of Nature', *Journal of the History of Ideas* 56 (1995), 531–53.

by the fact that many of his religious contemporaries shared some of the contents of this conceptual toolkit, and some at least were willing to conduct the debate on those terms. In this case the relevant point goes to an important change in how religious belief was conceptualised that was shared by advocates and critics alike.

Third is Hume's conclusion that 'A miracle can never be proved to be the foundation of a system of religion.' Here the unexamined assumption is that religion is a 'system' consisting of propositions for which a particular form of justification is required. Miracles, in this scheme of things, are meant to act as 'proofs' for the propositions that constitute the substance of a religion. Like Hume's stipulative conception of 'laws of nature', however, the very idea that Christianity was a 'religion' constituted by its propositional content was a product of the early modern period, and not a notion to which pre-modern individuals subscribed.[16] So again, this line of argument operates with a rather abstract understanding of the phenomenon that it purports to be addressing. It is certainly true that during this period we encounter religiously motivated defences of Christianity that exhibit a similar understanding of the issues. Apologetic appeals to miracles, along these lines, were responsible for eliciting Hume's critique. But again, the more general point here is that the new understanding of the nature of miracles and the evidential role ascribed to them tells us something important about new understandings of religious belief. These will be discussed in more detail in the next chapter.

The final element of Hume' case is this: miracles are supposed to serve as evidence for the truth of propositional beliefs that constitute religion, and all religions claim to be true based on their own proprietary miracles. However, the various religions, understood in this propositional sense, posit conflicting truth claims. It would then follow that *either* the miracles appealed to as evidence for competing religions did not occur, *or* even if they did, that they could not logically serve to guarantee the truth of incompatible systems of religious truths. The difficulty here, related to the point above, is the assumption that there are plural 'religions', modelled on Christianity, that can be understood in terms of mutually incompatible belief systems. Yet again, this represented a new way of understanding religious phenomena that first arose in the early modern period. What is significant about Hume's point is that it highlights how the appearance of multiple Christian confessions in the wake of the Protestant Reformation led to a reconceptualising of the religious life and its justifications.

---

[16] Harrison, *Territories*, passim; *'Religion' and the Religions*; Wilfred Cantwell Smith, *The Meaning and End of Religion* (London: SPCK, 1978). See also Chapter 2, n. 35.

There is also an element of the pot calling the kettle black in Hume's reference to the embarrassments of religious pluralism. René Descartes observed of the state of philosophy that 'it had been cultivated for many ages by the most distinguished men, and that yet there is not a single matter within its sphere which is not still in dispute'.[17] The ancient schools of Scepticism were a direct response to this 'known problem' within philosophy. For their part, modern philosophers have belatedly realised that the state of their own field is itself worthy of philosophical analysis and the philosophy of disagreement has become a lively topic in the last two decades. Needless to say, perhaps, philosophers have been reluctant to conclude, on the basis of the fact that many of them hold mutually exclusive positions, that philosophy is an irrational activity. The so-called 'steadfast view', for example, provides reasons for thinking that it is rational to stick to your guns, even in the face of strong peer disagreement.[18] In the comparable case of religion, even if we do regard religions as systems of propositional beliefs, as Hume seems to, the implications of disagreement among them might not be as destructive as he seems to think. Some of the problems associated with philosophical disagreements go away if we think of philosophy more as an activity than a set of theoretical commitments. The potential parallels with religion need not be laboured. The way in which religion was reconceptualised in the early modern period, coming to be understood in terms of beliefs to be supported by particular kinds of evidence, was at least partly responsible for generating the pluralistic predicament to which Hume drew attention in this final line of criticism.

In sum, Hume's celebrated argument helpfully exemplifies a number of the key issues that arise in attempts to understand the historical roots

---

[17] Descartes, *Discourse on the Method*, CSM I, pp. 114f. See also Augustine, *City of God* 19.1, 18.4; Basil, *Hexameron* 1.11; Tertullian, *Treatise on the Soul* 3; *Ad nations* 2.1.

[18] For the philosophy of disagreement see Bryan Frances, *Disagreement* (Cambridge: Polity Press, 2014); Jonathan Matheson, *The Epistemic Significance of Disagreement* (London: Palgrave Macmillan, 2015); Richard J. Colledge, 'Rethinking Disagreement: Philosophical Incommensurability and Meta-Philosophy', *Symposium* 18 (2014), 33–55. Peter van Inwagen is an advocate of the steadfast view, 'It Is Wrong, Always, Everywhere, and for Anyone, to Believe Anything, Upon Insufficient Evidence', in *Faith, Freedom, and Rationality*, ed. J. Jordan and D. Howard-Snyder (Lanham: Rowman & Littlefield, 1996), pp. 137–54; Thomas Kelly and Sarah McGrath, 'Are There Any Successful Philosophical Arguments?', in *Being, Freedom, and Method: Themes from the Philosophy of Peter van Inwagen*, ed. John A. Keller (Oxford: Oxford University Press, 2017), pp. 324–42. See also Joshua Thurow, 'Does Religious Disagreement Actually Aid the Case for Theism?', in *Probability in the Philosophy of Religion*, ed. Jake Chandler and Victoria Harrison (Oxford: Oxford University Press, 2012), pp. 209–24; Helen De Cruz, *Religious Disagreement* (Cambridge: Cambridge University Press, 2019). These issues also impinge upon 'the ethics of belief', see Chapter 3.

of modern naturalism. These determine the structure of what follows. Restating that order in terms of the discussion above, the historical fortunes of the ideas of faith and belief will be treated in the next two chapters. The question of how rational proofs relate to the religious beliefs, and how that relation has changed over time will be dealt with in Chapter 4. The fifth chapter will focus on the historical origins of the now familiar natural/supernatural distinction, along with the emergence of the accompanying notions of naturalism and supernaturalism. Chapter 6 will provide an account of how naturalism came to be written into accounts of historical progress.

2

LANGUAGES OF BELIEF

Is the word ever actually used in this way in the language game which is its original home? – What *we* do is to bring words back from their metaphysical to their everyday use.

                Wittgenstein, *Philosophical Investigations*

Something can be incandescently obvious but still utterly unintelligible to us if we lack the conceptual grammar required to interpret it.

                David Bentley Hart, *The Experience of God*[1]

2.1 Lost in Translation

In the winter of 1672, the Provincial of the Jesuits in Paris, Pierre Coton, received a despairing letter from a mission in Port Royal, Acadia (now Annapolis Royal, Nova Scotia). His correspondent, Pierre Biard, reported that the objects of his missionary endeavours – the Mi'kmaq people – were completely lacking in abstract, internal, and spiritual conceptions. They had no sense of metaphysical notions such as 'substance', and distinctions between the virtues of wisdom, fidelity, justice, mercy, gratitude, and piety were largely incomprehensible to them. Most worrying of all, they were innocent of anything that resembled a conventional notion of belief: 'we are still disputing, after a great deal of research and labor, whether they have any word to correspond directly to the word *Credo*, I believe.' Just imagine, Biard continued, what follows for attempts to school the Mi'kmaq in the Creed and the fundamentals of Christianity.[2] Conversion could not

---

[1] Epigraphs: Ludwig Wittgenstein, *Philosophical Investigations*, 2nd ed., trans. G. E. M. Anscombe (Oxford: Blackwell, 1963), §116 (p. 48); David Bentley Hart, *The Experience of God* (New Haven: Yale University Press, 2013), p. 13, reproduced with permission of Yale University Press through PLSclear.

[2] Pierre Biard, 'Lettre au R.P. Provincial, à Paris. Port Royal, January 31, 1612'. *The Jesuit Relations and Allied Documents*, 73 vols., ed. Reuben Gold Thwaites (Cleveland: Burrows

be a matter of persuading the Mi'kmaq to relinquish one set of beliefs and replace them with another. They seemed to have neither competing beliefs, nor a notion of what a belief was.

Not all seventeenth-century missionaries to the Americas regarded the translation of basic Western religious conceptions into native vocabularies an intractable problem. Puritan minister Roger Williams (1603–83) was the founder of the colony of Rhode Island, an abolitionist, and a strong advocate for indigenous rights. He was also a talented linguist and produced the first book on the Narragansett language, including a separate chapter on religion. Here he provides Narragansett equivalents of basic theological concepts – 'God', 'the soul', 'prayer', 'hell' – and even offers a kind a catechism rendered into the native tongue.[3] However, Williams's ambitious translation project was informed by his conviction that the American first peoples had descended from Adam and Noah some five-and-a-half thousand years before. On the basis of this contracted genealogy he also imagined that he had discovered in Narragansett vocabulary etymological links to various Hebrew expressions and, in keeping with this, customs that resembled ancient Jewish practices.[4] All of this was consistent with a relatively common view in the seventeenth century that 'heathen religions' were corrupted and degenerate forms of the original monotheism practised

---

Bros. 1896–1901), vol. 2, pp. 7–11. I am indebted to Ethan H. Shagan for this example and its historical significance. See his informative treatment of this episode in *Birth of Modern Belief*, pp. 195–9. For an account of problems of untranslatability of indigenous American languages, with many further examples, see Sarah Rivett, *Unscripted America: Indigenous Languages and the Origins of a Literary Nature* (Oxford: Oxford University Press, 2017), esp. pp. 11–14, 18, 42–5.

[3] Roger Williams, *A Key into the Languages of America* (London, 1643), pp. 114–32. On the different approaches of French Catholics and English Protestants to indigenous American languages see Gordon Sayre, *Les Sauvages Américains: Representations of Native Americans in French and English Colonial Literature* (Chapel Hill: University of North Carolina Press, 1997); Daniel Wasserman, *Truth in Many Tongues: Religious Conversion and the Languages of the Early Spanish Empire* (University Park: Pennsylvania State University Press, 2020).

[4] Williams, *A Key into the Languages of America*, To the Reader, p. 131. John Eliot's *The Indian Grammar Begun* (Cambridge, MA, 1666) shares similar assumptions. For other examples of the 'Hebraic hypothesis' see Harrison, '*Religion' and the Religions*, pp. 152f., 233f., n. 151; Rivett, *Unscripted America*, pp. 7–8, 12. A related thesis postulated the divine origin of human language, and hence a theoretical unity of languages. This was the prime target of Johann Gottfried von Herder's *Treatise on the Origin of Language* [1772], in *Philosophical Writings*, ed. Michael N. Forster (Cambridge: Cambridge University Press, 2008), pp. 65–164. Directly relevant to our general thesis, Johann Georg Hamann contended that this debate was predicated on a false dichotomy between natural and supernatural. 'The Last Will and Testament of the Knight of the Rose-Cross', in *Writings on Philosophy and Language*, ed. Kenneth Haynes (Cambridge: Cambridge University Press, 2007), pp. 96–110, esp. pp. 99f.

by Adam and the biblical patriarchs.[5] This idea underpinned the earliest forms of comparative religion which, in addition to their acceptance of the universal history set out in the pages of Genesis, also involved the projection onto indigenous cultures of a new early modern conception of religion that focused on beliefs and practices.[6]

These assumptions came under sustained pressure during the eighteenth century with challenges to the authority of the universal history set out in Genesis, along with a growing body of empirical evidence that cast doubt upon the idea of a common origin of all religious beliefs and practices. John Locke's *Essay concerning Human Understanding* (1689) makes reference to travel relations that attest to the existence of whole nations – both civilised and 'uncultivated', that 'want the idea and knowledge of God altogether'.[7] Huguenot philosopher Pierre Bayle argued similarly for the existence of nations of atheists.[8] In the following century, in his *Natural History of Religion* (1757), David Hume flatly rejected the idea that all extant religions were to be understood as either degenerate forms of, or elaborations upon, a primeval monotheism. In short, it was Biard's perspective, rather than that of Williams, that became typical of the understandings of subsequent missionaries and field anthropologists, and which reflected a significant body of opinion among philosophers.[9]

---

[5] Harrison, *'Religion' and the Religions*, pp. 131–9.

[6] For a classic example see William Turner, *The history of all religions in the world, from the creation down to this present* (London, 1695). The alternative explanation of primitive monotheism, favoured by many of the deists, was that there was an original, universal, natural religion. Early universal language schemes of the seventeenth century tended to rely on similar assumptions, bolstered by the Aristotelian conception of language according to which words corresponded directly to mental conceptions which in turn mapped the universal forms or essences of things. See Rhodri Lewis, *Language, Mind, and Nature: Artificial Languages in England from Bacon to Locke* (Cambridge: Cambridge University Press, 2007).

[7] Locke, *Essay* 1.4.8 (pp. 87f.). Also Richard Bentley, *The Folly and Unreasonableness of Atheism*, 4th ed. (London, 1699), pp. 31f. Locke's sources were not entirely reliable, however. For contemporary criticisms of his position see Charles Gildon, 'To Dr R. B– Of a God', in Charles Blount, *Miscellaneous Works* (London, 1695), p. 180; Anthony Earl of Shaftesbury, Letter 8 [1709], *Characteristics of Men, Manners, Opinions, Times*, 3 vols. (Basel, 1790), vol. 1, pp. 345f.; Henry Lee, *Anti-Scepticism: or, Notes upon each Chapter of Mr. Lock's Essay concerning Humane Understanding* (London, 1702), pp. 33–8. For further discussion see 'The Forgotten Proof', Chapter 4, below.

[8] Pierre Bayle, *Oeuvres Diverses de M. Pierre Bayle*, 4 vols. (The Hague: 1727–31), vol. 3, pp. 109a–110b.

[9] Thus Herder: 'All missionaries in all parts of the world complain about the difficulty of communicating Christian concepts to savages in their own languages .... If one is not willing to believe the missionaries, then let one read the philosophers: de la Condamine in *Peru* and on the *Amazon river*, Maupertius in Lapland, etc. *Time, duration, space, essence, matter, body, virtue, justice, freedom, gratitude* do not exist in the tongue of the Peruvians ....' *Origin*

Reports from nineteenth-century missions to the Pacific are replete with observations about a 'lack of any expressions for abstract things' in 'barbaric' and 'uncivilized' languages.[10] The first of the German *Neuendettelsau* missionaries to Papua New Guinea, Johann Flierl, wrote of the language of Kâte people that they have virtually 'no words into and with which to be able to express spiritual and religious concepts'.[11] Lutheran missionaries like Flierl had a particular investment in vernacular languages, since they often sought to translate the Bible, or parts of it, Martin Luther's 1534 German translation of the Bible having provided a powerful precedent. Accordingly, their efforts have played a significant role in the preservation of indigenous languages in New Guinea and Australia.[12] But the lack of a familiar religious terminology inevitably generated significant difficulties of translation (along with some spectacular mis-renderings, as when, to the amusement of his

---

of Language, in *Philosophical Writings*, pp. 118–19. Cf. Paul Broca, early anthropologist and polygenist: 'certain peoples have absolutely no notion of God and the soul and their languages have no point of contact with ours.' *Recherches sur l'hybridité animale en général et sur l'hybridité humaine* (Paris, 1860), p. 656. John Lubbock: 'What Spix and Martius tell us about the Brazilian tribes appears also to be true of many, if not of most, savage races ... they are entirely deficient in words for abstract ideas.' It followed that 'those who assert that even the lowest savages believe in a Supreme Deity, affirm that which is entirely contrary to the evidence'. *Prehistoric Times*, 4th ed. (London: Frederick Norgate, 1878), pp. 586f., 594.

[10] 'Auch eine Schwierigkeit bei der Missionsarbeit', *Kirchliche Mitteilungen aus und über Nordamerika, Australien und Neu-Guinea* 10 (1888), 77, quoted in Daniel Midena, 'Wine into Wineskins: The Neuendettelsau Missionaries' Encounter with Language and Myth in New Guinea', in *Savage Worlds: German Encounters Abroad, 1798–1914*, ed. Matthew Fitzpatrick and Peter Monteath (Manchester: Manchester University Press, 2018), pp. 86–104 (p. 88). I am grateful to Daniel for drawing my attention to these examples. In the nineteenth century these complaints would extend to scientific terminology. See Thomas Babington Macaulay, 'Minute on Indian Education' [1835], in *Speeches, with his Minute on Indian Education*, ed. G. M. Young (Oxford: Oxford University Press, 1935), p. 348.

[11] Johann Flierl, 'Vom Sattelberg', *Kirchliche Mitteilung* 11 (1897), 84, quoted in Midena, 'Wine into Wineskins', p. 90. Kâte is spoken in the Morobe Province, located on the north-eastern coast of Papua New Guinea.

[12] For examples, see Christian Teichelmann and Clamor Schürmann, *Outlines of a Grammar: Vocabulary and Phraseology of the Aboriginal Language of South Australia* (Adelaide, 1840); Clamor Schürmann, *A Vocabulary of the Parnkalla Language, Spoken by the Natives inhabiting the Western Shores of Spencer's Gulf* [1844], facsimile ed. (Adelaide: Public Library of Australia, 1962). Also Mary-Anne Gale, *Dhangum Djorra'wuy Dhäwu: A History of Writing in Aboriginal Languages* (Adelaide: Aboriginal Research Institute, University of South Australia, 1997); Rob Amery, 'Beyond their Expectations: Teichelmann and Schürmann's Efforts to Preserve the Kaurna Language Continue to Bear Fruit', in *The Struggle for Souls and Science – Constructing the Fifth Continent: German Missionaries and Scientists in Australia*, ed. Walter Veit (Alice Springs: Strehlow Research Centre Occasional Paper, 2004), pp. 9–28. For similar preservation efforts in New Zealand, see Paul Moon, 'Missionaries and Māori Language in Nineteenth-Century New Zealand: A Mixed Inheritance', *Journal of Religious History* 43 (2019), 495–510.

Pitjantjatjara auditors, Ronald Trudinger described the coming of the Holy of Spirit recorded in Acts 2:3 as a 'deluge of wallabies' rather than the more canonical 'tongues of fire').[13] More directly to the point, correspondence from the *Neuendettelsau* missionaries reveals a list a problematic terms that closely match those identified by Biard. Antipodean indigenous languages apparently had no way of accommodating 'spiritual concepts', 'higher concepts', and 'Christian notions'. Specifically, there were no equivalents to 'belief', 'Spirit of God', 'blessed', 'miracle', and the verbs 'to love' and 'to worship'.[14]

Moving to the other side of the Pacific and more recent history, the Wari' (or Pakaa Nova) people of the Amazon basin seem similarly bereft of a terminology of belief. The Wari' first became known to the outside world at the beginning of the twentieth century, owing to their attacks on workers constructing the ill-fated, and now long abandoned Madeira-Mamoré railway, undertaken in the hope of affording Bolivian rubber growers access to the Atlantic. Following this unhappy start, more peaceful contacts were made by Protestant missionaries in the 1950s. Translators found in the native language what they thought was an acceptable expression for belief in God in the word *howa* – 'to accept', 'to agree', or 'to think that something is true'. But for the Wari' themselves, the term used for experience of the other dimension of reality was not cognitive, but visual: 'to see'.[15] Their shamans were the ones who 'saw', while Catholic priests and Protestant missionaries were those who 'believed'. Conversion to Christian belief necessarily meant something quite different to those on the two sides of this linguistic divide. Anthropologist Aparecida Vilaça, attempting to offer an explanation for the apparently odd fluctuations in the religious beliefs of this group, concludes: 'the idea of belief to express a relationship to the "supernatural" is, I think, alien to the Wari'.[16]

---

[13] Richard Guilliatt, 'How a Bible Translation Is Preserving the Pitjantjatjara Language', http://ourlanguages.org.au/how-a-bible-translation-is-preserving-the-pitjantjatjara-language-2/, accessed 29 March 2019.

[14] '*Glauben*', '*Geist*', '*Gottes*', '*selig*', '*Wunder*', '*lieben*', '*anbeten*'. Examples from Midena, 'Wine into Wineskins', pp. 98–9.

[15] Hans Blumenberg regards the association of knowledge with vision as a transcultural 'absolute metaphor'. *Paradigms for a Metaphorology*, trans. Robert Savage (Ithaca: Cornell University Press, 2010), pp. 6–7, 35, 62–3; 'Light as a Metaphor for Truth: At the Preliminary Stage of Philosophical Concept Formation', trans. Joel Anderson, in *Modernity and the Hegemony of Vision*, ed. David Michael Levin (Berkeley: University of California Press, 1993), pp. 30–86.

[16] Aparecida Vilaça, 'Christians without Faith: Some Aspects of the Conversion of the Wari' (Pakaa Nova)', *Ethnos* 62 (1997), 91–115 (97).

The cattle herding Dinka tribes of South Sudan (or the Jieng, as they refer to themselves) offer yet another example. In his ground-breaking study of the religion of the Dinka, Godfrey Lienhardt informs us that 'it is not a simple matter to divide the Dinka believer ... from what he believes in, and to describe the latter then in isolation from him as the object of belief'. This relates to the fact that the Dinka, on Lienhardt's account, lack a concept of mind comparable to that of modern Westerners. Inevitably, then, their experiences of non-human 'powers' are not adequately described as 'beliefs', not least because it is these 'powers' that structure their experience.[17] The Western conception of belief, Lienhardt suggests, calls for a distinctive theory of mind that we cannot assume is widely shared.

The cumulative weight of reports such as these has prompted speculation among some anthropologists about whether absence of a notion of belief is less the exception than the rule. Perhaps the Western notion of 'belief', in the big scheme of things, is the odd one out. Social anthropologist Rodney Needham has maintained that 'there are numerous linguistic traditions which make no provision for the expression of belief and which do not recognise such a condition in their psychological assessments'. Belief, in our sense, he concludes, 'is a relatively modern linguistic invention, and it does not correspond, under any aspect, to a real, constant, and distinct resource of the self'.[18] 'Belief' heads Marshall Sahlins's list of ethnographic

---

[17] Godfrey Lienhardt, *Divinity and Experience: The Religion of the Dinka* (Oxford: Clarendon Press, 1961), pp. 155, 149, 170. Cf. *Social Anthropology* (Oxford: Oxford University Press, 1964), p. 141.

[18] Rodney Needham, *Circumstantial Deliveries* (Berkeley: University of California Press, 1982), p. 78. The argument for this thesis is set out in detail in Needham's *Belief, Language and Experience* (Oxford: Blackwell, 1972). See also Jean Pouillon, *Le Cru et le Su* (Paris: Éditions du Seuil, 1993), pp. 17–36; Eduardo Viveiros de Castro, 'The Relative Native', *Hau: Journal of Ethnographic Theory* 3 (2013), 473–502, esp. 490; Wyatt MacGaffey, *Religion and Society in Central Africa: The BaKongo of Lower Zaire* (Chicago: University of Chicago Press, 1986), p. 1; Malcolm Ruel, 'Christians as Believers', in *Religious Organization and Religious Experience*, ed. J. Davis (London: Academic Press, 1982), pp. 9–31; Galina Lindquist and Simon Coleman, 'Introduction: Against Belief?', *Social Analysis* 52 (2008), 1–18; Andrew Buckser, 'Cultural Change and the Meanings of Being Jewish in Copenhagen', *Social Analysis* 52 (2008), 39–55; Catherine Bell, '"The Chinese believe in spirits": Belief and Believing in the Study of Religion', in *Radical Interpretation in Religion*, ed. N. Frankenberry (Cambridge: Cambridge University Press, 2002), pp. 100–28; Jonathan Mair, 'Cultures of Belief', *Anthropological Theory* 12 (2012), 448–66; William F. Hanks, *Converting Words: Maya in the Age of the Cross* (Berkeley: University of California Press, 2010), pp. 131f.; Lisa Landoe Hedrick, 'The Ontological Turn's New Animists and the Concept of Belief', *The Journal of Religion* 103 (2023), 257–82. For a recent defence of a more moderate version of Needham's contention about belief see Arif Ahmepp, 'Belief and Religious "Belief"', *Religious Studies* 56 (2020), 80–94.

terms standing in need of 'considerable rectification'.[19] In evolving a sense of belief, understood as assenting to particular propositions, it looks as though the modern West has taken a unique turn.[20]

How does all of this bear upon the issue of 'belief in the supernatural' and the Humean tendency to regard such belief as an irrational holdover from the past? One thing we might say is that it puts pressure on our assumption that belief – understood as agreeing with, or giving assent to, some proposition – is natural and universal, or that it offers the best way of characterising the ways of knowing and being of those who are not modern and Western. This all the more so when 'belief' is dismissively conjoined with 'the supernatural' – another concept that is conspicuously absent from the vocabularies of many non-Western peoples.[21] (Indeed, as we will see in Chapter 5, the term 'supernatural' was also missing from the Western lexicon until the Middle Ages.) Anthropologist Martin Holbraad has accordingly suggested that to speak of the 'irrational beliefs' of other cultures is 'to shirk analytical responsibility for the failures of our own categorical (or more broadly conceptual) repertoire'.[22] We find a similar

---

[19] Sahlins, *New Science*, p. 12.

[20] Coming at this from a rather different angle, philosopher Martin Heidegger contends that fundamental concepts of Western philosophy – in his specific case, 'Being' – have their own histories and predetermine the kinds of understandings that it is possible for us to arrive at. Martin Heidegger, *Being and Time*, trans. John Macquarrie and Edward Robinson (New York: HarperCollins, 2008), p. 30, and *passim*.

[21] Thus E. E. Evans-Pritchard: 'To us supernatural means very much the same as abnormal or extraordinary. Azande certainly have no such notions of reality. They have no conception of "natural" as we understand it, and therefore neither of the "supernatural" as we understand it. Witchcraft is to Azande an ordinary and not an extraordinary, even though it may in some circumstances be an infrequent, event. It is a normal, and not an abnormal happening.' *Witchcraft, Oracles and Magic among the Azande* (Oxford: Clarendon Press, 1976), p. 80. Cf. Émile Durkheim, *The Elementary Forms of the Religious Life*, trans. Carol Cosman (Oxford: Oxford University Press, 2008), p. 24. For further discussion see 'The Birth of the Supernatural', Chapter 5, below.

[22] Martin Holbraad, 'The Contingency of Concepts', in *Comparative Metaphysics*, ed. Pierre Charbonnier, Gildas Salmon, and Peter Skafish (Lanham: Rowman & Littlefield, 2016), pp. 133–58 (p. 139). Historian Seth Schwartz offers a similar observation about the limitations of our contemporary conceptual apparatus in relation to past religious cultures: 'our modern western language is necessarily inadequate to describe the realities of a radically different culture'. 'How Many Judaisms Were There? A Critique of Neusner and Smith on Definition and Mason and Boyarin on Categorization', *Journal of Ancient Judaism* 2 (2011), 208–38. On this theme also see Daniel Boyarin, 'The Concept of Cultural Translation in American Religious Studies', *Critical Inquiry* 44 (2017), 17–39. For similar treatments in the anthropology literature see Godfrey Lienhardt, 'Modes of Thought', in *The Institutions of Primitive Society, a Series of Broadcast Talks*, ed. E. E. Evans-Pritchard et al. (Glencoe: Free Press, 1954), pp. 96–7; Michael W. Scott, 'The Anthropology of Ontology (Religious Science?)', *Journal of the Royal Anthropological*

sentiment in Marshall Sahlins's characterisation of much of 'received ethnography', said to operate with 'a misleading conceptual apparatus composed of nearly equal parts of transcendentalist equivocation and colonialist condescension'.[23] More directly relevant to Western history, Greg Anderson, in his fascinating account of the beliefs and practices of ancient Athenians, has asked us to consider whether Athenian encounters with the gods might arise not as a consequence of Athenians having a different or distorted perception of the world, but of their world being ontologically different to ours.[24] More generally, he hints that when we dismiss the 'supernatural' experiences of peoples of the past or, by implication, those of other cultures, this is a consequence of uncritically assuming the superiority of our own conceptions of reality.

It follows that the supposedly primitive commitments of others might represent less a systematic failure of their rationality than a symptom of the inadequacy of our own conceptual apparatus. There has been a belated recognition of the parochial and historically contingent nature of Western conceptions of, say, land ownership and private property. Accompanying this has been a growing realisation that the consistency of these conceptions with the relationships to land and country of many indigenous peoples cannot be resolved simply by declaring that modern Western understandings must trump all others. Something similar may well hold true for the repertoire of cherished philosophical concepts that we imagine to be natural and universal but which, no less than our ideas about private property and ownership, have complicated histories of their own. Categories of philosophical analysis such as 'belief', 'natural', and 'supernatural' are neither simply given, nor the unique discoveries of the modern West. The puzzles that we encounter in attempting to understand other cultures – and, indeed, own past – should ideally motivate us to think carefully about the role of our present vocabularies and analytical tools in generating those puzzles. The tendency of modern psychology to concentrate its investigative endeavours almost solely on WEIRD populations (Western, educated, industrialised,

---

Institute 19 (2013), 859–72; Tim Ingold, 'Dreaming of Dragons: On the Imagination of Real Life', *Journal of the Royal Anthropological Institute* 19 (2013), 734–52; Mario Schmidt, 'Godfrey Lienhardt as a Skeptic; or, Anthropology as Conceptual Puzzle-Solving', *HAU: Journal of Ethnographic Theory* 7 (2017), 351–75; and, most recently and relating to the context of Oceania, Anne Ross, 'Challenging Metanarratives: The Past Lives in the Present', *Archaeology in Oceania* 55 (2020), 65–71. Also see other articles in this special issue.

[23] Sahlins, *New Science*, p. 11.

[24] Greg Anderson, *The Realness of Things Past: Ancient Greece and Ontological History* (Oxford: Oxford University Press, 2018).

rich, democratic) does not help, since generalisations based upon this idiosyncratic sample will hardly hold good universally.[25]

As it directly pertains to the issue of 'belief', it turns out that this is not just a straightforward matter of the West versus the rest. Our modern Western understandings of faith and belief have also evolved significantly over time. It is not too much of an exaggeration to say that first-century Jews, Christians, and Pagans, like Biard's Mi'kmaq, had no conception of belief either, at least in our modern sense.[26] When we look carefully at the closest Greek and Latin equivalents to our modern English terms 'faith' and 'belief', it becomes clear that they bear different and more wide-ranging meanings than those we presently attach to them. We are more distant from past believers than we think, and the idea that we share with them a common epistemological vocabulary arises out of mistaken assumptions about the stability of meaning of terms like faith' and 'belief'. At the same time, it is possible to engage in a partial reconstruction of the past meanings of these terms. This enables us to identify some of the crucial historical turning points that have contributed to the formation of what I am suggesting is a distinctive conceptual category that decisively shapes how we now view religious phenomena.

2.2 Faith as Trust

This is not the occasion for an exhaustive history of understandings of 'faith' and 'belief' in the Western intellectual tradition.[27] But we can point to specific moments in the evolution of these ideas that reveal just how distinctive and path-dependent our modern conceptions are. Far and away the most important factor in shaping our modern, Western understandings of belief have been the fortunes of this concept in the emergence and development

---

[25] Literature reviews of the field of experimental psychology reveal that 96 per cent of the research subjects come from Northern Europe, North America, Australia, or Israel. Approximately 70 per cent of this number are American undergraduates. J. Arnett, 'The Neglected 95%: Why American Psychology Needs to Become Less American', *American Psychologist* 63 (2008), 602–14; Joseph Henrich, Steven J. Heine, and Ara Norenzayan, 'The Weirdest People in the World?', *Behavioral and Brain Sciences* 33 (2010), 1–75.

[26] Wilfred Cantwell Smith proposed that no word in the Christian scriptures should be translated by the English 'believe' or belief'. *Faith and Belief* (Princeton: Princeton University Press, 1979), p. 247, n. 3.

[27] Richard A. Muller's *Dictionary of Latin and Greek Theological Terms*, 2nd ed. (Grand Rapids: Baker Books, 2017), offers some 22 different variants and subsets of *fides: fides historica, fides temporaria, fides miraculosa, fides salvifica*, etc. The story is thus a complicated one. See the discussions in Smith, *Faith and Belief*; Shagan, *Birth of Modern Belief*.

of Christianity. The key terms in the first century were the Greek *pistis* and Latin *fides*, which are typically rendered into English as 'faith' or 'belief'.[28] This terminology was central to early Christianity and distinguishes it from both first-century Judaism and the contemporary Graeco-Roman religions. As Teresa Morgan has now established in her magisterial *Roman Faith and Christian Faith* (2015), the primary meanings of the *pistis/fides* lexicon in the first century centre on trust.[29]

---

[28] It is now generally agreed that *pistis* and *fides* are synonymous. See E. Gruen, 'Greek *pistis* and Roman *fides*', *Athenaeum*, new series, 60 (1982), 50–68. However, an important difference between the Greek and the Latin is that while Latin *fides* translates the noun form of the Greek *pistis*, the unrelated verb *credere* (to believe in, trust in) was used to render *pisteuo* (the verb form of *pistis*). See Charleton T. Lewis and Charles Short, *A Latin Dictionary* (Oxford: Clarendon Press, 1962), s.v. *fides* (p. 746). Thus in Latin and English, and in contrast to Greek, there are separate words for 'faith' and 'belief'. German parallels the Greek in having a single root for both forms: *der Glaube, glauben*, while the Romance languages follow the Latin: French *croire, Foi*; Italian *credere, fede*; Spanish *creer, fe*. That said, the English verb 'believe' is a direct cognate of the German *glauben*. See *OED*, s.v. 'believe', v., and Smith, *Faith and Belief*, pp. 103–27. Smith suggests an equivalence between the English 'believe' and the German *belieben* (to love, hold dear), but in spite of the apparent resemblance the connection is not firmly established. *Belief and History* (Charlottesville: University Press of Virginia, 1977), pp. 41–5. Other Latin terms could lay some claim to be related to 'beliefs', each with its own subtly distinct connotations: *assensio, opinio, notitia, persuasio, confidentia, fiducia, credendum*. These partial synonyms are relevant because of later controversies about whether the Latin Vulgate had correctly conveyed the meaning of the original sense of *pistis*, particularly as it related to the weight to be placed upon trust (*fides* and *fiducia*) as opposed to intellectual assent (*assensio* and *notitia*). For examples see Shagan, *Birth of Modern Belief*, pp. 16–19. I am grateful to Adam Bowles for discussions about these issues and for his gentle reminder that etymology does not determine meaning.

[29] Teresa Morgan, *Roman Faith and Christian Faith: Pistis and Fides in the Early Roman Empire and Early Churches* (Oxford: Oxford University Press, 2015). The relevant Greek terms are *pistis* (n. faith, faithfulness trust, confidence); *pistos* (adj. trustworthy); *pisteuo* (v. to trust, have faith in, believe). For lexical and biblical studies see Rudolf Bultmann and Artur Weiser, 'πιστεύω, πίστις, etc.', in *Theological Dictionary of the New Testament*, 10 vols., ed. Gerhard Kittel and Gerhard Friedrich (Grand Rapids: Eerdmans, 1977), vol. 6, pp. 174–228; Peter Oakes, '*Pistis* as Relational Way of Life in Galatians', *Journal for the Study of the New Testament* 40 (2018), 255–75; Matthew W. Bates, 'The External-Relational Shift in Faith (*Pistis*) in New Testament Research: Romans 1 as Gospel-Allegiance Test Case', *Currents in Biblical Research* 18 (2020), 176–202; James L. Kinneavy, *Greek Rhetorical Origins of Christian Faith: An Inquiry* (New York: Oxford University Press, 1987); Ruel, 'Christians as Believers'; Olga Weijers, 'Some Notes on *Fides* and Related Words in Medieval Latin', *Archivum Latinitatis Medii Aevi* 40 (1977), 77–192. Historical and theological accounts include G. Freyberger, *Fides: étude sémantique et religieuse depuis les origines jusqu'à l'époque Augustéenne*, 2nd ed. (Paris: Société d'Édition Les Belles Lettres, 2009); Marie George, 'Aquinas on the Nature of Trust', *Thomist: A Speculative Quarterly Review* 70 (2006), 103–23, esp. 105; Karl Barth, *Church Dogmatics*, ed. Thomas F. Torrance and Geoffrey Bromiley, 13 vols. (Edinburgh: T&T Clark, 1979), vol. I/1, pp. 228–47; Paul Tyson, *Faith's Knowledge* (Eugene: Pickwick, 2013), pp. 59–82; Graham Ward, *Unbelievable: Why We Believe and Why We Don't* (London: I. B. Tauris, 2014). Philosophical discussions that focus on these

This recognition of the centrality of trust only gets us so far, however, because our natural tendency is to subject 'trust' to further analysis and ask after the extent to which it might be understood as a cognitive attitude, an emotion, a virtue, or a set of social relations. First-century sources evince no such distinctions. As Morgan puts it, faith is treated as 'simultaneously cognitive and affective, active and relational'.[30] The relational aspect of faith, which is the most central, extended to the trustworthiness of God, to trust or confidence in God, trust in the person of Jesus, and trust among persons in the Christian community. Faith was also understood as a divine gift, and one that demanded a response of obedience. It was linked to a set of behaviours and obligations. There is little evidence that faith was understood primarily as right belief, or as assenting to propositions. Neither, at first, was there a conception of '*the* faith', a body of doctrines to which orthodox Christians subscribed.[31]

All this is reflected in how the earliest Christians thought of themselves – not as a community set apart by the unique set of propositional beliefs to which they subscribed, but as 'those who trust' or 'the faithful'.[32] Second-century Christian self-identifications expand into a range of expressions, but still retain something of this sense. Christians embody a form of 'godliness', a 'mode of worship', a 'new race', 'a new way of life' – self-conceptions that also emphasise the relational and non-cognitive.[33] The descriptor 'Christian',

---

issues include William Lad Sessions, *The Concept of Faith: A Philosophical Investigation* (Ithaca: Cornell University Press, 1994); Michael Pace and Daniel J. McLaughlin, 'Judaeo-Christian Faith as Trust and Loyalty', *Religious Studies* 58 (2022), 30–60; John Bishop; *Believing by Faith: An Essay in the Epistemology and Ethics of Religious Belief* (New York: Oxford University Press, 2007); J. L. Kvanvig, 'The Idea of Faith as Trust: Lessons in Noncognitivist Approaches to Faith', in *Reason and Faith: Themes from Richard Swinburne*, ed. M. Bergmann and J. Brower (Oxford: Oxford University Press, 2016), pp. 4–26.

[30] Morgan, *Roman Faith and Christian Faith*, p. 19.

[31] 'Propositionality', Morgan observes, 'is often less important than has often been assumed' (*Roman Faith and Christian Faith*, p. 30). On the connection of *pistis* to explicit belief, she observes that 'no Greek speaker would have coined the term *hoi pistoi* to mean "those who believe"' (p. 240). Further: 'to interpret *hē pistis* as "the faith" in anything like the modern sense in the New Testament is anachronistic' (p. 504). See also C. Kavin Rowe, *One True Life: The Stoics and Early Christians as Rival Traditions* (New Haven: Yale University Press, 2015), p. 104. For an earlier and opposing view see J. Fitzmeyer, 'The Designations of Christians in Acts and their Significance', in *Unité et Diversité dans l'eglise* (Vatican City: Editrice Vaticana, 1989), pp. 223–36. It may be relevant in this connection, that in the Geneva Bible (1599) and King James Version (1611) the noun 'belief' appears only once (albeit on different occasions in each, respectively Daniel 3:1 and 2 Thess. 2:13). The word 'faith' appears in those translations, respectively, 250 and 160 times.

[32] *Hoi pisteuontes/pistoi*. Morgan, *Roman Faith and Christian Faith*, pp. 234–41.

[33] *Epistle to Diognetus* 1.1. Cf. 1 Peter 2:9; Tertullian, *Against the Nations* 1.8; Minucius Felix, *Octavius* 5.1; Eusebius, *Preparation for the Gospel* 1.2. For discussion of early

we should remind ourselves, was initially an outsider's term and remained so for some time. Extending well into the Middle Ages, and in keeping with the New Testament terminology, the expression that Christian communities most often used for themselves was 'the faithful' (*fideles*) rather than 'Christians' (*christiani*).[34] It is significant in all of this (as I and others have argued at length elsewhere) that there was no concept 'religion' available at this time – or at least not one that equates to our modern conception. The idea of distinct religions, characterised by sets of beliefs and practices, is also a development that is peculiar to the modern West.[35]

While there was undoubtedly something novel in these understandings of faith in early Christianity, there were also important continuities with the usages in classical and Hebrew literature that are worth briefly mentioning. Looking to the closest equivalents of *pistis* in the Hebrew Bible, we encounter the idea of confidence in God based on his past acts, along

---

Christian identity see Denise Kimber Buell, *Why This New Race? Ethnic Reasoning within Early Christianity* (New York: Columbia University Press, 2005), pp. 23ff.; A. P. Johnson, *Ethnicity and Argument in Eusebius' "Praeparatio Evangelica"* (Oxford: Oxford University Press, 2006); Judith Lieu, *Christian Identity in the Jewish and Graeco-Roman World* (Oxford: Oxford University Press, 2004); Philip Harland, *Dynamics of Identity in the World of the Early Christians* (London: T&T Clark, 2009); Matthew Thiessen, *Contesting Conversion: Genealogy, Circumcision, and Identity in Ancient Judaism and Christianity* (Oxford: Oxford University Press, 2011), esp. pp. 143–8; Harrison, *Territories*, pp. 34–8. See also Christoph Markschies, *Kaiserzeitliche Christliche Theologie und ihre Insitutionen: Prolegomena zur einer Geschichte der antiken christlichen Theologie* (Tübingen: Mohr Siebeck, 2007).

[34] Elias J. Bickerman, 'The Name of Christians', *Harvard Theological Review* 42 (1949), 109–24; Simon C. Mimouni, 'Qu'est-ce qu'un "chrétien" aux Ier et IIe siècles? Identité ou conscience?', *Annali di storia dell' esegesi* 267 (2010), 11–34. John Van Engen points out that in Thomas Aquinas the ratio of uses of *christiani* (nominative plural forms), to *fideles* is about 1:4. *Religion in the History of the Medieval West* (London: Routledge, 2004), p. 50, n. 7. For changes in the traditional use of the term *fideles* at the time of the Reformation, see Scott H. Hendrix, *Ecclesia in Via* (Leiden: Brill, 1974), pp. 155–215.

[35] On the question of when Christianity became a religion see Harrison, *Territories*, pp. 34–44, and *passim*; 'Religion' and the Religions; Edwin Judge, 'Was Christianity a Religion?', in *The First Christians in the Roman World*, ed. James R. Harrison (Tübingen: Mohr Siebeck, 2008), pp. 404–9; Larry Hurtado, *Destroyer of the Gods: Early Christian Distinctiveness in the Roman World* (Waco: Baylor University Press, 2016), pp. xi–xiv, 37–44. On the concept of religion more generally, see Smith, *Meaning and End of Religion*; Harrison, 'Religion' and the Religions; Brent Nongbri, *Before Religion: A History of a Modern Concept* (New Haven: Yale University Press, 2013); Talal Asad, *Genealogies of Religion: Discipline and Reasons of Power in Christianity and Islam* (Baltimore: Johns Hopkins University Press, 1993); Guy Stroumsa, *A New Science: The Discovery of Religion in the Age of Reason* (Cambridge, MA: Harvard University Press, 2010); Carlin A. Barton and Daniel Boyarin, *Imagine No Religion: How Modern Abstractions Hide Ancient Realities* (New York: Fordham University Press, 2016); Nathan Ristuccia, '*Lex*: A Study on Medieval Terminology for Religion', *Journal of Religious History* 43 (2019), 532–48.

with connotations of trust in God's promises.[36] As already noted, the New Testament references also include an element of obedience, and these are even more prominent in the Hebrew.[37] Again, though, there is little emphasis on 'beliefs' (plural), or the idea of giving assent to doctrinal claims.[38]

Precedents in the classical Greek literature also have affinities with the New Testament references, with *pistis* referring primarily to confidence or trust, and particularly trust between persons.[39] In the philosophical works of Plato and Aristotle, because trust (*pistis*) was sometimes thought to entail a degree of uncertainty, it was occasionally contrasted with certain knowledge or 'science' (*epistēmē*).[40] In the *Republic*, Plato consigns *pistis* to the category of 'opinion' (*doxa*), which has a lower grade of certainty than 'science' (*epistēmē*). These are not understood as forms of knowledge, however, but affections of the soul, and part of Plato's intention is to downplay the significance of the world of the senses, to which belong the less certain affections of conjecture and opinion.[41] The basic thrust of Plato's position, then, is

---

[36] אמונה (*emunah*) is the term that is rendered '*pistis*' in the Septuagint (the Greek translation of the Hebrew Bible produced in the third and second centuries BCE).

[37] Bultmann and Weiser, 'πιστεύω, πίστις, etc.', pp. 182–96; Morgan, *Roman Faith and Christian Faith*, pp. 176–211; Emilio Di Somma, *Fides and Secularity: Beyond Charles Taylor's Open Faith* (Eugene: Pickwick, 2018), pp. 42–8.

[38] Smith, *Belief and History*, ch. 3; Kinneavy, *Greek Rhetorical Origins of Christian Faith*, pp. 6–7; Shagan, *Birth of Modern Belief*, pp. 15–16; Boyarin, 'The Concept of Cultural Translation in American Religious Studies'.

[39] Propositional belief seems not to have played much role in ancient Greek religion, although this claim has been challenged. Simon Price contends that belief was not an operative concept in Greek religion. *Rituals and Power: The Roman Imperial Cult in Asia Minor* (Cambridge: Cambridge University Press, 1984), pp. 10f. See his *Religions of the Ancient Greeks* (Cambridge: Cambridge University Press, 1999), pp. 126f. on the absence of creed and theology. Morgan provides more detail but also tends in this direction in *Roman Faith and Christian Faith*, pp. 75f., 120–2, 172–5. But cf. Henk Versnel, *Coping with the Gods: Wayward Readings in Greek Theology* (Leiden: Brill, 2011), pp. 544f. For both sides of the case see Thomas Harrison, 'Beyond the Polis? New Approaches to Greek Religion', *Journal of Hellenic Studies* 135 (2015), 165–80.

[40] In other contexts, however, *pistis* seems to exclude uncertainty. See Plato, *Republic* 505e; Aristotle, *De anima* 428a23–4. For Plotinus, too, it seems to signify a state of certainty: 'the contemplation, in one so conditioned, remains absorbed within as having acquired certainty [*pisteuein*] to rest upon. The brighter the certainty [*pistis*], the more tranquil is the contemplation.' Plotinus, *Enneads* 3.8.6, trans. Stephen MacKenna and B. S. Page (Chicago: William Benton, 1953), pp. 131–2, Greek in LCL 442, p. 378. On translating *epistēmē*, particularly in Aristotle, H. S. Thayer, 'Aristotle on the Meaning of Science', *Philosophical Inquiry* 1 (1979), 87–104; Robert Pasnau, *After Certainty: A History of Our Epistemic Ideals and Illusions* (Oxford: Oxford University Press, 2017), pp. 5, 142f.

[41] Plato ranks *pistis* as third out of four affections that relate to the truth and reality: science (*epistēmē*), understanding (*dianoia*), belief/trust (*pistis*), conjecture (*eikasia*). The first two are classified as intellection (*noesis*), the last two as opinion (*doxa*). *Republic* 533e–534a. In the *Republic* 511d–e the list is the same, with the exception that it begins with reason (*noesis*).

more or less opposite to what we now tend to hold: for us, it is natural to assume that more certainty is to be found in the material realm and in matters of empirical fact. Although Aristotle's priorities are different, he follows Plato in observing a distinction between knowledge and belief/opinion.[42]

Some of the Church Fathers sought to engage with these philosophical traditions, not least to deflect accusations that Christianity had abandoned any attempt at rational justification of its central claims. Clement of Alexandria (c.150–c.215), a convert to Christianity who was well versed in Greek philosophy, argued that while Christian faith was distinctively different from anything that had come before, it was not inconsistent with the principles of logic taught in the philosophical schools. Aristotle, for example, had proposed that genuine knowledge or 'science' (*epistēmē*) was based on logical demonstration. But he had also pointed out that the process of demonstration must begin somewhere. If an infinite regress is be avoided, and knowledge/science is possible at all, these must be premises that are themselves certain but undemonstrated.[43] Geometrical and logical axioms, common notions, the consensus of 'the wise', innate ideas or preconceptions (*prolēpseis*), were all proposed as possible first principles. Clement argued that 'faith' occupied a similarly foundational position for Christians, with its reliability guaranteed by its divine origins.[44] It followed that faith

---

Cf. *Timaeus* 29c. Opinion relates to the physical world, knowledge to the intelligible world. On the danger of equating Plato's *pistis* with the later Christian conception see Paul Shorley's comments in Plato, *The Republic, Books 6–10*, LCL 276, p. 117. See also Ward, *Unbelievable*, pp. 23–6.

[42] Aristotle, *Posterior Analytics* 88a3–89b5. This is a straightforward contrast between *epistēmē* and *doxa*. For a comparison of Plato and Aristotle on this issue see Gail Fine, 'Aristotle's Two Worlds: Knowledge and Belief in "Posterior Analytics" 1.33', *Proceedings of the Aristotelian Society*, new series, 110 (2010), 323–46. The terminology of 'belief' in Aristotle is as complicated as that of 'knowledge' and 'science'. Fred D. Miller observes: 'Many of Aristotle's key terms are hard to translate, but the topic of belief presents exceptional challenges especially for Greekless readers, because Aristotle uses a wide variety of terms for belief, each of which is translated in different ways. The problem is compounded by the fact that he wields a panoply of terms for knowledge as well.' 'Aristotle on Belief and Knowledge', in *Reason and Analysis in Ancient Greek Philosophy*, ed. Georgios Anagnostopoulos and Fred D. Miller (Dordrecht: Springer, 2013), pp. 285–307 (p. 305); cf. Lloyd P. Gerson, *Ancient Epistemology* (Cambridge: Cambridge University Press, 2012), p. 2.

[43] Aristotle, *Posterior Analytics* 72b5–7. In *Topics* Aristotle explains that such premises 'command belief through themselves and not through anything else; for regarding the first principles of science it is unnecessary to ask any further question as to "why"'. *Topics* 100b18–19 (LCL 391, p. 273).

[44] 'In point of fact, the philosophers admit that the first principles of all things are indemonstrable. So that if there is demonstration at all, there is an absolute necessity that there be something that is self-evident, which is called primary and indemonstrable. Consequently all demonstration is traced up to indemonstrable faith.' *Stromata* 8.3 (ANF 12, 494). The

was not so much a lower grade of knowledge as the necessary foundation for the construction of any 'science'. Faith, for Clement, was the solution to a logical difficulty of which the philosophers had been well aware. At the same time, Clement insisted that knowing God is not simply a matter of reasoning from the correct premises: there are moral impediments that must first be cleared away. It is the 'pure in heart' who see God.[45] This, too, was contiguous with the contemporary understanding of philosophy as primarily a moral enterprise involving spiritual exercises.

It would be a mistake, then, to think that there was an ancient 'philosophical' literature with its own technical epistemological vocabulary that might be placed into a simple relation to a comparable 'religious' terminology. In the first century the philosophical traditions present themselves as competing ways of life. In so far as they have doctrinal content, that content is to be grasped within the mode of living prescribed by the relevant school. Christianity and Stoicism, for example, might seem to be offering rival truth claims about the world, but these are better understood, as C. Kavin Rowe has persuasively argued, not as 'individual statements to be taken as true or false, as just justified or not, case by case' but as 'summoning people to a different pattern of being in the world'.[46] It was not, then, a simple matter of weighing up rival truth claims, along with relevant supporting arguments, since the force of the respective truths becomes apparent only through the adoption of the prescribed way of life. Christian 'faith', then, is not easily translatable into a generic philosophical language, or slotted into

---

source of faith, in turn was the divine *Logos* (reason) and the scriptures. *Stromata* 7.16.95, 8.3.7. For Clement's views on faith as a first principle see Andrew Radde-Gallwitz, *Basil of Caesarea, Gregory of Nyssa, and the Transformation of Divine Simplicity* (Oxford: Oxford University Press, 2009), pp. 38–66; Eric Osborn, 'Arguments for Faith in Clement of Alexandria', *Vigiliae Christianae* 48 (1994), 1–24; Andrei Giulea Dragos, 'Apprehending "Demonstrations" from the First Principle: Clement of Alexandria's Phenomenology of Faith', *The Journal of Religion* 89 (2009), 187–213.

[45] Clement, *Stromata* 1.12; 5.1.11; 5.4.25. Cf. Matthew 5:8.

[46] Rowe, *One True Life*, p. 244. The classic treatment of philosophy as a way of life is Pierre Hadot, *Philosophy as a Way of Life: Spiritual Exercises from Socrates to Foucault*, trans. Arnold I. Davidson (Oxford: Blackwell, 1995) and *What Is Ancient Philosophy?*, trans. Michael Chase (Cambridge, MA: Harvard University Press, 2002). Hadot's *'formes de vie'* is also related to Wittgenstein's *Lebensformen*. See *Philosophy as a Way of Life*, pp. 17f., 280; *Wittgenstein et les limites du langage* (Paris: Vrin, 2004). Other works on this theme include Alexander Nehamas, *The Art of Living: Socratic Reflections from Plato to Foucault* (Berkeley: University of California Press, 1998); John Sellars, *The Art of Living: The Stoics on the Nature and Function of Philosophy* (Aldershot: Ashgate, 2003); Berold Thomassen, *Metaphysik als Lebensform: Untersuchungen zur Grundlegung der Metaphysik im Metaphysikkommentar Alberts des Grossen* (Münster: Aschendorff, 1985); Michel Foucault, *The Care of the Self*, vol. 3 of *The History of Sexuality*, trans. Robert Hurley (New York: Vintage, 1986), esp. pp. 39–68.

a continuum of epistemological categories, or graded in terms of its relative certainty in relation to other species of knowledge.

That was to change when the full canon of the Aristotelian corpus found its way back into Western Europe in the twelfth and thirteenth centuries. But during this later period philosophy presented itself in a different guise. No longer a living tradition able to compete with Christianity as an alternative way of life, it became instead a resource for dialectical reasoning, a toolkit that could assist with the systematic articulation of a new Christian 'theology'. Philosophical doctrines and techniques, detached from their original therapeutic context, were accorded a kind of neutral instrumentality. What look like the epistemological categories of the ancients were thrust into prominence as scholastic thinkers began to grapple with such questions as how Christian faith relates to Aristotelian understandings of 'science' (*epistēmē*, now rendered into the Latin *scientia*).[47] Subsequently, when trust became marginalised in discussions of faith, as in a number of early modern treatments, the prospect for regarding faith and belief as deficient forms of knowledge arose for the first time.[48] From the seventeenth century onwards, then, belief was folded into what we now call epistemology (although the word itself did not make an appearance until the mid-nineteenth century) with genuine knowledge understood as true belief *plus* some justificatory condition.[49] This gave rise to a commonplace

---

[47] On this category in Aristotle see Harrison, *Territories*, pp. 16–18. In the tenth century, al-Fārābī had already begun to discuss the conditions for certain knowledge, drawing on Aristotle's *Posterior Analytics*. See Deborah L. Black, 'Knowledge (*'Ilm*) and Certainty (*Yaqīn*) in al-Fārābī's Epistemology', *Arabic Sciences and Philosophy* 14 (2006), 11–45. (The Arabic *'ilm* translates the Greek *epistēmē*.) See also Pasnau, *After Certainty*, pp. 27–8, 176–7.

[48] Precedents for this are already evident in some second-century Pagan critiques of Christian faith. Celsus thus complained that Christians did not support their beliefs with reason: 'Some do not even want to give or to receive a reason for what they believe, and use such expressions as "Do not ask questions: just believe".' Origen of Alexandria, *Contra Celsum* 1.9, trans. Henry Chadwick (Cambridge: Cambridge University Press, 1980), p. 12. Galen offered a similar remark in Εἰς τὸ πρῶτον κινοῦν ἀκίνητον, quoted in Richard Walzer, *Galen on Jews and Christians* (London: Oxford University Press, 1949), p. 14.

[49] For the coining of the English 'epistemology' see *The Eclectic Magazine of Foreign Literature, Science, and Art*, vol. 12 (November 1847), p. 317, note, where 'epistemology' is suggested as a translation of Fichte's '*Wissenschaftslehre*'. Earlier, Alexander G. Baumgarten had used another possible contender, '*gnoseologia*' in his *Sciagraphia encyclopaediae philosophicae* (Halle an der Saale, 1769). By 1854, James F. Ferrier could state that epistemology and ontology together constitute the main branches of metaphysics. *Institutes of Metaphysic* (Edinburgh: William Blackwood and Sons, 1854), p. 46, and *passim*. Google ngrams suggest a steady rise in frequency of the term from the 1850s, with an exponential increase from 1960, peaking in 1997. 'Ontology', incidentally, is of earlier coinage (seventeenth century), and with the ascendancy of 'epistemology' and experimental natural philosophy is regarded

philosophical definition of knowledge as 'justified true belief' which is then often read back into ancient philosophical texts and indeed frequently attributed to Plato.[50] In fact, for both Plato and Aristotle, knowledge (*epistēmē*) and belief (*doxa*) seem to have different objects, complicating readings that regard one as a subset of the other. (And this, even if we disregard further difficulties of translation.) For now, though, suffice it to say that observing some distance between faith and belief on the one hand, and propositional knowledge on the other, was not peculiar to the canonical documents of the Jewish and Christian traditions. Only much later was faith relocated from a social sphere in which trust was at the centre into an epistemological framework in which it comes to be understood primarily in terms of its relation to generic and disembodied ways of knowing.

There were, however, even in the first century, indications of the potential for this kind of transition. In spite of the dominance of the relational aspects of faith over the cognitive, we encounter instances of what Morgan has termed the 'reification' of *pistis/fides*, in which the trust relationship is objectified or given expression in some tangible form. Examples include oaths of allegiance, letters of credit, and, in the religious context, the idea of the formal covenant.[51] Necessarily, moreover, trust does not exist without something being held to be true about the objects of trust (even if held implicitly or tacitly). To trust in God is to be committed to the view that God is trustworthy: belief *in* implies belief *that*, in modern philosophical parlance. The idea that *pistis/fides* should entail an element of doctrinal commitment became more prominent as divisions arose within early Christian communities. While these were often to do with practices, doctrinal diversity and 'false teaching' also became a matter of increasing concern. Addressing himself to the dangers of schism in the early Church, Ignatius of Antioch (b. *c.* AD 50) insisted that possession of genuine Christian faith entailed the affirmation that Jesus was the Son of God, born of a virgin, crucified by

---

with increasing suspicion. For discussion of the novelty of the term, and its significance for understanding the history of philosophy, see Pasnau, *After Certainty*, pp. 139–41. See also Jan Woleński, 'History of Epistemology', in *Handbook of Epistemology*, ed. I. Niiniluoto, M. Sintonen, and J. Woleński (Berlin: Springer, 2004), pp. 3–54, esp. p. 3.

[50] Plato, *Theaetetus* 201c–d. For an extended critique of this anachronistic reading of Plato see Gerson, *Ancient Epistemology*, pp. 27–61. The exact formula 'justified true belief' dates only from the twentieth century, and difficulties with it were definitively set out by Edmund Gettier, 'Is Justified True Belief Knowledge?', *Analysis* 23 (1963), 121–3. On the history of the justified true belief condition see Mark Kaplan, 'It's Not What You Know that Counts', *The Journal of Philosophy* 82 (1985), 350–63; and Julien Dutant, 'The Legend of the Justified True Belief Analysis', *Philosophical Perspectives* 29 (2015), 95–145.

[51] Morgan, *Roman Faith and Christian Faith*, pp. 120–3, 181, 267, 291–2.

Pontius Pilate and Herod, and resurrected from the dead.[52] This tendency to codify the content of Christian belief, which culminates in the composition of formal creedal statements in the fourth and fifth centuries, is a prominent instance of the reification of *pistis/fides*.

The beginnings of the reification of faith were inseparable from changes in the authority structures of the early Church, which can be understood along the lines of Max Weber's notion of 'the routinization of charisma'.[53] Weber adopted the term 'charisma' directly from the Greek of the Pauline epistles, where it refers to gifts bestowed by God on the Christian community (one of which, incidentally, was the gift of faith). On the Weberian account, personal charismatic authority is inherently unstable on account of the natural lifespan of the individuals in whom it is vested. A successful transition of authority therefore requires a process of 'routinisation' in which personal charisma is transmuted into more enduring structures. Typically, charismatic authority devolves onto traditional leadership structures, legal-rational bureaucracies, or some combination of both. In the case of the Christian Church we witness these two elements in the idea of an apostolic succession and in the development of a hierarchical priesthood that enjoyed an inherited authority and the charisma of office. Ignatius, again, offers an instructive description of these adjustments in the evolving authority structures of the early Church: 'the bishop presiding in the place of God, and with the presbyters in the place of the council of the apostles, and with the deacons, who are most dear to me, entrusted with the business of Jesus Christ'.[54] The bureaucratic elements consisted not only in the gradual establishment of the structures of the Church and formalisation of its rituals, but also in the composition of creedal formulations that answer to the rationally established norms, decrees, and rules that for Weber characterise legal-rational bureaucracies. (Looking ahead, we will witness an analogous process in early modern formalisations of 'scientific' knowledge, when *scientia* ceased to be characteristic of an individual mind and became cumulative, corporate, and transgenerational.) These objectifying tendencies converge in the promulgation of the formal creeds and symbols of the fourth and fifth centuries – the Nicene Creed (325, 381) and the Symbol of Chalcedon (451).

---

[52] Ignatius, *Epistle to the Smyrnaeans* 1. 'Immovable faith' (ἀκινήτῳ πίστει) consists in being 'fully persuaded' (πεπληροφορημένους) of these truths. *Apostolic Fathers* (LCL), 2 vols., vol. 1, p. 296. See also Morgan, *Roman Faith and Christian Faith*, pp. 512–13.

[53] Max Weber, *Theory of Social and Economic Organization*, trans. A. R. Anderson and Talcott Parsons (New York: Free Press, 1947), pp. 363ff. Weber adopted the term 'charisma' from the Greek of the Pauline epistles in which it refers to divinely bestowed 'gifts'.

[54] Ignatius, *Letter to the Magnesians* 2, 6 (LCL 24, pp. 246f.).

2.3 Creedal Commitments

In the summer of 325, the first of the Christian emperors, Constantine the Great, convened a council in Nicaea (now Iznik, north-western Turkey) to settle matters of contested doctrine and fix the date of Easter. He invited some 1,800 bishops from across the Roman Empire, with some 300 eventually making the all-expenses-paid journey.[55] On 19 June, after a month of sitting, the council promulgated the original Nicene Creed, consisting of twelve doctrinal articles prefaced by the phrase 'We believe'.[56] While, as the example of Ignatius makes plain, informal creedal statements had been around long before this, the Nicene Creed has come to be regarded as the definitive statement of Christian belief and is typically understood as embodying the propositional essence of Christianity.[57]

Constantine, it must be said, had been less concerned with the precise content of Christian doctrines than with the preservation of social order throughout his empire. In the period leading up to the council he had been troubled by reports of civil unrest in Alexandria occasioned by doctrinal disputes. Writing to the bishops concerned, he expressed his fears of 'tumults' and 'sedition' and chastised them for placing their 'minute investigations' of 'unimportant matters' above the unity of 'one faith, one sentiment, and one covenant of the Godhead'. His own preference was to privilege a unity of worship, with the bishops keeping their potentially divisive theological speculations to themselves.[58] In the end, that did not happen. Constantine

---

[55] Estimates of attendees vary from 250 to 318. Socrates, *Ecclesiastical History* 1.9; Eusebius, *Life of Constantine* 3.7; Theodoret, *Ecclesiastical History* 1.7. For the history of the council see J. N. D. Kelly, *Early Christian Creeds*, 3rd ed. (London: Routledge, 1972), pp. 205–30.

[56] 'We believe ...' (Gk. Πιστεύομεν, Lat. *Credimus*). For versions of the Nicene Creed, see Kelly, *Early Christian Creeds*. Greek and Latin texts in Heinrich Denzinger (ed.), *Enchiridion Symbolorum*, 34th ed. (Freiburg: Herder, 1965), §§125–6 (pp. 52f.). The plural form implies not simply a personal confession, but a statement of communal identity.

[57] For earlier creedal statements see Alastair C. Stewart, 'The Early Alexandrian Baptismal Creed: Interrogative or Declaratory ... or Both?', *Questions liturgiques* 95 (2014), 237–53; Wolfram Kinzig, 'The Creed in Liturgy: Prayer or Hymn?', in *Jewish and Christian Liturgy and Worship*, ed. Albert Gerhards and Clemens Leonard (Leiden: Brill, 2007), pp. 229–46; and, more generally, Kelly, *Creeds of the Churches*, chs. 1–6. The original statement produced at Nicaea was subsequently modified at the Council of Constantinople (381) to produce the Niceno-Constantinopolitan creed, which is now known simply as 'the Nicene Creed'. It is accepted as authoritative by the Roman Catholic Church, the Eastern Orthodox Church, and most Protestant denominations.

[58] 'Let not this diversity of opinion, which has excited dissension among you, by any means cause discord and schism .... Let there be one faith, one sentiment and one covenant of the Godhead: but those minute investigations which ye enter into among yourselves with so much nicety ... should remain in the secret recesses of the mind.' Socrates, *Ecclesiastical History* 1.7 (*NPNF* II, vol. 2, pp. 6–7). Also Photius, *Bibliotheca* 127 (*NPNF* II,

2.3 CREEDAL COMMITMENTS

was compelled to convene the historic council and, fatefully, matters that he had deemed minute and unimportant became enshrined in the Christian creeds as core articles of belief. It should be said, parenthetically, that while Constantine is sometimes criticised for his theological naïvety and indifference to the specifics of Christian belief, he represented a long-standing tradition in which state religion was primarily about the promotion of cohesion and unity – typically expressed through ritual acts – rather than doctrinal conformity. 'Religion' in this sense, was rightly directed worship, not correct belief.

It is natural for us to think of these creeds as sets of propositions that constitute the content of the 'Christian faith' or the 'Christian religion'. Belief, understood in this way, is about understanding and agreeing with, or 'assenting' to, the propositions set out in the creed. On the face of it, moreover, the creeds specify precisely what counts as orthodox Christianity and what should be regarded as heretical. The practice of marginalising and persecuting heretics reinforces this perception that at its heart Christianity is about believing a set of propositions. The fact that the North African bishops were prepared to resist the imposition of Constantine's practice-oriented understanding of Christianity also suggests that the conciliar period represents a new phase in Christian understandings of faith and belief.

Yet, while these creedal statements place a premium on the importance of lending intellectual assent to propositions, they also preserve some of the original elements of trust that were associated with faith and belief.[59] The formulaic opening profession 'We believe' can still be taken to mean 'We place our trust in …' rather than 'We believe in the existence of …'.[60]

---

vol. 1, p. 71). Sozomen, *Ecclesiastical History* 1.16 (*NPNF* II, vol. 2, p. 252). This was consistent with a traditional view of religion (*religio*) as rightly directed worship, rather than doctrinal conformity.

[59] Consider, also, some theological discussions of creedal formula which suggest that they aim at the preservation of mystery, over against more rationalising heretical formulations. See Andrew Louth, *Discerning the Mystery: An Essay on the Nature of Theology* (Oxford: Clarendon Press, 1983), p. 71; Rowan Williams, *On Christian Theology* (Oxford: Wiley Blackwell, 2000), p. 101.

[60] Augustine tells us that to 'believe in God' [*credere in*] is 'to love Him, by believing to esteem highly, by believing to go into Him and be incorporated into His members'. '*Quid est ergo credere in eum? Credendo amare, credendo diligere, credendo in eum ire, et eius membris incorporari.*' *PL* 35: 1631. English translation in Augustine, *Homilies on the Gospel of John*, Tractate 29, 6 (*NPNF* I, vol. 7, p. 185); *Expositions of the Psalms* 77, 8 in *Works*, vol. III/18, p. 98. See also Augustine, Sermon 14a, 3, in *The Works of Saint Augustine*, 20 vols., ed. John Rotelle (New York, 1991–), vol. III/11, p. 26. Cf. Faustus of Riez: '*In Deum ergo credere, hoc est fideliter eum quaerere, est lota in eum dilectione transire. Credo ergo in illum, hoc est dicere, confiteor illum, colo illum, adore illum, totum me is jus ejus ac dominum trado alque transfundo.*' Faustus

The additional descriptors, 'maker of heaven and earth', and so on, would then be ways of identifying or otherwise specifying the nature of the primary objects in which trust of confidence is being expressed. This certainly seems to be the sense of the later articles of the creeds. 'We believe in ... one, holy, catholic and apostolic Church' is clearly not intended to be profession of belief in the existence of the Church, but rather a statement of allegiance to it, confidence in its authority, and commitment to maintaining its unity. Again, recall that the Latin *fides* had no verb form and hence no possibility for the expression 'I faith'.[61] The modern tendency to use the first person singular 'I', along with the use of a separate verb *credo* (I believe) lends itself to the construction 'I believe *that*' in a way that can stress the propositional content, rather than the stance of the believer.[62] Faith/belief can then be understood to have separate subjective and objective components.

It may seem that Augustine of Hippo (354–430) had something like this in mind when he proposed a distinction between 'the faith *by which* it is believed' (*fides qua creduntur*) and 'the faith *which is* believed' (*fides quae creduntur*).[63] This dichotomy was revived in the seventeenth century and invoked to support the idea that faith could be distributed in a binary way on the basis of its supposedly subjective and objective aspects.[64] But this is not what

---

of Riez, *De spiritu sancto* I.1 (*PL* 62: 10c–d), trans. in Henri de Lubac, *The Splendor of the Church* (San Francisco: Ignatius Press, 1999), p. 35. This sense was still articulated in the seventeenth century. Hence, Walter Franke: 'This is the Creed, whose summe, and sense is this: I doe confide, and put my hope of blisse, In one Christ crucifi'd.' *An Epitome of Divinitie* (London, 1655).

[61] The equivalent term in Buddhism *saddhā* (Sanskrit), *śraddhā* (Pali) is usually rendered 'faith, confidence, trust in'. Robert E. Buswell and Donald Lopez Jr., *Princeton Dictionary of Buddhism* (Princeton: Princeton University Press, 2013), pp. 847–8.

[62] It is interesting that in classical Latin *credo* is typically used with the dative case with persons that are believed in, but with accusative for things. The latter sometimes involves a preposition – *credo in*. In the Latin version of the Nicene Creed, the preposition is used for the persons of the Trinity (possibly translating the Greek article in [εἰς]?) but not for the Church: '*Et unam, sanctam, catholicam et apostolicam Ecclesiam*'.

[63] '*sed aliud sunt ea quae creduntur, aliud fides qua creduntur*'. *De Trinitate* 13.2.5, *PL* 42: 1016–17. On this distinction see Denis Villepelet, *L'avenir de la Catéchèse* (Paris: Éditions de l'Atelier, 2003), pp. 90–2. As far as I know, Augustine makes this distinction on just this one occasion.

[64] For Protestant references Johann Gerhard, *Loci Theologici* [1610–25] 16.66, 9 vols., ed. Eduard Preuss (Berlin, 1863–75), vol. 3, p. 350; Andrew Willet, *Hexapla* (London, 1611), p. 526; William Scott, *The Course of Conformity* (Amsterdam, 1622), p. 109; William Ames, *Medulla S.S. Theologiæ* (London, 1629), pp. 436f.; Edward Leigh, *Annotations upon all the New Testament* (London, 1650), p. 575; James Crawford, *Haereseo-Machea* (London, 1646), p. 8; Francis Fuller, *A Treatise of Faith and Repentance* (London, 1685), p. 1; Christopher Cartwright, *The Doctrine of Faith* (London, 1650), p. 2; Ralph Robinson, *Panoplia. Universa arma. Hieron* (London, 1656), p. 211. Richard Baxter made the distinction equivalent to that between 'subjective' and 'objective' religion, the latter referring to true doctrines. *The Safe*

the phrases connoted for Augustine and this modern interpretation is inconsistent with the general picture of faith that we encounter during this earlier period in which elements of willing, trusting, acting, obedience, commitment, and knowledge in some form, are all closely conjoined.[65] Augustine's position is somewhat analogous to what Plato had argued about the object of love (*eros*) in the *Symposium*: the act of love can be understood only in relation to what is loved; the two cannot be separated.[66] For Augustine the 'faith' that is believed, cannot be considered independently of the 'faith' by which it is believed. This was to change in the early modern period.

The liturgical function of creeds also complicates the idea that they are solely to do with assenting to propositions.[67] Professions of belief had been integral to baptismal rites from very early in the history of the Christian Church.[68] The creeds, as John Henry Newman would later observe, 'are devotional acts, and of the nature of prayers addressed to God'.[69] This ritual

---

Religion (1657), pp. 6, 18. On Roman Catholic side, see Gaspar do Casal, *De quadripertita iustitia, libri tres* (Venice, 1563), p. 194v. Karl Barth offers an illuminating history of the distinction. That said, he proposed that Gerhard was the first to use the distinction in the modern sense, while several sixteenth-century Catholic theologians, including Casal, refer to it. Barth, *Church Dogmatics* I/1, pp. 230–6.

[65] Olivier Riaudel, '*Fides qua creditur et Fides quae creditur*: Retour sur une distinction qui n'est pas chez Augustin', *Revue théologique de Louvain* 43 (2012), 169–94. Like Riaudel, Barth and Rudolf Bultmann caution against identifying *fides quae creditur* with a body of doctrines. Barth, *Church Dogmatics* IV/1, §63 (p. 741); Bultmann, 'Theology as Science', in *New Testament Mythology and Other Basic Writings*, ed. Schubert M. Ogden (Philadelphia: Fortress Press, 1984), pp. 45–68 (pp. 52–4). The classic modern account of the belief in/belief that distinction was offered in the 1960 Gifford Lectures of H. H. Price, published as *Belief* (London: George Allen & Unwin, 1969), esp. ch. 9.

[66] Marina Berzins McCoy, 'Eros, Woundedness, and Creativity in Plato's Symposium', in *Wounded Heroes: Vulnerability as a Virtue in Ancient Greek Philosophy and Literature* (Oxford: Oxford University Press, 2013), pp. 115–39 (p. 116). But cf. Gregory Vlastos, 'The Individual as an Object of Love in Plato', in *Platonic Studies*, 2nd ed. (Princeton: Princeton University Press, 1981), pp. 3–42 (p. 39). Rudolf Bultmann offered similar observations about faith: 'faith and its object cannot be seen in their unity from any standpoint outside faith'. 'Theology as Science', p. 54.

[67] For what it is worth, some evidence from recent neuroscience reinforces the idea that liturgical acts, including creedal recitation, entail more than merely the verbal assertion of propositional claims, but are more like formative technologies that 'synchronize affective, perceptual-cognitive, and motor processes within the central nervous system'. Eugene d'Aquili and Charles Laughlin, 'The Biopsychological Determinants of Religious Ritual Behavior', *Zygon* 10 (1975), 32–58 (35). For discussion of this and similar studies, and their implications for an understanding of faith/belief see Sarah Lane Ritchie, 'Integrated Physicality and the Absence of God: Spiritual Technologies in Theological Context', *Modern Theology* 37 (2021), 296–315.

[68] Stewart, 'The Early Alexandrian Baptismal Creed'; Kinzig, 'The Creed in Liturgy'.

[69] John Henry Newman, *An Essay in Aid of a Grammar of Assent* (London: Longmans, Green and Co., 1870), p. 132.

context is suggestive of creedal declarations as what we now refer to as 'speech acts' or 'performative utterances'.[70] J. L. Austin, one of the leading ordinary language philosophers of the last century, contended that philosophical understandings of language and meaning had been distorted by a preoccupation with propositional assertion. One of the more revealing examples he used to contest that tendency was the formulaic declarations of a traditional wedding ceremony: 'I take you to be my lawfully wedded husband/wife ...'; 'I now pronounce you man and wife'; and so on. Clearly, these are not so much assertions of some truth about the world as the performance of actions that bring into being a new state of affairs. One way of thinking about how the verb 'to believe' operates within the creedal context, then, is to categorise it with these 'illocutionary' speech acts.[71] Again, this is not to claim that these statements make no reference at all to objective features of the world or historical events. But like wedding vows, creedal recitation assumes, rather than asserts, the existence of the relevant parties.

It is also worth noting that the objects of speech acts such as wedding vows are not fully specified: this is the force of the familiar phrases 'for richer or poorer, in sickness and in health'. What is being committed to is not, and cannot, be definitively established in advance. Complete knowledge of the other person in the relation, or of the various circumstances likely to obtain in the future, are not prerequisites for commitment. On the contrary,

---

[70] Justin Martyr, *First Apology* 61; Hippolytus, *The Apostolic Tradition of Hippolytus*, 21. For suggestions along similar lines see J. J. Schaller, 'Performative Language Theory: An Exercise in the Analysis of Ritual', *Worship* 62 (1988), 415–32; G. Wainwright, 'The Language of Worship', in *The Study of Liturgy*, 2nd ed., ed. C. Jones, G. Wainwright, and E. Yarnold (London: SPCK, 1992), pp. 519–28. More common are applications to biblical interpretation. See Dietmar Neufeld, *Reconceiving Texts as Speech Acts: An Analysis of John 1* (Leiden: Brill, 1994); Richard S. Briggs, *Words and Actions: Speech-Act Theory and Biblical Interpretation* (Edinburgh: T&T Clark, 2001), esp. pp. 183–215; 'Getting Involved: Speech Acts and Biblical Interpretation', *Anvil* 20 (2003), 25–34; Anthony C. Thiselton, *New Horizons in Hermeneutics* (Grand Rapids: Zondervan, 1992), pp. 283–311; 'Speech-Act Theory and the Claim that God Speaks', *Scottish Journal of Theology* 50 (1997), 97–110. See also Nicholas Wolterstorff, *Divine Discourse* (Cambridge: Cambridge University Press, 1995).

[71] Consider, for example, three of Austin's subdivisions of illocutionary acts: the 'Exercitive' (appointing, dismissing, naming, commanding, praying, enacting, dedicating); the 'Commissive' (committing the speaker to a course of action, such as promising, contracting, pledging, oath taking), and the 'Expositive' (expounding a position and clarifying specific usages and references). J. L. Austin, *How to Do Things with Words*, 2nd ed. (Cambridge, MA: Harvard University Press, 1975), pp. 155–63. See also Walter H. Beale, 'Rhetorical Performative Discourse: A New Theory of Epideictic', *Philosophy and Rhetoric* 11 (1978), 221–46. For a direct application of Austin's thought to religious claims see Donald D. Evans, *The Logic of Self Involvement: A Philosophical Study of Everyday Language with Special Reference to the Christian Use of Language about God as Creator* (London: SCM, 1963).

commitment, in a way, becomes a prerequisite for a deeper knowledge.[72] In this sense, marriage, if taken to be a sacrament, parallels the sacrament of infant baptism, in which an infant is initiated into a communal setting which it is envisaged will provide the context for a more fully developed and explicit knowledge. There are also analogies here to the maxims associated respectively with Augustine who repeatedly maintained that 'unless you believe you will not understand', and Anselm of Canterbury whose famous maxim was 'faith seeking understanding'.[73] These assume forms of knowledge that are unattainable without at least some degree of prior commitment, and that these commitments also involve actions and behaviours along with participation in the life of a community.

None of this is to deny that creeds had an exclusionary function and that their articulation made possible formal definitions of heresy and heterodoxy, typically understood as believing – assenting to – erroneous propositions. It is tempting to think that the category of heresy, along with the practice of persecution of heretics, offers a compelling example of why we ought to think of religious faith and belief in terms of individuals giving assent to doctrinal statements.[74] But again it is more complicated than this. Among the perceived dangers of heresy were social instability and rejection of the authority of temporal or ecclesiastical powers. As already observed, what initially prompted a reluctant Constantine to convene the Council of Nicaea was a concern about civil unrest in the Empire rather than a theological interest in promoting a specific version of Trinitarian Christianity. During this period, as J. Rebecca Lyman has observed, heresy 'was increasingly no longer only an ecclesiastical matter or a serious theological challenge, but a problem of public safety, since correct belief and worship ensured the unity and stability of society'. The articulation of heresiological categories was 'often a means to establish or maintain common boundaries'.[75]

---

[72] Marriage was commonly used as a metaphor of the relation between Christ and the Church, and in the Hebrew Bible, between Yahweh and Israel. David G. Hunter, 'The Virgin, the Bride, and the Church: Reading Psalm 45 in Ambrose, Jerome, and Augustine', *Church History* 69 (2000), 281–303; Hans Wolff, *Hosea*, trans. G. Stanswell (Philadelphia: Fortress Press, 1974), esp. p. xxvi; Sebastian Smolarz, *Covenant and the Metaphor of Divine Marriage* (Eugene: Wipf and Stock, 2010).

[73] Variously, '*Nullus quippe credit aliquid, nisi prius cogitaverit esse credendum*', PL 44: 963; '*credo ut intelligam*'; '*fides quaerens intellectum*', etc. See also Richard of St Victor, *On the Trinity* 1.1–3. This is similar to Newman's subsequent contesting of the principle that 'Truth is to be approached without homage', and W. H. Auden's poem, 'Leap before you Look'.

[74] Aquinas raises this issue in *Quaestiones disputatae de veritate*, q. 14, art. 11, sed contra 5.

[75] J. Rebecca Lyman, 'Heresiology: The Invention of "Heresy" and Schism'', in *The Cambridge History of the Christian Church*, vol. 2, ed. Augustin Casiday and Frederick W. Norris (Cambridge: Cambridge University Press, 2014), pp. 296–313.

Accordingly, under the Christian emperors, penal laws effectively classified heresy as a crime against the state.[76] Subsequently, heresy came to be considered an instance of *laesa majestas* (injured majesty), a concept that originates from Roman legal definitions of treason.[77]

The same would be true for heterodox belief in the Middle Ages. Arguably the perceived danger of medieval heresies lay less in individuals believing the wrong things (in our sense) than in the potential for heretical movements to challenge temporal and ecclesiastical authorities. There was certainly no lack of heretical groups during the Middle Ages: the Apostolic Brethren, Arnoldists, Brethren of the Free Spirit, Bogomils, Cathars, Fraticelli, Henricans, Humiliati, Lollards, Neo-Adamites, Paulicians, Petrobrusians, and Waldensians, to name the more prominent. While, on a parallel with our modern understandings of plural religions, such groups are often defined in terms of the heterodox beliefs to which their adherents supposedly subscribed, what they shared was a common concern with perceived ecclesiastical abuses and corruptions, and resistance to aspects of the prevailing social order. The policing of correct propositional belief was often secondary to the need to supress movements imagined to constitute a threat to the legitimacy of both the Church and temporal rulers.[78]

Some historians have gone so far as to contend that the putatively heterodox beliefs of groups such as the Cathars and Bogomils were the construction of committed churchmen, and that the doctrinal deviations of the heretics lay largely in the imaginations of Inquisitors.[79] Medievalist

---

[76] While religious matters had rarely played a prominent role in Roman legal documents, this did not represent an entirely new, and specifically Christian, intolerance of religious diversity. The preceding persecution of Christians themselves is an obvious counterinstance. Moreover, the legislator of Plato's *Laws* makes provision for the suppression and punishment of blasphemy, heresy, and atheism (X.907d–910d), and this text very likely influenced the framing of the Theodosian and Justinian Codes. Sebastian Schmidt-Hofner, 'Plato and the Theodosian Code', *Early Medieval Europe* 7 (2019), 35–60; Cf. J. M. Schott, 'Founding Platonopolis: The Platonic πολιτεία in Eusebius, Porphyry, and Iamblichus', *Journal of Early Christian Studies* 11 (2003), 501–31.

[77] See Takashi Shogimen, 'Re-thinking Heresy as a Category of Analysis', *Journal of the American Academy of Religion* 88 (2020), 726–48.

[78] David Stagman, 'Piet Fransen's Research on *Fides et Mores*', *Theological Studies* 64 (2003), 69–77 (73).

[79] See R. I. Moore, *The Formation of a Persecuting Society: Authority and Deviance in Western Europe, 950–1250* (Oxford: Blackwell, 2007); *The War on Heresy: Faith and Power in Medieval Europe* (London: Profile Books, 2012); Mark Pegg, *The Corruption of Angels: The Great Inquisition of 1245–1246* (Princeton: Princeton University Press, 2001). See also the collection edited by Monique Zerner, *Inventer l'hérésie?* (Nice: Presses Universitaires de Nice, 1998); Uwe Brunn, *Des contestataires aux 'Cathares'* (Paris: Collection des Études Augustiniennes, Série Moyen Âge et Temps Modernes, 41, 2006); and Hilbert Chiu's 2009

Mark Pegg tells us that 'there were no pre-existing heresies in the twelfth and early thirteenth centuries until the thinking of Latin Christian intellectuals invented them'.[80] According to this account, medieval heresy was constructed by projecting the opinions of historical heretical 'types' and heresiarchs – Marcion, Mani, Arius – onto marginal social groups. As was the case for these earlier emblematic heresies, political considerations were at the fore. Robert Moore proposes that we think of the persecution of medieval heretics as a general social phenomenon and of a piece with the persecution of Jews, lepers, homosexuals, and prostitutes – in short, those perceived to lie on the margins of Christian society. Their suppression was not about 'belief' in our sense at all, but a mechanism to shore up the social cohesion of medieval societies.[81] The medieval 'war on heresy' was thus analogous in some respects to the more recent notion of a 'war on terror' and the idea of an 'axis of evil'. This latter identification had more to do with a domestic US audience than a geopolitical reality.

Even if we are sceptical of the 'invention of medieval heresy' hypothesis it should be clear that heretics, whatever their imagined doctrinal commitments, were guilty by definition of a failure to believe in, in the sense of *trusting* in, 'one holy, catholic, and apostolic Church' in as much as they contested its authority and threatened its unity. They could hardly fail to believe in its existence, without which the exercise of its powers of coercion would be impossible. Their transgression consisted in a stubborn adherence to their own opinions out of mistrust, pride, and obstinacy. Hence the insistence of medieval thinkers that the guilt of heretics arose out of a remediable moral failing rather than sincere but mistaken beliefs. From the twelfth century onwards, medieval thinkers had specifically

---

University of Sydney MPhil thesis, 'The Intellectual Origins of Medieval Dualism'. For a dissenting view see Peter Biller, review of *The War on Heresy: Faith and Power in Medieval Europe* (review no. 1546), https://reviews.history.ac.uk/review/1546, accessed 28 August 2019. Deborah Shulevitz provides a good overview of the debate in 'Historiography of Heresy: The Debate over "Catharism" in Medieval Languedoc', *History Compass* 17 (2019), e12513, https://doi.org/10.1111/hic3.12513, accessed 23 November 2023. See also John H. Arnold, 'Voicing Dissent: Heresy Trials in Later Medieval England', *Past and Present* 245 (2019), 3–37.

[80] Mark Gregory Pegg, 'The Paradigm of Catharism: or, the Historians' Illusion', in *Cathars in Question*, ed. Antonio Sennis (York: York Medieval Press, 2016), pp. 21–54 (p. 44).

[81] R. I. Moore, 'The Cathar Middle Ages as an Historiographical Problem', in *Christianity and Culture in the Middle Ages: Essays to Honor John Van Engen*, ed. D. C. Mengel and L. Wolverton (Notre Dame: University of Notre Dame Press, 2015), pp. 58–86, esp. pp. 72–4; and 'The Debate of April 2013 in Retrospect', in *Cathars in Question*, ed. Sennis, pp. 257–73. On heresy as a political crime see David Abulafia, *Frederick II: A Medieval Emperor* (Oxford: Oxford University Press, 1988), pp. 211–13.

identified 'pertinacity' as the defining vice of heretics.[82] Aquinas would link this vice back to pride and covetousness, which headed the list of the seven deadly sins.[83] All of this comports with an understanding of *pistis/fides* as not simply an epistemological category, but a broader moral, social, and relational phenomenon.

2.4 Belief without Knowledge?

When Constantine the Great embarked upon his ultimately unsuccessful mission to dissuade the North African bishops from what he regarded as dispute-engendering doctrinal hair-splitting, he had suggested that the subtle distinctions at issue were beyond the comprehension of most of the faithful: 'how few are capable either of adequately expounding, or even accurately understanding the import of matters so vast and profound!'[84] He had a point. The philosophical complexity of the articles of the Christian creeds poses a further problem for the idea of belief as simple knowledge of and assent to propositions. The relational predicates in the Nicene Creed, for example, specify that the Son is 'eternally begotten of the Father' and the Spirit 'proceeds from the Father and the Son'. But what does 'eternally begotten' actually mean, and how is it different to 'proceeding from'? While members of councils responsible for the vocabulary of the creeds may have had some notion of what they were intending to convey – and, importantly, what they were ruling out – this could hardly have been true for the vast bulk of the Christian community many of whom would have lacked the philosophical sophistication necessary to fully comprehend these articles.[85]

---

[82] Irene Bueno, *Defining Heresy: Inquisition, Theology, and Papal Policy in the Time of Jacques Fournier* (Leiden: Brill, 2015), pp. 187–9; Shogimen, 'Re-thinking Heresy as a Category of Analysis'.

[83] Aquinas, *ST* 2a2ae. 11, 1. Compare with the adage commonly attributed to Augustine: *Errare possum, haereticus esse nolo* – 'I may be in error, but I lack the will to be heretical' (Augustine did not use this exact wording, but says something like it in *De Gratia Christi et de Peccato Originali* 2.23.26 (*PL* 44: 397)). The etymology of 'heresy' from the Greek *hairesis* – 'a taking or choosing for oneself' – also points us in this direction, as Aquinas points out.

[84] Constantine's letter to Alexander and Arius, in Socrates, *Ecclesiastical History* 1.7 (*NPNF* II, vol. 2, p. 6).

[85] John Locke would draw attention to this problem in his *A Third Letter concerning Toleration* (London, 1692), pp. 232f.: 'If ever you were acquainted with a Country-Parish, you must needs have a strange Opinion of them, if you think all the Plough-Men and Milk-Maids at Church, understood all the Propositions in *Athanasius*'s Creed.' Cf. *Reasonableness of Christianity*, ed. John Higgins-Biddle (Oxford: Clarendon Press, 1999), p. 169. As, too, Newman, *Grammar of Assent*, p. 146.

2.4 BELIEF WITHOUT KNOWLEDGE? 51

Strictly speaking, moreover, what is being affirmed in the original Greek is not quite the same as what is being affirmed in the Latin. The Father is 'ruler of all' in the Greek, but 'omnipotent' or 'almighty' in the Latin. Jesus is 'of one *being* with the Father' in the Greek, but in Latin, 'of one *substance*'.[86] Arguably, these expressions reflect slightly different ontological commitments – the latter seeming to require, for example, some kind of metaphysics of substance. None of this is intended as a normative judgement on the validity of the creeds, but it does point to the fact that full comprehension and assent to their literal, propositional content could not have been the condition for genuine faith, or membership of the Church, for the simple reason that for most of the faithful this would have practically unachievable.

How then, was belief supposed to work in relation to these creedal formulae? For the bulk of the faithful, belief had to be a matter of trusting in the Church and in those charged with the business of getting the doctrinal details correct.[87] Belief in (that is, *trust* in) the one Holy, catholic, and apostolic church amounts to confidence that the councils of the Church have got the more abstruse propositions right. The third-century maxim that there

---

[86] 'Ruler of all' (Gk. *Pantocrator*, παντοκράτορα), cf. 'omnipotent' (Lat. *omnipotentem*). 'Of one *being*' (Gk. *homoousion*, ὁμοούσιον], cf. 'of one *substance*' (Lat. *consubstantialum*). Latin and Greek in Denzinger (ed.), *Enchiridion Symbolorum*, §§125–6 (pp. 52f.). See Graham Ward, *How the Light Gets In: Ethical Life 1* (Oxford: Oxford University Press, 2016), pp. 8–34, esp. p. 13. István Pásztori-Kupán argues that the Latin equivalent of *ousia* is not *substantia* but *essentia* and claims that the better translation of *homoousios* is *coessential*. *Theodoret of Cyrus* (London: Routledge, 2006), p. 59. The origins of these technical distinctions are well understood and were originally set out in order to oppose formulations thought to be erroneous – the use of *homoousion* (of the same being) as an explicit rejection of the 'semi-Arian' *homoiousion* (of similar being), is one example. But arguably these terms meant different things to Greek and Latin speakers. See Catherine Mowry LaCugna, 'Philosophers and Theologians on the Trinity', *Modern Theology* 2 (1986), 169–81, esp. 176; N. Jacobs, 'On "Not Three Gods"—Again: Can a Primary-Secondary Substance Reading of *ousia* and *hypostasis* Avoid Tritheism?', *Modern Theology* 24 (2008), 331–58; Jean-Yves Lacoste 'Homoousios et homoousios: La substance entre théologie et philosophie', *Recherches de Science Religieuse* 98 (2010), 85–100. Also relevant here are fundamental questions about the representational capacities of language and the possibility of translation. For Martin Heidegger's remarks on this theme and his view of the differing capacities of Latin and Greek see Heidegger, *An Introduction to Metaphysics*, trans. Ralph Manheim (New Haven: Yale University Press, 1959), pp. 62–5, and 'The Onto-Theo-Logical Nature of Metaphysics', in *Essays in Metaphysics* (New York: Philosophical Library, 2015), pp. 18–30.

[87] '... simple souls, even when they are incapable of comprehending deep mysteries, are near to the great, inasmuch as they account the excellencies of their brethren to be their own also by force of charity ... duller minds, when joined with the wise, are fed by their understanding'. Thus, Gregory the Great, *Moralia in Job* 2. 49, 3 vols., trans. James Bliss (Jackson, MI: Ex Fontibus, 2015), vol. 1, pp. 95f. Gregory was later cited by Aquinas in his treatment of implicit faith. *ST* 2a.2ae, 2, 6.

is 'no salvation outside the church' (*extra Ecclesiam nulla salus*) reinforces this understanding.[88] Salvation was not a matter, primarily, of explicitly assenting to the right set of propositions, but of being incorporated into the body of the Church through the medium of the sacraments. The specialised task of getting the doctrines right was left to theological authorities. Looking ahead, the most unambiguous statement of this position would be reiterated in the decrees of the Council of Trent (1545–63), at precisely the historical moment when this view of faith faced its most serious challenge : 'We believe all "that which is contained in the word of God, written or handed down, *and which the Church proposes for belief* as divinely revealed".'[89] Of course, if there were two (or more) churches offering competing proposals for belief this option would become problematic. This was the difficulty that became acute following the Protestant Reformation. The predicament generated by competing magisterial contributed to the rise of an instrumental conception of reason intended to provide the criterion for justified belief (where 'belief' is understood to be a form of knowledge). Along with this notion came the insistence that we take personal responsibility for what we affirm and do so in possession of all of the evidential grounds upon which we affirm it. But these epistemic ideals, as we will see, have problems of their own and, arguably, turn out to be impractical and unobtainable.

In the fourth century, an issue related to the conceptual complexity of creedal formulae was the status of biblical patriarchs and prophets who, on the basis of biblical authority, were generally thought to have been saved on account of their 'faith'.[90] Clearly, then, the object of that faith could not have been the articles of the creeds. Indeed, this would also have been true of the disciples and the first generation of Christians who lived before the promulgation of the creeds.[91] Augustine of Hippo (354–430), writing in the period that followed the Council of Nicaea, grappled with this

---

[88] Originally '*Salus extra Ecclesiam non est*'. Cyprian of Carthage, Epistle 72, 21 (*ANF* 5, p. 384; *PL* 3: 1123). The context was a discussion of the efficacy of baptism rites conducted by heretics.

[89] Tridentine Roman Catechism: §182, www.vatican.va/archive/ENG0015/__P12.HTM, accessed 23 November 2023. Articles on faith are given in §§166–84 (my emphasis). Newman would rehearse this in *Grammar of Assent*, pp. 150f. Similarly: 'Nothing would be more theoretical and unreal than to suppose the true Faith cannot exist except when moulded upon a Creed.' *Fifteen Sermons preached before the University of Oxford*, 3rd ed. (London: Rivingtons, 1872), pp. 253f.

[90] In Romans 4 we are informed that righteousness was imputed to Abraham on account of his faith. Hebrews 11 provides a long list of characters in the Hebrew Bible who acted according to faith.

[91] As James K. A. Smith points out: 'Before Christians had systematic theologies and world-views, they were singing hymns and psalms, saying prayers, celebrating the Eucharist,

question, concluding that 'true religion' had existed since the beginning of the world. With the coming of Christ, this religion was for the first time called 'Christian religion'.[92] True religion, on this account, had always had adherents, even if explicit assent to fundamental Christian doctrines would have been impossible for them.[93] Augustine thought that there had always been 'one faith', but over historical time a growth in knowledge. Medieval thinkers subsequently drew parallels between the faith of infants and the unlearned, and pre-Christian patriarchs and prophets. While neither would have been able to read the Bible or offer an account of the articles of the creed, they were nonetheless thought to have been capable of saving faith.[94] This faith became known as 'implicit faith'.

We shall return to Augustine shortly to consider his ideas on the status of second-hand knowledge. For now, and looking well ahead, the formal category of implicit faith was developed by successive thinkers at the abbey of St Victor during the high Middle Ages. Founded early in the twelfth century and located at the foot of Montagne Sainte-Geneviève on the outskirts of Paris, the abbey became one of the main centres of intellectual life in medieval Europe. Along with the schools of Ste Geneviève and Notre-Dame de Paris, it provided the foundation for the University of Paris, established around 1150 and generally regarded as the second-oldest university in Europe. Its most influential leader was Hugh of St Victor (c.1096–1141) whose *De sacramentis christianae fidei* ('On the Sacraments of Christian Faith') was one of the first systematic theological treatises of the Middle Ages. In his seven questions on faith, Hugh followed Augustine in proposing that 'right faith' had in some sense been in evidence from the beginning of the world. This faith consisted in trust in God along with a diffuse apprehension of a future redemption. In these earlier times, as in the present, 'the faith of the simple minded' consisted in their trust in those whose expectations were more fully formed. All had the same faith, but not the same knowledge.[95]

---

sharing their property, and becoming a people marked by a desire for God's coming kingdom.' *Desiring the Kingdom: Worship, Worldview, and Cultural Formation* (Grand Rapids: Baker, 2009), p. 139.

[92] Augustine, *Retractionum* 1.13.3, in *Augustine: Early Writings*, p. 218 (*PL* 32: 603). Cf. Augustine, Letter 102, Augustine to Deogratias 19, *Works*, vol. II/2, p. 30. For the relevance of this to the concept 'religion' see Harrison, *Territories*, pp. 8–10.

[93] 'it was the self-same faith in the Mediator which saved the saints of old'. Augustine, *On Marriage and Concupiscence*, bk. 2, ch. 24, *NPNF* I, vol. 5, p. 292.

[94] Owen Chadwick, *From Bossuet to Newman*, 2nd ed. (Cambridge: Cambridge University Press, 1987), pp. 22–5.

[95] Hugh of St Victor, *De Sacramentis* 10.7 (*Hugh of St Victor on the Sacraments of the Christian Faith*, trans. Roy J. Deferrari (Eugene: Wipf and Stock, 1951), p. 178). John Marenbon

Peter Lombard (c.1096–1160), whose *Sentences* overtook Hugh's *De sacramentis* to become the standard theological textbook during the high and later Middle Ages, also addressed this issue, concluding similarly that there were those, both before the coming of Christ and in his own time, who 'believe what they do not know'.[96] These individuals had what he calls a 'veiled faith'. Lombard's 'veiled faith' would subsequently evolve into the more formal 'implicit faith' (*fides implicita*), which became a standard category for scholastic philosophers.[97] When Thomas Aquinas came to take up this issue he conceded that there were degrees of knowledge and that it was sufficient for those not in the business of philosophy to assent to 'primary articles of faith' and to have an 'implicit faith' in the rest. This meant, in essence, cultivating an attitude of trust in God and in his earthly representatives.[98] The biblical patriarchs were also included in the number for whom implicit faith was regarded as efficacious.[99] Aquinas deals with implicit faith in a number of

---

explains Hugh's position in this way: 'People can have faith in what is affirmed by a proposition *p*, without holding or even contemplating *p*, if they accept a general proposition of which *p* is an instantiation, and they also place their trust in people who believe *p*.' *Pagans and Philosophers: The Problem of Paganism from Augustine to Leibniz* (Princeton: Princeton University Press, 2015), p. 161. See also Karein Ganss, 'Affectivity and Knowledge Lead to Devotion to God', in *A Companion to the Abbey of Saint Victor in Paris*, ed. Hugh Feiss and Juliet Mousseau (Leiden: Brill, 2017), pp. 422–68, esp. pp. 439–43.

[96] Peter Lombard, *Sententiarum libri quatuor*, bk. 3, dist. 25, ch. 2, *PL* 192: 810. There was a parallel principle that we must love what we do not know. Hence Gregory the Great: 'the love she [the soul] feels for what she knows, teaches her to love what she does not know', *Homilies on the Gospels* 11 (*PL* 76: 1115); and Aquinas: 'From the things it knows the soul learns to love what it knows not.' *ST* 2a.2ae. 27, 3. This sentiment is repeated by Pascal: 'the saints on the contrary say in speaking of divine things that it is necessary to love them in order to know them, and that we only enter truth through charity'. 'The Art of Persuasion', in *Great Shorter Works of Pascal*, trans. Emile Cailliet and John C. Blankenagel (Eugene: Wipf and Stock, 2018), p. 203.

[97] Alexander of Hales, *Summa theologica* 3, inq. 2, tr. 2, q. 1, ch. 4, art. 1 (Quaracchi: Collegium S. Bonaventurae, 1924–48), vol. 4, p. 1120; Bonaventure, *Commentaria in Quatuor Libros Sententiarum* 3, d. 25, a. 1, q. 2 (Quaracchi: Collegium S. Bonaventurae, 1882–1902), vol. 3, p. 540; Durandus of St-Pourçain, *Super sententias theologiae Petri Lombardi commentariorum libri quatuor* (Venice, 1571), p. 258.; Richard of Middleton, *Super Quatuor Libros Sententiarum* 3, d. 25, q. 1 (Brescia, 1591), pp. 277–9. For brief historical treatments of this conception see Marenbon, *Pagans and Philosophers*, esp. pp. 160–3; Chadwick, *From Bossuet to Newman*, pp. 23–6. For theological accounts, see Albrecht Ritschl, *Fides implicita: Eine Untersuchung über Köhlerglauben, Wissen und Glauben, Glauben und Kirche* (Bonn: Adolph Marcus, 1890).

[98] Aquinas, *ST* 2a2ae. 2, 5–6.

[99] Aquinas, *Disputed questions on Truth*, q. 14, art. 11, in *Truth*, 3 vols., trans. James V. McGlynn (Indianapolis: Hackett, 1964), vol. 2, pp. 260–2. Aquinas also pondered the plight of those 'living in the forest', or raised by wild beasts. In the wake of the second Vatican Council (1962–5) and the publication of the conciliar document *Lumen Gentium* (1964) a number of Catholic theologians, most prominently Karl Rahner, adopted broad

his works, offering a more complete treatment than any of his contemporaries. One way in which he imagines implicit faith to work is analogous to the way in which, if we have knowledge of a general principle, we will have implicit knowledge of its specific applications.[100] (For example, we may not ever think explicitly about the prime number 104,729 or contemplate its properties. But if we know what a prime number is, there is a sense in which we know implicitly that 104,729 is divisible by only itself and one.)

Requiring others to believe on our behalf may seem to be a problem that we only get ourselves into when we seek to justify one particular kind of belief – that is, religious belief, or belief that transcends the sensory realm, or is in some sense 'above reason'. Indeed, for some, this encapsulates the whole problem with religious belief. However, reliance on authorities goes beyond the religious sphere, and a moment's reflection will reveal that we rely upon others for much, if not most, of what we think we know. Aristotle had observed that 'some trust/faith [*pisteuein*] is necessary for whoever wants to learn'.[101] But it was not until Augustine that we encounter an extended treatment of this principle, and of how it might be rational to believe on the basis of authority. In the *Confessions*, he offers these reflections on all of the things he knows on the basis of trust:

> I began to consider the countless things I believed in though I could not see them and had not been present when they took place, such as the many events in the history of the nations, so many of them to do with places and cities that I had not seen; and so many things I learned from

---

definitions of implicit faith, arguing that salvation extended well beyond the visible boundaries of the Catholic Church. See, e.g., Geffrey B. Kelly, '"Unconscious Christianity" and the "Anonymous Christian" in the Theology of Dietrich Bonhoeffer and Karl Rahner', *Philosophy and Theology* 9 (1995), 117–49; Lamadrid Lucas, 'Anonymous or Analogous Christians? Rahner and Von Balthasar on Naming the Non-Christian', *Modern Theology* 11 (1995), 363–84; Stephen Bullivant, *The Salvation of Atheists and Catholic Dogmatic Theology* (Oxford: Oxford University Press, 2012).

[100] Aquinas, *Commentary on the Sentences* 3, d. 25, q. 2, a. 1. Aquinas is aware that analogies like these are imperfect because implicit faith resides in a person not a principle. But because the articles of faith are not ultimately derived from innate, self-evident principles, but from teaching, he suggests that it is appropriate to have faith in the knowledge of another. These considerations are also relevant to the broader problem of the development of doctrine (how there could be 'one faith' if the Church kept adding to it) for which logical inference provided a model. See Chadwick, *From Bossuet to Newman*, p. 35. Aquinas also argues that God has not revealed every implication of the articles of faith, and hence that these can be arrived at through study. *ST* 1a. 1, 6. Thomas Hobbes, while generally opposed to the notion of implicit faith, nevertheless allows that certain doctrines are implicit in others, in the sense that they can be deduced from it. *Leviathan*, 3 vols., ed. Noel Malcolm (Oxford: Clarendon Press, 2012), vol. 3, ch. 43, p. 948.

[101] Aristotle, *Sophistical Refutations* 2, 165b3.

friends, doctors, all sorts and conditions of people. Unless we believed in them [*quae nisi crederentur*], we would never take action of any kind in this life .... Finally, there was my unshakeable conviction about the parents who had begotten me, which I could not know [*scire*] except by hearing and believing it.[102]

These sentiments amount to a kind of sociology of knowledge in which Augustine sets aside theoretical, epistemological considerations to focus instead on how in practice we come to know things. He points to the fact that reliance upon authorities of various kinds is necessary for much of our knowledge and that leading a normal life would be impossible without it.[103] The warrant for holding such knowledge is twofold: practical necessity and the trustworthiness of our sources. Religious belief, one case of such knowledge, relies upon both.

In *De ordine* (On Order), written towards the end of the fourth century when the Western Empire was on the verge of disintegration, Augustine had already suggested a two-stage path to knowledge, in which authority

---

[102] Augustine, *Confessions* 6.5.7 (LCL 26, 250–1). A more extended treatment is offered in *De magistro*. The claim for *knowledge* based upon testimony takes Augustine beyond claims in earlier works that require stricter Platonic criteria for knowledge ('grasping something by the sure reason of mind'). In *On the Usefulness of Belief*, 25, e.g., he declares that 'What we understand, we owe to reason; what we believe, to authority; what we have an opinion on, to error .... Every one who understands also believes ...', 25 (*NPNF* I, vol. 3, p. 359). Cf. *Retractions* 1.14.3. See Peter King and Nathan Ballantyne, 'Augustine on Testimony', *Canadian Journal of Philosophy* 39 (2009), 195–214; John M. Rist, *Augustine: Ancient Thought Baptized* (Cambridge: Cambridge University Press, 1994), pp. 56–63. Famously, for Augustine, the authority of scripture was dependent upon the authority of the Church: 'I should not believe the gospel except as moved by the authority of the Catholic Church.' Augustine offers a parallel set of considerations for believing in what cannot be seen in *Concerning Faith of Things not Seen* where he uses the example of other minds, and argues that society could not subsist without belief in invisible realities. *NPNF* I, vol. 3.

[103] More recent philosophical discussions of 'extended epistemology' offer a related perspective. In his classic 1973 paper 'Meaning and Reference' (*The Journal of Philosophy* 70 (1973), 699–711) Hilary Putnam observed that in spite of his own inability to distinguish an elm from a beech, when he deploys the terms 'elm' and 'beech' he really *means* elm and beech. Those meanings are determined not on account of anything that he knows, but because he is a member of a linguistic community that includes experts who *can* make the relevant distinction. All of us, in innumerable everyday usages, implicitly defer to experts whose knowledge suffices for us to make sense. This linguistic deference is endemic in normal discourse. See also J. Adam Carter, Andy Clark, Jesper Kallestrup, S. Orestis Palermos, and Duncan Pritchard (eds.), *Socially Extended Epistemology* (Oxford: Oxford University Press, 2018), esp. the chapter by Cathal O'Madagain, 'Outsourcing Concepts: Social Externalism, The Extended Mind, and the Expansion of Our Epistemic Capacity' (pp. 24–35); Jennifer Lackey, 'Socially Extended Knowledge', *Philosophical Issues* 24 (2014), 282–98.

comes first, followed by reason. What this transition required, however, was not so much a training in philosophical dialectic as the leading of a good life. Only after individuals live out what they believe, says Augustine, 'do they appreciate how reasonable were the notions they learned before understanding them'.[104] The adoption of a particular form of life is also important for gauging the reliability of human authorities. Here the criterion is whether the lives of authorities are consistent with their teachings.[105] Augustine also acknowledges a difference between 'the uninstructed crowd' and 'the learned', the former being more reliant on authority than the latter. What is more important for those who have no talent for higher learning is that 'they live a clean life of upright desires'. This will be the basis upon they will judged, Augustine surmises, when they leave this present life.[106] In sum, for Augustine, not only do we need to believe things that we cannot understand, but belief (in the sense of trust) is actually a prerequisite for understanding. This brings us back to his dictum that 'unless you believe, you will not understand'.[107]

Augustine's reflections about the distinctiveness of Christian believing were also informed by the contrasting cases of classical philosophy and Judaism. The question of the relation between Christianity and the philosophical schools was a long-standing one. St Paul's identification of philosophy as 'the wisdom of the world', along with his observation that the gospel was folly to the Greeks and a stumbling block to the Jews gives some weight

---

[104] Augustine, *De ordine*, trans. Silvano Borrusco (South Bend: St Augustine's Press, 2007), bk. 2, ch. 9, p. 87. The notion of lived faith is also implied by the Augustinian phrase '*fides et mores*' (*Epistles* 54, 55). See Piet Fransen, 'A Short History of the Expression "Fides et Mores"', in *Hermeneutics of the Councils and Other Studies*, ed. H. E. Mertens and F. De Graeve (Leuven: Leuven University Press, 1985), pp. 287–318.

[105] Augustine, *De ordine*, bk. 2, ch. 9, p. 87. Cf. *Divine Providence and the Problem of Evil* 10.27 (*FC*, vol. 5, pp. 304–5).

[106] Augustine wonders whether such people can be truly happy, but insists that when they leave this life they will judged 'in direct proportion to the effort they have put into living a good life.' Augustine, *De ordine*, bk. 2, ch. 9, p. 87.

[107] Augustine, *Against the Academics* 3.20.43; *De Libero Arbitrio* II.2. Also 'For we believe in order that we may know (*cognoscamus*), we do not know in order that we may believe' (*Tract. in Joh.* XL, n. 9 [*PL* 35: 1690]). 'Believe so that you may understand [plural *you*]. For "unless you believe, you will not understand" (Is. 7:9, Vulgate)' (*Sermons* CCXII, n. 1 [*PL* 38: 1059]). 'But so that we may understand, first let us believe. For "unless you believe, you will not understand" (Is. 7:9, Vulgate)' (*Sermons* LXXXIX, n. 4 [*PL* 38: 556]). 'Therefore since we wish to understand the eternity of the Trinity, we must believe before we may understand' (*De Trin.* l. VIII, c. V, n. 8 [*PL* 42: 952]). No one 'believes anything unless he has first thought that it is to be believed'. *Nullus quippe credit aliquid, nisi prius cogitaverit esse credendum PL* 44, col. 963. *On the Predestination of the Saints* 2.5, *PL* 44: 963. *NPNF* I, vol. 5, p. 499. See discussion in Rist, *Augustine*, pp. 56–63.

to the thesis that the relationship was conceived, on the Christian side at least, as primarily oppositional.[108] But his address to an Athenian audience at the Areopagus, recounted in Acts 17, takes a more conciliatory line – Christianity as the fulfilment of the inchoate aspirations of ancient philosophy. The more eirenic of the Church Fathers adopted a similar perspective, viewing both Judaism and Christianity as, in some sense, a 'preparation' for the Christian gospel.[109] In all of this, the relation to Christianity was not conceived of primarily in terms of competing sets of doctrines: rather, the philosophical schools were seen as offering alternative prescriptions for the attainment of happiness and the leading of a fulfilled life.[110] At the same time, doctrines, teachings, and cosmological assumptions were integral to these ways of life.[111]

In the long prelude to his conversion to Christianity Augustine had explored two philosophical schools in depth – Academic Scepticism and Platonism – and his reflections on these traditions are directly relevant to the question of the role of belief in the Christian life. A core element of Scepticism was the withholding of assent from what could not be known with certainty. This practice of the suspension of belief was supposed to lead to the goal of tranquillity of mind. In our terms it thus had a psychological or moral, rather than an epistemological aim. Because the Sceptics held that little, if anything, could be known with certainty, the ultimate ambition of this school was, quite literally, 'a life without belief'.[112] This was clearly inconsistent with Christianity and Augustine accordingly mounted a number of arguments against Scepticism, some of which René Descartes would later adopt in the seventeenth century.[113] But Augustine was adamant that

---

[108] I Cor. 1:19–27. Tertullian is usually taken to typify this oppositional stance (although his attitude to Greek learning was considerably nuanced). For the oppositional motifs, see *Ad nationes* 4, *De presciptione haereticorum* 7.

[109] Justin Martyr, *First Apology* 46; Clement of Alexandria, *Stromata* 1.9, 13; *Exhortation to the Heathen* 6.

[110] Hadot, *Philosophy as a Way of Life*; John Peter Kenney, '"None Come Closer to Us than These": Augustine and the Platonists', *Religions* 7 (2016), 1–16; Harrison, *Territories*, pp. 26–34.

[111] See Harrison, *Territories*, pp. 26–34; Paul R. Kolbet, *Augustine and the Cure of Souls: Revising a Classical Ideal* (Notre Dame: University of Notre Dame Press, 2010), pp. 41–64.

[112] Katja Vogt, 'Ancient Skepticism', *SEP*, https://plato.stanford.edu/archives/fall2018/entries/skepticism-ancient/.

[113] Descartes's contemporary Antoine Arnauld pointed out the similarities, which Descartes seemed reluctant to acknowledge. *Objections and Replies*, CSM 2, p. 139. See discussions in Stephen Menn, *Descartes and Augustine* (Cambridge: Cambridge University Press, 1998), pp. 4f.; Gareth B. Matthews, *Thought's Ego in Augustine and Descartes* (Ithaca: Cornell University Press, 1992), ch. 3; Richard Sorabji, *Self: Ancient and Modern Insights about Individuality, Life, and Death* (Oxford: Oxford University Press, 2008), pp. 217–19.

there are things that we need to affirm if we are to attain genuine happiness, and we must commit to these things even if we do not fully know or understand them: 'If assent is taken away, faith goes too, for without assent there can be no belief. And there are truths, even if they are not seen, which must be believed if we would attain to a happy life.'[114] In the late nineteenth century, William James would take a similar line in his celebrated lecture, 'The Will to Believe'.[115] The success of the schools of sceptical philosophy in antiquity reflects the goal they shared with Christianity – the attainment of the happy life, or beatitude.

Apart from Augustine and the Church Fathers, the other key philosophical conversation partner for medieval thinkers was Aristotle, although his influence would not be fully felt in the Christian West until the translation projects of the twelfth century.[116] With the eventual appearance in the mid-twelfth century of a Latin version of the *Posterior Analytics* – in which Aristotle discusses the criteria for 'scientific' knowledge – the full complement of Aristotle's logical works, collectively known as the *Organon*,

---

[114] Augustine, *Enchiridion* 20, *PL* 40: 212. Aquinas will similarly propose that what is known is 'seen', and that the object of faith is something unseen. *ST* 2a2ae 1, 4 and 5. Augustine's stance bears a resemblance to Immanuel Kant's 'postulates of practical reason'; a postulate being 'a *theoretical* proposition, though one not demonstrable as such, insofar as it is attached inseparably to an a priori unconditionally valid *practical* law' (5:122). In relation to morality, or the question of how we should live, the specific Kantian postulates were immortality and the existence of God. Immanuel Kant, *Critique of Practical Reason* 5:122–32, in *Practical Philosophy*, ed. and trans. Mary Gregor (Cambridge: Cambridge University Press, 1996), pp. 238–46. Augustine's position even more directly resembles that set out by William James, in *The Will to Believe*.

[115] James writes: 'Our passional nature not only lawfully may, but must, decide an option between propositions, whenever it is a genuine option that cannot by its nature be decided on intellectual grounds; for to say under such circumstances, "Do not decide, but leave the question open," is itself a passional decision – just like deciding yes or not – and is attended with the same risk of losing truth.' *The Will to Believe* [1897] *and other Essays in Popular Philosophy* (Cambridge: Cambridge University Press, 2014), p. 11.

[116] In late antiquity, John Philoponus had written commentaries on both the *Prior Analytics* and the *Posterior Analytics*, but these were in Greek. Philoponus, *On Aristotle: Prior Analytics 1.1–8*, trans. Richard D. McKirahan (London: Duckworth, 2008), pp. 1–8; Mariska Leunissen and Marije Martijn (eds.), *Interpreting Aristotle's Posterior Analytics in Late Antiquity and Beyond* (Leiden: Brill, 2011), esp. the chapter by Owen Goldin, 'Two Traditions in the Ancient *Posterior Analytics* Commentaries' (pp. 155–82). And as noted earlier, in the tenth century al-Fārābī had already discussed the Aristotelian understanding of certitude in some depth in a number of writings, including his *Epitome of the Posterior Analytics*. Certainty, in the Aristotelian sense, was also important for subsequent medieval Arabic writers. See Black, 'Knowledge (*'Ilm*) and Certainty (*Yaqīn*)'; Michael Marmura, 'The *Fortuna* of the *Posterior Analytics* in the Arabic Middle Ages', in *Knowledge and the Sciences in Medieval Philosophy*, 3 vols., ed. M. Asztalos, J. E. Murdoch, and I. Niiniluoto (Helsinki: Acta Philosophica Fennica, 1990), vol. 1, pp. 85–103; Pasnau,

became available to Latin scholars for the first time.[117] The condition for certain knowledge, or science, that the Greek philosopher set out in these logical writings prompted a new conversation about the scientific status of Christian theology and the nature of faith. This took place largely in a new venue that was purpose-built for such discussions – the medieval university.

What Aristotle meant by 'science' is quite different from our present understandings of the term. In fact, the English 'science' did not take on its now familiar meaning until the nineteenth century.[118] As already noted, for Aristotle genuine scientific knowledge was arrived at by means of logical demonstration from incontrovertible principles and it bore the highest degree of certainty.[119] This, at least, was the ideal, since it was recognised that in reality only a deductive mathematical system would fully meet those criteria.[120] Because most Christian doctrines were clearly not arrived at by a process of logical demonstration, this raised the question of their certainty and scientific status. The brilliant logician Peter Abelard (d. 1142), perhaps best known today on account of his ill-fated romantic liaison with Héloïse, was one of the first to bring discussions of the nature of faith into the orbit of Aristotelian classifications of knowledge, concluding that faith was to be located between science and opinion.[121] While some critics found fault with the assessment, worrying that it placed faith too close to opinion, most

---

After Certainty, pp. 27–8, 176–7; Jon McGinnis, 'Avicenna's Naturalised Epistemology and Scientific Method', in *The Unity of Science in the Arabic Tradition*, ed. Shahid Rahman, Tony Street, and Hassan Tahiri (Dordrecht: Springer, 2008), pp. 129–52.

[117] Lat. *Scientia*, Gk. *epistēmē*. Boethius had translated the *Posterior Analytics* in the sixth century as part of his mission to preserve classical philosophy. However, this work was lost. Subsequently James of Venice retranslated the work in mid-twelfth century. See C. H. Lohr, 'The Medieval Interpretation of Aristotle', in *The Cambridge History of Later Medieval Philosophy*, ed. Norman Kretzmann, Anthony Kenny, and Jan Pinborg (Cambridge: Cambridge University Press, 1982), pp. 80–98; Robert Pasnau, 'The Latin Aristotle', in *The Oxford Handbook of Aristotle*, ed. Christopher Shields (Oxford: Oxford University Press, 2012), pp. 665–89.

[118] 'Science' – Gk. *epistēmē*; Lat. *scientia*.

[119] Aristotle, *Posterior Analytics* 78a22–79a33, cf. Aquinas, *ST* Ia. 1, 2. For the modern idea of 'science', see Harrison, *Territories*, pp. 11–15, 153–70.

[120] Pasnau, *After Certainty*, p. 7, and *passim*.

[121] This comports with the hierarchies of Plato and Aristotle, but Abelard sought to capture the special status of *fides* with the term *existimatio* (judgement, right opinion). Peter Abelard, *Epitome Theologiae Christianae* 1, *PL* 178: 695. On *existimatio* see Constant J. Mews, 'Faith as *Existimatio rerum non apparentium*: Intellect, Imagination and Faith in the Philosophy of Peter Abelard', in *Intellect and Imagination in Medieval Philosophy*, ed. M. C. Pacheco and J. Meirinhos (Turnhout: Brepols, 2006), pp. 915–26. Cf. Anselm of Canterbury, who sought a knowledge of Christian truths that was 'midway between faith and revelation'. *Why God became Man*, in *The Major Works*, ed. Brian G. Davies and G. R. Evans (Oxford: Oxford University Press, 1998), pp. 260–356 (p. 260).

scholastic thinkers conceded the point that faith was less certain than 'science', as Aristotle had conceived it. Hugh of St Victor agreed with Abelard that 'Faith is a form of certitude of mind concerning things not present, which stands as greater than opinion, but less than science.'[122] Thomas Aquinas followed suit. Citing with approval Augustine's definition of faith as 'thinking with assent', Aquinas maintained that assent, being an act of the will, is required precisely because faith falls short of certainty and lies between science and opinion.[123] And like both science and opinion, faith concerns propositions.[124] As for the scientific status of theological truths, Aquinas squared that circle by proposing that theology (*sacra doctrina* was his expression) was indeed a science for God, but a 'subordinate science' for us, since its principles were not self-evident, but required God (for whom they were self-evident) to reveal them to us.[125]

These developments signal the beginnings of a new dialectical approach to Christian belief. In the eleventh century, Anselm of Canterbury (1033/4–1109) had already sought to articulate the logic of ideas long cherished by

---

[122] Hugh of St Victor, *De sacramentis* I, 10, PL 176: 330. Aquinas cites this source on a number of occasions. See Appendix 4 to *Summa Theologiae*: Volume 31, Faith: 2a2ae. 1–7.

[123] Aquinas, *ST* 2a2ae. 1, 2; 1, 4. But unlike opinion, faith does not entertain the possibility of the falsity of what is accepted. On Augustine's definition of 'thinking with assent', *credere est assensione cogitarei*, see Aquinas, *ST* 2a2ae. 2, 1. Cf. Augustine, *Predestination of the Saints* 2.5. But thinking [*cogitare*] means something different for Augustine and requires the activity of God. The scholastics will read this in a more Aristotelian fashion. See G. Verbeke, 'Pensée et discernement chez saint Augustin: Quelques réflexions sur le sens du terme "cogitare"', *Recherche Augustiniennes* 2 (Paris, 1962), 59–80; Emmanuel Bermon, *Le Cogito dans la Pensées de Saint Augustin* (Paris: Vrin, 2001), pp. 77–80. For summary accounts of Aquinas on faith, see Victor Preller, *Divine Science and the Science of God: A Reformulation of Thomas Aquinas* (Princeton: Princeton University Press, 1967), esp. pp. 179–265, and John Bishop, 'Faith', *SEP*, https://plato.stanford.edu/archives/win2016/entries/faith/.

[124] Aquinas, *ST* 2a2ae 1, 2. Cf. *Disputed questions on Truth*, q. 14, art. 12 (trans. McGlynn, vol. 2, p. 265).

[125] Subordinate or subalternate sciences (*scientiae subalternatae*), in the Aristotelian tradition, were sciences in which the premises were derived from another science. Aquinas would sometimes use the term 'middle sciences' (*scientiae mediae*). The principles of optics, for example, were drawn from the deductive science of geometry. *Posterior Analytics* 75b15. See Richard D. McKirahan Jr., 'Aristotle's Subordinate Sciences', *British Journal for the History of Science* 11 (1978), 197–220. Aquinas allows that scientific knowledge of some preambles of faith is possible – the unity of the Godhead, e.g., – but for most individuals revelation of truths of faith is required (*ST* 1a. 1, 1; *ST* 2a2ae. 1, 5). 'Sacred doctrine' in its completeness is self-evident only to God, who reveals its principles to us. For this reason, while it ultimately has scientific status, it is a subordinate or subalternate science for us. See, e.g., Geoffrey Turner, 'Aquinas on the "Scientific" Status of Theology', *New Blackfriars* 78 (1997), 464–76; Eleonore Stump, *Aquinas* (London: Routledge, 2003), pp. 29–32.

the Christian community on the basis of faith and practice. In a practical realisation of his motto, 'faith seeking understanding', he produced works such as *Why God Became Man* which sought to explicate the logic of the Incarnation and the sacrificial nature of Christ's death.[126] Before this, as Jaroslav Pelikan has argued, the idea of Christ's atoning sacrifice was not embedded in doctrinal statements but rather 'was left to the liturgy of the Mass, above all to the interpretation of the Eucharist as sacrifice, to the hymns and prayers, and to the sacramental life of the Church'.[127] Anselm offered instead a step-by-step argument for the Incarnation that, in his own words, was 'logical and incontrovertible' and, in principle, could address even the concerns of Jews, Muslims, and Pagans that taking human form was unfitting for the Deity.[128] With works such as these, we see the beginning of a relocation of the substance of faith from the practices of the Church, including its liturgical performances and contemplation of its sacred texts, to more formal theology.

Increasing use of the term 'theology' is a marker of this trend towards the systematisation of belief. Until the innovations of Peter Abelard, the key expressions for the substance of Christian beliefs were *doctrina*, which reflected the pastoral activities of preaching and teaching, and *lectio divina*, which referred to the practice of the spiritual exegesis of scripture involving prayer and meditation.[129] 'Theology' (*theologia*) had something of a dubious reputation, typically being reserved as a label for Pagan thinking about the gods.[130] Abelard's application of Aristotelian logic to Christian teaching represented further steps towards a formal theology, and he was the first to deploy the term in a positive sense in the titles of some of his writings.

---

[126] Anselm, *Major Works*, esp. pp. 261f., 355f.

[127] Jaroslav Pelikan, *The Spirit of Medieval Theology* (Toronto: Pontifical Institute of Medieval Studies, 1985), p. 14. (I am grateful to Willemian Otten for drawing my attention to the significance of Anslem in this context and to Pelikan's assessment of his contribution.)

[128] '*Infideles*' – not really 'unbelievers', as commonly translated, rather those who believe in God but do not share the Christian faith. Anselm, *Libri duo cur deus homo*, 1.1, ed. Hugo Laemmer (Berlin, 1857), p. 1; cf. *Major Works*, p. 355.

[129] Jean Leclercq, *The Love of Learning and the Desire for God*, trans. Catherine Misrahi (New York: Fordham University Press, 2008), pp. 15–17, and *passim*; Brian Stock, *After Augustine: The Meditative Reader and the Text* (Philadelphia: University of Pennsylvania Press, 2001), esp. pp. 105–8.

[130] Plato was likely the first to use the term '*theologia*', *Republic* 379a. See Werner Jaeger, *The Theology of the Early Greek Philosophers* (Oxford: Clarendon Press 1948), p. 4. Augustine subsequently used *theologia* to refer to Pagan speculations about divinity. *City of God* 6.5. See also Stephen Brown, 'Key Terms in Medieval Theological Vocabulary', in *Méthodes et instruments du travail intellectuel au moyen âge*, ed. Olga Weijers (Turnhout: Brepols, 1990), pp. 82–97.

These innovations were not greeted with universal approbation. Bernard of Clairvaux complained that Abelard was 'an old Master turned theologian', offering some insight into the negative connotations of the latter designation and its reputation for logic chopping.[131] Part of what was at issue here was the desirability of a shift in emphasis away from contemplative practices to dialectical disputation. This transition was accompanied by changes in institutional settings as the locus of doctrinal reflection moved from monasteries to cathedral schools and then to the first universities. Even when general agreement had been reached on the legitimacy of theology as a 'scientific' activity, there remained significant differences over whether it was a practical science oriented towards goodness, or a speculative science oriented towards truth.[132]

Aquinas's insistence on the scientific status of theology was not intended to reduce Christianity to its propositional contents. Faith was not *just* about propositions. Ultimately, the real object of faith was God himself, who is the 'first truth', and not some proposition.[133] Moreover, because an act of the will is involved – Aquinas's 'inner assent' – belief is to some extent under voluntary control. Aquinas explains that this enables us to account for the fact that while two individuals might witness the same miraculous event, or hear the same sermon, only one might believe or have faith as a consequence.[134] At the same time, this assent is not simply a matter of

---

[131] G. R. Evans, *Old Arts and New Theology: The Beginning of Theology as an Academic Discipline* (Oxford: Clarendon Press, 1980); Turner, 'Aquinas on Theology'.

[132] Franciscans typically opted for the former. Bonaventure argued that theological science was a habit that had as its chief end 'that we become good'. *Commentary on the Sentences* 1.13. Dominicans, such as Aquinas, suggested that theology was primarily a theoretical science, that aimed at truth. For Aquinas the focus of theology is God, rather than human activities. *ST* 1a. 1, 4 cf. 1a. 1, 6. Brian Davies, 'Is "Sacra Doctrina" Theology?', *New Blackfriars* 71 (1990), 141–7.

[133] The 'first truth' (*veritas prima*). Aquinas, *ST* 2a2ae. 1, 1. Cf. *SCG* 1.16.15, and *De veritate* 1.7. On this general notion see William Wood, 'Thomas Aquinas on the Claim that God is Truth', *Journal of the History of Philosophy* 51 (2013), 21–47. 'Proposition' here rendering *enuntiatio* which, in turn, is Aquinas's translation of Aristotle's ἀπόφανσις (*apophansis*), the technical meaning of which is set out in Aristotle's *On Interpretation*. Arguably, 'assertion' is a better translation of both terms. For discussion of the Aristotelian terminology, see Mika Perälä, 'Affirmation and Denial in Aristotle's *De interpretatione*', *Topoi* 39 (2020), 645–56. In distinguishing between God and propositions about God Aquinas speaks of God as the formal object of faith, and the propositions as the material objects of faith. This distinction also informs accounts of implicit faith, with faith typically having to be explicit in relation to its formal object (God) but potentially implicit in relation to its material objects (propositions about God).

[134] This maps onto Augustine's distinction between *fides historica* (characteristic of 'the Jews') and *fides spiritualis*, which entails a conviction about the significance of some witnessed event.

exercising free will but also calls for the operation of 'a supernatural principle', whereby God moves man inwardly by grace.[135] This was a more technical restatement of the New Testament idea that faith was a divine gift. In yet another apparent complication, however, Aquinas also speaks of faith as a kind of interior 'instinct'.[136] But, of course, our instincts originally come from God, too. While having faith is not something that simply arises from our natures, in the sense that it is a gift from God, it is entirely consistent with the natural operations of the mind. This enables Aquinas to conclude that 'unbelief is contrary to nature'.[137]

For our purposes, the most important thing to note is that the first significant deployment of the term 'supernatural' (*supernaturalis*) occurs in these discussions. What Aquinas meant by 'supernatural' and the long-term consequences of this coinage have been the subject of considerable discussion, and will be considered in more detail in Chapter 5.[138] What is clear, however, is that Aquinas is not setting out a two-tier understanding of reality. Neither does he have in mind the kind of exclusive disjunction between natural and supernatural that is characteristic of modern usages. In a sense, Aquinas is offering a naturalistic account of faith, in so far as he assumes that part of the justification for believing comes from the fact that belief arises out of the proper operations of our natural instincts: we have both a natural orientation towards God and a natural belief-forming propensity.[139] The difference between this position and what presently counts as a naturalised epistemology

---

[135] By means of a '*supernaturali principio*' man is raised to things which are *above his nature* [*Elevetur in ea quae sunt supra naturam*]. *ST* 2a2ae. 6, 1.

[136] The believer 'is moved ... by the inward instinct of Divine invitation [*interior instinctu Dei invitantis*]'. *ST* 2a2ae. 2, 9. See commentary in Max Seckler, *Instinkt und Glaubenswille nach Thomas von Aquin* (Mainz: Matthias-Grünewald, 1961); Howard P. Kainz, *The Existence of God and the Faith-Instinct* (Cranbury, NJ: Susquehanna University Press, 2010), esp. pp. 90–101; Lawrence Feingold, *The Natural Desire to See God according to Thomas Aquinas and His Interpreters*, 2nd ed. (Ave Maria, FL: Sapientia Press, 2010).

[137] Aquinas, *ST* 2a2ae. 10, 1.

[138] The classic statement of the problematic comes in Henri de Lubac's *Surnaturel: Études historiques* (Paris: Aubier, 1946), discussed in more detail in Chapter 5. For an overview of an extensive literature see Johannes Mayer, 'Man Is Inclined to His Last End by Nature, though He Cannot Reach It by Nature but Only by Grace: The Principle of the Debate about Nature and Grace in Thomas Aquinas, Thomism and Henri de Lubac', *Angelicum* 88 (2011), 887–939.

[139] 'Though man is naturally inclined to his final end, he cannot attain it naturally, but only by grace.' *Commentary on Boethius: On the Trinity* 1 q. 2, ad. 4. a. 5. For an argument supporting Aquinas as a naturalist in relation to belief see Mark Boespflug, 'Thomistic Faith Naturalized? The Epistemic Significance of Aquinas's Appeal to Doxastic Instinct', *Faith and Philosophy* 38 (2021), 245–61. That said, there has been considerable debate about how Aquinas is to be interpreted on this issue.

hangs crucially on our understanding of 'natural' and 'supernatural', and that is what has changed between the thirteenth century and now.

All of this gives us what appears to be a very complicated picture. These apparent complications were then more manageable because our medieval forebears were operating with a multi-layered understanding of non-competing causes that could make sense of these doctrinal claims. Admittedly, there was an incipient tension between what was to be attributed to divine grace and what to human free will. This would later become the central point of contention in Reformation debates about the nature of justification. The relevant point is that during this period we do not have a disjunction between two separate realms of activity – natural and supernatural. For the scholastics, it was 'natural' for God to work in his creatures, even though his activity went beyond what the creatures could effect through their own natural powers. The term 'supernatural', in these first usages, thus operates within a causal economy that is unfamiliar to modern minds. We might also observe that there was a grain of truth in David Hume's ironic remark at the conclusion of 'Of Miracles' – 'the *Christian Religion* not only was at first attended with miracles, but even at this day cannot be believed by any reasonable person without one' – at least in terms of medieval understanding of the workings of faith. In faith, the movement of the will to lend its assent calls for something beyond natural human powers.[140] But as we will see, the same could also be said of more mundane mental operations.

These connections between the idea of the supernatural and genuine faith will be explored in more detail in Chapter 5. For now, though, we can sum up the key features of this history. First, we encounter new and distinctive usages of 'faith' (*pistis*) in the New Testament that stress the primacy of trust and focus on its social, relational, and affective dimensions. There follows the emergence of creedal formulae that promote consideration of how faith and belief now relate to doctrines set out in propositional form. We witness the influential attempt, in the writings of Augustine, to formalise the relations between trust, propositional belief, and authority. Finally, in the high Middle Ages, we have attempts to relate Christian faith to Aristotelian ideals of knowledge provided by the newly translated works of Aristotle. This last development is nothing less than the inception of theology. It was accompanied by the compensatory mechanism of implicit faith, which relieved the majority of Christians of the burden of having a full knowledge of theological doctrines. This sketch is hardly exhaustive. But it sets out some of the key aspects of pre-modern understandings of faith/belief, sufficient

---

[140] Hume, *Enquiries*, p. 131.

to provide a sense of how they begin to take on a new complexion in the modern period, beginning with the Protestant Reformation.

Looking ahead, the sixteenth-century Reformation brought a decisive end to the institutionally mediated trust relations that had been central to early Christian and medieval conceptions of faith. The shattering of the doctrinal monopoly of the medieval Church confounded appeals to ecclesiastical authority since there were now competing authorities offering divergent doctrinal prescriptions. It was no longer possible simply to reside trust in 'the Church' because there were multiple churches each with their own distinctive teachings. As a consequence, faith necessarily became a more personal matter, with individuals assuming for themselves the burden of understanding and assenting to sets of beliefs. The traditional resort to 'implicit faith' became increasingly suspect, and its critics articulated a new understanding of Christianity that required an explicit knowledge of, and agreement with, a set of doctrines.

The loss of a unitary ecclesiastical authority also motivated the quest for alternative, universal criteria for religious truth, now understood in propositional terms. 'Reason' or 'the light of nature' came to assume a much more prominent role in determining what truth claims individuals should assent to. So, too, did experience or 'experiment' (the Latin *experimentum* meaning 'practical experience'). These developments ceded to the increasingly independent enterprises of philosophy and the natural sciences the power to adjudicate matters of belief. While there was some precedent for this in the scholastic positioning of 'faith' within a broader framework of modified Aristotelian understandings of scientific knowledge (*scientia*), this compromise became difficult to sustain when the whole edifice of Aristotelian philosophy came under assault in the early modern period.[141] The new experimental science offered a different epistemic context against which faith was to be calibrated, even though the new science had itself surreptitiously borrowed a conception of experimental testing from the religious sphere and was no less reliant upon networks of trust.[142] At the same time, the general precedent of thinking about faith in relation to Aristotelian

---

[141] In addition to attempting to calibrate faith in relation to Aristotle's conception of *scientia* (see *ST* 1a. 1) Aquinas's account of faith draws upon Aristotelian formal and material causes, and the idea of a virtue as the 'mean', in this instance between science and opinion. *ST* 2a2ae. 1, 1; 1, 2.

[142] See especially Steven Shapin, *A Social History of Truth: Science and Civility in Seventeenth-Century England* (Chicago: University of Chicago Press, 1994); Peter Harrison, 'Experimental Religion and Experimental Science in Early Modern England', *Intellectual History Review* 21 (2011), 413–33.

thought meant that theological notions of 'faith' continued to be answerable to philosophical conceptions of knowledge and belief, although these were now inflected by the new experimental natural philosophy. 'Reason' and its variants 'natural light', 'natural reason', or 'right reason' would be proposed as either an adjunct to, or replacement for, ecclesiastical authority and the operation of divine grace in moving the faithful to assent to the truths of revelation. Reason had traditionally been understood as a divine gift that naturally disposed the soul to accept legitimate truths of revelation. It was 'natural' in the sense that God had ordained it to be integral to the nature of human beings. Fatefully, reason was destined to become 'natural' in a totally different sense, one that directly opposed it to 'supernatural' and hence placed it in opposition to putatively revealed truths.

Together, these trends are often construed as Christianity's ceding of its epistemic authority to the independent arbiter of philosophy, this being just another exemplification of a general trend of secularisation. More accurately, the religious crisis of the sixteenth and seventeenth centuries focused attention on the problem of knowledge and its justification in an unprecedented way. This, in turn, enabled the development of a new understanding of philosophy as an independent enterprise that has as one its central concerns what we now call epistemology. It is not a complete exaggeration to suggest that modern epistemology was invented to address the problem of the justification of religious beliefs in early modern Europe.[143] This is because religious belief, along with the social and political implications of religious divisions, was the main intellectual preoccupation of the period. The religious predicament of the Latin West subsequently came to determine the agenda of modern philosophy with its distinctive focus on knowledge and its justification. But the precondition for this new kind of philosophy was a problematic that arose within a divided Christendom in which correct propositional belief emerged as a central concern.

---

[143] Nicholas Wolterstorff makes a similar suggestion about Locke, whose epistemology is said to have been directly addressed to the cataclysm of the Reformation. *John Locke and the Ethics of Belief* (Cambridge: Cambridge University Press, 1996), pp. 227, 246.

3

INVENTING EPISTEMOLOGY

All knowers know God implicitly in all that they know.

Thomas Aquinas, *De veritate* q. 22, a. 2, ad. 1

Q. What do you believe?
A. I believe what the Church believes.
Q. What does the Church believe?
A. The Church believes what I believe.
Q. Well, then, what is it that both you and the Church believe?
A. We both believe the very same thing.

The Collier's Catechism

If we compare the changes to which *Religion* has bin always subject, with the present face of things, we may safely conclude, that whatever vicissitude shall happen about it in our time, it will probably neither be to the advantage of *implicit Faith*, nor of *Enthusiasm*, but of *Reason* .... The universal disposition of this *Age* is bent upon a rational religion.

Thomas Sprat, *History of the Royal Society*[1]

3.1 Making Europe Christian

When Père Biard despaired of converting the Mi'kmaq to Christianity on account of their apparent lack of a basic conception of belief, there was a sense in which he was confronting not one foreign culture, but two. In addition to the alien thought-world of the indigenous Americans he had

---

[1] Epigraphs: Collier's Catechism in James Wylie, *The Papacy: Its History, Dogmas, Genius, and Prospects* (Edinburgh, 1851), p. 198; Thomas Sprat, *History of the Royal Society* (London, 1667), p. 366.

also to deal with the residues of medieval notions of implicit faith that had informed the proselytising endeavours of his predecessors in Port Royal. The very first missionaries to Acadia had negotiated the problem of creedal belief by the simple expedient of baptising the willing, rather than inculcating the doctrinal truths of Catholic Christianity. This approach drew upon the idea of implicit faith and reflected the conviction that membership of the Church was bestowed through the rite of baptism. Augustine had maintained that through the sacrament of baptism the infant becomes 'a believer' even though, needless to say, they are unable to assent to any doctrines.[2] A subsequent and explicit affirmation of the truth represented by the sacrament would normally be expected when the 'believer' reached the age of reason, but baptism provided the first step. In keeping with this sentiment, throughout the Middle Ages the verb 'christen', in both its Latin equivalent and in the older European languages, meant 'to Christianise' or 'make someone a Christian'.[3] Biard, however, refused to emulate what he regarded as the lax approach of his predecessors and, to the consternation of many of his charges, withheld baptism from those unable to articulate core Christian doctrines unless they were on death's doorstep.[4] This stance reflected a significant change of attitude within the Catholic Church, as part of the Counter-Reformation response to the challenges issued by Protestants, on the fundamental question of who is counted as a true Christian. At the heart of this change were questions about what had to be explicitly believed, what was entailed by 'believing', and how central believing was to the Christian life.

While there is a widespread popular assumption that the medieval period was pre-eminently an age of Christian faith, historians vary in their assessments of just how Christian medieval Europe was.[5] These assessments are

---

[2] '*Itaque parvulum, etsi nondum fides illa quae in credentium voluntate consistit, jam tamen ipsius fidei sacramentum fidelem facit.*' Letter 98.10, *PL* 33: 364; ET *NPNF* I, vol. 1, p. 206. That said, Augustine also observed a distinction between those who were Christians on account of their baptism (*numero*) and those who genuinely merited the designation (*merito*). *Tractates on John* 61.2 [*PL* 35: 1799]. Luther, along with other early modern sources, also made reference to this distinction. Luther, WA 4, 240.6–25; Thomas Grantham: 'some are only *Numero*, some are *Numero & Merito*, some are *Numero, Merito, & Electio*'. *Christianismus Primitivus* (London, 1678), p. 3.

[3] 'christen, v.' *OED* (accessed 13 November 2020). See also Nathan Ristuccia, *Christianization and Commonwealth in Early Medieval Europe: A Ritual Interpretation* (Oxford: Oxford University Press, 2018), pp. 13–15.

[4] Roger Williams would adopt a similar position in his *Christenings Make Not Christians* [1645], ed. Henry Martyn Dexter (Providence, 1881).

[5] Jean Delumeau, in particular, has made a strong case that the notion of 'the Christian Middle Ages' is a highly dubious one, particularly if the label was meant to apply to rural

complicated by different criteria for what counts as being a Christian. There is little doubt that in the late Middle Ages the lives of most Europeans were governed by the cultic practices of Catholic Christianity, the divisions of time set out in the liturgical calendar, and notions of sacred and consecrated space. There is also clear evidence of widespread religious devotion and personal piety.[6] It is less obvious that there was a universal and explicit knowledge of core Christian doctrines, and this was true even for many of the clergy. Christianisation in early medieval Europe was not understood in terms of the adoption of a distinctive set of Christian beliefs. Instead, as one historian has recently observed, 'it was primarily, though not exclusively, a ritual performance: the integration of individuals into Church communities through mandatory rituals'.[7] This was entirely consistent with Augustine's

---

populations. *Catholicism between Luther and Voltaire* (London: Burns and Oates, 1977). See also Robert Muchembled, *Popular Culture and Elite Culture in France: 1400–1750*, trans. Lydia Cochcrane (Baton Rouge: Louisiana State University Press, 1985). For critiques or refinements of Delumeau's thesis see John Bossy, *Christianity in the West 1400–1700* (Oxford: Oxford University Press, 1985); John Van Engen, 'The Christian Middle Ages as an Historiographical Problem', *American Historical Review* 91 (1986), 519–52; Eamon Duffy, *The Stripping of the Altars: Traditional Religion in England, 1400–1580* (New Haven: Yale University Press, 1992); Richard Fletcher, *The Barbarian Conversion: From Paganism to Christianity* (Berkeley: University of California Press, 1999); C. J. Watkins, *History and the Supernatural in Medieval England* (Cambridge: Cambridge University Press, 2007). Delumeau has since nuanced his original position: 'The Journey of a Historian', *Catholic Historical Review* 96 (2010), 435–48.

[6] Van Engen, 'The Christian Middle Ages as an Historiographical Problem'; William Montner, 'Popular Piety in Late Medieval Europe', in *Ritual, Myth and Magic in Early Modern Europe* (Athens: Ohio University Press, 1983), pp. 6–22.

[7] Ristuccia, *Christianization and Commonwealth*, p. 2. 'Ritual' admittedly, can be a difficult category, partly because the historian must interpret it largely through texts. See Philippe Buc, *The Dangers of Ritual: Between Early Medieval Texts and Social Scientific Theory* (Princeton: Princeton University Press, 2001). There are important parallels between the original sense of 'Christianise' and 'Judaise' (Gk. *ioudaïzō*), with the latter meaning to adopt Jewish practices and observances. See Hurtado, *Destroyer of the Gods*, p. 41. Compare this with some anthropological accounts of conversion in non-Western contexts. 'When a Wari' says of himself that he is a believer or a convert to Protestant Christianity, he is, above all, saying that he is a member of a given community. For this it is necessary for him to perform certain rituals, which does not mean that he had understood or accepted any of the Christian doctrine.' Vilaça, 'Christians without Faith', 112, n. 12. For similar examples, respectively, among the Pitjantjara and Pico, see A. A. Yengoyan, 'Religion, Morality, and Prophetic Traditions: Conversion among the Pitjantjara of Central Australia', in *Conversion to Christianity*, ed. R. W. Hefner (Berkeley: University of California Press, 1993), pp. 233–57 (p. 243); Peter Gow, 'Forgetting Conversion: The Summer Institute of Linguistics Mission in the Piro Lived World', in *The Anthropology of Christianity*, ed. Fenella Cannell (Durham, NC: Duke University Press, 2006), pp. 211–39. See also R. W. Hefner, 'World-Building and the Rationality of Conversion', in *Conversion to Christianity*, ed. Hefner, pp. 3–46: 'religious conversion always involves [an] authoritative acceptance of as yet unknown or unknowable religious truths' (p. 18).

suggestion that one becomes a 'believer' through baptism. We encounter a related idea in the principle articulated by Augustine's disciple Prosper of Aquitaine (c.390–c.455 AD) who in the formula *lex orandi, lex credenda* (the law of prayer is the law of belief) suggested that liturgy and worship are, in a sense, constitutive of 'belief'.[8] It is against this background that we are to understand the new consensus, across the spectrum of sixteenth-century religious reformers, that Europe needed to be re-Christianised. Integral to this programme of Christianisation was a mission to inculcate the populace with explicit doctrinal knowledge.[9] But for all the talk of *re*-Christianising, this programme amounted to the implementation of a new idea of what it was to be Christian.

Martin Luther complained in 1520 that 'the Christian life' is 'unknown throughout the world. It is neither preached about nor sought after; we are altogether ignorant of our own name and do not know why we are Christian or bear the name of Christians.'[10] Much of this ignorance was credited to the scourge of implicit faith. Luther insisted that 'every man is responsible for his own faith', pointing out that just as no one can go to heaven or hell for me, neither can anyone believe or disbelieve for me.[11] In a similar vein, John Calvin lamented that his Roman Catholic adversaries 'deem it of little moment what each man believes concerning God and Christ, or disbelieves, provided he submits to the judgment of the Church with what they call implicit faith'. Implicit faith, he maintained, deludes the general populace: it 'not only buries true faith, but entirely destroys it'.[12] These observations bear more than a passing resemblance to Biard's characterisation of the first Christian converts that he had encountered in

---

[8] Prosper of Aquitaine, *PL* 51: 209–10. 'Let us consider the sacraments of priestly prayers, which having been passed down by the apostles and celebrated uniformly throughout the whole world and in every Catholic Church so that the law of praying might establish the law of believing.' Cf. John Henry Newman, *Grammar of Assent*, p. 134.

[9] Thus Stuart Clark: 'there is scarcely any doubt that "Christianizing" was what reformers of all the major churches *thought* they were doing'. *Thinking with Demons* (Oxford: Oxford University Press, 1997), p. 530. See also Scott H. Hendrix, *Recultivating the Vineyard: The Reformation Agendas of Christianization* (Louisville: Westminster John Knox Press, 2004), esp. pp. 17–24; Ann Marie Johnson and John A. Maxfield (eds.), *The Reformation as Christianization* (Tübingen: Mohr Siebeck, 2012).

[10] Martin Luther, *The Freedom of a Christian*, *LW* 31, 368. Cf. 'Receiving both kinds in the Sacrament', *LW* 36, 264.

[11] Luther, *Temporal Authority*, *LW* 45, 108.

[12] Calvin, *Institutes*, Prefatory Address, vol. 1, p. 7. For his more nuanced position see *Institutes* 3.2.2, vol. 1, pp. 470–1. Seen also Richard Muller, '*Fides* and *Cognitio* in Relation to the Problem of Intellect and Will in the Theology of John Calvin', *Calvin Theological Journal* 25 (1990), 207–24.

America: their baptism notwithstanding, they knew no prayers or articles of faith, attended services only out of curiosity, and had barely a passing familiarity with the word 'Christian'.[13]

As Biard's observations also make apparent, with the passage of time the insistence of Luther and Calvin that Christians have an explicit knowledge of what they believed came to be shared, at least to some degree, by Catholic reformers. The Catholic response to the Protestant Reformation, in the form of the protracted Council of Trent (1545–63), sought to bring greater attention to doctrinal and disciplinary matters. Historian Brad Gregory writes that the decrees and anathemas of the council represent an 'unprecedented emphasis on interior assent to the propositional content of doctrinal truth claims'.[14] This shift towards doctrinal knowledge was reinforced by a new determination to promote religious literacy, especially among the clergy, and the recognition that sacramental practices should be accompanied by knowledge of Christian doctrines. Europe itself thus became a mission field, with Catholic and Protestant clergy alike seeking to school the laity, particularly rural populations, in the basic teachings of Christianity.[15]

In all of this, faith became a much more individual matter, especially for Protestants. While Luther (like Calvin) strongly maintained that faith amounted to personal trust in God, that trust was less dependent upon communal practices or rituals. Faith was not attained through spiritual exercises – 'Masses, ceremonies, vows, fasts, hair shirts, and the like'.[16] What was required was individual resolve, albeit aided by God's grace. Faith was uprooted from a broader ecclesial and social context, making it more a matter

---

[13] *Jesuit Relations*, vol. 3, p. 146.

[14] Brad S. Gregory, *The Unintended Reformation: How a Religious Revolution Secularized Society* (Cambridge, MA: Harvard University Press, 2012), p. 155. In the seventeenth century, Jansenist theologians and philosophers took a hard line against implicit faith. Antoine Arnauld declared implicit faith to be 'chimerical and imaginary'. *De le nécessité de la foi en Jésus-Christ pour être suavéi*, Oeuvres, vol. 10 (Paris, 1777), p. 86. Arnauld was contesting the claim of François de La Mothe le Vayer that Pagans who live virtuous lives might merit salvation. La Mothe le Vayer, *De la vertu des payens* (Paris, 1642), esp. pp. 24f. For discussion see Michael Moriarty, *Disguised Vices: Theories of Virtue in Early Modern French Thought* (Oxford: Oxford University Press, 2011), pp. 211–15; Marenbon, *Pagans and Philosophers*, pp. 276–9.

[15] Delumeau, 'The Journey of a Historian', p. 444; Louis Châtellier, *Tradition chrétienne et renouveau catholique dans le cadre de l'ancien diocèse de Strasbourg (1650–1724)* (Paris: S.E.V.P.E.N., 1964); Gregory, *Unintended Reformation*, pp. 155–7. For the Protestant side see Gerald Strauss, *Luther's House of Learning: Indoctrination of the Young in the German Reformation* (Baltimore: Johns Hopkins University Press, 1978); Raymond A. Mentzer, 'The Persistence of "Superstition and Idolatry" among Rural French Calvinists', *Church History* 65 (1996), 220–33.

[16] Luther, *Lectures on Galatians*, LW 26, 41, cf. pp. 32, 312, 330.

of the individual's direct relationship to God. Indeed, it has been argued, with some justification, that Luther introduced modern individualism into the West.[17] This resistance to the ecclesiastical governance of all aspects of the religious life would have other, far-reaching consequences.[18] It signalled the beginning of a new relationship between the faithful and the institution that had presided over the ritual performances in which belief was enacted. That same institution had also been the custodian of religious knowledge and guarantor of its truth. The radical rupture of that institution wrought by the Protestant Reformation necessitated new understandings of religious authority and the faith once vested in it. At the same time, and quite independently of the reformers' intentions, it became possible to think of practice and belief as separate aspects of the religious life, even to the point where the relation could be seen as one of opposition – mindless ritual as an inferior substitute

---

[17] There is an extensive literature on this question. Jacques Maritain, *Three Reformers: Luther, Descartes, Rousseau* (New York: Charles Scribner, 1950), pp. 14–25; Martin E. Marty, 'Luther's Living Legacy', *Christian History* 39 (1993), 51–3; Derek Wilson, *Out of the Storm: The Life and Legacy of Martin Luther* (New York: Macmillan, 2008), p. 344; Rob Sorensen, *Martin Luther and the German Reformation* (London: Anthem Press, 2016), pp. 93–4. Famously, Max Weber had made a case for the influence of Calvinism on the emergence of a pessimistic individualism that for him underpinned capitalism. *The Protestant Ethic and the Spirit of Capitalism*, trans. Stephen Kalberg (London: Routledge, 2012), esp. pp. 58–61. See also Wolfgang Schluchter, *The Rise of Western Rationalism: Max Weber's Developmental History*, trans. Guenther Roth (Berkeley: University of California Press, 1981), esp. p. 169. Weber's Heidelberg colleague Ernst Troeltsch also saw in aspects of the Protestant Reformation the seeds of modernity, although these were unintended and again Calvin was given a more prominent role than Luther. *Protestantism and Progress: The Significance of Protestantism for the Rise of the Modern World* (Philadelphia: Fortress Press, 1986), esp. pp. 43f. Cf. A. Dakin, *Calvinism* (London: Duckworth, 1940), p. 134. In the nineteenth century Michael Pupin maintained that the religious individualism of the reformers paved the way for a new 'scientific individualism'. *The New Reformation: From Physical to Spiritual Realities* (New York: Charles Scribner's Sons, 1927), pp. 3–4. Charles Taylor gives Descartes a more prominent role. *Secular Age*, p. 26; *Sources of the Self: The Making of the Modern Identity* (Cambridge, MA: Harvard University Press, 1992), pp. 143–209. Larry Seidentop argues for an earlier, yet intrinsically Christian, emergence of the notion of the individual, *Inventing the Individual* (Cambridge, MA: Belknap Press, 2014) as, too, Karl Weintraub, who traces notions of Christian individualism to Augustine's autobiographical *Confessions*. *The Value of the Individual: Self and Circumstance in Autobiography* (Chicago: University of Chicago Press, 1978), pp. 18–48. Most recently, Joseph Henrich has claimed that Protestantism gave a 'booster shot' to the incipient individualism of medieval Catholicism. *The WEIRDest People in the World: How the West Became Psychologically Peculiar and Particularly Prosperous* (New York: Farrar, Straus & Giroux, 2020), ch. 12.

[18] The flip-side of this, arguably, was the application of monastic disciplines to the secular realm. On this theme see Taylor, *Secular Age*, pp. 90–145; Philip S. Gorski, *The Disciplinary Revolution: Calvinism and the Rise of the State in Early Modern Europe* (Chicago: University of Chicago Press, 2003); Gregory, *Unintended Reformation*, pp. 209–10; Michel Foucault, *Discipline and Punish*, trans. Alan Sheridan (New York: Vintage, 1979), p. 141, and *passim*.

for genuine religious knowledge. Again, this move was consistent with the appearance of new notions of religion and of plural religions. 'Religion', once understood as a virtue, a form of piety, was reified, enabling the category of plural 'religions' which were understood in terms of their distinctive beliefs and practices.[19] This development is also distantly reflected in the modern sociological distinction between 'believing' and 'belonging'.[20]

Accompanying this dismantling of a central ecclesiastical authority was a sustained attack on the Catholic clergy. The priesthood had been one of the prime targets of Luther's reforming zeal. He denied that priests and monks were different in kind to anyone else. Individuals might be allocated different offices, but all share the same spiritual estate.[21] Calvin agreed that all Christians belong to a royal priesthood, a status conferred not by the Church, but by God.[22] While church organisation was important for Calvin, neither the Church nor its ministers mediated between God and the elect. New forms of Church polity necessarily impacted on practices of believing that had previously been distributed across the institution of the one holy and apostolic Church. These changes were accompanied by a loss of trust in the priestly order, the extreme manifestation of which was the emergence of the early modern idea of 'priestcraft'. For those who subscribed to this notion, priests were regarded as members of a universal 'type' whose signal characteristic was the opposite of trustworthiness. Priestcraft entailed systematic deception and imposition on overly credulous populations.[23]

---

[19] Thus Robert Ferguson, 'All that Relates to Religion may be reduced either to faith or obedience; to what we are to *believe,* or what we are to *perform.* Faith and practice engross the whole of mans duty. *Credenda & agenda* constitute the System of Religion.' *A Sober Enquiry into the Nature, Measure, and Principle of Moral Virtue* (London, 1673), p. 169. In the Middle Ages, 'religions' had referred to different monastic orders.

[20] Grace Davie, 'Believing without Belonging: Is This the Future of Religion in Britain?', *Social Compass* 37 (1990), 455–69.

[21] Martin Luther, *To the Christian Nobility of the German Nation* (1520), LW 44, 127–8. This entailed a rejection of the medieval hierarchical social order premised on three distinct estates: clergy, aristocracy, laity. See Rosemary O'Day, 'The Clergy of the Church of England', in *The Professions in Early Modern England*, ed. Wilfred Prest (London: Routledge, 1987), pp. 25–63. For the Catholic position see The Council of Trent, Session 23, ch. 4.

[22] '… we are all through his grace made priests …'. John Calvin, *Commentaries on the Epistle of Paul to the Romans*, in *Calvin's Commentaries*, 22 vols., trans. John Owen (Grand Rapids: Baker, 2003), vol. 19, p. 452. See also John R. Crawford, 'Calvin and the Priesthood of all Believers', *Scottish Journal of Theology* 21 (1968), 145–56.

[23] Justin Champion, *The Pillars of Priestcraft Shaken: The Church of England and Its Enemies, 1660–1730* (Cambridge: Cambridge University Press, 1992). See also the special issue of *Intellectual History Review* 28/1 (2018), edited by James A. T. Lancaster and Andrew McKenzie-McHarg, on the theme 'Priestcraft: Early Modern Variations on the Theme of Sacerdotal Imposture'.

As a consequence of these linked developments – attacks on implicit faith, denial of the Roman Church's authority in matters of doctrine, the separation of practice and belief, the undermining of the office of the priesthood – the burden for knowing and defending doctrinal details fell increasingly upon the individual rather than being distributed, on the basis of trust relations, across the community of the faithful. Jesuit Cardinal Robert Bellarmine, who in the late sixteenth century compiled the first systematic catalogue of key differences between Catholics and Protestants, pointed to the novelty of the reformers' stance on this issue. Our present-day heretics (i.e., the Protestants), he charged, permit 'private persons to be judges in matters of faith'.[24] Insistence on the right to make private judgements, as we have seen, was the vice that lay at the heart of heresy. Essayist and philosopher Michel de Montaigne, writing around the same time as Bellarmine, offered a similar appraisal of the aftermath of Protestant attacks on Catholic religion:

> once you have thrown into the balance of doubt and uncertainty any articles of their religion, they soon cast all the rest of their beliefs into similar uncertainty. They had no more authority for them, no more foundation, than for those you have just undermined .... They then take it upon themselves to accept nothing on which they have not pronounced their approval, subjecting it to their individual assent.[25]

In a post-Enlightenment age we typically celebrate this development. For Bellarmine and Montaigne, it was deeply regrettable.[26]

---

[24] Robert Bellarmine, *Disputationes de Controversiis Christianae Fidei* (Ingolstadii, 1586), I, 1, 3, 3 (cols. 170–2). Bellarmine provided specific examples from the writings of Martin Luther, Philip Melanchthon, Johannes Brenz, John Calvin, and Martin Chemnitz.

[25] Michel de Montaigne, 'Apology for Raymond Sebond' [1576], in *The Complete Essays*, ed. and trans. M. A. Screech (London: Penguin, 2003), p. 439.

[26] This difference would continue to feature in competing confessional histories discussed in Chapter 6. Counter-revolutionary Catholic writer Louis de Bonald declared that the Protestant 'right of examination and interpretation' had led to a succession of social and political catastrophes in Europe. 'De l'unité religieuse en Europe', *Mercure de France* [1806], in *Oeuvres complètes*, vol. 10 (Geneva, 1982), pp. 229–83 (p. 260). Joseph de Maistre wrote in a similar vein that the Reformation principle of private judgement had caused numerous revolutions and massacres. *Considerations on France* [1796], ed. and trans. R. Lebrun (Cambridge: Cambridge University Press, 2000), p. 27. Subsequently, Catholic historian Jaime Balmes declared that: 'if there be any thing constant in Protestantism, it is undoubtedly the substitution of private judgment for public and lawful authority'. This principle was 'lamentable and disastrous'. *Protestantism and Catholicism Compared, With Respect to European Civilization*, 2nd ed. (Baltimore: John Murphy, 1851), p. 26.

3.2 Implicit Faith and the Ethics of Belief

In his *Lectures on the Philosophy of History* (1822–30) the philosopher G. W. F. Hegel (1770–1831) observes that the 'essential content' of the Protestant Reformation is this: 'man sets himself to be free'.[27] Hegel's historical pronouncements, it must be conceded, need to be treated with a degree of caution. But in this case he has a point. Arguably, one of the most iconic historical instances of the assertion of individual autonomy was Martin Luther's appearance before the Imperial Diet at Worms in April 1521. In June of the previous year, Pope Leo had issued the bull *Exsurge domine*, threatening Luther with excommunication and demanding that he recant his teachings within sixty days. He had also ordered, for good measure, that Luther's offending writings be sought out and burned in public.[28] On the sixtieth day, 10 December 1521, Luther responded in kind, burning the papal bull along with a number of books of canon law. He was duly excommunicated. Under pressure from the German princes to end the standoff, Emperor Charles V called an assembly of the Holy Roman Empire in the Imperial Free city of Worms and invited Luther to attend under promise of safe passage. The emperor and the Church were looking for Luther to recant his teaching and writings; a number of the German princes secretly hoped that he would not, seeing in this occasion the opportunity to establish their independence from Rome. When confronted with his allegedly heretical views Luther was invited to recant. Unconvinced by the arguments against him and, crucially, the criteria that were in play, Luther offered the celebrated response: 'Unless I am convinced by the testimony of the Scriptures or by clear reason (for I do not trust either in the pope or in councils alone .... I cannot and I will not recant anything, since it is neither safe nor right to go against conscience.' Tradition has it that he went on to say: 'Here I stand, I can do no other.'[29]

---

[27] G. W. F. Hegel, *Lectures on the Philosophy of History*, trans. Ruben Alvarado (Aalten: Wordbridge, 2011), p. 376. Cf. *Hegel's Lectures on the History of Philosophy*, 3 vols. in 1, trans. E. S. Haldane and Frances H. Simpson (Delhi: Lector House, 2020), pp. 614f.; *The Positivity of the Christian Religion* [1795], in *Early Theological Writings*, trans. Richard Kroner (Philadelphia: University of Pennsylvania Press, 1975), pp. 128, 146; *On the Tercentenary of the Augsburg Confession*, in *Hegel: Political Writings*, ed. Lawrence Dickey and H. B. Nisbet (Cambridge: Cambridge University Press, 1999), pp. 186–96.

[28] '*Exsurge domine*' (Rome, 1520) in Peter Fabisch and Erwin Iserloh (eds.), *Dokumente zur Causa Lutheri (1517–1521)*, 2 vols. (Münster: Aschendorff, 1988–91), vol. 2, p. 394.

[29] 'Luther at the Diet of Worms', *LW* 32, 112. Luther argued, partly on the authority of Nicholas of Tudesco (Panormitanus, 1386–1445), that in matters of faith individuals are above the pope, provided that they use better authority and reason. *LW* 31, 365f., cf. *LW*

3.2 IMPLICIT FAITH AND THE ETHICS OF BELIEF

In this symbolic moment we witness what appears to be a clear rejection of a corporate and institutional understanding of belief. Luther substituted individual conviction for trust in the Church and its councils, and elevated the alternative authorities of individual conscience, scripture, and reason (although he envisaged a carefully circumscribed role for the latter). Subsequently addressing the topic of 'the freedom of the Christian', he would expand membership of this tribunal to include a third authority – experience or, literally, 'experiment'.[30] This episode marks the inauguration of what has become a distinctive characteristic of the modern West – the principle that individuals ought to take responsibility for what they believe. This means not only being able to articulate the precise content of what is believed but, equally importantly, being able to offer a justification for what is held to be true. One of the major drivers of this new attitude to belief, as noted above, was the concerted Protestant campaign against implicit belief.[31] Indeed, the nub of the Protestant/Catholic divide, as one Protestant controversialist expressed it, could be understood in these terms: 'whether they shall follow their own reason and judgment, or give up themselves to follow a Guide with a blind and implicite faith'.[32] In *The*

32, 81, n. 99. Hegel described this event as 'the great foundation of Protestant freedom, the Palladium of the Protestant Church'. *The Positivity of the Christian Religion*, in *Early Theological Writings*, p. 121.

[30] Luther's *On the Freedom of the Christian* opens with this statement: 'To many, Christian faith has appeared to be an easy thing; indeed not a few reckon it among the social virtues, as it were, because they have not tested [or proved] it experimentally [*qui nullo experiment eam probauerunt*].' Martin Luther, *De libertate christiana* (n.p., 1520), sig. biiir.

[31] For theological treatments of implicit faith from a Protestant perspective, see Ritschl, *Fides implicita*; Georg Hoffmann, *Die Lehre von der Fides implicita* (Leipzig: Hinrichs, 1906); and, more recently, Ralf K. Wüstenberg, '*Fides implicita* "revisited": Versuch eines evangelischen Zugangs', *Neue Zeitschrift für Systematiche Theologie* 49 (2007), 71–85.

[32] William Sherlock, *A Vindication of both parts of the Preservative against Popery* (London, 1688), p. 8. The discussion above will reference primarily English language critiques of implicit faith, but these were characteristic of the reformed traditions across Europe. German critics include the Reformed theologian and one of the principal authors of the Heidelberg Catechism, Zacharias Ursinus, who declared that 'The Papists' implicit faith is not faith at all, but blind opinion.' *Corpus doctrinae Christianae* (Heidelberg, 1621), p. 143. Hartmann Creide maintained that 'Believing what the Church believes', amounts not to genuine faith but 'blind ignorance'. *Querela medela cautela*, 2 vols. (Frankfurt, 1666), vol. 2, p. 397. See also Andreas Kesler, *Pabsthumb. Gründlicher Bericht, von der Papisten Vrsprung, Lehre vnd Leben* (Coburg, 1630), p. 133. Daniel Toussain, a Huguenot author who wrote in Latin and German, referred to implicit faith as 'a confused belief, a dizziness'. *Warhaffter Bericht von der vorgenommenen Verbesserung in Kirchen* (Utrecht, 1584), p. 71. For other Huguenot critiques of implicit fait see Jean Daillé, *Sermons sur l'epître de l'apôtre saint Pauls aux Colossiens, seconde partie* (Paris, 1648), p. 147; Jean Valleton, *Le Réveille-matin des apostats sur la révolte de Jaques Illaire, ou la reutation des escrits publiez au nom d'icelui sous le faux et fantastique titre de conversion des Huguenots à la Foy Catholique* (Geneva, 1608), p. 529; Pierre Allix, *Douze sermons sur*

Religion of Protestants (1637/1687), a popular seventeenth-century work and favourite of the philosopher John Locke, William Chillingworth had similarly concluded that the Protestant creed called for the rational judgement of the individual rather than a simple acceptance of things on trust:

> Not willing I confess to take anything upon trust, and to believe it without asking myself why; no, nor able to command myself (were I never so willing) to follow, like a sheep, every shepheard that should take upon him to guide me; or every Flock that should chance to go before me; but most apt and most willing to be led by reason.[33]

There were several facets to the early modern critique of implicit faith. A common charge was that the medieval Church had substituted religious practice for the holding of correct beliefs, and that genuine Christianity was impossible without the latter. Preaching in 1684 on the theme of 'rational service' to a congregation of old Etonians, Joseph Layton asked his auditors to 'turn your Eye to the Men of implicit Faith: ... you shall see them creeping before Images, adoring of Wafers, paying Pensions for Purgatory, and Traffiquing for the price of Sins. In the midst of all this Pageantry, and this Nonsense, Their comfort is, they believe as the Church believes.'[34] Religious devotion, at least the kind that was evidenced in 'papist' rituals, was said to go hand in hand with religious ignorance. It was a commonplace among Protestant controversialists that their Catholic opponents actively promoted the principle that 'ignorance is the mother of devotion'.[35] This

---

divers textes, 2nd ed. (Rotterdam, 1685), pp. 199–200; J. D., *Le tableau de la nouvelle Jérusalem* (Geneva, 1690), p. 16.

[33] William Chillingworth, *The Religion of Protestants a Safe Way to Salvation* [1737], 6th ed. (London, 1687), p. 2. For Locke's approval see Victor Nuovo, *John Locke: The Philosopher as Christian Virtuoso* (Oxford: Oxford University Press, 2017), p. 220.

[34] Joseph Layton, *A sermon preached at the anniversary meeting of the Eaton-scholars* (London, 1684), p. 19.

[35] John Caldwell, *A Sermon preached before the right honorable Earle of Darbie* (London, 1577), sig. C.iiir. For similar remarks see Francis Bunny, *A comparison betweene the aunctient fayth of the Romans, and the new Romish religion* (n.p., 1595), p. 10; Thomas Beard, *A retractiue from the Romish religion* (London, 1616), p. 34; Baxter, *The Safe Religion*, p. 25; Robert Burton, *Anatomy of Melancholy* [1621], 3 vols., ed. Holbrook Jackson (London: Folio, 2005), 3.4.1.2, vol. 3, p. 374; Charles Blount, *A Just Vindication of Learning* (London, 1679), p. 13; Theophilus Gale, *The Anatomie of Infidelitie* (London, 1672), p. 90; Hugh Binning, *The Common Principles of Christian Religion* (Glasgow, 1667), p. 112. It is more difficult to find this principle actually being asserted by Catholic authors. Perhaps, out of context, Aquinas, *ST* 2a2ae. 82, 3: '*scientia ... quandoque occaisonaliter devotionem impenduit*' (Science ... sometimes occasions a hindrance to devotion), although this was hardly representative. Hume later reprised the maxim in the conclusion of his *Natural History of Religion*, ed. H. E. Root (Stanford: Stanford University Press, 1957), p. 75.

3.2 IMPLICIT FAITH AND THE ETHICS OF BELIEF 79

maxim implied an inverse relationship between devotional fervour and religious knowledge, along with the necessity of a proper balance between practice and belief. The *theory* of Roman rites was a related target, and in particular, teachings about transubstantiation. According to Protestant critics, this irrational doctrine could subsist only because it was accepted without question.[36] Huguenot controversialist Moïse Amyraut argued against 'blind, brutal acquiescence', insisting upon the 'necessity of examination' of all doctrines. To accept a dogma without understanding how it was grounded in scripture or rationally implied by some other well-founded doctrine was to fail to believe in it at all. Christians who uncritically receive what is taught, he concluded, are merely Christians by an accident of birth, in the same way that Turks are Mahommedans.[37]

The category of implicit faith was also alleged to have been a device invented by scholastic philosophers to justify their regrettable tolerance for nescience among the general population. Part of the problem with this scholastic version of the doctrine was its reliance upon an Aristotelian distinction between formal and material – specifically the 'formal' and 'material' objects of faith.[38] For those who no longer subscribed to an Aristotelian metaphysics it became more challenging to provide a philosophically plausible account of how implicit faith operated.[39] A more general critique was that it was a fancy label for ignorance: mere 'ignorance garnish'd and set off with a plausible word, that has no meaning'; a pretext for '*simple grosse ignorance*'; synonymous with 'virtual Unbelief'.[40] Protestants were to deploy their own derisory designation for this kind of uncritical belief: the 'faith of the collier' (or charcoal burner). This was the vacuous commitment of the rustic simpleton who knew nothing except the need to reside trust in

---

[36] See e.g., Thomas Bedford, *A Treatise of the Sacraments* (London, 1638), pp. 82–3; Robert Nelson, *Transubstantiation contrary to Scripture* (London, 1688), p. 2; Thomas Tenison, *A friendly debate between a Roman Catholick and a Protestant* (London, 1688), p. 29; Sherlock, *A Vindication*, pp. 100–1.

[37] Moïse Amyraut, *De l'élévation de la foi et de l'abaissement de la raison* (Saumur, 1640), pp. 75–6. See also Philippe du Marnix, *Traicte du Sacrement* (Saumur, 1601), p. 25; Michel le Faucheur, *Traitté de la Cène du Seigneur, où est monstré que c'est qu'il faut croire de la nature et de l'usage de ce saint sacrament* (Geneva, 1635), p. 799.

[38] For the formal/material distinction see Aquinas, *ST* 2a2ae. 1, 1. Simply put, the material objects of faith are doctrines, the formal object of faith is God.

[39] See, e.g., Theophilus Gale, *Christ's tears for Jerusalems unbelief and ruine* (London, 1679), p. 122.

[40] Anthony Burgess, *Expository Sermons upon the Whole 17th Chapter of the Gospel according to St. John* (London, 1656), pp. 123, 639. Cf. William Perkins, *A Commentarie or exposition, vpon the fiue first chapters of the Epistle to the Galatians* (London, 1617), p. 142; Sampson Estwick, *A Sermon preached at the Cathedral-Church of St. Paul* (London, 1698), p. 14.

the teachings of the Church.[41] Huguenot writers also spoke dismissively of the '*foi du charbonnier*', an expression that in various European idioms was in continual use until at least the mid-nineteenth century.[42] All of this signals a shift of attention, in conceptions of faith, to the content of belief and its justification, and away from an attitude of trust and the devotional practices that sustained it.

Unquestioning obedience and atrophy of the capacity for rational deliberation were also claimed to be the side-effects of implicit faith. There was a significant political dimension here, since the relevant trust relations and the accompanying demands on obedience ultimately led back to Rome. As one writer put it, implicit faith promotes 'indisputable obedience, & absolute dependence on the Church and Court of *Rome*'.[43] It was a device 'to keep men under their obedience', explained another.[44] Critiques of implicit faith were thus related to both religious and political freedoms. Susceptibility to religious imposture was another undesirable consequence of acquiescent belief. Samuel Estwick contended that implicit faith 'discards all Reasons and Motives of Credibility, closes and seals up the eyes and lips of the Votary, and thereby exposes him to all the fancies and extravagancies that Seducers can suggest to him'.[45] In so far as implicit faith entailed the surrender of rational

---

[41] Latin: *fides carbonaria*. See, e.g., Thomas Morton, *A Catholike Appeale for Protestants* (London, 1609), p. 676; Beard, *A retractiue from the Romish religion*, pp. 348–50; Barnaby Rich, *The Irish Hubbub* (London, 1618), p. 52; John White, *A Defence of the Way to the True Church* (London, 1614), pp. 191, 194, 200; Thomas Helveys, *Persecution for religion judg'd and condemned* (London, 1662), pp. 53f.; Thomas Barlow, *Brutum fulmen* (London, 1681), pp. 201f.; John Norris, *An Account of Reason and Faith: in Relation to the Mysteries of Christianity* [1697], 12th ed. (London, 1724), p. 77; Henry Stubbe, *A Censure upon certaine passages contained in the history of the Royal Society* (Oxford, 1670), p. 12; James Dupont, *Three Sermons* (London, 1676), p. 55; Wylie, *The Papacy*, p. 198.

[42] See, e.g., Philippe du Marnix, *Le tableau des différens de la religion* (Leiden, 1603), vol. 1, p. 9; Nicolas Vignier, *Theatre de l'Antichrist* (Geneva, 1613), vol. 1, p. 638; Fleury de Bellingen, *L'etymologie ou Explication des proverbes François* (La Haye, 1656), p. 252; Honoré de Balzac, *La messe de l'athée* (Brussels, 1836), p. 189. For examples of the German 'Köhlerglaube' see Arnold Mengering, *Scrutinium conscientiae catecheticum* (Leipzig, 1687), p. 182; Christian Thomasius, *Vollständige Erläuterung Der Kirchen-Rechts-Gelahrtheit*, 2 vols. (Frankfurt and Leipzig, 1738), vol. 1, p. 268; Carl Vogt, *Köhlerglaube und Wissenschaft* (Giessen, 1855), a derisive riposte to Rudolph Wagner's *Menschenschöpfung und Seelensubstanz* (Göttingen, 1854).

[43] T. A., *Religio Clerici* (London, 1681), p. 92. This connection could also be exploited to argue for religious and political freedoms in England. See William Penn, *England's great interest in the choice of this new Parliament* (London, 1669); Anon., *A Certain Way to Save England* (London, 1681), p. 17; Joseph Pennyman, *A Looking Glass for the Quakers* (London, 1689), p. 5; John Horn, *An Appeal to the Impartial & Judicious Reader* (London, 1660), p. 30.

[44] Anon., *Liberty of Conscience, Explicated and Vindicated* (London, 1689), p. 16. Cf. Richard Baxter, *A Moral Prognostication* (London, 1680), p. 33.

[45] Estwick, *A Sermon*, p. 15.

3.2 IMPLICIT FAITH AND THE ETHICS OF BELIEF

autonomy – often regarded as the distinguishing feature of human beings – it was said to reduce its adherents to a bestial servility. In his *Antidote against the poyson of popery* (1679), Christopher Ness declared that implicit faith 'is a mere bruitish unreasonable thing; ... like the motion of a Beast that is ordered by his Driver, but knows neither whither nor wherefore'.[46]

Common to virtually all critiques of implicit faith was the conviction that individuals had a religious duty to be able to give a reasoned account of what they believed and why. It was argued to be a sin against God-given reason to subcontract to an institution the responsibility for believing.[47] 'God calls upon us to employ our Talent', contended Joseph Layton, 'to Exercise our selves in these things, to *Build up our selves in our most holy Faith*, and to *Stand fast in the Liberty wherewith Christ has made us Free*'.[48] God requires of us 'a distinct knowledge of the points of our faith', agreed John White, so that we are able 'to expound, & manifest them'. 'Having given us reason', maintained Isaac Barrow, God requires it 'as a matter of duty' to exercise it in matters of faith.[49] It was thus held to be a religious obligation to have ready reasons for holding particular beliefs and this imperative was supported by appeals to a range of biblical passages.[50] In sum, being a true

---

[46] Christopher Ness, *A Protestant antidote against the poyson of popery* (London, 1679), p. 171. See also Theophilus Gale, *Christ's tears*, pp. 90f., 122; Layton, *A sermon*, p. 5.

[47] One of the standard proof texts for this argument was reference to 'reasonable service' or 'rational worship' (λογικὴν λατρείαν) in Romans 12:1. See Joseph Glanvill, *Logou thrēskeia, Or, A Seasonable Recommendation and Defence of Reason in the Affairs of Religion* (London, 1670), pp. 28, 33, and *passim*; Layton, *A sermon*, *passim*; John Cook, *What the Independents would Have* (London, 1647), p. 3; Anon., *A Catholic pill to purge Popery* (London, 1677), p. 9; Albert Warren, *An Apology for the Discourse of Humane Reason* (London, 1680), Preface (unpaginated); Charles Wolseley, *The Reasonableness of Scripture-Beleif* [sic] (London, 1672), Preface; John Goodman, *Seven Sermons Preach'd upon Several Occasions* (London, 1697), p. 222; Bentley, *Unreasonableness of Atheism*, p. 26.

[48] Layton, *A sermon*, p. 19; White, *Defence of the Way to the True Church*, p. 202.

[49] Isaac Barrow, 'Of Faith', in *The Theological Works of Isaac Barrow*, 8 vols. (Oxford: Oxford University Press, 1830), vol. 4, p. 267. For further examples see George Rust, *A Discourse of the Use of Reason in Matters of Religion* (London, 1683), pp. 17, 24, 46f.; William Bramston, *A Sermon preached at the opening of the Lecture at Maldon* (London, 1697), p. 17; Richard Kidder, *The Judgment of Private Discretion in Matters of Religion Defended* (London, 1687), p. 10; Anon., *A Protestant's Resolution: shewing reasons why he will not be a Papist* (London 1679), pp. 7–8; William Durham, *A Serious Exhortation to the Necessary Duties of Family and Person Instruction* (London, 1659), pp. 66–9; Samuel Johnson, *A Sermon Preach'd before the Lord Mayor* (London, 1684), pp. 12–13, 15–16; Warren, *An Apology*, p. 40; Martin Clifford, *Discourse of Humane Reason* (London, 1690), p. 46; James Canaries, *A Discourse representing the Sufficient Manifestation of the Will of God* (Edinburgh, 1684), p. 163.

[50] Most commonly 1 Peter 3:15: 'and be ready always to give an answer to every man that asketh you a reason of the hope that is in you'. Also Romans 12:1 on reasonable worship, referenced above, and Acts 17:11.

Christian was now thought to involve not only the explicit profession of certain beliefs, but also being cognizant of their content and capable of providing a justification for holding them.[51]

Since the late nineteenth century this basic principle, stripped of its historical context and original theological justifications, has been known in philosophical circles as 'the ethics of belief' – the idea that we have a moral duty to be able to provide good evidence for holding the beliefs we do. In the 1877 paper that introduced that phrase into the philosophical lexicon the Cambridge philosopher William Kingdon Clifford summed up the basic idea in these words: 'it is wrong always, everywhere, and for any one, to believe anything upon insufficient evidence'.[52] It should now be clear that something closely akin to this principle had been fundamental to critiques of implicit faith from the sixteenth century onwards. To the extent that the archaeology of this epistemic imperative has been excavated, John Locke has been proposed as its modern philosophical progenitor.[53] It is certainly true that Locke does articulate something like this principle and seems to have been the first to expound it systematically in a philosophical context. Yet, in effect, he was formalising an impulse that had characterised Protestant critiques of implicit faith for well over a century. For this reason, implicit faith is Locke's stock example of how *not* to arrive at reliable knowledge: 'whilst some (and those the most) taking things upon trust, misemploy their power of assent, by lazily enslaving their minds to the dictates and dominion of others in doctrines, which it is their duty carefully to examine, and

---

[51] There remained, however, even in Protestant circles, some concessions to the necessity of relying upon the judgements of others, not least for the same reasons that scholastics had originally proposed the idea – namely, the theological complexity of some key doctrines. See Jeremy Taylor, Θεολογία ἐκλεκτική. *A discourse on freedom of thinking in matters of Religion* [1647] (Oxford, 1763), pp. 77f.; William Bridge, *The truth of the times vindicated* (London, 1643), p. 51; George Keith, *Truth and innocency defended against calumny and defamation* (Philadelphia, 1692), p. 17; Norris, *Reason and Faith*, pp. 90–4. But it was typically stressed that this entailed faith in God, and not in the Church. Catholic writers also charged Protestants with having implicit faith in scripture – asserting its authority without explicit knowledge of the contents of every verse. See W. S. [William Stuart], *Presbyteries Triall* (Paris, 1657), p. 42; Charles Leslie, *The Case Stated between the Church of Rome and the Church of England in a Second Conversation* (n.p., 1721).

[52] William Kingdon Clifford, 'The Ethics of Belief' [1877] in W. K. Clifford, *Lectures and Essays*, 2nd ed., ed. Leslie Stephen and Frederick Pollock (London: Macmillan, 1886), pp. 339–63 (p. 346). Clifford goes on to invoke John Milton's criticism of implicit faith from *Areopagitica*, in *Prose Works of John Milton*, 5 vols. (London: Henry Bohn, 1848), vol. 2, p. 85. In a second essay, 'The Ethics of Religion', Clifford applied to principle directly to religious beliefs: 'Religious beliefs must be founded on evidence; if they are not so founded, it is wrong to hold them.' *Lectures and Essays*, p. 369.

[53] The key work is Wolterstorff, *Locke and the Ethics of Belief*.

not blindly, with an implicit faith, to swallow'.[54] A key problem to which Locke's epistemology had been addressed was the resolution of competing knowledge claims, the most acute form of which, during the period, lay in religious differences.[55] While an 'ethics of belief', as articulated by Clifford, was intended as a critique of religious convictions in general, the idea itself was hardly an innovation of the nineteenth century. It had its origins in confessional disputes of the early modern period when it was first wielded by Protestant controversialists.

Locke's positive prescriptions for combating the evils of implicit belief are similarly to be understood against the background of contemporary theological discussions. Examination of the grounds of one's beliefs was for Locke a divinely mandated duty: 'He that believes, without having any Reason for believing ... neither seeks Truth as he ought, nor pays the Obedience due to his Maker, who would have him use those discerning Faculties he has given him.' The Christian has a 'Duty as a rational creature' to use the faculties with which God has endowed them.[56] Reason, then, was to provide the means by which the holding of particular beliefs could be justified. Our duty is to believe or disbelieve 'as reason directs'. Reason 'must be our

---

[54] Locke, *Essay* 1.4.22 (p. 99). Locke begins the *Essay* with an appeal to readers to make use of their own thoughts and not 'to take things on trust from others' (Epistle to the Reader, p. 7). Elsewhere: the way to improve our knowledge is not 'blindly, and with an implicit faith, to receive and swallow principles'. *Essay* 4.12.6 (p. 642). 'For he that takes up the opinions of any Church in the lump, without examining them, has truly neither searched after, nor found truth, but has only found those that he thinks have found truth, and so receives what they say with an implicit faith, and so pays them the homage that is due only to God.' 'Error', from Locke's commonplace book, in *The Life of John Locke, with extracts from his Correspondence, Journals and Common-Place Books*, ed. Peter Lord King (London, 1829), pp. 281f. It is a miscarriage of reason to 'think according to the example of others, whether parents, neighbours, ministers, of who else they are pleased to make choice of to have an implicit faith in, for the saving of themselves the pains and trouble of thinking and examining for themselves'. *Of the Conduct of the Understanding*, new edition (London, 1801), pp. 9–10. '[E]ach must understand for himself, the best he can.' *Vindications of the Reasonableness of Christianity*, ed. Victor Nuovo (Oxford: Clarendon Press, 2012), p. 82, cf. pp. 59, 73–4, 123, 127. See also *A Third Letter for Toleration*, in *The Works of John Locke*, 12th ed., 9 vols. (London, 1824), vol. 6, pp. 152, 187, 407. Cf Hobbes: 'our Senses, and Experience; nor (that which is the undoubted Word of God) our Naturall Reason ... are not to be folded up in the Napkin of an Implicite Faith'. *Leviathan*, ch. 32 (vol. 3, p. 576), but cf. ch. 43 (vol. 3, p. 948). Locke does find a role for implicit faith, however, one that is necessitated by his minimalist approach to creedal beliefs. See *Third Letter concerning Toleration* (1692), pp. 232f.

[55] As Wolterstorff rightly puts it: 'Locke intended his epistemology as a solution to the crisis of the fracturing of the moral and religious tradition of Europe at the beginnings of modernity.' *Locke and the Ethics of Belief*, p. 227.

[56] Locke, *Essay* 4.17.24 (pp. 687f.).

last judge and guide in everything'. As for faith, it was now understood by Locke to be nothing other than assent 'based on the highest reason'.[57] All of this assumed that reason itself was a divinely sanctioned organ of critical judgement.

It is one thing to propose that the free exercise of the faculty of reason offers the best prospect for resolving dispute-engendering religious differences. It is quite another to establish what 'reason' is, and how it is to be applied. In something of an understatement, the literary historian Douglas Bush has observed that 'the meanings of "reason" in the seventeenth century admit a wide solution'.[58] It would ambitious, in the span of a few pages, to attempt to offer a satisfactory account of the full variety of ways in which 'reason' was conceptualised in the early modern period, far less in the centuries that followed. For now, it suffices to identify two ends of a broad spectrum, along with a gradual shift in one direction. One version of reason retains a strong continuity with preceding traditions that emphasise its divine origins, a scope that encompasses both moral and epistemological concerns, and a substantive content along the lines of 'innate ideas'. At this end of the spectrum, genuine religion was understood as more or less continuous with the cultivation of reason; hence the involvement of reason with matters of faith was imagined to be entirely natural and was justified on theological grounds. At the other end we encounter a narrower and more instrumental conception of reason, one that equates it with a calculative faculty of ratiocination that is capable of analysis but has no substantive content of its own. This established the conditions for a rather different relationship between faith and reason in which reason comes to act as a kind of independent arbiter of religious truth. In this role it could be supportive or critical. Over the course of the seventeenth and eighteenth centuries this latter conception becomes increasingly prominent.[59] Paradoxically, though, this

---

[57] Locke, *Essay* 4.17.24 (p. 688); *Essay* 4.18.14 (p. 704); *Essay* 4.16.14 (p. 668).

[58] Douglas Bush, 'Two Roads to Truth: Science and Religion in the Early Seventeenth Century', *ELH* 8 (1941), 81–102 (96). Seventeenth-century thinkers were themselves acutely aware of this. See Locke, *Essay* 4.14.1 (p. 668); Robert Boyle, *Christian Virtuoso 1*, *Works*, vol. 12, p. 423; 'Reason', in Ephraim Chambers, *Cyclopaedia, or, An Universal Dictionary of Arts and Sciences*, 2 vols. (London, 1728), vol. 2, pp. 964f.; 'Raison', in *Encyclopédie ou Dictionnaire raisonné des sciences, des arts et des métiers*, ed. Denis Diderot and Jean le Rond d'Alembert, 28 vols. (Paris, 1765), vol. 13, pp. 773f.

[59] S. L. Bethell spoke in similar terms of 'old' and 'new' reason. *The Cultural Revolution of the Seventeenth Century* (London: D. Dobson, 1951), pp. 63f. Immanuel Kant's distinction between pure and practical reason is also relevant. *Critique of Practical Reason* 5:90–3, in *Practical Philosophy*, pp. 212–14. So, too, are Frankfurt School critiques of 'instrumental reason' and Charles Taylor's distinction between 'substantive' and 'procedural' rationality. See

secularisation and instrumentalisation of reason was also initially informed by theological considerations, and hence the gradual shift in emphasis from one conception of reason to the other is the result of competing theological assessments of the proper scope of reason and its post-lapsarian capacities.

In sum, the Protestant critique of implicit faith represents the first articulation of a tightly connected set of principles that are now almost universally endorsed in the West: that individuals should be left to make up their own minds in the spheres of religion, morals, and politics; that claims about important matters of fact should not be taken on the basis of authority alone; that we have an obligation not to hold beliefs without being able to offer some kind of justification for them. This led to new attention being focused on the operations of reason and its role in providing the requisite support for beliefs.

3.3 God and the Light of Nature

In their popular, eleven-volume *Story of Civilization*, Will and Ariel Durant designate the period from 1550–1650 the 'Age of Reason', the period during which Europe set out on 'the bumpy road toward the Enlightenment'.[60] While the Durants did not present it in these terms, this age of reason is sometimes contrasted with a preceding 'age of faith', with the triumph of human reason representing a victory over the forces of darkness and superstition.[61] It is often thought, then, that the rise of philosophical rationalism in the seventeenth century is to be understood primarily as a challenge to traditional authorities. However, the championing of reason did not necessarily amount to a more naturalistic, secular alternative to ecclesiastical authority. For many thinkers, and particularly those influenced by traditions of Christian Platonism, the justification for ceding authority to reason ultimately derived from assumptions about its divine origin. Clearly, this complicates any simple story about an opposition between reason and religious faith.

Max Horkheimer, *Critique of Instrumental Reason*, trans. Matthew J. O'Connell (London: Verso, 2014); Taylor, *Sources of the Self*, pp. 121–4, 242–7. See also Wolterstorff, *Locke and the Ethics of Belief*, pp. 238–42. More generally on the history of reason see Robert Hoopes, *Right Reason in the English Renaissance* (Cambridge, MA: Harvard University Press, 1961); Barbara J. Shapiro, *Probability and Certainty in Seventeenth-Century England* (Princeton: Princeton University Press, 1983); Martin Jay, *Reason after Its Eclipse: On Late Critical Theory* (Madison: University of Wisconsin Press, 2016), esp. pp. 34f.

[60] Will Durant and Ariel Durant, *The Age of Reason Begins* (New York: Simon & Schuster, 1961).
[61] This, e.g., is how John William Draper sets things up in *A History of the Intellectual Development of Europe*, revised ed., 2 vols. (New York: Harper, 1875), vol. 1, p. 20.

The individual most often depicted as the quintessential rationalist, René Descartes (1596–1650), offers an instructive example. The standard 'birth of modern philosophy' narrative has him eschewing all preceding philosophical traditions and starting anew solely on the basis of reason – as one wit has recently suggested, a kind of turning philosophy off and then back on again.[62] Until relatively recently it was not uncommon for university courses in the history of philosophy to leap from the ancient Greeks to Descartes as if nothing of philosophical import had been transacted in the intervening eighteen centuries. This state of affairs was based on the identification of philosophy with modern epistemology, along with a mistaken assumption that the ancients shared something like a modern set of philosophical preoccupations. That said, it is significant that Descartes himself presented his programme as revolutionary. His quiet resolution to start afresh, detailed in the *Meditations* (1641), is akin in some respects to Luther's earlier and more public attempt to reconfigure the whole basis of religious authority and in the received version of the history of philosophy was no less momentous.[63] Yet Descartes's reliance on his scholastic forebears remained strong, and when we examine exactly what he understood by 'reason', for example, we find him reasserting what in many respects is a quite conventional religious understanding of this human capacity. He describes reason as 'a sort of spark of the divine, in which the first seeds of useful ways of thinking are sown', employing Augustine's image of 'the mark of the craftsman stamped on his work'.[64] He also consistently refers to reason as a 'natural light', by which he means not so much a capacity that is natural in a sense that opposes it to 'supernatural', but a light that is proper to our natures as human beings because God has bestowed it upon us.

---

[62] In Descartes's own words: 'to demolish everything completely and start again right from the foundations'. *Meditations* 1, CSM 2, p. 12. Hegel expresses it a little differently: 'with Descartes the culture of modern times, the thought of modern philosophy, really begins to appear, after a long and tedious journey'. *Lectures on the History of Philosophy*, p. 653. Descartes was constructed as the father of modern philosophy by nineteenth-century figures such as Kuno Fischer, *Geschichte der neueren Philosophie*, 6 vols. (Berlin, 1852–77). The English translation of the Descartes volume appeared as Kuno Fischer, *Descartes and his School*, ed. Noah Porter, trans. John P. Gordy (London: T. F. Unwin, 1890). For secondary accounts, see Stephen Gaukroger, *Descartes: An Intellectual Biography* (Oxford: Oxford University Press, 2005), pp. 5–8.

[63] Contemporaries remarked upon this: 'if some bold Defender, such as *Cartes* and others, had not interpos'd, we had been led by implicit Faith, in all the Objects of Knowledge as well as in all the Objects of Faith'. George Mackenzie, *Reason: An Essay* (London, 1690), pp. 89f.

[64] Descartes, *Rules*, IV, CSM 1, p. 17; *Meditations*, CSM 2, p. 35. See also *Discourse* II, CSM 2, 124; 'Early Writings', CSM 1, p. 4. Cf. Augustine, *Expositions of the Psalms*, 4:7, *Works* III/15, 89. For Aquinas's references to reason as a natural light see *ST* 1a. 12, 13; 88, 3; 106, 1.

Descartes's self-proclaimed originality notwithstanding, the overlap of human and divine in the processes of understanding, along with the use of the light metaphor for knowledge, had been a philosophical commonplace. The rational faculty or capacity to reason, on these understandings, was the divine component of the human being, and the recipient of the 'light' of eternal truths. These ideas had a pedigree that extended back to Presocratic thinkers. Around 500 BCE, Heraclitus had described reason as that 'which is in common and divine, and by participation in which we become rational'.[65] His successors put forward variations on this theme. Plato taught that 'God gave the sovereign part of the human soul to be the divinity of each one.' Accordingly, the pursuit of knowledge and wisdom leads to 'thoughts immortal and divine'. Aristotle declared (in an admittedly ambiguous passage) that the active intellect is 'immortal and eternal'. 'The starting point of reason', he tells us in the *Eudemian Ethics*, is God. In the conclusion to *Nicomachean Ethics* he describes the intellect as 'divine' and commends the cultivation of the divine within as the ultimate goal of life.[66] The Stoic philosopher Seneca taught that reason 'is nothing else than a portion of the divine spirit set in a human body', and 'a common attribute of both gods and men'.[67] In the same vein, Epictetus taught that while humans have a body in common with the beasts, they also have reason and intelligence 'in common with the gods'.[68] For Plotinus, the third-century founder of Neoplatonism, the 'higher soul', in which the particular excellence of human beings resides, contains 'some effluence from the Divine Reason'.[69] In the periods of late antiquity, and into the Middle Ages and

---

[65] Heraclitus, R 59, *Early Greek Philosophy*, vol. 3, LCL 526, p. 267 (rendering *logos* as 'reason').

[66] Plato, *Timaeus* 90a–d; Aristotle, *De anima* 430a17–23, cf. *Metaphysics* 12.7–10, 1072a–1076a; *Eudemian Ethics* 1248a21–9 (*logos*); *Nicomachean Ethics* 1177b27–34, 1178b20–4. The difficult passage in Aristotle's *De anima* has attracted varying interpretations. See, e.g., Victor Caston, 'Aristotle's Two Intellects: A Modest Proposal', *Phronesis* 44 (1999), 199–227; Octave Hamelin, *La théorie de l'intellect d'après Aristote et ses commentateurs* (Paris: Vrin, 1948), esp. pp. 29–31; Robert Pasnau, 'Divine Illumination', *SEP*, https://plato.stanford.edu/archives/spr2020/entries/illumination/. Whatever Aristotle meant by it, the medieval Islamic philosopher Averroes was to speak of an 'active intellect' that was shared by all human minds and was, to that extent, immortal. Stephen Gaukroger has alerted us to the similarities between this position and Descartes's idea that the mind is an incorporeal thinking substance (*res cogitans*). *Descartes: An Intellectual Biography*, pp. 646–8.

[67] Seneca, *Epistles* 66.12 (LCL 76, pp. 8–11); 92.27 (LCL 76, p. 465); Diogenes Laertius, VII, 87, 134.

[68] Epictetus, *Discourses*, 1.3.3 (LCL 131, p. 25). Cf. *Discourses* 1.14.6, 1.14.13–14, 2.8.11–13 (LCL 131, pp. 101, 103, 255–7).

[69] Plotinus, *Enneads* 2.1.5 (p. 37).

Renaissance, Platonic and Aristotelian thinkers, Greek, Latin, and Islamic, built upon these ideas.[70]

A persistent theme in the Platonic tradition was that the goal of life was to cultivate or restore that portion of divinity within, with the goal of becoming god-like. The cultivation of reason would then be identical to leading a religious life. Classicist David Sedley has suggested that were we to enquire of any educated Roman what Plato held as the goal of philosophy they would unhesitatingly cite the *Theaetetus*: 'becoming like a god so far as is possible'.[71] Platonist thinkers of the early Christian era certainly made this the central feature of their philosophy. Plotinus explains that we have fallen away from 'our resemblance to the divine'. This is to be restored through the exercise of 'the reasoning part of [our] nature' which will secure the likeness to God of which Plato spoke.[72] The fourth-century Platonist Hierocles of Alexandria accordingly defined philosophy as 'a purification and perfection of human life: a purification from our irrational, material nature and the mortal form of the body, a perfection by the recovery of our proper happiness, leading to a likeness with the divine'.[73] Full realisation of the potential of reason was thus both the goal of philosophy and a religious

---

[70] See, e.g., Stephen Gersh, *From Iamblichus to Eriugena: An Investigation of the Prehistory and Evolution of the Pseudo-Dionysian Tradition* (Leiden: Brill, 1978); John Walbridge, *The Science of Mystic Lights: Qutb al-Din Shirazi and the Illuminationist Tradition in Islamic Philosophy* (Cambridge: Cambridge University Press, 1992).

[71] Plato, *Theaetetus* 176a–b. Cf. Plato, *Timaeus*, 90c–d. David Sedley, 'The Ideal of Godlikeness', in *Plato 2: Ethics, Politics, Religion, and the Soul*, ed. Gail Fine (Oxford: Oxford University Press, 1999), pp. 309–28 (p. 309). While the proposal that this passage in the *Theaetetus* dominated the reception of Platonic philosophy in the ancient world is relatively uncontroversial, there has been considerable debate since the nineteenth century that it captures the essence of Plato's philosophy, a common argument being that the *Theaetetus* is just a prolegomenon to later epistemological dialogues (i.e., 'real' philosophy). See, e.g., Rachel Rue, 'The Philosopher in Flight: The Digression in Plato's *Theaetetus*', *Oxford Studies in Ancient Philosophy* 11 (1993), 71–100. Those who share Sedley's emphasis include Julia Annas, 'Becoming Like God: Ethics, Human Nature, and the Divine', in *Platonic Ethics, Old and New* (Ithaca: Cornell University Press, 1999), pp. 52–71; Daniel C. Russell, 'Virtue as "Likeness to God" in Plato and Seneca', *Journal of the History of Philosophy* 44 (2004), 241–60. For a recent overview of interpretations of the *Theaetetus* passage see Jens Kristian Larson, 'Measuring Humans against Gods: On the Digression of Plato's *Theaetetus*', *Archiv für Geschichte der Philosophie* 101 (2019), https://doi-org.ezproxy.library.uq.edu.au/10.1515/agph-2019-1001, accessed 23 November 2023. See also Michelle Jenkins, 'Plato's Godlike Philosopher', *Classical Philology* 111 (2016), 330–52.

[72] *Enneads* 1.6.5, 1.8.10, 2.7.5–6. In spite of Plotinus's hostility towards gnostic thinkers, we encounter a related idea in gnostic literature. See Lautaro Roig Lanzillotta, 'A Way of Salvation: Becoming Like God in Nag Hammadi', *Numen* 60 (2013), 71–102.

[73] *Commentary on the Golden Verses of the Pythagoreans*, Proem, 1–2, XX, 7, both cited in Hermann S. Schibli, *Hierocles of Alexandria* (Oxford: Oxford University Press, 2002), p. 42.

quest. The Aristotelian tradition was consonant with this to a large degree, with Aristotle regarding rational contemplation as the activity most proper to human beings and an emulation of, or participation in, the contemplative activity of the gods.[74]

The notion of deification subsequently became a central aspect of the Greek patristic tradition, and indeed for Greek Orthodoxy thereafter. An oft-repeated description of the purpose of the Incarnation among the Greek Church Fathers was that God became human so that humans might become gods.[75] An important parallel to the philosophical idea of reason as the divine within was provided by the biblical human beings as created in the image and likeness of God (Gen. 1:26).[76] The goal of the Christian life could thus be understood as the full realisation (or restoration) of this indwelling likeness to the divine. Maximus the Confessor (580–662) wrote: 'If we are made, as we are, in the image of God (Gen. 1 :27), let us become the image both of ourselves and of God ... so that we may consort with God and become gods, receiving from God our existence as gods.'[77] For thinkers of the Latin West, admittedly, this programme was complicated by the fact that while human beings may have originally been created in God's

---

[74] Aristotle, *Nicomachean Ethics* 1174b; *Metaphysics*, 1072b13–30. Commentators differ, however, on whether the divine and human contemplation are the same in kind. See Bryan C. Reese, 'Aristotle on Divine and Human Contemplation', *Ergo* 7/4 (2020), https://doi.org/10.3998/ergo.12405314.0007.004, accessed 27 April 2023.

[75] Irenaeus, *Against Heresies* 5. Preface (*ANF* 1, p. 526). Clement of Alexandria, *Exhortation to the Greeks* 1 (*ANF* 2, p. 174); Athanasius, *Incarnation of the Word* 54.3 (*NPNF* II, vol. 4, p. 65). See also Norman Russell, *The Doctrine of Deification in the Greek Patristic Tradition* (New York: Oxford University Press, 2004). The Latin West is typically thought to have emphasised to a much greater extent Fall/Redemption theology as an alternative to the Greek Orthodox *theosis*, although it has been argued that the differences between East and West on this issue have been exaggerated. See., e.g., Carl Mosser, 'The Greatest Possible Blessing: Calvin and Deification', *Scottish Journal of Theology* 55 (2002), 36–57; Carl E. Braaten and Robert W. Jenson (eds.), *Union with Christ: The New Finnish Interpretation of Luther* (Grand Rapids: Eerdmans, 1998); Joshua Bloor, 'New Directions in Western Soteriology', *Theology* 118 (2015), 179–87.

[76] A direct bridge between philosophical conceptions of divine reason and Jewish and Christian thought was provided by Philo of Alexandria, the Gospel of John, and the Greek fathers. Manuel Alexandre, Jr., 'Twofold Human Logos in Philo of Alexandria', in *Pouvoir et puissances chez Philon d'Alexandrie*, ed. Francesca Calabi, Olivier Munnich, Gretchen Reydams-Schils, and Emmanuele Vimercati (Turnhout: Brepols, 2016), pp. 37–59; W. E. Helleman, 'Philo of Alexandria on Deification and Assimilation to God, *Studia Philonica Annual* 2 (1990), 51–71.

[77] Maximus the Confessor, 'Various Texts', *Philokalia*, vol. 2, trans. G. E.H. Palmer, Philip Sherrard, and Kallistos Ware (New York: Farrar, Straus & Giroux, 1990), p. 171. Cf. Origen: 'Let us, therefore, contemplate that image of God that we can be transformed to his likeness.' *Homilies on Genesis* 1.13 (*FC*, vol. 71, p. 66).

image and likeness, important questions remained about just how much of that image persisted in our present fallen condition. Varying answers to these questions provide a point of difference between Christian and Platonic traditions, and a source of disagreement among Christian thinkers. Yet as it relates to discussions of reason in the early modern period, there are noteworthy convergences of Platonist and Christian understandings of reason as likeness to God, along with the goal of restoring that likeness. These informed discussions about the nature of reason and of its relation to faith. Broadly speaking, reason, in this rich and expansive sense, could never be opposed to true religion, but was in fact integral to its realisation.

Descartes's reference to the '*light* of nature' is also consistent with a tradition of deploying light metaphors in relation to the operations of reason.[78] Again, the key source is Plato who, in the *Republic*, set out the analogy of the sun: 'just as we see objects when they are illuminated by the light of the sun, so the mind sees truths when they are illuminated by the Good'.[79] The most celebrated elaboration of this insight was Augustine's theory of divine illumination. Puzzling in the *Confessions* over how human minds have the capacity to grasp shared truths, Augustine tells the reader how he came to the realisation that his mind 'needed enlightenment from some other light source in order to participate in the truth'. That light was God.[80] While there are Platonic resonances here, Augustine also drew upon various biblical sources, prominent among them the incipit of Psalm 27, 'The Lord is my light', which will be familiar to some as the motto of the University of Oxford – *Dominus illuminatio mea*.[81]

---

[78] For patristic references linking light, knowledge, and the image of God, see Clement of Alexandria, *Exhortation to the Heathen* 10; Origen, *Against Celsus* 4.86. More generally, see Blumenberg, 'Light as a Metaphor for Truth'.

[79] Plato, *Republic*, 500–17, esp. 508b; Cf. *Timaeus* 90a–b. If we take at face value Aristotle's statement in *De anima* that the active intellect is divine, then he can also be construed as advocating some kind of divine illumination (and was so interpreted by medieval commentators such as William of Auvergne and Roger Marston). See Étienne Gilson, 'Pourquoi Saint Thomas a critiqué Saint Augustin', *Archives d'Histoire Doctrinale et Littéraire du Moyen Âge* 1 (1927), 5–127; 'Roger Marston: Un cas d'Augustinisme Avicennisant', *Archives d'Histoire Doctrinale et Littéraire du Moyen Age* 8 (1933), 37–42.

[80] *Confessions*, IV.xv.25 (Loeb ed., vol. 1, p. 175). Cf. X.ii.2, XII.xxv.35; *De Magistro*, 12.40. Lydia Schumacher speaks of five aspects to Augustine's position: divine illumination as cognitive capacity; cognitive content; cognitive process; cognitive certitude; and knowledge of God. *Divine Illumination: The History and Future of Augustine's Theory of Knowledge* (Oxford: Wiley Blackwell, 2011), pp. 4–7.

[81] On light metaphors in the Psalms, see B. Janowski, 'Das Licht des Lebens: Zur Lichtmetaphorik in den Psalmen', in *Metaphors in the Psalms*, ed. Pierre Van Hecke and Antje Labahn (Leuven: Peeters, 2010), pp. 87–113; and more generally, Blumenberg, 'Light as a Metaphor for Truth'.

3.3 GOD AND THE LIGHT OF NATURE

There have been differing views about the precise nature of Augustine's theory of illumination and about its subsequent fortunes. What is not in doubt is that the language of divine illumination was commonplace up until the thirteenth century and, as we will see, persisted into the seventeenth century.[82] Usually regarded as the chief spokesman for the doctrine in the high Middle Ages, Franciscan friar Bonaventure (1221–74) taught that 'nothing can be understood at all unless God immediately illumines the subject of knowledge by means of the eternal divine truth'.[83] Henry of Ghent (c.1217–93), the leading theologian at the University of Paris in the period following Aquinas's tenure, maintained similarly that 'Pure truth ... or perhaps any truth at all, cannot be known without God himself doing the teaching.'[84] Even Thomas Aquinas, who is often regarded as having dispensed with the Augustinian model, retains key elements of the basic idea: 'the intellectual light itself which is in us, is nothing else than a participated likeness of the uncreated light'.[85] These sentiments would continue to inform the epistemology of Renaissance Platonists such as Marcilio Ficino (1433–99), who stresses that the reliability of our knowledge is related to its divine origins: 'our minds bear the same relationship to God as our sight to the light of the Sun, and ... therefore they can never understand anything without the light of God'.[86]

---

[82] For differing accounts of the history of divine illumination see Steven Marrone, *The Light of Thy Countenance: Science and Knowledge of God in the Thirteenth Century* (Leiden: Brill, 2001); Robert Pasnau, 'Henry of Ghent and the Twilight of Divine Illumination', *Review of Metaphysics* 49 (1995), 49–75; Schumacher, *Divine Illumination*.

[83] Bonaventure, *Collationes in Hexaëmeron et Bonaventuriana quaedam selecta* 12.11, quoted in Schumacher, *Divine Illumination*, p. 142.

[84] Henry of Ghent, *Summa* 1.7 ad. 1m, quoted in Pasnau, 'Twilight of Divine Illumination', p. 55. Both Bonaventure and Henry go well beyond rehearsal of the Augustinian position, under the influence of both Aristotle and Avicenna.

[85] Aquinas, *ST* 1a. 84, 5. Cf. *ST* 3a. 5, 4; *De veritate* 11.1c. The fortunes of divine illumination are usually thought to have waned in the late Middle Ages, owing to alternative theories of cognition espoused by Thomas Aquinas and others. See Pasnau, 'Twilight of Divine Illumination', who argues for a naturalising move in Aquinas's discussion of divine grace, where he proposes that man 'does not need a new light in addition to his natural light, in order to know the truth in all things' (*ST* 1a2ae. 109, 1). Aquinas insists, nonetheless, that 'for the knowledge of any truth whatsoever, man needs divine help, that the intellect may be moved by God to its act' (*ST* 1a2ae. 109, 1). This is entirely consistent with his understanding of 'natural' causation, which specifies the necessity of God's involvement in any motion in the universe.

[86] It is important not to forget, in addition, that there were a number of prominent Renaissance Platonists who bridge the gap between the late medieval advocates of divine illumination and the moderns. Chief among them was Marsilio Ficino: 'our minds bear the same relationship to God as our sight to the light of the Sun, and ... therefore they can never understand anything without the light of God'. *Platonic Theology*, Proem, 6 vols.,

Modern readers may find this widespread assumption that human knowledge relied upon God's presence, that it was in some sense 'miraculous', rather odd. But part of this puzzlement arises from our present assumption of an exclusive disjunction between 'natural' and 'supernatural'. For Augustine, and indeed many of the ancients, it was perfectly natural (in his sense) for the porous human soul to be a site of divine activity. God, Augustine insists, is 'the first principle *of our nature*'.[87] Our natural desire for truth (and happiness) is simply an indication of this. Augustine pointed out that the Platonists had also held this view: that God is 'the principle of reason, and the rule of life', 'the light by which things become known, and the good for which things are done'.[88] Accordingly, Augustine did not imagine himself to be authoring an idiosyncratic and theologically extravagant theory of knowledge, but adding a Christian refinement to a long-standing philosophical tradition which held that when the mind makes a true judgement it is in contact with something that is eternal and unchanging.[89] The ubiquity of this cluster of ideas – in Plato, Aristotle, Neoplatonism, medieval Christianity and Islam – suggests that it was perfectly 'natural' to assume that human knowledge and right living required, at a theoretical level, some transcendental grounding and, at a practical level, a process of mental training (or *askesis*) that would facilitate access to the transcendent. The prominence of this idea of divine illumination in the Western tradition might prompt us to reflect upon how difficult it is to provide an adequate naturalistic (in our modern sense of the term) account of how our minds might come to share common convictions that certain things are true, and that these things are, in fact, true. That problem

---

ed. James Hankins, trans. Michael J. B Allen (Cambridge, MA: Harvard University Press, 2001–6), vol. 1, p. 9. Cf. 'our mind illuminated by God's ray, understands in that ray the rational principles of all things'. *Platonic Theology* 12.1 (vol. 4, p. 23).

[87] '*quod ab illo nobis sit et principium naturae*', *City of God* 8.9 (my emphasis) (LCL 413, p. 42). This is also echoed in Augustine's celebrated '*interior intimo meo et superior summo meo*' ('You were deeper within me than the most secret part of me, and greater than the best of me'). *Confessions* 3.6.11 (LCL 86, p. 110). Luther would later generalise this to encompass every creature: 'There can be nothing more present, nothing more intimately connected with every creature than God and his power.' WA 23, 134. Robert Pasnau, in his excellent *SEP* entry on 'Divine Illumination', begins by stating that divine illumination is 'the oldest and most influential alternative to naturalism in the areas of mind and knowledge'. We may see it that way now, but naturalism, in this sense, was not available to proponents of divine illumination and they would not have understood it as breaching any explanatory desideratum. The modern naturalist/non-naturalist distinction is in any case difficult to apply to ancient epistemologies. See Gerson, *Ancient Epistemology*, pp. 152–65.

[88] Augustine, *City of God* 8.9, 8.4 (LCL 413, pp. 42, 20). See also *Tractates on John* 19.12.

[89] What is explicitly Christian about Augustine's position is his suggestion, set out in *De Trinitate*, that the operations of the mind are to be understood on the basis of analogies to the Trinity. See Schumacher, *Divine Illumination*, pp. 62–5.

has never really gone away and neither the neurosciences nor cognitive psychology have made this less puzzling. From the perspective of our predecessors, it would be an astonishing coincidence, verging on the miraculous, that creatures who evolved through blind natural processes might end up being able to access truths that had nothing to do with their mere physical survival.

All of this is by way of pointing to the fact that an early modern appeal to 'reason' does not initially rest on a hard and fast distinction between (natural) reason and (supernatural) revelation, since reason is already deeply theologically inflected. This relates to a more general thesis about the late historical emergence of a natural/supernatural divide. The initial turn towards reason already assumed its divine origin and natural receptivity to revelation. However, there would also be theological challenges to traditional understandings of reason, not least on account of a renewed emphasis on the fallen condition of human minds. In the end, a modern version of 'reason' would be severed from its theological roots and forced into the role of independent arbiter of religious claims. This would be an instrumental reason that passed judgement upon the theological assumptions upon which, paradoxically, its own reliability had originally been grounded.

It is tempting to think that metaphysical talk of an interior 'divine light' would be swept away with the inception of modern philosophy. Older models of the history of philosophy, which jump directly from antiquity to Descartes, tend to assume this, with the options of 'rationalism' and 'empiricism' offering non-theological and relatively unproblematic secular foundations for knowledge. However, as is already evident, Descartes regularly invokes the idea of natural light, along with concomitant notions of innate ideas and the image of God. These, in turn, inform his ontological arguments for the existence of God, with God subsequently acting as a guarantor of the reliability of our knowledge.

The theme of illumination is especially conspicuous in the thought of Descartes's most famous follower – the philosopher and priest Nicholas Malebranche (1638–1715) – who espoused what is an unmistakably Augustinian view of divine illumination, albeit in a Cartesian guise. While now relegated to the second division of philosophical thinkers, Malebranche was highly regarded in his own time. His contemporary Pierre Bayle, who was not easily impressed, lauded him as 'the premier philosopher of our age' and if Malebranche drew upon Augustine and Descartes, he also authored novel and influential solutions to philosophical problems.[90] He is perhaps

---

[90] Quoted in Tad Schmaltz, *Early Modern Cartesianisms* (Oxford: Oxford University Press, 2017), p. 154.

best known for his championing of occasionalism, the doctrine that God is the only true cause (although this idea has a much longer history going back to the medieval Ash'arite school of Islamic philosophy and was espoused by medieval Christian thinkers such as Nicholas of Autrecourt).[91] Equally prominent in his philosophy was the related idea that knowledge is possible only because human minds participate in God's knowledge. Malebranche insisted that God must be responsible for our ideas since our immaterial minds could be susceptible only to the influence of some other immaterial substance. He also repeated Augustine's argument that since all minds intuit the same set of necessary truths, they must all be illuminated by the same light.[92] While Malebranche is the best-known representative of this view, he was not the only one. In England, the philosopher John Norris also maintained that in so far as we know anything at all, we do so by participating in ideas in the divine mind.[93] This stance would also inform the idealism of Bishop George Berkeley (1685–1753) who, as is well known, argued for the counterintuitive thesis that minds and ideas are the only things to exist.

Thinkers who may have been reluctant to go all the way with Malebranche's version of divine illumination nonetheless endorsed the key principle that reason was reliable on account of its divine origins. Among the most prominent advocates of this idea were the 'Cambridge Platonists' (with whom John Norris was well acquainted).[94] Benjamin Whichcote,

---

[91] Nicholas Malebranche, *Search after Truth*, ed. and trans. Thomas Lennon and Paul Olscamp (Cambridge: Cambridge University Press, 1997), p. 448; *Dialogues on Metaphysics and Religion* [1688], ed. Nicholas Jolley, trans. David Scott (Cambridge: Cambridge University Press, 1997), pp. 59f.; D. Perler and U. Rudolph, *Occasionalismus: Theorien der Kausalität in arabisch-islamischen und im europäischen Denken* (Göttingen: Vandenhoeck & Ruprecht, 2000); Michael Marmura, 'Al-Ghazālī', in *The Cambridge Companion to Arabic Philosophy*, ed. Peter Adamson and Richard C. Taylor (Cambridge: Cambridge University Press, 2005), pp. 137–54. Hume's doctrine of causation looks a lot like Malebranche minus God. See M. Bell, 'Hume and Causal Power: The Influences of Malebranche and Newton', *British Journal for the History of Philosophy* 5 (1997), 68–86; Peter Kail, 'On Hume's Appropriation of Malebranche: Causation and Self', *European Journal of Philosophy* 16 (2007), 55–80. For Malebranche's medieval sources, see D. Connell, *The Vision in God: Malebranche's Scholastic Sources* (Louvain: Nauwelaerts, 1967).

[92] Malebranche, *Search after Truth*, p. 232; *Dialogues*, p. 141.

[93] John Norris, *An Essay Towards the Theory of the Ideal or Intelligible World, Part 1* (London, 1701), p. 451; *Cursory Reflections upon a Book called An Essay concerning Human Understanding* [1690] (London, 1713), p. 31. On John Norris, and the relation between his ideas and those of Malebranche, see William J. Mander, *The Philosophy of John Norris* (Oxford: Oxford University Press, 2008). William Collier set out similar ideas in his *Clavis Universalis, or A New Inquiry after Truth, being a Demonstration of the Non-Existence or Impossibility of an External World* [1713] (Edinburgh, 1836).

[94] It has been pointed out that 'the Cambridge Platonists' were not all Platonists, and not all based at Cambridge. See, e.g., Dmitri Levitin, *Ancient Wisdom in the Age of the New*

regarded as the intellectual father of the group, had described reason as 'God's mansion', the 'impression of God', 'the image of the Creator, copied out in the creature'.[95] This was the common view of his fellow Platonists who, following Whichcote, repeatedly made the claim that reason was 'the candle of the Lord'.[96]

Reason, understood as the 'light of nature', was thus 'natural' in the way that 'laws of nature' were – at least as the latter were originally conceived. Both notions concern the powers with which God imbues nature, or which he stamps upon it. Reason is natural in the sense that it is proper to our natures, but it was a light given by God and authoritative in proportion to its retention of an original, created integrity.[97] In an Aristotelian framework, which assumed a teleological order to things, reason worked because it was naturally oriented towards the discovery of truth. For Aristotle, that is just how things are. Whichcote defers to this general principle when he remarks that: 'It is natural and proper, for mind and understanding in man, to tend towards God, as for heavy things to tend towards their centre .... All understandings seek after God, and have a sense and feeling of God; and the mind and spirit of man is a candle in man lighted by God and doth

---

Science (Cambridge: Cambridge University Press, 2015), p. 16, but similar kinds of objections obtain for almost any convenient historical grouping. For a defence of the label see David Leech, 'Some Reflections on the Category "Cambridge Platonism"', *The Cambridge Platonist Research Group*, https://cprg.hypotheses.org/517, accessed 5 March 2020.

[95] Benjamin Whichcote, *Select Sermons of Dr. Whichcot [sic] in two parts* (London, 1698), p. 267.

[96] Based upon Proverbs 20:27: 'The spirit of man is the candle of the Lord' (KJV). Nathaniel Culverwell uses the expression almost 100 times in his modestly entitled *An Elegant and Learned Discourse of the Light of Nature* [1652], ed. Robert A. Greene and Hugh MacCallum (Indianapolis: Liberty Fund, 2001). See also Henry More, *Ad V.C. epistola altera*, in *Opera Omnia*, vol. 1 (London, 1679), pp. 600f.; Glanvill, *Logou thrēskeia*, p. 24, and *The Vanity of Dogmatizing* (London, 1661), p. 104; Peter Sterry, *The spirit convincing of sinne* (London, 1645), pp. 10–11; Philologus, *A seasonable discourse of the right use and abuse of reason in matters of religion* (London, 1676), p. 7. Similar allusions may be found in Walter Cross, *The Instrumentality of Faith* (London, 1695), pp. 25f.; Ireneus Freeman, *Logikē latreia the reasonablenesse of divine service* (London, 1661), p. 9; Henry Hallywell, *The Excellency of Moral Virtue* (London, 1692), p. 29. Quaker writers had their own, controversial, version of this idea. See e.g., Isaac Penington, *The ancient principle of truth, or, The light within asserted* (London, 1672), p. 19, and *passim*, and Henry More's comments, referenced above, were directed against them. George Rust helpfully sets out some of different senses in which the expression was used in *The remains of that reverend and learned prelate, Dr. George Rust* (London, 1686), pp. 21–43.

[97] Arguments about the extent to which, in a fallen world, reason had retained its integrity were very much at the forefront of discussions of the reliability of reason, and of what kind of balance should be struck between experience and reason. See Peter Harrison, *The Fall of Man and the Foundations of Science* (Cambridge: Cambridge University Press, 2007) and 'Original Sin and the Problem of Knowledge in Early Modern Europe', *Journal of the History of Ideas* 63 (2002), 239–59.

discover God.'⁹⁸ Such teleological assumptions, still deeply embedded in much thinking about *human* nature, were reinforced by the biblical idea that persons were created in the image of God. It was the supposition of a natural affinity between revelation and an internal, God-given reason that made it possible for reason to be the judge of supposedly revealed truths. As Whichcote put it: 'reason is the recipient of whatever God declares', reprising Aquinas's contention that because the soul is the image of God, it is *naturally* capable of grace.⁹⁹ As the natural intersection of divine and human, then, the mind is the place where 'spirituals and naturals join in and mingle' making it impossible to distinguish between religion and reason.¹⁰⁰ Reason was thus the site of human permeability to the divine.¹⁰¹

In view of these considerations we can say that the familiar story about Descartes, the birth of modern philosophy, and the rise of a reason and a foundationalist view of knowledge (the idea that all of our knowledge rests upon some non-inferential knowledge or indubitable belief), has a significant element of truth: it is just that the ultimate foundation of rational knowledge, on this broad conception of reason, turns out to be God. To some degree, then, the transition from implicit beliefs grounded in authority to explicit beliefs grounded in reason amounts to a shift in emphasis from one kind of religious source of knowledge to another.

Acknowledgement of the theistic grounding of knowledge was commonplace in the early modern period. Descartes himself remarked that 'man cannot achieve correct knowledge of natural things so long as he does not know God'.¹⁰² 'It is necessary to know God', Malebranche agreed, 'if we

---

[98] Benjamin Whichcote, *The Works of the Learned Benjamin Whichcote, D.D.*, 4 vols. (Aberdeen, 1751), vol. 3, p. 144. Elsewhere he remarks that 'All Mind and Understanding hath Tendency towards God. It was well said by the Philosopher [Simplicius], *God is more Essential to us, than that that is most ourselves; and is Supream to that which is in us Sovereign.*' *Select Sermons*, p. 265 (cf. Augustine, *Confessions* 3.6.11). For similar remarks on the cooperation of God-given reason with the truths of revelation, see John Smith, *Select Discourses* (London, 1660), p. 382; Robert Boyle, *Christian Virtuoso 1*, *Works*, vol. 12, p. 422.

[99] Whichcote, *Works*, vol. 3, p. 163; *Moral and Religious Aphorisms* (London: Matthews and Morrot, 1930), §76. Cf. Aquinas, *ST* 1a2ae. 113, 10.

[100] Whichcote, *Works*, vol. 3, p. 182. '... if a man can be once in a true state of religion, he cannot distinguish between religion and the reason of his mind; so that his religion is the reason of his mind, and the reason of his mind is his religion'. *Works*, vol. 4, p. 147.

[101] Robert Boyle took a similar position, stating that reason could be understood in three ways: as a receptable of innate ideas; as a discursive faculty; and as that part of the mind that is the natural recipient of revealed truths. Reason, he says, 'is capable of receiving a higher and more excellent information by supernatural revelations and discoveries'. *Appendix to the first part of the Christian Virtuoso* in *Works*, vol. 12, p. 682.

[102] Descartes, *Objections and Replies*, CSM 2, p. 290. See also *Meditations*, IV, CSM 2, pp. 37–43. In *Meditations* V he states that: 'The certainty and truth of all knowledge [*scientia*]

want to be fully convinced that the most certain sciences ... are true sciences'.[103] Leibniz, too, insisted that 'the same God who is the source of all goods is also the principle of all knowledge'.[104] For François Fénelon, 'the superior reason that resides in Man, is God himself'.[105] In England, the physician and natural philosopher Walter Charleton (1620–1707) declared that 'no one thing in Nature can be known, unless the Author of Nature be first knowne'.[106] Cambridge Platonist Ralph Cudworth spoke similarly of God as 'the *First Original Knowledge or Mind*, from whence all other *Knowledges* and *Minds* are derived'.[107] On this view, it was less a matter of reason providing grounds for believing in God, than it was God providing grounds for believing in reason.[108]

Others drew the obvious implication that without some faith in a providential Deity we would have no reason to reside confidence in the reliability of our mental faculties. Here the connection between knowledge and the divine was less direct, but equally crucial. According to Isaac Barrow (1630–77), the gifted mathematician, theologian, and classicist who preceded Isaac Newton in the Lucasian Chair at Cambridge, the dependability of the mind's logical operations 'does in some sort suppose the Existence of God'.[109] Anglican divine, Fellow of the Royal Society, and subsequently Archbishop of Canterbury, John Tillotson agreed that our confidence in the reliability of our clear and distinct ideas is grounded in the conviction that

depends uniquely on my awareness of the true God'. CSM 2, p. 49. It is interesting that one of the last medieval advocates of divine illumination, John of Rodington (1290–1348?), rehearsed a number of sceptical arguments – the senses deceive us, God could make one thing appear to be another – before concluding that such arguments would be valid were it not for divine illumination: 'without a special illumination ... no object whatever can be perfectly known'. See Étienne Gilson, *Christian Philosophy: An Introduction*, trans. Armand Maurer (Toronto: Pontifical Institute of Medieval Studies, 1993), p. 453. So the invocation of God – or at least of the natural order instantiated by God – had long been proposed as a defence against scepticism.

[103] Malebranche, *Search after Truth* 6.2.6 (p. 481).
[104] Leibniz, 'Letter to Countess Elizabeth?', in *Philosophical Essays*, trans. Roger Ariew and Daniel Garber (Indianapolis: Hackett, 1989), p. 237.
[105] François Fénelon, *Demonstration de l'Existence de Dieu*, 2nd ed. (Paris, 1713), p. 203.
[106] Walter Charleton, *The Darknes of Atheism Dispelled by the Light of Nature. A Physico-theological Treatise* (London, 1652), sig. a2v. For Charleton's praise of Descartes's approach in the *Meditations*, see sigs. B3r–v.
[107] Ralph Cudworth, *The True Intellectual System of the Universe* (London, 1678), p. 733.
[108] Cf. Aquinas's notion of God as 'first truth' (*ST* 2a2ae. 1, 1), and Bonaventure's assertion that 'All correct understanding proves and concludes to the truth of the divine being.' Bonaventure, *Commentary on the Sentences* 3.1.8.1.1.2 (ET, p. 181); 3.1.8.1.1.1 (ET, p. 102).
[109] Isaac Barrow, *The Usefulness of Mathematical Learning Explained and Demonstrated*, trans. John Kirby (London, 1734), pp. 109f.

God imbued us with trustworthy faculties. God guarantees the trustworthiness of 'the frame of our understandings'.[110] Even without subscribing to a fully developed theory of divine illumination, then, many early modern thinkers could still hold that the reliability of reason called for a divine guarantor.

Understood as a portal to the transcendent, reason was also thought to encompass moral considerations and fundamental religious truths.[111] The common early modern expression 'right reason' signals the moral orientation of human rationality. Again, this drew on a long tradition extending back to Plato's insistence on the convergence of knowledge and virtue.[112] The Stoics, in turn, had developed this understanding further, connecting reason to the idea of natural law and introducing the terminology of 'right

---

[110] John Tillotson, *The Works of the Most Reverend Dr John Tillotson*, 3rd ed., 2 vols. (London, 1722), vol. 1, p. 658. For further examples of God as the source of knowledge and guarantor of the operation of our cognitive faculties see George Rust, *A Discourse on Truth* (London, 1677), pp. 33–4; Matthew Barker, *Natural Theology* (London, 1674), p. 62; Edward Stillingfleet, *Origines Sacrae*, 4th ed. (London, 1675), p. 232. There is, of course, a difference between God acting as a guarantor for the general reliability of the mind, and consciously acknowledging that God plays such a role. An atheist can thus happily affirm that the three angles of a triangle are equal to two right angles (Descartes's example). However, this would not be genuinely 'scientific' knowledge, since it can still be rendered doubtful. *Objections and Replies*, CSM 2, p. 101. See discussion in Pasnau, *After Certainty*, pp. 22–6, 153–5. Compare Aristotle's criteria for 'scientific knowledge' which require not simply knowledge of the fact, but knowledge of the reasoned fact, or knowledge of its ultimate cause. *Posterior Analytics* 1.13. There are parallel arguments about the foundations of morality, namely, that our moral intuitions are difficult to justify outside of a theistic framework. Kant expressed this most forcefully, but this position has attracted many defenders. See, e.g., David Baggett and Jerry L. Walls, *Good God: The Theistic Foundations of Morality* (Oxford: Oxford University Press, 2012). Again, it does not follow that atheists cannot be moral; just that it is difficult to establish the basis of their moral obligations.

[111] The light within, says Robert South, has 'two grand and principal offices; to wit, one to inform and direct, and the other to command or oblige'. *Sermons preached upon Several Occasions*, 5 vols. (New York: Hurd and Houghton, 1872), vol. 2, p. 28. These offices comprise *recta ratio*.

[112] Plato, *Meno* 87c; *Timaeus* 47c; *Theaetetus* 176b. On the concept and its history see Hoopes, *Right Reason*; John Spurr, 'Rational Religion in Restoration England', *Journal of the History of Ideas* 49 (1988), 563–85; Lotte Mulligan, '"Reason," "Right Reason," and "Revelation" in Mid-Seventeenth-Century England', in *Occult and Scientific Mentalities in the Renaissance*, ed. Brian Vickers (Cambridge: Cambridge University Press, 1984), pp. 375–401; Anthony J. Lisska, 'Right Reason in Natural Law Moral Theory', in *Reason, Religion, and Natural Law from Plato to Spinoza*, ed. Jonathan A. Jacobs (Oxford: Oxford University Press, 2012), pp. 155–74. Also see the special issue 'Right Reason in Western Ethics', *The Monist* 66 (1983), 1–163. Dafydd Mills Daniel traces the secularisation of this notion in *Ethical Rationalism and Secularization in the British Enlightenment* (London: Palgrave Macmillan, 2020).

reason'. Cicero, for example, proposed that 'virtue is nothing other than right reason (*recta ratio*)'.[113] Aquinas subsequently linked right reason with God's eternal law. Human beings participated in the eternal law by virtue of the light of nature, which was itself an imprint of the divine light.[114]

In the early modern period, Richard Hooker (1554–1600), one of the most articulate defenders of the use of reason in matters of religion, explained that everyone, excepting children, innocents, and madmen, has the capacity to discern right from wrong though the exercise of right reason.[115] As we will see, in the wake of the Reformation, there was considerable discussion about the reliability of right reason on account of the fallen human condition. But it was usually allowed that right reason continued to function to some degree, especially in a sanctified state and with the assistance of divine grace. Calvinist divine George Hakewill thus spoke of 'the torch of right reason, yet left amongst the remainders of Gods image in man'.[116] John Donne used the expression 'rectified reason', suggesting that it was a natural partner for faith: 'They are not continuall, but they are contiguous, they flow not from one another, but they touch one another, they are not both of a peece, but they enwrap one another, Faith and Reason.' Ultimately, he would conclude that 'rectified Reason is Religion'.[117]

It follows that when many early modern thinkers sought to mobilise reason in the sphere of religion, they did not imagine themselves to be calling upon some 'external' or 'neutral' human capacity that was competent to pass judgement on the validity of various religious propositions. If anything, the appeal to reason was motivated by the assumption that it could provide a more direct channel to the divine than the fallible institutions and councils of the Church. It was not simply a natural (in our sense) cognitive

---

[113] Cicero, *Tusculan Disputations* 4.15.34 (LCL 141, 1945), p. 362. See also Seneca: 'if a man has brought his reason to perfection, he is praiseworthy and has reached the end suited to his nature. This perfect reason is called virtue, and is likewise that which is honourable.' *Epistulae Morales* 76.10 (LCL 76, 152–3).

[114] Aquinas, *ST* 1a2ae. 93, 2; 93, 3; 91, 2. Aquinas also assimilated right reason to the virtue of prudence, the capacity not merely to know the content of the natural law, but the wisdom to know how it applies to specific circumstances. Aquinas, *ST* 2a2ae. 47, 4. Lisska, 'Right Reason in Natural Law Moral Theory'.

[115] Richard Hooker, *The Works of that Learned and Judicious Divine Mr. Richard Hooker*, 3 vols. (Oxford: Clarendon Press, 1888), vol. 1, p. 222.

[116] George Hakewill, *King Dauids Vow for Reformation of Himselfe* (London, 1621), p. 52. Hakewill's right reason is a component of human wisdom which remains subordinate to a 'divine, holy, and heavenly wisdom'. Right reason was also contrasted with 'carnal reason'. Edward Reynolds, *The Lord's Property in his Redeemed People* (London, 1660), p. 12.

[117] John Donne, *LXXX Sermons* (London, 1640), pp. 448, 178, 729. Donne refers to reason that is 'rectified, refreshed, restored, reestablished by the seales of Gods pardon' (p. 132).

instrument, moreover, but was the bearer of the divine image, a receptable of innate truths, and already attuned to revelation.[118] This amicable partnership between reason and revelation was destined for a troubled future, however, with the emergence of more narrow and instrumentalist understandings of reason. Reason was set to be pried loose from its metaphysical and theological foundations, emptied of substantive content, and forged into a device for rational calculation. This 'secular' understanding of rationality first arose from a competing theological account of human rationality.

3.4 Reason Secularised

Luther's impassioned appeal at the Diet of Worms to scripture *and clear reason* may come as a surprise to some because Luther is commonly depicted as an implacable opponent of reason. For his harshest critics he was an embodiment of irrationality: a 'crass ignoramus' (Heinrich Denifle), a man 'wholly and systematically ruled by his affective and appetitive faculties' (Jacques Maritain), an unintelligent rabble-rouser (Goethe), a philistine (Thomas Arnold), the coarse and foul-mouthed leader of a revolution (Ralph Inge), etc.[119] In recent popular (albeit historically unreliable) writings Luther has been presented as the personification of an opposition between reason and

---

[118] It is important in this context to recall the 'objective' and 'subjective' versions of naturalism outlined in the introduction. Non-naturalistic epistemology, on these understandings, does not entail invoking the supernatural, but rather the claim that epistemology can be understood quite independently of empirical matters, and relies on conceptual analysis. Admitting the possibility of a priori knowledge is typically taken as a marker of a non-naturalistic approach (but cf. Philip Kitcher, 'A Priori Knowledge', *The Philosophical Review* 86 (1980), 3–23). See, e.g., the essays by W. V. Quine, Jaegwon Kim, and Hilary Putnam in *Epistemology: An Anthology*, ed. E. Sosa and J. Kim (Oxford: Blackwell, 2004). The early modern examples discussed above confound the naturalist/non-naturalist distinction in that they invoke what look like anthropological considerations, including those belonging to theological anthropology, to account for innate ideas, and which in turn provide an account of what it is to hold a justified belief.

[119] Examples taken from Brand Blanshard, *Reason and Belief* (London: George Allen & Unwin, 1974), ch. 4. Further examples in philosophical writings are provided by Oswald Beyer, 'Philosophical Modes of Thought of Luther's Theology as an Object of Inquiry', in *The Devil's Whore: Reason and Philosophy in the Lutheran Tradition*, ed. Jennifer Hockenbery Dragseth (Philadelphia: Augsburg Fortress, 2011), pp. 13–21 (p. 14). For more nuanced accounts of Luther on reason see Brian Gerrish, *Grace and Reason: A Study in the Theology of Luther* (Oxford: Clarendon Press, 1962); Paul Althaus, *The Theology of Martin Luther*, trans. Robert C. Schultz (Philadelphia: Fortress Press, 1966), pp. 64–70; Denis R. Janz, 'Whore or Handmaid? Luther and Aquinas on the Function of Reason in Theology', in *The Devil's Whore*, ed. Dragseth, pp. 47–52; David Andersen, *Martin Luther: The Problem of Faith and Reason* (Bonn: Verlag für Kultur und Wissenschaft, 2009).

religious faith.[120] In his less temperate moments, of which there were more than a few, Luther certainly provides some justification for these assessments. Reason was 'a mangy, leprous whore' and 'the devil's bride', 'the greatest enemy that faith has'.[121] This sceptical outlook was motivated partly by an identification of reason with aspects of Aristotelian philosophy, partly by Luther's emphasis on the fallen condition of humanity and his reckoning of the damage wreaked upon human reason by the Fall. Both Luther and Calvin maintained that the degree of rationality that we now possess is but a pale shadow of the original gift of reason granted to Adam. On the one hand, we retain some of the powers of the original gift of reason, in so far as the divine image was not completely effaced by the Fall. Its residual powers are sufficient for us to govern human affairs and make modest advances in the sciences. On the other hand, and comparatively speaking, these residual powers of reason were deemed to be 'leprous and dull' (Luther) or 'seriously injured' (Calvin).[122]

Luther and Calvin sought to distinguish their assessments of human reason from those of their scholastic predecessors who, in their view, had overestimated the integrity and scope of fallen reason – not least on account of the undue influence of the Pagan philosopher Aristotle.[123] The key implication, for Luther in particular, was diametrically opposed to the quasi-Platonist positions set out above: unaided human reason cannot provide us with direct access to the divine.[124] Its limitations extended even to our knowledge of the natural world. A truly scientific knowledge of nature, as Aristotle had imagined it, was for Luther a lost cause: the operations of

---

[120] See, e.g., Dawkins, *God Delusion*, p. 221; Jerry Coyne, *Faith versus Fact: Why Science and Religion Are Incompatible* (London: Penguin, 2015), p. 69.

[121] Luther, *Luther's Last Sermon in Wittenberg ... 17 January 1546*, LW 51, 374, 376; *Table Talk*, ed. and trans. William Hazlitt (Fearn: Christian Heritage, 2003), pp. 252f., §353. Cf. *The Bondage of the Will*, LW 33, 120f.; *Against the Heavenly Prophets*, LW 40, 174–5.

[122] Luther, *Lectures on Genesis*, LW 1, 66, cf. 113f.; Calvin, *Institutes* 2.2.4, vol. 1, p. 225.

[123] Luther, *Lectures on Genesis, 1–5*, LW 1, pp. 65, 142, 167; Calvin, *Commentaries on Ezekiel*, I, 375, *Institutes* 1.15.4, vol. 1, p. 164. Cf. Aquinas, *SCG* I.7. For similar points in subsequent Protestant authors see Edward Reynolds, *A Treatise of the Passions* (London, 1647), pp. 5, 44, 483; William Perkins, *An Exposition of the Symbole or Creed of the Apostles* (Cambridge, 1595), p. 81; Burton, *Anatomy of Melancholy*, 1.1.1.1, vol. 1, p. 143.

[124] Martin Luther, *Exegetica opera Latina*, vol. 19 (Erlangen, 1847), p. 10. Calvin has a slightly more complicated position, wishing to assert that everyone has an inbuilt 'sense of the Divine' (*sensus divinitatis*). *Institutes* 1.3.1, vol. 1, p. 43. This, however, needs 'the spectacles of scripture' in order to focus the knowledge of God that otherwise lies 'confused in our minds'. Calvin, *Institutes* 1.6.1, vol. 1, p. 64. See, e.g., Paul Helm, 'John Calvin, the *Sensus Divinitatis*, and the Noetic Effects of Sin', *International Journal for Philosophy of Religion* 43 (1998), 87–107; Edward Adams, 'Calvin's View of Natural Knowledge of God', *International Journal of Systematic Theology* 3 (2001), 280–92.

nature have become a mystery to us after the Fall of Adam, on account of the 'perversion' of reason.[125] This more sceptical assessment of the powers of reason thus also distinguished Luther, Calvin, and their followers from those early modern Platonists and rationalists who, as we have seen, discounted the impact of original sin and focused more on the traditional connection between human reason and its divine source.[126]

That said, Luther carved out a space for the operations of this attenuated reason. In keeping with virtually all early modern thinkers, Luther understood reason to have originally been a gift from God and he would describe it as 'the most important and the highest in rank among all things ... the best and something divine'. As his declaration at Worms illustrates, reason could also serve as a criterion for our judgement, too.[127] Crucially, though, reason was gifted to us in order to assist in our *secular* callings. It was 'the inventor and mentor of all the arts, medicine, laws, and of whatever wisdom, power, virtue, and glory men possess *in this life*'.[128] Reason, in spite of its fallen state, would thus enable us to muddle through in a world that shared its fallen condition.

Calvin adopted a similar stance. While reason was 'weak and immersed in darkness', there remained 'some residue of intelligence and judgement' which made it possible for human beings to establish stable social orders and glean some knowledge of the operations of nature. In delimiting the scope of reason, Calvin made a crucial distinction: 'we have one kind of intelligence of earthly things, and another of heaven things'. Mere reason was deemed largely incompetent in the higher spiritual realm and when applied to matters concerning the future life. When it came to knowledge of God and his favour towards us, even the most ingenious are 'blinder than moles'.[129] But reason could operate tolerably well in the present life – when applied to the spheres of 'policy and economy, all mechanical arts and liberal

---

[125] Martin Luther, *Complete Sermons*, 7 vols., ed. John Nicholas Lenker (Grand Rapids: Baker Books, 2000), vol. 1.1, p. 329.
[126] Harrison, 'Original Sin and the Problem of Knowledge'.
[127] 'If anything is really contrary to reason, it is certainly very much more against God also.' Luther, *Der Kleine Katechismus*, WA, 30/1, 248. Cf. Theodore G. Tappert (ed. and trans.), *Book of Concord* (Philadelphia: Fortress Press, 1959), p. 345; *Lectures on Genesis, LW* 1, 62–3, 112; Luther, *Disputation concerning Man, LW* 34, 137; *The Judgement of Martin Luther on Monastic Vows*, WA 8, 629, *LW* 44, 336. Luther could thus be held up as a champion of reason: 'And if *Luther* had not follow'd his own Reason, the Reformation would not have been, in all humane Probability, brought to pass.' Warren, *An Apology*, p. 46.
[128] Luther, *Disputation concerning Man, LW* 34, 137 (my emphasis). For similar remarks from Philip Melanchthon see *Orations on Philosophy and Education*, ed. Sachiko Kusukawa, trans. Christine F. Salazar (Cambridge: Cambridge University Press, 1999), p. 23.
[129] Calvin, *Institutes* 2.2.18, vol. 1, p. 238.

studies'.[130] The secular world was the legitimate sphere of operations for what, in essence, was a natural or secular reason – literally a reason fit for use in the *saeculum*, the imperfect in-between age that occupied the unstable temporal space between the Incarnation and the end of the world. While the original intention of Luther and Calvin had been to *limit* the scope of reason to mere 'earthly things', their efforts would eventually have the opposite effect. Once the domain of the here-and-now took precedence over the more remote region of 'heavenly things', there would be a corresponding expansion in the scope and status of natural reason. If the secular realm is all that there is, then reason tends to become omnipotent.

Attempting to delimit the scope of reason was by no means the sole preserve of Protestant thinkers. Catholic thinkers with strong Augustinian commitments were also inclined to reflect on the consequences of the impact of sin on the operations of reason. The basic strategy of Nicholas Malebranche's *Search after Truth* (1674–5) was thus to reflect upon 'the order found in the faculties and passions of our first father in his original state, as well as the changes and disorder that befell him after his sin'.[131] The Jansenist philosopher and mathematician Blaise Pascal wrote that 'if man had never been corrupted, he would, in his innocence, confidently enjoy both truth and felicity'. In our present state, however, we are unhappily suspended between 'absolute ignorance and certain knowledge; so obvious is it that we once enjoyed a degree of perfection from which we have unhappily fallen'.[132] Pascal rated the efforts of the ancient philosophers similarly: 'they knew the excellence of man, they were ignorant of his corruption; so that they easily avoided sloth, but fell into pride'.[133] The sanguine assumptions of Plato and Aristotle about the capacities of human reason were thus judged to have been misplaced on account of their ignorance of the fallen state

---

[130] Calvin, *Institutes* 2.2.12–13, vol. 1, pp. 233, 234.

[131] Malebranche, *Search after Truth*, I.5 (p. 19). For similar observations of Anglophone writers on the need to understand the impact of the Fall in assessing the operations of reason see Thomas Wright, *Passions of the Mind* (London, 1601), pp. 2–3. See also Burton, *Anatomy of Melancholy*, 1.1.1.1, vol. 1, pp. 143–50; Reynolds, *Treatise of the Passions*, pp. 483, 5–6. This general theme is developed in more detail in Harrison, *Fall of Man*.

[132] Blaise Pascal, *Pensées* L 131 (B 434), trans. A. J. Krailsheimer (London: Penguin, 1966), p. 65. This edition uses the Lafuma (L) numbering. Square bracketed numbers [B] refer to the Brunschvicg numbering for cross-referencing. Cf. L 45, L 199, L 401 [B 84, B 72, B 437], pp. 42, 88–95, 146.

[133] Pascal, *Pensées* L 208 [B 435], p. 96. This avenue of criticism was pursued most enthusiastically by Protestants. See Luther, *Lectures on Genesis*, LW 1, 166; Calvin, *Institutes* 2.7.6, vol. 1, p. 355. On characterisations of Aristotelian science as proud and 'puffed up' knowledge see Peter Harrison, 'Curiosity, Forbidden Knowledge, and the Reformation of Natural Philosophy in Early-Modern England', *Isis* 92 (2001), 257–78.

of humanity. The ancient sceptics had gone to the other extreme, lacking any sense of human beings created in the divine image. Pascal would reach the conclusion that: 'Reason's last step is the recognition that there are an infinite number of things which are beyond it ... and if natural things are beyond it, what are we to say about supernatural things?'[134] Again we see an emphasis on the limits of reason and a key distinction between earthly and heavenly spheres of competence.[135]

Theological anthropology and the narrative of the Fall were not the only sources for early modern efforts to delimit the operations and scope of reason. Metaphysical considerations were also important – especially the far-reaching influence of the nominalism of the late Middle Ages. In essence, nominalism was a denial of the existence of universals – those shared properties of individual things such as 'redness' or 'beauty'. Plato's theory of the forms is the most influential exemplification of the conviction that universals are real. Against this approach, William of Ockham (1285–1347) maintained that universals played a role only in the realm of logic, and should be understood only as abstractions from individual things.[136] Ockham also held the view, later adopted by Locke, that the mind, at birth, was a blank slate or *tabula rasa*.[137] We do not come into the world with eternal truths or intuitions of the forms written into our souls. Cutting a very long story short, on this view of things, the proper business of reason lies in the performance of logical operations, and not participation in eternal truths. Reason did not, indeed could not, be involved in unearthing and giving expression to innate ideas, since these did not exist. There was no necessary connection between this stance on universals and negative views of reason arising out of a particular interpretation of the Fall, although clearly they could be mutually reinforcing.[138]

---

[134] Pascal, *Penseés*, L 188 [B 267], p. 85.
[135] This will later be echoed in Kant's *Critique of Pure Reason* (1781).
[136] Stephen Tornay, *Ockham: Studies and Selections* (La Salle: Open Court, 1938), p. 5.
[137] Marilyn McCord Adams, *William Ockham*, 2 vols. (Notre Dame: University of Notre Dame Press, 1987), vol. 1, p. 495. Luther also followed Ockham on this point. Andersen, *Martin Luther*, pp. 6f.
[138] Ockham was relatively sanguine about natural human powers. Gregory of Rimini, while also regarded as a nominalist, took a strongly Augustinian view about human capabilities in a fallen world. It is possible that Luther had imbibed the version of nominalism associated with Gregory's *schola Augustiniana moderna* (as it was known) in which the doctrine of original sin combined with nominalism to fuel a powerful set of reservations of the operations of reason. See Heiko A. Oberman, 'Headwaters of the Reformation', in *The Dawn of the Reformation* (Edinburgh: T&T Clark, 1986), pp. 39–83; Alister McGrath, *Reformation Thought* (Oxford: Blackwell, 1993), pp. 78–80; Gordon Leff, 'Gregory of Rimini', *Revue d'Études Augustiniennes et Patristiques* 7 (1961), 153–70; Andersen, *Martin Luther*, pp. 56–71.

The story of the impact of these considerations on the trajectory of the modern West has been told many times, albeit in different versions, none of which need be rehearsed in detail here.[139] In essence, from the thirteenth century onwards, a strong emphasis on divine omnipotence led to questions about whether God was limited by putatively universal principles of reason and morality. Nominalists responded to this question in the negative. God was radically free to will any state of affairs that he chose, and to legislate what was right and wrong. This provides a link between nominalism and voluntarism, with the latter emphasising the priority of the divine will. It followed that what had once been thought of as eternal and immutable

[139] Michael Allen Gillespie, *The Theological Origins of Modernity* (Chicago: University of Chicago Press, 2008); John Milbank, *Theology and Social Theory: Beyond Secular Reason*, 2nd ed. (Oxford: Blackwell, 2006), pp. 13–18; Louis Dupré, *Passage to Modernity* (New Haven: Yale University Press, 1993), esp. pp. 39–41; Thomas Pfau, *Minding the Modern: Human Agency, Intellectual Traditions, and Responsible Knowledge* (Notre Dame: University of Notre Dame Press, 2013), pp. 160–82. For the related influence of *voluntarism* on the emergence of science, see Amos Funkenstein, *Theology and the Scientific Imagination* (Princeton: Princeton University Press, 1986); M. B. Foster, 'The Christian Doctrine of Creation and the Rise of Modern Natural Science', *Mind*, new series, 18 (1934), 446–68; P. M. Heimann, 'Voluntarism and Immanence: Conceptions of Nature in Eighteenth-Century Thought', *Journal of the History of Ideas* 39 (1978), 271–83; Henry Guerlac, 'Theological Voluntarism and Biological Analogies in Newton's Physical Thought', *Journal of the History of Ideas* 44 (1983) 219–29; Francis Oakley, 'Christian Theology and the Newtonian Science: The Rise of the Concept of Laws of Nature', *Church History* 30 (1961), 433–57; Margaret J. Osler, *Divine Will and the Mechanical Philosophy: Gassendi and Descartes on Contingency and Necessity in the Created World* (Cambridge: Cambridge University Press, 1994); 'Fortune, Fate, and Divination: Gassendi's Voluntarist Theology and the Baptism of Epicureanism', in *Atoms, Pneuma, and Tranquillity: Epicurean and Stoic Themes in European Thought*, ed. Margaret Osler (Cambridge: Cambridge University Press, 1991), pp. 155–74; John Henry, 'Henry More versus Robert Boyle', in *Henry More (1614–87): Tercentenary Essays*, ed. Sarah Hutton (Dordrecht: Kluwer, 1990), pp. 55–76; James E. Force and Richard H. Popkin, *Essays on the Context, Nature, and Influence of Isaac Newton's Theology* (Dordrecht: Kluwer, 1990); Antoni Malet, 'Isaac Barrow on the Mathematization of Nature: Theological Voluntarism and the Rise of Geometrical Optics', *Journal of the History of Ideas* 58 (1997), 265–87. My own intervention into this discussion has often been taken to be a rejection of the voluntarism and science thesis, whereas it was mostly intended to correct an unhelpful dichotomy between 'voluntarists' and 'intellectualists' and the identification of Descartes with the latter rather than the former. See Peter Harrison, 'Voluntarism and Early Modern Science', *History of Science* 40 (2002), 63–89; 'Was Newton a Voluntarist?', in *Newton and Newtonianism: New Studies*, ed. James E. Force and Sarah Hutton (Dordrecht: Kluwer, 2004), pp. 39–64; 'Voluntarism and the Origins of Modern Science: A Reply to John Henry', *History of Science* 47 (2009), 223–31. Cf. John Henry, 'Voluntarist Theology at the Origins of Modern Science: A Response to Peter Harrison', *History of Science* 47 (2009), 79–113; Francis Oakley, 'Voluntarist Theology and Early-Modern Science: The Matter of the Divine Power, Absolute and Ordained', *History of Science* 56 (2018), 72–96 with both of whom I mostly agree about the importance of voluntarism for the emergence of modern science.

features of the world were to be understood either as arbitrary divine commands, or as human creations that help us navigate the world. Universals have no transcendental status and serve merely as signs. Controversially, the same was often held true for moral universals, too. Expressing the implications of this position simply, if there are no eternal and unchangeable notions of the good and the true, a model of knowledge that has human reason participating in these universals is no longer viable. Nominalism, in combination with voluntarism, was thus destined to leave an indelible mark on subsequent theology, politics, and the natural sciences. It also promoted a revised understanding of human reason.

Thomas Hobbes offers a good indication of how such commitments would play out in early modern philosophy. Perceptively characterised by the polymath philosopher G. W. Leibniz, as 'a super-nominalist', Hobbes proposed in the *Leviathan* (1651) that reason 'is nothing but *Reckoning* (that is, Adding and Subtracting) of the Consequences of general names agreed upon, for the *marking* and *signifying* of our thoughts'.[140] Given Hobbes's commitment to mechanistic understandings of the world, this amounted to a view of reason as a straightforward calculating device. The appeal to common consent also received short shrift: 'no mans Reason, nor the Reason of any one number of men, makes the certaintie; no more than an account is there well cast up, because a great many men have unanimously approved it'.[141] Hobbes expressed a similarly deflationary approach to 'right reason'. Right reason was simply 'the act of reasoning, that is, the peculiar and true ratiocination of every man concerning those actions of his, which may either redound to the damage or benefit of his neighbours'.[142] This was a clear anticipation of the hedonistic calculus of later utilitarians who understand moral judgement as a computing of the balance of benefits and harms caused by particular acts, but without any overriding conception of the good (which right reason had traditionally been thought to provide). With

---

[140] G. W. Leibniz, 'Preface to an Edition of Nizolius', in *Philosophical Papers and Letters*, 2nd ed., ed. L. E. Loemker (Dordrecht: Kluwer, 1969), pp. 121–30 (p. 128); Hobbes, *Leviathan*, pt. 1, ch. 5, vol. 2, p. 64. Hobbes nonetheless allows that reason is 'the undoubted Word of God'. *Leviathan*, pt. 3, 32.2, vol. 3, p. 576.

[141] Hobbes, *Leviathan*, pt. 1, ch. 5, vol. 2, p. 66.

[142] Hobbes, *Philosophical Rudiments concerning Government and Society*, [*De Cive*] in *The English Works of Thomas Hobbes*, 11 vols., ed. William Molesworth (London: Bohn, 1851), vol. 2, p. 16, note. In places Hobbes seems to invoke right reason, but his final position is unmistakably negative. See Robert A. Greene, 'Thomas Hobbes and the Term "Right Reason": Participation to Calculation', *History of European Ideas* 41 (2015), 997–1028. Richard Cumberland produced *De legibus naturae* (London, 1672) in large part to refute Hobbes's dismissal of right reason.

3.4 REASON SECULARISED

substantive matters now lying outside the scope of a merely calculative reason, Hobbes referred issues of morals and religion to the determination of a human judge.[143] This is clearly a step towards the secularisation of reason. For Hobbes, as Peter Dear observes, 'the supernatural has been quietly replaced with civil authority, which provides the absolute criterion for reason'.[144] But all of this was originally motivated by a particular understanding of divine omnipotence.

John Locke represents a further example of the way in which reason came to be reconceptualised. While he retained the traditional descriptions of reason as a 'spark of the divine nature', 'the candle of the Lord', and 'the voice of God', he also took pains to stress 'the weakness of our faculties in this state of mediocrity'.[145] Crucially, for Locke, reason had no substantive content. Against the 'established opinion' that there were innate principles attested to by universal consent, Locke contended that the mind was a blank slate that could be written upon only by experience. This is one of the central messages of the *Essay concerning Human Understanding* (1689), a foundational source for modern epistemology. It is significant that a primary target of the book was Herbert of Cherbury's 'common notions' and the tradition that they represented.[146] (This tradition will be discussed in more detail in Chapter 4.) For Locke, reason is a content-free engine of inference and calculation – the capacity to make deductions and judgements of probability based on ideas that ultimately derived from sensations.[147] Reason in this

---

[143] 'And therfore, as when there is a controversy in an account, the parties must by their own accord, set up for right Reason, the Reason of some Arbitrator, or Judge, to whose sentence they will both stand, or their controversie must either come to blowes, or be undecided, for want of a right Reason constituted by Nature; so is it also in all debates of what kind soever.' *Leviathan*, pt. 1, ch. 5, vol. 2, p. 66.

[144] Peter Dear, 'Divine Illumination, Mechanical Calculators, and the Roots of Modern Reason', *Science in Context* 23 (2010), 351–66 (363). See also Gregory S. Kavka, 'Right Reason and Natural Law in Hobbes's Ethics', *The Monist* 66 (1983), 120–33. In a sense, this is Hobbes's version of a new kind of implicit faith.

[145] Locke, *Reasonableness of Christianity*, pp. 139f.; *Two Treatises of Government*, ed. Peter Laslett (Cambridge: Cambridge University Press, 2003), p. 205; *Essay* 4.12.10 (p. 645). In the *Essay* Locke also calls reason 'a natural revelation' (again confounding modern understandings of revelation as essentially supernatural). *Essay* 4.19.4 (p. 698). As Shaftesbury pointed out, it is not clear that the innate ideas that Locke rejects correspond to the connate principles, *koinai ennoiai* and the *prolêpsis* held by the Cambridge Platonists. See Friedrich A. Uehlein, 'Whichcote, Shaftesbury and Locke: Shaftesbury's Critique of Locke's Epistemology and Moral Philosophy', *British Journal for the History of Philosophy* 25 (2017), 1031–48.

[146] Locke, *Essay* I, 3, 15; I.4.13 (pp. 77, 92).

[147] Reason involves 'the perception of the connexion there is between the *Ideas* in each step of the deduction, whereby the Mind comes to see, either the certain Agreement or

sense had the potential to act as a kind of arbiter in matters of faith, which was increasingly understood as the act of assenting to propositions. What God reveals is undoubtedly true, Locke allows, but whether it is a true revelation '*Reason* must judge.'[148] With Locke, reason moves from being intimately connected to divine revelation to being an independent judge of what actually counts as revelation in the first place.[149]

Again, Locke's intention was to place constraints upon reason. With its modest reach, it was sufficient for our activities in the present world, God having equipped us for 'the conveniences of life and the business we have to do here'.[150] And even our knowledge of the natural world is significantly circumscribed: 'what a darkness we are involved in, how little it is of being, and the things that are, that we are capable to know'. We know nothing of the true nature of the universe and remain ignorant about physical bodies and the causes of events. Our faculties, Locke wrote, 'are not fitted to penetrate into the internal fabric and real essences of bodies' and the knowledge that our senses provide yields 'but judgment and opinion, not knowledge and certainty'. They might allow us to 'draw advantages of ease and health, and increase our stock of conveniences for this life', but fall well short of providing us with genuine science.[151] Again, reason serves well enough for secular purposes in the here and now.

This restrained vision of reason fitted well with an experimental programme of science that had as its primary aim the relief of the human

---

Disagreement of any two *Ideas*'. *Essay* 4.17.2 (p. 669). Further on, reason is 'the discovery of the certainty or probability of such propositions or truths, which the mind arrives at by deduction made from such ideas, as it has got by the use of its natural faculties; viz, by the use of sensation or reflection'. Locke, *Essay* 4.8.2 (p. 689).

[148] Locke, *Essay* 4.18.10 (p. 695). Thomas Reid argued similarly in his 'Lectures on Natural Religion', 5.17–18, in *Thomas Reid on Religion*, ed. James J. S. Foster, introduction by Nicholas Wolterstorff (Edinburgh: Library of Scottish Philosophy, 2017), unpaginated.

[149] But Locke does not deny that some matters of faith may be above reason and its authority derives from the fact it is a light that God has given us. *Essay* 4.18.8 (p. 694).

[150] Locke, *Essay* 2.23.12 (p. 302). For Locke's complicated position in relation to the reformers' pessimistic assessments of the capacities of reason, see Harrison, *Fall of Man*, pp. 221–33; W. M. Spellman, *John Locke and the Problem of Depravity* (Oxford: Clarendon Press, 1988).

[151] Locke, *Essay* 4.12.10 (p. 645). 'Science' here in the sense of Aristotelian *scientia* which entailed demonstrative certainty. Locke's position is an interesting echo of Nicholas of Cusa: 'The quiddity of things, which is the truth of beings, is unattainable in its purity; though it is sought by all philosophers, it is found by no one as it is. And the more deeply we are instructed in this ignorance, the closer we approach the truth.' Nicholas of Cusa, *On Learned Ignorance*, 1.3.10, in *Selected Spiritual Writings*, trans. H. Lawrence Bond (New York: Paulist Press, 1997), p. 91. Cf. also Joseph Glanvill, *Scepsis Scientifica: Or, Confest Ignorance, the Way to Science* (London, 1665).

condition in the present world. Francis Bacon had earlier outlined how, once human knowledge-making confronted the limitations imposed by the Fall, it might be oriented towards the charitable goal of human welfare: 'knowledge being now discharged of that venom which the serpent infused into it, and which makes the mind of man to swell, we may not be wise above measure and sobriety, but cultivate truth in charity'.[152] This approach informed the mission of the early Royal Society and its programme of experimental natural philosophy. Robert Hooke, the Society's first curator of experiments, thus noted that on account of an innate corruption, human beings were prone to error and misfortune. Experimental science was addressed to a partial rectification of those errors and to ameliorating 'the mischiefs, and imperfection, mankind has drawn upon it self'.[153] On this understanding, which is some distance from later assessments, science (or, more strictly, natural philosophy) was a kind of consolation prize, and the human faculties that enabled it were accorded a status that was correspondingly modest.[154]

In sum, over the course of the sixteenth and seventeenth centuries, much of the discussion of the powers of reason and its status in comparison to other authorities (experience, tradition, scripture), was linked to specific theological commitments. In relation to human nature, these can be correlated with differing interpretations of the biblical Fall and along varying assessments of the damage to reason that it had wrought. In relation to the divine nature, the question was whether divine omnipotence could be trammelled by human conceptions or was ultimately inscrutable. More generous appraisals of reason, characteristic of the Cambridge Platonists and, before them, many scholastic thinkers, were linked to relatively sanguine readings of the Fall along with the assumption that predicates such as 'goodness' could be reliably applied to the Godhead. But for those who argued that more severe and comprehensive losses had attended Adam's lapse, and who also stressed the inscrutability of the divine will, reason and its operations were thought to be seriously compromised and limited in their reach. It was

---

[152] Bacon, *The Great Instauration*, in *Works*, vol. 4, p. 20. Bacon's estimation of the potential accomplishments of human knowledge-makers is more optimistic than that of Locke, in part because of the eschatological context in which it was originally articulated and understood. Following the Restoration, however, more exuberant visions of scientific progress were treated with a degree of suspicion.

[153] Robert Hooke, *Micrographia* (London, 1665), Preface (unpaginated).

[154] How science moves from this position of relative inferiority to become a central feature of European cultures is addressed in a magisterial series of volumes written by Stephen Gaukroger, beginning with *The Emergence of a Scientific Culture* (Oxford: Oxford University Press, 2006).

the latter stance that advanced the secularisation of reason, now understood to be a diminished natural power and not a luminous divine presence in the human mind.

3.5 The Eclipse of Trust

The Lockean proposal that instrumental reason, in spite of its limitations, could provide a more reliable guide to religious truths than trust in fallible authorities led to a new understanding of what counted as 'reasonable religion'. As Thomas Sprat declared in 1667: 'The universal disposition of this *Age* is bent upon a *rational religion.*'[155] The vogue for rational religion was of a piece with criticisms of unreflective, implicit faith. But given the range of understandings of reason, what counted as 'rational religion' varied widely. At one end of the scale, those who shared the Cambridge Platonists' generous and broad assessment of human rationality, essentially regarded the perfecting of reason, understood as the image of the divine within, as one of the chief aims of the religious life. Henry Hallywell summed up this approach with his observation that 'Christianity is not only agreeable to, but perfective of our Rational Powers.'[156] Many of his contemporaries endorsed this view.[157] Importantly, the specification of *Christian* religion meant that believing revealed truths and the mysteries of Christianity was included in the package.

At the other end of the scale, however, for those who regarded reason as an instrument of calculation – reason as ratiocination – rational religion might be understood as a minimalist religion consisting only in those truths that were rationally comprehensible and supported by argument. This

---

[155] Sprat, *History of the Royal Society*, p. 366.
[156] Henry Hallywell, *The Sacred Method of Saving Humane Souls* (London, 1677), p. 78. Cf.: 'For the Christian Religion is a manifestation of the highest Reason that ever the World had any cognizance of, and all its Parts and Doctrines are every way fitted to Rational Capacities' (p. 69).
[157] Joseph Glanvill: '*The belief of our reasons is an exercise of Faith, and Faith is an act of Reason.*' *Logou thrēskeia*, p. 24; Benjamin Whichcote: 'The Perfection of the Happiness of Humane Nature, consists in the right Use of our Rational Faculties; in the vigorous and intense Exercise of them, about their Proper and proportionable Object; which is God.' Aphorism 296, *Select Sermons*, p. 451; Bentley, *Unreasonableness of Atheism*, p. 26; Robert South: 'Reason is that into which all Religion is at last resolved.' 'The Doctrine of the Blessed Trinity Asserted', *Sermons*, vol. 2, p. 404; Daniel Nicols: 'True Religion is most rational, answering the Philosophy of Man's Nature, and the Ends of Discourse.' *A Sermon Preached in the Cathedral of Lincoln* (London, 1681), p. 14; John Jenny: 'there being nothing in the world more rational then Religion and the Worship of a Deity', *A Sermon Preached at the Funeral of Lady Frances Padget* (London, 1697), p. 9.

was the position associated with an (admittedly diverse) group of 'deists'.[158] One of the prominent deists, the Irish freethinker John Toland, notoriously insisted that no true religious doctrine could be 'above reason' or 'against reason'. This, he contended, was an implication of the principle, urged by both Locke and the Cambridge Platonists, that reason was 'the candle of the Lord'. For Toland, this reason was the measure of the intrinsic reasonableness of any purported doctrine.[159] As he expressed it: 'For as 'tis by Reason we arrive at the Certainty of God's own Existence, so we cannot otherwise discern his *Revelations* but by their Conformity with our own natural Notices of Him.'[160]

Again, critique of implicit faith and the ethics of belief were central concerns. Toland insisted that if we are to be morally responsible for what we hold to be true, we must fully comprehend its content: 'as long as he conceives not what he believes, he cannot sincerely acquiesce in it'.[161] Arguing that Christianity cannot enjoin belief in things that are above or against reason, Toland pointed to what was at stake: if salvation depends upon belief, then 'the Subject of Faith must be intelligible to all'. But this logic assumed a quite new understanding of faith. Medieval thinkers endorsed the premise, but drew the different conclusion that for many, if not most, faith must be implicit and involve an attitude of trust. Such faith was the precondition for knowledge. Toland demurred: 'I stand by it that Faith *is* knowledg.'[162] A new kind of moral commitment would necessarily attend this reconstrued 'faith': not trust in others, but a capacity on the part of each individual to fully comprehend and provide reasons for holding those propositions that now constituted religious faith.

It may seem that the principle of deploying reason to determine the veracity of revelation seems simply a repetition of Locke's view with echoes of the Cambridge Platonists. But Locke had still been committed to

---

[158] On the problem of defining deism see Harrison, *'Religion' and the Religions*, p. 62.

[159] 'for *Reason* is not less from God than *Revelation;* 'tis the Candle, the Guide, the Judge he has lodg'd within every Man that cometh into this World'. John Toland, *Christianity not Mysterious* (London, 1696), pp. 140f.

[160] Toland, *Christianity not Mysterious*, p. 30. Other deistical writers expressed the same sentiment. Thomas Chubb: 'Reason is the judge of the meaning and sense of the divine revelation. Reason ought to be the judge of *every part* of that revelation.' *The Comparative Excellence and Obligation of Moral and Positive Duties* (London, 1730), p. 26; Thomas Morgan: 'The moral Truth, Reason, of Fitness ... is the only Mark of Criterion of any Doctrine as coming from God, or as making any Part of true Religion.' *The Moral Philosopher*, vol. 1 (London, 1737), p. viii.

[161] Toland, *Christianity not Mysterious*, p. 36.

[162] Toland, *Christianity not Mysterious*, pp. 134, 139 (my emphasis).

the principle that many things exceeded the scope of reason, and that such things might be revealed. It was given to reason to judge the reliability of the *source* of revealed truths rather than judge their intrinsic intelligibility.[163] The tendency of the deists was to omit this key step, which had still allowed for the possibility that reason might judge it necessary to accept things that went beyond its scope. This takes us to the broader question of 'evidences' for Christianity and rational judgements of the trustworthiness of sources of revelation (which will be considered in the next chapter).

For now, it should be clear that the dismantling of implicit faith required a new understanding of faith in which the role of trust was reassessed and diminished, while reason, however conceived, was elevated. The question of the role of trust in relation to belief had been tackled head-on by Thomas Hobbes. In his no-nonsense analysis of 'believing *in*' and how, if at all, it differs from 'believing *that*', Hobbes insisted that 'by *Beleeving in*, as in the Creed, is meant, not trust in the Person; but Confession and acknowledgement of the Doctrine'.[164] In direct opposition to first-century understandings, Hobbes contended that to believe in God is not to put one's trust in God, but rather to give intellectual assent to the proposition 'God exists'. Hobbes's collapse of the distinction between belief-in and belief-that, and his exclusion of the trust relations, became increasingly common in the late seventeenth century, even among those less theologically suspect than Hobbes.

The classicist Meric Casaubon observed that some who had written on belief and unbelief 'have chiefly, under that title, insisted upon *trust*, or *trusting*'. Casaubon was having none of it, making it clear that for him belief was about histories of things done and credited as true.[165] We find comparable assessments among many orthodox religious thinkers. Isaac Barrow maintained that faith and belief are the same thing, referencing Aristotle's *Topics*. To reinforce the point, he offers this definition: 'To believe πιστεύειν [*pisteuein*] is the effect ... of a persuasive argument, and the result of ratiocination.' The object of faith, he goes on to say, is not a person or institution but 'a proposition, deduced from others by discourse'. It follows that 'to

---

[163] Locke, *Essay* 4.18.8 (pp. 694f.).
[164] Hobbes, *Leviathan*, ch. 7, vol. 2, p. 102. Cf. ch. 32, appendix, vol. 3, pp. 576, 1142. As discussed earlier, there is a comparable distinction in Augustine, and subsequently discussed in Aquinas, *ST* 2a.2ae. 2, 2. 'Believing God, believing in a God, believing in God'. For seventeenth-century treatments of Augustine's distinction which oppose Hobbes's interpretation see John Cromp, *Collections out of St Augustine* (London, 1638), p. 29; Christopher Cartwright, *A Brief and Plain Exposition of the Creed* (London, 1649), pp. 8f.
[165] Meric Casaubon, *A TREATISE PROVING Spirits, Witches, AND Supernatural Operations* (London, 1672), p. 6.

3.5 THE ECLIPSE OF TRUST

believe on a person, or thing' is just a 'figurative manner of speaking' that can be reduced to 'the being persuaded of the truth of some proposition relating in one way, or other, to that person'.[166] We find a similar view of faith and belief being advocated by the Anglican divine and popular preacher Edward Stillingfleet. In his aptly entitled *Rational Account of the Grounds of the Protestant Religion* (1664) Stillingfleet tells us that faith is '*a rational and discursive act* of the mind ... an *assent* upon *evidence*, or *reason* inducing the mind to assent'. Whenever God requires us to believe anything as true, Stillingfleet maintained, 'he gives us *evidence* that it is so'.[167] Matters of faith are not simply a matter of taking someone's word for it. Faith was essentially a form of knowledge in which justificatory reasons played a stronger role than interpersonal trust.[168] John Tillotson was in agreement. Faith, he declared, 'is an assent of the mind to something as revealed by God'. All such assent, he continues, 'must be grounded on evidence; that is, no man can believe anything, unless he have, or think he hath, some reason to do so'.[169] The shift is from trust to an appeal to the evidence. On these new understandings, to believe in God or Christ was not so much to reside trust in them as persons, but to believe their edicts and utterances on the basis of some independent evidence. To the extent that faith might seem to require a degree of trust, determining the trustworthiness of a source was the business of reason.

John Locke set out a similar position on belief and its objects. To 'believe', Locke suggests in the *Reasonableness of Christianity* (1695), is to 'assent to the Truth of Propositions'.[170] This assertion effectively repeats a stance already taken in the *Essay*, according to which '*Faith*, as we use the word, has to do with ... Propositions ... which are supposed to be divinely revealed.'[171]

---

[166] Isaac Barrow, 'Of Justifying Faith' [c.1669], in *Theological Works*, vol. 4, pp. 327, 329, 330. The reference is to Aristotle, *Topics* 4.5 126b29–126a2. In his definition, Barrow gives the present, active infinite form of πιστεύω, which is used five times in the New Testament including one reference to 'believe on him' [εἰς αὐτὸν πιστεύειν] (Philippians 1:29). Barrow goes on to annex obedience to this faith, attempting to show that faith is not mere intellectual assent. Yet he concedes that this extension is 'beyond its [i.e., faith's] natural and primary force' (p. 341). He also explicitly rejects Calvin's understanding of faith as a 'firm and certain knowledge of God's eternal good-will toward us' (p. 350).

[167] Edward Stillingfleet, *A Rational account of the grounds of Protestant Religion* (London, 1665), pp. 203, 139. Stillingfleet's repute as a preacher was such that Samuel Pepys records on one occasion not being able get into the parish church at Westminster to hear him, and having to settle instead for a meal of herring at a nearby pub: Entry for Wednesday, 10 October 1666, www.pepysdiary.com/diary/1666/10/10/, accessed 23 November 2023.

[168] 'There is no *contrariety* between the *foundation of faith* and *knowledge*, as the *schoolmen* have perswaded the *world*; we see both of them *proceed* on the same *foundation* ....' Stillingfleet, *Origines Sacrae*, 4th ed., p. 232.

[169] Tillotson, *Works*, vol. 1, p. 18. [170] Locke, *Third Letter concerning Toleration*, p. 233.

[171] Locke, *Essay* 4.18.6 (p. 693).

Specifically, to become a Christian one need only assent to the proposition that 'Jesus is the Messiah'.[172] Locke, admittedly, holds that other things must be believed after one has become a Christian, and in other contexts would admit that faith was also in some sense a gift that required obedience.[173] But he could easily be construed as proposing that what faith consisted in was an objective belief in a single article.[174] Locke thus shared with Herbert of Cherbury a concern to identify the fundamental propositional beliefs necessary for salvation, but rather than turning to innate ideas he looked instead to the doctrinal content of the gospels.

The demise of implicit faith and the accompanying emphasis on rational determination of the content of belief on the part of the individual will be parsed differently depending on the extent to which reason is itself evacuated of theological significance. But the direction of travel is clear, as narrower, more secular conceptions of reason gained currency. The theological origins of these new conceptions of reason notwithstanding, increasingly they will no longer mesh neatly with revelation but will rather stand over against it. If we move to the middle decades of the eighteenth century we get a good sense of where these developments are headed by considering the definitions of reason set out in the *Encyclopédie* (1765) of Diderot and d'Alembert.[175] The relevant entry in this monument of Enlightenment scholarship offers us four meanings of 'reason' which fortuitously divide

---

[172] Locke, *Reasonableness of Christianity*, pp. 23, 30, 168f. Cf. p. xvii. Whether intentional or not, this comes interestingly close to Hobbes's own formulation in the *Leviathan*: 'The (*Vnam Necessarium*) Onely article of Faith, which the Scripture maketh simply Necessary to Salvation, is this, that JESUS IS THE CHRIST' (pt. 3, ch. 43, vol. 3, p. 938). The editor of this Hobbes edition, Noel Malcolm, points out that *Unam Necessarium* appears to be a reference to Luke 11:42 (Vulgate). Intriguingly Hobbes goes on to say that other articles of the creed are 'contained in this one' and held 'implicitly' by those not skilled enough to discern its full implications (vol. 3, p. 948).

[173] Locke, *Reasonableness of Christianity*, pp. xvii–xviii; *A Second Letter concerning Toleration* (London, 1690), pp. 18, 22; *Third Letter concerning Toleration*, p. 221.

[174] Even Locke's supporters conceded this. Samuel Bold thus admitted that Locke's 'enquiry and search was not concerning *Christian Faith*, considered *Subjectively*, but *Objectively*'. *Some Passages in the Reasonableness of Christianity* (London, 1697), p. 31.

[175] 'Raison', in *Encyclopédie ou Dictionnaire raisonné des sciences, des arts et des métiers*, vol. 13, pp. 773–4. I have been unable to determine the author of this article, but the treatment is well informed by theological considerations. In definition (3), for example, processes of instrumental reason are said to be fallible on account of the depravity of reason. In definition (4) the difference between a priori and a posteriori is explained in terms of God's choices. A priori truths could not have been otherwise, and their contradiction implies absurdity. But a posteriori truths are the consequence of God's freely choosing to create particular states of affairs. Hence, 'the general laws that God established when creating the universe' could have been otherwise, and can be known only through experience.

neatly along the lines of the two conceptions of reason under consideration. The first two refer to the more expansive understandings: (1) 'natural faculty with which God endowed us to know the truth', followed by (2) 'notions which we have from birth, and common to all men of the world'. The next two, however, suggest a more restrictive, calculative reason: (3) reason as a faculty or reasoning process; and (4) sequences of truths that can be known 'without being assisted by the light of faith'. Reason, in these latter senses, is divorced from faith and invested with the authority to render judgement on putative truths of faith, now understood in propositional terms. Over the course of the eighteenth and nineteenth centuries we witness the ascendancy of the last two, secular, instrumental conceptions of reason. Today, the first two senses of reason are now almost virtually unrecognisable except as historical relics. Reason in the two new senses might either challenge religious beliefs or lend support to them. But either way, reason is separated out from religious convictions that are now understood as consisting in knowledge claims of the kind that stand in need of the external confirmation that reason might provide.

The ensuing discussion in the *Encyclopédie* makes the implications of these developments plain. Reason is now 'the true competent judge' of all things of which we have clear and distinct ideas. It must exercise 'jurisdiction over religion'.[176] Even for those who cherished religious commitments, plural religions could be regarded as one of the most common manifestations of irrationality, excepting only one's own religion, which was typically imagined to uniquely enjoy the support of rational judgement. For critics of religion in general, however, the accusation of irrationality could be extended to all manifestations of religion without exception. Such critique became a common feature of one strand of the Enlightenment and emerges as an implication of the first position. But across the board, reason was understood less as a participatory act or sharing in the ideas in the divine mind. Neither did it consist in a set of common notions that attracted universal assent. Reason was now a natural faculty that enabled individual judgement – albeit judgement that supposedly drew upon universally held principles.[177] The putative universality of the judgement of reason was the

---

[176] This becomes the common refrain of the British deists. See, e.g., Toland, *Christianity not Mysterious*, p. 230; Chubb, *Excellence and Obligation of Moral and Positive Duties*, pp. 15, 26; Morgan, *Moral Philosopher*, p. 8.

[177] This is not to say that broader conceptions of reason were completely eclipsed by instrumental or 'Enlightenment' versions of reason. Gotthold Lessing, for example, persisted with the notion of reason as a kind of receptacle for divine revelation, the latter being necessary for the 'education' of the human race (discussed further in Chapter 7).

one thing that carried over into these understandings, even as the original theological justifications for that universality silently fell away. This now made possible an opposition between faith and reason that would have been largely incomprehensible before.

Immanuel Kant would later nuance the sharp divide between reason and faith with his distinction between speculative and practical reason, stressing the limitations of the former when it came to moral and religious matters. To some degree, this is a continuation of the long-standing Protestant restriction of reason to the secular sphere. But in the meantime, considerable effort was also expended in exercises that sought show why instrumental reason was not necessarily hostile to traditional Christianity. One of the more conspicuous consequences of the ascendancy of instrumental reason and an ethics of belief was the development of new forms of natural theology. This consisted in rational proofs for God's existence, developed in response to demands that core theistic commitments be embraced on the basis of evidence and not authority. These transitions will be the subject of the next chapter. Before turning to these proofs and their new role in providing foundations for religious belief, it is important to consider, albeit briefly, the place of early modern science in relation to these new understandings of rationality and evidence-based knowledge.

3.6 Slogans of Modernity

There is a sense in which religion was the main game in town for sixteenth- and seventeenth-century Europe. But it was not the only one. Another emerging cultural phenomenon also raised acute questions about the foundations of knowledge. This was the new science or, as the historical actors referred to it, 'experimental natural philosophy'. Just as the Reformation had thrown open the question of the nature of religious commitment and its foundations, so the scientific revolution necessitated a re-examination of how scientific knowledge is acquired and justified, paralleling the challenges to implicit faith and trust in traditions that had taken place in the religious sphere. This is not the occasion for a full account of the rise of modern science or even of the religious factors involved in its emergence

---

Lessing's reason remains 'religiously grounded'. See Arno Schilson, *Geschichte im Horizont der Vorsehung: G. E. Lessings Beitrag zu einer Theologie der Geschichte* (Mainz: Matthias-Grünewald-Verlag, 1974), p. 124; Günter Rohrmoser, *Emanzipation und Freiheit* (Munich: Wilhelm Goldmann Verlag, 1970), p. 50; Toshimasa Yasukata, *Lessing's Philosophy of Religion and the German Enlightenment* (Oxford: Oxford University Press, 2003), p. 142.

and consolidation.[178] But there are intriguing parallels between the treatments of implicit faith and appeals to reason and experience in the two spheres and these cast a long shadow over subsequent developments.

One parallel lies in the appeal to first-hand experience or experimental knowledge. 'Experiment' is a term that we naturally associate with the methods of the sciences. However, when we examine the use of the expressions 'experiment' and 'experimental' in seventeenth-century English sources, it is striking that by a significant margin the most frequent references occur not in connection with scientific matters but in various genres of religious literature. Most common is the phrase 'experimental knowledge of God', but we also regularly encounter 'experimental apprehension of God', 'inward experimental feeling', 'experimental prayer', 'experimental reading of scripture', 'experimental witnesses', and 'experimental divines'.[179] This terminology has its origin in the Latin *experimentum*, which denoted 'experience', 'trial', or 'test'. A simple translation of '*experimental* knowledge of God' would thus be '*experiential* knowledge of God', but the connotations of 'trial' and 'test' were also present, as was a contrast with 'speculative' knowledge.

In the context of the epistemic crisis precipitated by the Reformation, this emphasis on experimental religion emerged as an alternative to reliance upon authority, tradition, book learning, and speculative metaphysics.[180] Martin Luther maintained that only those with 'experimental proof' of Christian faith were qualified to know what it is and speak authoritatively about it.[181] Seventeenth-century Puritan writers also emphasised the priority of experiment in the religious life. John Downame would propose that 'experimental divinity needeth not so much reading and studying ... as conference, observation and experience'.[182] First-hand 'experimental'

---

[178] For accounts of religious factors, see Peter Harrison, *The Bible, Protestantism and the Rise of Natural Science* (Cambridge: Cambridge University Press, 1998); *Fall of Man*; and, more generally, Gaukroger, *Emergence of a Scientific Culture*.

[179] Harrison, 'Experimental Religion', on which the argument that follows is based.

[180] That said, the distinction between speculative and experimental goes back to medieval sources. Aquinas, e.g., distinguished between speculative and experiment knowledge of God's will. *ST* 2a2ae. 97, 2. Jean Gerson spoke of the division between speculative and experimental theology, 'Sermon on Saint Bernard', in *Early Works*, trans. Brian McGuire (New York: Paulist Press, 1998), p. 132.

[181] '*Facilis res multis est uisa, Christiana fides, quam & non pauci inter uirtutes ceu socias numerant, quod faciunt, qui nullo experiment eam probauerunt ...*' (To many, Christian faith has appeared to be an easy thing; indeed not a few reckon it among the social virtues, as it were, because they have not tested [or proved] it experimentally ...). *De libertate christiana*, sig. biiir.

[182] John Downame, *The Christian Warfare* (London, 1634), p. 15.

knowledge of God, according to another Puritan divine, Francis Roberts, contrasts with 'speculative' knowledge which is 'remote, general, confused, consisting in certain empty, comfortlesse, swimming notions, arising from natural or artificial abilities'. Roberts went on to explain, in what were standard tropes in this literature, that the distinction is akin to what physicians learn from books as opposed to direct experience with their patients, or what scholars know of distant lands from maps as opposed to what travellers encounter when they get there.[183] Anthony Burgess linked the distinction to his critique of implicit faith, contrasting 'dogmatical assent' to speculative knowledge with 'a *practical, and experimental receiving of holy Truths*'.[184]

The religious literature has abundant examples of these usages and the significance of parallel usages in the scientific context did not go unnoticed. Johnathan Edwards observed that 'as that is called experimental philosophy, which brings opinions and notions to the test of fact; so is that properly called experimental religion, which brings religious affections and intentions to the like test'.[185] More generally, it seems clear that the speculative/experimental distinction, borrowed from the religious context, was the way in which seventeenth-century thinkers conceptualised what we now think of as the rationalist/empiricist divide, a distinction that was retrospectively applied to the early modern period by later Kantian historians of philosophy.[186]

---

[183] Francis Roberts, *A Communicant Instructed* (London, 1659), p. 100.
[184] Anthony Burgess, *A Treatise of original sin* (London, 1658), p. 212.
[185] Jonathan Edwards, *A Treatise concerning Religion Affections* [1746], in *The Works of Jonathan Edwards*, 2 vols. (Peabody, MA: Hendrickson, 1998), vol. 1, p. 333.
[186] See especially Peter Anstey, 'Experimental Versus Speculative Natural Philosophy', in *The Science of Nature in the Seventeenth Century*, ed. Peter Anstey and J. A. Schuster (Dordrecht: Springer, 2005), pp. 215–42. Cf. Harrison, 'Experimental Religion', 422–5. The construction of the common rationalist vs. empiricist divide was largely the work of Wilhelm Gottlieb Tennemann, author of *Grundriß der Geschichte der Philosophie*, 2nd ed. (Leipzig: Barth, 1816) (ET, *A Manual of the History of Philosophy*, trans. Arthur Johnson (Oxford: Talboys, 1832), rev. J. R. Morell (London: Bohn, 1852)) and Johann Gottlieb Buhle, *Lehrbuch der Geschichte der Philosophie* (Göttingen: Vandenhoeck & Ruprecht, 1796–1804). The histories of philosophy of Kuno Fischer and Friedrich Ueberweg then helped introduce this story into the English-speaking world, where it became the dominant narrative. See, e.g., Ueberweg, *A History of Philosophy*, trans. G. S. Morris (London: Hodder & Stoughton, 1872–3). For secondary discussions see Alberto Vanza, 'Empiricism and Rationalism in Nineteenth-Century Histories of Philosophy', *Journal of the History of Ideas* 77 (2016), 253–82; 'Kant on Empiricism and Rationalism', *History of Philosophy Quarterly* 30 (2013), 53–74; Peter Anstey and Alberto Vanza, 'The Origins of Early Modern Experimental Philosophy', *Intellectual History Review* 22 (2012), 499–518; K. Walsh and A. Currie, 'Caricatures, Myths and White Lies', *Metaphilosophy* 46 (2015), 414–35; David Fate Norton, 'The Myth of British Empiricism', *History of European Ideas* 1 (1981), 331–44.

3.6 SLOGANS OF MODERNITY

The sentiment that one should discover things for oneself and seek assurances for what one held to be true thus became part of the self-understanding and rhetoric of the new experimental philosophy. In keeping with this sentiment, the motto adopted by the Royal Society, founded in 1660, was *nullius in verba* – 'take no one's word for it' or, expanding on its original context, 'I pledge allegiance to the authority of no master'.[187] Leaving aside the irony that the advice to take no one's word for it is borrowed from an ancient authority (the Roman poet Horace), this is a clear articulation of a principle that runs directly parallel to Protestant critiques of implicit faith and reliance on authority. In this case, like advocacies of experimental knowledge, the injunction is to ignore the voice of authority and satisfy oneself about knowledge claims on the basis of first-hand evidence. The parallel becomes even more conspicuous when we consider the fact that the epigram from Horace had already been deployed in a religious context to support the rejection of implicit faith.[188] This again suggests the temporal priority of religious discussions of knowledge and its justification.

An even deeper irony than the borrowing of the epigram from Horace and previous religious sources is that the new scientific enterprise was just as dependent on a version of implicit faith as medieval Christianity. The corporate and cumulative character of the new natural and experimental philosophy meant that reliance upon the testimony of others and acceptance of 'historical' records of observations and experiments was foundational to the whole enterprise. Even today, and notwithstanding popular misconceptions about 'the scientific method', virtually everything we know about the natural world comes to us second-hand. Given an increasing specialisation of knowledge and division of labour this is true even, and perhaps especially, for natural scientists themselves. Wittgenstein has remarked in this context that justification is a *social* practice.[189] Speaking more specifically about the public acceptance of the science of climate change, Bruno Latour

---

[187] Horace, *Epistles* 1.1.14. The Society's website informs us that the motto is 'an expression of the determination of Fellows to withstand the domination of authority and to verify all statements by an appeal to facts determined by experiment'. https://royalsociety.org/about-us/history/, accessed 3 February 2022.

[188] See, e.g., Clement Walker, *The Mystery of the two ιυntos, Presbyterian and Independent* (n.p., 1647), p. 4. On the other side, Robert Burton, in *The Anatomy of Melancholy*, cites this principle as characteristic of heretics: 'Common as madness, folly, pride, insolency, arrogancy, singularity, peevishness, obstinacy, impudence, scorn and contempt of all other sects: *Nullius addicti jurare in verba magistri*; they will approve of naught but what they invent themselves.' 3.4.1.3, vol. 3, p. 401.

[189] On the congruity between Sellars and Wittgenstein on this point, see Richard Rorty's introduction to Sellars, *Empiricism and the Philosophy of Mind*, pp. 1–12.

has similarly insisted that scientific facts remain robust only when they are supported by 'a common culture' and 'by institutions that can be trusted'.[190]

In the seventeenth century, with knowledge acquisition becoming a corporate and collaborative affair, natural historians and natural philosophers had to determine whose observations and experimental reports they would regard as reliable. Then as now, scientific knowledge, as Steven Shapin has demonstrated, had an ineradicable social dimension, resting upon protocols about which individuals and groups could be regarded as trustworthy. Shapin rightly points out that 'no practice has accomplished the rejection of testimony and authority and that no cultural practice recognizable as such could do so'.[191] Augustine had said as much in the fifth century, and de Tocqueville repeated it in the nineteenth: 'There is in this world no philosopher so great that he does not believe a million things on the faith of others, and who does not assume more truths than he establishes.'[192] There is a largely unacknowledged disparity, then, between the ostensibly unmediated rational and empirical foundations of natural science that is part of its public image, and the on-the-ground reality of needing to trust in others, especially when what is reported is counterintuitive and contrary to mundane experience.

On occasion, and despite a motto that suggested otherwise, this was acknowledged by the relevant parties, especially those concerned to show affinities between scientific and religious forms of knowing. Robert Boyle pointed out that when Galileo described the craters on the moon it was received by others in the astronomical community 'upon an implicit faith, upon his authority'.[193] Because this was a scientifically heterodox claim, based on the unsubstantiated observations of a single individual, Galileo's status as a reliable observer was a key factor in determining the credibility of his reports. Boyle also pointed out that an ordinary seaman travelling with Columbus could have furnished the learned of Europe with knowledge of the new world capable of rectifying 'divers Erroneous Presumptions and Mistakes, which till then they thought very agreeable to ... Sciences, and so to Reason'.[194] In a third example, Boyle compared experimental reports to the information conveyed by a deep sea diver who has unique access to objects that 'lye conceal'd from other men's Sight and Reach'. Boyle

---

[190] Bruno Latour, *Down to Earth: Politics in the New Climatic Regime*, trans. Catherine Porter (Cambridge: Polity Press, 2018), p. 23.
[191] Shapin, *A Social History of Truth*, p. xxv.
[192] Alexis de Tocqueville, *Democracy in America*, II.1.2, ed. and trans. Harvey C. Mansfield and Delba Winthrop (Chicago: University of Chicago Press, 2000), p. 408.
[193] Boyle, *Reflections on a Theological Distinction, Works*, vol. 11, pp. 339f.
[194] Boyle, *Christian Virtuoso, I, Works*, vol. 11, p. 314.

3.6 SLOGANS OF MODERNITY

admitted that he had revised his own views about 'submarine parts' on the basis of such reports. He went on to suggest that the depths of God are similar to the depths of the ocean in that our opinions on divine matters need to be informed and rectified by 'preachers of the Gospel'.[195]

Boyle also conceded that he relied heavily upon his assistant Denis Papin to conduct and record the outcomes of experiments because 'I had cause enough to *trust* his skill and diligence'.[196] Papin's contributions were rarely acknowledged in the official accounts of experiments (which themselves were typically written by amanuenses who were equally invisible). These parallels between complex scientific networks of authority and trust, and a medieval epistemic ecosystem that relied upon implicit faith, are to some extent obscured by the rhetoric of modern science and official versions of its history.[197] The nineteenth-century emergence of the idea of 'the scientific method' has tended to make scientific practitioners invisible – with the exception of the rare celebrity scientist – with an apparently impersonal set of procedures providing science with the requisite epistemic legitimacy.[198]

---

[195] Boyle, *Christian Virtuoso I, Works*, vol. 11, pp. 314f. Similar observations in *Some Considerations about the Reconcileableness of Reason and Religion, Works*, vol. 8, p. 293, and in Norris, *Reason and Faith*, pp. 106–8.

[196] Boyle, *Spring of the Air: Second Continuation, Works*, vol. 9, p. 125 (my emphasis). On the invisibility of certain forms of scientific labour see Steven Shapin, 'The Invisible Technician', *American Scientist* 77 (1989), 554–63.

[197] A good example of such idealisation is the notion of the individual scientist as a kind of systematic sceptic, exemplified in Karl Popper's notion of falsifiability. For Popper, a genuine scientific claim must be one that is, in principle, empirically falsifiable. Science progresses, on this view, not by verifying favoured scientific hypotheses, but by falsifying the alternatives. See *Conjectures and Refutations* (London: Routledge & Kegan Paul, 1963). This attempt at demarcating genuine science from pseudoscience (which indirectly owes its origins to positivist notions of verification) has not found much favour among historians and philosophers of science. But it continues to play a role in the self-conception of many scientists and popularisers of science. One deeply misleading aspect of this notion is its failure to grasp the degree to which scientific knowledge is dependent upon networks of trust and credibility. The image of science that we often presented with – as an exemplary rational activity driven by systematic scepticism – is an unrealistic as the rational-calculator model assumed by neoclassical economics. This is relevant to the historical parallels between two quite similar notions of implicit faith because the contrast that is sometimes drawn between a rational, self-correcting, and sceptical science on the one hand, and a credulous and irrational religion on the other overlooks the hidden role played by trust and authority in both of these communities.

[198] There is extensive literature, relevant to this point, on how modern scientists come to accept new theories and knowledge claims. It has been argued that these are akin to faith (or 'acceptance') in important respects. Just a few examples: Thomas Kuhn controversially suggested that choices between competing paradigms 'can only be made on faith'. *The Structure of Scientific Revolutions*, 4th ed. (Chicago: University of Chicago Press, 2012), p. 157; Bas Van Fraassen defends 'the traditional epistemological view in the philosophy

Yet another parallel between religious and scientific modes of knowing concerns the comprehensibility of what is being assented to. Again, it was Boyle who pointed to the fact that even naturalists must 'admit several things, wherof they cannot clearly explicate'.[199] A case in point was the hidden mechanical operations postulated as explanations of natural effects. These remained hypothetical because similar effects could be produced by different underlying mechanisms, as the contemporary example of mechanical clocks with their diverse modes of operation demonstrated.[200] (This situation falls under what philosophers of science refer to as the problem of underdetermination: incompatible explanations of phenomena are often empirically equivalent.[201]) Boyle also thought that the precise nature of certain laws – such as those determining mind–body interactions – were unknown and perhaps ultimately unknowable.[202] Gravity offered another example of a phenomenon whose effects could be described with considerable mathematical precision, but whose ultimate nature remained a mystery. Newton offered (largely private) speculations about what gravity was, but this was never settled definitively.[203] His successors eventually came to be comfortable with ignorance about the nature of gravity and how it

---

of science' that we may rationally believe theories that are not entailed by the evidence. 'Belief and the Will', *Journal of Philosophy* 81 (1984), 235–56 (255). Margaret Gilbert speaks of 'collective beliefs'. 'Modelling Collective Beliefs', *Synthese* 73 (1987), 185–204; W. Brad Wray describes these in terms of 'acceptance' rather than 'belief'. 'Collective Belief and Acceptance', *Synthese* 129 (2001), 319–33.

[199] Boyle, *Reason and Religion*, Works, vol. 8, p. 264.

[200] J. J. Macintosh (ed.), *Boyle on Atheism* (Toronto: University of Toronto Press, 2006), §3.5.19, p. 255. Cf. Boyle, *Disquisition about the Final Causes*, Works, vol. 11, pp. 111f.

[201] First formulated by Pierre Duhem, *The Aim and Structure of Physical Theory* [1914], trans. P. W. Wiener (Princeton: Princeton University Press, 1954), there is now an extensive literature on this issue. See, e.g., P. Kyle Stanford, *Exceeding Our Grasp: Science, History, and the Problem of Unconceived Alternatives* (New York: Oxford University Press, 2006); Thomas Bonk, *Underdetermination: An Essay on Evidence and the Limits of Natural Knowledge* (Dordrecht: Springer, 2008).

[202] Macintosh, *Boyle on Atheism*, §3.5.1, pp. 247f. For Boyle's discussion of believing what is 'not fully intelligible to the assenting faculty' in both scientific and religious spheres, see *The Christian Virtuoso I, Appendix*, Works, vol. 12, pp. 380–3. In the following century Abbé Pluche would make the same point: 'God obliges me to believe certain Doctrines in Nature, as well as Religion, of which he has not thought fit to impart me an adequate Comprehension.' Noël Antoine Pluche, *Spectacle de le Nature: Or, Nature Display'd*, 8th ed., 4 vols. (London, 1757), vol. 1, p. 226. The contemporary philosophical stance positing that the nature of mind–body interactions might be, in principle, unknowable, is known as 'mysterianism', and is associated with the philosopher Colin McGinn, 'Can We Solve the Mind-Body Problem?', *Mind* 98 (1989), 349–66. See also Owen Flanagan, *The Science of Mind* (Cambridge, MA: MIT Press, 1991), p. 313.

[203] Eugenia Torrance, 'God of the Gaps, or the "God of Design and Dominion": Revisiting Newton's Theology', *Zygon* 58 (2023), 64–79.

worked, and this again exemplifies the little commented upon contraction of explanatory ambitions that characterised the new natural philosophy. The insistence that we must fully understand the things to which we lend intellectual assent, which seems quite reasonable at first sight, has never been a realistic aspiration for those within the experimental sciences, far less those outside the scientific community. Boyle was fully aware of this as, too, was the astute Jonathan Swift, who observed that while God might command us to believe things that we do not understand: 'this is no more than what we do every day in the works of nature, upon the credit of men of learning'.[204] Swift's judgement notwithstanding, reliance on the much-derided implicit faith became one of modern science's best-kept secrets.

It is not unreasonable to conclude, then, that while suspicion of implicit faith radically altered the religious landscape, it continued to play a covert role in the one context where we might least expect it. Knowledge did not cease to be embedded in networks of trust. It was just that the networks were different ones, established outside fractured ecclesiastical structures in the newly formed institutions of the experimental sciences.[205] Scientific societies strived to establish universal criteria for making knowledge claims while at the same time avoiding religious controversies that seemed to militate against consensus.[206] It was gentlemanly virtue, especially that of the Christian virtuoso, rather than ecclesiastical office, that conferred the necessary authority and grounded the new trust relations. Robert Boyle's remarks on the topic of the 'scientist as priest' are revealing in this context. The activity of the natural philosopher, he proposed, 'is a more acceptable act of religion, than the burning of sacrifices or perfumes upon his altars'.[207]

---

[204] Swift, 'On the Trinity', in *The Works of Dr Jonathan Swift*, 8 vols. (Edinburgh, 1761), vol. 1, p. 264. See also Norris, *Reason and Faith*, p. 259.

[205] According to Shapin: 'The justifications changed, but the outcome was recognizably the same: the distribution of imputed credit and reliability followed the contours of authority and power.' *A Social History of Truth*, p. 69.

[206] Thomas Sprat: 'The Royal Society is abundantly cautious not to intermeddle in *Spiritual things*' and its members 'meddle no otherwise with divine things'. *History of the Royal Society*, pp. 347, 82; Robert Moray, Letter to Christiaan Huygens, 1665, quoted in Henry Lyons, *The Royal Society, 1660–1940: A History of Its Administration under Its Charters* (Cambridge: Cambridge University Press, 1944), p. 56; Michael Hunter, *Science and the Shape of Orthodoxy* (Woodbridge: Boydell, 1995), p. 171. Sprat's caveat pertained to controversial doctrinal matters and was consistent with the broader religious goals of exploring 'the Power, Wisdom, and Goodness of the Creator [as] display'd in the admirable order, and workman-ship of the Creatures'. Sprat, *History of the Royal Society*, p. 82.

[207] Boyle, *Some Considerations touching the Usefulness of Experimental Natural Philosophy, Works*, vol. 3, p. 279. For more on the scientist/priest trope see H. Fisch, 'The Scientist as Priest: A Note on Robert Boyle's Natural Theology', *Isis* 44 (1953), 252–65.

Christian natural philosophers could be trusted as theological authorities; the priestly class, not so much. Yet all of this was disguised beneath a rhetoric that stressed reason, experience, and liberation from authority – a rhetoric necessitated by the tainted associations of implicit faith with the early modern travails of faith-based religion.

Historical amnesia about the borrowings of the new sciences from the sphere of religion is paralleled in the subsequent sloganising of Enlightenment thinkers. As we will see in more detail in Chapter 6, Enlightenment *philosophes* appropriated for themselves what was originally a Reformation image of an age of light after darkness. The same is true for the famous Enlightenment slogan that appears in Immanuel Kant's celebrated essay 'What is Enlightenment?' (1784): *Sapere aude* ('dare to know' or 'have the courage to use your own reason'). Again, this is taken from Horace, who seems to have been the first port of call for moderns in search of mottoes.[208] Kant's usage turns out to have been doubly unoriginal. In 1518, on the eve of the Protestant Reformation, Philip Melanchthon alluded to the maxim in his inaugural address to the University of Wittenberg, implying that the principle 'dare to know' accurately characterised the mood of both Renaissance humanism and the impending religious reformation.[209] Subsequently in the seventeenth century, Catholic priest and early advocate of Epicureanism Pierre Gassendi adopted the phrase as his personal motto, imprinting it on his published works. Gassendi's rejection of scholastic Aristotelianism and his championing of empiricism and atomism make him a seminal figure in the development of early modern science.[210] It is likely that Kant first encountered the phrase in one of these writers. But the larger point concerns what these earlier usages signal, namely that the slogans adopted by Enlightenment thinkers had already been deployed in characterisations of the earlier movements of the Reformation and scientific revolution. Much Enlightenment rhetoric thus consists in 'a transformed appropriation of Christian-reformatory insights' as Edgar Thaidigsmann has put it.[211]

---

[208] Horace, *Epistulae* 2.1.40, in a context recommending eclecticism rather than rejection of all authority.

[209] Edgar Thaidigsmann, '"Sapere aude": Auflärung und Theologie bei Melanchthon und Kant', *Zeitschrift für Theologie und Kirche* 111 (2014), 389–415.

[210] Franco Venturi, 'Sapere Aude!', *Revista storica italiana* 71 (1959), 119–28; Barry Brundell, *Pierre Gassendi: From Aristotelianism to a New Natural Philosophy* (Dordrecht: Reidel, 1987); Osler, *Divine Will and the Mechanical Philosophy*.

[211] Thaidigsmann, '"Sapere aude"', 415. Jean-Claude Vuillemin maintains that the motto characterises the Baroque period just as well as the Enlightenment. *Épistémè baroque. Le mot et la chose* (Paris: Hermann, 2013). On the connection between Luther's theological

3.6 SLOGANS OF MODERNITY

Some nineteenth-century thinkers, in closer proximity than us to both the Reformation and the Enlightenment, also drew this conclusion. On numerous occasions Hegel identified the Protestant Reformation as a decisive moment in the evolution of human freedom. Gotthold Lessing also maintained that the true spirit of Lutheranism 'requires that *no* man may be prevented from advancing in knowledge of the truth according to his own judgment'.[212] Theologian and philosopher of religion Ernst Troeltsch (1865–1923) would agree that Protestantism is 'the religion of conscience and conviction, without dogmatic compulsion'.[213] These were not merely expressions of the nationalistic pride of German authors. Scottish essayist and historian Thomas Carlyle announced that Luther's declaration at the Diet of Worms was 'the greatest scene in Modern European History ... from which the whole subsequent history of civilization takes its rise'.[214] In his influential and widely read *History of Civilization in Europe*, the brilliant French historian François Guizot described the Protestant Reformation as 'a great movement of the liberty of the human mind, a new necessity for freely thinking and judging its own account, and with its own power'.[215] While in more recent times 'the Enlightenment' would lay sole claim to this impulse, and (in its French manifestations in particular) set itself over and against religion, it is not unreasonable to argue that the first and decisive move towards the principle of thinking for oneself (for better or worse) came with the Protestant rejection of implicit faith.

If those in the early modern period thought in terms of 'grand challenges' and 'wicked problems', as many do today, at the top of their list would have been the problem of religious pluralism and confessional conflict. At a personal level, the eternal destiny of the individual soul came to be understood as vitally dependent upon the adoption of correct beliefs and practices. But which beliefs and practices? As Herbert of Cherbury had poignantly

---

conception of freedom and subsequent secular conceptions of religious freedom see Martin Heckel, 'Luthers Traktat "Von der Freiheit eines Christenmenschen" als Markstein des Kirchen- und Staatskirchenrechts', *Zeitschrift für Theologie und Kirche* 109 (2012), 122–52; Marius Timmann Mjaaland (ed.), *The Reformation of Philosophy* (Berlin: Mohr Siebeck, 2020).

[212] Lessing, *Anti-Goetze*, in *Gotthold Ephraim Lessing's Sämmtliche Schriften*, vol. 10, ed. Karl Lachman (Leipzig, 1856), p. 161.

[213] 'die Religion des Gewissens und der Überzeugung ohne dogmatischen Zwang'. Ernst Troeltsch, *Die Bedeutung des Protestantismus für die Entstehung der modernen Welt* (Munich and Berlin: R. Oldenbourg, 1911; reprint, Aalen: Otto Zeller, 1963), p. 97, trans. and quoted in Yasakuta, *Lessing's Philosophy of Religion*, p. 141.

[214] Thomas Carlyle, *On Heroes and Hero Worship* (London: Ward, Lock and Co., 1910), p. 99.

[215] François Guizot, *General History of Civilization in Europe*, ed. George Wells Knight (New York: Appleton, 1896), p. 225.

expressed it: 'What ... shall the layman, encompassed by the terrors of divers churches militant throughout the world, decide as to the best religion? For there is ... none almost that does not deny possibility of salvation outside its own pale.'[216] At the political level, moreover, religious uniformity had long underpinned social stability. Not only did post-Reformation religious diversity generate psychological uncertainty and distress, it was also accompanied by warfare, bloodshed, and suffering.[217]

Looking well ahead to the nineteenth century (and to Chapter 6), the fledgling social sciences would eventually seek to articulate rational, scientific principles that could compensate for the loss of the cohesive power of a single, unifying religion. In the interim, however, there emerged pragmatic, juridical procedures to manage the anomic political consequences of religious pluralism. These involved setting aside the truth claims of the competing traditions and seeking legislative solutions to secure a compromised but peaceful coexistence.[218] On one account, these solutions amount to nothing less than the formation of the modern nation-state.[219] Arguably, this de facto side-lining of religious truth claims promoted secularisation, allowing a pluralism of partly incompatible beliefs to quietly foster a scepticism about whether any of them might be true. At the same time, it had the practical consequence of quarantining religious differences by consigning them to the private sphere, again facilitating the emergence of a putatively neutral, public, secular space. This solution represented the importation into the political and legal sphere of a form of methodological naturalism. While initially a kind of legal heuristic that attracted the support of the religiously

---

[216] Herbert of Cherbury, *De religione laici* [1645], ed. and trans. Harold R. Hutcheson (New Haven: Yale University Press, 1944), p. 87. Cf. Jean Bodin, *Colloquium heptaplomores de rerum sublimium arcanis abditis* [1588], ed. L. Noack (Schwerin, 1857), p. 56.

[217] This is not necessarily to endorse the common view that religion caused the so-called 'wars of religion'. See William T. Cavanaugh, *The Myth of Religious Violence: Secular Ideology and the Roots of Modern Conflict* (New York: Oxford University Press, 2009). If anything, the modern concept 'religion' was one of the products of these conflicts rather than a root cause.

[218] Martin Heckel, *Vom Religionskonflikt zur Ausgleichsordnung: Der Sonderweg des deutschen Staatskirchenrechts vom Augsburger Religionsfrieden 1555 bis zur Gegenwart* (Munich: C. H. Beck, 2007); Cf. Wolterstorff, *Locke and the Ethics of Belief*, p. 246.

[219] This view has been especially prevalent in the field of International Relations. For an overview and critical discussions of this thesis see Jason Farr, 'Point: Westphalia Legacy and the Modern Nation-State', *International Social Science Review* 80 (2005), 156–9; Stephen D. Krasner, 'Westphalia and All That', in *Ideas and Foreign Policy: Beliefs, Institutions, and Political Change*, ed. Judith Goldstein and Robert O. Keohane (Ithaca: Cornell University Press, 1993), pp. 235–64; Andreas Osiander, 'Sovereignty, International Relations, and the Westphalian Myth', *International Organization* 55 (2001), 251–87.

committed, it had longer-term practical implications for the status of the religious truth claims to which they all subscribed.²²⁰

Whatever their political benefits, legal-procedural solutions were the wrong instrument for the alleviation of intense personal anxieties about what needed to be explicitly believed in order to secure salvation. In this new context, implicit faith offered little comfort, either. On the contrary, rather than providing a solution, it was often regarded as central to the problem. As a consequence, systematic approaches to propositional belief and its justification – what we now call epistemology – arose in tandem with a new understanding of Christianity in which a kind of evidence-based belief came to be elevated over a communal, trust-based, faith. Religious truths were now rendered into propositional form and defended or critiqued outside of the ecclesial and ritual contexts that had been their native environment. Early modern discussions about the ethics of belief thus first appear in the context of debates about implicit faith. An unintended consequence of thinking about religious faith in this way was the distillation of the modern idea of religion (and plural 'religions') understood as constituted by propositional beliefs, the holding of which required some form of rational justification. At the same time, this contributed to the birth of a modern version of philosophy in which questions to do with the foundations and justification of knowledge became a central preoccupation. This development is especially evident in the trajectory of Anglophone philosophy from Herbert to Locke. While on opposite sides of what we now call the rationalist-empiricist divide, both were responding to a new problem of religious pluralism precipitated by the perceived limitations of implicit faith.²²¹

It must be said, in all of this, that while the overall trend is clear, the traffic was not one-way. Some Catholic thinkers continued to defend implicit faith, especially during the sixteenth and early seventeenth centuries. The doctrine even found qualified support among a few Protestant thinkers, not least because the difficulties to which implicit faith had originally been addressed had not gone away.²²² The element of trust originally attached to

---

²²⁰ Wolterstorff, *Locke and the Ethics of Belief*, p. 246.
²²¹ Thomas Hobbes can also be placed into this trajectory, as a representative of the alternative that sought refuge less in epistemology than in temporal authority, with a sovereign (or sovereign body) making determinations on matters of public religion. His focus on social stability thus led him in the direction of political philosophy, as opposed to Hebert who had been more preoccupied with the issue of truth, as the title of his *De veritate* suggests.
²²² For Catholic defences see, e.g., Stanislaus Hortius, *Confutatio prolegomenon Brentii, quae primum scripsit adversus* (Antverpiae, 1561), p. 62v; Robert Persons, *The Warn-word to Sir Francis Hastinges Wast-word* (n.p., 1602), pp. 49r–53r; Francisci Toleti, *Summa casuum*

faith was also strongly defended in certain quarters, not least by the reformers themselves.[223] In the eighteenth century, John Wesley was a conspicuous example, reacting against what he considered to be over-intellectualised versions of Christianity. Wesley invoked the authority of Luther to define faith as 'a lively and a steadfast trust in the favour of God, wherewith we commit ourselves altogether unto God'. Genuine faith, he protested, 'is not barely a speculative, rational thing, a cold, lifeless assent, a train of ideas in the head; but also a disposition of the heart'.[224] It is crucial, then, to observe a distinction between the teachings of the Protestant reformers on the one hand, and the epistemic crisis engendered by the Reformation on the other. The understanding of faith preached by the reformers, in combination with their rejection of implicit faith, turned out to be unable to bear the weight of the justificatory demands now placed upon it in the new context of religious pluralism. There was a mismatch, in other words, between the central thrust of some Reformation doctrines and the social and epistemic conditions to which the Reformation gave rise.

Overall, the Reformation and its aftermath represent a key stage in the evolution of a distinctively modern and Western notion of belief and, indeed, of religion. The older conception of faith/belief was to become isolated from its social and institutional context and the role played by trust diminished and derided. This placed a new moral burden on the individual believer – to be in a position to articulate evidential support, typically on the basis of reason and experience, for what was believed. At the same time, the increasingly differentiated enterprises of philosophy and science

---

conscientiæ absolutissima (Duaci, 1622), pp. 555–6; Laurenz Forer, *Indifferentismvs: Oder Allerley Gattung Kyrch* (Ingolstadt, 1656), p. 56. Some Protestants also supported versions of implicit faith. See, e.g., Norris, *Reason and Faith*, pp. 90–3.

[223] Thus Luther, faith is 'a living, daring confidence in God's grace', a 'kind of trust in and knowledge of God's grace'. *Prefaces to the New Testament*, trans. Charles M. Jacobs (St Louis: Concordia, 2010), p. 18. See also Lancelot Andrewes *The pattern of catechistical doctrine at large* (London, 1650), pp. 13f.; John Baker, *Lectures of I.B. vpon the xii. Articles of our Christian faith* (London, 1581), sig. Ciiiiv; Jeremy Taylor, *The Righteousness Evangelicall Describ'd* (Dublin, 1663), p. 205.

[224] John Wesley, 'Salvation by Faith: Sermon Preached at Saint Mary's, Oxford, before the University, 18 June 1738', in *The Works of the Rev. John Wesley*, 3rd ed., 7 vols., ed. John Emory (New York: Carlton and Porter, 1856), vol. 1, p. 14. The Wesleys had been strongly influenced by William Law's works, especially *A Serious Call to a Devout and Holy Life* (London, 1729). For Law's rejection of faith as intellectual assent see *The Way to Divine Knowledge* (London, 1752), pp. 169–76. More generally on the eighteenth-century reaction against over-intellectualised faith see Phyllis Mack, *Heart Religion in the British Enlightenment* (Cambridge: Cambridge University Press, 2008) and David Hempton, *Methodism: Empire of the Spirit* (New Haven: Yale University Press, 2005).

came to assume authority in these respective domains, making religious beliefs answerable to external authorities. These would come to be regarded as neutral epistemic spaces, paralleling the creation of a religiously neutral political sphere. Between the sixteenth and eighteenth centuries, this rarely constituted a problem for the legitimacy of religious belief as such, since the core propositions of Christianity were widely held to be consistent with the demands of reason and experience, and hence of philosophy and science. But all of this represented a momentous shift in the nature of belief and a key stage in the evolution of this distinctively Western, modern conception.

One way of tracking the significance of these transitions is to consider the changing nature and status of proofs for the existence of God upon which, for some accounts at least, the evidential basis of religious belief rests. Standard treatments of proofs tend to assume a set repertoire of arguments and that these arguments are to be understood against a uniform background of fixed evidentiary expectations. However, if the demise of implicit faith and accompanying rise of ethics of belief is an early modern phenomenon, and one that placed entirely new evidential demands on religious believers, 'proofs' must have served different functions in the pre-modern period. Along the same lines, if it were impossible not to believe in God in the medieval period, proving God's existence would seem to be a rather pointless exercise. The next chapter explores traditional arguments for the existence of God with a view to showing how their significance radically changes in the post-Reformation period.

4

THE AGE OF EVIDENCES

The last century, a time when love was cold, is noted as being especially the Age of Evidences .... For is not this the error, the common and fatal error, of the world, to think itself a judge of Religious Truth without preparation of heart?

John Henry Newman, *Sermons*

It was not by dialectic that it pleased God to save his people.

Ambrose of Milan, *De fide*[1]

IF MEDIEVAL CHRISTIAN BELIEF WAS MORE ABOUT PERSONAL TRUST and communal commitment than assenting to propositions on the basis of evidence, it makes sense to enquire after the purpose of medieval proofs for the existence of God and the reasons for the apparent flourishing of a natural theology. Was it not the case that scholastic philosophers spent considerable time and effort articulating rational arguments for God's existence and, more generally, seeking to bring together faith and reason? And do these activities not suggest that they were just as concerned to provide rational evidence for propositional beliefs as their early modern successors? The short answer is no. The well-known medieval proofs for God's existence were not devised to fulfil any significant evidential function; neither was there anything like a medieval natural theology, understood as a philosophical exercise conducted from neutral premises and uninformed by religious presuppositions. Careful consideration of classical and medieval 'proofs' for God's existence is thus important for gaining an understanding of the distinctive and novel character of modern forms of such arguments and of the significant change in the understanding of religious belief that

---

[1] Epigraphs: John Henry Newman, *Sermons, chiefly on the Theory of Religious Belief* (London: Rivingtons, 1843), pp. 198–201; Ambrose of Milan, *De fide* 1.5.42.

this new style of rational defence signals. Our natural assumption that beliefs should be supported by a specific kind of rational justification has often led us to construct medieval arguments along those lines, resulting in an elision of the context and purpose of these arguments. As will become apparent, these differences concern what for classical and medieval thinkers were the interpenetration of the natural and supernatural, their assumptions about the starting point of rational arguments, and their views about what arguments for God's existence were thought to accomplish.

4.1 Arguments for Atheists?

Before his death on New Year's Eve, 1691, the devout natural philosopher Robert Boyle had made provision in his will for a series of public lectures (strictly speaking, sermons) devoted to 'the proof of the Christian religion' against 'Atheists, Theists [i.e., deists], Pagans, Jews and Mahometans'.[2] Consistent with the Protestant position on implicit faith, Boyle had often expressed a concern that Christians be able to offer rational grounds for their beliefs, presumably against largely theoretical objections that might be raised. Boyle was also worried that ancient forms of disbelief might be revived and form alliances with new philosophical and scientific developments. Given this prospect he sought to show how the new sciences, rightly understood, strongly supported Christian belief.[3] Boyle was hardly alone in expressing anxieties about atheism. Earlier in the century, the Cambridge Platonist Henry More wrote a complete work on this topic – *An Antidote against Atheisme* (1653). More's disquiet arose out of the recent religious divisions of Europe and his *Antidote* begins with a frank admission that the Protestant Reformation had exposed Christianity to a new vulnerability. Medieval religion was charged with having promoted adherence to religion 'in a meere externall way, either for fashion [sic] sake, or in a blind obedience to the Authority of a Church'. The reformers had removed the blindfold, freeing individuals to exercise their own judgements in the religious sphere. But More was now worried that this new-found religious freedom might lead to the opposite extreme. Atheism now beckoned those recently

---

[2] *The Works of the Honourable Robert Boyle*, 6 vols., ed. T. Birch (London, 1772), vol. 1, pp. cxxxviii–cxxxix.
[3] Macintosh, *Boyle on Atheism*, §3.7.5, pp. 301–2. Boyle's 'Essay of the Holy Scriptures' connects these two concerns beginning with the problem of Catholic 'Implicite Fayth', and going on to identify various forms of atheism, ancient and modern: Aristotle, Galen, Seneca, Epicurus, Lucretius, and the moderns Machiavelli and Pietro Pomponazzi. *Works*, vol. 13, pp. 175, 187. Cf. *Usefulness of Natural Philosophy*, *Works*, vol. 3, pp. 244–61.

liberated from superstition, threatening to transpose them 'out of one darke prison into another'.[4] More's proposed remedy was to offer detailed elaboration of a series of proofs for the existence of God intended to fortify the faithful.

If More had expressed a measured concern about the unintended consequences of the Protestant Reformation, some of his Catholic counterparts were less restrained. The reformers were accused of outright atheism, while others alleged that they had indirectly encouraged it.[5] In the 1620s, Marin Mersenne contended that Luther and Calvin had so devalued reason that they had undermined the rationality of religious belief, enabling atheism to take root and flourish.[6] In what seems an improbable estimate, Mersenne reckoned that Paris alone was home to 50,000 atheists.[7]

While the anxieties of More and Mersenne may have been expressed quite differently, they converged on a similar solution. Mersenne's response was to stock the arsenal of Christian defences with no fewer than thirty-five proofs for God's existence, building on arguments already circulating in the Theology Faculty of the Sorbonne.[8] The articulation of these arguments had also been motivated by the spectre of atheism.[9] New arguments for God's existence would subsequently be set out by Descartes, Spinoza, and

---

[4] Henry More, *An Antidote against Atheisme: Or, an Appeal to the Natural Faculties of the Mind of Man whether there be not a God* (London, 1653), pp. 1–2. More assumes the commonplace that genuine religion is a mean between atheism and superstition, a tradition that goes back to Plutarch's *On Superstition*.

[5] Nicolas Chichon, *L'atheism e des pretendus reformes* (Poitiers, 1620). Jesuit author François Garasse identified Luther as a 'complete atheist', while Calvin and his disciples Zwingli and Beza made the list of also-rans. *La doctrine curieuse des beaux esprits de ce temps ou prétendus* (Paris, 1623), pp. 1, 11, 39–46.

[6] Marin Mersenne, *L'impiete des deistes, athees et libertins de ce temps, combatue et renversee*, 2 vols. (Paris, 1624).

[7] Marin Mersenne, *Quaestiones Celeberrimae in Genesim* (Paris, 1623), col. 671. The estimated population of Paris at the time was 300,000.

[8] Mersenne, *Quaestiones in Genesim*, cols. 25–6, 29–34. In 1617 the Leuven-based Jesuit theologian Leonardus Lessius had provided a more modest list of fifteen arguments. *De providentia numinis* (Antwerp, 1617), pp. 9–10. Lessius addressed his arguments to ancient atheists, but they bore a curious resemblance to Protestants in elevating their 'own private judgment above the judgement of the whole world and all times' (pp. 14–15). A translation of the work, published by one of English Jesuit colleges on the Continent, appeared in 1631, bearing the title: *Rawleigh his Ghost. Or a feigned apparition of Syr Walter Rawleigh to a friend of his* ..., trans. A. B. (Saint-Omer, 1631).

[9] For the sources of Mersenne's proofs see Jean-Robert Armogathe, '"An sit deus". Les preuves de Dieu chez Marin Mersenne', *Les études philosophiques* 1 (1994), 161–70. For the influence of Suárez, see Igor Agostini, 'Descartes' Proofs of God and the Crisis of Thomas Aquinas's Five Ways in Early Modern Thomism', *Harvard Theological Review* 108 (2015), 235–62.

Leibniz. The two centuries following the religious division of Christendom thus saw both sides of the confessional divide develop something of a new argument industry. This was not a continuation of some medieval tradition of 'natural theology' and it was not yet the modern philosophy of religion. But it led to an age of evidences that represented a crucial new phase in the shifting boundaries of what was believable.

The apparent prevalence of atheism, as More suggests, was related to the new ethics of belief. If we bear moral responsibility for what we believe, there must be an element of free choice involved. While that choice was initially restricted to a range of Christian confessions, there was no reason, in principle, that it could not extend further to the question of whether or not God even existed. Genuine disbelief in God had long been regarded as an impossibility. This is why Charles Taylor rightly proposes that the distinctive feature of the modern, secular age lies in the theoretical possibility of disbelief. It is significant in this context that the terms 'atheist' and 'atheism' did not even enter the English lexicon until the latter decades of the sixteenth century, with a similar pattern of emergence in the other European languages.[10] This heightened linguistic activity signals a widespread new interest in the phenomenon or, perhaps more correctly, its creation. Even then, their 'atheism' was not quite the same as ours. The modern propensity to construct everything that relates to religion in terms of propositional belief suggests a simple equation between 'atheism' and 'lack of belief in God', but 'godless' might be a better definition for earlier periods. Some ancient Greek usages suggest the condition of having been abandoned by the gods – more a matter of being one in whom the gods did not believe than the reverse. In the early modern period the term also had a wide range of connotations.[11]

---

[10] The term does not appear in the standard philosophical dictionary of the period, Rudolph Goclenius's *Lexicon Philosophicum* (Frankfurt, 1613), but there are brief entries in Johannes Micraelius, *Lexicon Philosophicum* (Stettin, 1662) and Theodoricus Hackspan, *Termini distinctiones et divisiones philosophico theologicae* (Altdorff, 1664). In the Romance languages, French *athée* appears in noun form in 1543, as an adjective 1680; Spanish *ateo*, 1595; Italian *ateo*, 1650; Portuguese *ateu*, 1671; Romanian *ateu*, 1694. See Philip Durkin, 'Linguistic History of the Terms "Atheism" and "Atheist"', in *The Cambridge History of Atheism*, 2 vols., ed. Stephen Bullivant and Michael Ruse (Cambridge: Cambridge University Press, 2021), vol. 1, pp. 11–13. For early Greek senses see Tim Whitmarsh, *Battling the Gods: Atheism in the Ancient World* (New York: Alfred A. Knopf, 2015), pp. 116–17.

[11] On broad understandings of 'atheism' in this period see Shagan, *Birth of Modern Belief*, pp. 101–5; Michael Hunter, 'The Problem of "Atheism" in Early Modern England', *Transactions of the Royal Historical Society* 35 (1985), 135–57; Hans-Martin Barth, *Atheismus und Orthodoxie: Analysen und Modelle christlicher Apologetik im 17. Jahrhundert* (Göttingen: Vandenhoeck & Ruprecht, 1971), pp. 144f.; Alan Charles Kors, *Atheism in France,*

A series of 1639 disputations on the topic of atheism by the Calvinist theologian Gisbertus Voetius (1589–1676), best known to posterity as one of Descartes's most hostile opponents, offers a guide to the variety of contemporary meanings of atheism.[12] At the outset Voetius acknowledges that the label was frequently used simply to slander opponents – the Pagan accusation that the first Christians were atheists being a notable instance. Such accusations were not to be taken at face value. Nonetheless, Voetius regarded atheism as a substantive category with several subdivisions: those who outright deny the existence of God; those who worship false gods; those who have a deficient conception of God. There were also 'practical' atheists – those who neglect worship or who worship in a false way, along with those who lead immoral lives as if there were no God and no post-mortem consequences. Practical atheists would thus include a number of those on Boyle's list (Theists [i.e., deists], Pagans, Jews, and Mahometans) together with heretics and those who led dissolute lives. Finally, there were 'indirect' atheists who deny particular attributes of God or key Christian doctrines. Epicureans were thus atheists on account of their denial of providence; Catholics since they supposedly refused to accept the authority of scripture; sceptics because of their failure to acknowledge the reliability of the (God-given) natural light of reason. For their part, Catholic authors would often include Protestants in the last category, accusing them of undermining the integrity of reason in which, according to the common understanding, was apprehended a natural conception of the Deity. Voetius's classification of the forms of atheism thus demonstrates it to be a rather capacious category,

---

1650–1729, Volume 1: The Orthodox Sources of Disbelief (Princeton: Princeton University Press, 1990); Kenneth Sheppard, *Anti-Atheism in Early Modern England 1580–1720* (Leiden: Brill, 2015), esp. pp. 14–40; Gianluca Mori, *Early Modern Atheism from Spinoza to D'Holbach* (Liverpool: Liverpool University Press, 2021); Nathan G. Alexander, 'Defining and Redefining Atheism: Dictionary and Encyclopedia Entries for "Atheism" and their Critics in the Anglophone World from the Early Modern Period to the Present', *Intellectual History Review* 30 (2020), 253–71. For the previous century see Lucien Febvre, *The Problem of Unbelief in the Sixteenth Century: The Religion of Rabelais*, trans. Beatrice Gottlieb (Cambridge, MA: Harvard University Press, 1982). The first instances of explicit and confessed atheism, in Britain at least, date from the mid-eighteenth century. Roger Maioli, 'The First Avowed British Atheist: Lord Hervey?', *Eighteenth Century Studies* 54 (2021), 357–79.

[12] Gisbertus Voetius, *De atheismo*, in *Selectae Disputationes Theologicae*, 5 vols. (Utrecht, 1648–69), vol. 1, pp. 114–226. There are helpful discussions of Voetius in Theo Verbeek, 'Descartes and the Problem of Atheism: The Utrecht Crisis', *Nederlands archief voor kerkgeschiedenis / Dutch Review of Church History* 71 (1991), 211–23, and Henri Krop, 'Spinoza and the Low Countries', in *The Cambridge History of Atheism*, ed. Bullivant and Ruse, vol. 1, pp. 223–41.

one that makes Mersenne's estimates of the extent of atheism look conservative. If Catholic and Protestant definitions were combined, pretty much everyone would be an atheist and this partly accounts for the sharp increase in interest in atheism in the wake of the Reformation. But if the breadth of the category provides an explanation of the moral panic generated by this putatively pervasive phenomenon, it is less helpful in understanding how 'proofs' were intended to refute it.

The Boyle Lecturers would provide more straightforward definitions and explanations of atheism, adapted to the proofs that would follow. Samuel Clarke, who delivered the lectures in the years 1704 and 1705, identified three kinds of atheist, omitting much of the confessional polemic that had characterised earlier works in the genre. First, were those who 'being extremely ignorant and stupid ... have never duly considered any thing at all, nor made any just use of their natural reason'. Here, the ethics-of-belief requirement is in play, suggesting that individuals who properly exercise their own reason and judgement will irresistibly assent to the truth of theism. The second category of atheists were those who were 'totally debauched and corrupted in their practice [and who] have by a vicious and degenerate life corrupted the principles of their nature and defaced the reason of their own minds'. Atheism, in this instance, amounted to a moral failing that had knock-on effects for the operations of reason. The third group were said to have relied upon 'speculative reasoning' and the 'principles of philosophy' to deny the being and attributes of God.[13] Clarke had specific targets in mind here – Thomas Hobbes and Baruch Spinoza – both of whom make regular appearances as the villains of the piece in early modern anti-atheist literature.

These characterisations of atheism help account for the wildly varying estimates of its prevalence. Writing a century after Mersenne's reckoning of 'fifty thousand atheists in Paris', Rice Adams also crunched the numbers, identifying a mere 'two or three' historical atheists from a literature that spanned 4,000 years, adding to their number another three from the modern

---

[13] Samuel Clarke, *A Demonstration of the Being and Attributes of God, and Other Writings*, ed. Ezio Vailati (Cambridge: Cambridge University Press, 1998), p. 3. A variation on these types combined the second and third motivations, as in the case of the so-called 'erudite libertines' (*libertinage érudit*) thought to have been influenced by heterodox Renaissance thinkers such as Pietro Pompanazzi, Girolamo Cardano, Tommaso Campanella, Guilio Vanini, and, in the political sphere, Niccolò Machiavelli. The category is the invention of René Pintard, *Le libertinage érudit dans la première moitié du XVIIe siècle* [1943] (Geneva and Paris: Slatkine, 1983). Like all such categories its helpfulness has been challenged. See Jean-Pierre Cavaillé, 'L'histoire des "libertins" reste à faire', *Les Dossiers du Grihl*, 18 October 2010, http://journals.openedition.org/dossiersgrihl/4498, accessed 26 February 2021.

age: Lucilio Vanini and the usual suspects, Spinoza and Hobbes.[14] This more modest estimate represents a narrowing of the criteria to something much closer to Clarke's 'speculative atheism', and captures what would count as atheism today – that is, a literal rejection of belief in God. Such a position was exceptionally rare (and was almost certainly not true even of Hobbes or Spinoza). Given this, the real puzzle was not to account for the existence of God, but the very possibility of atheism. Earlier disputations on the question 'Whether there is a God?' would often begin with the observation that the topic was hardly worth pursuing given the universal testimony to the affirmative.[15] Voetius, in spite of his elaborate typology, thought that ultimately speculative atheism required thinking an impossibility.[16] For Nicolas Malebranche, one need only think of God in order 'to know that he exists'.[17] François Fénelon agreed that in so far as we are conscious of our own existence, we are conscious of the existence of God. He concluded that it is certain that 'there are no real atheists'.[18] One writer thus spoke of 'the mystery of atheism'. Perhaps this is why the title of Richard Bentley's Boyle Lectures promises not a demonstration of God's existence, but 'of the folly and unreasonableness of atheism'.[19] As we will see, these are essentially appeals to what was regarded as the clinching argument against atheism – the universality and naturalness of belief in God.

Yet explanations for the existence of atheism were offered, tailored to the different categories of atheist.[20] The difficulty of dealing with the first two groups had already been identified by the inaugural Boyle Lecturer, Richard Bentley. Atheists, Bentley observed, fail to '*seek after God*'; they

---

[14] Rice Adams, *Some Discourses: Wherein the Being of God, and of his Watchful Providence … are Asserted* (London, 1736), p. 10.

[15] Lambert Daneau, *Christianae Isagoges ad Christianorum Theologorum Locos Communes* (Geneva, 1583), fol. 3r; Sibrandus Lubbertus, *Thesis Prima* [1616] in L. Guedtman, *Illustrium exercitationum* (Leeuwarden, 1669).

[16] Voetius, *Selectae disputationes*, vol. 1, p. 140. Cf. Jean-Alphonse Turretin, *Cogitationes et dissertationes theologicae* (Geneva, 1737), p. 68.

[17] Malebranche, *Dialogues*, p. 19.

[18] Fénelon, *L'Existence de Dieu*, Preface.

[19] [A. B.], *The Mystery of Atheism* (London, 1699).

[20] The explanations provided did not exhaust the genuine options, omitting key moral and affect-related factors. Genuine anguish about the eternal state of one's soul could promote atheistic ideation, and not just for those who led dissolute lives. Moral objections to Calvinist predestination and matters of theodicy more generally are likely to have been contributing factors, too. For a sympathetic corrective to over-intellectualised accounts of early modern atheism, see Alec Ryrie, *Unbelievers: An Emotional History of Doubt* (Cambridge, MA: Belknap Press, 2019). Also stressing the moral aspect of disbelief are Nick Spencer, *Atheists: The Origin of the Species* (London: Bloomsbury, 2014) and Dominic Erdozain, *The Soul of Doubt* (Oxford: Oxford University Press, 2016).

have *no knowledge*, nor any desire of it'; 'they are not led astray by their Reasoning, but led captive by their Lusts to the denial of God'. It follows from this 'there's small hope of reclaiming them by arguments of Reason'.[21] In keeping with the new ethics of belief, then, it was proposed that some atheists failed to deploy their reason correctly. For others – in effect a subset of Voetius's 'practical atheists' – atheism had been reverse-engineered from base desires. Wishing to lead debauched lives, it suited them to deny the existence of God in order to assuage anxieties in the present life about what might happen in the next.[22] For the first group, the prescription was to help them come to their senses and spur them into a recognition of what should have come naturally. For the second group, moral exhortation was in order. As we will see, many of the early modern 'proofs' contain both of these elements, especially those arguments based on observations of nature.

The third group – those who had reasoned themselves into atheism on account of their philosophical opinions or views about the natural world – represent something quite new. This version of atheism had a genuine cognitive content and a degree of sophistication lacking in the first two types. Not the result primarily of any epistemic or moral failing, although these were always implicated to some degree, it was a reasoned position supported by 'philosophy', including natural philosophy. Though the numbers of speculative atheists might be minuscule, the concern was that as new philosophical and scientific viewpoints became more predominant they might be accompanied by a rise in infidelity. Philosophical atheists could be countered only by philosophical reasoning and/or by arguments demonstrating that the sciences had no implications that pointed in the direction of atheism and that, on the contrary, they were uniformly supportive of orthodox piety. Responses to philosophical atheism thus drew upon two sources: speculative philosophy which focused on metaphysical topics such

[21] Bentley, *Unreasonableness of Atheism*, pp. 13f. Boyle himself had stated as much in an unpublished tract on atheism: 'The Vitious Affections & Habits and the depravd frame of mind to be met with in most Atheists do very much indispose them to be convinc'd by the proofes of a Deity that might other wise be sufficient.' Macintosh, *Boyle on Atheism*, §1.1, p. 49; cf. §4.6.9, p. 384. See also Voetius, *De atheismo*, Selectae Disputationes, vol. 1, pp. 140–2; vol. 5, pp. 457–9. Other Boyle Lecturers endorsed this assessment. John Harris: '*Immorality* and *Pride* are the great Causes of the Growth of Atheism amongst us.' *The Atheistical objections against the being of God and his attributes fully considered and fully refuted* (London, 1698), Sermon 1, p. 2; William Derham, *Physico-Theology: or, A Demonstration of the Being and Attributes of God, from his Works of Creation*, 4th ed. (London, 1716), pp. 428f.

[22] Thus More: 'they have a mind there should be [no God], that they may be free from all wringings of conscience, trouble of correcting their lives, and feare of being accountable before that great Tribunall'. *Antidote*, pp. 1–2. See also South, *Sermons*, vol. 1, p. 122; [A. B.], *Mystery of Atheism*, pp. 2, 4; Harris, *Atheistical objections*, Sermon 1, p. 22.

as necessary and contingent existence and the principle of sufficient reason, and 'science'-based arguments that took in the new findings of natural philosophy and natural history. The more speculative, metaphysical avenues of argument would later be distinguished as 'the ontological argument' and 'the cosmological argument'. Those defences that drew upon the sciences, were taken up in the enterprise of physico-theology, later unhelpfully redescribed as 'the teleological argument' or 'the design argument'.

Introductory philosophy of religion texts will typically identify three kinds of argument: ontological, cosmological, and teleological. Briefly, the *ontological* argument reasons from the idea of a perfect being to the necessary existence of that being. According to the *cosmological* argument the existence of contingent beings points to the existence of a necessary being. Stated in terms of causation, the argument is that casual chains imply a first, uncaused, cause (including 'first' in the sense of foundational, rather than 'first' in a temporal sense). The *teleological* argument, also referred to as 'the physico-theological argument' or 'the argument from design', argues from evidence of purpose and design in the world to a powerful and wise designer. The specific details of these arguments are less important than the fact that this threefold taxonomy and its associated terminology arrived late in the piece, in the wake of Kant's influential analysis of the proofs for God's existence (discussed in more detail later in the chapter). Its retrospective application to earlier periods amounts to the shoehorning of past discourses into one of three essential 'types', while also obscuring important differences between the contexts and aims of the arguments as articulated in different historical periods.

Another set of interpretative issues arises out of the related assumption that the proofs belong to some perennial endeavour called 'natural theology'. Natural theology is presently defined as 'the enterprise of providing support for religious beliefs by starting from premises that neither are nor presuppose any religious beliefs'.[23] Understood in these terms, the rational proofs for God's existence are philosophical exercises that take place on neutral ground such that, in principle, their persuasive force will be felt equally by believer and non-believer. This impression is reinforced by the misplaced (but understandable) assumption that proofs in the past were intended to persuade atheists or agnostics. As with the taxonomy of proofs, however, this idea of an agnostic starting point almost completely

---

[23] William P. Alston, *Perceiving God: The Epistemology of Religious Experience* (Ithaca: Cornell University Press, 1991), p. 289. Alister McGrath calls this the 'established conception of natural theology'. *Re-Imagining Nature: The Promise of Christian Natural Theology* (Oxford: Wiley Blackwell, 2016), pp. 16, 181. Cf. Peter Harrison, 'What Is Natural Theology? And Should We Dispense with It?', *Zygon* 57 (2022), 114–40.

mischaracterises medieval proofs and, to a lesser extent, early modern ones as well, once again raising the question of what work they were intended to do and for whom. This chapter explores how the new early modern understanding of faith/belief, along with the insistence that religious commitment be supported by independent evidence and reason, radically altered the context and purpose of traditional proofs and shifted the grounds upon which the discussion was conducted.

One of the clearest indications of the changing status of proofs of God's existence lies in the fact that what was once touted as the foremost argument has now been almost completely forgotten. This was the *consensus gentium* principle, according to which all nations and in every age have affirmed the existence of God.

4.2 The Forgotten Proof

Among Robert Boyle's unfinished writing projects was an outline for work devoted to the topic of atheism. Perhaps it was this ambition, combined with a consciousness of his failing health, that prompted him to make provision in his will for the celebrated Boyle Lectures which were to be devoted to the same subject. Among the notes that Boyle left for this unfinished work was a list of arguments against atheism. It is headed by two items: 'The innate Idea of a Deity' and 'The general Consent of mankind. (To one of which or both may be referrd the Epicurean Anticipation.)'[24] While these items may not seem particularly compelling to modern readers, Boyle's placing them at the top of his list reflects the priorities of the period. Earlier in the century, when the Flemish Jesuit scholar Leonardus Lessius (1554–1623) set out to argue for the existence of God against atheists and 'politicians', he began with the argument 'from the general confession of all nations and the wise'. Mersenne's inventory of thirty-five proofs for God's existence is also headed up with the claim that 'the existence of God is something that all men have affirmed'.[25] Early modern surveys of the proofs

---

[24] Macintosh, *Boyle on Atheism*, §1.1, p. 50.
[25] Lessius, *De providentia numinis*, p. 9; Mersenne, *Quaestiones in Genesim*, cols. 25–6, 29–34. For the background of Mersenne's proofs see Armogathe, '"*An sit deus*"'. Among the relatively few treatments of the argument in the secondary literature see especially Jasper Reid, 'The Common Consent Argument from Herbert to Hume', *Journal of the History of Philosophy* 53 (2015), 401–33 and Kors, *Atheism in France*. Other commentary includes Jakob Roover, 'Incurably Religious? Consensus Gentium and the Cultural Universality of Religion', *Numen* 61 (2014), 5–32; Walter H. O'Briant, 'Is There an Argument "Consensus Gentium"?', *International Journal for Philosophy of Religion* 18 (1985), 73–9; Paul Edwards, 'Common Consent Arguments for the Existence of God', in *The Encyclopedia*

would usually note the prominence of this principle, known as the *consensus gentium* (the agreement of the nations). At the beginning of the eighteenth century, Henry Lee observed that 'the first and most popular Argument, which is generally brought for proving the Existence of God, is, the *universal Consent of Mankind*'.[26] John Stuart Mill could still endorse this assessment almost 200 years later, stating that 'no argument for the truth of theism is more commonly invoked or more confidently relied on, than the general assent of mankind'.[27]

These claims may strike the modern reader as puzzling. As already noted, this 'most popular' argument rarely receives a mention in contemporary discussions of the proofs for God's existence. Further, and perhaps related to this, it is not immediately obvious what makes this an argument at all. At best, it sounds more like a questionable anthropological observation; at worst, an egregious instance of begging the question. It is worth establishing, then, just how prominent this principle was over the course of history, exploring the reasons why many early modern thinkers ranked it as the first and most important proof, and why it fell from favour. If in fact this argument was once as prominent as these commentators suggest, its demise would signal how the burden of proof has gradually shifted over the past four centuries so that belief in the existence of God, rather than atheism, is thought to require rational justification. Related to this, study of the different understandings of universal consent in relation to God's existence can shed light on the emergence of a distinctive feature of secular modernity, in which belief in the existence of God has become just one possibility among others.

Strictly speaking, as Boyle's enumeration implies, there are two connected proposals here. One is that the idea of God is innate or in some way embedded in the structure of thought, such that denying God's existence is akin to denying one of the axioms of logic or geometry. The other is the empirical claim that as a matter of fact no nation on earth has

---

of Philosophy, 8 vols., ed. Paul Edwards (New York: Macmillan, 1967), vol. 2, pp. 147–55; Linda Zagzebski, 'Epistemic Self-Trust and the Consensus Gentium Argument', in *Evidence and Religious Belief*, ed. Kelly James Clark and Raymond J. VanArragon (Oxford: Oxford University Press, 2011), pp. 22–36; Thomas Kelly, '*Consensus Gentium*: Reflections on the "Common Consent" Argument for the Existence of God', in *Evidence and Religious Belief*, ed. Clark and VanArragon, pp. 135–56.

[26] Lee, *Anti-Scepticism*, p. 31. (I am indebted to Reid, 'The Common Consent Argument', for this reference.) See also John Milner, *An Account of Mr Lock's Religion* (London, 1703), p. 3.

[27] J. S. Mill, 'Theism', in *The Collected Works of John Stuart Mill*, 10 vols., ed. J. M. Robson (Indianapolis: Liberty Fund, 2006), vol. 10, p. 430.

ever consistently denied the existence of God. Each component is typically thought to entail the other and historically the two elements usually appear together. That said, universal consent might be accounted for in other ways: as the result of a shared historical tradition, for example, or common patterns of reasoning to the existence of God from the ordered phenomena of nature.[28] On the other side, an exception to the rule of general consent might be accounted for in terms of a failure of the relevant innate principle to be fully expressed. To some degree, the idea of unitary and perennial 'proof' obscures the variety of positions that have been associated with the principle of universal consent. Moreover, as will become apparent, prior to the modern period, the *consensus gentium* principle was not typically articulated as a formal proof or demonstration of God's existence. Rather, it tended to be presented as a simple truth that rendered any further justification superfluous.

The principle was, in fact, common among classical philosophers. Plato observed that 'it looks easy enough to speak the truth in saying that gods exist .... All mankind, Greeks and non-Greeks alike, believe in the existence of gods.' Aristotle remarked similarly that 'all men have a conception of gods, and assign the highest place to the divine'.[29] We encounter a more developed argument in the Stoic philosophers Cicero and Seneca, who show a concern to refute the claim that the gods were a political invention. Both thinkers insisted that belief in the gods was natural rather than conventional. In a passage that made an almost obligatory appearance in early modern discussions, Cicero linked universal consensus, innateness, and necessary truth: 'Belief in the gods has not been established by authority, custom, or law, but rests on the unanimous and abiding consensus of mankind; their existence is therefore a necessary inference, since we possess an instinctive or rather an innate concept of them.'[30]

The inference to the truth of universal beliefs – the move from the ubiquity of the belief to its truth – was informed by logical considerations. In the *Topics* Aristotle proposed that dialectic begins from premises that consist in propositions that are commonly held (or are held by the most wise). The *Posterior Analytics* argued along similar lines that 'science' begins with

---

[28] Boyle himself entertained this second option. *The Christian Virtuoso II*, *Works*, vol. 12, p. 436.
[29] Plato, *Laws* 886a (Hamilton and Cairns, p. 1441); Aristotle, *On the Heavens* 270b6–7 (LCL 338, p. 25). Cf. *Metaphysics* 1074b.
[30] Cicero, *De natura Deorum* 1.17 (LCL 268, p. 45). Cf. *Tusculan Disputations* 1.13 (LCL 141, 37), *Topics* 7 (LCL 38, p. 405). Seneca offers a similar argument: 'For instance, we infer that the gods exist, for this reason, among others – that there is implanted in everyone an idea concerning deity ....' *Epistles* 117 (LCL 77, p. 341), Cf. *On Benefits* 4.4 (LCL 310, p. 211).

undemonstrated but true propositions. These propositions provide the foundation for subsequent demonstrations and include 'common principles'.[31] On this view, universal consent provides the axiomatic foundations upon which subsequent arguments are built. There was a similar form to these foundations in the spheres of mathematics, morals, and religion. Euclid, for example, had included five 'common notions' among the axiomatic foundations of his geometry.[32]

Epicurean and Stoic philosophers had comparable views about the truth of what was universally consented to. Epicurus suggested that the mind contains natural 'preconceptions' (*prolêpseis*) that provide a criterion for truth.[33] The Stoics supplemented this idea of *prolepsis* with a related conception of 'common notions' which, again, were taken to be necessarily true.[34] Chrysippus tells us that we receive common notions from nature 'as chief

---

[31] 'Those opinions [*endoxa*, ἔνδοξα] are reputable which are accepted by everyone or by the majority or by the wise.' Aristotle, *Topics* 100b20–3 (cf. LCL 139, p. 272). *Posterior Analytics* 73a, 75a–b. Cf. *Nicomachean Ethics* 1098b27. For varying interpretations of Aristotle's 'endoxa' see the discussions in Tobias Reinhardt, 'On Endoxa in Aristotle's Topics', *Rheinisches Museum für Philologie*, Neue Folge, 158. Bd., H. 3/4 (2015), pp. 225–46; Dirk Obbink, 'What All Men Believe – Must Be True: Common Conceptions and *consensio omnium* in Aristotle and Hellenistic Philosophy', *Oxford Studies in Ancient Philosophy* 10 (1992), 193–231. In the *Eudemian Ethics* 1248a21–4, Aristotle proposes that divine inspiration can be the starting point of reasoning (LCL 285, p. 467). Universal moral principles were similarly said to be 'divined' [μαντεύομαι]. *Rhetoric* 1373b4–8.

[32] These include, e.g., 'that the whole is greater than the part'. Euclid, *Elements*, bk. 1 (LCL 335, pp. 444f.). 'Common notions' rendering the standard expression κοιναὶ ἔννοιαι. On their status in the *Elements*, see Vincenzo di Risi, 'Euclid's Common Notions and the Theory of Equivalency', *Foundations of Science* (2020), https://doi.org/10.1007/s10699-020-09694-w, accessed 23 November 2023.

[33] Diogenes Laertius 10.31–2 (LCL 185, pp. 560–1). Henry Dyson describes these Epicurean preconceptions as 'analytically true claims embedded within one's ordinary conceptual scheme'. *Prolepsis and Ennoia in the Early Stoa* (Berlin: De Gruyter, 2009). But there is some discussion in the secondary sources about the role played by perception in triggering these common notions. See Robert M. Van Den Berg, 'As we are always speaking of them and using their names on every occasion. Plotinus, *Enn*. III.7 [45]: Language, Experience and the Philosophy of Time in Neoplatonism', in *Physics and Philosophy of Nature in Greek Neoplatonism*, ed. Riccardo Chiaradonna and Franco Trabattoni (Leiden: Brill, 2009), pp. 101–20; J. Phillips, 'Stoic "Common Notions" in Plotinus', *Dionysius* 11 (1987), 40–1.

[34] Matt Jackson-McCabe, 'The Stoic Theory of Implanted Conceptions', *Phronesis* 49 (2004), 323–47; Ralph Doty, 'Ennoēmata, Prolēpseis, and Common Notions', *Southwestern Journal of Philosophy* 7 (1976), 143–8. On the relation between prolepsis and the common notions see Robert B. Todd, 'The Stoic Common Notions: A Re-examination and Reinterpretation', *Symbolae Osloenses* 48 (1993), 47–75. For the later combination of Stoic and Epicurean concepts with Aristotelian logic see Frans A. J. De Haas, 'Deduction and Common Notions in Alexander's Commentary on Aristotle's *Metaphysics* A 1–2', *History of Philosophy and Logical Analysis* 74 (2021), 71–102.

4.2 THE FORGOTTEN PROOF

criteria for truth'.[35] Cicero expressed the same sentiment in his maxim that 'in every enquiry the unanimity of races of the world must be regarded as a law of nature'.[36] Given unanimity about the existence of God it followed that belief in the supernatural was 'natural' and since, on the Stoic reading, nature was the ultimate source of normative truths, this rendered the general consensus true. These classical and patristic understandings — and, in particular, versions of the Stoic/Epicurean idea of a preconception or prolepsis of God — informed much of the early modern discussion of 'common notions' or 'innate ideas' of God.[37]

During the first centuries of the Common Era these notions fed into Christian and Neoplatonic discussions of the innate sense of Deity. Justin Martyr spoke of the idea of God 'implanted in the nature of men'.[38] Tertullian declared that 'the conscience of all men' acknowledges God as the supreme being. He also cited Plato on the universality of belief in God and made reference to the Stoic idea of 'seeds within the soul'.[39] Clement of Alexandria (c.150–c.215) drew particular attention to affinities between the Pagan notion of *prolepsis* and Christian 'faith', making the case for a theological science that necessarily rested upon principles that were themselves indemonstrable (although for him the first principles included scripture).[40] Plotinus (c.204–70), the Neoplatonic philosopher whose writings exerted a profound influence on Augustine and much of the Middle Ages, insisted that 'all men instinctively affirm the god in each of us to be one, the same in all'.[41] In the same vein, Augustine declared that God 'cannot be altogether and utterly hidden from any rational creature, so long as it makes use of its

---

[35] Hans von Arnim (ed.), *Stoicorum Veterum Fragmenta* [SVF], 4 vols. (Stuttgart: Teubner, 1903–5), vol. 2, §473 (pp. 254, 29–30).

[36] '*omni autem in re consensio omnium gentium lex naturae putanda est*'. Cicero, *Tusculan Disputations* 1.13 (LCL 141, p. 37), and again '*omnium consensus naturae vox est*', *Tusculan Disputations* 1.15 (LCL 141, p. 40).

[37] There is a much longer story about the place of scholastic 'sensible and intelligible species', and their gradual displacement by the modern category of idea and principles. See, e.g., Leen Spruit, *Species Intelligibilis: From Perception to Knowledge*, vol. 2 (Leiden: Brill, 1995).

[38] Justin Martyr, *Second Apology* 6.3 (*ANF* 1, p. 190).

[39] Tertullian, *Against Marcion* 1.3, 5.16; *On the Resurrection of the Flesh* 3, 5 (*ANF* 3, pp. 273, 463; p. 547). Carlo Tibiletti, 'Tertulliano e la dottrina dell'anima "naturaliter christiana"', *Atti della Accademia delle scienze di Torino, tom. 2: Classe di scienze morali storiche e filologiche* 88 (1953–4), 84–117, esp. 109–15. For the Church Fathers' use of common notions see M. Spannent, *Le Stoïcisme des Pères de l'Église* (Paris, 1957).

[40] Clement of Alexandria, *Stromata* 7.16.95, 8.3.7, 6.8.67, 6.17.153. See Radde-Gallwitz, *Basil of Caesarea*, pp. 38–66; Osborn, 'Arguments for Faith'; Dragos, 'Apprehending "Demonstrations"'.

[41] Plotinus, *Enneads* 6.5.1.

reason'.[42] A century later, Boethius (d. 524) would repeat these sentiments. Common consent amounted to a proof of God's being and nature: 'That God, the principle of all things, is good is proved by the common concept of all men's minds.'[43]

As already noted, the principle of *consensus gentium* is not usually numbered among the classical demonstrations of God's existence and accordingly receives relatively little attention in treatments of medieval proofs. But elements of the idea are certainly present during this period and have an important bearing on better-known arguments such as Anselm's ontological argument and Aquinas's classic 'five ways'. Anselm famously argued that God cannot be conceived not to exist since to conceive of the greatest possible being (strictly speaking, 'something than which nothing greater can be thought') is to conceive of something that exists necessarily.[44] In a sense, this means that God's existence is self-evident. Aquinas expressed doubts about whether the existence of God was formally self-evident but nonetheless conceded that 'man possesses a natural aptitude for understanding and loving God, and this aptitude consists in the very nature of the mind, which is common to all men'.[45] Aquinas concludes each of his five proofs with the formula 'and this everyone holds to be God', implying that the proofs are intended to give additional content to a conception of God that is already entertained by all.[46] Bonaventure, who was more sympathetic to Anselm's ontological argument than Aquinas, claimed that, 'absolutely speaking', it was impossible to think that God could not exist.[47] Siger of

---

[42] Augustine, *Homilies on the Gospel of John*, NPNF I, vol. 7, p. 685. Cf. *The Trinity* 14.2.9.

[43] Clement of Alexandria, *Stromata* 2.2.8; Lactantius, *Divine Institutes* 3.10; Boethius, *Consolation of Philosophy* 3.10 (LCL 74, pp. 276f.). Elsewhere Boethius appeals to 'the common judgement [*commune iudicium*] of all who live by reason' to establish God's eternity. *Consolation of Philosophy* 5.6 (LCL 74, pp. 422f.). The relevant general principle is set out in the first axiom of his *De hebdomadibus* 1 <18>: 'A conception belonging to the common understanding is a statement that anyone approves once it has been heard.' There are two modes of these conceptions, those that command immediate assent (axiomatic truths of logic and mathematics) and those agreed upon by the learned. Trans. in Scott MacDonald (ed.), *Being and Goodness* (Ithaca: Cornell University Press, 1999), pp. 299–300.

[44] Anselm, *Proslogion*, 3.

[45] Aquinas, *ST* 1a. 93, 4. Cf. 'There is a certain general and vague knowledge of God in the minds of practically all men, whether it be by the fact of God's existence being a self-evident truth, as some think ... or, as seems more likely, because natural reasoning leads a man promptly to some sort of knowledge of God: for men seeing that natural things follow a certain course and order, and further considering that order cannot be without an ordainer, they perceive generally that there is some ordainer of the things which we see.' Aquinas, *SCG* 3.38.

[46] Aquinas, *ST* 1a. 2, 3.

[47] Bonaventure, *In I Sent.* d. 8, a. 1, q. 2 (p. 107). Bonaventure cites Hugh of St Victor to the same effect, referring to *De Sacramentis* 1.3.1 (PL 176: 217a).

Brabant (1240–84) took a similar view of the logical impropriety of theoretical atheism, listing the non-existence of God in a short disputation dealing with 'impossible things' and considering it to be more or less equivalent to denying the principle of contradiction.[48]

Another strand of the argument that found its way into medieval discussions of God's existence was the Platonic notion of reminiscence of the divine and the idea of the soul's natural affinity for God. North African apologist Lactantius (c.250–c.325), dubbed 'the Christian Cicero' by his Renaissance admirers, said of the innate sense of Deity that it prompted the minds of individuals to recall the divine source whence they had sprung. A number of medieval and Renaissance thinkers followed suit in speaking of the inherent striving of the human soul for reunion with its divine place of origin. This was accompanied by the Aristotelian assumption that the ends towards which things strive must be real, following the maxim that 'nature does nothing in vain'. Accordingly, the natural orientation of the human being towards the divine was taken as evidence of the necessary existence of the object of its desire. In the poignant opening lines of the *Confessions*, Augustine spoke of this inherent orientation towards God: 'you have made us for yourself, and our hearts are restless until they find their rest in you'.[49] Less eloquently, but to the same point, Aquinas stated that 'Every intellect naturally desires the vision of the divine substance.'[50] Nicholas of Cusa (1401–64) extended this sentiment to every created being: 'every creature knows and, in its own self-sufficient way, recognises his omnipotent Creator'.[51]

---

[48] Siger of Brabant, *Impossibilia*, in B. Bazán and A. Zimmermann (eds.), *Siger de Brabant: Écrits de logique, de morale et de physique* (Louvain: Publications Universitaires, 1974), pp. 67–97 (pp. 67–73). In a cosmological style proof, Siger proposed that the denial of a non-caused first cause would render all existing things contingent, which would make them unable to come into existence.

[49] '*quia fecisti nos ad te*', which could be rendered 'made us *towards* yourself'. *Confessions* 1.1.1 (LCL 26, p. 2).

[50] Aquinas, *SCG* 3, 57. In detail: 'It is impossible for natural desire to be empty, for nature does nothing in vain. Now, a natural desire would be in vain if it could never be fulfilled. Therefore, man's natural desire is capable of fulfillment.' *SCG* 3.48. Following Aristotle, *Nicomachean Ethics* 1.2. In the twentieth century C. S. Lewis would develop a related 'argument from desire'. *Mere Christianity* (London: HarperCollins, 2002), pp. 136–7. See John Beversluis, *C. S. Lewis and the Search for Rational Religion*, rev. ed. (Amherst: Prometheus, 2007), pp. 33–80.

[51] Nicholas of Cusa, *De venatione sapientiae*, cap. 19, 12–13; ed. Raymond Klibansky and Hans G. Senger (Hamburg: Felix Meiner, 1982) [*Opera Omnia*, vol. 12], p. 51. The idea that *all* creatures have some natural orientation towards God appears again in Mersenne, *Quaestiones in Genesim*, col. 25; Godfrey Goodman, *The Creatures Praysing God: Or, the Religion of Dumb Creatures* (London, 1622), p. 8; Edward Pelling, *A Discourse concerning the Existence of God* (London 1696), pp. 352–85.

Renaissance Platonist Marsilio Ficino (1433–99) spoke of a kind of religious instinct common to all peoples. This instinct, rather than discursive reason or language use, was the feature that distinguished human beings from other creatures. It was 'as natural to men almost as neighing is to horses or barking to dogs'.[52]

Taken together, these pre-modern references to the innateness and universality of a God concept yield the impression that the *consensus gentium* notion was to be understood less as the conclusion of an argument and more as an unassailable premise or a logical principle.[53] This goes to one aspect of our present puzzlement about what makes the *consensus gentium* an argument. For a good deal of its history it was not really an argument at all, if by 'argument' is meant arriving at a logical conclusion through a series of steps from sound premises. Rather it was a specific instance of the kind of premise or principle that made a chain of reasoning possible at all.

Related to this was an accompanying assumption that our mental faculties and intuitions, generally speaking, should be taken to be reliable. Stated in Aristotelian terms, our cognitive faculties are naturally oriented towards the truth. Both Aristotelian teleology and Neoplatonic notions of the soul's return to God had been overlaid during the Middle Ages with a more explicitly Christian gloss, with the innate God-idea being linked to the indwelling image of God. Generally speaking, human desires, rightly ordered, were directed towards the ultimate source of truth, God. Augustine would propose, accordingly, that 'One who knows *the truth*' knows the eternal light of God.[54] In the thirteenth century, Bonaventure would develop this insight further, proposing that 'All true understanding proves and concludes to the truth of the divine being, for knowledge of the divine truth is impressed on every

---

[52] Ficino, *Platonic Theology* 14.9 (vol. 4, pp. 293–5). In *De christiana religion*, ch. 1, Ficino speaks of '*communis omnium gentium religio*'. On Cusa and Ficino see Harrison, 'Religion' and the Religions, pp. 11–14; Smith, *Meaning and End of Religion*, pp. 32–4.

[53] 'Principles' is another relevant conception in this context. Franciscus Junius (the Elder): 'We call principles those things which are known *per se* by the light of nature, which are known immediately, and which are unmoved or immutable, such that from them at last definite knowledge arises.' Junius, *A Treatise on True Theology* [1594], trans. David C. Noe (Grand Rapids: Reformation Heritage Books, 2014), p. 146. Elsewhere Junius would directly identify common notions of God with 'principles'. *Opera theologica*, 2 vols. (Geneva, 1607), vol. 1, col. 1777. However, principles were typically understood in relation to the foundations of the sciences, and the term subsequently took on quite different meanings during the seventeenth century. For a concise overview see Peter Anstey (ed.), *The Idea of Principles in Early Modern Thought* (London: Routledge, 2017), Introduction, pp. 1–15.

[54] Augustine, *Confessions* 7.10 (LCL 26, p. 329).

soul.'⁵⁵ The assumptions that underpin this conclusion – if not the conclusion itself – bear an interesting resemblance to a school of modern philosophical thought known as 'reliabilism' – discussed in more detail below.

All that said, if the *consensus gentium* had not traditionally been understood as an argument, it was destined to become one in the early modern period. What enabled that transition was a new context in which theoretical atheism was imagined to be a live possibility. At first, the *consensus gentium* principle was deployed as 'a demonstration of the folly and unreasonableness of atheism' to allude again to the title of the first of the Boyle Lectures offered by Richard Bentley. It was thus a rather indirect demonstration of God's existence. But it was gradually transformed into a positive proof of God's existence suggesting that the burden of proof had begun to shift from imagined atheists to theists.

While the *consensus gentium* principle was a commonplace during the early modern period, two treatments were especially influential – those of John Calvin and Herbert of Cherbury.⁵⁶ Establishing an important precedent for subsequent reformed thinkers, Calvin incorporated elements of the earlier traditions into his conception of the 'sense of the divine' (*sensus divinitatis*): 'That there exists in the human mind, and indeed by some natural instinct some sense of the Divinity, we hold to be beyond dispute ....'⁵⁷ This sense is 'indelibly engraven on the human heart', 'naturally engendered in all', 'a remembrance of God ... spontaneously suggested from within by natural sense'.⁵⁸ Admittedly, for Calvin, the manifestations of this sense were often

---

⁵⁵ Bonaventure, *Commentary on the Sentences: Philosophy of God*, d. 8, pars 1, art. 1, q. 2, ed. and trans. R. E. Houser and Timothy B. Noone (St. Bonaventure, NY: Franciscan Institute Publications, 2013), p. 108. Houser comments: '... because knowledge of the divine truth is impressed on every soul, and all knowledge comes about through the divine truth. Every affirmative proposition proves and concludes to that truth. For every such proposition posits something. And when something is posited, the *true* is posited; and when the true is posited that *truth* which is the cause of the true is also posited.' Principles are 'self-evident' (cf. Aristotle, *Topics* 100a31–b21). In the second of Aristotle's modes of '*per se*' (Aristotle, *Posterior Analytics* 73a34–b3), the essence of the subject *causes* the predicate. This provided Bonaventure with an ingenious explanation of why principles are self-evident: 'We know principles to the extent that we understand the terms which make them up, because the cause of the predicate *is included in* the subject' (Introduction, p. xlii).

⁵⁶ On common notions more generally during this period see Andreas Blanck and Dana Jalobeanu, 'Common Notions: An Overview', *Journal of Early Modern Studies* 8 (2019), 9–24, which makes reference to the thought of Pierre Gassendi, Kenelm Digby, Thomas White, and Walter Charleton.

⁵⁷ Calvin, *Institutes* 1.3.1, vol. 1, p. 43. For secondary treatments see J. Caleb Clanton, 'John Calvin and John Locke on the *Sensus Divinitatis* and Innatism', *Religions* 8 (2017), 1–14; Helm, 'Calvin and the Noetic Effects of Sin'.

⁵⁸ Calvin, *Institutes* 1.3.3, vol. 1, p. 44; 1.4.2, vol. 1, p. 47. Calvin cites as sources Romans 1:20: 'Ever since the creation of the world his eternal power and divine nature, invisible

distorted by sin, leading to idolatry and superstition. But in their own ways, even these deformed versions of religion bore testimony to this innate sense. The notion of an instinctive God-idea was espoused by both Calvinist and Lutheran thinkers.[59]

In the following century, a more comprehensive advocacy of the idea is to be found in Herbert of Cherbury's *De veritate* ('On Truth', 1624).[60] Herbert identified a number of mental faculties, the most fundamental of which he called 'natural instinct'. This instinct produces common notions, which are independent of both external perceptions and rational deliberation.[61] They provide the conditions for having any experiences at all, and they enable us to distinguish truth from falsehood.[62] In the former respect they are akin to the Kantian a priori forms of sensible intuition. Herbert enumerated five such notions, the very first of which is that there is a

though they are, have been understood and seen through the things he has made. So they are without excuse'; and the oft quoted passage from Cicero, *De natura Deorum* 1.17.

[59] Philip Melanchthon maintained that God's existence is known from 'the law of nature' and his enumeration of arguments for God's existence begins with the innate God-idea. *Loci communes* (1521 edition), *Corpus Reformatorum* (Braunschweig, 1854), vol. 21, col. 117, cf. col. 116; *Loci communes* (1535 edition), *Corpus Reformatorum*, vol. 21, col. 566. Cf. Martin Luther, *Lectures on Romans*, trans. W. Pauck (Louisville: Westminster John Knox Press, 1961), pp. 23f. For similarities between Calvin and Melanchthon on this issue see David C. Steinmetz, *Calvin in Context* (Oxford: Oxford University Press, 1995), pp. 23–39. For Melanchthon's arguments for God's existence see John Platt, *Reformed Thought and Scholasticism* (Leiden: Brill, 1982), pp. 10–33. Franciscus Junius speaks of *notitia* (notions, conceptions) invoking Cicero (cf. '*notitiam habera dei*', *De Legibus* 1.8.24) and the Greek concepts of *ennoia* (common notions) and *katalepsis* (grasp, insight). *True Theology*, p. 148. Calvin used the slightly different terminology of '*cognitio*' of God (rather than '*notitia*') and does not refer to *ennoia*. *Institutes* 1.1 (*Joannis Calvini Opera Selecta*, 5 vols., ed. P. Barth and W. Niesel (Munich: C. Kaiser, 1957), vol. 3, p. 31). Other sources include Johannes Kuchlinus, *Ecclesiarum Hollandicarum* (Geneva, 1612), pp. 207f.; Sibrandus Lubbertus, *Commentarius in Catechesin Palatino-Beligicam* (Franker, 1618), pp. 217f.; Amyraut, *De l'élévation de la foi*, pp. 43–9; and R. T. te Velde and Riemer Faber (eds.), *Synopsis Purioris Theologia* [1625], 3 vols. (Leiden: Brill, 2014–19), vol. 1, p. 153. For Voetius's appeal to the argument, see Andreas J. Beck, 'Melanchthonian Thought in Gisbertus Voetius' Scholastic Doctrine of God', in *Scholasticism Reformed*, ed. Maarten Wisse, Marcel Sarot, and Willemien Otten (Leiden: Brill, 2010), pp. 107–26.

[60] Herbert of Cherbury, *De veritate, prout distinguitur a Revelatione, a Verisimile, a Possibili, et a Falso* (Paris, 1624), with subsequent Latin editions published in London in 1633, 1645, and 1656. Mersenne thought it an important work, producing an anonymous French translation in 1639. (The Latin edition had been placed on the Index of forbidden books in 1634.) See Jacqueline Lagrée, 'Mersenne traducteur d'Herbert de Cherbury', *Les Études philosophiques* 1/2 (1994), 25–40. English translation Herbert of Cherbury, *De Veritate*, trans. Meyrick H. Carre (Bristol: J. W. Arrowsmith, 1937). References below are to the English translation.

[61] 'natural instinct' (*instinctus naturalis*); 'general consent' (*consensu generalis*).

[62] Herbert, *De Veritate*, pp. 132, 105f.

supreme being.⁶³ While evidence for these notions comes from reflection on one's own faculties, Herbert regards the unanimous verdict of history as further confirmation of their innateness and immediacy. The appeal to common notions is also directly opposed to implicit faith in 'an infallible Church or its priesthood', pointing to the fact that Herbert's motivation for writing *De veritate* was connected to the epistemic crisis precipitated by the Reformation.⁶⁴

Herbert has often been associated with the rise of English deism on account of his insistence on the sufficiency of the common notions and the implication that revelation and ecclesiastical tradition were superfluous to salvific requirements. In this respect, his motivation was very different from that of Calvin. The Genevan reformer had articulated the principle of the *sensus divinitatis* partly to justify the claim that the reprobate were 'without excuse' (in keeping with the locus classicus Rom. 1:20). For Herbert, by way of contrast, the common notions were intended to provide an alternative route to salvation, one that largely bypassed tradition and revelation.⁶⁵ However, Herbert's incipient deism did not prevent the adoption of the idea of common notions by those whose orthodoxy was not in question. In the middle decades of the seventeenth century the 'Cambridge Platonists' were particularly taken with the argument. Henry More's *Antidote*, for example, drew a parallel between this a priori recognition of the existence of God and the way we come to a realisation of the truths of geometry:

> And therefore if there were any Nations that were destitute of the knowledge of a *God*, as they might be, it is likely, of the Rudiments of *Geometry*, so long as they will admit of the knowledge of one as well as of the other, upon due and fit proposal; the acknowledgement of a *God* is as well to be said to be according to the *light of nature*, as the knowledge of *Geometry* which they thus receive.⁶⁶

---

⁶³ Herbert, *De Veritate*, p. 122.
⁶⁴ Herbert, *De Veritate*, pp. 115, 44, 154, 291. Further discussion in Harrison, 'Religion' and the Religions, pp. 34–9, 65–73.
⁶⁵ Common notions constituted 'saving knowledge' and were 'the only Catholic and uniform Church' through which salvation was possible. Herbert invokes here a version of the principle *extra Ecclesiam nulla salus* – no salvation outside the Church. *De Veritate*, p. 303.
⁶⁶ More, *Antidote*, pp. 31f. The *consensus gentium* was thus compatible with the possibility of nations of atheists. Cudworth, similarly: 'For since Humane Nature is so Mutable and Depravable, as that notwithstanding the *Connate Idea* and *Prolepsis* of God in the Minds of Men, some unquestionably do degenerate and lapse into Atheism.' *True Intellectual System*, p. 631.

More thus endorsed the principle while at the same time explaining why it might not be uniformly manifested among all peoples. Ralph Cudworth followed a similar line to More, but specifically appealed to the Epicurean and Stoic idea of a cognitive pre-apprehension: 'the Generality of mankind, have constantly had a certain *Prolepsis* or *Anticipation* in their Minds, concerning the *Actual Existence* of a *God*, according to the *True Idea* of him'.[67] Cudworth spends many pages of his *True Intellectual System* (1678) citing ancient authors to this effect. Such arguments were commonplace, not only in the circle of the Cambridge Platonists, but also in a variety of religious and philosophical works of the period.[68]

The argument was also strongly represented on the other side of the confessional divide. As already noted, it appears in the writings of Lessius and Mersenne. One of the more enthusiastic presentations of the argument comes in the four-volume *Natural Theology* (1633–8) of Capuchin theologian Yves of Paris. Seeking to establish the rationality of belief in God against fideists and erudite libertines, Yves opens by insisting that a sense of God's existence (*sentiment naturel de Dieu*) is essential to our natures and is universally acknowledged. This sentiment is of the order of the principle that 'the whole is greater than the sum of the parts', was imprinted in us by God, and was 'common to all nations', including those recently discovered.[69] Other Catholic thinkers of the seventeenth and early eighteenth centuries would also reference the argument, albeit in less detail.[70] Among

---

[67] Cudworth, *True Intellectual System*, Preface, cf. pp. 634, 665, 691, 834.

[68] Whichcote, *Works*, vol. 3, p. 187; Joseph Glanvill, 'The Agreement of Reason and Religion', in *Essays on Several Important Subjects* (London, 1676), p. 5; Culverwell, *Treatise of the Light of Nature*, esp. pp. 71–8; Margaret Cavendish, 'Philosophical Letters' [1664], in *Essential Writings*, ed. David Cunning (Oxford: Oxford University Press, 2019), pp. 75, 83; Edward Stillingfleet, *Origines Sacrae*, 1st ed. (London, 1662), pp. 360, 365, 384; Theophilus Gale, *The Court of the Gentiles*, part IV (London, 1667), p. 223; [A. B.], *The Mystery of Atheism*, p. 34; Charles Wolseley, *The Unreasonablenesse of Atheism Made Manifest*, 2nd ed. (London, 1669), p. 66; Bentley, *Unreasonableness of Atheism*, pp. 4, 168–9; Harris, *Atheistical objections*, Sermon 3, pp. 26–31; John Tillotson, *Several discourses upon the attributes of God* (London, 1699), p. 216; South, *Sermons*, vol. 1, p. 381; John Warly, *The Natural Fanatick* (London, 1676), p. 59; Pelling, *Existence of God*, p. 54; Isaac Barrow, 'The Being of God proved by Universal Consent', *Theological Works*, vol. 4, pp. 448–50; Adams, *Some Discourses*, p. 9. Further sources may be found in Reid, 'The Common Consent Argument'.

[69] Yves de Paris, *La Théologie Naturelle* [1633–8], 4 vols. (Paris, 1640), vol. 1, pp. 50–89.

[70] See, e.g., Emmanuel Maignan, *Philosophia sacra*, 2 pts. (Toulouse, 1661; Lyons, 1672), pt. 1, pp. 60f.; Jean-Claude Sommier, *Histoire dogmatique de la religion ou La religion prouvée par l'autorité divine & humaine, & par les lumières de la raison*, 3 vols. (Paris, 1708–11), vol. 1, pp. 61–6; Fénelon, *L'Existence de Dieu*, Preface, pp. 215f., 303, 309 (Fénelon generally preferred design arguments, however); Pierre-Daniel Huet, *Demonstratio Evangelica* [1673], 6th ed. (Frankfurt, 1722), p. 4; Félicité Robert de Lamennais, *Essai sur l'indifférence en matière*

the philosophers, Pierre Gassendi, despite some initial reservations about the thesis, came to the mature view that there were two powerful arguments for God's existence, the argument from a universal and inherent 'anticipation' (in essence, the Epicurean *prolepsis*), and the argument based on the wonders of nature.[71] Descartes would also strongly endorse one element of the argument – the innate idea of God – although, as we will see, he was reluctant to make much of universal consent.

While the context of the early modern arguments was different, the persuasive force as a form of argument still drew upon traditional classical and medieval justifications relating to the proper functioning of the mind. Lessius, for example, stated that nature never plants anything in the mind that is false, and hence that the truth of implanted ideas can be taken for granted. Truth is understood to be the 'health of the mind'.[72] This orientation included a natural tendency towards knowledge of God. Yves of Paris spoke of a 'natural curiosity' that is quenched only when it encounters the ultimate explanation for things in God. Our common inclinations are oriented only towards 'legitimate ends', which is to say really existing objects.[73] As we have already seen, Benjamin Whichcote proposed that the mind naturally tended towards God just as heavy objects tend towards the earth.[74]

One way of understanding the force of this position is to cast it as a version of what has recently become known as 'reliabilist' epistemology. The basic principle is that rather than beliefs being warranted by means of argument and extrinsic *evidence* – what is known as 'evidentialism' – it is a matter of their being the outcome of reliable cognitive *processes*.[75] Ironically, this is now usually taken to be a naturalistic understanding of knowledge

---

de religion, 2 vols. (Paris, 1817, 1820), vol. 1, p. 498. De Lamennais built a complete epistemology around common consent, which he opposed to the philosophical schools of empiricism (Locke), idealism (Berkeley and Kant), and rationalism (Descartes). See esp. *Essai sur l'indifférence*, vol. 2.

[71] Pierre Gassendi, *Opera omnia*, 6 vols. (Lyon, 1658), vol. 1, p. 311a. Gassendi had criticised Herbert of Cherbury's reliance upon the *consensus gentium* principle but modified his position in the *Syntagma*. See Marcelino Rodríguez Donís, 'Consensus Gentium et prolepsis dans la philosophie de Gassendi', in *Gassendi et la Modernité*, ed. S. Taussig (Turnhout: Brepols, 2008), pp. 261–78; Richard Serjeantson, 'Herbert of Cherbury before Deism: The Early Reception of the *De veritate*', *The Seventeenth Century* 16 (2001), 217–38.

[72] Lessius, *De providentia numinis*, p. 11.

[73] Yves de Paris, *La Théologie Naturelle*, vol. 1, pp. 45f., 55.

[74] Whichcote, *Works*, vol. 3, p. 144.

[75] For reliabilists, the justification of a belief is to be understood in terms of the history of the processes that cause the belief and their reliability. I would be justified, e.g., in claiming that the sky is blue in the event that my eyes and visual cortex are operating reliably. For an overview of this position see Alvin I. Goldman, *Epistemology and Cognition* (Cambridge, MA: Harvard University Press, 1986).

production and, indeed, this is one of its touted advantages. The medieval and early modern examples alluded to above, needless to say, are not naturalistic in a sense that is opposed to the supernatural. On the contrary, it is theistic assumptions that put the 'reliable' into reliabilism in this earlier context. God, in other words, certifies the trustworthiness of our most fundamental intuitions. Something close to reliabilism (*avant la lettre*) was the default position in the pre-modern West until derailed by the sceptical challenges of the post-Reformation period, to which Cartesian foundationalism and the way of ideas (inner ideas as representing some 'external' reality) were responses.

To digress briefly, the common sense philosophy of the Scottish Enlightenment, which stressed the necessity of our reliance upon innate and common notions, can be understood as an attempt to reinstate a reliabilist approach. Thomas Reid's (1710–96) ambition for his philosophical project, for example, was to get philosophy back on track in the wake of Descartes's sceptical diversion.[76] In normal usage, according to Reid, having an idea simply meant thinking about something, implying a mind that thinks, an act of thinking, and an object of thought. Since Descartes, philosophers had added a fourth thing – the idea in the mind, which replaces the 'external' object as the immediate object of perception.[77] According to Reid, this inevitably leads to scepticism in relation to objects external to the mind, with Hume's philosophy representing the logical conclusion of the Cartesian project. Reid maintained that we can obviate elaborate justificatory exercises that seek to establish the existence of our minds, the external world, and God, simply by trusting the deliverances of our faculties unless we have compelling reasons not to do so. Reid, in any case, dismissed these attempted justifications as utterly unconvincing. Ratiocination must begin with first principles for which no reason can be given other than 'by the constitution of our nature, we are under a necessity of assenting to them'. If we are mistaken in these things 'we are deceived by Him that made us, and there is no remedy'.[78]

---

[76] For Reid as an antecedent of present-day reliabilism see Philip de Bary, *Thomas Reid and Scepticism: His Reliabilist Response* (London: Routledge, 2002).

[77] Thomas Reid, *Essays on the Intellectual Powers of Man*, ed. Derek R. Brookes (Edinburgh: Edinburgh University Press, 2002), 1.1; 2.7 (pp. 31, 105). In the twentieth century, Richard Rorty expressed similar doubt about the direction of modern philosophy. *Philosophy and the Mirror of Nature* (Princeton: Princeton University Press, 1981). Arguably, representational 'ideas' have their origins in Duns Scotus's *ens objectivum* – the object of knowledge in our minds, which replaced the older conception of knowledge by means of 'intelligible species'. This transition accompanied the demise of the analogical understanding of the relation of the mind to the world.

[78] Thomas Reid, *An Inquiry into the Human Mind on the Principles of Common Sense* 5.7, ed. Derek R. Brookes (Edinburgh: Edinburgh University Press, 1997), pp. 71f. Some interpreters have argued, implausibly in my view, that Reid allows for rational knowledge in

Reid's younger contemporary Adam Ferguson (1723–1816) argued specifically for the rationality of belief in God on the basis of its universality and inevitability. Human nature is constituted in such a way that we naturally assume that effects have causes. Belief in God is a similar case, following necessarily from a perception of ends or intentions in the works of nature. 'No argument', says Ferguson, 'is required to prove where nature determined that we shall continue to believe'.[79] Another member of the school, James Beattie (1735–1803), pointed out that Scottish common sense philosophy was part of a long historical tradition that went back to Aristotle and had been most strongly championed by the Stoics. The key ideas were common notions, universal consensus, right reason, and natural instinct.[80] Beattie writes that 'except we believe many things without proof, we never can believe any thing at all …. Common sense is the ultimate judge of truth, to which reason must continually act in subordination.'[81] John Henry Newman would argue along similar lines that without a general confidence in the fidelity of our reasoning powers (and in spite of the fallibility of sense, memory, and reason) we would be unable to conduct ourselves in the world. On the same basis we can assume the general reliability of religious faith and our 'instinctive apprehension of the Omnipresence of God'.[82] More recently, philosophers such as Nicholas Wolterstorff and Alvin Plantinga have adopted a Reidian approach, proposing that we have (God-given) faculties that generate reliable intuitions with respect to such things as the existence of the external world, other minds, and, crucially, God.[83]

the absence of a divine guarantor. See, e.g., Keith Lehrer and Bradley Warner, 'Reid, God and Epistemology', *American Catholic Philosophical Quarterly* 74 (2000), 357–72; James Sommerville, *The Enigmatic Parting Shot: What was Hume's "Compleat Answer to Dr Reid and to that Bigotted Silly Fellow, Beattie"* (Aldershot: Avery Press, 1987).

[79] Adam Ferguson, *Institutes of Moral Philosophy*, 2nd ed. (Edinburgh, 1773), pp. 116–17.

[80] Beattie, *Essay*, pp. 38–40. More recently Hans-Georg Gadamer has also drawn attention to the history of the notion of *sensus communis*, and its pervasive philosophical influence. *Truth and Method*, rev. 2nd ed. (London: Bloomsbury, 2004), pp. 18–32. For the subsequent influence of common sense philosophy on the development of critical philosophy in Germany, see Manfred Kuehn, *Scottish Common Sense in Germany* (Montreal: McGill-Queen's University Press, 1987), esp. pp. 251–74.

[81] Beattie, *Essay*, pp. 54f. Beattie had already insisted, with Hume in mind, that 'implicit confidence in testimony' is a natural part of the epistemic ecosystem (p. 130).

[82] Newman, 'The Nature of Faith in Relation to Reason', *Fifteen Sermons*, p. 214. Newman shares Reid's epistemological naturalism, but with the difference that first principles are to be discovered inductively, rather than intuitively. Newman will speak of 'illative sense' rather than 'common sense' especially in his *Grammar of Assent*. On the connection between the two thinkers, see M. Jamie Ferreira, *Scepticism and Reasonable Doubt: The British Naturalist Tradition in Wilkins, Hume, Reid, and Newman* (Oxford: Clarendon Press, 1986).

[83] For a succinct statement, see Alvin Plantinga and Michael Tooley, *Knowledge of God* (Oxford: Blackwell, 2008), pp. 7–8. See also Nicholas Wolterstorff, 'Can Belief in God

Returning to the early modern period and its version of reliabilism, Herbert regarded the common notions as a gift imparted to us by God for the regulation and preservation of our lives. This rendered them trustworthy.[84] The role of God as guarantor of the reliability of our shared intuitions and reasonings was, in fact, an early modern commonplace. John Tillotson would state the principle in these terms: 'If God be a *God of truth*, then this gives us assurance that he doth not deceive us, that the faculties which he hath given us are not false.'[85] These connections help explain the consistent equation of atheism with a self-defeating irrationality, since the only thing that assured the reliability of our ratiocination was a connection to the divine.[86] Descartes offered another version of this principle, proposing a rule 'that everything we conceive very clearly and very distinctly is true' and, further, that 'our ideas or notions, being real things and coming from God, cannot be anything but true, in every respect in which they are clear and distinct'.[87] But in this instance the focus is on the content of *ideas* and their correspondence with reality, as opposed to the reliability of our *faculties* and this makes a crucial difference.[88]

The principle of universal consent was also reinforced by a distinctively early modern preoccupation: the historical thesis of 'primitive monotheism'. This was the view that the ancients had all worshipped a single supreme being and that this tradition, which could be traced back to the very first humans, had subsequently been transmitted to the whole human race. This compressed history, spanning less than 6,000 years, was read directly out of the Pentateuch. It began with Adam and Eve and was followed by the dispersion of the human race following the deluge, through the lineage of the

---

Be Rational if It Has No Foundations?', in *Faith and Rationality*, ed. Alvin Plantinga and Nicholas Wolterstorff (Notre Dame: University of Notre Dame Press, 1983), pp. 135–86. Reference to Reid on pp. 149–53. Alvin Plantinga, 'Reason and Belief in God', also in *Faith and Rationality*, pp. 16–93; *Warrant: The Current Debate* (New York: Oxford University Press, 1993).

[84] Herbert, *De Veritate*, pp. 118, 122. Herbert remarks in the same context that universal consent is 'the sole test of truth' (p. 118).

[85] John Tillotson, 'The Truth of God', in *Works*, vol. 1, p. 658. Admittedly, Tillotson speaks of faculties rather than ideas.

[86] By the same token, there is an element of circularity to this reasoning. On a more charitable interpretation the position is one of internal coherence.

[87] Descartes, *Discourse*, CSM 1, p. 130. Spinoza offers a similar justification: 'All ideas are in God (Pr. 15, 1) and insofar as they are related to God, they are true (Pr. 32, II).' *Ethics*, pt. II, Proposition 36, *CW*, p. 264. While Thomas Reid agreed that God ultimately guarantees the reliability of our fundamental intuitions, he thought that the Cartesian process of arriving at that conclusion was extravagant: 'A man that disbelieves his own existence, is surely as unfit to be reasoned with, as a man that believes he is made of glass.' *Inquiry* 1.3, p. 16.

[88] Reid, *Essays* 2.20 (pp. 226–33).

4.2 THE FORGOTTEN PROOF

sons of Noah. Moses was the 'divine historian' who had recorded all of this and served as the primary written source of knowledge and wisdom for all of the ancient civilisations.[89] Isaac Newton would speak for this tradition when he referred to 'the Religion of Adam, Enoch, Noah, Abraham Moses Christ & all the saints'.[90] There were less reliable oral traditions as well. The religious beliefs and customs of the various races were thus to be understood as fragmented versions of an original, pure monotheism. Viewed through this historical lens, common notions could be both innate *and* the result of cultural transmission.[91] These dual sources would contribute to a universal consensus.

What happened to this 'first and most popular' argument? First, predictably, Protestant critiques of implicit faith also tended to undermine the logic of reliance upon the consent of the nations. The idea that common knowledge might provide a criterion of truth seemed perilously close to Catholic appeals to 'tradition'. The classic definition had been provided by Vincent of Lérins (d. *c*.445) for whom (Catholic) tradition is constituted by what has been believed 'everywhere, always, by all'.[92] This sounds a lot like universal consent, provided that 'universal' is limited to Christendom. It is true that Protestants might still affirm the principle while arguing that medieval Catholicism embodied a protracted deviation from it.[93] But so long as questions could be asked about what aspects of tradition actually met the criterion, its capacity to serve as a reliable benchmark was compromised.

---

[89] For examples see Jean de Léry, *The History of a Voyage to the Land of Brazil* [1574], trans. Janet Whatley (Berkeley and Los Angeles: University of California Press, 1990), p. 151; Robert Fludd, *Mosaicall Philosophy* (London, 1659); Henry More, *Conjectura Cabbalistica* (London, 1653); Robert Jenkin, *The Reasonableness and Certainty of the Christian Religion* (London, 1698), pp. 58, 64f., 129–38; Huet, *Demonstratio Evangelica*, pp. 44f., and *passim*; John Leland, *The Advantage and Necessity of the Christian Revelation*, 3rd ed., 2 vols. (Dublin, 1776), vol. 1, p. 68. For secondary treatments see Harrison, 'Religion' and the Religions, pp. 130–8; D. P. Walker, *The Ancient Theology* (Ithaca: Cornell University Press, 1972).

[90] Isaac Newton, 'A short Schem of true Religion', Keynes MS 7, 1r, King's College, Cambridge, www.newtonproject.ox.ac.uk/view/texts/normalized/THEM00007, accessed 4 April 2022.

[91] See, e.g., Barrow, *Theological Works*, vol. 4, pp. 448–50; Bentley, *Unreasonableness of Atheism*, pp. 31f., 44, cf. p. 5; Jacques Bernard, 'Article 1: Continuation des Pensées diverses', *Nouvelles de la république des lettres* (1705), pp. 123–53 (p. 138), cited in Reid, 'The Common Consent Argument', 423.

[92] Vincent of Lérins, *Vincentius Lerinensis, Commonitorium* 2.3, ed. Reginald Stewart Moxon (Cambridge: Cambridge University Press, 1915), p. 10. Cardinal Jacques Davy du Perron, for example, conflated the consensus of Church councils with the *consensus gentium* in his defence of transubstantiation against the Protestants. *Traitté du Sainct Sacrement de l'Eucharistie* (Paris, 1622), p. 1015.

[93] Chillingworth, *Religion of Protestants*, p. 169.

Thus, the demand that individuals decide on matters of belief for themselves counted against deferring to tradition which, under another description, could simply be the aggregated opinions of others.⁹⁴ The Jesuit Lessius, betraying his confessional allegiance, darkly hinted at this in his observation that rejecting universal consent would amount to elevating 'a man's own private judgement above the verdict of the whole world'.⁹⁵

There was also an inherent instability in versions of the argument articulated by those who held to a strong version of original sin and its consequences – especially Calvinists and Jansenists. As we have seen, these groups had significant reservations about the scope and powers of fallen human minds. Any vestigial notion of God remaining in the human soul was said to be feeble and dull, and incapable of providing, on its own, any reliable knowledge of God.⁹⁶ This stance informed a standard criticism of Descartes's arguments for God's existence which required that the mind have a 'clear and distinct' idea of God lodged within it. A number of Descartes's critics upheld the innateness of some notion of God but argued that it was vague and imprecise.⁹⁷

Parallel developments in philosophy and the sciences also placed the notion of common consent uncomfortably close to the less respectable category of 'received opinions' (or even 'vulgar opinions'). Uncritical acceptance of received opinions increasingly came to be regarded as a barrier to progress, especially in the realm of natural philosophy. Given the long-standing role played by common notions in logic, this necessitated the revision of long-accepted principles of logic, reasoning, and rhetoric, and indeed a questioning of the role of logic in knowledge acquisition. Francis

---

⁹⁴ For Pierre Bayle's criticisms along these lines see Reid, 'The Common Consent Argument', 426; Kors, *Atheism in France*, pp. 140–2.

⁹⁵ Lessius, *De providentia numinis*, pp. 14f.

⁹⁶ Luther, *Complete Sermons*, vol. 4.2, p. 8. Philip Melanchthon, *Loci Communes* (1543 edition), trans. J. A. O. Preus (St Louis: Concordia, 1992), p. 18.

⁹⁷ Descartes, *Discourse*, CSM 1, pp. 128f.; *Meditations*, CSM 2, pp. 31–6, 44–9. For critiques of this position see *Objections and Replies*, CSM 2, pp. 70, 133, 152, 200. Samuel Parker, *Tentamina physico-theologica de Deo* (Oxford, 1665), p. 164. For Calvinist critique see Verbeek, 'Descartes and the Problem of Atheism'. In response Descartes had stressed that God is an 'incomprehensible power'. CSMK, pp. 23, 25; *Objections and Replies*, CSM 2, p. 80. See also Jean-Luc Marion, *On the Ego and on God: Further Cartesian Questions*, trans. Christina Gschwandtner (New York: Fordham University Press, 2007), pp. 170–2. Leibniz and Wolff would later address this issue by seeking first to establish the *possibility* of the idea of the most perfect being. Leibniz, 'Meditations on Knowledge, Truth, and Ideas', in *Philosophical Essays*, pp. 25–7; Christian Wolff, *De differentia nexus rerum sapientis et fatalis necessitatis* [1724], 2nd ed. (Halle, 1734), §5, pp. 9–13. This issue goes back to Aquinas's critique of Anselm's 'ontological argument'. *ST* Ia. 2, 1; *De veritate*, 10.12.3.

4.2 THE FORGOTTEN PROOF

Bacon alleged in his *Novum Organum* (1620) that 'the logic now in use serves rather to fix and give stability to the errors which have their foundation in *commonly received notions* than to help the search after truth'. Logic, he concluded, 'does more harm than good'.[98] At the time, the traditional logic curriculum was built around Aristotle's logical writings, including the *Topics*, which had instated common notions as the starting point of arguments. These works were collectively known as the *Organon*, which Bacon clearly intended to replace with his *Novum Organum* – a 'new' *Organon*.[99] Descartes and Locke voiced similar criticisms of logic and particularly the role that it was accorded in scientific discovery.[100]

In keeping with these sentiments Descartes had resolved to make a completely new beginning – 'to demolish everything completely and start again right from the foundations' – a strategy that was incompatible with acceptance of received wisdom, however unanimous it may have been.[101] Descartes's demolition of received truths initially extended even to the existence of God. Notwithstanding that the idea of God is in some sense innate, establishing God's existence became something that needed to be demonstrated rather than directly intuited. In the address to the Sorbonne that prefaces his *Meditations*, Descartes points to his arguments for God's existence as one of the work's selling points. If we are to convince unbelievers, he argues, what is needed are 'demonstrative proofs'.[102] This distinguishes his position from that of Herbert of Cherbury. Descartes was familiar with Herbert's *De veritate*, having read both the Latin original and the French translation, independently sent to him by the century's great 'intelligencers', Samuel Hartlib and Marin Mersenne.[103] In the *Discourse* and the *Meditations*, Descartes would maintain that we encounter in our minds the idea of an infinite, eternal,

---

[98] Bacon, *Novum Organum*, bk. 1, §§11, 12, *Works*, vol. 4, pp. 48f. (my emphasis).
[99] Logic texts of the seventeenth century, such as Robert Sanderson's *Logicae Artis Compendium* (Oxford, 1614) were typically structured around Aristotle's *Organon*. There were, admittedly, theological defences of logic by figures such as Johannes Alsted and Bartholomew Keckermann, according to whom it had a role in rectifying fallen reason. Howard Hotson, *Johann Heinrich Alsted, 1588–1638: Between Renaissance, Reformation, and Universal Reform* (Oxford: Oxford University Press, 2000), pp. 66–8; Richard A. Muller, *Post-Reformation Reformed Dogmatics*, 4 vols. (Grand Rapids: Baker, 2005), vol. 1, p. 279.
[100] Descartes, *Rules for the Direction of the Mind*, Rule 10, CSM 1, p. 36; Locke, *Essay* 3.10.6 (p. 494). Locke further argued that 'giving up our assent to commonly received notions' was a requirement of taking personal and moral responsibility for what we believe. *Essay* 4.20.17 (pp. 718f.).
[101] Descartes, *Meditations*, CSM 2, p. 17.   [102] Descartes, *Meditations*, CSM 2, p. 3.
[103] Mattia Mantovani, 'Herbert of Cherbury, Descartes and Locke on Innate Ideas and Universal Consent', *Journal of Early Modern Studies* 8 (2019), 83–115; Desmond M. Clarke, *Descartes: A Biography* (Cambridge: Cambridge University Press, 2006), p. 185.

perfect being which could only have come from God himself. This seems very close to the first of Herbert's common notions.[104] However, Descartes does not take the innate conception of God to be sufficient of itself to warrant belief. Rather, the *idea* of God becomes the premise of an argument that then establishes his *existence*. The difference may be subtle, but it is relevant since the Cartesian positing of 'ideas', understood as mental representations, called for an additional step that established the connection between the idea and real existence. This would become true for all mental representations.

Simply put, Descartes gives us an argument, whereas Herbert had sought to draw attention to an inalienable aspect of human cognition. This amounts to a difference between an indemonstrable *principle* or *notion*, established on the basis of universal consent, and an *idea*, the certainty of which rested on an internal criterion of clarity and distinctness.[105] Descartes's argument was thus purely philosophical, making no reference to historical precedents, the opinions of the wise, or universal consent. In fact, Descartes argues that because God has given us a light to distinguish truth from falsehood, we owe it to ourselves to ignore the opinions of others and rely upon our own judgement.[106] The proper gauge of truth is the clarity and distinctness of the ideas that God has implanted within our minds, rather than the historical convergence of opinions. The move from principles to ideas set up a potential tension between two once-unified criteria of truth – universality and innateness. After Descartes what had been two tightly intertwined aspects of a single powerful argument began to come apart.

One outcome of Descartes's foundationalist approach was the inauguration of 'the way of ideas', in which ideas *represent* reality. But this raises

---

[104] Descartes, *Discourse*, CSM 1, pp. 128f. Similar arguments are presented in the *Meditations*, CSM 2, pp. 31–6, 44–9.

[105] Descartes thus inaugurates the 'way of ideas' which John Locke, in spite of his criticisms of Descartes, subsequently adopted. See John Yolton, *John Locke and the Way of Ideas* (New York: Oxford University Press, 1956). Edward Stillingfleet would identify the novelty of this approach in his criticism of Locke who denied not only innate ideas, but also innate *principles*: 'But your Way of Certainty by Ideas is so wholly New, that here we have no general Principles ....' According to Stillingfleet, 'the Way of Reason hath been always supposed to proceed upon *General Principles*; and you assert them to be *Vseless* and *Dangerous*'. He went on to charge Locke with having laid the foundations of scepticism. *The Bishop of Worcester's Answer to Mr. Locke's Second Letter* (London, 1698), pp. 120, 106f. These concerns would be echoed in Thomas Reid's subsequent criticisms of Descartes, Malebranche, and Locke. Descartes posits God as an idea, rather than a principle, the latter being closer to Herbert's conception.

[106] Descartes, *Discourse*, CSM 1, p. 124; *Meditations*, CSM 2, pp. 8, 15. For English writers who tended to separate the logic of innateness from common consent, see Reid, 'The Common Consent Argument', 414–16.

4.2 THE FORGOTTEN PROOF

the issue of the reliability of these mediating representations, which in turn necessitates additional arguments to establish the existence of the external world, other minds, and God. With the existence of God no longer enjoying axiomatic status, it now rested on the validity (or not) of arguments that were based upon other principles. In the philosophical theology of Spinoza and Leibniz, for example, the 'principle of sufficient reason' would assume the foundational role once occupied by the common notion of God. In Spinoza's original formulation the principle takes this form: 'Of every thing that exists, it can be asked what is the cause or reason why it exists.'[107] Leibniz would give this principle its familiar name, and propose that along with the principle of contradiction it was one of the necessary truths of reason.[108] Wolff considered it to be a self-evident logical axiom.[109] The new argument based on this principle proceeds from the question of how contingent things come to exist if the only things that exist do so contingently. This leads to the question of why anything exists at all. The explanation was that some thing must exist necessarily: God.[110] In speculative arguments for God's existence the principle of sufficient reason provided the foundation for new forms of the cosmological argument. Like Descartes's arguments, the principle of sufficient reason had the added advantage, as 'a necessary truth of reason' as Leibniz categorised it, of being of a different order to 'matters of fact'.[111] This again rendered it immune to falsification on empirical grounds, an advantage that the *consensus gentium* principle did not seem to enjoy. By the same token, the existence of God now became dependent upon the validity of specific philosophical arguments.

While Descartes and Locke shared a commitment to 'the way of ideas', they provided very different answers to the question of where these ideas

---

[107] Spinoza, *Principles of Cartesian Philosophy*, pt. I axiom II, CW, p. 133.
[108] Leibniz, *Monadology*, §32, in *Philosophical Writings*, ed. G. H. R Parkinson (London: Dent, 1934), p. 8. The principle of contradiction is the principle 'by virtue of which we judge to be false everything that involves a contradiction' (§31). For Leibniz, along with the principle of contradiction, the principle of sufficient reason (PSR) provided the foundation for all of our reasonings (§33, *Philosophical Writings*, p. 8).
[109] Christian Wolff, *Philosophia prima sive ontologia* (Frankfurt and Leipzig, 1730), §§56–78 (pp. 39–61). Wolff agrees with Leibniz that the law of contradiction is also foundational, but adds two further self-evident principles, the principle of excluded middle and the principle of certitude (§§52–5, pp. 35–9).
[110] Leibniz, *Monadology*, §§36–8 (pp. 9–10). For Wolff's application of the PSR in a proof of God based on the existence of the soul see *Theologia naturalis scientifica pertractata*, 2 vols. (Frankfurt, 1736–7), vol. 1, §24. Spinoza's arguments are less straightforward. See Martin Lin, 'Spinoza's Arguments for the Existence of God', *Philosophy and Phenomenological Research* 75 (2007), 269–97.
[111] Leibniz, *Monadology*, §§33–7 (p. 9).

originate. Locke offered penetrating criticisms of the thesis that the mind contains any innate principles or ideas. His magnum opus, *An Essay concerning Human Understanding* (1689), begins with an attack on Herbert's view that there are 'truths imprinted on the soul' – an attack that by extension would also apply to aspects of Descartes's programme. Locke pointed out that children, idiots, savages, and the illiterate – those whose minds were least likely to have been overwritten by culture or education – do not acknowledge such truths. But such acknowledgement would have been a prediction of the theory. As for the defence that our minds have a *propensity* to affirm certain propositions given particular conditions, this, Locke contended, is arguably indistinguishable from the mind's discovering them as a consequence of those conditions alone.[112] Arguments against innate ideas per se necessarily applied to the specific case of an inherent God-idea. Again, Locke's reasons for attacking this doctrine are related to his 'ethics of belief' commitments. Acceptance of innate ideas and the ruling consensus relieved the intellectually indolent of the burden of thinking for themselves.[113]

Moving from philosophy to anthropology, it was still possible to salvage universal consensus in the absence of innate principles by appealing to historical and anthropological considerations alone and positing alternative mechanisms to account for the universality of religion.[114] As noted in Chapter 2, Locke went the extra mile and sought to rule out this option as well. Reports from explorers, missionaries, and colonists fed back to Europe intelligence about peoples who seemed to entertain no conceptions of a Deity. Locke drew upon such reports to suggest that religious belief was not as ubiquitous as had typically been claimed. 'In these latter Ages', he contended, we have discovered 'whole Nations … amongst whom was to be found no Notion of a God, no Religion'.[115] This was not a new objection, given

---

[112] Locke, *Essay* 1.2.5, 1.2.12 (pp. 49–50, 53). Descartes had anticipated the first objection, explaining to Hobbes in the Third Set of Replies: 'when we say that an idea is innate in us, we do not mean that it is always there before us. This would mean that no idea was innate. We simply mean that we have within ourselves the faculty of summoning up the idea.' CSM 2, p. 132. Cf. *Comments on a Certain Broadsheet*, CSM 1, p. 304.

[113] Locke, *Essay* 1.4.24 (p. 101).

[114] Jean Le Clerc thus accepted his friend's position on innate ideas, but still upheld the idea of a *consensus gentium* on the basis on inherited tradition or individuals' arriving at common conclusions. See Reid, 'The Common Consent Argument', 418–20.

[115] Locke, *Essay* 1.4.8 (pp. 87f.). Richard Bentley agreed that there were instances of 'a whole Nation of Atheists' also denying on this basis the argument from innate theism. *Unreasonableness of Atheism*, pp. 31f., cf. p. 5. Part of Locke's motivation to deny universal consent and innate ideas was not only to correct what he regarded as a philosophical error, but also to ensure that the doctrine of innate ideas did not provide a refuge for those

contemporary anthropological discussions about theistic belief among exotic peoples, but this meant that there were already standard responses to it.[116] As we have seen, one was to contend that such societies represented such an unnatural depravity that they did not count against the main proposition.[117] Others simply denied that there were or could be nations of atheists, pointing out – often quite correctly – that explorers and colonisers lacked the linguistic ability and cultural sensitivity to discern the true beliefs of native peoples.[118] Pierre Bayle was on more secure ground when he came to make a case for the possible existence of 'societies of atheists'.[119] A key data-point for Bayle came from Jesuit missions to the Far East and their encounters with what would later become known as Buddhism.[120] In his dictionary article on Spinoza, whom he characterised as a 'systematic atheist', Bayle

---

seeking to shield cherished conceptions from rational scrutiny. See Nicholas Jolley, *Locke: His Philosophical Thought* (New York: Oxford University Press, 1999), p. 32.

[116] For a summary of this literature and a caution against attributing too much originality on this point to figures such as Locke and Pierre Bayle, see Kors, *Atheism in France*, pp. 146–50.

[117] Yves de Paris, *La Théologie Naturelle*, vol. 1, pp. 53f.; Robert Ferguson, *The Interest of Reason in Religion* (London, 1675), pp. 53–5. Specifically in response to Locke, see John Edwards, *The Eternal and Intrinsick Reasons of Good and Evil* (Cambridge, 1699), p. 18; Milner, *An Account of Mr Locks Religion*, p. 9, and *passim*.

[118] These included Locke's own source, the Huguenot missionary Jean de Léry, *Histoire d'un voyage faict en la terre du Brésil, autrement dite Amérique* (La Rochelle, 1578), who while initially questioning the Ciceronian principle of a *consensus gentium*, went on to concede that 'Cicero's adage is verified through them [the Brazilians] after all'. *History of a Voyage*, pp. 138f., cf. p. 134. See also Yves de Paris, *La Théologie Naturelle*, vol. 1, p. 82. Jesuit missionary and ethnologist Joseph François Lafitau made similar remarks about the putative atheism of native North Americans. *Moeurs des sauvages Américains*, 2 vols. (Paris, 1724), vol. 1, p. 29. See also René Joseph Tournemine, *Réflexions sur l'athéisme attribué à quelques peuples par les premiers missionnaires qui leur ont annoncé l'Evangile* in *Mémoires de Trévoux* (n.p., 1717). For similar objections from English writers, see Pelling, *Existence of God*, pp. 70–3; John Hancock, *Arguments to Prove the Being of God* (London, 1706), pp. 18–20; Leland, *Advantage and Necessity of the Christian Revelation*, vol. 1, pp. 65f. On the role of the *consensus gentium* doctrine in missionary activities of the period see Michael Schulz, 'Natural Knowledge of God in Early American Protestant and Catholic Theology', in *Philosophy of Religion in Latin America and Europe*, ed. Michael Schulz and Roberto Hofmeister Pich (Göttingen: Bonn University Press, 2020), pp. 51–74.

[119] Bayle, *Oeuvres Diverses*, vol. 3, pp. 109a–110b. For discussions of Bayle and responses to his position see Reid, 'The Common Consent Argument', 404–8; Kors, *Atheism in France*, pp. 139–55.

[120] The key source was the Jesuit *Confucius Sinarum Philosophus* (1687), which provided the first Latin translations of Chinese classics. Jesuit writings made reference to the Buddha, identified as 'Fo or Shija' and described as 'a most degenerate imposter and Prince of Atheism' who had 'led the literati and more intelligent people into atheism'. 'The Life of Confucius', in *Confucius Sinarum Philosophus*, trans. Thierry Meynard (Rome: Institutum Historicum Societatis Iesu, 2011), p. 239.

makes reference to Buddhism, suggesting that Spinoza's philosophy shared common features with 'several other ancient and modern philosophers, both European and Oriental'.[121] According to Bayle, while atheism may have been uncommon, there were sufficient historical instances to cast doubt on the universal consensus argument. Bayle's musings on this topic had a pervasive influence on the *philosophes* of the French Enlightenment.[122]

More generally, gains in knowledge from the voyages of discovery were matched with new scientific discoveries, including those based on telescopic and microscopic investigations. These also made it clear that just as cherished authorities had been wrong about such matters as whether the antipodes were inhabited, they had also been mistaken about the arrangement of the heavens. Bayle pointed out that before the seventeenth century the universal consensus was that the earth was at rest in the centre of the universe, again suggesting that in the sphere of natural philosophy, at least, the principle of universal consent was attended with fatal difficulties.[123] Where empirical questions were concerned, humanistic appeals to a general consensus, or even the past agreement of the learned – as epitomised in Cudworth's painstaking scholarship – no longer carried the day. All of this led to the re-evaluation of a long-standing prejudice against novelty, once regarded as a sure sign of unreliability.[124]

---

[121] Pierre Bayle, *Historical and Critical Dictionary: Selections*, ed. Richard H. Popkin (Indianapolis: Bobbs Merrill, 1965), s.v. 'Spinoza', n. B (pp. 288–93). On Bayle and Spinoza see Thijs Weststeijn, '*Spinoza sinicus*: An Asian Paragraph in the History of the Radical Enlightenment', *Journal of the History of Ideas* 68 (2007), 537–61. For Bayle's sources see Philip C. Almond, *The Buddha from East to West* (Cambridge: Cambridge University Press, 2024).

[122] It has been argued that Bayle's depictions of an implicitly desirable atheist East were motivated more by domestic concerns, including the 1685 revocation of the Edict of Nantes, than by an interest in anthropological precision. See Virgile Pinot, *La Chine et la formation de l'esprit philosophique en France (1640–1740)* (Geneva: Slatkine Reprints, 1971), p. 314. Gianluca Mori, however, suggests that Bayle sought to represent atheism as a viable theological option and one that, unlike Christianity, was compatible with 'common notions'. 'Pierre Bayle on Scepticism and "Common Notions"', in *The Return of Scepticism: From Hobbes and Descartes to Bayle*, ed. Gianni Paganini (Dordrecht: Kluwer, 2003), pp. 393–413; also, *Bayle philosophe* (Paris: Champion, 1999), pp. 50, 18.

[123] Bayle, *Oeuvres Diverses*, vol. 3, p. 692a.

[124] The label '*novatore*' – a peddler of the novel rather than the true – had borne strong negative connotations. Catholics thus alleged that Protestants were 'novatours' who had rejected 'the uniform ancient doctrine of the universal [Church]'. John Hamilton, *A Facile Traictise* (Leuven, 1600), pp. 32, 35. But '*novatore*' was to change valence during the early modern period, and become a badge of pride, especially in the sphere of the natural sciences. See Daniel Garber, 'Descartes among the Novatores', *Res Philosophica* 92 (2015), 1–19; 'Telesio Among the Novatores: Telesio's Reception in the Seventeenth Century', in *Early Modern Philosophers and the Renaissance Legacy*, ed. C. Muratori and G. Paganini (Dordrecht: Springer, 2016), pp. 119–33.

Finally, this period also saw the emergence of alternative explanations for the apparent universality of religiosity. Chief among them were fear theory and clerical or political imposture.[125] Fear theory goes as far back as Democritus, who argued that primitive humans were frightened by phenomena such as thunder and lightning, and invented the gods to account for them.[126] Fear and ignorance came to play a central role in theories of religion espoused by Hobbes, Vico, and Hume.[127] What follows from reductionist theories of this kind is that religion does not arise out of some primary religious instinct, but is instead a secondary phenomenon that results from the misapplication of a more fundamental human impulse or passion. In the early modern period, as with imposture, this theory was often presented as accounting for the corruption of religion, rather than its origin. But unalloyed versions of these arguments called the primacy of the religious instinct into question. While entertained by only a small minority, fear theory anticipated later reductionist, naturalising treatments of religion that became prevalent from the nineteenth century onwards.

Imposture theorists maintained that religion was the invention of priests and politicians. (Hence Lessius's proof of God's existence against 'politicians'.) The theory attributed Machiavellian motives to those in power, alleging that they had invented religion in order to maintain social control. Imposture and priestcraft theories were prevalent among the English deists.[128] Religion, on this view, had a cultural rather than a natural origin. It had already been argued, again as a consequence of early modern contact with numerous other cultures, that long-standing assumptions typically attributed to nature might actually be artefacts of culture. Michel de Montaigne (1533–92) had suggested in his essay 'Of Custom' that cultural conditioning can lead us to confuse habits with what is natural and universal: 'the *common notions* that we find in credit around us and infused into our soul by our fathers' seed, these seem to be the universal and natural ones'. As a consequence, 'what is off the hinges of custom, people believe to be off

---

[125] For these theories see Harrison, *'Religion' and the Religions*, pp. 14–18, 73–85. Euhemerism was another theory according to which religion had begun as a form of hero worship, with dead kings and heroes being elevated to divine status. *'Religion' and the Religions*, pp. 17f., 75.

[126] Sextus Empiricus, *Against the Physicists* 1.24 (LCL 311, p. 13).

[127] Hobbes, *Leviathan*, ch. 12, vol. 1, p. 166; Giambattista Vico, *The New Science* [1725], trans. T. G. Bergin and M. H. Frisch (Ithaca: Cornell University Press, 1948), §337; Hume, *Natural History of Religion*, pp. 27f.

[128] See, e.g., Charles Blount, 'Great is Diana of the Ephesians', in *Miscellaneous Works*, pp. 3, 7–14; *Oracles of Reason* (London, 1693), p. 125; John Toland, *Letters to Serena* (London, 1704), pp. 9, 130; Champion, *Pillars of Priestcraft Shaken*.

the hinges of reason'.[129] His compatriot Blaise Pascal (1623–62) agreed that 'natural principles' may simply be 'habitual principles', and that changes of habits will produce 'different natural principles'. It followed, as he famously remarked, that what was true on this side of the Pyrenees could be false on the other.[130]

In sum, multiple factors contributed to the declining popularity of the notion of a *consensus gentium*. For our purposes what the demise of this 'argument' signals is a portentous shift in the burden of proof, from the assumption that the existence of God is 'natural' and a default position, to the view that it was a proposition that needed to be argued for. It was this change of perspective that made the *consensus gentium* argument appear to post-seventeenth-century observers as if it were begging the question by assuming at the outset what had to be proven.

By the late eighteenth century, the argument based on universal consensus scarcely warranted a mention in systematic treatments of proofs for God's existence. Enlightenment thinkers either ignored it or summarily dismissed it. In Johannes Eberhard's authoritative 1781 overview of the arguments for God's existence, the 'proof based on the consensus of peoples' makes a brief appearance only to be rejected. Eberhard contended, albeit mistakenly, that the argument had been disputed 'from time immemorial'. But he also made reference to the objections of Locke and Bayle, which he regarded as decisive.[131] Eberhard was an important source for Kant, who also dismissed the argument in a brace of question-begging sentences. The proof 'from *the agreement of all nations* ... would not work at all'. This is because history teaches that all nations have believed in ghosts and witches, and still believe in them.[132] This conveniently meant that Kant did not have to fit it into his threefold classification of the proofs, which had no way of

---

[129] Michel de Montaigne, 'Of Custom', in *Complete Essays*, trans. Donald Frame (Stanford: Stanford University Press, 1958), p. 83. The French *coutume* has the meanings of both 'custom' and 'habit'.

[130] Pascal, *Pensées*, L60 [B 294] p. 46. Pascal, though ambivalent about Montaigne, had been influenced by him. Pierre Force, 'Innovation as Spiritual Exercise: Montaigne and Pascal', *Journal of the History of Ideas* 66 (2005), 17–35.

[131] Eberhard argued that both major and minor premises of the argument were dubious (major: whatever receives universal consent is true; minor; all nations believe in God). He offers no evidence for ongoing disputes about its status beyond referring to debates in Cicero. J. A. Eberhard and I. Kant, *Preparation for Natural Theology: With Kant's Notes and the Danzig Rational Theology Transcript*, ed. and trans. Courtney D. Fugate and John Hymers (London: Bloomsbury, 2016), p. 41.

[132] Immanuel Kant, *Lectures on the Philosophical Doctrine of Religion*, in *Religion and Rational Theology*, ed. and trans. Allen W. Wood and George Di Giovanni (Cambridge: Cambridge University Press, 1996), p. 354.

logically accommodating it.¹³³ Such was the influence of the Kantian classification that subsequent historical surveys – at least those conducted by philosophers – tend to omit reference to consensus arguments altogether.

Kant's critical philosophy was relevant in another crucial way. Kant granted the existence of a priori categories of thought, conceding that the principle of sufficient reason, like the categories of space and time, was one of the grounds of the possibility of experience. But this meant that its application was restricted to the sensible realm and that it could not be used to establish the existence of transcendental realities such as God.¹³⁴ The traditional proofs, on this reading, were illicit ventures into the realm of the supersensible.¹³⁵ Kant's, influential classification was thus shaped by his own agenda, that of establishing the limits of speculative reason and relocating the question of God into the sphere of practical reason. This set the scene for his alternative 'proof': God (along with human freedom and immortality) is 'an absolutely necessary presupposition for reason's most essential ends'.¹³⁶

Two nineteenth-century references to the argument, those of Hegel and John Stuart Mill, are also revealing about its fate. As might be expected, Hegel's explanation for the demise of the *consensus gentium* again illustrates the dominance of a particular version of the ethics of belief, namely, that individuals were now expected to arrive at their own conclusions about religious matters without being swayed by majority opinion: 'Cicero makes copious use of the *consensus gentium*; in more modern times this appeal has been more or less left alone, since the individual subject has to rest upon himself.'¹³⁷ Hegel refers to an identifiable change in historical consciousness – speaking of 'modern times' – in keeping with his own understanding of dialectical historical development. This is less an attack on the logic of the argument than an observation that moderns draw upon different resources to justify their beliefs. Why these are to be preferred comes down to Hegel's

---

¹³³ Immanuel Kant, *Critique of Pure Reason*, A591/B619, trans. Paul Guyer and Allen W. Wood (Cambridge: Cambridge University Press, 1998), p. 563. See also *Lectures on the Philosophical Doctrine of Religion* in *Religion and Rational Theology*, p. 354.
¹³⁴ Kant, *Critique of Pure Reason*, A201/B246 (p. 311).
¹³⁵ Kant, *Critique of Pure Reason*, A591/B619–A630/B658 (pp. 563–83).
¹³⁶ Kant, *Critique of Pure Reason*, A818/B846 (p. 684).
¹³⁷ Hegel, *Lectures on the History of Philosophy*, p. 5. Earlier Hegel had also suggested that there was empirical evidence against the universality of belief in God. *The Encyclopaedia Logic*, pt. 1, §71 [1817], trans. T. F. Geraets, W. A. Suchting, and H. S. Harris (Indianapolis: Hackett, 1991), pp. 118–19. Hegel nonetheless insists that religion must rest upon the immediate consciousness of God but implies that universal consent would then follow on from this and hence could not in itself be a justification for adopting religious belief.

vision of historical development as successive stages in the realisation of human freedom.[138]

John Stuart Mill's appraisal of the argument from universal consent also evinces the importance of the historical framing of the structure of arguments (a theme that will be explored in more detail in Chapter 6). As we have seen, Mill acknowledges the popularity of the *consensus gentium* proof. But he immediately proceeds to dismiss it on the grounds that 'historical treatment' of belief in God needs to make way for an approach that evaluates theistic claims 'by the same scientific methods, and on the same principles as those of any of the speculative conclusions drawn by physical science'. It is philosophy and the sciences – not history and scholarship, not tradition – that provide the resources for evaluating beliefs. This is consistent with the 'outsourcing' strategies of the previous period, but to a rather different end. Mill tells us that 'the religious traditions of mankind … are natural growths of the human mind, in particular stages of its career, destined to disappear and give place to other convictions of a more advanced age'.[139] The larger frame is itself a historical one – in this instance an assumption of progressive cultural evolution – that licenses the jettisoning of one mode of justification and its replacement by another. It is this background historical commitment, rather than any philosophical argument as such, that then warrants the displacement of the appeal to universal consent by a more 'advanced' scientific philosophy. Judgements of this kind are part of a general pattern of justifications for modern naturalism which, not to put too fine a point on it, might be said to reduce to forms of historical prejudice.

The reinstatement of the *consensus gentium* principle to its proper place of historical prominence is not simply a matter of adding a forgotten proof to the standard inventory, so that instead of the three classical proofs – ontological, cosmological, and teleological – we now have four. Grasping the significance of this principle adds a new dimension to our understandings of these other 'proofs' and how their evidentiary status changes in the early modern period. The obvious question to ask of this earlier period is that if belief in God was regarded as natural and universal, what purpose was served by the development of additional rational arguments to the same effect? Here we need to understand that while the sense of Deity might have been regarded as innate, it was also agreed to have been a rather diffuse and even confused conception, and one that fallible human creatures

---

[138] G. W. F. Hegel, *Lectures on the Philosophy of World History*, trans. H. B. Nisbet (Cambridge: Cambridge University Press, 1975), pp. 62–3.
[139] Mill, 'Theism', in *Collected Works*, vol. 10, pp. 430–1.

might on occasion have neglected. Some pre-modern 'proofs' can be understood as spiritual exercises intended to foster a deeper, contemplative understanding of God's nature. Others seek to provide additional logical substance to the rather vague sense of Deity to which the consent of the nations attested.

4.3 Subterranean Homesick Blues

In a fragment of one of Aristotle's many lost works, fortuitously preserved by Cicero, we are offered the following thought experiment:

> Suppose there were men who had lived always underground, in good and well-lighted dwellings, adorned with statues and pictures, and furnished with everything in which those who are thought happy abound. Suppose, however, that they had never gone above ground, but had learned by report and hearsay that there is a divine authority and power. Suppose that then, at some time, the jaws of the earth opened, and they were able to escape and make their way from those hidden dwellings into these regions which we inhabit. When they suddenly saw earth and seas and sky, when they learned the grandeur of clouds and the power of winds, when they saw the sun and learned his grandeur and beauty and the power shown in his filling the sky with light and making day; when, again, night darkened the lands and they saw the whole sky picked out and adorned with stars, and the varying lights of the moon as it waxes and wanes, and the risings and settings of all these bodies, and their courses settled and immutable to all eternity; when they saw those things, most certainly they would have judged both that there are gods and that these great works are the works of gods.[140]

---

[140] Aristotle, [De philosophia] F 12, Complete Works, vol. 2, p. 2392. Quoted in Cicero, De natura Deorum 2.37, 95–9. For commentary on this passage see A. P. Bos, Cosmic and Metacosmic Theology in Aristotle's Lost Dialogues (Leiden: Brill, 1989), ch. 13 (pp. 174–84); Eric Schliesser, 'On Aristotle's Cave', Digressions&Impressions, 18 January 2019, https://digressionsnimpressions.typepad.com/digressionsimpressions/2019/01/on-aristotles-cave-on-platos-cave-via-ahh-yes-cicero.html, accessed 19 January 2019. There is a similar passage in Philo of Alexandria, in which he speaks of men who 'have advanced upwards from below' into the world, and 'being struck with awe and amazement at these things, they are come to form notions consistent with what they behold, that all these beautiful things, excessive as they are, and of such admirable arrangement and contrivance, were not produced spontaneously but were the work of some maker, the Creator of the whole world ....' On Rewards and Punishments 7.41–3, in The Works of Philo, trans. C. D. Yonge (Peabody, MA: Hendrickson, 1993), p. 668. In the seventeenth century John Wilkins offered a variation of Aristotle's thought experiment, with a single subterranean dweller who, on being exposed to the surface world, needs to rely upon the consensus of others to understand that the natural world had been created. Of the Principles and Duties of Natural Religion (London, 1675), pp. 59–61.

The conceit of people living in a world beneath our own has been a recurring literary motif since antiquity. Much of the attraction of these stories comes from the possibility of drawing a contrast between ourselves and our underworld counterparts, and the narrative usually pivots on an incursion of the inhabitants of one world into the other. The allegory of Plato's cave is the best-known ancient version of this narrative, and moving to the Renaissance, Dante's *Inferno* is at least distantly related to this genre.[141] From the nineteenth century onwards, numerous works of science fiction have exploited this premise.

It is tempting to read Aristotle's parable as a version of the 'design argument'.[142] On that interpretation, the intended contrast is between the condition of those living in subterranean caverns and left to rely upon reports and hearsay for their evidence of divine power and authority, and that of those who escape from the limited perspective of their underground world and are able to see the order of the cosmos for themselves. Equipped with an evidence base denied to those left behind, the new arrivals are in a position to draw the correct logical inference from appearances of purpose in the world. But another way of thinking about this story is to imagine a different contrast being set up: one between those who have always dwelt under the sun and have ceased to marvel at the spectacle of nature and the new subterranean arrivals who are immediately struck by its wonders.

Cicero's commentary on the passage points us in the direction of the second reading: 'From daily habit our minds and eyes have become accustomed to this sight, and we no longer wonder at it, or seek a reason for something we have always known.'[143] In this version of events, we are prompted to

---

[141] The setting of the cave as the scene of a primordial event has precedents in Empedocles (Diels B 120, Loeb, R 56 (LCL 528, p. 661)). Hans Blumenberg explains that for later Neoplatonists 'the cave' becomes what he calls 'an absolute metaphor', representing a cosmos that is 'cut off from a realm of sheer transcendence that can no longer be reached by paideutic means', while for the Church Fathers, it becomes the site of a soteriological event. *Paradigms for a Metaphorology*, pp. 79–80. Blumenberg gives an extended treatment of the cave parable and its legacy in *Höhlenausgänge* (Frankfurt: Suhrkamp, 1989). See also Ward, *Unbelievable*, pp. 26–8. Nietzsche neatly inverts the standard metaphor in his preface to *Morgenröthe* (*Dawn*), describing himself as '*einen Bohrenden, Grabenden, Untergrabenden*' (a tunneller, miner, underminer) and characterising his philosophical labours as necessarily 'subterranean'. *Dawn*, §1, trans. Brittain Smith, *Complete Works*, vol. 5 (Stanford: Stanford University Press, 2011), p. 1.

[142] It may look like a teleological argument, but because Aristotle is not committed to divine design on the part of a creating Deity it is causal order that he draws attention to. And in any case, we may take the teleological argument to be a special case of the cosmological argument.

[143] Cicero, *De natura Deorum* 2.96 (LCL 268, p. 45). Strictly speaking it is Cicero's Stoic protagonist Balbus making this case. Plato will also refer to 'habituation' (Συνηθείας) in his

acknowledge what we ought to have seen all along. Others, over the centuries, made similar observations. Augustine would reprise this sentiment in his ruminations on the miraculous nature of the ordinary events of nature: 'Isn't the daily course of nature itself a miracle, something to be wondered at? Everything is full of marvels and miracles, but they are so common that we regard them as cheap and of no account.'[144] For John Calvin, too, the theatre of the world was an ongoing miracle that familiarity and ingratitude had rendered uninteresting and mundane.[145] Robert Boyle thought that 'the magnificent Fabrick of the Universe' would transport us 'with Wonder and Joy' were 'we not lulled asleep by Custom or Sensuality'.[146] In these instances, wonder is not just posited as the beginning of philosophy, as both Plato and Aristotle had observed, but of a related theistic understanding of the world and its operations.[147]

Aristotle's myth also brings to mind the lessons of Plato's more familiar allegory of the cave, which seeks to convey the importance of escaping the illusions foisted upon us by our bodily existence in a material world and to spur us into a recollection or reminiscence (*anamnesis*) of eternal truths lodged within our minds. This bears a resemblance to the Epicurean, Stoic, and Neoplatonic notions, discussed above, of an innate preconception or anticipation of God. Cicero's retelling of Aristotle's parable draws directly upon this idea, suggesting that sometimes the mind needs to be jolted into a conscious recognition of what in some sense has been known all along. Augustine would later use a similar description of how the image of God resides 'in the recesses of the mind', and that we may need reminding and prompting to bring it 'into the open'.[148]

Aristotle's tale further suggests that experiencing the reality of the gods is a matter of discernment and perspective, rather than argument and inference: a matter of 'seeing-as' to use a more recent philosophical coinage.[149] Again, Aristotle's primary purpose on this reading is not to present us with

---

relation of the allegory. *Republic* 516a, 517b (LCL 276, pp. 112–14). Yet another reading is that Aristotle is seeking to counter the contention that people only believe in the gods because of tradition.

[144] Augustine, *Sermons* 247, *Works*, III/7, p. 109.
[145] Calvin, *Institutes* 1.5.2, vol. 1, pp. 51f.; 'miracle' rendering the Lat. *mirificam signa*. Cf. *Commentary on the Psalms* 22, 104, *Calvin's Commentaries*, vol. 4, p. 369; vol. 6, pp. 149f.
[146] Boyle, *Usefulness of Natural Philosophy*, in *Works*, vol. 3, p. 204.
[147] Plato, *Theaetetus* 155d; Aristotle, *Metaphysics* 982b.
[148] Augustine, *On the Trinity* 14.2.9, *Works*, vol. 5, p. 377.
[149] The expression is associated with Wittgenstein, *Philosophical Investigations*, pt. 2, §11 (pp. 193–230). The task of philosophy, for Wittgenstein, is to come to see things from a particular point of view. Ludwig Wittgenstein, *Culture and Value*, trans. Peter Winch (Chicago: University of Chicago Press, 1984), p. 16. For Wittgenstein himself, this was a 'religious' point of view. See Norman Malcolm, *Wittgenstein: A Religious Point of View?*

his own version of one of the classical 'arguments for the existence of God', but rather to suggest that the reality of the divine is obvious to all whose sensibilities have not been dulled or overwritten by some form of aberrant cultural conditioning.[150] On this interpretation, Aristotle stands closer to the Psalmist of the Hebrew Bible than to modern exponents of 'the design argument'. While the latter propose that we think of the operations of nature as analogous to those of a watch and draw the inference that there must be a divine watchmaker, the Psalmist simply announces: 'The heavens declare the glory of God, and the firmament shows his handiwork, day unto day utters speech, and night unto night shows knowledge.'[151] Aristotle's cave-dwellers immediately *see* that nature is under the superintendence of the gods. Indirect inference and weighing of probabilities, in Aristotle's story, was the resort of those tenants of the subterranean world who, until their above-ground epiphany, were reliant upon 'report and hearsay'. What to modern readers may at first sight appear to be a kind of argument from design is more a commentary on how the world looks if viewed from a certain point of view. Arriving at the correct perspective, as Aristotle's parable implies, may call for some preparatory mental exercises.

The allegories of Plato and Aristotle suggest that things which ought to be obvious to the human mind, for various reasons, often are not. For Plato, embodiment was the problem. For Aristotle (on Cicero's reading), the problem lay in a kind of desensitisation to the wonders of nature through overfamiliarity. Aristotle also reflected upon the inherent limitations of human reason (again with a subterranean reference): 'as the eyes of bats are to the blaze of day, so is the reason in our soul to those things which are by nature the most evident of all'.[152] Christian thinkers would speak of the fallen condition of human beings – a broad recognition that the conditions of human finitude and the circumstances of earthly existence bring with them inescapable limitations. We now see through a glass, darkly.[153] These obstacles

---

(London: Routledge, 1993). For applications to religion see John Hick, 'Seeing-as and Religious Experience', in *Problems of Religious Pluralism* (New York: St. Martin's Press, 1985), pp. 16–27; N. K. Verbin 'Religious Beliefs and Aspect Seeing', *Religious Studies* 36 (2000), 1–23; J. Kellenberger, '"Seeing-as" in Religion: Discovery and Community', *Religious Studies* 38 (2002), 101–8. On parallels to the immediacy of native language use see Stephen Mulhall, *On Being in the World: Wittgenstein and Heidegger on Seeing Aspects* (London: Routledge, 1993), chs. 1–3.

[150] Cicero's Balbus offers a further thought experiment to reinforce this point. *De natura Deorum* 2.96.

[151] Psalm 19:1.   [152] Aristotle, *Metaphysics* 993b, *Works*, vol. 2, p. 1570.

[153] I Cor 13:12 KJV. The idea that philosophical exercises provide a means of avoiding error persisted into the modern period. Francis Bacon spoke of the obstacles presented by 'idols

were thought of in both moral and epistemological terms: our original orientation towards goodness *and* truth have been disrupted. The common theme is that unless our minds undergo some kind of preparatory regimen, the truth is likely to escape us. Imagined neutrality or disinterestedness are neither the starting point nor the goal. Rather it is a matter of being moved to a position where one can 'see' (or recollect) the truth, either from the mind's internal resources, or from an encounter with nature, or both. In short, some transformative process of intellectual and spiritual formation is called for. This, in turn, leads to a further process of intellectual enlightenment. For Plato, the right kind of engagement with the cosmos was an encounter that ultimately made the knower more god-like.[154] This was a common theme for both Neoplatonist philosophers and those Christian thinkers influenced by them.[155] Some of the traditional 'proofs', then, might be better understood as offering a regimen for changing one's perspective so that certain truths reveal themselves. Anselm's celebrated 'proof' of God's existence can be understood in this way.

Anselm of Canterbury (1033–1109) is best known today as the originator of 'the ontological argument'. When we begin to read this 'argument' for God's existence, however, we find ourselves in terrain that is some distance from the usual territory of philosophical argumentation. Here are parts of

---

of the mind'; Descartes and many others of the influence of the passions on reason. In the present, we have the 'critical thinking' phenomenon and psychological accounts of cognitive biases. Whether learning about logical fallacies and cognitive biases protects against committing them is an empirical question that remains open. For both sides see, e.g., D. Kahneman *Thinking, Fast and Slow* (New York: Farrar, Straus & Giroux, 2011); H. Arkes 'Cost and Benefits of Judgement Errors: Implications for Debiasing', *Psychological Bulletin* 110 (1992), 486–98; cf. Anne-Laure Sellier, Irene Scopelliti, and Carey K. Morewedge, 'Debiasing Training Improves Decision Making in the Field', *Psychological Science* 30 (2019), 1371–9. Of course, the problem with such psychological studies is that we tend only to learn of those with results that meet rather modest requirements for statistical significance.

[154] Plato, *Timaeus* 90d; f. 47b. Sedley, 'The Ideal of Godlikeness'.
[155] See Origen, *In Cantica Canticorum: Prologus* 3, *PG* 13: 73–5 (*ACW*, vol. 26, pp. 39–42); cf. Clement, *Stromata* 1.28; IX; Gregory Thaumaturgus, *Address of Thanksgiving* 8–9 (*FC* 109f.); John Cassian, *The Conferences* III.vi.4 (*ACW*, vol. 57, p. 125); Evagrius Ponticus, *Scholia on Proverbs* 247 (*Sources chrétiennes* 340, trans. Paul Géhin (Paris: Cerf, 1987), p. 343). For secondary treatments see Jean Daniélou, *Platonisme et théologie mystique*, 2nd ed. (Paris: Éditions Montaigne, 1953), pp. 17–26; Paul M. Blowers, '"Entering This Sublime and Blessed Amphitheatre": Contemplation of Nature and Interpretation of the Bible in the Patristic Period', in *Nature and Scripture in the Abrahamic Traditions*, vol. 1: *To 1700*, ed. Scott Mandelbrote and Jitse van de Meer (Leiden: Brill, 2008), pp. 147–77, esp. p. 162; Pui Him Ip, 'Physics as Spiritual Exercise', in *After Science and Religion: Fresh Perspectives from Philosophy and Theology*, ed. Peter Harrison and John Milbank (Cambridge: Cambridge University Press, 2022), pp. 282–98.

the opening sections of the *Proslogion*, the work in which the argument is to be found – with apologies for the lengthy quotation:

> turn aside for a while from your daily employment, escape for a moment from the tumult of your thoughts. Put aside your weighty cares, let our burdensome distractions wait, free yourself a while for God and rest awhile in him. Enter the inner chamber of your soul, shut out everything except God and that which can help you in seeking him, and when you have shut the door, seek him. Now, my whole heart, say to God, 'I seek your face, Lord, it is your face I seek'.
>
> How wretched is the fate of man when he has lost that for which he was created. How hard and cruel was the Fall .... He has lost the blessedness for which he was made and he has found wretchedness for which he was not made.
>
> I do desire to understand a little of your truth which my heart already believes and loves. I do not seek to understand so that I might believe, but I believe so that I may understand.[156]

Reading on to what is regarded as the kernel of the 'proof' itself, the culmination of this contemplative process comes with the recognition that if we rightly conceive of the nature of God, understood as 'a being than which none greater can be conceived', we will come to understand that the greatest possible being necessarily exists (since if the being we are imagining fails to exist, then there is a greater being, namely one that has the property of necessary existence). This, in brief, is the 'argument'.[157]

How do we assess the force of this putative proof? For a start, it seems obvious that Anselm is not attempting to provide a demonstration that will satisfy the atheist or agnostic. It is more a matter of seeking to explicate that nature of a God already known by faith and the mode of his existence. This leads to an understanding of God as a necessarily existing being. Moreover, Anselm's 'proof' has something in common with Aristotle's parable. Both imply that a certain amount of preparatory work is needed if the mind is to be in a position to grasp the truth. For Aristotle, the failure to grasp the

---

[156] Anselm, *Proslogion* 1.2–14, 50–3, 55–6, 154–5, in *The Prayers and Meditations of Saint Anselm, with the Proslogion*, trans. Benedicta Ward (Harmondsworth: Penguin, 1953), pp. 239, 241, 244. The original title for this piece, *Fides quaerens intellectum* (faith seeking understanding), conveys a sense of the starting point for the meditation.

[157] Some commentators have suggested that Anselm offers us two arguments, the second of which invokes necessary existence as a greater perfection than contingent existence. This would then provide a connection with one version of the cosmological argument. Norman Malcolm, 'Anselm's Ontological Arguments', *The Philosophical Review* 69 (1960), 41–62; A. D. Smith, *Anselm's Other Argument* (Cambridge, MA: Harvard University Press, 2014).

divine grounding of the cosmos arises out of an over-familiarity with the operations of nature that dulls our sensitivities. Accordingly, his exercise seeks to 'reset' our perceptions to jolt us into seeing again what we have forgotten. Plato's allegory of the cave seems also to prescribe a kind of reset with the intention of triggering a reminiscence of truths that are already known (albeit from a previous disembodied state). For Plato and, after him, Plotinus, the darkness of the cave stands in for the body and the material world which conspire against our accessing the truth. In the Christian tradition, as already noted, it is the sinful condition of humanity that constitutes the primary barrier between fallen human beings and God. In these examples, discovery of the truth is not accomplished through a naïve application of an unrectified reason. In fact, both Christians and Neoplatonists spoke of a 'fall' away from a pristine condition, so that regaining access to the transcendent is beset with obstacles.[158] Granting this, grasping the truth calls for a therapeutic process aimed at remedying the deficiencies of the mind in its present state.[159]

For these reasons Anselm frames his account with a preparatory reference to a fall from an original condition. We were created to *see* God, he says, but on account of sin are now unable to do so directly. Anselm is not setting out an argument to show that the existence of God should be immediately self-evident to all, as is sometimes claimed.[160] Instead he

---

[158] A link between the Christian notion of the Fall and the Platonic conception is provided by the Plotinian notion of a 'fall' into bodies. See Robert J. O'Connell, 'The Plotinian Fall of the Soul in St. Augustine', *Traditio* 19 (1963), 1–35.

[159] For a parallel argument to the effect that Anselm's 'argument' is to be understood as a form of *excitatio mentis* see Willemien Otten, 'Religion as *Excitatio Mentis*: A Case for Theology as a Humanist Discipline', in *Essays Offered to Arjo Vanderjagt on the Occasion of His Sixtieth Birthday*, ed. Z. R. W. M. von Martels and A. MacDonald (Leiden: Brill, 2009), pp. 60–73. The title of the first section of the *Proslogion* is *Excitatio mentis ad contemplandum deum* (exhortation of the mind to the contemplation of God). Otten explains *excitation mentis* as 'a series of mental exercises geared towards the mind's preparation for contemplation' (p. 64). See also Ward, *How the Light Gets In*, pp. 225–45; Lydia Schumacher, 'The Lost Legacy of Anselm's Argument: Re-thinking the Purpose for the Proofs of the Existence of God', *Modern Theology* 27 (2011), 87–101.

[160] Thomas Aquinas rejected the idea that the existence of God is self-evident *to us* on the basis that while we know *that* God is, we do not fully know *who* he is (i.e., we do not know his essence) and hence cannot reason from his essence to his existence. *ST* Ia 2, 1; *SCG* I.10–11. Schumacher has suggested that the argument being denied is Bonaventure's rather than Anselm's. Schumacher, *Divine Illumination*, p. 149. An important background question is 'what makes something self-evident?' and why what is immediately evident to some is not to others. Heidegger posed this question in relation to the fundamental categories of ontology, proclaiming that it was not enough simply to assert that some categories are self-evident. *Being and Time*, pp. 23, 37. It is relevant to the question of the burden of proof and, as we shall see, the 'proof' for God's existence from innate ideas.

suggests that in order to at least partially regain our original capacity to see God, we must commit ourselves to the task of finding God, set aside burdensome cares, rely on divine assistance, and so on. It is also necessary for God to do his part. Given that none of these conditions constitutes a prerequisite for contemporary philosophers engaging in an assessment of the validity of 'the ontological argument', it should not come as a complete surprise that Anselm's 'argument' is generally regarded by today's philosophical community as ingenious but unpersuasive. For his part, Anselm could reasonably respond that this situation arises not out of any deficiency in the logic of his argument, but out of a straightforward failure to follow the directions.

Anselm is not attempting a kind of 'view from nowhere' argument. This proof assumes a particular starting place – as Anselm explicitly states: 'from the point of view of one trying to raise his mind to contemplate God and seeking to understand what he believes'. For this reason, he gave the work the title 'faith seeking understanding' (*fides quaerens intellectum*). In the body of the *Proslogion*, as we have seen, he would repeat this sentiment: 'I do not seek to understand so that I may believe; but I believe so that I may understand.'[161] These, then, are conditions for 'getting' the argument, which cannot really be a 'proof' as we presently understand it. Alternatively, we might say that proofs, in the common usage, actually rely more on unstated presuppositions and uncritical starting points than we normally suppose.

Situating 'proofs' within an explicit faith context was common throughout the Middle Ages. The 'argument' of Augustine's classic *On the Trinity* is a sustained reflection on what he imagines to be the triune structures of human consciousness. The premise upon which Augustine operates is that by reflecting on this aspect of the divine image within we gain knowledge of both ourselves and God. The starting point cannot be one of dispassionate and disinterested neutrality, but rather a second-order desire to know God.[162] As Augustine expressed it, in language similar to that later deployed by Anselm: 'Teach me how to come to you. I have nothing else but the will

---

[161] *Proslogion*, Preface (pp. 238–9); 1.154–5 (p. 244). '*Neque enim quaero intelligere ut credam, sed credo ut intelligam*'. Latin version from *Anselmus Cantuariensis, Proslogion* 1, The Latin Library, www.thelatinlibrary.com/anselmproslogion.html#capi, accessed 2 February 2018.

[162] Augustine assumes that we can desire God without knowing him. As Jean-Luc Marion expresses it, referring to various passages in *De Trinitate*: 'Desire does not here presuppose the knowledge of what it loves but precedes it, and precedes it because it begets it.' *In the Self's Place: The Approach of St Augustine*, trans. Jeffrey L. Kosky (Stanford: Stanford University Press, 2012), p. 107.

4.3 SUBTERRANEAN HOMESICK BLUES

to come .... Show me. Provide for my journey.'[163] Aquinas's contemporary Bonaventure, the most prominent Augustinian thinker of the thirteenth century, begins his *Journey of the Mind to God* with a preamble that recalls both Augustine and Anselm: 'As I begin I call upon the First Beginning: The Father of Lights from whom all illumination descends.' In order to know God, he proposes, we must counter the effects of 'nature-deforming sin' and train the natural powers through prayer, living a good life, and contemplation.[164] These passages in Augustine and Bonaventure seem to have been less susceptible to modern reconstruction as 'proofs', presumably because the overtly theological context in which they occur was too obvious for even modern analytic philosophers to ignore.

It is tempting to think that these preparatory exercises are just instances of special pleading of a kind only required in the case of dubious theological arguments. But there is a strong case – articulated most persuasively by the French philosopher and historian Pierre Hadot – that most ancient philosophy had as its primary concern the practice of spiritual exercises and a way of life, as opposed to a focus on dialectic and doctrine.[165] It is these exercises that facilitate access to divine truth. If we look carefully at key discussions in Plato and Aristotle, for example, it becomes clear that they assume some connection between the direct intuition of the divine source of the motions of the cosmos and the leading of a properly ordered, *philosophical* life. Common to most ancient accounts of natural philosophy was the idea that the whole point of grasping the regularities of the cosmos was to direct this knowledge towards the regulation of one's own life. The study of order and purpose in the natural world was not aimed at providing an argument, it was not a search for evidence, but part of spiritual discipline.[166]

In the *Timaeus* Plato observes that 'God invented and gave us sight to the end that we might behold the courses of intelligence in the heavens, and apply them to the courses of our intelligence.' The idea of a direct

---

[163] Augustine, *Soliloquies* 1.1.5. Schumacher links this to divine illumination: 'Augustine regarded divine illumination as the source of an intrinsic intellectual ability, which is gradually salvaged from the effects of the fall as the mind re-learns to think in unifying terms in view of the existence of one God.' This re-learning involves the formation of 'a habit of reasoning in faith' *Divine Illumination*, p. 235.

[164] Bonaventure, *Itinerarium*, Prologue, 1.8, in *Works*, vol. 1, pp. 5, 12.

[165] Hadot, *Philosophy as a Way of Life*. See also John M. Cooper, *Pursuits of Wisdom: Six Ways of Life in Ancient Philosophy, from Socrates to Plotinus* (Princeton: Princeton University Press, 2012).

[166] See Rémi Brague, *The Wisdom of the World: The Human Experience of the Universe in Western Thought*, trans. Teresa Fagan (Chicago: University of Chicago Press, 2003); Hadot, *What is Ancient Philosophy?*; Harrison, *Territories*, pp. 26–34.

affinity between the divine regularities of the heavens and the motions of the human soul is reprised in a number of the Platonic dialogues. This 'philosophical way' is contrasted with the 'graceless ways that prevail amongst mankind generally'.[167] Comparable ideas were developed by Stoics and Middle Platonists.[168] The Alexandrian polymath Claudius Ptolemy (*c.*100–*c.*170 CE), whose astronomical and geographical writings provided core texts for medieval science, offers an uncompromising statement of the principle in the preface of his famous *Almagest*. The study of the heavens is to be pursued because it 'prepares understanding persons with respect to nobleness of actions and character by means of the sameness, good order, due proportion, and simple directness contemplated in divine things, making its followers lovers of that divine beauty, and making habitual in them, and as it were natural, a like condition of the soul'.[169] The Neoplatonist philosopher Simplicius (*c.*480–560 CE) followed this logic in his commentary on Aristotle's *Physics*. The study of physics is to be pursued not merely on account of the practical benefits that it promises, but most importantly because it contributes to 'the perfection of the soul, leads us towards knowledge of God, and enkindles within us acts of piety and thanksgiving'.[170] In these discussions it is clear that neither philosophy nor 'science' are understood in terms of disinterested doctrines – not 'justified true beliefs' – but involve a dialectical process that calls for an adjustment and ordering of the individual's life in order to encounter more intimately a reality that is divine, or infused with the divine.

In terms of the standard classification of proofs, these Platonic treatments are more suggestive of 'design' arguments than 'ontological' arguments. But this interpretative frame should not prevent us from seeing the common formative elements in these exercises. Anselm's prologue is not just pious and idiosyncratic window dressing but draws upon a long-standing

---

[167] Plato, *Timaeus*, 47a–e, *Collected Dialogues*, p. 1175. Cf. 'And the motions which are naturally akin to the divine principle within us are the thoughts and revolutions of the universe. These each man should follow, and by learning the harmonies and revolutions of the universe, should correct the courses of the head which were corrupted at our birth, and should assimilate the thinking being to the thought, renewing his original nature.' *Timaeus* 90d (p. 1209). See also *Republic* VI, 500d; *Laws* IV 716a–d, X, 904d–e; *Phaedrus* 246d, 248a; *Theaetetus* 176a–d; *Republic* X, 613b.

[168] Gretchen Reydams-Schils, '"Becoming like God" in Platonism and Stoicism', in *From Stoicism to Platonism: The Development of Philosophy, 100 BCE–100 CE*, ed. T. Engberg-Pedersen (Cambridge: Cambridge University Press, 2017), pp. 142–58.

[169] *Ptolemy's Almagest* 1.1. trans. R. Catesby Taliaferro (Chicago: Encyclopedia Britannica, 1952), p. 6.

[170] Simplicius, *In Physica*, quoted in Brague, *Wisdom of the World*, p. 115.

philosophical tradition in which accessing the truth calls for a certain preparatory work to be conducted upon the self. Augustine regarded Socrates as exemplary in this respect: 'he believed that the first and highest cause exists in nothing but the will of the one supreme God; hence that the causation of the universe could be grasped only by a purified mind'.[171]

The example of Socrates adds another, perhaps unexpected, dimension to this discussion about how the truth is to be approached. Socrates frequently recounted how his own philosophical endeavours had been guided by a *daimonion* – variously understood by commentators as divine sign, spiritual monitor, an inner voice.[172] The difficulties that beset the translator in rendering this entity intelligible to the modern reader arise out of Socrates' casual and unselfconscious references to a guiding divine voice juxtaposed with his reputation as the progenitor of a supposedly rational Western philosophical tradition.[173] Socrates clearly thought that it was entirely natural that he be guided by an inner divine voice. Such guidance could be understood as another kind of preparatory or rehabilitating process, and as lending additional authority to the Socratic message.

Treating mysterious voices, apparitions, and dreams as sources of philosophical inspiration was commonplace until well into the modern period. Socrates again offers a precedent, reporting a recurring dream that he understood as exhorting him to the study of philosophy.[174] Boethius (477–524), the translator of Plato and Aristotle and chief intermediary between the classical and the early medieval worlds, offers a further striking example. In the opening passage of *The Consolation of Philosophy*, a work that would become one of the most prized texts of the Middle Ages, we encounter our downcast and disheartened protagonist, unjustly imprisoned for treason by the Ostrogothic King Theodoric and destined for execution. He receives an unexpected visit

---

[171] Augustine, *City of God* 8.3.
[172] 'δαιμόνιον'. Plato, *Apology* 31d, 40a–c; 41c–d; *Euthyphro* 3b; *Phaedrus* 242b–d; *Republic* 496c; *Theaetetus* 151a; *Euthydemus* 272e–273a; *Theages* 128d–129e. Cf. Xenophon, *Memorabilia* 1.1.1–5; Cicero, *De Divinatione* 1.54.
[173] For discussions of Socrates' *daimonion*, which vary in their attempts to naturalise it, see John Bussanich, 'Socrates and Religious Experience', in *A Companion to Socrates*, ed. Sara Ahbel-Rappe and Rachana Kamtekar (New York: Wiley, 2009), pp. 200–13; Mark L. McPherran, 'Socratic Religion', in *The Cambridge Companion to Socrates*, ed. Donald R. Morrison (Cambridge: Cambridge University Press, 2011), pp. 111–37; John M. Rist, 'Plotinus and the *Daimonion* of Socrates', *Phoenix* 17 (1963), 13–24; Osamu Muramoto and Walter G. Englert, 'Socrates and Temporal Lobe Epilepsy', *Epilepsia* 47 (2006), 652–4; Anna Lännström, 'Trusting the Divine Voice: Socrates and His Daimonion', *Apeiron* 45 (2012), 32–49.
[174] Plato, *Phaedo* 60c–61a.

from the Lady Philosophy: 'While I was pondering thus in silence, there appeared standing over my head a woman's form, whose countenance was full of majesty, whose eyes shone as with fire, and whose power of insight surpassed that of all men.' Lady Philosophy says to him: 'I understand the cause of your sickness – you have forgotten who you are .... It is what you cannot remember that causes you to feel lost, and grieve about your exile.' She then prompts Boethius to remember 'the universal end to which all nature is directed' and assures him that the divine reason that governs the world is also a 'divine spark' within him, and from which his recovery may be kindled.[175]

Like Anselm's prologue, this is not a component of philosophical reasoning that receives much attention in contemporary philosophy of religion texts: a psychologically fragile man, languishing in prison, taking philosophical counsel from an imaginary woman. It would take some courage to begin a modern work of philosophy with this kind of prolegomenon. But its affinity to other stage-setting exercises for the philosophical quest is clear: Boethius' state of incarceration brings to mind both the Pythagorean/Platonic formula of the body as the prison (from the alliterative Greek *soma sema*) and the allegorical 'caves' of Plato and Aristotle.[176] He has 'forgotten' who he is, echoing the Platonic theme of philosophising as a form of recollection, and the Aristotelian motif of the underground dwellers coming to their senses.

In the thirteenth century, Roger Bacon (c.1214–94), often regarded as a precocious forerunner of early modern experimental science, also conceded the philosophical role played by divine inspiration. Bacon maintained that knowledge by experience comes in two forms: external and internal. The former comes via the senses but gives rise only to partial knowledge. The

---

[175] Boethius, *The Consolation of Philosophy* 1.1 (LCL 74, pp. 133–7).
[176] Literally, the body, a grave. Plato, *Phaedrus* 250c; *Phaedo* 67d–e. Compare Al-Ghazali who describes a sceptical episode followed by divine illumination, in language not too distant from Augustine, and later rehearsed in Descartes's *Meditations*: 'This malady was mysterious and it lasted for nearly two months. During that time I was sceptic in fact, but not in utterance or doctrine. At length God Most High cured me of that sickness. My soul regained its health and equilibrium and once again I accepted the self-evident data of reason and relied on them with safety and certainty. But this was not achieved by constructing a proof or putting together an argument. On the contrary, it was the effect of a light which God Most High cast into my breast. And that light is the key to most knowledge.' Muhammad-i Al-Ghazali, *Al-Ghazali's Path to Sufism: His Deliverance from Error (al-Munqidh min al-Dalal)*, trans. R. J. McCarthy (Louisville, KY: Fons Vitae, 2000), p. 66. I can't vouch for this translation, and 'self-evident data of reason' sounds a little anachronistic. For commentary and comparison to Descartes, see Mahmoud Zakzouk, *Al-Ghazālīs philosophie im vergleich mit Descartes* (Frankfurt: Peter Lang, 1992); Tamara Albertini, 'Crisis and Certainty of Knowledge in Al-Ghazali and Descartes', *Philosophy East and West* 55 (2005), 1–14.

latter, a form of spiritual experience, yields a more complete knowledge even about corporeal things. Accordingly, the patriarchs and prophets who 'first gave science to the world' gained their knowledge by means of an 'inner light'. So, too, many Christians since. 'Divine inspiration', Bacon concludes, pertains not just 'to spiritual things but also to the physical and philosophical sciences'.[177]

This was not just a mystical medieval belief. 'Supernatural' visitations would continue to provide inspiration for philosophers and experimenters until well into the early modern period. Herbert of Cherbury recalled in his autobiography that the publication of *De veritate* had received a direct divine sanction: 'a Loud though yet Gentle noise came from the Heavens (for it was like nothing on Earth) ... whereupon also I resolved to print my Book'.[178] Dreams and visions were not uncommon sources for alchemical experimenters such as Jan Baptista Van Helmont and George Starkey.[179] Robert Boyle, whose approach towards chemical experimentation was influenced by the Van Helmont circle, was more reticent to admit the possibility of such communications – not out of any scepticism but, to the contrary, on account of his fears of magic, malevolent spirits, and the idolatrous worship of good angels. But even Boyle allowed that God did 'promote some Mens Proficiency in the study of Nature' by providing some with 'happy and pregnant hints'.[180]

---

[177] Roger Bacon, *The Opus Majus of Roger Bacon*, 2 vols., ed. Roger Bridges (Oxford: Clarendon Press, 1897), vol. 2, p. 169.

[178] Herbert of Cherbury, *The Life of Edward, Lord Herbert of Cherbury*, ed. J. M. Shuttleworth (Oxford: Oxford University Press, 1976), p. 120.

[179] Starkey to Boyle, 26 Jan. 1652, in George Starkey, *Alchemical Laboratory Notebooks and Correspondence*, ed. William R. Newman and Lawrence M. Principe (Chicago: University of Chicago Press, 2004), p. 69.

[180] Robert Boyle, *Usefulness of Natural Philosophy*, Works, vol. 3, p. 276. Boyle references Jacob's dream in Genesis 30. See n. 181 below. For discussion of Boyle and his relation to Van Helmont and Starkey see William R. Newman and Lawrence M. Principe, *Alchemy Tried in the Fire* (Chicago: University of Chicago Press, 2002), pp. 198–206, and William R. Newman, 'Spirits in the Laboratory: Some Helmontian Collaborators of Robert Boyle', in *For the Sake of Learning: Essays in Honor of Anthony Grafton*, ed. Ann Blair and Anja-Silvia Goeing (Leiden: Brill, 2016), pp. 621–40. More recently, organic chemist Auguste Kekulé was said to have come upon the hexagonal ring structure of Benzene following a dream involving a snake devouring its own tail (an ouroboros). This anecdote is very likely apocryphal. Alan J. Rocke, *Image and Reality: Kekulé, Kopp, and the Scientific Imagination* (Chicago: University of Chicago Press, 2010), pp. 194, 312f. Likewise, the story of Dmitri Mendeleev's formulation of the period table, and Otto Loewi's discovery of neurochemical transmission, both said to have resulted from dreams. Better attested is Cantor's contention that God had directly communicated to him the theory of transfinite numbers. See Joseph Dauben, *Georg Cantor* (Princeton: Princeton University Press, 1990), pp. 239, 290. Srinivasa Ramanujan also contended that many of his mathematical proofs had been communicated to him, in dreams, by the Hindu goddess Namagiri.

Along the same lines, the touted founder of modern philosophy, René Descartes, recounts that his whole philosophical vocation was inspired by a 'night of dreams' on St Martin's Eve, 10 November 1619.[181] The young Descartes was convinced that this series of visions 'could have come only from on high' and interpreted them as portending that he would found a new and comprehensive mathematical science. He further reports that he turned to God, asking him to reveal his will and 'conduct him in the search for truth' and vowed to the Virgin that he would visit her shrine at Loretto.[182] Descartes follows this up with specific meditative prescriptions in the canonical works that are now mandatory reading for fledgling philosophers. These prescriptions are often simply passed over in silence by those focused on the content of the arguments, but for the attentive reader they are difficult to miss. They also mark a point of difference from typical works of metaphysics for which the standard genre was the disputation or formal treatise.[183] In the *Discourse on the Method* and *Meditations* we encounter an attenuated version of the kind of meditational prelude that Anselm invites his readers to undertake. The *Discourse* (1635) provides the reader with a set of directions, accompanied by what by modern standards is a surfeit of gratuitous biographical material.

[181] The idea of dreams as divine communications has a long history. Socrates was reported to have had a recurring dream in which he was urged to cultivate the art of philosophy. Plato, *Phaedo* 60e–61b. Aristotle spoke of 'the melancholy men the dreamers of what is true'. *Eudemian Ethics* 1248a40. (Although in *On Divination in Sleep* 458b10–15 he seems more sceptical.) Michael J. Woods, 'Aristotle on Sleep and Dreams', *Apeiron* 25 (1992), 179–88. Genesis 31 tells of how Joseph gained knowledge of sheep breeding in a dream, which gave biblical licence to the idea of the divine origin of at least some dreams. Philo of Alexandria also referred to such dream stories in the Hebrew Bible in *De somniis* 1–2, distinguishing three different kinds of dream, the first of which were said to have been sent by God. See M. J. Reddoch, 'Enigmatic Dreams and Onirocritical Skill in *De somniis* 2', *The Studia Philonica Annual* 25 (2013), 1–16. See also Troels Engberg-Pedersen, 'Philo's *De vita contemplativa* as a Philosopher's Dream', *Journal for the Study of Judaism in the Persian, Hellenistic, and Roman Period* 30 (1999), 40–64.

[182] 'le conduire dans la recherche de la vérité'. The report of the dream is provided by Descartes's first biographer, Adrien Baillet, *La Vie de M. Des-Cartes*, 2 vols. (Paris, 1691), vol. 1, pp. 80–6, in AT X, 180–5. See also Descartes, *Early Writings*, §216, CSM 1, p. 4. See Paul Mahoney, 'Christian Inspiration in Descartes' Olympic Dreams', *Heythrop Journal* 54 (2013), 371–84. Gilson, Gouhier, and Lewis argue that divine inspiration underpins Cartesian philosophy. See Richard Kennington, 'Descartes' Olympia', in *On Modern Origins: Essays on Early Modern Philosophy*, ed. P. Kraus and F. Hunt (New York: Lexington Books, 2004), pp. 79–100.

[183] There were, however, contemporary precedents for the meditative approach in Marin Mersenne's *L'usage de la raison* (Paris, 1623). There are also significant meditative elements in Pierre Charron, *De la Sagesse livres trois* (Bourdeaux, 1601) and Jean de Silhon, *L'immortalité de l'âme* (Paris, 1634). See Matt Hetche, 'Descartes and the Augustinian Tradition of Devotional Meditation: Tracing a Minim Connection', *Journal of the History of Philosophy* 48 (2010), 283–311.

Descartes's claim for these instructions is more modest than that of Anselm. These steps worked for him, he tells us, and we can follow them if we choose:

> My present design, then, is not to teach the method which each ought to follow for the right conduct of his reason, but solely to describe the way in which I have endeavored to conduct my own. ... But as this tract is put forth merely as a history, or, if you will, as a tale, in which, amid some examples worthy of imitation, there will be found, perhaps, as many more which it were advisable not to follow, I hope it will prove useful to some without being hurtful to any, and that my openness will find some favor with all.

Descartes will offer a version of the ontological argument in this work and present it again in his *Meditations*. The latter work also offer some preparatory instructions: 'Today, then, since I have opportunely freed my mind from all cares' (compare Anselm's 'cast aside your burdensome cares') 'and am happily disturbed by no passions, and since I am in the secure passion of leisure in a peaceable retirement, I will at length apply myself earnestly and freely ...' etc.[184] Descartes is quite specific in offering instructions to prospective readers, recommending the book only to 'those who are able and willing to meditate seriously with me'. Foreseeing fussy philosophical objections, Descartes urged potential critics to follow his meditative path, convinced that this would allay 'carping' and 'quibbling'. Again, the 'argument' requires that we adhere to the instructions.[185] The title, moreover, was deliberately chosen, and calls to mind the traditional genre of spiritual exercises.[186] The *Meditations* can be read as a set of practical prescriptions

---

[184] Meditation 1. Relying here on John Veitch's translation, in *The Method, Meditations and Philosophy of Descartes* (Washington, DC: M. Walter Dunne, 1901), Meditation 1, p. 219; Cf. CSM 2, p. 12.

[185] Descartes, CSM 2, p. 8.

[186] Numerous commentators have pointed to the significance of this connection. See, e.g., Pierre Mesnard, 'L'Arbre de la sagesse', *Descartes, Cahiers de Royaumont, Philosophy* II (Paris, 1957), 336–49, and discussion, 350–9; Hadot, *Ancient Philosophy*, pp. 264f.; L. J. Beck, *The Metaphysics of Descartes: A Study of the Meditations* (Oxford: Oxford University Press, 1965), 28–38; Matthew Jones, 'Descartes's Geometry as Spiritual Exercise', *Critical Inquiry* 28 (2001), 40–72; Amélie O. Rorty, 'The Structure of Descartes' Meditations', in *Essays on Descartes' Meditations*, ed. Amélie O. Rorty (Berkeley: University of California Press, 1986), pp. 1–20, and in the same volume Gary Hatfield, 'The Senses and the Fleshless Eye: The Meditations as Cognitive Exercises', pp. 45–79; Walter Stohrer, 'Descartes and Ignatius Loyola: La Flèche and Manresa Revisited', *Journal of the History of Philosophy* 17 (1979), 11–27; Arthur Thomson, 'Ignace de Loyola et Descartes: L'influence des exercises spirituels sur les oeuvres philosophiques de Descartes', *Archivs de philosophie* 35 (1972), 61–85; Z. Vendler, 'Descartes' Exercises', *Canadian Journal of Philosophy* 19 (1989), 193–224; Dennis Sepper, 'The Texture of Thought: Why Descartes'

for purging philosophical prejudices. 'My habitual opinions kept coming back, and despite my wishes they capture my belief', Descartes tells us.[187] Hyperbolic doubt is an example of one strategy that Descartes deploys to overcome habitual philosophical prejudices. He eventually progresses to the ontological argument, bringing the meditator to a position where God's necessary existence can be grasped clearly and distinctly.[188] This then provides the secure foundation that he needs for his philosophical enterprise: 'now that I have perceived that God exists ... I have drawn the conclusion that everything which I clearly and distinctly perceive is of necessity true'.[189] Such immediate perceptions are the end-product of the meditative process. As we will see, there are important differences between the framing of Anselm's argument and Descartes's more attenuated prescriptions. But they share, to a degree, the process of setting out the preparatory steps required to move the mind to a position where it can grasp the truth.

Descartes's contemporary, Blaise Pascal, offers another example of locating a 'proof' of God's existence within an explicitly religious context. Pascal was one of Descartes's staunchest critics and was strenuously opposed to what he called 'the God of the philosophers' – a theoretical Deity whose existence could be established by reason.[190] Yet Pascal is usually taken to have offered his own, alternative, justification for believing in the existence of God – 'the wager'. This is often understood as a prudential argument for belief, based upon a weighing up of probabilities. In a nutshell: what is

---

Meditationes Is Meditational, and Why It Matters', in *Descartes' Natural Philosophy*, ed. Stephen Gaukroger, John Schuster, and John Sutton (London: Routledge, 2000), pp. 736–50. More sceptical about the link between Descartes's work and the traditional spiritual exercises is Bradley Rubidge, 'Descartes's *Meditations* and Devotional Meditations', *Journal of the History of Ideas* 51 (1990), 27–49. Descartes himself explained that he wished to avoid the more common title 'Disputations' because he wanted to stress the importance of readers' joining him in meditation. *Objections and Replies*, CSM 2, p. 112.

[187] Descartes, *Meditations*, CSM 2, p. 15.
[188] For an argument to this effect see Lawrence Nolan, 'The Ontological Argument as an Exercise in Cartesian Therapy', *Canadian Journal of Philosophy* 35 (2005), 521–62. Nolan proposes that 'proof' for Descartes 'is not a matter of having a certain logical form, not an expression of logical relations between propositions, but a psychological process whereby prejudices which have been contingently formed are dispelled to produce clear and distinct ideas' (559).
[189] Descartes, *Meditations*, CSM 2, p. 48. And further: 'Thus I see plainly that the certainty and truth of all knowledge depends uniquely on my awareness of the true God' (p. 49). It is also worth noting that the innate idea of God again makes an appearance here: 'the mark of the craftsman stamped on his work' which is nothing other than God's image and likeness. *Meditations*, CSM 2, p. 35, cf. Descartes, *Rules*, IV, CSM 1, p. 17; *Discourse* II, CSM 1, p. 124; 'Early Writings', CSM 1, p. 4.
[190] Pascal, *Pensées*, L 913, p. 309.

gained by believing in God is infinite – eternal life; what is gained by not believing, if anything, can only be finite. Weighing up potential gains and losses, the prudential decision must be for belief.[191] But the true moral of the wager follows this discussion, with Pascal's insistence that genuine belief is not motivated by reasons nor by prudential calculations, but emerges out of rightly ordered desire and religious practice. It is possible for the faithless to acquire beliefs, but only through participation in a religious form of life:

> You want to find faith and do not know the road. You want to be cured of unbelief and you ask for the remedy: learn from those who were once bound like you, and who now wager all they have. These are people who know the road you wish to follow, who have been cured of the affliction of which you wish to be cured: follow the way by which they began. They behaved just as if they did believe, taking holy water, having masses said, and so on. This will make you believe quite naturally.[192]

There are obvious parallels here with the method set out by Anselm, for whom the starting point is not agnosticism with respect to the outcome of the argument, but an attitude of trust in the source of truth. Pascal begins a step before this, not with faith, but with a second-order desire to have faith.[193] Behind all of this lies Pascal's celebrated 'reasons of the heart', not intended as a mawkish metaphor, but as a strong claim for an alternative order of evidence grounded in love and based in the will.[194] The overall approach, like that of Descartes, comports with a central theme of ancient philosophy, understood as a way of life. But it also suggests that an imagined disinterestedness is the wrong place to start and that, contra Descartes and the ancient Stoics, freeing oneself from the passions may take one to a different destination.

Returning to the Middle Ages, it must be conceded that not all arguments for God's existence are prefaced by the kind of elaborate stage-setting that we encounter in Anselm. The most celebrated medieval arguments for God's existence – the 'five ways' of Thomas Aquinas – seem to be presented with little fanfare and few preparatory demands being placed upon the reader. Indeed, Aquinas is often regarded as having initiated an uncompromising brand of natural theology, understood, in the sense already

---

[191] Pascal, *Pensées*, L 418 [B 233], pp. 149–53. [192] Pascal, *Pensées*, L 418 [B 233], p. 152.
[193] A second-order desire is a desire about our desires. See Harry Frankfurt, 'Freedom of the Will and the Concept of a Person', *The Journal of Philosophy* 68 (1971), 5–20. Second-order desires are sometimes said to be a distinguishing feature of human beings.
[194] For a comparison of Pascal and Descartes on this issue see Marion, *On the Ego and on God*, pp. 63–79.

provided, as arguments that provide support for religious beliefs by starting from premises that are non-religious or neutral.[195] But no one at the time could have begun from such premises, which would have seemed unintelligible. Simply to establish the remote theoretical possibility of someone not believing in the existence of God Aquinas had to appeal to scripture.[196] In any case, Aquinas clearly *does* begin with theological presuppositions for his celebrated arguments in the article that proceeds their enumeration. Here the question is posed: 'Whether it can be demonstrated that God exists?' The enquiry is directed to whether the existence of a being already known and worshipped can be demonstrated. Aquinas answers in the affirmative, but on the basis that we know this from what is revealed in scripture.[197] It turns out to be an article of *faith* that the existence of God can be proved by *reason*, and it is this that prompts Aquinas to seek demonstrations. It is at least conceivable, then, that we might hold God's existence to be provable without being in possession of any actual proofs. In the previous century, Richard of St Victor seems to suggest just this: 'I believe that arguments are not lacking for explaining those things that exist necessarily; not just probable arguments, but necessary ones, *even if our efforts have not yet uncovered them.*'[198] At any rate, Aquinas's position is not inconsistent with Anselm's principle of 'faith seeking understanding' and Augustine's suggestion that we 'believe in order to understand'. Nothing foundational hangs on the proofs, which Aquinas explores partly as the exposition of a biblical text.

---

[195] This is typically argued on the basis of the opening sections of *Summa contra gentiles*, where Aquinas seems to make a distinction between what knowledge can be obtained by natural reason and philosophy alone and what by divine revelation (*SCG* 1.2). See, e.g., Norman Kretzmann, *The Metaphysics of Creation: Aquinas's Natural Theology in Summa Contra Gentiles* (Oxford: Oxford University Press, 1998). But as we have seen, philosophy and reason are already understood in theistic and teleological terms. Philosophy is thus the activity that promotes the ultimate end of the human intellect 'as intended by the first author or mover', and the whole universe has as its end 'the good of the intellect' or truth. Yet again our present naturalistic understanding of 'natural' can get in the way of the interpretative process.

[196] Aquinas, *ST* 1a. 2, 1. 'The Fool says in his heart: "There is no God"'. Ps. 14:1.

[197] Aquinas cites Romans 1:19–20a: The context is not an apologetic attempt to persuade unbelievers, but commentary on two biblical passages that seem slightly at odds with each other, i.e., Ps. 14:1 and Rom. 1:19–20.

[198] Richard of St Victor, *On the Trinity* 1.4 (*PL* 196: 892) (my emphasis). Aquinas makes a related point at the very beginning of the *Summa theologiae*, when he contends that theology is not a genuine science for us, since we do not enjoy the kind of knowledge of God that he has of himself. Theology is thus a subordinate science, deriving its principles from the higher science of God's self-knowledge. *ST* 1a. 1, 2.

Some commentators have suggested, moreover, that in spite of the absence of the kind of pious preamble that we encounter in Anselm's *Proslogion*, Aquinas's five ways do bear important similarities to the earlier argument, and that they can be seen as a form of contemplative practice. Lydia Schumacher contends that the arguments 'promote the constant vision of God through experiences in the world, which presupposes the abandonment of the fallen assumption that anything in the world including the self is as important as God'.[199] Leo Elders has suggested that the five ways can be mapped onto the 'three ways' of ascent to God set out by Dionysius (*via negationis, via causalitatis, via eminentiae*).[200] These stages have been detected in Descartes's *Meditations*, too.[201]

Aquinas's terminology is also informative. As just noted, the use of 'ways' (*viae*) calls to mind the language of spiritual exercises and mystical ascent to God.[202] Aquinas's expressions for 'proof' also move around. When he first poses the question of whether God's existence can be demonstrated he uses the Latin *demonstrabile*, which suggests a logical or mathematical proof, but when enumerating the 'proofs' he switches to the weaker *probāre* (or even *ostendere* –to show, or illustrate).[203] Just as the English 'prove' has meanings that extend beyond 'logical demonstration', *probāre* can mean 'to demonstrate through the work of the mind what is already the case' or 'to try, test, examine, inspect, judge of any thing in respect of its goodness'.[204] As already

---

[199] Schumacher, *Divine Illumination*, p. 172; 'The Lost Legacy of Anselm's Argument', 98. See also Fergus Kerr, *After Aquinas: Versions of Thomism* (Oxford: Blackwell, 2002), pp. 68–72. Kerr analyses Aquinas's discussion of Augustine's distinctions between *credere Deo* (believing God), *credere Deum* (believing that God exists), and *credere in Deum* (believing into God). 2a2ae. 2, 2. Aquinas's remark at this point seems to suggest that the proposition 'God exists' does not mean the same thing for believers and non-believers. For further discussion on this point, see n. 205, below.

[200] Leo Elders, 'Justification des "cinq voies"', *Revue Thomiste* 61 (1961), 207–25. For Elders, admittedly, they are not to be understood *only* in this sense. Leo Elders, *Philosophical Theology of Aquinas* (Leiden: Brill, 1990), pp. 132–3. See also Cornelius Ernst, 'Metaphor and Ontology in *Sacra Doctrina*', *The Thomist* 38 (1974), 403–25; Rowan Williams, *The Edge of Words* (London: Continuum, 2015), pp. 1–34, esp. pp. 3f.

[201] Hetche, 'Descartes and the Augustinian Tradition', 295f.

[202] On the 'three ways' and their history, see Fran O'Rourke, 'The Triplex Via of Naming God', *The Review of Metaphysics* 69 (2016), 519–54.

[203] See also *SCG* 1.12–13. Aquinas also uses *ostendere* (to show, or illustrate), translated in my edition as 'prove'. *SCG* 1.14 (vol. 11, p. 25). Aquinas deals with different senses of *demonstratio* in his *Commentary on the Posterior Analytics of Aristotle*, trans. F. R. Larcher (Albany, NY: Magi Books, 1970).

[204] Laurence Paul Hemming and Susan Frank Parsons, *Restoring Faith in Reason* (Notre Dame: University of Notre Dame Press, 2003), p. ix; Lewis and Short, *Latin Dictionary*, s.v. 'probo' (p. 1449b). Subsequently, for John Duns Scotus, not all proofs would count as demonstrations. Scotus would also observe a relevant distinction between authoritative

noted, it is also significant that after the brief statement of each 'proof' Aquinas concludes with a common formula: 'and this everyone understands to be God'; 'to which everyone gives the name God'; 'this all men speak of as God', and so on. For Aquinas, 'everyone' thus already holds that God exists, consistent with his earlier remark that all have implanted within them knowledge of God, albeit 'in a general and confused way'.[205] The function of the 'proofs', then, is not to provide rational evidence for a proposition that might otherwise be in doubt – not, in other words to satisfy some 'ethics of belief' requirement about the existence of God – but to provide insights into a conception of God that is held universally, if vaguely. Neither does the process necessarily dispel that vagueness, and indeed Aquinas's five ways have been read as an exercise in negative theology, as guiding the intellect through a series of stages that lead to an encounter with something that escapes adequate conceptualisation. The paradoxical outcome is the discovery that 'the human intellect is ordered to a reality that it cannot know, and is seeking an intelligibility that it cannot understand'.[206]

As a brief aside, we might consider an example from recent history that may help give us a better idea of the significance of 'proofs' in this context. For more than 350 years Pierre de Fermat's celebrated 'last theorem' represented one of the greatest unsolved problems of mathematics. (The theorem states that there is no solution to the equation $a^n + b^n = c^n$ for values of n that are greater than 2, and where a, b, and c are positive integers.) Fermat had set the hares running in the 1630s when he tantalisingly scribbled into the pages of an ancient mathematical work that he had a proof of the theorem but that it was too long to write in the margin. Numerous attempts to devise a proof were unsuccessful and after more than three centuries of failed efforts the 1995 *The Guinness Book of World Records* judged

proofs and argumentative proofs. Proofs (*probationes*) could thus be understood in terms of authoritative texts (*auctoritate*) or rational arguments (*ratione*). See Antonie Vos, *The Philosophy of John Duns Scotus* (Edinburgh: Edinburgh University Press, 2012), pp. 341–7.

[205] *ST* 1a. 2, 1. Leo Elders has suggested that this is Aquinas repeating an Aristotelian claim. *Philosophical Theology of Aquinas*, p. 130. Cf. Aristotle, *Physics* 203b 14–15, *On the Heavens* 270b6–7. Another consideration is that there are two distinct ways of believing in the existence of God. Reflecting on Augustine's distinction between *credere Deo* (believing God), *credere Deum* (believing that God exists), and *credere in Deum* (believing into God), Aquinas contends in relation to the second formula that unbelievers do not truly believe that God exists in the same way that the faithful do, since the latter do not believe it 'under the conditions which faith determines'. *ST* 2a2ae. 2, 2 (with 'unbeliever' translating *infidelis*). See the discussion in Kerr, *After Aquinas*, p. 67. On Augustine's distinction see Th. Camelot, '*Credere deo, credere deum, credere in deum* pour l'histoire d'une formule traditionnelle', *Revue des Sciences philosophiques et théologique* (1940–1), 149–55.

[206] Preller, *Divine Science*, p. 179.

Fermat's conjecture to be 'the most difficult mathematical problem' of all. Eventually in 1993 the British mathematician Andrew Wiles formulated the first successful proof, widely lauded as one of the great mathematical accomplishments of the century. It is telling that, prior to this breakthrough, the succession of unsuccessful proofs presented no challenge to the acceptability of Fermat's conjecture and had Wiles's efforts ultimately proved fruitless this would have rendered it no less believable. There are many things that we know to be true without proofs (and, strange as it may seem, for formal mathematical systems we can prove this).[207] Sometimes it is our certainty that things are true that motivates the quest for formal proofs.

4.4 Divine Designs and First Causes

While the status of the classical proofs undergoes an important change in the early modern period, from something like spiritual exercises to the provision of rational evidence, it is significant that some of the formative elements of the earlier arguments persist. This is evident in instances of what appear to be design arguments conjoined with innate belief arguments. In the sixteenth century, the Protestant reformer Philip Melanchthon would speak of the wonders of nature enervating the *prolepsis* of God implanted within human minds. The existence and wisdom of God were not so much logical inferences based on a dispassionate survey of nature as the awakening of a God-given propensity that had been dulled by sin.[208] Minds are already

---

[207] One of the other great mathematical accomplishments of the twentieth century, Gödel's incompleteness theorems, are relevant here, in that they established that in a formal mathematical system there will always be statements about natural numbers that are true but unprovable within the system.

[208] '*Et illa mirabilia spectacula rerum in natura sunt signa, quae commonefaciunt mentes, ut de Deo cogitent ac illam* πρόληψιν *excitent.*' Philip Melanchthon, *Commentarii Epistolam Pauli ad Romanos* (Wittenberg, 1532), p. 72. Voetius referred to 'cognition and knowledge, which the natural man receives from God by observing and perceiving the creatures'. *Catechisatie* 46, quoted in Beck, 'Melanchthonian Thought', p. 122. Junius's student, Franciscus Gomarus (1563–1641) also described an 'implanted reason aroused to true attention through the senses ... like a natural eye for reading and contemplation'. Thesis 36, *Opera theologica*, 3 vols. (Amsterdam, 1644), vol. 3, p. 2, cited in Platt, *Reformed Thought and Scholasticism*, p. 146. Gomarus sought to distinguish this from Platonic reminiscence although the difference is subtle: 'The notion of these is not acquired by recollection (ἀνάμνησις), nor from the senses and induction, granted that it is strengthened and refined by these): but arises from the latent natural seed of reason and religion' (cited in Platt, *Reformed Thought and Scholasticism*, pp. 144f.). Francis Turretin suggests a similar combination – 'partly implanted' as in a form of conscience, and 'partly acquired' from rational reflection on the book of Creatures. *Institutio Theologiae Elencticae*, 3 vols. (Geneva, 1679–85), I.iii.4.

primed to believe in God when they encounter the beauty and order of nature. Yves of Paris described in similar terms how the stars on a beautiful evening, or the solitude of the forest, could awaken the inner sense of Deity.[209] These experiences did not count as proofs or design arguments, but were rather an immediate apprehension of 'truths that our minds comprehend without ratiocination'. Yves would go on to suggest that our natural instinct of God works together with reason, which can be thought of as a 'second light'.[210] Herbert of Cherbury used the image of innate notions as a kind of 'closed book' that could be opened by experience. For him the common notions, while not being derived from experience, were not fully independent of it either. In this regard he differs from Descartes, who seeks to use the meditative method to draw the mind *away* from the world of sense-experience.[211] These examples suggest that the now standard division of arguments for God's existence into a priori and a posteriori forms is not entirely helpful when applied to historical arguments.[212]

Works of physico-theology also exhibit a degree of continuity with traditional spiritual exercises. William Derham's first series of Boyle Lectures introduced the term 'physico-theology' into the English lexicon in the eighteenth century.[213] Kant's subsequent identification of '*the*

---

[209] Yves de Paris, *La Théologie Naturelle*, vol. 1, p. 67. Cf. Fénelon, who also contended that God should be evident in nature from a 'first glance' and without the need for metaphysical subtleties. *L'Existence de Dieu*, p. 239. Sin accounts for those to whom these things are not immediately obvious (pp. 305–7).

[210] Yves de Paris, *La Théologie Naturelle*, vol. 1, pp. 68, 107. Yves argued that given the naturalness of the sense of Deity, to ask for additional rational proofs was an exhibition of bad faith (vol. 1, p. 51).

[211] Herbert, *De Veritate*, p. 125; Descartes, *Meditations*, CSM 2, p. 10.

[212] Some Protestant theologians observed a distinction between *theologia naturalis innata* and *theologia natural acquisita*, the former referring to innate notions, the latter arrived at by 'observing and perceiving the creatures of God'. However, this 'acquired' theology was still dependent upon an innate capacity to see the world as a divine creation. Neither could be fully understood outside the confines of revealed theology. Junius, *True Theology*, pp. 200f.; Voetius, *Selectae Disputationes*, vol. 1, p. 140; Beck, 'Melanchthonian Thought', pp. 120–2. On the Catholic side, Pierre Gassendi had a similar understanding of the interaction between the natural world and innate principles. See Antonia LoLordo, *Pierre Gassendi and the Birth of Early Modern Philosophy* (Cambridge: Cambridge University Press, 2007), pp. 239–42. Also worth noting is the fact that Samuel Clarke's use of the a priori and a posteriori in relation to arguments for God's existence does not map onto the modern distinction, with Clarke regarding his cosmological argument to be an argument a priori.

[213] The adjective 'physico-theological' had already been in use for some time. On the origins and nature of physico-theology see Peter Harrison, 'Physico-Theology and the Mixed Sciences: The Role of Theology in Early Modern Natural Philosophy', in *The Science of Nature in the Seventeenth Century*, ed. Anstey and Schuster, pp. 165–83, and 'What's in a Name? Physico-Theology in Seventeenth-Century England', in *Physico-Theology: Religion*

4.4 DIVINE DESIGNS AND FIRST CAUSES

physico-theological *argument*' has led to the assumption that physico-theology can simply be equated with a generic argument from design. But for many of its eighteenth-century proponents, physico-theology was understood more as the business of training (or re-training) the mind to perceive God in the things of nature. In this respect it had important affinities to the more traditional spiritual exercises and to medieval 'proofs', rightly understood. While physico-theology continued to offer an interpretative strategy for seeing God in the book of nature, it was novel in that it was informed by new scientific approaches.[214] To this extent, it displaces the early medieval contemplative approach that was based on the theological symbolism of natural objects.[215] But at the same time, it continued to be attentive to formative, moral, and devotional goals.

Robert Boyle proposed on numerous occasions that the study of nature inspires 'true Sentiments both of Devotion and of particular Vertues'.[216] In the foremost English work of natural theology of the seventeenth century, *The Wisdom of God Manifested in the Works of Creation* (1691), John Ray, the pioneering botanist and Fellow of the Royal Society, agreed that, properly conducted, the study of the creation would 'Stir up and Increase in us the Affections and habits of Admiration, Humility, and Gratitude'.[217] This sentiment reflects the origins of the work, which had been compiled from morning divinity exercises delivered in the chapel of Trinity College, Cambridge.

---

and Science in Europe 1650–1750, ed. Ann Blair and Kaspar von Greyerz (Baltimore: Johns Hopkins University Press, 2020), pp. 39–51.

[214] It was also novel in representing a new combination of what, in the Aristotelian classification, had been two distinct speculative sciences, theology and natural philosophy. This combination of sciences broke an Aristotelian prohibition on such combinations (*metabasis*), the exception being the model of subordinate or 'mixed' sciences. Harrison, 'Physico-Theology and the Mixed Sciences'. On *metabasis* see Funkenstein, *Theology and the Scientific Imagination*, pp. 35–7, 303–7.

[215] For the displacement of symbolic forms of contemplation by a new natural history and natural philosophy, see Harrison, *Bible and the Rise of Science*. On the persistence of the idea of the natural world as a communicative medium for religious truths in the modern period see Peter N. Jordan, *Naturalism in the Christian Imagination: Providence and Causality in Early Modern England* (Cambridge: Cambridge University Press, 2022), pp. 42–3, 183.

[216] Boyle, *A Disquisition about the Final Causes of Natural Things*, *Works*, vol. 11, p. 114. Cf. *Usefulness of Natural Philosophy*, *Works*, vol. 3, pp. 200, 203, 213; *The Christian Virtuoso II*, *Works*, vol. 12, pp. 431, 481. In this latter work Boyle lists some of these virtues: admiration, humility, gratitude, and love (pp. 483, 490, 491, 495). See also Peter Harrison, 'Sentiments of Devotion and Experimental Philosophy in Seventeenth-Century England', *Journal of Medieval and Early Modern Studies* 44 (2014), 113–33; Courtney Weiss Smith, *Empiricist Devotions: Science, Religion, and Poetry in Early Eighteenth-Century England* (Charlottesville: University of Virginia Press, 2016).

[217] John Ray, *The Wisdom of God Manifested in the Works of Creation* (London, 1691), Preface.

Derham took a similar line in his Boyle Lectures, claiming that the study of nature inspires fear and obedience, thankfulness, and devotion to God. We also learn of our 'duties and moral obligations' from nature.[218] In the eighteenth century's best-selling multi-volume work of physico-theology, *Le spectacle de la nature* (1732–42), Noël Antoine Pluche similarly proposed, on his title page, that a central goal of physico-theology was 'the formation of the minds of the youth'.[219] Pluche explicitly rejected the goal of proving the existence of God as 'at best unprofitable and needless' since in reality there are no atheists. The point of the exercise was not to offer a demonstrative proof, but 'to open our Eyes, and receive Instruction'.[220] Even William Paley's classic *Natural Theology* (1802), now regarded as the epitome of an extended argument from design, informed its readers that the purpose of the exercise was to inculcate 'a habitual sentiment of our minds' that would serve as 'the foundation of every thing that is religious'.[221] The emphasis would continue in the series of works often thought of as a nineteenth-century successor to the Boyle Lectures, the Bridgewater Treatises. William Whewell, one of the contributors to the series, wrote that when a man contemplates nature, 'there springs up in his breast, *unbidden and irresistibly*, the thought of superintending intelligence'.[222] For Whewell, it was not just a matter of offering inferential or analogical arguments. As Jonathan Topham has established, while

---

[218] Derham, *Physico-Theology*, pp. 431, 442–3 (the pagination of this edition duplicates the page numbers 430–3). William Derham, *Astrotheology or, A Demonstration of the Being and Attributes of God, from a Survey of the Heavens*, 2nd ed. (London, 1715). 'Thus, as the Heathen have by the Light of Nature deduced the Existence and Attributes of God from his Works, and particularly those of the Heavens; so have they at the same time collected what the principal Duties are which Men owe to God; so reasonable, so natural, so manifest they are to all mankind' (p. 226).

[219] Noël Antoine Pluche, *Le spectacle de la nature, ou Entretiens sur les particularités de l'histoire naturelle, qui ont paru les plus propres à rendre les jeunes gens curieux, et à leur former l'esprit*, 9 vols. (Paris, 1732–42), vol. 1 (1732).

[220] Pluche, *Spectacle de la Nature or Nature Display'd* (1757), vol. 3, p. 304. On the preceding page Pluche demolished what would become Paley's famous watch-maker analogy: 'were any Man to dispute whether my Watch had a Maker, I should not think it worth while to convince him'. All of this is consistent with Pluche's Jansenist sympathies. See Ann Blair, 'Noël Antoine Pluche as a Jansenist Natural Theologian', *Intellectual History Review* 26 (2016), 91–9; Nicolas Brucker, 'What Abbé Pluche Owed to Early Modern Physico-Theologians', in *Physico-Theology*, ed. Blair and von Greyerz, pp. 183–93.

[221] William Paley, *Natural Theology*, in *The Works of William Paley, D.D.*, 7 vols. (London, 1875), vol. 5, pp. 374f. This partly accounts for why Paley could continue to advocate a physico-theological approach *after* what have often been regarded as the devastating refutations of the design argument laid out in David Hume's *Dialogues concerning Natural Religion* (London, 1779).

[222] William Whewell, *Astronomy and General Physics considered with reference to Natural Theology*, 2nd ed. (London: William Pickering, 1833), p. 299 (my emphasis).

4.4 DIVINE DESIGNS AND FIRST CAUSES

these Treatises might seem primarily to be written as scientifically informed accounts of divine design, when read as a form of devotional literature they were more to do with 'the management of religious habits, associations and feelings than ... theological reasoning or argument'.[223]

The problem with atheism, on these analyses, was less a failure to draw the correct logical inferences from features of nature and more a careless forgetfulness and an absence of the right interpretative framework. Exercises in physico-theology were intended to train the mind so that it was primed to respond to nature with reverence, piety, and gratitude. The apparently repetitive character of many works of physico-theology, with their seemingly tedious enumeration of instances of design, is to be understood in this light. It was not a matter of accumulating evidence but engaging in a practice of iterative conditioning, now necessary for fallen or desensitised minds. The aim was to show how virtually every aspect of nature, even the most unlikely, could be interpreted in ways that fortified religious faith. This remains some distance from a dispassionate 'design argument', based purely on empirical evidence and logical inference, and intended to prove the existence of God to the religious sceptic. That said, however physico-theology was conceived by its first proponents, its content was such that it *could* be reduced to an 'argument from design' when read through the lens of later notions of natural theology and philosophy of religion.

The modern 'philosophy of religion' approach to these texts not only diverts attention from their contemplative and devotional context, it also renders some elements of their content invisible. It is difficult to accommodate, say, Aquinas's five ways within Kant's procrustean tripartite taxonomy: we get what appear to be three cosmological proofs, and one teleological or physico-theological proof. But the fourth way, on degrees of perfection, now needs to be passed over as a peculiar vestige of a defunct Neoplatonic worldview. The retrospective application of this commonplace threefold division promotes the conclusion that these older accounts are either underdeveloped versions of our modern arguments or just historical curiosities devoid of any genuine philosophical substance, the *consensus gentium* argument being a case of the latter. We have seen how this was true of the 'ontological' and 'teleological/design' arguments. It also applies to aspects of the 'cosmological arguments' based upon the causal order of the universe.

Medieval arguments based on the notion of a first cause were typically indebted to versions of Aristotle's fourfold schema of causes (material,

---

[223] Jonathan R. Topham, *Reading the Book of Nature* (Chicago: University of Chicago Press, 2023), p. 330.

formal, efficient, and final). Accounting for things in terms of these causes amounted to a comprehensive explanation: what material they are made of (material); what form that material takes (formal); external sources of their motion and change (efficient); and their ultimate purpose or inherent tendency to motion (final). These were supplemented with notions of causation by emanation and fluxus, and the idea of exemplary causation.[224] Of the multiple causes today only the efficient cause remains, the paradigm instance being an object in motion (the cause) acting directly and externally on another to produce some change (the effect). Causation for modern thinkers is to do with discrete events that are constantly conjoined. Because by 'cause' we now mean only 'efficient cause' we are operating with what from a medieval standpoint is a somewhat impoverished understanding of causation. In modern scientific explanations, moreover, even efficient causation has disappeared to a large degree, replaced by a mathematical description of regularities. Newtonianism is the classical example, with mathematical laws coming to stand in for causal explanations. Hume belatedly grasped this, articulating the fact that a world governed by laws of nature was a world in which causation was no longer required. Getting ahead of ourselves, for theistic interpreters of nature, God's role in this scheme of things would be limited to ordaining and upholding laws of nature, rather than being involved in the broader range of causal relations postulated by medieval thinkers.

For medieval Christian thinkers, God was intimately involved at the level of each of the causes.[225] He was the source of primary matter (although not its material cause); the efficient cause of all things in so far as they were understood to derive their being from him; the final cause, the end to which all things tended; and their formal cause in as much as their specific natures were modelled on divine ideas. Aquinas tells us that 'God is the efficient, the exemplar [i.e., formal] and the final cause of all things'.[226] Bonaventure

---

[224] Albert the Great, *Liber de causis* in *B. Alberti Magni ... Opera omnia*, 38 vols., ed. Auguste Borgnet (Paris: Louis Vivès, 1890–5), vol. 10; Aquinas, *Disputed questions on Truth*, q. 3, art. 1 (trans. McGlynn, vol. 1, p. 138); Isabelle Moulin and David Twetten, 'Causality and Emanation in Albert', in *A Companion to Albert the Great*, ed. Irven M. Resnick (Leiden: Brill 2013), pp. 694–721.

[225] This because the creatures do not derive their material substance from God, being created *ex nihilo*. Aquinas, *ST* Ia. 44, 2.

[226] Aquinas, *ST* Ia. 44, 4. Even earlier, John of Damascus (675–749 CE) had made these identifications: 'For, *toward* Him all things tend [final causation], and in Him they have their *existence* [efficient causation], and to all things He communicates their being in accordance with the *nature of each* [formal causation]. He is the being of all things that are, the life of the living, the reason of the rational, and the intelligence of intelligent beings ... [and yet,

says something similar: 'God is origin [efficient cause], mode [formal cause], and goal [final cause] of every creature.'²²⁷ Aquinas's relatively unfamiliar terminology of 'exemplar' causes points to the fact that created things to some degree *resemble* their causes. This notion goes back at least as far as Plato, who tells us that the creator 'desired that all things should be as like himself as they could be'.²²⁸ In the Christian tradition this resemblance to the creator is most conspicuous in the human person who is said to be the bearer of the image and likeness of God. But resemblances were said to be evident in all creatures. The third-century Christian Platonist Origen wrote that just as God made man in his image, 'so also did He create the other creatures after the likeness of some heavenly patterns' resulting in a 'correspondence between all things on earth and their celestial prototypes'.²²⁹ These reflections of divine ideas in the creation established the possibility of a kind of direct, as opposed to inferential, knowledge of God through the creation. The late fourth- and early fifth-century Neoplatonic theologian Pseudo-Dionysius explained it this way: 'we know not God by His Nature (for this is unknowable and beyond the reach of all Reason and Intuition), yet by means of that ordering of all things which (being as it were projected out of Him) possesses certain images and semblances of His Divine Exemplars'.²³⁰ The ordering of nature, on this understanding, was not just about billiard ball-style causal interactions, or William Paley-style design, but about images, reflections, and analogies. This explains how, for the ancients, knowledge of the operations of nature, and indeed the imitation of nature, could be connected to moral and religious formation.

he] surpasses intelligence, reason, life, and essence.' *On the Orthodox Faith* 1.14, quoted in Andrew Davison, *Participation in God* (Cambridge: Cambridge University Press, 2019). Davison's book offers an excellent account of scholastic understandings of causation in relation to the Christian doctrine of creation.

²²⁷ Bonaventure, *Itinerarium* 2.12, *Works*, vol. 1, p. 26. Davison writes that for Bonaventure God is the creature's source (*ortus*), manner (*modus*), and fulfilment (*fructus*)'. *Participation in God*, pp. 58, 63–4.

²²⁸ Plato, *Timaeus* 30a (*Collected Dialogues*, p. 1162), cf. 92c. Also this remark in the Parmenides: 'these forms are as it were patterns fixed in the nature of things. The other things are made in their image and are likenesses, and this participation they come to have in the forms is nothing but their being made their image.' *Parmenides* 132d (p. 927). The hermetic literature contains similar ideas. 'The sensible world is the image of God', *Asclepius* 8; cf. *Corpus Hermeticum* 12.15. Aristotle, who has no doctrine of creation, nonetheless offers this principle: 'like produces what is like itself'. *On the Soul* 415a29. Aquinas cites this in support of his notion of exemplary causation *Super Libros Sententiarum* 36.2.3, 2 vols., ed. R. P. Mandonnet (Paris, 1929), vol. 1, p. 844.

²²⁹ Origen, *The Song of Songs, Commentary and Homilies*, ACW, vol. 26, pp. 218f.

²³⁰ Pseudo-Dionysius, *On the Divine Names and the Mystical Theology*, 7.3, trans. C. E. Rold (London: SPCK, 1920), pp. 151–2.

Aquinas tells us that God's wisdom is evident in the creatures because 'by a kind of communication of his likeness it is spread abroad in the things he has made'.[231] A paradigm case would be biological reproduction, in which the offspring resemble the parents.[232] This should not be mistaken for what we would now call a design argument. Neither does it fit the pattern of cosmological arguments. For Aquinas, exemplary causes are a kind of extrinsic final cause (and one that also involves both efficient and formal causes).[233] Bonaventure set out a similar conception, explaining that every effect is 'a *sign* of its cause'. All creatures, he concludes, are 'a certain image and likeness of the Eternal Wisdom'.[234] The claim is that there is a kind of qualitative representation of God in the world which is less to be inferred than directly intuited. Study of the creatures, moreover, could assist in the restoration of the vitiated image of God in the human observer, since it involved a partial recovery of the divine nature – this in so far as the human mind grasped the original ideas (or exemplars) of the creatures as they existed in the divine mind.[235]

This mindset was related to the commonplace idea that the world was a book authored by God. While the 'book of nature' trope is a familiar one, it has meant quite different things in different historical periods. For some medieval thinkers this metaphor was taken almost literally, such that the

---

[231] Aquinas, *SCG* 2.2. In *ST* 1a. 44, he speaks of the '*procession* of the creatures from God'. Albert the Great has a stronger conception of the emanation of beings from God. Thérèse Bonin, *Creation as Emanation: The Origin of Diversity in Albert the Great's On the Causes and the Procession of the Universe* (Notre Dame: University of Notre Dame Press, 2001).

[232] Aquinas, *ST* 1a. 4, 3.

[233] 'God is the efficient and final cause of things. Hence, He is also their formal cause – but as an exemplary cause, since He cannot be a form that is part of a creature.' *Disputed questions on Truth*, q. 3, art. 1 (trans. McGlynn, vol. 1, p. 138). See also *SCG* 1.21, and *Commentary on Metaphysics*, bk. 5, L2, 764 (trans. John P. Rowan, *Latin/English Edition of the Works of Thomas Aquinas* (Lander: Aquinas Institute, 2020), vol. 50, p. 381). For a definitive account see Gregory T. Doolan, *Aquinas on the Divine Ideas as Exemplary Causes* (Washington, DC: Catholic University of America Press, 2008); also Davison, *Participation in God*, pp. 84–112.

[234] Bonaventure, *Itinerarium* 2, 11–13, *Works*, vol. 1, pp. 26–7. Elsewhere in this work: 'Taking perceptible things as a mirror, we see God THROUGH them – through his traces so to speak; but we also see him IN them.' *Itinerarium* 2.1, *Works*, vol. 1, p. 18. Also see *Commentary on the Sentences* 7.1.35.1; *Quaestiones disputatae de scientia Christi*, q. 2, *Opera Omnia*, vol. 9.

[235] Philosophy, for Hugh of St Victor, is able 'to restore within us the divine likeness, a likeness which to us is a form but to God it is his nature. The more we are conformed to the divine nature, the more do we possess Wisdom, for then there begins to shine forth again in us what has forever existed in the divine Idea or Pattern, coming and going in us but standing changeless in God.' *Didascalicon* 2.1, trans. Jerome Taylor (New York: Columbia University Press, 1991), p. 61.

4.4 DIVINE DESIGNS AND FIRST CAUSES

nature of God could be directly 'read' in creatures that represented divine ideas. Hugh of St Victor (1096–1141) insists that the triune nature of God can be known through meditation upon the magnitude, beauty, and utility of the creation.[236] Bonaventure maintained something similar: 'The creature of the world is like a book in which the creative Trinity is reflected, represented, and written.'[237] German mystic Meister Eckhart (1260–1328) contended that if we fully knew only the creatures, it would be unnecessary to attend even a single sermon, since 'every creature is full of God and is a book'.[238] In the early fifteenth century, the Catalan scholar Raymond of Sebunde (1385–1436) wrote a book bearing the title 'Natural Theology or the Book of the Creatures', in which he, too, proclaimed that what we can learn from the book of nature, including the triune nature of God, almost exactly parallels what can be known from scripture.[239] The fact that God was imagined to operate in terms of three kinds of cause was taken to be another natural reflection of the Trinity.[240] Despite his title – and this is the first time that 'natural theology' appears in a book title – this is not natural theology in the established sense, since it apprehends aspects of God that go beyond what can be known through reason alone. The 'natural' here refers to a divinely infused nature, not natural as opposed to 'revealed'.

As with Aristotelian parable and the Anselmian prologue, the discernment of the meanings of nature called for a certain preparedness of the mind. Hugh of St Victor pointed out that just as literacy was requisite in order to read and understand books, the unenlightened intellect might remain blind to the transcendent meanings of the natural world: the stupid and 'animal man' who 'does not perceive the things of God', may see the outward appearance of these visible creatures, but does not understand

---

[236] Hugh of Saint Victor, *De tribus deibus*, passim (PL 176: 811–38). In the *Didascalicon*, Hugh states that created things are 'a resemblance of the divine Idea' and that 'every nature tells of God'. 5.3, 6.5 (pp. 122, 145). On the book of nature metaphor, from an extensive literature, see K. van Berkel and Arjo Vanderjagt (eds.), *The Book of Nature in Early Modern and Modern History* (Leuven: Peeters, 2006); Harrison, *Bible and the Rise of Science*, pp. 44–56.

[237] 'creatura mundi est quasi quidam liber in quo relucet, repraesentatur et legitur Trinitatis fabricatrix'. Bonaventure, *Breviloquium* 2.12 (*Opera Omnia*, vol. 7, p. 270). Bonaventure's reference to 'reflection' recalls the parallel metaphor of nature as a mirror, which reflected the Godhead.

[238] Meister Eckhart, Sermon 67, *The Complete Mystical Works of Meister Eckhart*, trans. Maurice O'C. Walshe (New York: Crossroad, 2009), p. 345.

[239] Raymon Sibiuda [Raymond Sebunde], *Theologia naturalis, sive, liber creaturarum*, ed. F. Stegmüller (Stuttgart-Bad Canstatt: Frommann, 1966), Prologus. In 1559, the Prologue was placed on the Index of prohibited books, for its apparently bold elevation of the status of nature to that of scripture.

[240] See Davison, *Participation in God*, pp. 44–52.

the reason within.²⁴¹ One essential preparatory step to reading the book of nature was knowledge of the 'other book', scripture. This was grounded in the hermeneutical practice exemplified by Augustine and based on the principle that God communicates not only through words, but also things. The literal sense of scripture is understood, for Augustine, once we grasp the link between the words and the things to which the words refer. These things themselves have additional meanings with which God has invested them, and which also need to be understood.²⁴² Scripture read allegorically is thus a way of understanding the meanings of the natural world, proceeding from the literal sense to the allegorical sense.²⁴³ Hugh explained that 'in divine utterance not only words but even things have a meaning'. This is because 'the thing is a resemblance of the divine idea'.²⁴⁴ Aquinas addressed this question in his account of allegorical readings. God can express himself in things, and this makes possible allegorical readings of scripture – 'not because one word signifies several things, but because the things signified by the words can be themselves types of other things'.²⁴⁵ Reading the natural world thus requires both a certain attentiveness to the creatures along with a mind primed by the reading of scripture.

We can thus understand ancient and medieval 'proofs' to have a number of related functions: to prepare the mind to fully recognise what in a sense is already known; to seek a more reasoned account of that universally acknowledged, yet dimly apprehended, God-idea; to foster personal piety and help direct it towards its proper object; to exegete biblical texts that make reference to naturalness of belief and foolishness of atheism. During the early modern period we see changes to each of these aspects of medieval proofs. For a start, and at the risk of redundancy, there is a new emphasis on the need for the rational justification of beliefs which gives proofs for God's existence a distinctively modern, evidential function. This arose partly from the rejection of implicit faith and the new demand to justify propositional beliefs in terms of generally accepted rational arguments, and partly from the prospect of atheism against which it was thought necessary to prepare philosophical defences. The evidentiary demand placed on proofs meant that there was a growing tendency to assume the possibility of a putatively

---

[241] Hugh of St Victor, *De tribus deibus* 4 (PL 176: 814 B–C). See Wanda Cizewski, 'Reading the World as Scripture: Hugh of St. Victor's *De tribus diebus*', *Florilegium* 9 (1987), 65–88.
[242] Augustine, *On Christian Doctrine*, 1.2.2 (pp. 8f.). Also see Gerald L. Bruns, *Hermeneutics Ancient and Modern* (New Haven: Yale University Press, 1992), p. 141, and *passim*.
[243] On this general theme see Harrison, *Bible and the Rise of Science*, pp. 28–33, and *passim*.
[244] Hugh of St Victor, *Didascalicon* 5.4 (pp. 121f.).
[245] Aquinas, *ST* Ia, 1. 10; cf. *Quaestiones Quodlibetales* 7.6.15.

neutral starting point for argumentation, leading eventually to a conception of *natural* theology as an enterprise that involves no prior religious assumptions. That said, the 'neutrality' of the early modern starting point still took it for granted that theism was the default natural condition, with most arguments seeking to show how atheistic tendencies represented a deviation from this universal norm. 'Natural', in this sense, was thus not contrasted with 'supernatural', as it is now. Moreover, some articulations of the proofs still retain traditional elements of intellectual, moral, and religious formation, as we see in the case of Descartes's *Meditations*.

One major change in the content of the proofs was driven by early modern challenges to Aristotelian natural philosophy and the medieval system of causal relations built upon them. These challenges, especially as they related to new understandings of laws of nature, will be considered in more detail in the chapter that follows. For now, it can be said that while Aristotelian scholasticism persisted in various guises as a methodological approach, especially in the universities, the new physics of Descartes and Newton was grounded in the revival of an atomistic (or, strictly speaking, 'corpuscularian') ontology. This matter theory had historical connections with an unsavoury Epicureanism and its modern recovery raised the acute question of whether atheistic commitment was an accidental appendage or was somehow essential to it. Given that Aristotelian and scholastic ideas of causation were intrinsically 'theological' – for Aristotle metaphysics *was* theology or 'the divine science' – the new physics or 'natural philosophy' urgently needed its own theological legitimation along with a recalibration of God's relation to the world. This was worked out in the context of new sciences of nature, based on the new ideas of matter and causation, and conducted according to new experimental methods. The alliance of new proofs with the new sciences was thus partly aimed at establishing the theological respectability of an otherwise suspect Epicurean matter theory. At the same time, the loss of the notion of exemplary causation ruled out the possibility of *seeing* the divine image in the world; now God's power and wisdom could only be logically *inferred* from the intricate designs of the creatures and from the lawful order of the cosmos. God's presence became quantitative rather than qualitative.

A number of these new directions are exemplified in the work of Francis Bacon. On older models, Christian and classical, contemplation of the world was an exercise in religious and moral edification. For Bacon, the world is not to be passively contemplated, but actively investigated so that human power might be exercised over it. Descartes also touches upon this theme in his *Discourse*, proposing that 'the speculative philosophy of the schools' be replaced by a 'practical philosophy' that would be 'useful in life'. The goal of the new philosophy was 'to make us the lords and masters of nature'.[246] Bacon provided this new approach with an alternative religious justification, presenting it as both a re-establishment of the dominion over nature that the human race had lost in Eden, and an exercise in Christian charity aimed at relieving the human estate. The older 'reading' of nature for images and resemblances is in competition with a more active and intrusive attempt to master it – or at least this is how Bacon saw things. On Bacon's view, the aspect of God evident in the world that we need to imitate is his active power, which we attain through knowledge of how to manipulate nature. Relying on a rather anthropomorphic and mechanical understanding of the business of creation, Bacon thus insisted that we cannot discern God's image in nature – just the operations of his power.[247]

This was a direct rejection of a common medieval view. It also inverted the order of reasoning. For Aquinas the starting point was the idea of divine creation, one of the truths of faith, and from there he proposed that God's agency was communicated to the creatures by means of an exemplary causality. This retained a degree of distance between Creator and creation. Bacon began with the model of the human artificer and projected the analogy in the other direction. (This analogy was made possible only by abandoning another key tenet of Aristotelianism – a hard distinction between natural and artificial.) What resulted from this was the popular early modern conception of God as a designer and engineer. This anthropomorphic analogy, which turned out to be vulnerable to criticisms later identified by Hume, offered a less direct route to God and a significantly lower theological yield. From it we learn only of God's power and wisdom, and this by inference.

Bacon's deployment of the 'two books' metaphor follows a similar line, with a very clear distinction being posited between them: the book of

---

[246] Descartes, *Discourse on the Method*, CSM 1, p. 142.
[247] 'all works do show forth the power and skill of the workman, and not his image; so it is with the works of God which do shew the omnipotency and wisdom of the maker, *but not his image*'. Bacon, *Advancement of Learning, Works*, vol. 3, pp. 349f. (my emphasis). Cf. Noah Biggs: 'I am assured by faith, that neither is *man* the Image of *nature*, nor *Nature* the image of *man*.' *Mataetechnia Medicinae Praxeos* (London, 1651), p. 33. Descartes would also insist that mastery of the world is the aim of natural philosophy. Arguably, what we see is a shift in the conception of mastery itself, a move from an interior, mental self-governance, to an exterior, literal and material domination of other things. See Harrison, *Bible and the Rise of Science*, pp. 205–11; 'Reading the Passions: The Fall, the Passions, and Dominion over Nature', in *The Soft Underbelly of Reason: The Passions in the Seventeenth Century*, ed. Stephen Gaukroger (London: Routledge, 1998), pp. 49–78.

4.4 DIVINE DESIGNS AND FIRST CAUSES

scripture reveals God's will; the book of nature, *only his power*.[248] While some elements of the older exemplarist approach lingered, 'book of nature' metaphors from this period onwards will tend towards an *inference* to the existence of God, most commonly via an analogy relating to design. This contrasted with the medieval assumption that God can be almost literally 'read' from nature, and that accordingly the books of nature and scripture shared an overlapping content. Not unrelated to this, Bacon also advocated a more active approach to the natural world, characterised by a more aggressive set of experimental procedures. Again, along the lines of the traditional division between action and contemplation, this utilitarian approach was contrasted with a meditative, contemplative mindset that was focused more on changing the investigator than changing the world.[249]

The question of the purpose of the natural world leads to another area of significant disagreement about the new God–world relationship. This was the discussion of final causes. Whereas Aquinas had maintained that final causes were 'the cause of causes', scholastic thinkers in the later Middle Ages placed an increasing emphasis on efficient causes, and tended to resolve the operation of final causes into some form of efficient causality.[250] With

---

[248] Bacon, *Novum Organum* I, §89, *Works*, vol. 4, p. 89 (my emphasis). Bacon's insistence on this point is partly owing to fact that contemporaries were still finding images of God in nature. That said, there were survivals of this idea. These included alchemists and followers of Jacob Boehme. See Oswald Croll, *A Treatise of Oswaldus Crollius of Signatures* (London, 1669), Preface; Jacob Boehme, *Signatura Rerum, or the Signature of all Things* (London, 1651), p. 4; Barker, *Natural Theology*, p. 25; Richard Saunders, *Saunders Physiognomie and Chiromancie, Metoposcopie*, 2nd ed. (London, 1671), Preface. Others simply rehearsed the 'book of nature' metaphor with all of its medieval connotations. Edward Evans thus described 'the book of the world' as 'a Book of Golden Similitudes of GODS glory, yea and a Book gloriously garnished with the Images thereof'. *Verba Dierum* (Oxford, 1615). For other examples see Dennis R. Klinck, '*Vestigia Trinitatis* in Man and His Works in the English Renaissance', *Journal of the History of Ideas* 42 (1981), 13–27. John Donne took a middle position, approving of Sebonde's 'book of nature' trope but insisting that there were important truths in scripture not reflected in the book of nature. John Donne, *Essayes in Divinity*, ed. Evelyn Simpson (Oxford: Clarendon Press, 1952), pp. 17f.

[249] Bacon, *Valerius Terminus*, *Works*, vol. 3, p. 222; *Advancement of Learning*, *Works*, vol. 3, p. 294; *Great Instauration*, Preface, *Works*, vol. 4, p. 21. *Redargutio Philosophiarum* (1608), in B. Farrington, *The Philosophy of Francis Bacon* (Liverpool: Liverpool University Press, 1964), pp. 92f. Also see Harrison, *Territories*, pp. 117f.

[250] Aquinas, *De principiis naturae* §4.18–36, *Opera omnia*, Editio Leonina, vol. 43. For developments in late scholasticism, see, e.g., Anneliese Maier, 'Finalkausalität und Naturgesetz', in *Metaphysische Hintergründe der spätscholastischen Naturphilosophie* (Rome: Edizioni di Storia et Letteratura, 1955), pp. 273–335; Giles Olivo, 'L'efficience en cause: Suárez, Descartes et la question de la causalité', in *Descartes et le Moyen Âge*, ed. Joël Biard and Roshdi Rashed (Paris: Vrin, 1997), pp. 94–102; Vincent Carraud, *Causa sive Ratio. La raison de la cause de Suárez à Leibniz* (Paris: Presses Universitaires de France, 2002), pp. 145–8; Stephan Schmid, 'Finality without Final Causes? – Suárez's Account of Natural Teleology', *Ergo*

the introduction of a new corpuscular matter theory and the concomitant expulsion of inherent qualities and goal-directed behaviours from natural objects, final causes survived in a kind of vestigial form as divine intentions, purposes, or designs. But how these purposes could be discerned, and what explanatory role they should be accorded in natural philosophy, remained open questions. Bacon complained that the invocation of final causes had been a persistent barrier to the investigation of 'real and physical causes'. The examples he had in mind were statements such as: 'the leaves of trees are for protecting of the fruit' or 'the clouds are for watering of the earth'. Bacon maintained that while it might be legitimate to speak of the ends and purposes of human actions, such talk should be excluded from explanations of natural events. Final causes in this context were like holy virgins – dedicated to God, but barren.[251] The criticism may seem justified, since the instances of transcendental design to which Bacon alludes seem to divert attention away from the question of *how* it is that clouds provide rain. Here Bacon seems to be offering an argument parallel to Molière's subsequent mockery of formal causes: why does opium make one drowsy – it contains 'dormitive virtue', the nature of which is to induce drowsiness.[252] Yet these attacks were misplaced to a degree. The lame explanations that Bacon argued against turn out to be all that remains of 'final causation' once the more robust scholastic understanding had been dispensed with. In fact, Bacon's position amounts to the assertion of a new, and more restricted understanding of what counts as a satisfactory explanation in the sphere of natural philosophy – one that allows for the 'how' but excludes the 'why'.

This jettisoning of final and exemplary causes began a process that culminated in the later Newtonian approach, which further constrains what counts as genuine explanation by removing even efficient causes from the explanatory framework of science, leaving us with only descriptive laws. This circumscribed notion of explanation fits perfectly with Bacon's new view of why we should study nature which, as we have seen, amounts to a difference

---

2 (2016), https://doi.org/10.3998/ergo.12405314.0002.016, accessed 23 November 2023; Henrik Lagerlund, 'The Unity of Efficient and Final Causality: The Mind/Body Problem Reconsidered', *British Journal for the History of Philosophy* 19 (2011), 587–603.

[251] '*Nam Causarum Finalium inquisitio sterilis est, et, tanquam virgo Deo consecrata, nihil parit.*' Francis Bacon, *De augmentis scientiarum*, *Works*, vol. 7, p. 571. Despite subsequent paraphrases by Whewell and others, the Latin makes no reference to vestal virgins. Cf. William Whewell, *Astronomy and General Physics*, p. 355.

[252] Jean Baptiste Molière, *La Malade Imaginaire*, in *The Plays of Molière*, 8 vols., trans. A. R. Waller (Edinburgh: John Grant, 1926), vol. 8, p. 328. For a discussion of misplaced criticisms of scholastic qualities and virtues see Keith Hutchison, 'Dormitive Virtues, Scholastic Qualities, and the New Philosophies', *History of Science* 29 (1991), 245–78.

4.4 DIVINE DESIGNS AND FIRST CAUSES

between the contemplation of nature, and the study of its mechanical operations with a view to manipulating, changing, and mastering it. As for the role of divine purposes in natural history and natural philosophy, this was not fully resolved until the nineteenth century. At that time, the subsuming of natural philosophy and natural history under the modern notion of 'science', along with the appearance of an explicit category of 'scientific naturalism' and the ideal of a naturalistic scientific method, would more-or-less settle this question definitively. The twentieth-century adoption of methodological naturalism as the legitimate starting point for all scientific investigation represents the final step in the naturalisation of the scientific method.[253]

On the issue of final causes Bacon had important allies in Descartes and, less helpfully, Spinoza.[254] The French philosopher invoked the limitations of human reason and the inscrutability of the divine will to propose that God's purposes in the created order would necessarily be 'impenetrable'. This parallels Bacon's insistence that we cannot discern the image of God in the world. The common quest for final causes in the physical world he declared to be 'totally useless'.[255] But this also left rather large explanatory gaps, particularly in the realm of developmental biology. Attempts to show how mechanical laws of motion might account for embryological development, for example, met with little success.[256] A greater concern for many of Descartes's contemporaries was that a rejection of final causes could be read as a denial of divine providence. The new role of arguments as forms of evidence made this issue more acute. Pierre Gassendi put this directly to Descartes, complaining that ignoring final causes meant abandoning a key argument for God's existence: 'How or where will you be able to get better evidence for the existence of … God?'[257] Robert Boyle restated the same worry in a work solely devoted to a discussion of final causes. Descartes's neglect of final causes, he complained, would rule out 'one of the best and

---

[253] For a more complete account of these issues see Harrison, 'Physico-Theology and the Mixed Sciences'; *Territories*, pp. 145–8; Bernard Lightman, 'The Theology of Victorian Scientific Naturalists', in *Science without God?*, ed. Harrison and Roberts, pp. 235–53.

[254] For Spinoza's views, not discussed in detail here, see *Ethics*, pt. 1, appendix, *CW*, pp. 241f. For the case that the 'final causes' that Spinoza rejects were not actually final causes in the sense understood by Aristotle and Aquinas see Paul Hoffman, 'Final Causation in Spinoza', in *Final Causes and Teleological Explanation*, ed. Dominik Perler and Stephan Schmid (Leiden: Brill, 2011), pp. 40–50.

[255] Descartes, *Meditations*, CSM 2, p. 39. Cf. CSM 1, pp. 202f., CSMK, p. 341.

[256] For the classic statement of the issues see Jacques Roger, *The Life Sciences in Eighteenth-Century French Thought*, ed. Keith R. Benson, trans. Robert Ellrich (Stanford: Stanford University Press, 1998). See also Justin E. H. Smith (ed.), *The Problem of Animal Generation in Early Modern Philosophy* (Cambridge: Cambridge University Press, 2006).

[257] Gassendi, *Objections and Replies*, CSM 2, p. 215.

most successful Arguments, to convince Men, that there is a God'.[258] As for Spinoza, his scepticism about final causes contributed further to his reputation for atheism. Lurking in the background of these defences, again, was the long-standing association between Epicureanism and the denial of a providential order to nature. Arguments pointing to providential design showed that the world is not the result of random processes, as in classical Epicureanism, but divine counsel. Gassendi and Boyle, who were among the most prominent advocates of a neo-Epicurean physics, were particularly concerned to populate what might otherwise have been a random and purposeless world with providential purpose.

Overall, the war of attrition against the multiple layers of Aristotelian causes, along with a radical contraction of explanatory requirements for natural philosophy, laid the groundwork for a realm of nature that could be understood (in this new and comparatively circumscribed sense) without reference to God. This process was helped along by Immanuel Kant, who, prompted by Hume, proposed that efficient causes were not part of nature anyway, but were the mind's subjective contribution to our knowledge of nature – a kind of grid that exists in the mind but not in the world as it really is. This approach cut off any avenue from causation to the existence of a transcendental first cause, since causes were not part of the transcendental realm. In the seventeenth century these developments were still some distance away. In the meantime, there was a proliferation of works devoted to the defence of a theistic interpretation of nature that was adapted to the new scientific and religious circumstances of the early modern world.

4.5 A New Natural Theology

Another important aspect of the new status of proofs for God's existence concerns the way in which they could be used to support philosophical enterprises, including natural philosophy, by lending them religious legitimacy. Given the present status and authority of science it is natural to assume that the utilisation of scientific discoveries in early modern proofs represents the attempt to shore up support of an epistemically dubious enterprise – theology – by appealing to an experimental natural philosophy whose authority was comparatively more secure. At the time, however, the more vulnerable of the two enterprises, and by a considerable margin, was the new science. An important goal of the prospective partnership was

---

[258] Robert Boyle, *A Disquisition about the Final Causes of Natural Things*, Works, vol. 11, p. 94.

4.5 A NEW NATURAL THEOLOGY

to establish the religious respectability of novel approaches to the study of nature, especially those with a known historical association with atheism.

The new experimental science was subject to much critical scrutiny and even ridicule in early modern England. Best known, perhaps, is Jonathan Swift's savage satire of the Royal Society in *Gulliver's Travels*. But this was just one of a number of critical judgements passed on experimental natural philosophy.[259] These include considered and well-reasoned arguments to the effect that experimental science represented a distraction from the more dignified and edifying enterprises of theology and moral philosophy.[260] Inadvertently or otherwise, this might generate conditions conducive to one or other variety of atheism. For this reason, advocates of experimental philosophy went to considerable lengths to demonstrate its religious propriety, even to the point of arguing that it was an intrinsically moral and religious activity. This is why, following the precedent set by Richard Bentley, subsequent Boyle Lecturers would often defer to new scientific theories. The Lectures were thus able to serve a double function by training minds to see God in nature while establishing the religious usefulness and respectability of the new experimental science at the same time. Here again, then, the accommodation of physico-theological exercises to something like philosophy-of-religion style proofs misses something quite crucial.

The natural sciences would eventually achieve social legitimacy on their own terms, not least by successfully changing the criteria for what counted

---

[259] Jonathan Swift, *Travels into Several Remote Regions of the World* (London, 1726), pt. III, ch. 5. See also Thomas Shadwell, *The Virtuoso* (London, 1676), III, 49; V, 84; Samuel Pepys, *The Diary of Samuel Pepys*, 1 February 1663/4, 8 vols., ed. R. Latham and W. Matthews (London: Bell, 1971), vol. 5, p. 33; James Harrington, *The Prerogative of Popular Government* (London, 1658), Epistle Dedicatory. For attacks on the Royal Society and experimental science see Barbara M. Benedict, *Curiosity: A Cultural History of Early Modern Inquiry* (Chicago: University of Chicago Press, 2001), pp. 46–51; Michael Hunter, *Science and Society in Restoration England* (Cambridge: Cambridge University Press, 1981), p. 111; Stephen Gaukroger, 'Science, Religion and Modernity', *Critical Quarterly* 47 (2005), 1–31; R. H. Syfret, 'Some Early Critics of the Royal Society', *Notes and Records of the Royal Society of London* 8 (1950), 20–64; Peter Harrison, '"The Fashioned Image of Poetry or the Regular Instruction of Philosophy?" Truth, Utility, and the Natural Sciences in Early Modern England', in *Science, Literature, and Rhetoric in Early Modern England*, ed. D. Burchill and J. Cummins (Aldershot: Ashgate, 2008), pp. 15–36.

[260] See, e.g., Meric Casaubon, *A Letter of Meric Casaubon, D.D. &c. to Peter du Moulin D.D., concerning Natural Experimental Philosophie* (Cambridge, 1669), pp. 5, 6, 31; Henry Stubbe, *Legends no Histories: or a Specimen of some Animadversions upon the History of the Royal Society ... together with the Plus Ultra reduced to a Non-Plus* (London, 1670), Preface; *Campanella Revived* (London, 1670), p. 14. Sprat also references such complaints, *History of the Royal Society*, p. 27, as too, Boyle, *Usefulness of Natural Philosophy*, *Works*, vol. 3, p. 213.

as 'useful knowledge'. This was now understood in terms of a contribution to material welfare rather than the accomplishment of moral or religious goals. The independence of science would be signalled by a decline in the use of the compound 'physico-theology' from the nineteenth century onwards. But the initial partnership had established what in retrospect can look like a dependence of religion on science to provide justifications for its fundamental beliefs. Theistic commitment thus found itself in a more precarious position than before and subject to the possibility that future sciences might prove to be less enthusiastic in their support of the religious proposition.

Metaphysical proofs for God's existence – those that would later fall under the classification of ontological and cosmological arguments – share some of the features of the story of physico-theology. In the case of Descartes, for example, it is natural to assume that his more purely 'philosophical' works are attempts to provide foundations upon which to construct subsequent philosophical and scientific projects. Details of his biography suggest an alternative reading. In the late 1620s Descartes embarked upon a scientific project – *The World* – in which he began to develop his mechanical model of a Copernican world system. Learning of the Condemnation of Galileo in 1633, Descartes prudently withdrew the work from publication and turned his hand to the familiar methodological and metaphysical considerations that established his modern reputation as a philosopher. Arguably, however, the intention in the philosophical writings was to provide a post-facto philosophical justification for a set of existing scientific commitments.[261] While Descartes half-heartedly emulated the scholastic order of reasoning in his *Principles of Philosophy* (1644) – metaphysics first, then natural philosophy – this was the result of a reluctant realisation that his scientific ventures could only be successful if it were first established that at worst they were religiously innocuous. A physicist-turned-reluctant-metaphysician, Descartes became 'the father of modern philosophy' largely by accident.

Descartes also sought to establish the respectability of philosophy in a way that paralleled the legitimising endeavours of pious natural philosophers. In the dedicatory letter that prefaces his *Meditations*, he claimed that the topics of God and the soul 'are prime examples of subjects where demonstrative proofs ought to be given *with the aid of philosophy rather than theology*'. This is because while 'the faithful' hold both things true by faith, the 'unfaithful' will be unable to adopt true religion or virtue unless they are

---

[261] See especially Stephen Gaukroger, *Descartes' System of Natural Philosophy* (Cambridge: Cambridge University Press, 2002).

4.5 A NEW NATURAL THEOLOGY

first persuaded by natural reason to a belief in God and the soul.[262] While proofs are superfluous for the faithful, they are needed in order to persuade infidels of the truth and, indirectly, to guarantee social stability in the face of anomic behaviours of 'atheists' who might otherwise abandon religion and virtue. For that audience, appeals to revelation and religious tradition assumed as true the very things that were in dispute.

There are two noteworthy features of Descartes's strategy. First is the deployment of the category 'the unfaithful' to justify the project. This is part of a pattern in which early modern 'atheists' provide the occasion for rationalising enterprises that promise arguments that support fundamental religious claims. Given their intended audience, these arguments present themselves as requiring no prior religious commitments. To put it another way, they appeal to some religiously disinterested 'reason'. Second, and related to this, is Descartes's location of arguments for God's existence within the ambit of an independent philosophy. It is the independence of the operation that lends it credibility. Philosophy becomes the enterprise that can play the role of neutral arbiter. The audience for Descartes's proofs differs from that of the physico-theologians, suggesting a tension between the goals of the respective enterprises – persuading the unbeliever versus edifying the faithful. Proofs would increasingly be understood in terms of the first of these goals.

In spite of Descartes's uneasy relations with religious authorities on both sides of the confessional divide, his appeal to philosophy was consistent with the stance of many Catholic theologians of the period who looked to metaphysics to confront the apparent menace of scepticism and atheism, together with Calvinism and Jansenism (which, in their lights, was scepticism in a religious guise). The physicist-theologian Emmanuel Maignan argued that theology must rest upon the foundation of 'sacred philosophy', which could establish on rational grounds alone the existence of God and his providence.[263] Later in the century, the Benedictine philosopher Dom François Lamy maintained that certitude of faith depended on the science of metaphysics which could prove that there is God who is not a deceiver.[264]

---

[262] CSM 2, p. 3 (my emphasis). In the original Latin, 'we faithful' (*nobis fidelibus*) contrasted with 'the unfaithful' (*infidelibus*). AT VII, 1–2.

[263] Maignan, *Philosophia sacra*, pt. 1. pp. 59f.; cf. Prologue, sections 3–5. For discussion of Maignan and further examples see Alan Charles Kors, 'Scepticism and the Problem of Atheism', in *Scepticism and Irreligion in the Seventeenth and Eighteenth Centuries*, ed. Richard Popkin and Arjo Vanderjagt (Leiden: Brill, 1993), pp. 185–215.

[264] Dom François Lamy, *Le nouvel athéism renversé* (Paris, 1696), 5–8, cited in Kors, 'Scepticism and the Problem of Atheism', pp. 196–7.

Only with this assurance could the believer reside confident in the content of divine revelation. This rationalising trend was accompanied by a revival of interest in scholastic thinkers such as Aquinas, who was now interpreted as having set out a two-tier division of theology. This consisted in a foundational layer of natural theology that established the existence of God through reason alone, upon which was then constructed a second storey of revealed theology that added details specific to Christianity. Natural theology, consisting in proofs, became a necessary foundation for revealed theology.[265]

This was not the view of most Protestant thinkers who, despite using the expression 'natural theology', understood it neither as an independent exercise grounded in reason, nor as a preamble to revealed theology, but as an activity that could be legitimately conducted only within the ambit of revealed theology.[266] Melanchthon thus maintained that once the mind arrives at a right opinion of God from scripture it is *then* possible to seek 'vestiges of God in nature' and 'gather arguments that testify there is a God'.[267] This position was informed by an anthropology that stressed the relative impotence of unassisted reason in the wake of the Fall. This stance was shared by the Jansenists, a movement within early modern French Catholicism that emphasised original sin, predestination, and the primacy of divine grace. Blaise Pascal, the most celebrated representative of this group, contended that 'proofs' were largely pointless because 'the faithful, with living faith in their hearts *can certainly see at once* that everything which exists is entirely the work of the God they worship'. Arguments cannot be for them. As for the rest, when those deprived of faith and grace survey nature they find only 'obscurity and darkness'. Addressing arguments to them serves only to convince the faithless that the proofs of Christian religion are 'feeble'.[268]

---

[265] See, e.g., Théophile Raynaud, *Theologia naturalis* (Lyon, 1622). Kors, 'Scepticism and the Problem of Atheism', pp. 190f.; Marcia L. Colish, 'St. Thomas Aquinas in Historical Perspective: The Modern Period', *Church History* 44 (1975), 433–49.

[266] For a comprehensive overview see Muller, *Reformed Dogmatics*, vol. 1, pp. 270–310.

[267] Melanchthon, *Loci communes* (1535 edition), *Corpus Reformatorum*, vol. 21, col. 369. Calvin held similarly that the human mind, once restored by grace, could again begin to perceive God's revelation in the created order. See Susan E. Shriner, *The Theatre of His Glory: Nature and the Natural Order in the Thought of John Calvin* (Grand Rapids: Baker, 1991), p. 121. See also Junius, *True Theology*, pp. 96f.; *De Theologia*, in *Opuscula Theologia Selecta*, ed. Abraham Kuypers (Amsterdam, 1882), p. 47; Johann Heinrich Alsted, *Theologia Naturalis* (Frankfurt, 1615), p. 12; Johannes Wollebius, *Christianae theologiae compendium* (Basel, 1626), p. 1.

[268] Pascal, *Penseés*, L 781 [B 242], pp. 263f. (my emphasis). Pascal retained the idea of nature as bearing the divine image, but that it could be seen with the eye of faith. *Penseés*, L 199 [B 72], L 934 [B 580], pp. 91, 322. On Pascal's criticisms of contemporary arguments for the existence of God see Martine Pécharman, 'Pascal's Rejection of Natural Theology', in *Physico-Theology*, ed. Blair and von Greyerz, pp. 141–53.

That said, there was a gradual capitulation to the rationalising tendencies of the late seventeenth century among prominent Protestant thinkers and natural theology morphed into something much closer to received conception.[269] On occasion, Robert Boyle would suggest that revealed religion must be founded on a natural theology, in which the experimental sciences were to play an increasingly prominent role. For Boyle, the practices of experimental natural philosophy prepared the mind for the more elevated truths of revelation.[270] This was a slightly different stance to that of Calvin and Melanchthon for whom the truths of revelation enabled the correct interpretation of nature. On the more purely philosophical side, the influential philosopher and mathematician Christian Wolff (1679–1754) helped establish natural theology as a division of a free-standing philosophy. For Wolff, natural theology deals with what can be known of God '*only* through the natural light'.[271] Wolff's natural theology consisted of two speculative proofs for God's existence, one based on the fact that we exist and another proceeding from the idea of God as the most perfect being.[272] These proofs rely upon highly developed philosophical, rather than theological, conceptions. The proof from our existence is thus classified as an a posteriori proof that proceeds on the basis of the principle of sufficient reason; the proof based on the idea of God is a priori and moves from a notion of the *ens perfectissimum* (the most perfect being) to *ens realissimum* (the most real existing

---

[269] See, e.g., Franz Burman, *Synopsis theologiae et speciatim oeconomiae foederum Dei*, 2 vols. (Geneva, 1678, The Hague 1687), I.xiv.7; Abraham Heidanus, *Corpus theologiae Christianae*, 2 vols. (Leiden, 1654–9), vol. 1, pp. 8–10. On the change in the Protestant understanding of natural theology see Otto Zöckler, *Theologia naturalis. Entwurf einer systematischen naturtheologie vom offenbarungsgläubigen standpunkte aus*, vol. 1 (Frankfurt am Main: Heyder & Zimmer, 1860), p. 3. Zöckler argued in favour of the older conception (pp. iii, 1f.). See Bernhard Kleeberg, 'Vestiges of the Book of Nature: Religious Experience and Hermeneutic Practices in Protestant German Theology, ca. 1900', in *Historical Perspectives on Erklären and Verstehen*, ed. Uljana Feest (Dordrecht: Springer, 2010), pp. 37–60; Willem van Asselt, 'The Fundamental Meaning of Theology: Archetypal and Ectypal Theology in Seventeenth-Century Reformed Thought', *Westminster Theological Journal* 64 (2002/3), 319–35; Muller, *Reformed Dogmatics*, vol. 1, pp. 82–4, 122; vol. 4, pp. 401–3.
[270] Boyle, *The Christian Virtuoso I*, *Works*, vol. 11, pp. 298, 304.
[271] Wolff, *Theologia naturalis*, vol. 1, §1 (my emphasis). This is preceded by a rather idiosyncratic definition of natural theology as 'those things that are understood to be possible through God'. Wolffian theologians include Daniel Wyttenbach, Johann Friedrich Stapfer, and Jakob van Nuys Klinkenberg. See Muller, *Reformed Dogmatics*, vol. 1, pp. 82–4, 122.
[272] Wolff, *Theologia naturalis*, vol. 1, §24, vol. 2, §21. For more detail see Charles Anthony Corr, 'The Existence of God, Natural Theology and Christian Wolff', *International Journal for Philosophy of Religion* 4 (1973), 105–18; Gualtiero Lorini, '"Diversa Theologiae naturalis systemata": Christian Wolff's Ways to God', *Revista de Storia della Filosofia* 76 (2021), 760–81.

being). The lineage of these proofs includes the arguments of Descartes's *Meditations*, the sophisticated cosmological argument that Samuel Clarke developed in his Boyle Lectures, and the philosophical theology of Leibniz who, along with Spinoza, introduced the principle of sufficient reason into arguments for the existence of God.[273]

While both physico-theology and the more purely metaphysical proofs represent a trend to outsource defences of Christianity, there are important differences. The metaphysical proofs evince little of the emphasis on moral and religious formation that characterised physico-theology and rely more on the operations of a purely instrumental reason. It was frequently observed, with some justification, that physico-theology appealed more to the popular imagination, while the ontological and cosmological arguments had more intellectual rigour.[274] In terms of these differences, it is significant that Wolff did not even deal with physico-theology in his massive *Theologia naturalis*, regarding it as a kind of popularising addendum. On the other side, as noted earlier, the Jansenist Abbé Pluche could champion physico-theology and yet deny that rational proofs of God's existence were even possible. In his estimation, physico-theology was of a different order to the philosophical articulation of ontological and cosmological arguments. This was because he held to a different view of what natural theology should be. As we have seen, for a good number of its exponents, physico-theology was intended to lead the mind to more elevated truths of revelation. It was foundational in a formative, rather than a logical sense. For the metaphysical systematisers, on the other hand, natural theology was an independent philosophical enterprise that provided an indispensable, rational foundation for theology. The philosopher Alexander Baumgarten, who attended Wolff's lectures at Halle and was later read closely by Kant, typifies this transition. Natural theology, he writes, is 'the science of God insofar as he can be known *without faith*': it 'contains the first principles ... of revealed theology' and belongs to metaphysics.[275]

---

[273] Clarke, *A Demonstration*, pp. 8–12; Leibniz, *Monadology*, §32, §36, in *Philosophical Writings*, pp. 8f.; Spinoza, *Principles of Cartesian Philosophy*, pt. I axiom 11, *CW*, p. 133. The principle of sufficient reason is discussed in more detail below. For Wolff it has an equivalent status to the law of contradiction. *Ontologia*, §§54–78.

[274] See, e.g., Samuel Clarke, 'The Answer to a Seventh Letter', in *A Demonstration*, p. 119; Fénelon, *L'Existence de Dieu*, pp. 1–4.

[275] Alexander Baumgarten, *Metaphysics*, 4th ed. (Halle, 1757), §§800–1, ed. and trans. Courtney D. Fugate and John Hymers (London: Bloomsbury, 2014), p. 294. Cf. Daniel Wyttenbach, *Tentamen theologiæ dogmaticæ methodo scientifica pertractatæ* (Frankfurt am Main, 1747–9), Prologue. For further examples see Muller, *Reformed Dogmatics*, vol. 1, pp. 174, 306.

4.5 A NEW NATURAL THEOLOGY

The theology of nature approach never really went away, but the identification of natural theology as a branch of metaphysics gave the proofs a new disciplinary home and a new status. It was no coincidence that this relocation was accompanied by the appearance of the familiar threefold typology of proofs. In the first *Critique* Kant summarily announces that 'there are three modes of proving the existence of a Deity through reason, and three alone. These are the physico-theological argument, the cosmological argument and the ontological argument.'[276] The range of possibilities for proofs was now circumscribed by a particular conception of reason. Such has been the influence of Kant's treatment, especially in philosophical circles, that the history of proofs and arguments now tends to be constructed along the lines of this typology, with historical figures aligned with one or another of these three arguments. Together, these arguments were also assumed to constitute 'natural theology', in the sense first established in the rationalising philosophies and theologies of the eighteenth century.[277]

The dominance of the Kantian classification since the late eighteenth century has had unfortunate consequences for the historical understanding of the proofs and natural theology. As should be apparent, the reduction of the activity of physico-theology to '*the* physico-theological *argument*' has led to its being artificially aligned with exercises in speculative philosophy. The formative goals of the historical 'proofs' and the role played by preparatory contemplative exercises are also routinely overlooked. Another consequence of the dominance of this approach has been that once-prevalent proofs that are not easily accommodated within the threefold schema have largely been erased from the history of philosophy.[278] This is regrettable,

---

[276] Kant, *Critique of Pure Reason*, A591/B619 (p. 563). Also *Lectures on the Philosophical Doctrine of Religion* in *Religion and Rational Theology*, p. 354. The key labels also come into use for the first time during this period. Wolff invented the term 'teleology' in 1728, while 'physico-theology', as noted earlier, is the 1731 coinage of William Derham. 'Ontology' and 'cosmology' arose earlier, appearing in Greek characters in Goclenius, *Lexicon philosophicum*, p. 16. See Michaël Devaux and Marco Lamanna, 'The Rise and Early History of the Term Ontology (1606–1730)', *Quaestio* 9 (2009), 173–208. Virtually all specific references to ontological, cosmological, and teleological proofs or *arguments* come after Kant.

[277] Johann Eberhard's *Preparation for Natural Theology* (1781) thus neatly packages the proofs, first with a distinction between a priori and a posteriori arguments, followed by further subdivisions and references to the key historical authors. Physico-theology is defined as 'the science that contains the principles for coming to know the existence and attributes of God from the order of nature' (pp. 19–41). Following Wolff, Eberhard goes on to call this a science of final causes, teleology or *theologia experimentalis* (pp. 29–30).

[278] Examples would include Aquinas's fourth way (*ST* Ia. 2, 3); Bonaventure's arguments (see Christopher M. Cullen, *Bonaventure* (Oxford: Oxford University Press, 2006), pp. 63–6); and several of Mersenne's arguments (*Quaestiones in Genesim*, cols. 25–6, 29–34). The rigid

since understanding the appeal of these forgotten proofs and their gradual erasure sheds light on shifting notions of what belief consists in and how it is justified.

4.6 The Consent of Nations Revisited

The Kantian classification of the proofs was as influential as his delimitation of their sphere of operations to the realm of appearances. And while his typology had the practical consequence of defining the *consensus gentium* argument out of existence as a proof, his critical philosophy inadvertently provided a way to give it a new foundation. The post-Kantian philosopher Jakob Friedrich Fries (1773–1843) sought to reinstate the objectivity of a priori forms of intuition, insisting that Kant had been mistaken in thinking that a priori concepts such as space and time were only mind-contributed features of the phenomenal world and that notions of God and the soul were postulates or regulative ideals. Fries also thought that Kant had failed to correctly identify all of the a priori forms of intuition. This alleged failure arose out of the limitations of Kant's philosophical method which Fries sought to rectify with what he called anthropological critique – a kind of empirical investigation of mental processes which philosophy, thus far, had been too 'timid' to broach.[279] This investigation revealed that the mind had a specific capacity for apprehending religious truths, which Fries referred to as *Ahndung* (modern German, *Ahnung*), a form of religious-aesthetic intuition or premonition.[280] Belief in God, then, was not something arrived at indirectly on the basis of evidence. Rather, along the lines of a Kantian transcendental argument, it was a deduction from an analysis of the structures of thought. For Fries, however, this implied a reference to things as they really are, and not just to the phenomenal realm. Whereas Kant maintained that we have no sensations that correspond to the idea of God, Fries insisted that

---

classification also generates ahistorical debates about what counts as an a priori argument as in the cases of Spinoza and Clarke. Clarke thus regarded his 'cosmological proof' to be an argument a priori. For Spinoza see Lin, 'Spinoza's Arguments for the Existence of God'.

[279] Jakob Fries, *Neue oder anthropologische Kritik der Vernunft* [1807], 10th ed., 3 vols. (Heidelberg, 1828–31), vol. 1, pp. 31f. Thomas Reid argues for an analysis of natural history of the mind's operations that is similar in some respects. *Inquiry* 1.2, p. 15.

[280] This was one of three a priori categories of the mind, along with scientific knowledge (*Wissen*) and Faith/Belief (*Glauben*). Jakob Fries, *Wissen, Glauben, und Ahndung* (Jena, 1805), pp. 61–76. For an illuminating discussion see Philip C. Almond, *Rudolf Otto: An Introduction to his Philosophical Theology* (Chapel Hill: University of North Carolina Press, 1984), pp. 47–54; also Todd A. Gooch, *The Numinous and Modernity: An Interpretation of Rudolf Otto's Philosophy of Religion* (Berlin: De Gruyter, 2000), pp. 52–77.

4.6 THE CONSENT OF NATIONS REVISITED

we do, and that religious feelings were genuine intuitions of a real object. The goal was not to prove the existence of God, but to establish that 'every finite reason believes in God'.[281] The substantive claim was essentially the same as that made by advocates of the *consensus gentium* principle. But now it was given a new philosophical/psychological grounding.

A major philosophical figure in his own time, Fries is little known today.[282] If he is known for anything, it is not for his theory of religious experience but for the eponymous 'Fries' Trilemma' which suggests the impossibility of proving anything to be true (also called the 'Münchhausen trilemma', on account of the story of Baron Münchhausen pulling himself out of the mire by his own hair). The quandary lies in the fact that those seeking proofs must opt for one of three equally unsatisfactory options – infinite regression, in which a proof rests in turn on another proof, ad infinitum; circularity, in which the proof of some proposition assumes the truth of the proposition that is to be proven; and dogmatism, where the premises of the proof are dogmatically asserted. Fries contended that the way out of the trilemma was to base argument on forms of unimpeachable experience, religious apprehensions being one such example.[283] The trilemma is thus related to his position on religious experience.

Fries's reworking of Kant also had a major impact on the classic treatment of the religious sensibility set out by Rudolf Otto in *The Idea of the Holy* (1917). Otto criticised the tendency of contemporary rationalising theologies to produce 'one-sidedly intellectualistic' understandings of God.[284] On the other side, the efforts of philosopher-theologians such as Friedrich Schleiermacher to account for religion primarily in terms of 'feeling' (*Gefühl*) were characterised as 'the loose day-dreaming of a sensitive heart'.[285] As for Kant, his distinction between the ideal or phenomenal and

---

[281] Fries, *Kritik der Vernunft*, vol. 1, p. 343. In this passage Fries draws a parallel between belief in God and the Kantian example of belief in the persistence of substances. Kant, *Critique of Pure Reason*, A182/B225 (p. 299). This 'belief' would hold, even if the relevant subject did not consciously acknowledge the reality of the idea. *Kritik der Vernunft*, vol. 2, pp. 204f.

[282] Leonard Nelson did much to revive Friesian thinking in the early twentieth century. See esp. 'The Impossibility of the "Theory of Knowledge"', in *Socratic Method and Critical Philosophy, Selected Essays*, trans. T. Brown, III (New York: Dover, 1965).

[283] Fries's trilemma was influentially referenced by Karl Popper, who referred to Fries's solution as 'psychologism'. *The Logic of Scientific Discovery* (London: Routledge, 2002), p. 87.

[284] Rudolf Otto, *The Idea of the Holy* [1917], 2nd ed., trans. John W. Harvey (Oxford: Oxford University Press, 1958), p. 3.

[285] Rudolf Otto, *The Philosophy of Religion Based on Kant and Fries*, trans. E. B. Dicker (London: Williams and Norgate, 1931), p. 24. For differences between Schleiermacher and Otto see Andrew Dole, 'Schleiermacher and Otto on Religion', *Religious Studies* 40 (2004), 389–413.

'things in themselves' had led to his making the 'disastrous and basic error' that our knowledge of things under the constraints of the a priori categories of space and time were ideal or subjective.[286] For Otto, then, there is an objective reality – the 'holy', or the numinous – which is apprehended 'through the operation of an *a priori* category unique to it, which in its operation is a source of cognition'.[287] This is not reducible to feeling, or reason, or morality, but is its own thing. It is, as Otto would later say, *sui generis*. In moving the focus away from the notion of a monotheistic Deity to a less culturally specific 'numinous', Otto was able to return to a rather diffuse notion of a *consensus gentium* (although he does not use this expression) that was less susceptible to objections based on apparently atheistic religions. The history of religions was said to testify to the fact that the innate sense of the numinous was to be found in every time and every place.[288] This universality did not 'prove' the reality of the numinous but was rather an implication and verification of the religious a priori. Otto's idea of the a priori sense of the numinous had a pervasive impact on the study of religion in the twentieth century and beyond.[289]

A second philosophical survival of the *consensus gentium* principle, as already intimated, was based on Thomas Reid's appeal to common sense. For Reid, our beliefs rest upon '*first principles, principles of common sense, common notions, self-evident truths*'.[290] These are intuitive judgements that are no sooner understood than believed and are attested to by 'the consent of ages and nations, of the learned and unlearned'. Echoing Herbert, Reid states that these principles are 'necessary to all men for their being and preservation', and therefore are 'unconditionally given to all men by the Author of Nature'.[291] But Reid does not list a sense of Deity among these first principles, and neither does he rely upon a universal and innate conception of God in his natural theology.[292]

---

[286] Otto, *The Philosophy of Religion*, p. 19.   [287] Almond, *Rudolf Otto*, p. 83.

[288] Otto, *Idea of the Holy*, pp. 139–40. Otto would seek to apply this principle comparatively in his *Mysticism East and West: A Comparative Analysis of the Nature of Mysticism*, trans. Bertha L. Bracey and Richenda C. Payne (Eugene: Wipf and Stock, 2016). Carl Jung made the connection between Otto's 'numinous' and the *consensus gentium*. C. G. Jung, *Psychology and Religion, Collected Works*, 20 vols., ed. Herbert Reid, Michael Fordham, and Gerhard Adler (Princeton: Princeton University Press, 1953–91), vol. 11, p. 4891.

[289] Almond, *Rudolf Otto*, pp. 11–132.

[290] Reid, *Essays* 6.4, p. 452.

[291] Reid, *Essays* 6.4, p. 464; 4.6, p. 412; 1.2.7, p. 44.

[292] On Reid's failure to be 'Reidian' in relation to an innate sense of Deity see Wolterstorff's introduction to *Thomas Reid on Religion*. See also Ryan Nichols and Robert Callergård, 'Thomas Reid on Reidian Belief Forming Faculties', *The Modern Schoolman* 88 (2011), 329–47. Reid favoured cosmological and design arguments. His cosmological argument

4.6 THE CONSENT OF NATIONS REVISITED

Nonetheless, Reid's general approach lends itself to a more explicit invocation of a *consensus gentium* argument and contemporary philosophers such Nicholas Wolterstorff and Alvin Plantinga have developed his basic approach along these lines. Both thinkers marry Reid's 'first principles' to Calvin's *sensus divinitatis*, proposing that belief in God is not a conclusion to be argued to, but is more like an undemonstrated premise.[293] A distinctive feature of this so-called 'reformed epistemology' is Reid's reliabilism, according to which we are generally justified in accepting what our faculties present to us as true, provided that those faculties are operating as intended by nature (or, in Reid's case, God). Plantinga, for example, suggests that we are warranted in accepting a belief that 'has been produced ... by cognitive faculties that are working properly (functioning as they ought to, subject to no cognitive dysfunction) in a cognitive environment that is appropriate for my kinds of cognitive faculties'.[294] He then suggests that we may have a faculty, along the lines of Calvin's *sensus divinitatis*, which God has placed in us with the intention of generating true beliefs about him. Elsewhere he would describe such beliefs as 'properly basic', which means that they function as non-demonstrated starting points.[295] There are clear affinities here with pre-Cartesian understandings of the way in which the existence of God is built into the mind and the structures of thought. That said, Plantinga's focus on warrant still reflects a modern concern with the rational justification of religious beliefs. It is just that the justification is provided on reliabilist rather than evidentialist grounds.[296]

Closely related to this is a third survival of the *consensus gentium* principle which appears in a somewhat surprising quarter – the cognitive science of religion. Practitioners within this rather heterogeneous field have sought to identify the cognitive mechanisms responsible for religious belief. The underlying assumption is that religious belief is, in fact, universal,

---

rests on the principle of sufficient reason which *is* identified as one of the principles of common sense. *Essays*, pp. 497, 503.

[293] Alvin Plantinga, *Warranted Christian Belief* (New York: Oxford University Press, 2000), pp. 167–98.

[294] He goes on to specify two further conditions: '(2) the segment of the design plan governing the production of that belief is aimed at the production of true beliefs, and (3) there is a high statistical probability that a belief produced under those conditions will be true'. Alvin Plantinga, *Warrant and Proper Function* (Oxford: Oxford University Press, 1993), pp. 46–7.

[295] Plantinga, *Warrant: The Current Debate*, p. 86; *Warrant and Proper Function*, p. 61. However, this notion takes us in different direction to the *consensus gentium* principle, on account of Plantinga's suggestion that properly basic beliefs are different for different epistemic communities.

[296] The concern with justification is what distinguishes this position from fideism.

notwithstanding the advances made by secularisation in the West or the earlier claims of figures such as Locke and Bayle. In fact, the assertions of the latter about societies of atheists have not aged well and were under attack as early as the end of the nineteenth century. 'As every anthropologist knows', declared Frank Jevons in 1896, the debate about the existence of atheistic societies 'has now gone to the limbo of dead controversies'. Jevons went on to list eight of the leading anthropologists of his time, all of whom 'agree that there are no races, however rude, which are destitute of all ideas of religion'.[297] For sociologist Émile Durkheim (1858–1917), religion, albeit understood functionally, was actually constitutive of societies, rendering the expression 'non-religious society' an oxymoron.

Contemporary social scientists tend to be of the same view. According to psychologist Paul Bloom, 'Religious belief and religious practice are human universals. There are no atheist communities and, as far as we know, there never have been.'[298] This contention is supported by empirical research findings which suggest that children's cognitive systems are especially receptive to, or even generative of, God concepts. Children are said to be 'intuitive theists' or 'born believers'.[299] This research also points to innate

[297] Frank B. Jevons, *An Introduction to the History of Religion* (London: Methuen, 1896), p. 7. Cf. American anthropologist John H. King, *The Supernatural: Its Origin, Nature, and Evolution*, 2 vols. (London: Williams and Norgate, 1892), vol. 1, p. 4. This was also strongly maintained by theological advocates of natural theology. See W. R. Pirie, *Natural Theology* (London: Blackwood, 1867), pp. 53–68. Scientific naturalists such as John Lubbock and Frederick Harrison continued to attack the idea, however, wondering why intelligent individuals such as themselves were apparently devoid of such innate sentiments. Lubbock, *Prehistoric Times*, pp. 589–94; Lester F. Ward, *Dynamic Sociology*, 2 vols. (New York: Appleton, 1883), vol. 2, p. 263; Rev. F. W. Farrar, 'On the Universality of Belief in God, and in a Future State', *The Anthropological Review* 2 (1864), ccxvii–ccxxii. See also Bernard Lightman, 'Science at the Metaphysical Society', in *The Age of Scientific Naturalism: Tyndall and His Contemporaries*, ed. Bernard Lightman and Michael S. Reidy (Abingdon: Routledge, 2016), pp. 187–206 (pp. 198f.).

[298] Paul Bloom, 'Religious Belief as an Evolutionary Accident', in *The Believing Primate: Scientific, Philosophical, and Theological Reflections on the Origin of Religion*, ed. Jeffrey Schloss and Michael Murray (Oxford: Oxford University Press, 2009), pp. 118–27. Theravada Buddhism might seem to present an immediate obstacle to this contention. While this issue is too large a question to be canvassed here, briefly, it is possible to think of Theravada Buddhism as consistent with theism in the limited sense that it allows for finite gods, notwithstanding that attachment to belief in them may constitute a barrier to achieving enlightenment which lies beyond our concepts and beliefs. The Buddha himself was known, in Pali, as *devamanusyanam shasta* – the teacher of gods and humans: and so neither an atheist nor a believer in a monotheistic Deity.

[299] See esp. Justin L. Barrett and R. A. Richert, 'Anthropomorphism or Preparedness? Exploring Children's God Concepts', *Review of Religious Research* 44 (2003), 300–12; Deborah Kelemen, 'Are Children "Intuitive Theists"? Reasoning about Purpose and Design in Nature', *Psychological Science* 15 (2004), 295–301.

tendencies to interpret the world teleologically or subscribe to dualist theories of mind.[300] Locke's test case of the presence of the innate conception of God in children, granting the reliability of these studies, has thus turned out to count against him. Religious belief, on these accounts, can be said to be both 'natural' and at least potentially universal.[301]

The modern rediscovery of universal consent has mostly inspired efforts to explain religious belief away – directly contrary to the pre-modern assumption that naturalness constitutes evidence for the truth of the belief. The prevailing tendency, drawing upon evolutionary psychology, has been towards various forms of evolutionary debunking – religion not as the outcome of any unitary cognitive structure, but as a by-product or 'false positive' generated by mental mechanisms designed by natural selection for other adaptive purposes.[302] The trick, of course, is to debunk religious commitment without at the same undermining every product of human cognition (including evolutionary debunking itself).[303] However, against the general trend, some have pointed to affinities between this empirical research and Calvin's *sensus divinitatis*. In the spirit of early modern defences of the *consensus gentium* principle there is, then, a possible reading that might actually support the rationality of religious belief. This empirical approach

---

[300] Deborah Kelemen, 'British and American Children's Preferences for Teleo-Functional Explanations of the Natural World', *Cognition* 88 (2003), 201–21; Paul Bloom, 'Religion Is Natural', *Developmental Science* 10 (2007), 147–51.

[301] Justin Barrett, 'Exploring the Natural Foundations of Religion', *Trends in Cognitive Sciences* 4 (2000), 29–34, esp. 29; Robert N. McCauley and Emma Cohen, 'Cognitive Science and the Naturalness of Religion', *Philosophy Compass* 5 (2020), 779–92; Bloom, 'Religion Is Natural'. Scholars of religion are generally less enthusiastic than social scientists about such claims, with some suggesting that they involve naïve and uncritical conceptions of 'religion'. Some philosophers have also been hostile to the thesis. See John R. Shook, 'Are People Born to Be Believers, or Are Gods Born to Be Believed?', *Method & Theory in the Study of Religion* 29 (2017), 353–73, and further discussion in the same journal number.

[302] Advocates of evolutionary debunking arguments include Scott Atran, *In Gods We Trust: The Evolutionary Landscape of Religion* (New York: Oxford University Press, 2002); Pascal Boyer, *Religion Explained: The Evolutionary Origins of Religious Thought* (New York: Basic Books, 2001); Daniel Dennett, *Breaking the Spell: Religion as a Natural Phenomenon* (New York: Viking Penguin, 2006). For discussions of the effectiveness of such arguments, see Helen De Cruz and Johan De Smedt, *Natural History of Natural Theology: A Cognitive Science of Theology and Philosophy of Religion* (Cambridge, MA: MIT Press, 2014), pp. 184f., and *passim*; Michael J. Murray, 'Scientific Explanations of Religion and the Justification of Religious Belief', in *The Believing Primate*, ed. Schloss and Murray, pp. 168–79; Lari Launonen, 'Natural Religion in Science and Theology', PhD thesis, University of Helsinki, 2022, pp. 28–34.

[303] For an attempt to thread this needle see John S. Wilkins and Paul E. Griffiths, 'Evolutionary Debunking Arguments in Three Domains: Fact, Value, and Religion', in *A New Science of Religion*, ed. James McLaurin and Greg Dawes (London: Routledge, 2012), pp. 133–46.

also nicely complements the Reidian assumptions of the project of reformed epistemology.[304] So the appeal to universal consent lives on in different guises, although few now subscribe to the assumptions that once rendered it 'the first and most popular argument' for God's existence.

The changing content, status, and background assumptions of the proofs for God's existence in the modern period are revealing. It is clear that from the sixteenth century onwards the existence of God moved from being something that could be more-or-less taken for granted, to something for which supportive arguments needed to be provided. The burden of proof thus gradually shifted from largely imaginary atheists to defenders of theism. This new situation, as we have seen, was owing to a cluster of related developments: critiques of implicit faith and the growth of an ethics of belief; the appearance of a largely theoretical atheism which seemed to demand 'neutral' arguments'; the emergence of specialist domains of argumentation in the spheres of philosophy, natural philosophy, and natural theology. These changes meant that the rationality of religious belief came to rest upon new forms of contestable evidence and argument. Few at the time thought that these rational defences would prove to be inadequate. Yet, Descartes's Calvinist detractors may well have had a point when they accused him of advancing arguments for God's existence that were so feeble that they opened the way for atheism. Margaret Cavendish wondered likewise about the laboured proofs of Henry More's *Antidote*: whether in seeking 'to prove that which all men believe' the unintended result was 'to bring it into question'.[305] Along these same lines, the deist philosopher Anthony Collins mischievously suggested that no one thought to question the existence of God until the Boyle Lecturers set out to prove it, while the notorious materialist Julien de la Mettrie remarked that tiresome repetitions of the physico-theologians were 'more likely to strengthen than to undermine the foundations of atheism'.[306] The philosophy of religion, understood as an activity that was neutral with respect to religious commitments, was thus destined to oversee and make determinations on the rationality of religious belief, inheriting Kant's procrustean classification of proofs (but

---

[304] See, especially, Kelly James Clark and Justin L. Barrett, 'Reidian Religious Epistemology and the Cognitive Science of Religion', *Journal of the American Academy of Religion* 79 (2011), 639–75; Alvin Plantinga, *Where the Conflict Really Lies: Science, Religion, and Naturalism* (Oxford: Oxford University Press, 2011), pp. 60, 263–4, 312.

[305] Margaret Cavendish, 'Philosophical Letters', in *Essential Writings*, p. 75, cf. p. 86.

[306] Quoted in John Brooke and Geoffrey Cantor, *Reconstructing Nature: The Engagement of Science and Religion* (Edinburgh: T&T Clark, 1998), p. 198; Julien de la Mettrie, *Man a Machine* [1747] (La Salle: Open Court, 1912), p. 123.

largely ignoring his proposal that God be understood as a postulate or regulative ideal). When used as a lens through which to view the history of 'proofs' this led to the erasure of anything that did not fit the pattern of ontological, cosmological, or teleological arguments, with 'argument' now understood in a quite specific way. As it relates to changing conceptions of belief outlined in the previous section, this approach promotes an idea of knowledge as something like justified true belief, along with the assumption of a gap between knowledge and belief that is to be bridged with evidence.

These transitions did not go unprotested and there were powerful religious objections to the evidential role given to philosophical proofs. But these were necessarily internal to the Christian tradition and hence lacked the 'neutral' standpoint that evidentialism now required. At the same time, as is apparent in the Cartesian 'meditations' and at least some of the practices of physico-theology, the idea of 'proofs' as forms of spiritual exercise did not completely vanish either. Arguably, these formative elements linger on still, persisting to some degree in the pedagogical practices associated with training in the modern university disciplines. Their vestiges might be made visible through attentive study of the ways in which scientists and social scientists, for example, undergo disciplinary training. Now, of course, the goal is to inculcate a naturalistic mindset that seeks to eradicate any trace of teleological or theistic thinking, at least for the purposes of the disciplinary exercise. This, arguably, is what methodological naturalism consists in. From the early modern period to the present, then, we see a trajectory from theistic (understood as natural), to neutral, to philosophical and scientific. The latter are also understood as natural, but now in the completely opposite sense. This transformed understanding of the authority of 'the natural' takes place partly as a consequence of a new opposition between naturalism and supernaturalism.

5

THE BIRTH OF THE SUPERNATURAL

Moreover, the idea of the supernatural, as we understand it, arrived only yesterday; it presupposes, in fact, its opposite .... Now as long as this idea was absent or insufficiently established, there was nothing inconceivable in even the most marvellous events.

> Émile Durkheim, *Elementary Forms of the Religious Life*

Our modern world, on the contrary, after many centuries of tedious research, has attained a conviction, that all things are linked together by a chain of causes and effects, which suffers no interruption .... This conviction is so much a habit of thought with the modern world, that in actual life, the belief in a supernatural manifestation, an immediate divine agency, is at once attributed to ignorance or imposture.

> David Strauss, *Life of Jesus*

Indeed, what might have to be challenged here is the very distinction nature/supernature itself.

> Charles Taylor, *A Secular Age*[1]

In the closing decade of the nineteenth century, Thomas Henry Huxley, the fierce advocate of Darwinism and scientific naturalism, offered this overview of the course of human civilisation: 'From the earliest times of which we have any knowledge, Naturalism and Supernaturalism have consciously or unconsciously, competed and struggled with one another; and the varying fortunes of the contest are written in the records of the course of civilization.' Huxley went on to predict the ultimate victory of Naturalism. While 'Supernaturalism'

---

[1] Epigraphs: Émile Durkheim, *Les formes élémentaire de la vie religieuse, le système totémique en Australie* (Paris: Alcan, 1912), p. 36; David Strauss, *The Life of Jesus, critically examined*, 4th ed, trans. George Eliot (London: George Allen & Unwin, 1913), p. 78; *A Secular Age* by Charles Taylor, Cambridge, MA: The Belknap Press of Harvard University Press, p. 732. Copyright © 2007 by Charles Taylor. Used by permission. All rights reserved.

was acknowledged to have deep roots in human nature, making it difficult to eradicate, 'Naturalism' was embodied in the irresistible force of 'Science'. The triumph of science and naturalism was assured, and Huxley predicted that the authority of scientific naturalism would eventually extend 'to every region in which the Supernatural has hitherto been recognised'.[2]

While Huxley's vision of a naturalistic future turned out to be prescient in many respects, his assertions about the past were wide of the mark. The depiction of the history of civilisation as a perennial struggle between naturalism and supernaturalism would certainly have come as news to those on both sides of the imagined divide (leaving aside the fact that a history of *civilisation* is already a loaded exercise). More significant for our purposes is the fact that the concepts deployed by Huxley to frame this apparent conflict would have been utterly foreign to the historical actors whose commitments they were meant to represent. For pre-modern thinkers, and indeed for many in the early modern period, reality was simply not divided along the lines of a natural/supernatural dichotomy. Crucially, the terminology of 'the supernatural' did not begin to emerge in the West until the thirteenth century and even then it bore a very different meaning to the one that Huxley attached to it. The subsequent '-isms' to which Huxley refers – natural*ism* and supernatural*ism* – came even later, appearing at the close of the eighteenth century. The more general idea of history as an enduring struggle between competing ideologies or authorities is implicit in some post-Reformation and Enlightenment views of history, but again, only in the nineteenth century did it become a mainstream historical thesis expressed in terms of a tension between science and religion or naturalism and supernaturalism. This version of history played a central role in establishing the authority of the modern natural and social sciences, and to a large degree of twentieth-century analytic philosophy, too. More generally, it became a foundational motif for modernity's historical self-understanding. The details of how it did so will be dealt with in more detail in the next chapter.

What made these histories possible was a broad acceptance of the naturalism/supernaturalism dichotomy along the lines set out by Huxley and its retrospective application to history. Three aspects of the Huxley-style narrative require scrutiny. We need first to examine the actual practices and underlying assumptions of imagined historical practitioners of naturalism, paying attention to the ways in which they understood nature and its operations. Second, we must consider the concepts and terminology

---

[2] Thomas Henry Huxley, 'Essays upon some Controverted Questions' [1892], *CE*, vol. 5, pp. 5, 7, 32. Capitalisation is Huxley's.

used in these late nineteenth-century constructions of history – 'natural', 'naturalism', 'supernatural', 'supernaturalism' – in order to discover when individuals first began to think in terms of these categories, and then reflect upon what difference this makes to how the story of intellectual progress is told. Third, given what will become apparent from these analyses – the distance between Huxley's story and actual history – we can explore how the naturalism narrative first came into being, why it seemed plausible to his contemporaries, and why it persists in some form to this day.

5.1 Ionian Disenchantment?

It was common in nineteenth-century naturalism stories, and indeed for much commentary since, to locate the origin of scientific naturalism in Presocratic Greek thinkers of the sixth and fifth centuries BCE.[3] These thinkers are said to have moved away from explanations of natural events in terms of the actions of gods, seeking instead to identify underlying explanatory principles. There is some textual evidence for this familiar story. A number of early Greek thinkers can be read as seeking to account for nature's operations in terms of general principles and this was recognised by their immediate successors. Aristotle, for example, seems to identify the first of the Presocratic philosophers, Thales of Miletus (c.624–c.548 BCE), as the inaugurator of a new, philosophical, way of thinking about the world. For Aristotle, this distinguished him from earlier 'myth-makers'.[4] But the idea of Thales

---

[3] T. H. Huxley, 'The Progress of Science', *CE*, vol. 1, p. 43; cf. vol. 9, p. 104. For the same story in relatively recent popular histories of science see Bryan Bunch and Alexander Hellemans, *The History of Science and Technology* (Boston: Houghton Mifflin, 2004), pp. 1, 51f., 81, 93, 142; Charles Freeman, *The Closing of the Western Mind* (New York: Vintage, 2005), pp. xviii–xix, 4–6, and *passim*; Robert Wilson, *Astronomy through the Ages* (Princeton: Princeton University Press, 1997), p. 45; David Deming, *Science and Technology in World History*, 2 vols. (Jefferson, NC: McFarland, 2010), vol. 2, pp. 26–31; Andrew Ede and Lesley B. Cormack, *A History of Science in Society*, 2nd ed. (Toronto: University of Toronto Press, 2012), p. 10; E. O. Wilson, *Consilience: The Unity of Knowledge* (New York: Random House, 1998), pp. 4–5; and, most recently, Carlo Rovelli, *Anaximander and the Nature of Science* (London: Penguin, 2023). These views persist to some degree even in relatively recent scholarly commentary. See J. Warren, *Presocratics* (Berkeley: University of California Press, 2007), p. 24; K. Algra, 'The Beginnings of Cosmology', in *The Cambridge Companion to Early Greek Philosophy*, ed. A. A. Long (Cambridge: Cambridge University Press, 1999), pp. 45–65; D. Graham (ed. and trans.), *The Texts of Early Greek Philosophy* (Cambridge: Cambridge University Press, 2010), pp. 45–6; Peter Adamson, *Classical Philosophy: A History of Philosophy Without Any Gaps*, vol. 1 (Oxford: Oxford University Press, 2014), pp. 3–6. These stories also continue to inform the self-image of contemporary naturalistic philosophers. See Smith, 'Metaphilosophy of Naturalism'.

[4] Aristotle, *Metaphysics* 983b27–33.

as the progenitor of philosophy is more the invention of nineteenth-century historians of philosophy than it is an Aristotelian or ancient Greek tradition.[5] The questions of what gets counted as 'philosophy' and who gets the credit for having originated it will be examined in more detail in the next chapter. For now, however, we can ask whether the efforts of the Presocratic philosophers amount to a move in the direction of anything like modern naturalism. In a word – no. While we have only fragmentary textual evidence for the views of most of these thinkers, it is safe to say that the underlying explanatory principles that they identified were in a broad sense theistic. The relevant opposition was between nature as governed by the capricious activities of anthropomorphic deities versus nature as a manifestation of orderly divine principles. For Presocratic thinkers and virtually all of their Greek and Roman successors, the cosmos was thought to be permeated by the divine. The opposition in play is between competing theological conceptions.

Thales, for example, declared that 'all things are full of gods'. On discovering his celebrated mathematical theorem he is reported to have sacrificed an ox, presumably attributing his discovery to divine inspiration.[6] Anaxagoras (b. c.500 BCE) who was another of the 'Ionian school' (named for a Greek colony on the west coast of what is now modern Turkey) is also associated with the transition to naturalism, on account of his apparent denial of the divinity of some of the heavenly bodies. But he, too, contended that the world is governed by a divine principle (*nous* – mind or intellect).[7] This conception, which speaks to the inherent rationality of the natural world, found its way in different guises into the thinking of Plato, Aristotle, the Stoics, and the Neoplatonists.[8] Another unwitting Presocratic

---

[5] The ancient Greeks typically thought that philosophy had originated with earlier, non-Greek thinkers – Babylonians, Egyptians, Persians, or Phoenicians. Moreover, Aristotle's commonly invoked distinction between natural philosophers (*physiologoi/physikoi*) and theologians (*theologoi*) is often overdrawn. See esp. Lea Cantor, 'Thales – the "First Philosopher"? A Troubled Chapter in the Historiography of Philosophy', *British Journal for the History of Philosophy* 30 (2022), 727–50. The thesis of the Greek origins of Western philosophy will be discussed in more detail in the next chapter.

[6] Thales' theorem states that the diameter of a circle subtends a right angle to any point on the circumference. Sources for Thales' views include Aristotle, *De Anima* 411a9; Euclid, *Elements*, bk. 1, prop. 32. See also Sarah Broadie, 'Rational Theology', in *The Cambridge Companion to Early Greek Philosophy*, ed. Long, pp. 205–24; Robin Waterfield, *The First Philosophers* (Oxford: Oxford University Press, 2000), p. xxxiii.

[7] Anaxagoras R5/A47 (LCL 529, p. 133). Cf. Plato, *Phaedo* 97c; *Philebus* 28d; Aristotle, *Metaphysics* 984b15–18.

[8] For an argument that Aristotelian teleology is the logical development of this Presocratic tradition see, e.g., Edward Engelmann, 'Aristotelian Teleology, Presocratic Hylozoism, and 20th Century Interpretations', *American Catholic Philosophical Quarterly* 64 (1990), 297–312.

conscript to the cause of naturalism, Anaximander (c.610–c.546 BCE), seems to have held similarly that a divine lawmaker was responsible for the regularities of nature. Like most of his contemporaries he also believed that the heavens were divine.[9] Xenophanes of Colophon provides an even clearer example of the role played by theological considerations in these revised understandings of the natural world. He offers a mocking critique of the anthropomorphic gods depicted by the poets Homer and Hesiod. But his motivation arose not from some incipient 'naturalism' but rather a conviction that there is 'one God' who 'moves all things by the will of his mind'.[10] Given all this, it is unsurprising that classicist David Sedley has remarked that naturalist readings of these early thinkers, in spite of their ongoing currency among non-experts, represent 'a serious misperception of the Presocratic agenda'. Sedley suggests, to the contrary: 'that the world is governed by a divine power is a pervasive assumption of Presocratic thought'.[11] In keeping with this analysis Daryn Lehoux has recently observed that almost all Presocratic thinkers invoke deities in reference to the operations of nature.[12]

While the Presocratics are commonly imagined to represent the first turn towards something like naturalistic science, Aristotle might be regarded as the most influential of all scientific thinkers. Aristotelian approaches to natural philosophy dominated Western thinking for more than a millennium and arguably have never completely gone away.[13] In many respects, Aristotle continued the Presocratic indifference to any strong demarcation of natural and divine. As already noted, Aristotle taught that a complete explanation of change in the natural world involved recourse to four causes – material,

---

[9] Stobaeus, *Anthology* 1.1.29b. See Daryn Lehoux, '"All Things are Full of Gods": Naturalism in the Classical World', in *Science without God?*, ed. Harrison and Roberts, pp. 19–36. For Anaximander's naturalism see Algra, 'The Beginnings of Cosmology', p. 48.

[10] Xenophanes D 12–14; D 16–20 (LCL 526, pp. 29–31, 33–5).

[11] David Sedley, *Creationism and Its Critics in Antiquity* (Berkeley: University of California Press, 2007), p. 2. For the persistence of the mythopoetic worldview among Presocratic thinkers see the classic studies of F. M. Cornford, *From Philosophy to Religion* [1912] (Princeton: Princeton University Press, 1991), pp. 127–30; Jaeger, *Theology of the Early Greek Philosophers*; and, more recently, Adam Drozdek, *Greek Philosophers as Theologians: The Divine Arche* (Aldershot: Ashgate, 2007). See also Cantor, 'Thales – the "First Philosopher"?'

[12] Lehoux lists Thales, Anaxagoras, Anaximenes, Heraclitus, Empedocles, Diogenes of Apollonia, all the Pythagoreans, and Parmenides. 'Naturalism in the Classical World'.

[13] For its persistence see William M. R. Simpson, Robert C. Koons, and Nicholas J. Teh (eds.), *Neo-Aristotelian Perspectives on Contemporary Science* (London: Routledge, 2018); Edward Feser, *Aristotle's Revenge: The Metaphysical Foundations of Physical and Biological Science* (Neunkirchen-Seelscheid: Editiones Scholasticae, 2019).

formal, efficient, and final. The most eminent of these was the final cause, which is the ultimate source of all motion. The heavenly bodies, for example, move for the sake of a divine unmoved mover.[14] For Aristotle, moreover, as for his philosophical predecessors, the heavens are 'divine'. This meant that the study of celestial motions was a form of theology.[15] Human beings also have divine qualities – reason, intelligence, and a potential for moral perfection.[16] In *Parts of Animals* Aristotle thus contends that our 'nature and essence are divine'.[17] The general point is that for Aristotle the study of nature necessarily incorporates the divine (albeit 'divine' as he understood it). Philosopher Martin Heidegger informs us that for Aristotle nature (*physis*) 'originally means both heaven and earth, both the stone and the plant, both the animal and the human, and human history as the work of humans and gods, *and finally and first of all, it means the gods who themselves stand under destiny*'.[18] If Heidegger is right about this it makes little sense to locate Aristotelian science on the naturalistic side of some imagined divide between naturalism and supernaturalism. Aristotle was simply not operating with that kind of distinction in mind.[19] In fact, his typology of theoretical knowledge places 'theology' at the top of the hierarchy of the sciences, with

---

[14] Aristotle, *Metaphysics* 1072a26–27; *On the Heavens* 279a20–30. See Fabienne Baghdassarian, *La question du divin chez Aristote: Discours sur les dieux et science du principe* (Leuven: Peeters, 2016); Michael Frede and David Charles (eds.), *Aristotle's Metaphysics Lambda* (Oxford: Oxford University Press, 2000). Aristotle sometimes speaks of divine *movers* (plural). See Stephen Menn, 'Aristotle's Theology', in *The Oxford Handbook of Aristotle*, ed. Shields, pp. 422–64.

[15] Aristotle, *On the Heavens* 279a31f.; *Posterior Analytics* 644b25; *Metaphysics*, 1026a20.

[16] Aristotle, *Eudemian Ethics* 1248a25f.; *On the Soul*, 408b29; *Metaphysics* 1074b16; *Nicomachean Ethics* 1177a16.

[17] Aristotle, *Parts of Animals* 686a27–8. He also makes the curious remark in *Generation of Animals* 761a2–5 that bees possess something divine. See the fascinating discussion in Daryn Lehoux, 'Why Does Aristotle Think Bees Are Divine?', *British Journal for the History of Science* 52 (2019), 383–403.

[18] Heidegger, *Introduction to Metaphysics*, p. 16 (my emphasis). Compare Bruno Snell on 'natural' for the earlier Homeric period: 'The natural first sees the light of day in the Homeric poems; its emergence involves an intimate connexion between the life of man and the purpose of the gods.' *The Discovery of the Mind*, trans. T. G. Rosenmeyer (New York: Dover, 1982), p. 38. *Physis* is typically regarded as the ancient Greek term most analogous to our 'nature', but a case can also be made for *kosmos*, which refers to the ordered totality of all things, including the gods. See Julia Kerschensteiner, *Kosmos: Quellenkritische Untersuchungen zu den Vorsokratikern* (München: C. H. Beck, 1962); Gerard Naddaf, *The Greek Concept of Nature* (Albany, NY: SUNY Press, 2005); Julián Pacho, 'The Universe as Cosmos: On the Ontology of the Greek World Image', in *Concepts of Nature*, ed. Hans Ulrich Vogel and Günter Dux (Leiden: Brill, 2010), pp. 136–59.

[19] For Aristotle's definitions of nature (*physis*), see *Metaphysics* 1014b16–1015a19. Cf. Aquinas, *Commentary on Metaphysics*, 808–26.

natural philosophy and mathematics proposed as way stations.[20] Aristotle's failure to observe the natural/supernatural distinction is not a bug in the system, or an inability to fully realise the extent of his own incipient naturalism. The involvement of the divine in nature was foundational to the explanatory framework.

While Aristotle does not oppose natural to supernatural, one relevant contrast that he did offer is that between the natural and the *accidental*. For Aristotle, scientific explanation is not threatened by theistic considerations so much as by events that happen by chance or by accident.[21] These present a challenge to scientific explanation, as Aristotle understands it. Against the background of this assumption, and in what would become a fairly standard pattern for the subsequent history of science, divine beings or principles (or a single divine being) were regarded as the source of nature's regularity and intelligibility and hence as foundational to scientific explanation. Two other oppositions are important for Aristotelian philosophy: natural versus violent, and natural versus artificial.[22] These also had a bearing on later scientific developments. For Aristotle, human interference in natural processes renders them unnatural and 'violent' – as, for example, when an object is thrown upwards against its natural tendency to move downwards. This distinction accounts for the resistance with which experimental approaches were initially met by those wedded to this common sense Aristotelian distinction. The production of experimental effects by human agents rendered what was observed unnatural, and hence not truly revealing of nature itself. The natural/artificial distinction similarly ruled out the use of mechanical models for natural processes, since again such models were human constructions.[23] These distinctions comport with Aristotle's assertion of the eternity

---

[20] Aristotle, *Posterior Analytics* 75a38–39; *Metaphysics* 1025b19–1026a33; *On the Heavens* 299a2–20. This, of course, is 'theology' in Aristotle's sense of the word. See Harrison, *Territories*, pp. 31f. In a sense, it is Aristotle who first regarded theology as the queen of the sciences, although neither he nor subsequent medieval thinkers seemed to have used that exact expression. See Gijsbert van den Brink, 'How Theology Stopped Being *Regina Scientiarum*—and How Its Story Continues', *Studies in Christian Ethics* 34 (2019), 442–54.

[21] Aristotle, *Metaphysics* VI; *Physics* 197a31–35, 196b, 15–16. On chance and scientific explanation see Peter Harrison, 'What Was Historical about Natural History? Contingency and Explanation in the Science of Living Things', *Studies in History and Philosophy of Science* 58 (2015), 8–16.

[22] Aristotle, *Physics* 192b9–193b23; *On the Heavens* 268b27–270a13; *Nicomachean Ethics* 1134b18–1135a6.

[23] Fritz Krafft, 'Kunst und Natur. Die Heronische Frage und die Technik in der klassischen Antike', *Antike und Abendland* 19 (1973), 1–19. For a more nuanced interpretation see Mark J. Schiefsky, 'Art and Nature in Ancient Mechanics', in *The Artificial and the Natural: An Evolving Polarity*, ed. B. Bensaude-Vincent and W. R. Newman (Cambridge, MA: MIT

of the world which, although it depends upon a divine first cause, is not created in time. ('First' here referring to primacy rather than some temporal order.) This view of the eternity of the world was challenged by Jewish and Christian thinkers for whom the world was God's creation. This meant that it was, in effect, an artefact. This theological challenge to the natural/artificial distinction arguably enabled early modern thinkers to make the case that mechanics was relevant to understanding motion.[24]

Aristotle's exclusion of the accidental from the sphere of scientific study brings to mind the one group from classical antiquity who might with some justification be regarded as exemplars of a form of naturalism (*avant la lettre*) – the Epicureans. Epicureans held that the gods were uninterested in human affairs, implying that they could be safely ignored. They also subscribed to an atomistic materialism and proposed a speculative theory of evolution to account for the existence of the world and its human inhabitants. Yet an interesting tension lay at the heart of Epicurean physics. On the one hand, natural phenomena were to be understood in terms of the interactions of atoms moving in a void. On the other hand, in the deterministic, centreless Epicurean universe, atoms would be perpetually falling in parallel. Strictly speaking this meant that they would never interact, yielding a rather barren universe in which nothing could ever happen. In other words, there was no reason, internal to the Epicurean system, for atoms to deviate from their paths, and this deprived the theory of much of its explanatory power. An additional problem was that this view of things deprived human beings of free will. To negotiate these difficulties, Lucretius famously invoked the ad hoc device of 'the swerve', which has atoms deviating from their courses and giving rise to the interactions that were required for anything to happen in the universe.[25] It is not clear whether this was supposed to be a one-time occurrence, or a regular feature of the system. Either way, against the general thrust of ancient 'scientific' endeavours to expel random and chance events from the natural world, the Epicureans found it necessary to

---

Press, 2007), pp. 67–108; William Newman, 'Art, Nature and Experiment among some Aristotelian Alchemists', in *Texts and Contexts in Ancient and Medieval Science: Studies on the Occasion of John E. Murdoch's Seventieth Birthday*, ed. E. Sylla and M. McVaugh (Leiden: Brill, 1997), pp. 305–17.

[24] Johannes Kepler made a parallel theological case for the applicability of mathematics to natural philosophical questions. Opposing Aristotelian critics, he wrote: 'God the Creator, since he is a mind, and does what he wants, is not prohibited, in attributing powers and appointing circles, from having regard to things which are either immaterial or based on imagination.' Johannes Kepler, *Mysterium Cosmographicum*, trans. A. M. Duncan (Norwalk, CT: Abaris, 1999), p. 123.

[25] Lucretius, *De rerum natura* 2.216–93.

introduce one into the very heart of their physics. In a way, the capricious gods of the poets had their functional equivalent in the Epicurean swerve.[26]

As we will see shortly, key aspects of Epicurean natural philosophy would come to play an important role in the emergence of modern physics in the seventeenth century. This required the taming of Epicurean chance, made possible by relocating atomism into a framework of theological voluntarism and introducing a lawmaking Deity. It is also worth observing that the putative 'naturalism' of Epicurean physics, far from propelling it to the forefront of ancient understandings of the world, led to its being consigned to irrelevance — at least if measured by its popularity and explanatory power.[27] To be fair, naturalistic explanation was never the main objective, with physics being subservient to ethics. But if we are thinking, in an admittedly teleological fashion, of the trajectory that leads to modern science, we might say that in order to become scientifically fruitful Epicurean physics had first to be incorporated into the framework of a voluntarist theology. That did not occur, in Europe at least, until the seventeenth century.[28]

The other ancient philosophical schools reflect Aristotle's indifference to a sharp distinction between the natural and divine. Stoic writers thus spoke happily of a divinised nature. Seneca writes: 'The whole that encompasses

---

[26] Lehoux points out this paradox in 'Naturalism in the Classical World', pp. 33f. See also M. R. Johnson, 'Nature, Spontaneity, and Voluntary Action in Lucretius', in *Lucretius: Poetry, Philosophy, Science*, ed. D. Lehoux, A. D. Morrison, and A. Sharrock (Oxford: Oxford University Press, 2013), pp. 99–130.

[27] Thus Aquinas: 'Democritus and Empedocles attributed things to chance in most things. But by a more profound diligence in their contemplation of the truth later philosophers showed by evident proofs and reasons that natural things are set in motion by providence …. Therefore after the majority of men asserted the opinion that natural things did not happen by chance but by providence because of the order which clearly appears in them ….' *Commentary on the Book of Job*, Prologue (trans. Brain Mullady, *Latin/English Edition of the Works of Thomas Aquinas*, vol. 32 (Lander: Aquinas Institute, 2016), p. 7). Aquinas, *Disputed questions on Truth*, q. 5, art. 2 (trans. McGlynn, vol. 1, p. 210).

[28] Well before this, from the eighth century, Islamic theologian/philosophers (*mutakallimūn*) developed the science of *kalām*, which entailed an atomistic philosophy and an occasionalist understanding of causation. See A. I. Sabra, '*Kalam* Atomism as an Alternative Philosophy to Hellenizing *Falsafa*', in *Arabic Theology, Arabic Philosophy: From the Many to the One – Essays in Celebration of Richard M. Frank*, ed. J. E. Montgomery (Leuven: Peeters, 2006), pp. 199–272. For a comparison to Epicurean atomism see A. Dhanani, *The Physical Theory of Kalam: Atoms, Space, and Void in Basrian Mu'tazili Cosmology* (Leiden: Brill, 1994), pp. 191f. Medieval alchemical practices, possibly indebted to Arabic sources, also drew upon atomistic assumptions and are a likely influence on early modern developments. See William R. Newman, *Atoms and Alchemy: Chymistry and the Experimental Origins of the Scientific Revolution* (Chicago: University of Chicago Press, 2006); Christoph Lüthy, J. E. Murdoch, and William R. Newman (eds.), *Late Medieval and Early Modern Corpuscular Matter Theories* (Leiden: Brill, 2001).

us is one, and it is God.'[29] Elsewhere he would observe that 'the causes of things divine and things human are a part of the divine system'.[30] As for 'natural' operations, 'the whole of creation' was said to move 'as a result of the divine law'.[31] In Seneca's letters, C. Kavin Rowe writes, 'Nature' is 'virtually synonymous with the set of words we moderns tend to think of as more explicitly theological: *God/gods/divinity/divine*'.[32] Rowe goes so far as to suggest that if we wish to grasp what the Stoics think about nature as we presently understand it we should actually be attending to their deployments of the term 'God' (*theos/deus*).[33] None of this is to say that Aristotle and the Stoics entertained a sense of Deity that could be directly equated with the God of Jews and Christians.[34] But this goes to the point that attributing to them a natural/supernatural distinction as imagined by someone like Huxley is unhelpfully ahistorical and anachronistic.

Christian and Jewish concepts of divine creation – and especially creation out of nothing – brought a new dimension to these philosophical conceptions. Contrary to what we might expect, however, the positing of a divine and transcendent Creator gave rise to conceptions of nature that are closer in many respects to modern naturalism than to the speculations of the Greek philosophers. The sharp separation between Creator and creation suggested by the Hebrew Bible and inherited by Christianity effected a qualified desacralising of the cosmos and especially of the heavens.[35] Several of the Church Fathers pointed out that the natural philosophy inherited from the Greeks was pervaded by overly promiscuous theological explanations. Clement of Alexandria observed that the philosophers had been ignorant of 'the great First Cause, the Maker of all things, and Creator of those very first principles'. This had led some of them to deify nature, while others had mistakenly invested the stars and planets with divinity.[36] Lactantius

---

[29] Seneca, *Epistles* 92.30 (LCL 76, 466).
[30] Seneca, *Epistles* 89.5 (LCL 76, 381).
[31] Seneca, *Epistles* 86.23 (LCL 76, 161).
[32] Rowe, *One True Life*, p. 29.
[33] Rowe, *One True Life*, p. 227.
[34] Rowe thus proposes that for first-century Stoics to grasp what Christians meant by 'God' would require that they 'convert to the way of life that is bound to the grammar in which God gets its meaning .... The density of meaning surrounding the words *cosmos, physis, phantasia, sophia,* and so on – all this would change.' *One True Life*, p. 228.
[35] Philo of Alexandria was instrumental in combining Platonic thought, which already posited a more transcendent Deity than other philosophical schools, with biblical notions of creation. See Johannes Zachhuber, 'Nature', in *The Routledge Companion to Early Christian Philosophy*, ed. Mark Edwards (Abingdon: Routledge, 2021), pp. 27–40.
[36] Clement of Alexandria, *Exhortation to the Heathen* 5 (*ANF* 2, p. 190). Origen, characteristically, had a more colourful view that brought together Christian eschatology with traditional views of the divinity of the heavens. See Allan Scott, *Origen and the Life of the Stars* (Oxford: Clarendon Press, 1994), esp. ch. 8.

made a similar observation about the 'scientific' implications of monotheism: 'Therefore the motion of the stars is not voluntary, but of necessity, because they obey the laws appointed for them [by God].'[37] The lawfulness of nature was thus associated with a single divine lawgiver. On the other side, Pagan critics took the Christians' refusal to believe in a sufficient number of gods as evidence of impiety, lumping them together with sceptical Epicureans and accusing both parties of atheism.[38]

There is a plausible link between these theologically motivated critiques of Pagan natural philosophy and the eventual emergence of modern science. Perhaps the clearest example comes in the work of the Christian philosopher John Philoponus (c.490–c.570). An original and iconoclastic thinker who opposed central elements of the prevailing scientific orthodoxy, Philoponus rejected Aristotelian dynamics and put forward in its place a theory of impetus that resembles in many respects the modern theory of inertia. Philoponus followed earlier Christian writers in insisting that because there was only one Deity, the Christian God, the celestial bodies could not be divine. It also followed that they were not self-movers and needed an external source of motion. Related to this was the insight that if the world were the product of a single divine mind, it was reasonable to assume that celestial and terrestrial motions would be of the same kind. By way of contrast, Aristotle had insisted that different principles of motion apply to celestial and terrestrial objects, with the former moving eternally in circular orbits, the latter in a linear fashion with motions that will naturally come to rest. Philoponus went on to develop a theory of impetus informed by these theological commitments. All of this led to what appears to be a comparatively 'naturalistic' explanatory framework: the stars are no longer to be understood as self-moving divine bodies. This stance was accompanied by a unified theory of dynamics, similarly informed by his assumption of the 'supernatural' creation of the world in a single divine act.[39]

---

[37] Lactantius, *Divine Institutes* 2.5 (*ANF* 7, p. 48).
[38] 'Thus we are even called atheists. We do proclaim ourselves atheists as regards those whom you call gods, but not with respect to the most true God.' Justin Martyr, *First Apology* 6 (*FC*, vol. 6, pp. 38–9). See also Origen, *Contra Celsum* 5.7; Proclus, *Commentary on the Cratylus* 125. See also J. J. Walsh, 'On Christian Atheism', *Vigiliae Christianae* 45 (1991), 255–77; R. Jungkuntz, 'Fathers, Heretics and Epicureans', *Journal of Ecclesiastical History* 17 (1966), 3–10; A. D. Simpson, 'Epicureans, Christians, Atheists in the Second Century', *Transactions and Proceedings of the American Philological Association* 72 (1941), 372–81.
[39] Philoponus *contra Aristotelem ap.* Simplicium *in Cael.* 88, 28–34, in Richard Sorabji, *The Philosophy of the Commentators 200–600 AD*, vol. 2: *Physics* (London: Duckworth, 2003), p. 374. See also C. Wildberg, 'Impetus Theory and the Hermeneutics of Science in Simplicius and Philoponus', *Hyperboreus* 5 (1999), 107–24; C. Scholten, *Antike Naturphilosophie und*

While Philoponus was a controversial figure during his lifetime, his writings influenced a number of prominent medieval thinkers including Al-Kindi, Bonaventure, Buridan, and Oresme. A millennium after they were first produced, they were also read closely and cited by Galileo, who was attracted by Philoponus's criticisms of Aristotle and by his theory of dynamics. It was with some justification that French physicist and historian of science Pierre Duhem designated Philoponus 'one of the main precursors of modern science'.[40]

Muslim and Christian thinkers of the Middle Ages would develop their own versions of naturalism, although to some degree these were discontinuous with the patristic and Augustinian traditions. The Church Fathers had opposed a desacralising monotheism to an enchanted, polytheistic Paganism, and Philoponus had deployed Christian conceptions against Aristotelian doctrines. From the ninth century onwards, with the increasing circulation of Aristotelian texts in translation – first Arabic and then Latin – the Greek philosopher became more of an ally and the inspiration for a natural philosophy that was largely independent from theology (although usually consistent with it).[41] In the medieval Arabic speaking world, the earlier ninth-century traditions of *kalām* which combined atomistic physics with theological concerns were now accompanied by the parallel enterprise of *falsafa* that increasingly draw upon Aristotle's metaphysics and natural philosophy.[42] In the practice of *falsafa* Aristotle was acknowledged as the supreme authority when it came to questions about nature, and this inevitably gave rise to a body of knowledge that was distinct from theology. Nevertheless, the Arabic conception of nature (*ṭabī'a*) bore connotations that differed in important ways from the Greek equivalent (*phusis*). The

---

christliche Kosmologie in der Schrift "De opificio mundi" des Johannes Philoponos (Berlin: De Gruyter, 1996); Richard Sorabji (ed.), *Philoponus and the Rejection of Aristotelian Science* (Ithaca: Cornell University Press, 1987); Brian Stock, 'Science, Technology, and Economic Progress in the Early Middle Ages', in *Science in the Middle Ages*, ed. David C. Lindberg (Chicago: University of Chicago Press, 1978), pp. 1–51 (p. 11).

[40] Pierre Duhem, *Le système du monde*, vol. 1 (Paris: A. Hermann and Sons, 1913), p. 398.

[41] Albert the Great, e.g., would go so far as to reinstate intelligences and celestial souls as animators of heavenly bodies, in what was essentially a completion of the Aristotelian programme. *De causis* II.1.1. See David Twetten, 'The Emanation Scheme of Albert the Great and the Questions of Divine Free Will and Mediated Creation', in *Albert the Great and His Arabic Sources: Medieval Science between Inheritance and Emergence*, ed. Katja Krause and Richard C. Taylor (Turnhout: Brepols), in press.

[42] Jon McGinnis, 'Natural Knowledge in the Arabic Middle Ages', in *Wrestling with Nature: From Omens to Science*, ed. Peter Harrison, Ronald L. Numbers, and Michael H. Shank (Chicago: University of Chicago Press, 2011), pp. 59–82; Sabra, '*Kalam* Atomism as an Alternative Philosophy to Hellenizing *Falsafa*'.

latter, in typical Aristotelian usages, implies an internal principle of change whereas the former bears the sense of a nature that is imposed from without.[43] The Arabic conception was thus more hospitable to a doctrine of creation than Aristotle's. The Islamic 'naturalism' of this period was thus tied to a conception of nature that was theologically informed.

Thinkers of the twelfth and thirteenth centuries in the Latin West drew upon 'the Arab masters', as Adelard of Bath referred to them, as well as new translations of Aristotle, to arrive at their own version of an independent natural science.[44] As historian David Lindberg has observed, 'naturalism', in a particular sense, 'was one of the most salient features of twelfth-century natural philosophy'.[45] This trend was facilitated by the structure of the new medieval universities with their undergraduate Arts faculties that were increasingly devoted to the study of Aristotle. The Arts faculty was separate from the higher faculties of Medicine, Law, and Theology. The thirteenth century also witnessed the emergence of a terminological distinction between 'natural' and 'supernatural' (discussed in more detail in Chapter 6). For now, suffice it to say that the formal study of nature was generally understood to be an enterprise that excluded the miraculous. The teacher of Thomas Aquinas, Albert the Great (d. 1280), who did much to incorporate Aristotle's philosophy into the university curriculum, typifies this approach. The general approach adopted in his numerous scientific writings was to completely bracket out miraculous interventions: 'I am not concerned about the miracles of God, since I will discuss natural things.'[46]

In the next century, Nicole Oresme (c.1325–1382) adopted a similar approach to the subject of popular marvels and wonders. Oresme studied

---

[43] McGinnis, 'Natural Knowledge in the Arabic Middle Ages', p. 63.
[44] Charles Burnett (ed. and trans.), Adelard of Bath, *Conversations with His Nephew: 'On the Same and the Different', 'Questions on Natural Science', and 'On Birds'* (Cambridge: Cambridge University Press, 1998), p. xxix.
[45] David C. Lindberg, *The Beginnings of Western Science*, 2nd ed. (Chicago: University of Chicago Press, 2007), p. 210. For examples, see pp. 209–14.
[46] Albertus Magnus, *De generatione et corruptione* 1.1.22, in *Opera omnia*, vol. 4, p. 363. Siger of Brabant says something similar: 'But the miracles of God do not concern us now, since we will discuss natural things naturalistically (*de naturalibus naturaliter*).' *Quaestiones de anima intellectiva*, in Pierre Mandonnet (ed.), *Siger de Brabant et l'averroïsme latin au XIIIme siècle*, part 2, *Textes inédits*, 2nd ed. (Louvain: Institut Supérieur de Philosophie de l'Université, 1908), p. 154. For Albert's 'naturalism' see Michael J. Shank, 'Naturalist Tendencies in Medieval Science', in *Science without God?*, ed. Harrison and Roberts, pp. 37–57; Edward Grant, *The Nature of Natural Philosophy in the Late Middle Ages* (Washington, DC: The Catholic University of America Press, 2010), pp. 163–4, 251–2; Katja Krause and Richard C. Taylor, 'Albert's Philosophical *scientia*: Origins, Geneses, Emergences', in *Albert the Great and His Arabic Sources*, ed. Krause and Taylor.

arts and theology at the University of Paris and wrote influential works on scientific, philosophical, and theological topics. He is perhaps best known for a work that marshals arguments for and against the motion of the earth.[47] Interestingly, he concluded that were the earth in motion and the celestial spheres stationary, the calculations of astronomers would predict exactly what we presently see (although there were telling physical reasons why the earth could not be in motion).[48] Oresme's 'naturalism' is most evident in his *On the Causes of Marvels* which opens with a clear statement of intent: 'to show the causes of some effects which seem to be marvels and to show that the effects occur naturally .... There is no reason to take recourse to the heavens, the last refuge of the weak, or demons, or to our glorious God as if he would produce those effects directly more so than those effects whose causes we believe are well known.'[49]

The references to miracles by these thinkers betray a concern to observe a clear distinction between the usual course of events and the miraculous, and to restrict the scope of special supernatural activity to miracles. But it did not follow that God's power was not thought to be operative in natural events. On the contrary, changes in nature were thought to involve divine power that conserved natural things so that they continued to exist while also operating along with them when they exercised their natural powers. Scholastic views of nature were thus informed by the axiom, attributed to various ancient thinkers, that 'the work of nature is the work of intelligence'.[50] Within the framework of his 'naturalism', for example, Albert the Great could observe of sentient creatures that 'there is a certain noble natural and divine cause in all of them, because none of them was brought into being naturally in vain or without purpose'.[51] Neither was the observation of a distinction between the miraculous and the normal course of events solely to preserve the integrity of natural philosophy: religious considerations also

---

[47] Nicole Oresme, *Le Livre du ciel et du monde*, ed. and trans. A. D. Menut and A. J. Denomy (Madison: University of Wisconsin Press, 1968).

[48] Edward Grant, *Foundations of Modern Science in the Middle Ages* (Cambridge: Cambridge University Press, 1996), pp. 14–16.

[49] Bert Hansen, *Nicole Oresme and the Marvels of Nature: A Study of His De Causis Mirabilium with Critical Edition* (Toronto: Pontifical Institute of Medieval Studies, 1985), p. 137. For further examples of medieval 'naturalism' see Shank, 'Naturalist Tendencies in Medieval Science'.

[50] James A. Weisheipl, 'The Axiom "*Opus naturae est opus intelligentia*" and Its Origins', in *Albertus Magnus – Doctor Universalis 1280/1980*, ed. Gerbert Meyer and Albert Zimmermann (Mainz: Matthias-Grünewald-Verlag, 1980), pp. 441–63.

[51] Albertus Magnus, *De animalibus* XI.1.3, trans. in Katja Krause, 'Source Mining: Arabic Natural Philosophy and *experientia* in Albert the Great's Scientific Practices', in *Albert the Great and His Arabic Sources*, ed. Krause and Taylor.

played a role. Performance of a miracle was a criterion for sainthood and medieval canonisation proceedings required evaluation of the evidence that a miracle had taken place. The thirteenth century thus witnessed official attempts to define and circumscribe the miraculous.[52] Properly implementing this distinction was important for both scientific and theological reasons, ensuring that, in principle at least, there was no competition between naturalistic and supernaturalistic modes of explanation.[53]

In light of the examples considered to this point, Huxley's retrospective narrative looks rather doubtful. Before the Middle Ages no one was operating with a natural/supernatural distinction. To the extent that we might map the nineteenth-century category 'supernaturalism' onto something like 'a belief in God that occludes a proper understanding of the operations of nature', Huxley's version of events seems to get things exactly the wrong way around. The imagined ancient champions of naturalism turn out to have religious commitments that are directly implicated in their natural philosophies. The rise of Christianity, identified as having impeded what would otherwise have been the natural development of Greek science, turns out to have been the agent of naturalisation. As Hegel expressed it, 'Christianity has emptied Valhalla, felled the sacred groves.'[54] Moreover, if we were to seek some distant, pre-modern precedent for nineteenth-century naturalism, the

---

[52] Michael E. Goodich, *Miracles and Wonders: The Development of the Concept of Miracle, 1150–1350* (London: Routledge, 2007), p. 100. See also Laura Smoller, 'Defining the Boundaries of the Natural in Fifteenth Century Brittany: The Inquest into the Miracles of Saint Vincent Ferrer (d. 1419)', *Viator* 28 (1997), 333–59; Sari Katajala-Peltomaa, *Gender, Miracles, and Daily Life: The Evidence of Fourteenth-Century Canonization Processes* (Turnhout: Brepols, 2009); Neil Tarrant, *Defining Nature's Limits: The Roman Inquisition and the Boundaries of Science* (Chicago: University of Chicago Press, 2022), pp. 15–18. The Council of Trent further tightened procedures for determining whether claimed miracles could be sanctioned as genuine. See H. J. Schroeder (ed. and trans.), *Canons and Decrees of the Council of Trent* (London: Herder, 1941), p. 217.

[53] In practice, and especially at a popular level, this could prove difficult. Demonic possession constituted an especially complicated case. See Moshe Sluhovsky, *Believe Not Every Spirit: Possession, Mysticism, & Discernment in Early Modern Catholicism* (Chicago: University of Chicago Press, 2007), esp. pp. 14–16. The Catholic Church sought to address this situation in 1614, when it established the formal rite of Exorcism, setting out criteria that offered guidance for distinguishing supernatural possession from natural afflictions. '*De exorcizandis obsessis a Daemonio*' [1614] in *Rituale Romanum* (Baltimore: Murphy, 1873). The early modern period also witnessed parallel efforts on the part of the Catholic Church to distinguish between religious impostures and false wonders on the one hand, and true miracles on the other. See Andrew W. Keitt, *Inventing the Sacred: Imposture, Inquisition, and the Boundaries of the Supernatural in Golden Age Spain* (Leiden: Brill, 2005).

[54] Hegel, *The Positivity of the Christian Religion*, II, §1, in *Early Theological Writings*, pp. 145f. See also Karl Löwith, *Meaning in History* (Chicago: University of Chicago Press, 1949), p. 201; Hurtado, *Destroyer of the Gods*, passim.

closest analogue would not be Presocratic 'science', but the *falsafa* of figures such as Avicenna and Averroes, and the natural philosophy of Albert the Great and Oresme. As we will see below, these thinkers are closer in certain respects to Huxley than were the scientific innovators of the seventeenth century, although their conception of nature was much more capacious.

5.2 The Supernatural and the Scientific Revolution

To understand the remarkable efflorescence of scientific activity in seventeenth-century Europe it is worth revisiting the account of the origin of the world taught by the Epicurean poet and philosopher Lucretius (c.99–55 BCE). In his poem *De rerum natura*, Lucretius offers this account:

> This world was made by nature, and the seeds of things themselves of their own accord, knocking together by chance, clashed in all sorts of ways, heedless, without aim, without intention, until at length those combined which, suddenly thrown together, could become in each case the beginnings of mighty things, of earth and sea and sky and the generation of living creatures.[55]

Stated in this compressed manner the scenario seems rather implausible. It is not surprising, then, that for much of the modern period the reputation of Lucretius rested upon his poetic gifts rather than his scientific acumen. As already noted, the general historical consensus, at least until the time of Darwin, was that Epicurean cosmogony and physics in their original form were non-starters.[56] (And Darwin only pushed the question back to more fundamental levels of organisation.) As late as the nineteenth century, the eminent Victorian historian Thomas Babbington Macaulay would render this series of verdicts on Lucretius' physical theories: 'folly', 'nonsense', 'drivelling', 'exceeding absurd'.[57] That said, the universe of the Epicurean philosophers did have the advantage of being ontologically simple: it consisted only of microscopic particles of matter in motion. However, its reliance upon chance to account for the order of the world, its omission of reference to divine providence, and its rather desperate invocation of 'the swerve' to make the whole thing work at all, meant that whatever the attractions of

---

[55] Lucretius, *De rerum natura*, bk. 2, 1058–63 (LCL 181, p. 177).
[56] Cicero, *Nature of the Gods* 2.37; Lactantius, *On the Anger of God*, 10; Boyle, *Usefulness of Natural Philosophy*, *Works*, vol. 3, pp. 257–61; Glanvill, 'Usefulness of Real Philosophy', in *Essays*, p. 32; Ray, *Wisdom of God*, pp. 13–20; Kant, *Lectures on the Philosophical Doctrine of Religion*, in *Religion and Rational Theology*, p. 399.
[57] Quoted in Frank M. Turner, 'Lucretius among the Victorians', *Victorian Studies* 16 (1973), 329–49 (333).

its austere ontology, or its moral vision for that matter, it had never been in serious contention as an alternative to Platonism, Aristotelianism, Stoicism, or Christian teachings about creation.

It is remarkable, given all this, that key elements of its ontology were adopted by pious scientific innovators of the early modern period who developed a mechanical and experimental natural philosophy. This partial revival was testament to a latent explanatory potential, largely unrealised in earlier manifestations, along with the crucial addition of a divine oversight that provided the necessary compensation for its unpalatable and 'unscientific' reliance on chance. Initially, at least, the theistic component of the new atomism also lent it explanatory power and afforded it a more general intellectual legitimacy. It was also important that its explanatory scope be restricted to the material world. The basic premise was straightforward: macroscopic effects can be understood in terms of the motions of invisible particles, their configurations, or their shapes and sizes. This was obviously incompatible with the more complex Aristotelian causal regime, with its intrinsic qualities and virtues and the inherent tendencies of things to move towards their proper places. Aristotle's multiple causes were successively made redundant, at least in explanations of the operations of nature. The philosopher-priest Pierre Gassendi was one of the first to appreciate the promise of Epicurean physics, which was further modified by Robert Boyle and adopted by Newton.[58] Additional ingredients were provided by Descartes's mechanical philosophy and his notion of laws of nature.

There are important differences between the positions adopted by these figures. Descartes was a mechanical philosopher but not, strictly speaking, an atomist. While insisting that natural change in the physical world was to be understood in terms of the interactions of particles of inert matter, he denied some traditional tenets of atomism – the existence of the void and limits to the divisibility of matter. By the same token, while Newton adopted a version of atomism, he was not a thoroughgoing mechanist, since various natural operations – including that of gravity – were not ultimately mechanical.[59]

---

[58] Alan Chalmers, *The Scientist's Atom and the Philosopher's Stone: How Science Succeeded and Philosophy Failed to Gain Knowledge of Atoms* (Dordrecht: Springer, 2009), pp. 75–137; Osler (ed.), *Atoms, Pneuma, and Tranquillity*.

[59] There is a minority view that Newton's thought can be understood as a version of mechanical philosophy. Hylarie Kochiras, 'The Mechanical Philosophy and Newton's Mechanical Force', *Philosophy of Science* 80 (2013), 557–78; Peter Machamer, J. E. McGuire, and Hylarie Kochiras, 'Newton and the Mechanical Philosophy: Gravitation as the Balance of the Heavens', *Southern Journal of Philosophy* 50 (2012), 370–88.

What these thinkers shared, however, was the idea that all of the motion in the universe was to be attributed to God.

Descartes, for example, declared that natural phenomena 'can be explained without the need to suppose anything in their matter other than the motion, size, shape, and the arrangement of its parts'.[60] But these parts had been created and put into motion by God, who continued to govern their operations. This neatly removed the element of chance from the equation while at the same time solving the ancient problem of how to get particles to collide in ways that would ultimately produce an intelligible universe such as ours. In simple terms, if matter consisted of arrangements of intrinsically inert particles (or 'corpuscles'), the source of all motion in the universe must be God, whose ongoing lawful willing of events underpins all of the regularities of nature.[61] As Descartes expressed it: 'God imparted various motions to the parts of matter when he first created them, and he now preserves all this matter in the same way, and by the same process by which he originally created it.'[62]

The key innovation here is the idea of laws of nature, which Descartes introduced to account for the mathematical regularities that we observe in the world. These are not intrinsic to nature but arise solely out of God's arbitrary and immutable will. Referencing one of Augustine's favourite biblical passages Descartes explained: 'God himself has taught us that he has arranged all things in number, weight and measure.' All mathematical truths, he goes on to say, ultimately depend on the will of God, whose immutability also underwrites the constancy of nature's laws.[63] The order of nature, on this interpretation, is not a kind of emergent property that arises out of

---

[60] Descartes, *The World*, CSM 1, p. 89.
[61] For Descartes and the laws of nature see John Henry, 'Metaphysics and the Origins of Modern Science: Descartes and the Importance of Laws of Nature', *Early Science and Medicine* 9 (2004), 73–114; J. R. Milton, 'Laws of Nature', in *The Cambridge History of Seventeenth-Century Philosophy*, 2 vols., ed. Daniel Garber and Michael Ayers (Cambridge: Cambridge University Press, 1998), vol. 1, pp. 680–701; Friedrich Steinle, 'From Principles to Regularities: Tracing "Laws of Nature" in Early Modern Europe', in *Natural Law and Laws of Nature in Early Modern Europe*, ed. Lorraine Daston and Michael Stolleis (Aldershot: Ashgate, 2005), pp. 213–32; Peter Harrison, 'Laws of Nature in Seventeenth-Century England: From Cambridge Platonism to Newtonianism', in *The Divine Order, the Human Order, and the Order of Nature: Historical Perspectives*, ed. Eric Watkins (New York: Oxford University Press, 2013), pp. 127–48; 'Laws of God or Laws of Nature: Natural Order in the Early Modern Period', in *Science without God?*, ed. Harrison and Roberts, pp. 58–76.
[62] Descartes, *Principles of Philosophy*, §61, CSM 1, p. 240. See also *The World*, CSM 1, p. 96.
[63] Descartes, *The World*, CSM 1, p. 97, 'Descartes to Mersenne, 15 April 1630, CSMK, p. 23. The biblical reference is Wisdom 11.21, a passage to which Johannes Kepler often referred as well.

an ensemble of natural objects all acting in accordance with their essential natures in conjunction with the concurrence of the Creator. It is now identified with laws that are directly imposed on matter by God.[64] These derive their universality and immutability from their divine source. There were, admittedly, earlier historical references to 'laws of nature'. Mostly, although not invariably, these refer to the moral realm.[65] After Descartes, laws of nature become virtually the sole descriptor for those regularities that form the object of scientific enquiry.

There were controversial aspects to Descartes's proposals, but over the course of the seventeenth century many of his key innovations – corpuscular matter theory, God as the immediate source of motion, divinely authored laws of nature – came to be widely accepted. While English 'empiricists' are often taken to be implacable opponents of Cartesian 'rationalism', in fact there was considerable agreement on central issues including the basic understanding of laws of nature. Robert Boyle wrote that in the beginning 'God gave Motion to Matter … guided the various Motions of the parts of it, as to contrive them into the World he design'd they should compose … and establish'd those *Rules of Motion*, and that order amongst things Corporeal, which we are wont to call the *Laws of Nature*.'[66] Natural philosophers within Newton's orbit also spoke explicitly of laws of nature in these terms. William Whiston, the theologian and mathematician who succeeded Newton in the Lucasian Chair of mathematics at Cambridge, declared that 'the Effects of nature' are nothing but divine power 'acting according to fixt and certain laws'.[67] Richard Bentley, the brilliant classicist and Newton's personal choice for the first Boyle Lecturer, insisted

---

[64] On the traditional model, God is involved at the level of final cause, as the source of the harmony of the motions of the creatures, which are unable according to their own powers to act for rational ends. This is the gist of Aquinas's fifth way. *ST* 1a. 2, 3. So the order of nature appears to us as a kind of emergent property but is directly intended by God.

[65] For earlier references see Daryn Lehoux, 'Laws of Nature and Natural Laws', *Studies in History and Philosophy of Science, Part A* 37 (2006), 527–49. Lehoux cites a number of references to laws of nature (*leges naturae, foedera naturae*) in classical authors including Lucretius. For similar references, respectively in the Stoics and in medical literature, see Brad Inwood, *Reading Seneca* (Oxford: Oxford University Press, 2005), ch. 8; Heinrich von Staaden, 'The Rule and the Exception: Celsus on a Scientific Conundrum', in *Maladie et maladies dans les textes latins antiques et médiévaux*, ed. C. Deroux (Brussels: Latomus, 1998), pp. 105–28. These instances do not involve the occasionalist view that God directly wills ordered natural events.

[66] Robert Boyle, *About the excellency and Grounds of the Mechanical Hypothesis*, Works, vol. 8, p. 104. See also *Forms and Qualities*, Works, vol. 5, p. 306; *A Disquisition about the Final Causes of Natural Things*, Works, vol. 11, p. 111; *The Christian Virtuoso, II*, Works, vol. 5, p. 521.

[67] William Whiston, *A New Theory of the Earth* (London, 1696), pp. 6, 211.

that 'gravity, the great basis of all mechanism, is not itself mechanical, but the immediate *fiat* and finger of God, and the execution of divine law'.[68] Samuel Clarke, another of the Boyle Lecturers and the defender of the Newtonian system against the criticisms of Leibniz, agreed: 'The course of nature, truly and properly speaking, is nothing else but the will of God producing certain effects in a continued, regular, constant, and uniform manner.'[69] The missing ingredient of ancient Epicureanism, according to those responsible for its early modern revival, was God and the idea of laws of nature.

It follows that the common assumption of a scientific revolution premised on a break with the theological understandings of nature cherished by a medieval 'age of faith' is at best half-true. It is not that theological understandings were replaced by secular ones. Rather, a different set of theological understandings came to the fore. In an important sense, nature became more thoroughly 'supernatural' than it had ever been in the medieval period when natural things were invested with their own, inherent, causal agency (albeit one that relied upon God's concurrence with its exercise, along with his ongoing conservation of their being). As Samuel Clarke expressed it, once the full implications of the Newtonian picture of the universe are taken on board it becomes clear that 'there is no such thing, as what Men commonly call the *course of Nature*, or the *Power of Nature*'.[70] Every 'natural' event was directly produced by God.[71]

This reduction of all natural events to occasions for the operation of God's power looks like a serious diversion from a presumedly progressive path towards modern naturalism. From a historical perspective, nineteenth-century naturalism has more in common with the medieval naturalism of Avicenna and Albert the Great than with leading figures of the scientific revolution such as Boyle and Newton. If anything, the latter more closely resemble the Islamic occasionalists associated with the *kalām* tradition – figures such as Al-Ghazali (who is routinely charged with having derailed medieval Islamic science). Medieval science was relatively independent of

---

[68] Richard Bentley, *The Works of Richard Bentley, D.D.*, 3 vols., ed. Alexander Dyce (London: Macpherson, 1838), vol. 3, *Theological Writings*, pp. 74, 75.
[69] Samuel Clarke, *Truth and Certainty of the Christian Revelation*, in *The Works of Samuel Clarke, D.D.*, 2 vols. (London, 1738), vol. 2, pp. 697f.
[70] Samuel Clarke, 'The Evidences of Natural and Revealed Religion', in *Works*, vol. 2, p. 698.
[71] More generally, as Peter N. Jordan has shown, early modern Protestants would conceptualise providence in terms of divine 'government' even if they were reluctant to relinquish more traditional ideas of secondary causation. *Naturalism in the Christian Imagination*, pp. 28–37.

theology; early modern science is deeply entangled with it, complicating any neat linear trajectory towards modern naturalism.[72]

For all this, the scientific supernaturalism of the early modern period was an indispensable way station on the path towards a thoroughgoing metaphysical naturalism. The reduction of the complex, multi-layered, causal economy of the Middle Ages to a divine monopoly was susceptible to a hostile takeover in which God's immediate action could simply be redescribed in purely naturalistic terms. All that was required was for God's ongoing but immutable activity to be given a new label: 'nature'. This option was not fully realised until the nineteenth century when habituation to the notion of laws of nature led to an amnesia regarding its theological origins. At the same time, the Darwinian idea of natural selection lent a degree of plausibility to the ancient Lucretian thesis, although many of Darwin's initial supporters continued to believe that the process of evolution took place under divine superintendence.

In none of this did the successes of science constitute evidence for the truth of naturalism. What happened was that the modern development of the natural sciences as independent and specialised disciplines meant that broader questions about their own metaphysical and theological foundations gradually faded from view. Whereas the sciences are sometimes said to be based in curiosity, from the mid-twentieth century that curiosity rarely extended to fundamental questions about the metaphysical foundations of science, or of the intelligibility of the natural world. In this respect, as Wittgenstein aptly expressed it, science has 'put us to sleep'. This soporific effect applies especially to curiosity about where laws of nature come from.[73] The spectre of naturalism was already present in Descartes's radical elevation of God's power and will and in the broader application of this univocal voluntarism to physics and cosmogony.[74] Indeed it was partially realised in Spinoza, who agreed with Descartes and the Newtonians that while the vulgar might imagine two kinds of powers operating in nature,

---

[72] Thus, for Amos Funkenstein, figures such as Kepler and Newton were 'secular theologians', blending natural philosophy and theology in a way that medieval thinkers could not. *Theology and the Scientific Imagination.* See also Gaukroger, *Emergence of a Scientific Culture*, p. 23. This blending is exemplified in the practices of physico-theology. Harrison, 'Physico-Theology and the Mixed Sciences'.

[73] 'Man has to awaken to wonder – and so perhaps do peoples. Science is a way of sending him to sleep again.' *Culture and Value*, p. 5. And on laws of nature specifically, *Tractatus Logico-Philosophicus*, trans. D. F. Pears and B. F. McGuiness (London: Routledge & Kegan Paul, 1961), 6.371–2.

[74] On one common account the foundations had been laid by the late medieval nominalists, who are said to have introduced a univocal account of causation, thus already flattening

natural and supernatural, there was in reality only one. For Spinoza this power fell under the description 'God *or* Nature'.[75] Modern naturalists have simply plumped for the latter, often mistakenly identifying Spinoza as one of their own.[76]

The possibility of naturalism (in the modern sense) can already be discerned in the cosmogony laid out in *The World*. In a key passage Descartes writes that because God is immutable, changes that take place in nature cannot be attributed to God, whose action never changes. They must then be attributed to 'nature'.[77] While Descartes had insisted on the need for God's ongoing creative activity in upholding the cosmos at every moment, his approach left open questions about divine providence and miracles, and critics were prepared to ask them. This accounts for the accusations of atheism levelled against the French philosopher. Calvinist theologians at the University of Utrecht, for example, contended that Descartes's arguments for the existence of God were so feeble that they invited the assaults of religious sceptics – a double insult, since Descartes had boasted that his arguments were the best that could ever be devised.[78] A related charge was

---

the causal order into a single plane. There is considerable truth to this version of events, but the path into modernity for these recondite philosophical conceptions was partly the Protestant Reformation, which operationalised these ideas in its theological doctrines, and the scientific revolution, which operationalised them in the sphere of natural philosophy.

[75] Spinoza, *Ethics*, pt. 4, preface, *CW*, p. 321. Also: 'Nature's power is nothing but power of God ... so it is folly to have recourse to the power of God when we do not know the natural cause of some phenomenon – that is, when we do not know the power of God.' *Theologico-Political Treatise*, ch. 1, *CW*, p. 403.

[76] Spinoza is usually categorised as a pantheist or atheist. For an interesting argument that Spinoza was a panentheist (nature as contained in God, rather than equivalent to God), see Clare Carlisle, *Spinoza's Religion: A New Reading of the Ethics* (Princeton: Princeton University Press, 2021).

[77] Descartes, *The World*, CSM 1, p. 92. See also Theo Verbeek, 'The Invention of Nature: Descartes and Regius', in *Descartes' Natural Philosophy*, ed. Gaukroger et al., pp. 149–67; Harrison, 'Laws of Nature', pp. 136–9. Spinoza develops this same principle into an argument against miracles. *Tractatus Theologico-Philosophicus*, ch. 6, *CW*, pp. 445f.

[78] Descartes, Dedicatory Letter, *Meditations*, CSM 2, p. 4. Chief among Descartes's attackers were Gisbertus Voetius and Maarten Schoock. Their joint objections may be found in Schoock's *Admiranda Methodus novæ philosophiæ Renati Des Cartes* (Utrecht, 1643). Schoock argued that Descartes denied a valid argument – the cosmological – and replaced it with his own defective argument. Accusers from elsewhere include Theophil Spitzel, *Scrutinium atheismi historico-ætiologicum* (Augsburg, 1663); Jean Hardouin, *Athei detecti*, in *Opera varia* (Amsterdam, 1733), pp. 1–273. See Agostini, 'Descartes' Proofs'; Verbeek, 'Descartes and the Problem of Atheism'. Christian Wolff later elicited a similar response from Pietist theologians at Halle, when he substituted his own metaphysical arguments for what they regarded as the more secure approach of physico-theology. Gualtiero Lorini, '"Diversa Theologiae naturalis systemata"'.

that Descartes had relied upon God simply to set things up, after which the universe could continue on without the need for further providential superintendence. Blaise Pascal complained bitterly that Descartes would like to have dispensed with God altogether but needed him 'to set the world in motion'.[79]

A more systematic critique came from the English Platonists Henry More and Ralph Cudworth. Both had initially been enamoured of the philosophy of Descartes, but eventually came to be concerned about the theological and scientific implications of his view of nature. Henry More presciently worried that 'the sameness and immutableness of the Law of Nature' might serve as a refuge of atheists.[80] Cudworth went so far as to say that Aristotle's system of philosophy was more consistent with piety than that of Descartes.[81] Cudworth did not think that atomic philosophy should be abandoned, however. History had witnessed two different versions of atomism, he maintained, a pure form that had been taught by Moses, and a second, corrupted form espoused by Leucippus and Democritus. The latter was tainted with atheism. Descartes had revived the legitimate, Mosaic form, but had deviated from it in worrying ways – in rendering nature inert and unintelligent, in emphasising the necessary character of laws of nature, and in insisting that only matter had extension.[82]

There were more than metaphysical and theological concerns at stake here. The scientific issue – in so far as we can distinguish philosophy and science for this period – was whether merely mechanical interactions of particles were sufficient to account for all the phenomena of nature. There were hard cases, including not just the motions of the heavens, but phenomena such as magnetism, animal generation, and digestion. Descartes's own mechanical explanation of the orbits of planetary bodies involved vortices of invisible ethereal matter that carried the planets in their courses. While this satisfied the requirement of offering a mechanical account, it suffered from the fatal disadvantage of being inconsistent with observation. Given the paths of comets, for example, it was difficult to see how such

---

[79] Pascal, *Pensées*, attrib., p. 355.
[80] Henry More, *An Explanation of the Grand Mystery of Godliness* (London, 1660), p. 214. Thomas Baker expressed the same concern, *Reflections upon Learning* (London, 1708), pp. 97f.
[81] Cudworth, *True Intellectual System*, p. 54.
[82] Cudworth, *True Intellectual System*, pp. 174f. For More and Cudworth, spiritual substance could be extended in space. This had implications for both God's omnipresence and the nature of space, and forms part of the background of Newton's contention that space might be thought of as 'the sensorium of God'. This issue also provided the occasion for early modern discussions of angels sitting on pinheads. Peter Harrison, 'Angels on Pinheads and Needles' Points', *Notes and Queries* 63 (2016), 45–7.

a mechanism could work. This brought a second scientific issue into the frame: Descartes's alleged preference for grand hypotheses over modest experimentation, which drew the disapproval of his English detractors.

The Newtonian solution was to abandon both mechanical explanation and, in principle at least, hypothesising. Newton's laws of gravity were thus consistent with observed motions of planetary bodies. But a satisfactory mechanical account of those motions was lacking. Gravity was neither a property of bodies, nor a material agent of efficient causation. In fact, Newton was never able to specify exactly what it was – although, as we have seen, a good number in his circle identified it with God. In effect, Newton was prepared to dispense with causal explanation altogether and put in its place mathematical descriptions in terms of laws of nature. He was also willing, albeit reluctantly, to abandon the explanatory principle of mechanism when necessary. The former meant that scientific explanation ultimately relied upon God. This opened him up to the criticism of Leibniz, who perceptively observed that Newtonian gravity was just a scholastic 'occult virtue' by another name.[83] But this was a compromise that the Newtonians were apparently prepared to live with. The eventual triumph of Newtonianism represents the final stage of the elimination of all of Aristotle's causes from the sphere of physics, with efficient causation the last to go.

Before moving to the nineteenth century, when the theological foundation of laws begins to be quietly ignored, it is worth briefly considering just one example of a parallel development that took place in another context in which 'natural law' was operative – enquiries into *human* nature. The German jurist and political philosopher Samuel Pufendorf (1632–94), although not as well known today as he should be, was regarded by his contemporaries as the intellectual equal of such figures as Grotius, Locke, and Hobbes. Pufendorf's goal was to produce a political theory that avoided the difficulties of the 'atheistic' systems of Hobbes and Spinoza on the one hand and the overly rationalised proposals of scholastic philosophers, medieval and contemporary, on the other. His attempt to do this was grounded in a voluntaristic conception of laws of nature akin to that held by Newton and Boyle. In his description of the natural state of human beings Pufendorf declared that when we use the word 'natural' when speaking of human nature or natural law, we are not referring to some 'natural', inherent principle, nor to some human convention, but something 'imposed by the

---

[83] For Leibniz's criticisms of Newtonianism see John Hedley Brooke, *Science and Religion: Some Historical Perspectives* (Cambridge: Cambridge University Press, 1991), pp. 218–21.

Divine will'.[84] 'Nature' is thus understood as what God directly wills. It followed that natural law (in the moral and political sense) could not be intuited from rational reflection upon some imagined essence of human nature or derived from the theological notion of the divine image, human nature instead being imposed or 'superadded' by God. Moreover, because God's will was inscrutable, it followed that natural law could only be discovered through empirical investigation of how human beings actually conducted themselves in the social and political spheres.[85] The effect of Pufendorf's 'supernaturalisation' of natural law was thus, paradoxically, to relocate questions about human nature into the realm of secular history.

Pufendorf's logic neatly matches what we find in the Preface to the second edition of the *Principia*, which sets out the rationale of Newton's approach in the sphere of nature:

> Surely, this World ... could not have arisen except from the perfectly free will of God, who provides and governs all things. From this source, then, have all the laws that are called laws of nature come, in which many traces of the highest wisdom and counsel certainly appear, but no traces of necessity. Accordingly we should not seek these laws by using untrustworthy conjectures, but learn them by observing and experimenting.[86]

In both cases – physics and political philosophy – an emphasis on the primacy of the divine will encourages an empirical approach while also representing an incipient tendency towards naturalisation and secularisation.

5.3 Law and Order in the Nineteenth Century

In Britain, and to a large degree elsewhere, the theistic basis of laws of nature was taken for granted by virtually all practitioners of the sciences until well into the nineteenth century. Hume had certainly made a case for laws as mere constant conjunctions, while Kant had placed causal regularities in the sphere of the phenomenal. However, those wishing to uphold scientific realism – science as describing the world as it really is – tended

---

[84] Samuel Pufendorf, *De jure naturae et gentium* (Francofurti & Lipsiae, 1759), p. 4. For further commentary see Ian Hunter, 'Human Nature, the State of Nature, and Natural Law', in *The Cambridge Companion to Pufendorf*, ed. Knud Haakonssen and Ian Hunter (Cambridge: Cambridge University Press, 2023), pp. 109–39; Kari Saastamoinen, *The Morality of Fallen Man: Samuel Pufendorf on Natural Law* (Helsinki: Societas Historica Finlandiae, 1995).

[85] What Pufendorf had in mind here was not psychology in our sense, but examination of the cumulative historical record produced by learned sources. See Hunter, 'Human Nature'.

[86] Roger Cotes, Preface to the 2nd edition of the *Principia*. *Isaac Newton: The Principia*, trans. I. B. Cohen and A. Whitman (Berkeley: University of California Press, 1999), p. 397.

5.3 LAW AND ORDER IN THE NINETEENTH CENTURY 243

to argue that laws of nature were genuine features of reality rather than of human psychology. They typically maintained this by reiterating the arguments initially put forward in the seventeenth century, to the effect that laws of nature were edicts of God.

In what was widely acknowledged to be the period's most authoritative statement on the foundations and methods of science, the gifted polymath John Herschel (1792–1871) made much of the fact that science rests upon the uniformity of nature. That uniformity, in turn, was said to have arisen from 'the constant exercise of his [God's] direct power in maintaining the system of nature or the ultimate emanation of every energy which material agents exert from his immediate will, acting in conformity with his own laws'.[87] For Michael Faraday (1791–1867), the discoverer of electromagnetic induction (and more), God governs the world 'by means of *definite laws* resulting from the forces impressed on matter'. William Whewell (1794–1866), both an enthusiastic practising scientist and an eminent historian and philosopher of science, proposed the maxim that 'law implies mind'. It was impossible, he maintained, to imagine the universe being governed by general laws without at the same time positing 'an intelligent and conscious Deity, by whom these laws were originally contemplated, established, and applied'. Without committing himself to the idea, John Stuart Mill also observed in his 1846 *System of Logic* – a work that also addressed the methods of science – that 'the expression *law of nature* is generally employed by scientific men with a sort of tacit reference to the original sense of the word *law*, namely, the expression of the will of a superior; the superior, in this instance, being the ruler of the universe'.[88] Theologians, for the most part,

---

[87] John Herschel, *Preliminary Discourse on the Study of Natural Philosophy* [1830], new edition (London, 1851), p. 37. For American geologist Edward Hitchcock laws of nature were 'Nothing more nor less than the uniform mode in which divine power acts.' *Religion of Geology and its Connected Sciences* [1851] (London: James Blackwood, 1860), p. 183. See also Baden Powell: 'The laws of nature are … the thoughts of God.' 'The Uniformity of Nature', in *Essays on the Spirit of Inductive Philosophy, the Unity of Worlds, and the Philosophy of Creation* (London: Longman, Brown, Green and Longmans, 1855), p. 113. Powell is paraphrasing the Danish physicist Hans Christian Oersted, *Soul in Nature* (London: Bohn, 1852), pp. 20, 444. From the French literature, see also Constantin-François Volney, who opens his work on the law of nature with the statement that the law of nature is 'the regular and constant order of events by which God rules the universe'. Constantin-François Volney, *La Loi Naturelle*, in *Les Ruins, ou Méditation sur les Révolutions les Empires*, 11th ed. (Paris, 1822), p. 257.

[88] Faraday, quoted in Geoffrey Cantor, *Michael Faraday: Sandemanian and Scientist* (London: Macmillan, 1993), p. 202; Whewell, *Astronomy and General Physics*, pp. 293, 301; cf. p. 357; J. S. Mill, *A System of Logic, Collected Works*, vol. 7, pp. 316f. (reading from MS 43). Cf. Thomas Reid, for whom 'The laws of nature are the rules by which the Supreme Being governs the world.' Reid, *Essays*, p. 560, cf. p. 83.

agreed with this conception, and it was also widely communicated to the reading public.[89] The relevant 1817 *Encyclopaedia Britannica* entry offered a definition of laws of nature essentially no different from that set out by Descartes a century and a half earlier: 'God, when he created matter, and endued it with a principle of mobility, established certain rules for the perpetual direction of that motion.'[90]

Even during this later period, the expression 'law of nature' in its original theistic sense was no empty metaphor or pious gloss. It made a difference to how working scientists understood and formulated laws and principles. The uniformity of nature had been a clear implication of the original Cartesian formulation of laws. Nineteenth-century men of science also stressed the related notions of simplicity and harmony. The fruitfulness of this theological conception was also held, with some justification, to have been true of scientific innovation in the past. William Whewell connected the historical quest for simplification and unification to a belief in a single, divine

---

[89] Philip Doddridge wrote in his well-regarded *Lectures on Pneumatology*: 'When we assert a perpetual divine agency, we readily acknowledge that matters are so contrived, as not to need a divine interposition in a different manner, from that which it had been constantly exerted.' *The Works of the Rev. P. Doddridge, D.D.*, 10 vols. (Leeds, 1803), vol. 4, p. 382. To a similar end, the eminent Scottish theologian Thomas Chalmers wrote in the first of the Bridgewater Treatises: 'For the continuance of the system and of all its operations, we might imagine a sufficiency of the laws of nature; but it is the first construction of the system which so palpably calls for the intervention of an artificer or demonstrates to powerfully the fiat and finger of a God.' Chalmers sees this as consistent with Newton's views of laws of nature. *Of the Adaptation of External Nature to the Moral and Intellectual Constitution of Man*, 2 vols. (London: William Pickering, 1833), vol. 1, p. 27. See also Chalmers, 'The Constancy of God in His Works an Argument for the Faithfulness of God in His Word', in *The Select Works of Thomas Chalmers, D.D., LL.D.*, 4 vols. (New York, 1850), vol. 4, pp. 261–70, esp. p. 262; Newman, *Sermons, chiefly on the Theory of Religious Belief*, pp. 5f.; James Martineau, 'Is there any Axiom of Causality?', *Contemporary Review* 14 (April–July 1870), 636–44; F. D. Maurice, 'On the Words "Nature," "Natural," and "Supernatural"', in *The Papers of the Metaphysical Society, 1869–1880: A Critical Edition*, 3 vols., ed. Catherine Marshall, Bernard Lightman, and Richard England (Oxford: Oxford University Press, 2015), vol. 1, pp. 296–309, and 'On the Mode of Dealing with the Words which occur most Frequently in Treatises on Mental Philosophy', *The Contemporary Review* 19 (1871), 260–80 (277); Frederick Temple, *The Relations between Religion and Science* (New York: Macmillan, 1884), pp. 6–8, 19, 31–3.

[90] *Encyclopaedia Britannica*, 5th ed. (Edinburgh, 1817), vol. 11, s.v. 'Law', p. 582b. The same definition appears in F. M. Hodson, *Encyclopedia Mancuniensis*, 2 vols. (Manchester, 1815), vol. 2, s.v. 'Law', p. 354. See also William Benjamin Carpenter for whom laws of nature were 'the simplest and most direct expressions we possess, of the mode in which Deity operates on the material universe'. *Popular Cyclopaedia of Natural Science* (London, 1843), p. 470. For laws of nature in the nineteenth century see Matthew Stanley, 'God and the Uniformity of Nature: The Case of Nineteenth-Century Physics', in *Science without God?*, ed. Harrison and Roberts, pp. 97–109.

Creator. His chief examples were Kepler and Newton.[91] (As we have seen, this description also fits John Philoponus.) Whewell implied that, historically speaking, truly original scientific insight, associated with the reduction of diverse phenomena to more simple principles, was directly correlated with a strong belief in a monotheistic Deity. Theistic commitments, on his analysis, thus contributed positively to the progress of science and the stronger the commitment, the greater the scientific contribution.[92]

Contemporary examples also lent credence to Whewell's historical claims. Scottish physicist and mathematician James Clerk Maxwell (1831–79) laid the foundations for special relativity and quantum mechanics by establishing the connection between the apparently diverse phenomena of electricity, magnetism, and light. This feat is on a par with Newton's unification of terrestrial gravity and celestial astronomy. Maxwell dismissed suggestions that the laws of nature he was unifying were mere psychological associations.[93] Neither were they the result of some capricious Deity who might have instituted disparate sets of laws that did not genuinely interconnect. On the contrary, Maxwell insisted that 'the laws of nature are not mere arbitrary and unconnected decisions of Supreme Power, but … they form essential parts of one universal system'.[94] Confidence that there was thus a genuine connection between the various laws of forces of nature, including 'the convertibility and equivalence of all forms of Energy' flowed from his theological commitments.[95]

---

[91] Whewell, *Astronomy and General Physics*, pp. 306–17.

[92] Hence, Jean d'Alembert, Alexis Clairault, Leonhard Euler, Joseph-Louis Lagrange, and Pierre-Simon Laplace, while distinguished, were of a lesser rank than Newton (Whewell, *Astronomy and General Physics*, pp. 326–8). Excepting Euler, none was particularly enthusiastic when it came to religious matters. Whewell suggests here something like Thomas Kuhn's distinction between revolutionary science and normal science, with the Continental mathematicians exemplifying the latter.

[93] T. H. Huxley would later adopt precisely this interpretation: 'a law of nature, in the scientific sense, is the product of a mental operation upon the facts of nature which come under observation, and has no more existence outside the mind than colour has'. 'Pseudo-Scientific Realism', in *Science and Christian Tradition*, CE, vol. 5, pp. 59–89 (p. 76). Cf. James Ward, *Naturalism and Agnosticism*, 2nd ed., 2 vols. (London: Adam and Charles Black, 1903), vol. 2, pp. 259–66.

[94] James Clerk Maxwell, 'Inaugural Lecture to King's College London, October, 1860', in *Scientific Letters and Papers*, 3 vols. ed. P. M. Harman (Cambridge: Cambridge University Press, 2009), vol. 1, p. 670, cf. p. 673.

[95] Maxwell, 'Inaugural Lecture', p. 666. See esp. Matthew Stanley, 'By Design: James Clerk Maxwell and the Evangelical Unification of Science', *The British Journal for the History of Science* 45 (2012), 57–73. Crosbie Smith has shown how Maxwell was representative of a 'North British' group of physicists who resisted the naturalistic endeavours of 'metropolitan' physicists such as John Tyndal. *The Science of Energy* (Chicago: University of Chicago Press, 1998), chs. 9–11.

Nineteenth-century discussions of energy and its conservation were also strongly inflected with theological themes. The Welsh physicist William Robert Grove (1811–96) linked the principle that would become the first law of thermodynamics – 'neither matter nor force can be created or annihilated' – to the fact that 'Causation is the will, Creation the act, of God.'[96] Michael Faraday, whose pioneering work in electromagnetism laid the groundwork for Maxwell's equations, also held that the first law was underpinned by the fact that the creation and destruction of energy was reserved for God alone: it is 'only within the power of Him' to create or destroy force.[97] As in the case of other laws of nature, the consistency of this principle – responding to the question of what it is that does the conserving – was attributed to the steadfastness of God. James Joule (1818–89), in spite of differences with Faraday over specifics of the conservation of energy, agreed that force cannot be created or destroyed 'because it is manifestly absurd to suppose that the powers with which God has endowed matter can be destroyed any more than that they can be created by man's agency'.[98] The other nineteenth-century figure associated with the foundations of modern thermodynamics, William Thomson, Lord Kelvin (1824–1907) was similarly concerned to point out connections between advances in physics and a theistic conception of the universe. Thomson was convinced that the second law of thermodynamics (entropy increases – there is in the universe an ever-reducing amount of energy available for physical processes) implies a beginning and end of the universe. For him, this fundamental physical law was perfectly correlated with the Christian view of the beginning and end of the world, now understood in terms of a law of 'nature'.[99]

While the connections might be obvious in physics, it is tempting to think that it was a different matter in biology.[100] However, that was not

---

[96] William Robert Grove (1811–96), *The Correlation of Physical Forces* [1846], 3rd ed. (London: Longman, Brown, Green and Longmans, 1855), p. 218. Cf. p. 10.

[97] Cantor, *Michael Faraday*, p. 186. See also Smith, *The Science of Energy*, p. 63.

[98] James P. Joule, 'On the changes of temperature produced by the rarefaction and condensation of air', in *The Scientific Papers of James Prescott Joule*, 2 vols. (London, 1887), vol. 1, pp. 172–89, n. 90, p. 269; quoted in Cantor, *Michael Faraday*, p. 192. Cantor outlines the key differences between Faraday and Joules on the conservation of energy (pp. 185–90).

[99] Kelvin remarked that we now have 'the sober scientific certainty that heavens and earth shall "wax old as doth a garment" [Ps. 102.26]; and that this slow progress must gradually, by natural agencies which we see going on under fixed laws, bring about circumstances in which "the elements shall melt with fervent heat" [2 Pet. 3.10].' Crosbie Smith and M. Norton Wise, *Energy and Empire: A Biographical Study of Lord Kelvin* (Cambridge: Cambridge University Press, 1989), p. 535.

[100] A third area of the operation of laws of nature worth mentioning parenthetically was human society – e.g., Thomas Malthus's 'law of population' as a law imposed by God.

the case. One of the leading physiologists of the Victorian period, William Benjamin Carpenter (1813–85), drew upon Grove's idea of the 'correlation of forces' to suggest that a 'vital force' in living things could be correlated with the operation of forces in the physical world. Both were conserved in the same fashion and both were to be understood in terms of laws originally ordained by God.[101] 'Let it be borne in mind', wrote Carpenter in one of the standard physiology texts of the period, 'that when a *law* of Physics or of Vitality is mentioned, nothing more is really implied than a simple expression of the *mode* in which the Creator is *constantly* operating on inorganic matter, or on organised structures'.[102] Carpenter explicitly opposed the subjectivist understanding of laws of nature later promoted by Huxley and other naturalists.[103]

Initially, most prominent nineteenth-century proponents of evolution in Victorian Britain, like their counterparts in physics, sought to account for long-term changes in the realm of living things by making reference to unchanging *organic* laws. The first, controversial, attempt to introduce evolution to English readers was Robert Chambers's *Vestiges of the Natural*

See 'Population' [1824], *A Summary View of the Principle of Population* [1830], in *The Works of Thomas Robert Malthus*, vol. 4, ed. E. A. Wrigley and D. Souden (London: William Pickering, 1986), pp. 177–243 (p. 240). Also George Combe, 'God reigns, through the medium of fixed natural laws, in another department of human affairs–namely, that of population.' *On the Relation between Science and Religion*, 4th ed. (Edinburgh: MacLachlan and Stewart, 1857), p. xii. Combe also refers to Adam Smith in this context.

[101] '... many of the phenomena of living bodies may be placed in the same category with those of inanimate matter'. William Benjamin Carpenter, 'On the mutual relations of the vital and physical forces', *Philosophical Transactions of the Royal Society* 140 (1850), 727–57 (728). Cf. '... all *force* which does not emanate from the will of created sentient beings, directly and immediately proceeds from the Will of the Omnipotent and Omnipresent Creator ... and looking therefore at what we are accustomed to call the physical forces, as so many *modi operandi* of one and the same agency, the creative and sustaining will of the Deity'. For Carpenter's contributions to the principle of the conservation of energy see P. M. Heimann, 'Conversion of Forces and the Conservation of Energy', *Centaurus* 18 (1973–4), 147–61, esp. 149, and Vance M. D. Hall, 'The Contribution of the Physiologist, William Benjamin Carpenter (1813–1885), to the Development of the Principles of the Correlation of Forces and the Conservation of Energy', *Medical History* 23 (1979), 129–55.

[102] William Benjamin Carpenter, *Principles of General and Comparative Physiology* (London: John Churchill, 1839), p. 135.

[103] William Benjamin Carpenter, 'Of Mind and Will in Nature', *Papers of the Metaphysical Society*, vol. 1, pp. 47–66. Cf. Maurice, 'On the Words "Nature," "Natural," and "Supernatural"'; Ward, *Naturalism and Agnosticism*, vol. 2, p. 266. On Carpenter's theistic science see Piers Hale, 'Between Intuition and Empiricism: William Benjamin Carpenter on Man, Mind, and Moral Responsibility', in *The Metaphysical Society (1869–1880): Intellectual Life in Mid-Victorian England*, ed. Catherine Marshall, Bernard Lightman, and Richard England (Oxford: Oxford University Press, 2019), pp. 204–27.

History of Creation (1844).[104] Chambers took considerable pains to draw parallels between the theologically respectable law of gravitation and his own proposal for an analogous law of 'development' in the organic realm. Both laws, he opined – adverting to the principle of unification – might eventually be combined in 'one still more comprehensive law, the expression of a unity, flowing immediately from the One who is First and Last'.[105] In an extended note he went on to cite such pillars of the establishment as John Herschel, Dugald Stewart, William Paley, William Benjamin Carpenter, and Philip Doddridge, on laws of nature as divine volitions in order to establish the propriety of the idea that God accomplishes his purposes through general laws, rather than by means of 'interventions'.[106] This principle was now simply extended to the sphere of living things. The co-discoverer of natural selection, Alfred Russel Wallace (1823–1913), while by no means a conventional theist, also held that 'the origin of universal forces and laws' lies in 'the will or power of "one Supreme Intelligence"'.[107] That Intelligence had directed the course of evolutionary change, albeit by means of the operation of those laws.[108]

It is not surprising, then, that Charles Darwin would initially seek to locate his *Origin of Species* (1859) within this theistic context, bookending it with references to divine law. The epigraphs that faced the title page of the first edition include a citation from William Whewell's Bridgewater Treatise to the effect that 'events are brought about, not by insulated interpositions of divine power exerted in each particular case, but by the establishment of general laws'. In the second edition, published a year after the first, this was bolstered by an additional quotation from Joseph Butler's still-influential *Analogy of Religion* (1736), which also argues that what is 'natural', in the sense of ordered or settled, 'presupposes an intelligent agent to render it so'.[109] Darwin's clear intention was to propose that the diversity of life on

---

[104] For its reception see James A. Secord, *Victorian Sensation: The Extraordinary Publication, Reception, and Secret Authorship of Vestiges of the Natural History of Creation* (Chicago: University of Chicago Press, 2001).

[105] Robert Chambers, *Vestiges of the Natural History of Creation* [1844], 8th ed. (London: John Chambers, 1850), p. 269.

[106] Chambers, *Vestiges*, n. 6 (pp. 295–6).

[107] Alfred Russel Wallace, *Contributions to the Theory of Natural Selection: A Series of Essays*, 2nd ed. (London: Macmillan, 1871), p. 372 (my italics).

[108] Alfred Russel Wallace, 'Geological Climates and the Origin of Species', *The Quarterly Review* 126, no. 252 (1869), 359–94 (391). Wallace had sketched a plan for a book devoted to the law underlying evolutionary change. *The Organic Law of Change*, ed. James T. Costa (Cambridge, MA: Harvard University Press, 2013).

[109] The full Butler quote reads as follows: 'The only distinct meaning of the word "natural" is STATED, FIXED or SETTLED; since what is natural as much requires and presupposes

earth could be attributed to the operation of the law of natural selection, operating in a manner analogous to the law of gravity. The direct comparison is made in the closing lines of the work.[110] The move was to suggest that if God does not need to intervene to ensure the evolution and smooth running of the physical world, neither is he required to institute special measures in the realm of organic life.

Notwithstanding Darwin's efforts to co-opt establishment views about divine governance and the uniformity of nature, his relocation of natural laws onto the organic realm proved controversial, especially when it came to the origins of human beings. The Darwinian story of the development of life was certainly inconsistent with the chronology implied by a literal reading of Genesis. But this was a relatively minor concern at the time, not least because such inconsistency had been true in regard to generally accepted geological timescales for much of the century, 'the public mind', as Irish physicist John Tyndall put it, 'being rendered gradually tolerant of the idea that not for six thousand, nor for sixty thousand, nor for six thousand thousand thousand, but for aeons embracing untold millions of years, this earth has been the theatre of life and death'.[111] It was not until the twentieth century, with the rise of young earth creationism, that objections to evolution on such grounds were widely expressed. More worrying to Darwin's contemporaries were the issues of the uniqueness of human beings and the origins of their moral and religious capacities. Related to this was also the spectre of Epicurean chance lurking in the details of natural selection. It was not entirely clear, for example, how an unguided process of evolutionary development would guarantee the appearance of rational human creatures. Again, however, there was uncertainty about the primacy of natural selection as an evolutionary mechanism, and the genetic basis of natural selection would not be established for some decades. These considerations blunted the religious shock of evolution, allowing for the possibility of theistic and

---

an intelligent agent to render it so, i.e., to effect it continually or at stated times, as what is supernatural or miraculous.' Joseph Butler, *The Analogy of Religion*, ed. David McNaughton (Oxford: Oxford University Press, 2021), p. 21. In the original context Butler argues that what is natural is relative to our knowledge of consistencies in nature. He suggests that with sufficient knowledge, the whole Christian dispensation (i.e., the revealed tradition) would appear 'natural'.

[110] Charles Darwin, *On the Origin of Species by means of Natural Selection*, 2nd ed. (London: John Murray, 1860), p. 490. See also Darwin to Charles Lyell, 17 June 1860, Letter 2833, Darwin Correspondence Project, 'Letter no. 2833', www.darwinproject.ac.uk/letter/?docId=letters/DCP-LETT-2833.xml, accessed 9 August 2022.

[111] John Tyndall, 'The Belfast Address', in *Fragments of Science*, 6th ed. (New York: A. L. Burtt, n.d.), p. 470.

directional understandings of the history of life. Accordingly, Darwinism attracted religious supporters, as well as detractors.[112]

Returning again to the Huxley narrative, there is still very little in this survey of the history of science to suggest an enduring naturalism/supernaturalism conflict over the course of Western history. In one sense, the naturalist narrative is not even wrong, because for most of the relevant history there was no naturalism/supernaturalism disjunction functioning as a universal background assumption about how the world operates. But even if something like that disjunction could be forced onto the relevant history, what seems to be happening is that supernatural considerations – especially those focused on the creative power of single Deity – actually promoted advances in the sciences. These included a number of instances of the unification of apparently diverse phenomena under specific laws of nature. Something like this version of history had been taken for granted by figures such as William Whewell and William Benjamin Carpenter.[113]

It is true that the advent of the theory of evolution by natural selection, coming late in the piece, might now be taken as an important exception to the general rule. After all, this was a contemporary scientific theory that *could* be understood as accounting for biological diversity and adaptation without requiring the special creative activity of the Deity, despite the fact that Darwin himself initially took pains to imply that evolution rested upon the same kind of theistic presuppositions as laws of the physical world. It is relevant that Darwinism attracted prominent theological critics (although it is important not to forget that he also had significant support in some clerical circles). Given this, it was not implausible to regard the reception of Darwin's theory as an example of science versus theology.

But more was required, in addition to this largely isolated counterinstance, to establish the plausibility of the naturalism story that Huxley and others wished to tell. Crucially, the conception of laws of nature had to be de-coupled from its theological foundations. One way in which this could

---

[112] For theological supporters of Darwin see David N. Livingstone, *Darwin's Forgotten Defenders: The Encounter between Evangelical Theology and Evolutionary Theory* (Grand Rapids: Eerdmans, 1987); James R. Moore, *The Post-Darwinian Controversies* (Cambridge: Cambridge University Press, 1981); Brooke, *Science and Religion*, pp. 422–37.

[113] Whewell, *Astronomy and General Physics*, pp. 326–8. For Carpenter, 'the culminating point of Man's Intellectual Interpretation of Nature' was 'his recognition of the Unity of the Power of which her phenomena are diversified manifestations'. This dawning recognition began with 'the most enlightened of the Greek and Roman philosophers' among whom 'we find a distinct recognition of the idea of the Unity of the Directing Mind from which the Order of Nature proceeds'. *Presidential Address, 1872, Report of the Forty-Second Meeting of the British Association* (London: John Murray, 1873), p. lxxxiv.

5.3 LAW AND ORDER IN THE NINETEENTH CENTURY

be accomplished was by simply denying that laws of nature were genuine features of the world. Huxley, for example, suggested that laws of nature could be understood as a 'product of the mental operation upon the facts of nature which come under observation'. On this view they would have no 'existence outside the mind' being simply 'a record of experience'.[114] One of the period's leading English advocates of positivist philosophy, Frederick Harrison, agreed that laws of nature were 'subjective generalizations'.[115] The atheist and freethinking statistician Karl Pearson also insisted that 'man gives laws to nature' rather than the converse.[116] William Clifford went further and offered an evolutionary explanation, speculating that nature had selected for those individuals who believed in the uniformity of nature and that this accounted for the prevalence of the belief in 'the civilized world'.[117] These subjectivising moves were inconsistent with how most historical actors had imagined laws to operate (Hume being a notable exception). Neither did they accord with the work of unification that laws, realistically conceptualised, had effected.[118] Equally importantly, these moves also wrought significant collateral damage on one of the planks of scientific naturalism – the principle that scientific commitment was incompatible with belief in miracles. If laws of nature were human conventions, there was no in-principle difficulty with contraventions of such 'laws'. Conflict between scientific and religious doctrines requires that they both lay claim to be offering a realist account of things. For this reason, there was often a degree of equivocation in the naturalists' use of the conception.[119] In discussions of miracles, laws of nature were invoked to suggest the scientific impossibility of interventions into the natural order. When discussions turned to the theological basis of nature's regularities, however, resort was made to weaker conception of laws as psychological constructs or summaries of experience rather than divine edicts. This inevitably led to the dilemma that Hume had faced. Miracles cannot be ruled out in principle, since our assumptions about how

---

[114] Huxley, 'Pseudo-Scientific Realism', *CE*, vol. 5, pp. 76–8.
[115] 'The Relativity of Knowledge', *Papers of the Metaphysical Society*, vol. 1, pp. 160–73. See also Clifford, 'Aims and Instruments of Scientific Thought', *Lectures and Essays*, p. 95.
[116] Karl Pearson, *The Grammar of Science* (London: Walter Scott, 1892), p. 104.
[117] Clifford, 'The Philosophy of the Pure Sciences', *Lectures and Essays*, pp. 180–243 (p. 209). Cf. 'Aims and Instruments of Scientific Thought', *Lectures and Essays*, pp. 85–109 (p. 95).
[118] Huxley comes close to conceding this at times. 'The Progress of Science', *CE*, vol. 1, pp. 87, 94f.
[119] Huxley could speak of 'rules or so-called "laws of Nature," by which the relation of phenomena is truly defined [and is] true for all time'. Subsequently, scientific progress depends on 'belief in the universal validity of that orderly relation of facts which we express by the so-called "Laws of Nature"'. 'The Progress of Science', *CE*, vol. 1, pp.

nature operates are based upon cumulative testimony. But the appeal to testimony has then to confront the inconvenient fact of the historical and cultural universality of experiences of the supernatural. More generally, the move to a constructivist understanding of laws of nature looks like a retreat from scientific realism. If science is more a product of human psychology than an accurate depiction of the world as it really is, this would take the sting out of any imagined conflict between science and religion.

The triumph of naturalism was impossible while the long-standing historical alliance between belief in the supernatural and the principle of the uniformity and intelligibility of nature remained intact.[120] Proponents of naturalism promoted a twofold strategy that exploited existing tensions within Christianity. This required, first, the adoption of a sharp natural/supernatural divide, accompanied by an alignment of the former, rather than the latter, with the uniformity of nature. Instead of underwriting the uniformity of nature and its laws, 'the supernatural' might then be understood as fundamentally incompatible with uniformity.[121] This was a radical change of perspective, given the general consensus among the Victorian scientific establishment about laws of nature. An important factor behind the success of the naturalist vision of the world was simply to do with generational change and a concerted ideological campaign on the part of advocates of naturalism. As Matthew Stanley has shown, the naturalist camp was remarkably successful in gaining control over the training of scientists and in infiltrating the bastions of the scientific establishment.[122] But this strategy was accompanied by key conceptual innovations, of which the most

---

61, 96. Cf. the criticisms of James Ward: 'We find laws of Nature used in two very different senses by scientific writers. Sometimes such laws are spoken of as self-existent and as independent of the phenomena which they are said to govern and which of necessity conform to them .... [At other times] laws of nature only state the relations, they do not make them.' *Naturalism and Agnosticism*, vol. 2, pp. 259f. This point was also made in a roundabout way by F. D. Maurice, who identified such equivocation in Lucretius. 'On the Words "Nature," "Natural," and "Supernatural"'. Cf. the editorial commentary on p. 298 of *Papers of the Metaphysical Society*, vol. 1. See also Frederick Temple's first Bampton Lecture, *Relations between Religion and Science*, pp. 1–33.

[120] For a detailed account this issue, and of how the naturalists eventually 'won', see Matthew Stanley, *Huxley's Church and Maxwell's Demon: From Theistic Science to Naturalistic Science* (Chicago: University of Chicago Press, 2015).

[121] Thus Tyndall: 'science demands the radical extirpation of caprice and the absolute reliance upon law in nature'. This demands, in turn, the elimination of the 'mob of gods and demons'. Tyndall, 'Belfast Address', p. 444. Tyndall is nonetheless aware of the theistic implications of laws of nature, and references the ideas of Gassendi, Bishop Butler, and Maxwell (pp. 461f.).

[122] Stanley, *Huxley's Church*, pp. 243–8, 262f. Stanley also points to the naturalists' rewriting of history (pp. 256f.).

important was the construction of the category of 'supernatural*ism*' that could serve as the necessary counterpoint to naturalism. This was a further refinement of the modern natural/supernatural dichotomy. These conceptual developments did not originate, as we might expect, within the philosophy of the natural sciences but in the realm of theology – more specifically, the sphere of biblical criticism.

A second part of the strategy involved an application of this new naturalism/supernaturalism divide to history. The rise of modern science could then be identified with a more general triumph of naturalism. At the same time, a progressivist historical understanding could be used to discount the historical weight of testimony to the existence of the supernatural, by relegating religious experiences to an earlier, primitive phase of the intellectual development of the human race. The retrospective application of these concepts to history – which is difficult to square with the actual events – was facilitated by the fact that it could be accommodated to contemporary models of historical progress. With a few adjustments, and the application of the new dichotomy, Huxley's version of the history of science could be slotted into a well-worn historiographical groove that had been in the making since the time of the Protestant Reformation. These developments will be the main topic of the next chapter. For now, we are concerned with the appearance of the relevant framing concepts.

5.4 The History of the Supernatural

It can be difficult to fully apprehend the historical novelty of the natural/supernatural distinction, given its centrality to our present understandings of the world. Some of the historical episodes related in the previous sections point to alternative ways of conceptualising reality, much as anthropological observations also bear witness to the distinctively modern and Western nature of this divide.[123] The appearance and subsequent history of the term 'supernatural' in the West is a central part of this story.

In *Studies in Words*, a diverting book that has not enjoyed the readership of many of his more prominent writings, C. S. Lewis boldly tackled the polyvalent word 'nature'. His suggestion for dealing with the many

---

[123] See., e.g., Durkheim, *Elementary Forms of the Religious Life*, p. 24; Evans-Pritchard, *Witchcraft, Oracles, and Magic*; articles by Kenneth Morrison et al. on 'Native American Religions', in *Religion* 22, no. 3 (1992), 201–86; David Shorter, 'Binary Thinking and the Study of Yoeme Indian Lutu'uria/Truth', *Anthropological Forum* 13 (2003), 195–203; S. Dein, 'The Category of the Supernatural: A Valid Anthropological Term?', *Religion Compass* 10 (2016), 35–44; Sahlins, *New Science*, p. 6.

different meanings of 'nature' and its equivalents (Greek *physis*, Latin *natura*) was to think about 'what is the implied opposite to *nature*'.[124] The necessity of adopting such a strategy is clear if we look to the numerous senses of the word even when deployed in relatively formal philosophical contexts. In book V of the *Metaphysics*, for example, Aristotle set out six different meanings of 'nature' (*physis*) drawn from his philosophical precursors. His subsequent attempts to bring definitional clarity to the concept met with only qualified success, however, and there have been discussions ever since about exactly what is encompassed in his conception.[125] In the thirteenth century, Thomas Aquinas uses the expression in at least nine different ways in the *Summa theologiae*. The standard philosophical dictionary of the early modern period, compiled by Rudolph Glocenius, offers ten definitions.[126] The *Oxford English Dictionary* now lists thirteen distinct meanings of the English word, with numerous subdivisions of each.[127] All of this suggests that 'nature' is not itself a natural kind – a permanent, unchanging feature of reality that exists independently of human reasoning. Needless to say, perhaps, this generates difficulties for 'natura*lism*', if it is to be understood as a coherent set of philosophical commitments.[128]

---

[124] C. S. Lewis, *Studies in Words*, 2nd ed. (Cambridge: Cambridge University Press, 1967), p. 43.

[125] Aristotle, *Metaphysics* 1011 4b17–1015a19. Aristotle concludes that nature is 'the essence which things have in themselves ... the source of the movement of natural objects, being present in them somehow, either potentially or in complete reality'. 1015a14–19, *Complete Works*, vol. 2, p. 1603. The sixteenth-century Portuguese Jesuit Manuel de Góis picked out seven meanings of nature/*physis* in Aristotle's *Physics* alone, complaining that this hindered arriving at any clear understanding of the term. He concluded that 'the principle of motion and rest' of entities was the principal meaning (p. 220). *Commentarii Collegii Conimbricensus ... in octo libros Physicorum Aristotelis stagiritae* (Coimbra, 1592), pp. 217–18. For modern commentary, see Enrico Berti, 'Aristotle's Concept of Nature: Traditional Interpretation and Results of Recent Studies', Evolving Concepts of Nature, Pontifical Academy of Sciences, Acta 23, Vatican City 2016, www.accademiascienze.va/content/dam/accademia/pdf/acta23/acta23-berti.pdf, accessed 10 March 2020; W. W. Nicolas Fawcett, 'Aristotle's Concept of Nature: Three Tensions', PhD thesis, University of Western Ontario, 2011; Johannes Fritsche, 'Meaning and Function of Aristotle's Two Definitions of Nature (*Physics* B, 192b8–193a9), *Physics* B, and his Biology', *Revue de philosophie ancienne* 36 (2018), 215–87; William A. Wallace, 'Is Finality Included in Aristotle's Definition of Nature?', in *Final Causality in Nature and Human Affairs*, ed. Richard F. Hassing (Washington, DC: Catholic University of America Press, 1997), pp. 52–70.

[126] Roy J. Deferrari and M. Inviolata Barry, *A Lexicon of St. Thomas Aquinas* (Washington, DC: Catholic University of America Press, 1948–9), s.v. 'Nātūra', pp. 720–4. Also s.v. 'Nātūralis', pp. 724–5, with three main meanings and many subdivisions. Goclenius, *Lexicon philosophicum*, s.v. 'Natura', p. 739.

[127] OED, s.v 'Nature', n.

[128] On the problem of clearly defining naturalism see S. Stich, *Deconstructing the Mind* (Oxford: Oxford University Press, 1996), p. 197; Stroud, 'The Charm of Naturalism'; Bas van Fraassen, *The Empirical Stance* (New Haven: Yale University Press, 2002); Michael

5.4 THE HISTORY OF THE SUPERNATURAL

This difficulty is ameliorated somewhat by specifying naturalism in terms of what it is opposed to – that is, 'supernaturalism' – and this takes us back to Lewis's proposal that the specific senses of nature can be understood in terms of their implied opposite.

The crucial point is that the natural/supernatural disjunction arrives historically late in the West (and arguably appeared nowhere else).[129] It is instructive that Aristotle, as already noted, contrasts 'nature' and 'natural' not with an imagined 'supernatural' but with the artificial or the 'violent'. The other contrasts that we encounter in classical Greek authors include nature/convention, nature/law, nature/culture. Early Christian religious literature is similarly devoid of a contrast between natural and supernatural. The New Testament has no term for 'supernatural' and the same holds for the ancient Christian liturgies and the writings of the Church Fathers.[130] The more relevant distinction was between 'heavenly' and 'earthly', or between Creator and creation.[131] We occasionally encounter a pairing of 'nature' with the prepositions 'beside' or 'above'. In the fifth century, Cyril of Alexandria would thus speak of the elevation of the human dignity to

---

Rea, 'Naturalism and Material Objects', in *Naturalism: A Critical Analysis*, ed. William L. Craig and J. P. Moreland (London: Routledge, 2016), pp. 110–32; Hans Halvorson, 'What is Methodological Naturalism?', in *The Blackwell Companion to Naturalism*, ed. Kelly James Clark (Oxford: Blackwell, 2016), pp. 136–49.

[129] The significance of this distinction for an understanding of secular modernity was first raised by Henri de Lubac, in his ground-breaking study of the history of 'supernatural'. *Surnaturel: Études historiques*; 'Remarques sur l'histoire du mot *surnaturel*', *Nouvelle revue théologique* 61 (1934), 225–49. On the history of the concept see also August Deneffe, 'Geschichte des Wortes "supernaturalis"', *Zeitschrift für katholische Theologie* 46 (1922), 337–60; Michael Figura, 'Übernatürlich, I. Begriffsgeschichte', in *Lexikon für Theologie und Kirche*, 3. Auflage (Freiburg, 1993–2001), vol. 10, pp. 336–8; J. P. Kenny, *The Supernatural: Medieval Theological Concepts to Modern* (New York: Alba House, 1972); Robert Bartlett, *The Natural and the Supernatural in the Middle Ages* (Cambridge: Cambridge University Press, 2008); J. Weinhardt, 'Supranaturalismus', in *Theologische Realenzyklopädie*, ed. Gerhard Krause and Gerhard Muller (New York: De Gruyter, 2001), vol. 32, pp. 467–77; Graham Ward, 'Supernaturalism', in *Encyclopedia of Science and Religion*, ed. Wentzel van Huyssteen (New York: Macmillan, 2003), pp. 846–8.

[130] Kenny, *Supernatural*; Figura, 'Übernatürlich'.

[131] See, e.g., I Corinthians 15:46–9, Ephesians, 4:9–10. For commentary, see Risto Saarinen, 'Nature and Supernature', *Religion Past and Present* 9 (2010), 68–9. Saarinen also points to deployments of the constructions ὑπὲρ τὴν φύσιν/*hypér tēn phýsin* or *super naturam*. The heavenly/earthly distinction follows, to some extent, the earlier Greek notions of the heavens (*ouranios*) and the place above the heavens (*uperouranios*) from which the gods descend. See Ward, 'Supernaturalism', 846–7. Clement of Alexandria, for example, would develop a kind of celestial hierarchy based on supercelestial regions and their inhabitants. Bogdan G. Bucur, 'The Other Clement of Alexandria: Cosmic Hierarchy and Interiorized Apocalypticism', *Vigiliae Christianae* 60 (2006), 251–68.

a state 'above nature' (*hyper physis*).[132] But here the reference is not to a two-tiered ontology, but to the elevation of the human condition by means of divine grace. To state the matter plainly, authors of the canonical documents of Christianity are able to make perfect sense of the world and its relation to the divine without making reference to what we would recognise as natural/supernatural distinction.

The Latin *supernaturalis* first became known to medieval thinkers through Carolingian translations of Pseudo-Dionysius (fl. c.650–c.725 BCE), especially those of the Irish Neoplatonic philosopher and theologian John Scotus Eriugena (c.800–c.877). Eriugena did not himself adopt this concept as a way of dividing reality, however. On the contrary, in his classic work devoted to the divisions of nature the overriding distinction is between 'what creates and what is not created'. In this conceptual scheme, both the Creator and the creatures are encompassed within nature.[133] It is not until Thomas Aquinas that we encounter the word 'supernatural' occurring with any frequency. Even then, the word is relatively uncommon and bears different connotations to those we are familiar with.[134]

In Aquinas's writings, 'supernatural' appears in a few different contexts, almost always in adjectival or, occasionally, adverbal form: there is no settled sense of '*the* supernatural'. Aquinas explains that on the occasion of the conception of Christ the supernatural power of God was operative along with the usual natural powers.[135] In the Eucharist, the bread and wine become the body and blood of Christ not by a natural change, but by the supernatural power of God alone.[136] Other places in which Aquinas uses the

---

[132] Cyril of Alexandria, *In Joannis evangelium* 1:12 (PG 73: 153), with parallel Latin translation rendering this as '*supernaturalem*'. Earlier in this passage he would also speak of a condition beyond or beside nature (*para physis*). PG 73: 152. For similar references in Origen and Gregory of Nyssa see Deneffe, 'Geschichte des Wortes "supernaturalis"'. Aristotle used *para phusin*, contrasted with *kata phusin* (according to nature), to describe the violent, artificial, mechanical, and monstrous. *Physics* 197b 32–7; *On the Heavens* 300a 23; *Generation of Animals* 770b 9–17.

[133] John Scotus Eriugena, *De divisione naturae* 1.1. *Periphyseon: On the Division of Nature*, trans. Myra L. Uhlfelder (Eugene: Wipf and Stock, 1976), p. 2. Cf. Aquinas, *SCG* 4.11.1–5.

[134] Aquinas uses the term and variants only 336 times in a corpus of more than 8 million words. This compares, for example, to 'natural' which is used more than 15,000 times. Across his whole corpus, Aquinas uses 'supernatural' on average once every 26,000 words. I am indebted to Andrew Murray for this analysis: 'The Spiritual and Supernatural according to Thomas Aquinas', www.cis.catholic.edu.au/Files/Murray-SpiritualSupernatural.pdf, accessed 21 February 2018. Murray also helpfully summarises the different contexts in which Aquinas uses the expression. Deneffe, by way of contrast, remarks on how frequent Aquinas's use is, presumably in comparison to his scholastic predecessors. 'Geschichte des Wortes "supernaturalis"', 355.

[135] Aquinas, *ST* 3a. 31, 5.   [136] Aquinas, *ST* 3a. 74, 3.

expression 'supernatural' pertain to divine grace and the infusion of the theological virtues, faith, hope, and love. As the gift of God these things lie beyond or above the natural powers of human beings.[137] The creatures also have a 'supernatural' end – God – which they are unable to attain by virtue of their own (natural) powers. What is required is God's supernatural light or power.[138]

We might expect that Aquinas would use the descriptor 'supernatural' for miraculous events. However, the word does not appear in the formal discussion of miracles in his *Summa contra gentiles*. Here Aquinas speaks of miraculous events in terms of the effect that they have on human observers: miracles are so-called because they elicit wonder.[139] But miracles also differed from mundane events because they transcended the inherent powers of created things. The recurring descriptor for such events was not 'supernatural' but 'beside the order implanted in nature' (*praeter naturam* or 'preternatural').[140] Aquinas is at pains to stress that miracles are in no sense contrary to nature. They are not violations or interventions. Subsequently, in the *Summa theologiae*, we do encounter the expressions 'supernatural' and 'supernaturally' in relation to miracles. But the context here is the operation of divine grace within the miracle-worker, not the status of the events themselves. This usage is in keeping with Aquinas's use of 'supernatural' to describe the particular virtues and graces as gifts that come from God. Miraculous events, then, are not the primary site of manifestations of the

---

[137] Aquinas, ST 1a2ae. 63, 3. Sometimes referred to as 'praeternatural gifts'. See J. H. Murphy, *The Preternatural Gifts of our First Parents in the Fathers of the First Four Centuries* (Maynooth: St Patrick's College, 1947).

[138] Aquinas, SCG 3.52–7; 147–50.

[139] Aquinas, SCG 3.101. Here referring to the common etymology of the Latin *miro*: to be amazed. This bears comparison to Augustine's position that miracles are not above nature, but above our knowledge of nature. Augustine, *City of God* XXI.8; *Contra Faustum* XXVI.3 (*NPNF* I, vol. 4, pp. 321f.). Cf. *Sermons* VII, in *Works* III/2: 78, 86. Augustine implies a subjective understanding of the miraculous.

[140] Variously: 'apart from the order implanted in natural things by God' (*praeter ordinem naturalibus inditum rebus a Deo*), SCG 3.99; or, 'beside the order commonly observed in things' (*praeter ordinem communiter observatum in rebus*), SCG 3.100. To some extent this follows the earlier usage of Peter Lombard, for whom natural events come about by means of the joint operation of divine power concurring with the natural powers that God has implanted in things. Other events, however, are effected solely through the power of God. Lombard speaks in these latter cases of a power that is 'beside' or 'beyond' nature (*praeter naturam*). *Sententiarum*, bk. 2, dist. 19, ch. 7, *PL* 192: 689. This is consistent with the earlier usage of Ambrose of Milan who had referred to miracles performed by Moses as '*praeter naturum*'. *De mysteriis* 9.51, *PL* 16: 406. For uses of the expression and a possible later distinction from 'supernatural' see W. H. Principe, 'Preternatural', *New Catholic Encyclopedia*, 2nd ed. (Detroit: Gale, 2003), vol. 11, pp. 686–7.

supernatural. In another point of difference with later understandings, neither was their chief role that of providing an evidential basis for religious belief. Miracles do act as 'signs' – but typically signs of the sanctity of the miracle-worker.[141] This is consistent with the use of 'supernatural' to describe the gifts of grace, and with the practice of linking canonisation to the performance of miracles. What evidential role miracles do play is largely limited to their effect on those who are 'less perfect and less perceptive'.[142] Even in this context, they do not compel belief. The faithful, for their part, believe on the basis of authority.[143]

In all of this, 'supernatural' is a relative term – relative to the powers of the respective agent. This understanding is in keeping with the scholastic principle that 'every work of nature is the work of an intellect'.[144] There is a sense in which everything that God does is natural in so far as it is in keeping with his nature. Hence Aquinas's insistence that miracles are not contrary to nature. Even when God works changes in human beings – prompting them to faith, for example – this is a 'natural' activity for God, because it is integral to his nature to work in this way.[145] By the same token, it is natural for the human soul to be the recipient of divine grace. There is no puzzle, in any of this, about how God might 'act' or be an 'agent' in the natural world. Everything in nature requires God's ongoing conservation of natural agents and every event relies upon his concurrence in the exercise of their created causal powers.[146] In all of this, Aquinas retains something of the

---

[141] Aquinas, *ST* 1a. 43, 3; 1a2ae. 111, 5.
[142] Aquinas, *Commentary on the Gospel of Saint John*, ch. 6, lec. 1, sect. 843, trans. James A. Weisheipl and Fabien R. Larcher (Toronto: Pontifical Institute of Medieval Studies, 1980), p. 341.
[143] Those things that God requires us to believe 'which surpass human intelligence ... are to be proved by the authority of Holy Writ'. *SCG* 4.1. Cf. *ST* 1a.1, 8.
[144] '*Opus naturae est opus intelligentiae*'. Among numerous references see Aquinas, *SCG* 3.24; *Disputed questions on Truth*, q. 13, art. 1. Aquinas attributes the axiom to Aristotle, and to 'philosophers' generally, although the saying cannot be found in Aristotle in this precise formulation. See Weisheipl, 'The Axiom "*Opus naturae est opus intelligentia*"'; L. Hödl, '"*Opus naturae est opus intelligentia*": Ein neuplatonisches Axiom im aristotelischen Verständnis des Albertus Magnus Averroismus im Mittelalter', in *Averroismus im Mittelalter und in der Renaissance*, ed. Friedrich Niewöhner and Loris Sturlese (Zürich: Spur 1994), pp. 132–48.
[145] 'That which God does is not against nature, but is simply natural [*non est contra naturam, sed simpliciter est naturale*] .... So, too, since every creature is naturally subject to God, whatever God does in the creature is simply natural ....' *In Rom.* 11.24 in *Super Epistolas S. Pauli lectura*, 8th ed., 2 vols., ed. Raphael Cai (Turin: Marietti, 1953), §910b (vol. 1, p. 169). Cf. *Disputed questions on Truth*, q. 13, art. 1; *ST* 1a, 105. Cf. *SCG* 1.19; *SCG* 3.100. In this sense Aquinas is a thoroughgoing naturalist.
[146] There are two ways for God to be causally involved in natural occurrences: in a weaker sense, because God merely *conserves* in existence the relevant causal agents

Neoplatonic understanding of natural causation as involved the inflowing, or *influentia*, of divine power into secondary causes. God is not imagined simply as one species of cause among others.[147]

The application of the term 'supernatural' to agency rather than ontology carried over into the intermediate categories of the 'preternatural' and 'magic'. While the former was originally more or less synonymous with 'supernatural', in the later Middles Ages it took on a more precise meaning that connected it to acts performed by angels and demons, or with their assistance. These beings could produce wonderful effects on account of their superior knowledge of the operations of nature, but these were not truly miraculous. Aquinas would thus distinguish genuine miracles (*miracula*) from wonders (*mira*).[148] The performance of magic similarly involved superior knowledge of nature. Magicians could thus perform 'natural magic' because of their secret knowledge of how nature worked. 'Demonic magic', by way of contrast, relied upon the invocation of demons.[149] Not surprisingly, this activity was viewed rather dimly, although it was not always easy to distinguish from more innocuous magical performances. This situation thus raised acute questions about the limits of the natural powers of human, angelic, and demonic agents, about which a long story could be told.[150] For now, it can simply be concluded that an agential understanding of both supernatural and preternatural, combined

---

(conservationism); in a stronger sense, because God *concurs* with the causal activity of the natural agents (concurrentism). Most scholastic philosophers were concurrentists. Alfred Freddoso, 'God's General Concurrence with Secondary Causes: Why Conservation Is Not Enough', *Philosophical Perspectives* 5 (1991), 553–85. A third option is occasionalism, which collapses the ontological distinction between natural and supernatural. This was essentially the position adopted by Descartes and the Newtonians.

[147] Jacob Schmutz, 'The Medieval Doctrine of Causality and the Theology of Pure Nature (13th to 17th Centuries)', in *Surnaturel: A Controversy at the Heart of Twentieth-Century Thomistic Thought*, ed. Serge-Thomas Bonino, O.P., trans. Robert Williams, trans. rev. Matthew Levering (Ave Maria, FL: Sapientia Press of Ave Maria University, 2009), pp. 203–50, esp. pp. 215–30. Schmutz describes the shift in the understanding of *influentia* away from the influx of primary causes *into* secondary causes towards an understanding of primary causes acting *with* or *alongside* secondary causes. The distinction is subtle but the latter understanding leads to a more flattened view of 'causes amongst causes' rather than a hierarchical view of causation in which the higher causes inhere in the lower causes and act not *with* them but *in and through* them.

[148] Aquinas, *SCG* 3:104.

[149] Lorraine Daston, 'Marvellous Facts and Miraculous Evidence in Early Modern Europe', *Critical Inquiry* 18 (1991), 93–124; Lorraine Daston and Katherine Park, *Wonders and the Order of Nature* (New York: Zone Books, 1998), pp. 121–2; Principe, 'Preternatural'; Tarrant, *Defining Nature's Limits*, pp. 15f.; Clark, *Thinking with Demons*, pp. 152–60, 214f.

[150] See Tarrant, *Defining Nature's Limits*, pp. 56–72, and *passim*.

with an assumption of the hierarchy of being, conspired against the adoption of a simple, two-tiered ontology.

The next significant phase in the evolution of 'the supernatural' took place in the early modern period. Theological discussions in the wake of the Protestant Reformation led to a sharpening of the natural/supernatural disjunction, promoting the notion of two distinct ontological orders. In the sphere of natural philosophy, the gradual demise of Aristotelian understandings of causation also promoted an 'all-or-nothing' understanding of causation. This was accompanied by the gradual incorporation of the preternatural into the natural.[151] Increasingly events came to be understood as having either natural causes, or supernatural causes, with no middle ground between them. While these causes may have been different in origin, they were nonetheless understood to be essentially of the same type – efficient causation. These developments were also related to the modern conception of belief and the rise of an independent natural theology.

On the theological front, the twentieth-century Jesuit theologian Henri de Lubac, who first drew attention to the significance of a conception of the supernatural for understanding aspects of modernity, argued that the early modern construct of 'pure nature', along with the novel conception of the supernatural that it entailed, fostered the subsequent development of deistic conceptions of God–world interactions and licensed Enlightenment conceptions of human independence and autonomy. The story of how this is thought to have happened is not altogether straightforward. It is further complicated by the fact that de Lubac's thesis involved revisionary readings of canonical scholastic and neo-scholastic sources and had controversial implications for aspects of contemporary Catholic theology.[152]

For readers interested in the details, in essence, a key theological question in post-Reformation debates concerned the 'natural' condition of human beings and how divine grace operated upon human nature. Related to these debates were discussions of the primeval Fall and differences about

---

[151] On the naturalisation of the preternatural see esp. Daston, 'Marvellous Facts and Miraculous Evidence'.

[152] For the debates generated by de Lubac's thesis see Bonino (ed), *Surnaturel*; Denis J. M. Bradley, *Aquinas on the Twofold Human Good: Reason and Human Happiness in Aquinas's Moral Science* (Washington, DC: The Catholic University of America Press, 1997). Critical appraisals of de Lubac's argument include Feingold, *Natural Desire to See God*; Ralph McInerny, *Praeambula Fidei: Thomism and the God of the Philosophers* (Washington, DC: Catholic University of America Press, 2006); Steven A. Long, *Natura Pura: On the Recovery of Nature in the Doctrine of Grace* (New York: Fordham University Press, 2010); Bernard Mulcahy, *Aquinas's Notion of Pure Nature and the Christian Integralism of Henri de Lubac* (New York: Peter Lang, 2011).

what could be regarded as 'natural' to the human condition in its respective prelapsarian and fallen states. Catholic thinkers such as Thomas Cajetan (1469–1534), author of several theological works directed against Luther, along with the highly influential early modern scholastic philosopher Francisco Suárez (1548–1617), promoted the idea of a theoretical state of 'pure nature' without which, it was thought, too much would be granted to purveyors of more pessimistic anthropologies such as Luther and Calvin on the one hand, and heterodox Catholic thinkers such as Michael Baius on the other. In light of this conception, the standard question of whether human beings were naturally ordered to the divine was answered by positing two distinct human ends, one natural and one supernatural. According to de Lubac, as a consequence of this newly conceived division, the supernatural vocation became something extrinsic to the fulfilment of a relatively self-sufficient natural end.[153] The operation of divine grace in the human soul came to be understood as a kind of miraculous intervention into a discrete and relatively self-sufficient human nature. This differed from the traditional medieval position which, on de Lubac's account, characterised the human condition in terms of 'a natural desire for the supernatural'.[154] By way of contrast, Cajetan and Suárez proposed that the human desire for God was not natural but conditional or 'elicited'.[155]

Oversimplifying the issue somewhat, we might say that the medieval view had been that openness to the supernatural is the 'natural' condition of the world and its creatures.[156] In a sense, the natural world is not a self-subsistent reality but one that is at every moment dependent upon and oriented towards the supernatural. This applied to human creatures, too. On the modern view that developed in the wake of the controversies over 'pure nature', the operation of the supernatural came to be conceived as an incursion into, or even violation of, an order that could be understood

---

[153] Alasdair MacIntyre took up the next chapter of the story, proposing that during the Enlightenment even the conception of the *natural* ends of human life disappeared, so that any notion of 'man-as-he-could-be-if-he-realised-his-telos' disappeared. This led to a sharp 'is-ought' divide because now moral values could not be derived through the exercise of reason reflecting on natural human ends. This characteristic of modern moral thinking, on MacIntyre's analysis, led to the essential incoherence of modern meta-ethical discourse. *After Virtue*, 2nd ed. (Notre Dame: University of Notre Dame Press, 1984), pp. 52f.

[154] Henri de Lubac, *The Mystery of the Supernatural*, trans Rosemary Sheed, introduction by David L. Schindler (New York: Herder and Herder, 1998), pp. 54–5.

[155] For Suárez's position see Feingold, *Natural Desire to See God*, pp. 221–59.

[156] De Lubac spoke of 'a natural desire for the supernatural', in an explicit rejection of the positions of Cajetan and Suárez who had proposed that the human desire for God was not natural but conditional or 'elicited'. *Mystery of the Supernatural*, pp. 54–5.

on its own terms without reference to the transcendental. This divide promoted a situation in which philosophy and science came to be understood as enterprises that were independent of theology.[157] Extrapolating further, this generated a new problem of how God could act in a world whose operations seemed to be adequately accounted for by the natural sciences alone. Both providence and miracles became philosophically problematic. In the specific case of human individuals, this divide would coincide with the arrival of what Charles Taylor has termed 'the buffered self' – modern individuals who are no longer permeable to the influence of supernatural agencies.[158] It was de Lubac's contention that the late modern disappearance of a sense of the sacred could be traced to this early modern separation of natural and supernatural.[159] While this interpretation has not been without its critics, it is certainly consistent with the emergence of a more polarised conception of a natural/supernatural distinction during this period. At the very least, de Lubac showed that it was during the early modern period that the terminology of the 'supernatural' first became prevalent.[160]

The tendency to identify the 'supernatural' with the 'miraculous' was an integral part of these early modern transitions. This new usage signalled a shift of attention away from the site that Aquinas had identified as the primary locus of supernatural activity – the human person – to the natural

---

[157] De Lubac would thus conclude that the natural/supernatural distinction was a precondition for modern secularism. *Surnaturel*, p. 153.

[158] Taylor, *A Secular Age*, pp. 27, 37–42, 571. The 'buffered self' is contrasted with the 'porous self', which is vulnerable to spirits, demons, and cosmic forces (p. 38).

[159] Henri de Lubac, 'The Internal Causes of the Attenuation and Disappearance of the Sense of the Sacred', in *Theology in History* (San Franscisco: St Ignatius Press, 1996), pp. 223–40 (p. 230). See also David L. Schindler's introduction to De Lubac, *Mystery of the Supernatural*, pp. xvii–xix; John Milbank, *The Suspended Middle* (London: SCM, 2005); Randall S. Rosenberg, *The Givenness of Desire: Concrete Subjectivity and the Natural Desire to See God* (Toronto: University of Toronto Press, 2017), pp. 39–62; and, most recently, David Bentley Hart, *You Are Gods: On Nature and Supernature* (Notre Dame: University of Notre Dame Press, 2022), esp. ch. 1. De Lubac has a related story about the secularisation of political life in the West, which he attributes to changed conceptions of the notion of the 'mystical body' (*corpus mysticism*) in medieval scholasticism. See *Corpus Mysticum: The Eucharist and the Church in the Middle Ages*, trans. Gemma Simmonds with Richard Price and Christopher Stephens (Notre Dame: University of Notre Dame Press, 2007); Sarah Shortall, 'From the Three Bodies of Christ to the King's Two Bodies: The Theological Origins of Secularization', *Modern Intellectual History* 20 (2023), 785–807.

[160] It is significant, for example, that the first appearance of 'supernatural' in official Catholic documents was in 1567, where it is deployed in relation to theological debates about 'pure nature'. The context was Pius V's condemnation of Baius. Denzinger, *Enchiridion Symbolorum*, §§1921, 1923 (p. 431). The first reference to imply any sense of an opposition between natural and supernatural comes in the 1870 documents of the first Vatican Council, §3008 (p. 589). See Deneffe, 'Geschichte des Wortes "supernaturalis"', 358.

5.4 THE HISTORY OF THE SUPERNATURAL

world, leading to further changes in the status of belief and the operations of nature along the way. The requirement that religious beliefs – now understood as assenting to certain propositions – be supported by certain kinds of rational evidence was affected by these transitions in three ways. First, understandings of faith and belief increasingly shifted to the natural side of the natural/supernatural divide. If there were an obligation to provide grounds for one's religious convictions – and this was a requirement of the new 'ethics of belief' – it followed that faith could not be an undeserved supernatural gift, but was a conscious act for which believers were individually responsible. This was certainly not what Protestant reformers had taught, but it was a position that could be regarded as a logical consequence of their critiques of implicit faith. This facilitated the secularisation of faith/belief and its transformation into a secular, epistemic category.

Second, miracles, now understood as visible supernatural interventions into a relatively independent natural order, were proposed as evidences of the truth of the Christian revelation.[161] That is to say, they came to constitute the kind of evidence that one might adduce as a reason for believing. At times, this could descend to the specifics of offering rational support for holding to one Christian confession over another. Protestants, for example, allowed that the miracles of the apostolic period had been vital for the establishment of Christianity and that they demonstrated that the mission of Christ had supernatural sanction. As John Locke expressed it: 'The miracles that Christ did, are a proof of his being sent from God, and so his religion the true religion.'[162] However, as we see in more detail in the next chapter, Protestant thinkers were generally sceptical about the performance of contemporary miracles, and it was often alleged that the age of true miracles had long ceased. For Catholics, on the other hand, the ongoing performance of miracles served as a vindication of their version of Christianity.[163] Either way, the evidential role now allotted to miracles required that there be a

---

[161] For this change in the role and status of miracles see Peter Harrison, 'Miracles, Early Modern Science, and Rational Religion', *Church History* 75 (2006), 493–511.

[162] Locke, *Third Letter concerning Toleration*, p. 225. For further examples see Boyle, *The Christian Virtuoso, Works*, vol. 11, pp. 315–17; Samuel Clarke, 'The Evidences of Natural and Revealed Religion', in *Works*, vol. 2, p. 695; Jenkin, *Reasonableness and Certainty*, pp. 33–8; Sprat, *History of the Royal Society*, p. 352.

[163] Thus, e.g., Thomas Anderton: 'all the marks of the Catholik Church must be miraculous; otherwise they were not fit motiues for prudent men to submit their judgments to the testimony or ministery of that Church'. *A sovereign remedy against atheism and heresy* (n.p., 1672), pp. 53f.; John Warner: 'The Catholick Church must have supernatural signes and Miracles whereby it may be discerned from all Heretical Congregations.' *Dr. Stillingfleet's principles of Protestancy cleared, confuted, and retorted* (London, 1673), p. 33.

clear ontological difference between natural occurrences and the miraculous. The significance of the performance of miracles was now no longer related to the sanctity of the miracle-worker, but instead served as evidence for the truth of the doctrines that they espoused.

Third, another avenue for the justification of theistic belief came from natural theology which was increasingly understood as an activity that was independent of revealed theology. The natural theology/revealed theology divide mirrored the new natural/supernatural distinction. This led to a new role for 'proofs' (discussed in the previous section) understood as operating in the sphere of neutral rationality or as what can be discerned of God by means of a purely *natural* light. The required rational foundation for theistic commitment was provided by the independent enterprise of philosophy in the specific form of a newly conceptualised natural theology, in Alexander Baumgarten's sense of 'the science of God insofar as he can be known *without faith*'.[164] Again, the twofold provision of evidences for Christianity – miracles and prophecy for the revealed component, and rational proofs for the natural component – directly mapped onto the natural/supernatural distinction.

Natural philosophy played an important role in the provision of both kinds of evidences. While physico-theology, as we have seen, was more than just the amassing of evidence of divine design and involved elements of what we might call spiritual exercises, it was nonetheless reducible to a form of rational argument that was the primary purview of naturalists. Expertise in natural philosophy thus became requisite to the provision of evidences of two kinds. God's wisdom in nature may have been obvious to even the 'superficial' observer, wrote Robert Boyle, but 'how wise an agent he has in these works expressed himself to be, none but an experimental philosopher can well discern'.[165] Natural philosophers also played a role in the provision of external evidences on the basis that they were the ones who could most expertly determine the boundaries between natural and supernatural. Boyle, again, proposed that the natural philosopher 'will examine with more strictness and skill, than ordinary men are able, miracles, prophecies, or other proofs, said to be supernatural, that are alleged to evince a real religion'.[166] In an epistemological outsourcing exercise, practitioners of

---

[164] Baumgarten, *Metaphysics*, §§800–1 (p. 294). See also 'Théologie', in *Encyclopédie ou Dictionnaire raisonné des sciences, des arts et des métiers*, vol. 16, pp. 249–51.
[165] Boyle, *The Christian Virtuoso*, in *Works*, vol. 11, p. 297.
[166] Boyle, *The Christian Virtuoso*, in *Works*, vol. 11, p. 324. See also Anon., *A Short Discourse concerning Miracles* (London, 1702); Robert Filmer, *An Advertisement to the Jurymen of England touching Witches* (London, 1688); John Gaule, *Select Cases of Conscience touching Witches* (London, 1646).

the natural sciences were allotted the task of adjudicating on the rationality of religious belief. This led to a strongly co-dependent relationship between science and religion.

The new understandings of causality operative in natural philosophy were also highly significant. It may seem that the voluntarist and occasionalist bent of early modern Cartesian and Newtonian physics represents a significant counterinstance to the sharp natural/supernatural dichotomy that we see developing in the early modern period. If we take Samuel Clarke to be the official spokesman for a regnant Newtonianism, his declaration that all the operations of nature, philosophically considered, are in fact miraculous seems to cut against the two-tier ontology presupposed by the natural/supernatural divide. However, this position does not entail stepping back to a pre-modern mindset in which the natural/supernatural distinction was simply not operable. It represents instead an acceptance of the dichotomy in principle, but accompanied by a reduction of the natural to the supernatural. This provided the fateful precedent for a subsequent reductionist exercise that went in the other direction. Modern naturalism would then derive its primary meaning from the genus of the realities whose existence it denied, being typically described in terms of the rejection of supernatural or spiritual agents and their operations.[167] This requires that some sense be attached to the latter. The modern concept of the supernatural was thus an essential precondition for the emergence of contemporary naturalism.

5.5 '-isms'

The next phase in the development of the conceptions necessary for Huxley to articulate his version of history, and indeed for the rise of modern scientific naturalism, is the appearance of the categories of natural*ism* and supernatural*ism*. It is telling that Huxley makes reference to a historical divide characterised in terms of competing '-isms', since the use of that suffix is more often associated with polemical intent than dispassionate historical judgement. The sixteenth-century term 'atheism', as noted in the previous chapter, offers a good example. Not only does it mark the appearance of a creed that existed primarily in the imaginations of religious controversialists, it is also symptomatic of a more general tendency of the period to generate a panoply of new '-isms' related to competing religious belief systems.

---

[167] Recall the characterisations of naturalism proposed by philosophers David Papineau and Barry Stroud which oppose it directly to supernaturalism and refer to the denial of supernatural agencies. Introduction, note 11.

The suffix in question comes from Greek, was passed into Latin, and then subsequently distributed into the European vernaculars.[168] Originally it was used to form nouns of action from verbs. Some early occurrences, 'Judaism' for example, also marked out those committed to a particular way of life. Overall, however, its use was rare until the sixteenth century.[169] Following the religious controversies of the early modern period, however, we see a remarkable proliferation of new '-isms'. These now marked out bodies of doctrine rather than actions or ways of life.[170] Typically, the coining and deployment of the relevant '-ism' – Lutheranism, Calvinism, Papism, etc. – was the work of the opponents of the doctrines in question. All of this comports with the reification of religion and the alignment of Christian confessions with bodies of doctrine. It also suggests, more generally, that a degree of caution be exercised when approaching constructions of this kind, given the circumstances that typically attend their inception.

Scattered negative references to 'naturalism', used in a variety of senses, appear in the vernacular European languages during the second half of the eighteenth century. The English 'naturalism' first appears in the Chambers' *Cyclopaedia* (1738) where the term is used on a single occasion to characterise the position of Spinoza, equating it to something like pantheism.[171] In the 1750s and 1760s Bishop William Warburton used the expression to describe the commitments of Lord Bolingbroke and David Hume. But in this context 'naturalism' was understood as a form of natural religion or belief in a God who is a creator but not a providential ruler of the world's affairs.[172] Naturalism was also equated with deism or belief in the sufficiency

---

[168] Greek '-*ismos*' or '-*isma*'; Latin '*ismus*'; subsequently English '-isme', etc. See *OED*, '-ism'. Especially informative on the topic is H. M. Höpfl, 'Isms', *British Journal of Political Science* 13 (1983), 1–17. See also Jussi Kurunmäki and Jani Marjanen, 'A Rhetorical View of Isms: An Introduction', *Journal of Political Ideologies* 23 (2018), 241–55. I am grateful to Fred D'Agostino for drawing my attention to this source.

[169] Hence *baptismos* (baptise) from *baptizein* (to dip). As denoting ways of life, Gk. 'Judaismos' (Lat. '-*mus*'), 'Christianismos' (Lat. '-*mus*').

[170] Examples include Lutheranisme, Lutherisme (Fr. 1554), Calvinisme (Fr. 1562, Lat. 1575) Anabaptisme (Fr. 1564), papisme (1541); puritanism (1573), Romanism (1603), Protestantisme (1606). From Höpfl, 'Isms', p. 1, n. 2, and relevant *OED* entries.

[171] Chambers, *Cyclopaedia*, vol. 2, s.v. 'Spinozism'.

[172] Naturalism is 'the belief of a God as Creator and Physical Preserver, but not moral Governor of the World'. William Warburton and David Hurd, *Remarks on David Hume's Essay on the Natural History of Religion* (London, 1757), p. 9. Warburton nonetheless regards this as a form of atheism. See also Warburton, *A View of Lord Bolingbroke's Philosophy* (London, 1754), pp. 72, 75, 163–75; *The Principles of Natural and Revealed Religion* (Dublin, 1753), p. 30; *The Doctrine of Grace*, 2 vols. (London, 1763), vol 2, p. 284.

of natural religion.[173] Contemporary German authors would occasionally refer to 'natural*ists*'. For Alexander Baumgarten, 'naturalists' deny revelation and miracles but are not to be confused with atheists who deny the existence of God.[174] Christian Wolff also saw it as his mission to refute '*naturalismi*', again distinguished from '*atheismi*'.[175] Typically, however, 'naturalist' was an innocent descriptor for the studious enquirer into nature. Again, it was the '-ism' form that bore the more sinister connotations. The French 'naturalisme' receives a brief definition in the eighteenth-century *Dictionnaire de l'Académie Française*.[176] Here the sense given is suggestive of an interpretative framework – reading prodigies as natural events. By 1873, however, French sources begin to speak of 'the *system* of those who attribute everything to nature', although the exemplars are historical rather than contemporary figures.[177] Pius IX's reactionary 1864 encyclical, '*Quanta Cura*', condemned a number of developments of secular modernity, including an 'impious and absurd naturalism (*naturalismi*)', referring in this context to the principle 'that human society be conducted and governed without regard being had to religion any more than if it did not exist'.[178] In the nineteenth century, naturalism was more consistently associated with a specific set of metaphysical or scientific commitments, although as we will see, it was also equated with 'rationalism' with both terms having a quite specific meaning when understood in the context of biblical criticism.

The combination '*scientific* naturalism', often assumed to be the coinage of Thomas Huxley, begins to appear from about the 1820s, increasing

---

[173] Warburton and Hurd, *Remarks on David Hume*, p. 11; K. R. Hagenbach, *Text-book of the History of Doctrine*, 2 vols., trans. Henry B. Smith (New York: Sheldon and Co., 1869), vol. 2, §275 (pp. 378–82).

[174] Baumgarten, *Metaphysics* [1739], §999 (ET, p. 334) 4th ed. (1757). The usual pattern of linguistic innovation was for the '-ists' to precede the '-isms'.

[175] Wolff, *Theologia naturalis*, title page.

[176] 'Caractère de ce qui est naturel. *Le naturalisme d'un prétendu prodige*' (Character of what is natural. *The naturalism of an alleged* prodigy). *Le Dictionnaire de l'Académie Française*, 4th ed., 2 vols. (Paris, 1762), vol. 2, s.v. 'Naturalisme'. Cf. Jean-François Féraud, *Dictionnaire critique de la langue Français*, 3 vols. (Marseille, 1787), vol. 2, s.v. 'naturalisme'.

[177] *Dictionnaire de la Langue Française*, 5 vols. (Paris, 1883–4), vol. 3, s.v. 'naturalisme'. The 1798 edition of the *Dictionnaire de l'Académie Française* also gives the additional meaning of 'the system of those who attribute everything to nature as the first principle. *Strato's naturalism.*' From 1932 to the present, Lucretius replaces Strato as the one who exemplifies the 'system of naturalism'. https://academie.atilf.fr/9/consulter/ NATURALISME?options=motExact, accessed 1 February 2023.

[178] Papal Encyclicals Online, www.papalencyclicals.net/pius09/p9quanta.htm, accessed 19 July 2022. For an exposition of the distinction between political and philosophical naturalism, see 'The Encyclical of December 8, 1864', *The Dublin Review*, new series, 5 (July–October, 1865), 246–55.

in frequency in the middle decades of the century.[179] An intriguing early reference appears in the writings of the French philosopher and priest Félicité Robert de Lamennais (1782–1854). Lamennais was a proponent of a liberal and socially engaged form of Catholicism and an advocate for religious freedom of conscience. His *Essay on Indifference in Matters of Religion* (1818–23), a work that established his reputation in Europe, set out a theory of religion based upon common sense or universal consent. This foundation he related to the traditional Catholic notion of the rule of faith. In a later work, he lamented the legacies of the Protestant Reformation and modern philosophy which, in his eyes, had given rise to a split between 'two orders and two powers' – the natural power of reason and the supernatural power of the Church. In de Lamennais's vision of the future these would be resolved into a higher unity or a 'new synthesis' between Christian spiritualism and 'scientific naturalism'. He spoke in this context of 'Catholic Science'. This unity was understood as a return to a true original religion of which Catholicism was the pre-eminent historical manifestation.[180]

The sources of mid-century Anglophone references to scientific naturalism almost certainly lay elsewhere, in the religious periodical literature of North America. Bernard Lightman and Gowan Dawson have suggested the term was originally employed by American evangelicals as a pejorative descriptor for a range of secularist scientific publications that they found

---

[179] There is an early occurrence of the phrase in the German philosopher and poet C. A. H. Clodius, who regards scientific naturalism (*wissenshaftliche Naturalismus*) as one of the varieties of 'false naturalism'. He seems to mean by the term something like the idea of God as a prime mover. Aristotle is his example. C. A. H. Clodius, *Von Gott in der Natur, in der Menschengeschichte, und im Bewußtseyn*, 5 vols. (Leipzig, 1818), vol. 1, p. xvi. Closer to the familiar meaning is an 1833 reference to 'the scientific naturalism [*wissenshaftliche Naturalismus*] and atheism that prevailed in the age of Voltaire, Rousseau, and the Encyclopaedists'. Ernst Gersdorf (ed.), *Repertorium der gesammten deutschen Literatur*, vol. 15 [1833] (Leipzig, 1838), p. 503. The French *naturalisme scientifique* is attested from 1836, this time in relation to religions in antiquity. 'Scientific naturalism' is distinguished from 'popular naturalism' or the adoration of nature. Anon., 'Code Sacré', *L'ami de la religion: journal ecclésiastique, politique et littéraire* 89 (1836).

[180] Félicité Robert de Lamennais, *Du passe et de l'avenir du peuple* (Paris, 1841), pp. 100–4. Cf. *Essai sur l'indifférence en matière de religion*, vol. 2 (Paris, 1820). The phrase 'Catholic science' – 'Il est temps que la science catholique' – demonstrates his conviction that Catholicism was insufficiently scientific, and science insufficiently Catholic. *Des progrès de la Révolution et de la guerre contre l'Eglise* (Brussels, 1829), p. 253. See François Laplanche, *Le Bible en France entre mythe et critique, XVIe–XIXe siècle* (Paris: Albin Michel, 1994), pp. 112f.; Arthur McCalla, 'The Mennaisian "Catholic Science of Religion": Epistemology and History in Early Nineteenth-Century French Study of Religion', *Method and Theory in the Study of Religion* 21(2009), 285–309.

uncongenial.[181] The classicist and biblical scholar Tayler Lewis seems to have been the first to speak of scientific naturalism, which he associated with a denial of God's ongoing interactions with the natural world.[182] Subsequently, Robert Chambers' *Vestiges* was identified as a prominent exemplification of the principle.[183] The Congregationalist theologian Horace Bushnell was another early adopter of the phrase. His *Nature and Supernatural* (1858) sought to negotiate some of the difficulties raised for traditional Christian belief by Hume and the German biblical scholar David Strauss by pointing to limitations of the conceptions of natural and supernatural that they were operating with. Bushnell used the term in a way similar to Lewis: 'scientific naturalism' characterised the positions of those who denied the possibility of miracles.[184] More generally, these thinkers were concerned with what they saw as a growing mood of religious scepticism fuelled by interest in science. Lewis referred to 'the language of a generation, and of a thinking, immersed in the physical'. This he attributed to the rise in prominence of natural sciences: 'Science at the present day, in distinction from philosophy and theology, occupies a disproportioned, and therefore injurious space in

---

[181] Gowan Dawson and Bernard Lightman, 'Introduction', in *Victorian Scientific Naturalism: Community, Identity, Continuity*, ed. Dawson and Lightman (Chicago: University of Chicago Press, 2014), pp. 1–24, esp. pp. 4–5.

[182] Anon., 'Professor Lewis's Naturalism', *Literary World* 6 (1850), 559–61 (560), reporting on an 1859 lecture given by Lewis, subsequently published as *Nature, Progress, Ideas* (Schenectady, 1850). In Lewis's 1850 article 'Names for Soul', 'scientific naturalism' was identified with scepticism about the immortality of the soul. Lewis contended that scientific naturalism was in opposition to a universal consensus about the soul, encapsulated in the phrase *semper, ubique, et ab omnibus* (i.e., held always, everywhere, by everyone). *The Biblical Repository and Classical Review* 21 (1850), 674–703 (679). See also Lewis, 'Creation a Series of Supernatural Growths', *Methodist Quarterly Review* 47 (1865), 207–29 (219); and 'Two New Trinities', *Massachusetts Quarterly Review* 3 (1850) 191–200 (195). Lewis later provided a more systematic threefold typology of naturalism – 'blank naturalism', 'theistic naturalism or naturalism of science', and 'religious or supernatural naturalism'. The first 'admits nothing strictly divine'; the second naturalism 'brings in Deity or first cause … to start the machinery of the world'; the third, endorsed by Lewis, 'allows many divine *acts*, or beginnings in nature, by which a new life is imparted that did not exist before and which previous nature could never have developed, – or, a *series* of forces is *originated*'. *The Six Days of Creation* (Schenectady, 1855), pp. 36–40.

[183] Tayler Lewis, 'Hickok's Rational Psychology', *Bibliotheca Sacra* 8 (1851), 169–217, 346–77 (377).

[184] Horace Bushnell, *Nature and the Supernatural, as Together Constituting the One System of God* [1858], 4th ed. (New York: Charles Scribner, 1859), pp. 258, 334–8, 348. For similar references to the expression see Henry Witney Bellows, *A Sequel to 'The Suspense of Faith'* (New York: D. Appleton, 1859), p. 24 and Anon., 'The Church and Modern Thought', *Irish Ecclesiastical Record* 10 (March 1874), 56–62, 102–9, 237–45, which associates scientific naturalism with John Tyndall (243).

the public mind.'[185] From America, the expression found its way to Britain, making occasional appearances in the press from about the 1860s. Initially it was used in much the same way, as a negative characterisation of a growing list of scientifically minded sceptics who denied miracles and divine providence – figures such as Robert Chambers, Thomas Huxley, John Tyndall, William Kingdon Clifford, and even Charles Darwin.[186] Eventually, in the final decade of the century, Huxley was to own the term on behalf of those to whom it once disparagingly referred.[187]

There is another important source for these conceptions, indicated by Huxley's explicit opposition of naturalism to 'supernaturalism'. In the eighteenth century 'supernaturalism' had a far more precise meaning than 'naturalism'. The original context for this concept was neither philosophy nor the natural sciences but theology – specifically historical or 'higher' criticism. Here, the standard opposition was almost always between supernaturalism on the one hand, and naturalism or rationalism on the other.[188] Historical

---

[185] Tayler Lewis, *The Bible and Science; or, the World-Problem* (Schenectady, 1856), p. 42. Cf. p. 40.

[186] Dawson and Lightman, 'Introduction', *Victorian Scientific Naturalism*, p. 4.

[187] That said, the term was not necessarily widely adopted as a label. Paul White, 'The Conduct of Belief', in *Victorian Scientific Naturalism*, ed. Dawson and Lightman, pp. 220–42 (p. 220). On the usefulness of the expression as an actor's category in the late nineteenth century see Ruth Barton, *The X Club: Power and Authority in Victorian Science* (Chicago: University of Chicago Press, 2018), pp. 18–23.

[188] See, e.g., Daniel Jenisch, *Sollte Religion den Menschen jemals entbehrlich werden?* (Berlin, 1797), pp. 217f., 258f., and *passim*. The more common opposition in the earlier nineteenth century was that between 'rationalism' (*rationalismus*) and supernaturalism (*supernaturalismus*). See Johann Friedrich Röhr, *Briefe über den Rationalismus* (Aachen, 1813); Johann Tittmann, *Über Supranaturalismus, Rationalismus und Atheismus* (Leipzig, 1816); Christian Ferdinand Zöllich, *Briefe über den Supernaturalismus* (Sondershausen und Nordhausen, 1821); Carl Schwarz, *Zur Geschichte der neuesten Theologie*, 3rd ed. (Leipzig, 1864), pp. 4–7; Karl Friedrich Stäudlin, *Geschichte des Rationalismus und Supernaturalismus* (Göttingen, 1826); 'Naturalismus und Supranaturalismus', in *Kirchen-Lexikon oder Encyklopädie der katholischen Theologie und ihrer Hilfswissenschaften*, 12 vols., ed. Benedikt Welte and Heinrich Joseph Wetzer (Freiburg im Bresgau, 1853), vol. 10, pp. 478–85. Kant is a likely source for the original terminology with his brief reference in *Religion within the Boundaries of Mere Reason* [1793] to 'rationalists', 'naturalists', and 'supernaturalists'. *Religion and Rational Theology*, pp. 177f. These are not yet, '-isms', however. For Anglo-American sources see Anon., 'Theology', *The Christian Teacher*, new series, vol. 3, no. 12 (London: John Green, 1841), pp. 131–49; Anon., 'German Biblical Criticism', *The New York Review*, 2nd ed. (New York: George Dearborn, 1838), pp. 133–45; Theodore Parker, *A Discourse pertaining to Matters of Religion* (Boston, 1842), pp. 198–214; Edward E. Washburn, 'Parallel between the Philosophical Relations of Early and Modern Christianity', *Bibliotheca Sacra* 8 (1851), 34–57. Secondary treatments include Emanuel Hirsch, *Geschichte der neuern evangelischen Theologie*, 5 vols. (Gütersloh: Gerd Mohn, 1964), vol. 5; Kevin M. Vander Schel, *Embedded Grace: Christ, History, and the Reign of God in Schleiermacher's Dogmatics* (Minneapolis: Fortress Press, 2013), pp. 17–43.

criticism was an approach to the Bible that sought to determine the meaning of the text for its original audience, in part by attempting a historical reconstruction of the thought of the period in which the text was produced. This approach began in the early modern period, with the Protestant elevation of the authority of scripture which was accompanied by a focus on the Bible's literal or 'historical' sense. Historical approaches gradually replaced medieval practices of multi-layered interpretation in which both the world and the Bible were understood symbolically or allegorically.[189] For those deploying these earlier approaches, reading and interpreting the Bible was akin to a form of spiritual exercise. The new focus on the literal, doctrinal content of the Bible was in keeping with the early modern move towards evidentialism and the need to give explicit intellectual assent to the propositions thought to constitute religion.

In Protestant Germany especially, higher criticism was taken to be properly 'scientific'. It was an objective university discipline rather than a form of private devotion. One focus of historical criticism was the reports of miracles and wonders in the Bible, not least in light of Hume's question of why miracles were common in biblical times, but comparatively rare (or non-existent) in the present.[190] First appearing in late eighteenth-century German theological literature, the term 'supernaturalism' (*Supernaturalismus*) described the stance of those for whom the biblical miracles were historical events of genuinely supernatural character. The competing view was 'rationalism' (*Rationalismus*) – although 'naturalism' (*Naturalismus*) was also commonly used in this context.[191] Those who subscribed to supernaturalism

---

[189] The classic treatment is Henri de Lubac, *Medieval Exegesis: The Four Senses of Scripture* [1959–64], 3 vols., trans. Mark Sebanc and E. M. Macierowski (Grand Rapids: Eerdmans, 1998–2009). On the significance of this for scientific understandings of nature, see Harrison, *Bible and the Rise of Science*.

[190] The application of historical criticism to miracle accounts is often traced back to Spinoza and deist writings of the seventeenth century. However, it is important to understand that practice of historical criticism was largely internal to Christian theology.

[191] Röhr contends that 'rationalism' and 'naturalism' amount to the same thing. *Briefe über den Rationalismus*, p. 14. Stäudlin also notes different usages of *naturalismus* but maintains that it is usually synonymous with *rationalismus*. *Geschichte des Rationalismus und Supernaturalismus*, p. 1. However, the parallel development of 'naturalism' as a generic category for those who denied supernatural involvement with the world led some to distinguish 'naturalism' from 'rationalism'. Heinrich Tzschirner, for example, proposed that naturalists reject divine revelation, while rationalists accept it. The latter accept the basic facts of sacred history but insist that they be interpreted in a rational way. *Memorabilien für das Studium und die Amtsführung des Predigers*, 8 vols. (Leipzig, 1810–23), vol. 1, p. 13. Amand Saintes contended similarly that rationalism was accepting of divine revelation in a way that naturalism was not. *Histoire critique du rationalisme en Allemagne depuis son origine jusqu'à nos jours* (Paris: J. Renouard, 1841); ET, *A Critical History of Rationalism in Germany* (London,

(sometimes '*supranaturalism*') maintained that biblical miracle narratives need to be accepted on their own terms, as events that transcend the natural order and our scientific understandings of it. More generally, and in opposition to Kant, supernaturalists maintained that religion cannot be constrained within the limits of reason alone. For rationalists (or 'naturalists'), miracle narratives were honest attempts to accurately report the relevant events, even if the key witnesses were mistaken in characterising them as manifestations of the supernatural. According to rationalists/naturalists, given what we know about nature, namely, that it 'follows an invariable course', miraculous events must be understood in naturalistic terms.[192] (In the seventeenth century, Spinoza had controversially ventured a similar opinion about miracles.)[193] By their own account, rationalists were not seeking to undermine Christianity, but were rather defending it by showing how it might be consistent with modern historical and scientific developments.[194]

These categories were kept in play by the theological controversies generated by the biblical criticism of the Tübingen School inaugurated by F. C. Baur (1792–1860) and the subsequent publication of David Friedrich Strauss's controversial *Life of Jesus* (1835–6).[195] Baur's approach to history has significant parallels with that of Hegel, and his work represents an important further stage in the development of higher criticism. For our purposes his significance lies in the fact that he was thought to have produced, in the words of one of his critics, 'a theory which makes of Christianity a thing of purely *natural* origin'.[196] In other words, for Baur, the origins of Christianity were to be explained just like any other historical event. Baur's sometime pupil David Friedrich Strauss (1808–74) went one further, casting doubt on the literal historicity of much of the content of the gospel stories. Strauss had read Hume on miracles and concluded that it was impossible for events contrary to the laws of nature to have taken place. An event is

---

1849), p. 78. Saintes suggests that rationalism was a consequence of reformed theology and contrasts German rationalism with English naturalism and French deism (the latter two being less reconciled to revelation than rationalism). The French encyclopaedists are accused of 'gross naturalism' (p. 83). Hence 'many persons confound Naturalism, which openly avows itself the enemy of revealed religion, with Rationalism, which admits revelation' albeit that they tend to end up with the same consequences (p. 89, n.).

[192] 'Alles gehet einen naturgemäßen Gang'. Röhr, *Briefe über den Rationalismus*, p. 257.
[193] Spinoza, *Theological-Political Treatise*, ch. 6, *CW*, pp. 444–56.
[194] Röhr, *Briefe über den Rationalismus*, p. 342; David Strauss, *The Old Faith and the New: A Confession*, 2nd ed., trans. Mathilde Blind (London: Asher and Co., 1873), pp. 41f.
[195] David Strauss, *Das Leben Jesu, kritisch bearbeitet* (Tübingen, 1835–6).
[196] A. B. Bruce, 'F. C. Baur and his Theory of the Origin of Christianity and of the New Testament Writings', *Present Day Tracts* 38 (1885), 5 (my emphasis).

not historical, Strauss maintained, 'when it is irreconcilable with the known and universal laws which govern the universe'. Inhabitants of 'the modern world' know that all events are determined by an inviolable chain of closed causes. Accordingly, when we read accounts of events that are supernatural in character, we know immediately that they were not 'historical' events.[197] Again, it did not follow that the biblical authors had fabricated their accounts. Miracle stories for Strauss were not invented fictions but the product of a form of mythological thinking that Western Europeans had outgrown. Miracle reports originated in 'a period of civilization in which the imagination worked so powerfully, that its illusions were believed as realities.'[198] This was neither rationalism nor supernaturalism, but an attribution to ancient peoples of a different way of perceiving the world. Strauss thus posited that the interpretation of scripture must take into consideration what he regarded as the obsolete mindset of a pre-modern age.[199]

What we see in these developments is essentially the application of naturalistic principles, respectively, to the history of Christianity and the biblical text. In neither case did the specific findings of the natural sciences play a significant role. Instead, the focus was on historical reconstructions that were informed by speculations about the psychology of ancient peoples. These were accompanied, in what would become a standard pattern, by the assumption of a social evolution that divided the modern West from 'earlier' stages of civilisation. As the end-product of that process, advocates of rationalism and naturalism considered themselves to have left behind the illusory readings of natural and historical events characteristic of a more primitive era. At this level of generalisation, natural science did become a relevant consideration, but primarily as an example of the processes of social evolution, rather than as the primary driver of that process.[200] The distinction between naturalism and supernaturalism, in short, is initially

---

[197] Strauss, *Life of Jesus*, trans. Eliot, pp. 78, 88.

[198] Strauss, *Life of Jesus*, p. 83. Cf. pp. 130, 169. Spinoza has a similar view about ancient prophecy which he attributed to the 'imaginative faculty' of the prophets. *Theological-Political Treatise*, ch. 2, *CW*, p. 403. See also Shagan, *Birth of Modern Belief*, pp. 259–64.

[199] Strauss thus sought 'to substitute a new mode of considering the life of Jesus, in the place of the antiquated systems of supranaturalism and naturalism'. That new mode was 'the mythical point of view'. *Life of Jesus*, p. xxix (preface to the first edition).

[200] It is important to distinguish the natural sciences (*Naturwissenschaften*) from 'science' (*Wissenschaft*), which encompassed systematic knowledge in general, including theology and historical criticism. Strauss could thus speak of a conflict between faith and science in his *Glaubenslehre*, but the science he had in mind was modern historical criticism. *Die Christliche Glaubenslehre in ihrer geschichtlichen Entwicklung und in ihrem Kampf mit der modernen Wissenschaft*, 2 vols. (Tübingen, 1840–1), in English, *The Christian Doctrine of Faith in its Historical Development and in its Conflict with Modern Science*.

and most conspicuously manifested within debates internal to Christianity. References to 'supernaturalism' appear almost entirely within the sphere of biblical criticism and theology, with the contrast cases being naturalism and/or rationalism.[201] When these terms were first rendered into English, they were understood in much the same way. The 1886 *Encyclopaedia Britannica*, for example, informs us that: 'In modern usage the term "rationalism" is employed almost exclusively to denote a theological tendency, method, or system.' The author then goes on to explain that 'Rationalism had its antithesis on the one hand supernaturalism, and on the other naturalism or simple deism.'[202]

When late in the century Huxley opposed naturalism to supernaturalism he was adopting a terminology that had predominantly arisen within the 'science' of biblical criticism. That said, the addition of the qualification 'scientific' signalled an intention for these categories to be operative within a much broader context, providing a framework for understanding the whole course of history, including the development of modern science. With this new application of the dichotomy, theology was no longer understood as the primary site within which the naturalism/supernaturalism debate had taken place.[203] Instead, 'theology' *in toto* was placed on one side of the divide and simply identified with supernaturalism. For its part, natural science was elevated to a more prominent position in the conversation as the historical representative of a progressive naturalism. Part of what made this

---

[201] Or, occasionally, 'anti-supernaturalism'. William Hinks, *Anti-Supernaturalism considered* (London: John Green, 1841). Anti-supernaturalism could be further divided into three schools. First, sceptics who regarded miracle reports as false and fraudulent; second, the historico-rationalist school, which sought to offer naturalistic explanations of events reported as miraculous; third, the 'mythical school' of which Strauss was a representative, which denied miraculous phenomena, regarding them as mythical constructions, albeit motivated by genuine religious impulses. See also Philip Harward, *German Anti-Supernaturalism* (London, 1841), pp. 1–15.

[202] 'Rationalism', *Encyclopaedia Britannica*, 9th ed., 24 vols. (New York: Charles Scribner's Sons, 1886), vol. 20, pp. 289a–291a. Cf. *Encyclopedia Americana*, 14 vols. (Boston: B. B. Mussey & Co., 1851), vol. 12, p. 62: 'Supernaturalism, a word chiefly used in German theology, is contradistinguished to *rationalism*.' There is a similar entry in *The Popular Encyclopedia*, 7 vols. (Glasgow: Blackie and Son, 1830–41). See also C. A. Beckwith, 'Rationalism and Supernaturalism', in *The New Schaff-Herzog Encyclopedia of Religious Knowledge*, 15 vols. (Grand Rapids: Baker, 1977), vol. 9, pp. 393a–402a.

[203] For ecclesiastical history as the primary locus for this debate consider this statement: 'The history of the subject enables us to recognise in the early Church two tendencies which came into frequent conflict with each other ... in a later day they assumed the forms of rationalism and supernaturalism.' 'The Leading Tendencies of Theological Thought', in George R. Crooks and John F. Hurst (eds.), *Theological Encyclopaedia and Methodology* (New York: Hunt and Eaton, 1894), p. 100.

possible was the fact that in the Anglophone context 'science' was understood in the now familiar sense of 'natural science', while the more capacious German *Wissenschaft* still incorporated the human sciences. The latter had included the 'science' of biblical criticism.[204]

Huxley was well informed about developments in historical biblical criticism. He had read Strauss's *Old Faith and the New* (1873) in the original German and was familiar with the controversies concerning naturalism and supernaturalism, along with Strauss's attribution to biblical writers of a mythological mindset.[205] He had written intelligently on one of the standard challenges of higher criticism, 'the synoptic problem', which considers the relations among the first three Gospels and their apparent reliance on a common earlier source.[206] He also addressed the issue of New Testament miracles, drawing upon the scholarship of historical criticism. In his naturalistic treatment of the resurrection he was thus able to plead with some justification that he had drawn upon 'the works of scholars and theologians of the highest repute in … Holland and Germany'.[207] Although his stance, on this issue at least, was aligned with that of the theological naturalists, he retained Strauss's conviction that we need to be mindful of the fact that when reading the Bible we are dealing with the viewpoint of the 'rude inhabitants of Palestine' and the 'semi-barbarous Hebrew', to use his somewhat loaded descriptors. The implication was that present-day supernaturalism was a vestige of this outmoded worldview that had outlived its usefulness. Huxley's labels are also reminiscent of Hume's dismissive categorisation of the purveyors of tales of the supernatural.

---

[204] This had also been true for earlier Anglophone writers. Thus, for example, in Nicolas Wiseman's discussion of the connection between 'science' and revealed religion, comparative linguistics and biblical criticism appear on the side of the sciences. *Twelve Lectures on the Connexion between Science and Revealed Religion*, 2nd ed. (London: Joseph Booker, 1836). On the narrowing of the conception of science later in the century see Harrison, *Territories*, pp. 145–82.

[205] Leonard Huxley, *The Life and Letters of Thomas Henry Huxley*, 3 vols. (Cambridge: Cambridge University Press, 2012), vol. 3, p. 109.

[206] Matthew Day, 'Reading the Fossils of Faith: Thomas Henry Huxley and the Evolutionary Subtext of the Synoptic Problem', *Church History* 74 (2005), 534–56. He was also familiar with Ernest Renan's biblical criticism. See Huxley, 'Agnosticism and Christianity', *CE*, vol. 5, pp. 353–60.

[207] Huxley, 'Agnosticism: A Rejoinder' [1889], *CE*, vol. 5, p. 266. On the earlier occasion of Huxley's presentation of arguments about the resurrection to a meeting of the Metaphysical Society, his critic Hutton had pointed out that Huxley's position was identical to the German naturalistic exegetes of the first half of the century. See Gowan Dawson, '"The Cross-Examination of the Physiologist": T. H. Huxley and the Resurrection', in *The Metaphysical Society*, ed. Marshall et al., pp. 91–118.

Huxley's extra-curricular interest in theology and biblical criticism is revealing of the major intellectual preoccupations of the period. The centrality of theological issues in the debates of the day – as opposed to controversies relating to the science of evolutionary theory – is attested by two publishing phenomena that bracketed the appearance of Darwin's 1859 *Origin of Species* and to some degree overshadowed it. The first was Henry L. Mansel's Bampton Lectures of 1858, *On the Limits of Religious Thought*. Mansel was Waynflete Professor of Metaphysical Philosophy at Magdalen College, Oxford and subsequently Regius Professor of Ecclesiastical History at Christ Church and Dean of St Paul's. The Lectures drew large crowds and generated considerable controversy. The printed version ran to two editions in 1858, with a further two in the next year, followed by an expanded edition in 1867. In these works Mansel set out a defence of Christian belief based on a version of metaphysical agnosticism that took as its point of departure aspects of the philosophy of Kant and the now little-known English metaphysician Sir William Hamilton. In essence, Mansel advocated a form of negative theology, proposing that knowledge of God as he is in himself is impossible for finite human minds.[208] As Bernard Lightman has shown, the remarkable feature of the reception of the Lectures was that while Mansel generated little enthusiasm among his Christian co-religionists, his ideas had a profound influence on Thomas Henry Huxley, Herbert Spencer, John Tyndall, J. S. Mill, and others.[209] Huxley saw in Mansel an unwitting advocate of agnosticism and remarked in his correspondence that this ostensible defender of Christianity was in reality sawing off the branch upon which he was sitting.[210] He was particularly taken with Mansel's implication that theology should be less concerned with the issuing of dogmatic dicta and more with representing ineffable religious sentiment. In fairness to Mansel,

---

[208] Henry L. Mansel, *The Limits of Religious Thought*, 5th ed. (London: John Murray, 1867). See also Mansel, *The Philosophy of the Unconditioned* (London: Alexander Strahan, 1866). William Hamilton's 'Philosophy of the Unconditioned' [1829], repr. in *Kant's Thought in Britain: The Early Impact*, ed. Robert Adamson (London: Routledge/Thoemmes Press, 1999) presents an interesting mix of Reidian and Kantian ideas. For the relation between these thinkers, and for their subsequent influence in England see William J. Mander, *The Unknowable: A Study in Nineteenth-Century British Metaphysics* (Oxford: Oxford University Press, 2020), pp. 9–58.

[209] Bernard Lightman, 'Henry Longueville Mansel and the Genesis of Victorian Agnosticism', PhD thesis, Brandeis University, 1978.

[210] Huxley to Charles Kingsley, 23 September 1860, *Life and Letters*, vol. 1, p. 293. Huxley also remarked that in his youth he had read Hamilton's *On the Philosophy of the Unconditioned* which left an indelible expression on him. He later recalled the substance of Hamilton's essay on reading the 'eminently agnostic thinker', Henry Mansel. 'Agnosticism', *CE*, vol. 5, pp. 235f., and n.1.

the Lectures also contained an attenuated positive argument to the effect that the setting of a limit or boundary implies something that lies on the other side. In this sense, the argument was intended to make an indirect case for the existence of an ineffable Deity.[211] But Huxley was primarily interested in what Mansel was denying, not the possibility of some apophatic affirmation.[212]

The other work was *Essays and Reviews*, published in 1860, four months after the appearance of Darwin's *Origin*. Written by seven liberal Anglican thinkers – six clergyman and one layman (the 'seven against Christ', as they became known by their detractors) – this collection presented the case, based largely on principles drawn from German historical criticism, for naturalistic readings of biblical and pre-biblical history. Some measure of the impact of the book can be ascertained from the fact that it sold more copies in two years than Darwin's *Origin* did in twenty.[213] Frederick Harrison's influential review in the liberal *Westminster Quarterly* described the collection as marking 'an epoch in the history of opinion'. What characterised the common stance of the essayists, according to Harrison, was that 'the whole supernatural element is eliminated from belief'. It was acknowledged that the writers considered themselves to be friends of Christianity, imagining that they were defending it against its staunchest critics. But Harrison concluded that 'the mass of ordinary believers may well ask to be protected from such friends, as their worst and most dangerous enemies'. The final word of the review said it all – 'suicidal'.[214] Again, then, it seemed that opponents of supernaturalism were well served by arguments originally articulated by those who thought themselves to be on the other side.

---

[211] 'We thus learn ... that it is a duty, enjoined by Reason itself, to believe in that which we are unable to comprehend.' By the impotence of reason we are led 'to believe in the existence of that infinite which we cannot conceive; for the denial of its existence involves a contradiction'. Mansel, *Limits*, p. 69, and n. This bears comparison the Pascal's 'reason's last step is the recognition that there are an infinite number of things which are beyond it' (*Pensées* L 188 [B 267], p. 85) and to Wittgenstein's remark in the preface to the *Tractatus* that 'in order to be able to draw a limit to thought, we should have to find both sides of the limit of the thinkable' (Wittgenstein accordingly sought to draw limits to what could be said, not thought). *Tractatus Logico-Philosophicus*, p. 3.

[212] Mansel clearly subscribed to some notion of Christian evidences, including the idea that miracles supported the Christian revelation. Mansel, 'On Miracles as Evidences of Christianity', in *Aids to Faith: A Series of Theological Essays*, ed. William Thompson (London: John Murray, 1862), pp. 1–40.

[213] Adrian Desmond and James Moore, *Darwin* (London: Michael Joseph, 1991), p. 500.

[214] Frederic Harrison, 'Neo-Christianity', *The Westminster Review*, vol. 74, no. 146 (1 October 1860), 293–332 (293, 302, 295, 332).

Given this context, we might say that in the closing decades of the nineteenth century Huxley and his fellow travellers insinuated the natural sciences into a discussion that up until this moment had primarily been the province of theology and biblical criticism. This move was accomplished partly by arguing that a range of 'scientific' endeavours stood in opposition to 'supernaturalism'. According to Huxley, a genuine 'scientific method' for arriving at reliable knowledge was evident in the labours of 'the historians, the philologists, the Biblical critics, the geologists, and the biologists in the nineteenth century'.[215] Supernaturalism, for its part, was now ranged against a 'true scientific culture' that was manifested in a range of intellectual approaches: 'historical, philological, philosophical, or physical'. These were the vectors of naturalism that, for Huxley, would eventually bring about 'the end of theology'.[216] This ultimate goal necessarily meant that the broad coalition which included religiously sympathetic biblical scholars, historians, and theologians, was destined to be relatively short-lived. Once their position was more secure, single-minded naturalists, having co-opted the arguments of liberal Christian thinkers, ejected them from the nest. Naturalism came to be identified with science, supernaturalism with religion and theology.[217]

In taking on the once-derided label of 'scientific naturalist' Huxley also sought to invest it with a set of positive moral qualities and provide it with a respectable historical pedigree. On the first score, it was important that naturalism and its twin conception, agnosticism, be understood not in purely negative terms as amoral forms of religious scepticism. The

---

[215] Huxley, 'The Evolution of Theology', *CE*, vol. 4, p. 371. Elsewhere Huxley would speak of 'scientific investigation, historical or physical', of 'scientific historical criticism' and 'scientific physical criticism', and of 'physical and literary criticism'. 'Controverted Questions', *CE*, vol. 5, pp. 25, 32f., 36. This meant that 'scientific theology' – informed by the fruits of historical criticism – was not opposed to science generally. See 'Agnosticism and Christianity', *CE*, vol. 5, p. 312. For a detailed account of the reforming activities of Huxley and his circle see Barton, *The X Club*.

[216] Huxley, 'The Evolution of Theology', *CE*, vol. 4, pp. 371f. Renan had already said something similar in *L'Avenir de la Science, Pensées de 1848*, claiming variously that: 'Positive and experimental science only, by imbuing man with a strong sentiment of the reality of life, is capable of destroying supernaturalism'; that 'the task of modern criticism is to lay the axe to every system of belief tainted with supernaturalism'; and that 'All supernaturalism will receive its death-blow from philology.' *The Future of Science* [1848] (Boston: Roberts Brothers, 1893), pp. 41, 43, 135. Clearly, one way or another, supernaturalism was destined for destruction.

[217] Bernard Lightman has spoken perceptively in this context of a 'wedge strategy' adopted by scientific naturalists that left liberal theologians with no middle ground. 'The Nineteenth-Century Origins of the Problem: Naturalistic Metaphysics and the Dead Ends of Victorian Theology', in *After Science and Religion*, ed. Harrison and Milbank, pp. 35–58.

customary arguments for the pursuit and teaching of natural philosophy had appealed to the role of the natural sciences in moral edification and the inculcation of religious piety. This was said to be embodied in 'men of science' who, through most of the nineteenth century, were a locus of epistemic and moral authority. Against this, it was now argued that naturalism or agnosticism better exemplified the appropriate moral comportment for scientific practitioners than the more traditional theistic commitments that up until this point had informed their endeavours. Naturalism, for its advocates, entailed honest individuals putting their faith in 'scientific methods for ascertaining truth'. This was promoted as an ethical stance – the now familiar commitment to believe only on the basis of evidence.[218] Huxley described agnosticism as 'the essence of science, whether ancient or modern. It simply means that a man shall not say he knows or believes that which he has not scientific ground for professing to know or believe.' This was a principle 'as old as Socrates' but also said to be 'the foundation of the Reformation, which simply illustrated the axiom that every man should be able to give a reason for the faith that is in him'.[219] There was thus some recognition of the historical role played by Protestantism in insisting upon an ethics of belief. It was simply unfortunate for this and other religious creeds that in the long run the principle turned out to be 'destructive to the forms of supernaturalism which enter into the constitution of existing religions'.[220]

William Clifford, of course, had already made a direct argument to this effect, implying that traditional religious commitment was morally suspect because it was grounded in belief on the basis of insufficient evidence. For Clifford, our genuinely 'sacred' duty consists in putting knowledge claims to the test of experience and not believing on the basis of authority.[221] John Tyndall agreed that in the honest conduct of science 'moral qualities

---

[218] 'Agnosticism is not properly described as a "negative" creed, nor indeed as a creed of any kind, except in so far as it expresses absolute faith in the validity of a principle, which is *as much ethical as intellectual*.' Huxley, 'Agnosticism and Christianity', CE, vol. 5, p. 310 (my emphasis). For men of science, it was necessarily an either/or. Charles Lyell, for example, had argued in the 1820s that scientific training inculcated epistemic, moral, and religious virtues. 'State of the Universities', *The Quarterly Review* 36/71 (June 1827), 216–68.

[219] Huxley, 'Agnosticism', CE, vol. 5, pp. 245f. See also 'Mr Darwin's Critics', CE, vol. 2, pp. 148–50.

[220] Thomas Henry Huxley, 'Agnosticism, a Symposium', *Agnostic Annual* 1 (1884), 5–20 (5).

[221] Clifford, 'The Ethics of Belief', *Lectures and Essays*, p. 359. Cf. 'The Ethics of Religion', *Lectures and Essays*, p. 369; 'The Influence upon Morality of a Decline in Religious Belief', *Lectures and Essays*, p. 392. For similar remarks about science versus theology see Ernest Renan, *Vie de Jésus*, 13th ed. (Paris, 1867), pp. vi, xxviii.

were incessantly invoked', especially the need to follow the truth 'as it is in nature'.[222] Naturalism and agnosticism, for their late nineteenth-century champions, were thus understood not simply in terms of what they denied. On offer was an alternative moral conception of scientific endeavour which incorporated a minimal standard for the holding of beliefs to which all reasonable and ethical individuals could, and should, subscribe. This moral comportment was exemplified in a new generation of scientific role models. John Tyndall saw in the person of Charles Darwin the personification of these epistemic virtues. Darwin was 'the Abraham of scientific men – a searcher as obedient to the command of truth as was the patriarch to the command of God'.[223] Along similar lines, Tyndall and Clifford also sought to retain a space within the scientific endeavour for the continued expression of the passions of delight and wonder that had once been the preserve of physico-theology.[224]

By the second half of the nineteenth century two of the key prerequisites for the emergence of scientific naturalism were in place: a naturalism/supernaturalism binary and an accompanying epistemology that vested this

---

[222] Tyndall, 'Professor Virchow and Evolution', in *Fragments of Science*, p. 633. Tyndall compares this to the moral seriousness of theologians.

[223] Tyndall, 'Science and Man', in *Fragments of Science*, p. 622. See also his 'Belfast Address', p. 478. For a similar construction of the moral nature of scientific endeavour see Ernst Haeckel, *Monism as Connecting Religion and Science*, trans. J. Gilchrist (London: Adam and Charles Black, 1874), pp. vi–vii. Early biographies of Darwin often stressed his status as a secular saint. See Bernard Lightman, 'The Many Lives of Charles Darwin: Early Biographies and the Definitive Evolutionist', *Notes and Records of the Royal Society of London* 64 (2010), 339–58; Janet Browne, 'Charles Darwin as a Celebrity', *Science in Context* 16 (2003), 175–94.

[224] See Frank M. Turner, *Contesting Cultural Authority: Essays in Victorian Intellectual Life* (Cambridge: Cambridge University Press, 1993), pp. 131–50; Bernard Lightman, *The Origins of Agnosticism: Victorian Unbelief and the Limits of Knowledge* (Baltimore: Johns Hopkins University Press, 2019), pp. 146–76. Thomas Carlyle's phrase 'natural supernaturalism' in *Sartor Resartus* represents a relevant literary development in which the supernatural is said to be manifested in the natural. It has been remarked in this context that Romanticism represents a secularisation of Christian motifs and modes of experience. See M. H. Abrams, *Natural Supernaturalism: Tradition and Revolution in Romantic Literature* (New York: Norton, 1971). But cf. Alison Milbank, *God and the Gothic: Religion, Romance, and Reality in the English Literary Tradition* (Oxford: Oxford University Press, 2018), esp. pp. 247–68. Milbank substitutes for this subtraction story a more positive and creative form of alternative theologising. For Carlyle's influence on Tyndall see Frank M. Turner, 'Victorian Scientific Naturalism and Thomas Carlyle', *Victorian Studies* 18 (1975), 325–43; Ruth Barton, 'John Tyndall, Pantheist: A Re-Reading of the Belfast Address', *Osiris* 3 (1987), 111–34; Ursula DeYoung, *A Vision of Modern Science: John Tyndall and the Role of the Scientist in Victorian Culture* (Basingstoke: Palgrave Macmillan, 2011), pp. 60–9; Ian Hesketh, 'Technologies of the Scientific Self: John Tyndall and His Journal', *Isis* 110 (2019), 466–9.

dichotomy with moral and philosophical legitimacy. As we have seen, these prerequisites originated in debates internal to Christian theology rather than in deliberations about the proper foundations of science. Advocates of a new *scientific* naturalism simply imported them into their understandings of the natural sciences. As part of a nineteenth-century quest to establish the legitimacy of science and assert its independence from theological oversight it was now claimed that a contest between naturalism and supernaturalism had been integral to the history of science from the moment of its birth among the Presocratic natural philosophers of ancient Greece. 'Naturalism' would eventually come to be understood not as a belated import from the sphere of biblical criticism, nor a historically contingent development that had arisen from parochial controversies within Christian theology in the post-Reformation period, but as an abiding and essential feature of a putatively perennial 'science'. Thus understood, naturalism and its supernaturalist antithesis could be used to explain the fluctuating fortunes of science in a universal history of civilisation. Huxley would accordingly project the origins of this 'primitive dualism' between the natural and supernatural back to ancient times and construct history in terms of their imagined perennial antagonism.[225]

All of this required a disavowal of the disreputable monotheistic parentage of natural sciences and the construction of a new historical lineage. This new history would not only seek to erase the conspicuous pre-nineteenth-century alliances between theistic and scientific conceptions of the world but would also offer a means of discounting the weight of past testimony, in Europe and elsewhere, to the existence of divine entities and activities. It was Protestant apologists who pioneered the use of polemical histories as a means of securing the authenticity of their apparently 'new' religion. They also successfully wrote the Reformation into history. Along with the Renaissance and scientific revolution, it would come to be understood as an irreversible and epochal change that established, for the first time, the conditions for historical progress. This was accompanied by the deployment of the image of light following an age of darkness, establishing an important precedent for the rhetoric of Enlightenment thinkers. Biblical prophecy and apocalypticism also played key roles in the new historical consciousness, with eschatological hopes being projected onto history rather than being postponed until the hereafter. Finally, a key element in the Protestant periodisation of history was the proposal that at a particular historical juncture the working of genuine miracles had ceased. This established the

---

[225] Huxley, 'Controverted Questions', *CE*, vol. 5, p. 4.

momentous precedent of a historical periodisation scheme that not only restricted miracle-working to a specific period in the past, but also put into circulation a range of sceptical arguments about miracles that could be applied with somewhat less discrimination than their original authors had intended. Advocates of scientific naturalism simply helped themselves to the basic plotlines of these Protestant histories.

6

THE SHAPE OF HISTORY

The philosophy of history can be nothing but a religious metaphysic of history. The meaning of history cannot be immanent in history, it lies beyond the confines of history.
>   Nikolai Berdyaev, *The Beginning and the End*

We are living in a shadow ... on the perfume of an empty vase. Those who come after us will live in the shadow of a shadow.
>   Ernest Renan, Address to the French Academy[1]

6.1 History Wars

Of course, in the beginning, I was not at all knowledgeable about or expert in history, and attacked the papacy *a priori*, which is to say, on the basis of Holy Scripture. I am now wonderfully glad to see others do the same *a posteriori*, which is to say, on the basis of history.[2]

In 1536, almost twenty years after he had inadvertently precipitated the Reformation, Martin Luther reflected on a significant tactical shift that had taken place in Protestant battles with the papacy. Luther had come to realise that arguing on the basis of fidelity to scripture went only so far if one's opponents insisted that the authority to interpret holy writ rested with them. In any case, Luther's adversaries also rejected his insistence on the principle of *sola scriptura*, contending that this criterion represented but one source of religious authority. The Catholic claim to be the authentic church also rested

---

[1] Epigraphs: Nikolai Berdyaev, *The Beginning and the End* (New York: Harper, 1957), p. 199; Ernest Renan, *Disours de réception de M. V. Cherbuliez, Response de M. Ernest Renan* (Paris, 1882), p. 53.
[2] Luther's Epistle Dedicatory to Robert Barnes, *Vitae Romanorum Pontificum* [1536] (Basel, 1555), sig. a5r.

on a well-established historical lineage that connected it directly to the earliest churches, the apostles, and, ultimately, to the person of Christ himself. At the time, moreover, novelty was regarded as a hallmark of heresy. Advocates of religious reformation found themselves having to justify doctrinal and liturgical innovation in the face of claims that their reforms represented a heretical departure from established tradition. 'Where was your church before Luther?' was the pointed question repeatedly put to the reformers.[3] In light of this, Protestants sought to create historical narratives that established their continuity with an original, pristine Christianity while presenting Catholicism as an illicit deviation from it. Catholic historians responded in kind, giving rise to a new industry devoted to the production of competing histories.[4]

The genealogies developed by Protestants were necessarily varied, given the diverse national characters of the reform movements. In Geneva, for example, Calvin's successor Theodore Beza informed his flock that they were heirs to a long tradition of resistance to Roman corruptions, linking them back to the twelfth-century Waldensians of south-central Europe. This proto-Protestant sect had already traced its own origins back to the second century.[5] This genealogy provided Huguenots with a respectable path back to the apostolic age that conveniently bypassed the imagined corruptions of medieval Catholicism. The legend of Joseph of Arimathea's visit to England and his sojourn in Glastonbury provided English Christianity with its direct connection to the apostles. This version of events, later immortalised in William Blake's 'Jerusalem', prompted English bishop John Bale (known

---

[3] S. J. Barnett, 'Where Was Your Church before Luther? Claims for the Antiquity of Protestantism Examined', *Church History* 68 (1999), 14–41.

[4] Euan Cameron, *Interpreting Christian History: The Challenge of the Churches' Past* (Oxford: Oxford University Press, 2005), pp. 131–52; Avihu Zakai, 'Reformation, History, and Eschatology in English Protestantism', *History and Theory* 26 (1987), 300–18; Reinhard Schwarz, 'Die Wahrheit der Geschichte im Verständnis der Wittenberger Reformation', *Zeitschrift für Theologie und Kirche* 76 (1979), 159–90; Matthias Pohlig, *Zwischen Gelehrsamkeit und konfessioneller Identitätsstiftung: Lutherische Kirchen- und Universalgeschichtsschreibung 1546–1617* (Tübingen: Mohr Siebeck, 2007); Katherine Van Liere, Simon Ditchfield, and Howard Louthan (eds.), *Sacred History: Uses of the Christian Past in the Renaissance World* (Oxford: Oxford University Press, 2012).

[5] Theodore Beza, *Histoire Ecclesiastique* (1580), referenced in Barnett, 'Where Was Your Church', p. 20. See also Pierre Boyer, *Abrege de l'Histoire des Vaudois Ou On voit leur origine comme Dieu a consérvé la Religion Chrétienne en sa pureté parmi eux, dépuis le tems des Apôtres jusques à nos jours* (La Haye, 1691); Pekka Tolonen, 'Medieval Memories of the Origins of the Waldensian Movement' and Yves Krumenacker, 'The Use of History by French Protestants and its Impact on Protestant Historiography', both in *History and Religion: Narrating a Religious Past*, ed. Bernd-Christian Otto, Susanne Rau, and Jörg Rüpke (Berlin: De Gruyter, 2015), pp. 165–87, 189–201; Charlotte Methuen, 'History and Heresy in the Lutheran Reformation', *Renaissance and Reformation Review* 24 (2022), 3–22.

6.1 HISTORY WARS

as 'bilious Bale' for his quarrelsome disposition) to write that, contrary to the 'Italyane writers and of the subtylle deuysers of sāctes legendes', true religion in England came not from Rome, but 'from the schole of Christe hymselfe'.[6] In an alternative, but no less tenuous connection, Christianity was said to have arrived in England during the second century on the occasion of the conversion of 'King Lucius'.[7] Historical constructions such as these would subsequently feed into nascent European nationalisms, with Protestant nation-states understanding their identity in terms of an abiding struggle against Roman domination.[8]

If the lineages of the different Protestant confessions necessarily differed in detail, there was more agreement about what had gone wrong for the other side. Medieval Catholicism was said to have been a deviant and superstitious corruption of an originally pure Christianity. Again, the task of providing evidence for this thesis fell to historians, rather than biblical exegetes, feeding into a new industry of historical scholarship. The first, monumental product of this collaborative endeavour was the *Magdeburg Centuries* (1559–74), an impressively researched series of volumes of ecclesiastical history produced by 'several learned and pious men in the city of Magdeburg' led by the Croatian scholar Matthias Flacius Illyricus (1520–75).[9] The centuriators of Magdeburg – so called because they adopted the novel approach of setting out their histories century by century – argued that Western Europe had gone into a long period of degeneration and decline during the medieval period which had ended only with the religious reforms of Luther and Calvin. In keeping with the efforts of historians of specific confessions, the

---

[6] John Bale, *The vocaycon of Iohan Bale* (Rome, 1553), p. 12. See also Matthew Parker, *De antiquitate Britannicae ecclesiae et privilegiis ecclesiae Cantuariensis* (London, 1572). For Bale, and the development of apocalyptic readings of history during this period, see Richard Bauckham, *Tudor Apocalypse: Sixteenth Century Apocalypticism, Millenarianism and the English Reformation, from John Bale to John Foxe and Thomas Brightman* (Oxford: Oxford University Press, 1978); Katharine R. Firth, *The Apocalyptic Tradition in Reformation Britain: 1530–1645* (Oxford: Oxford University Press, 1979).

[7] Thomas Fuller, *Church-History of Britain* (London, 1655), pp. 9–14. Fuller is sceptical of the Joseph of Arimathea account (pp. 6–8).

[8] Donald R. Kelley, *Foundations of Modern Historical Scholarship* (New York: Columbia University Press, 1970), pp. 151–82; James T. Thompson, *A History of Historical Writing*, 2 vols. (New York: Macmillan, 1942), vol. 1, pp. 531–4.

[9] Flacius et al., *Ecclesiastica Historia*, 14 vols. (Basel, 1560–74). For the history of these volumes see Greg B. Lyon, 'Baudouin, Flacius, and the Plan for the Magdeburg Centuries', *Journal of the History of Ideas* 64 (2003), 253–72; Anthony Grafton, 'Where Was Salomon's House? Ecclesiastical History and the Intellectual Origins of Bacon's *New Atlantis*', in *Die Europäische Gelehrtenrepublik im Zeitalter des Konfessionalismus*, ed. Herbert Jaumann (Wiesbaden: Harrassowitz, 2001), pp. 21–38.

centuriators also sought to identify those advocates of true Christianity who in every age had struggled against forces of the Antichrist (typically identified as the papacy).

This first sally in the history wars of the sixteenth century was countered, from the other side, by the equally impressive *Annales Ecclesiastici* (1588–1607) produced by Cardinal Caesar Baronius.[10] As the Vatican Librarian, Baronius had unfettered access to a massive and largely untapped archive. The volumes he produced were no less polemical than those of his Protestant counterparts and arguably surpassed them in scholarly rigour, not least on account of the quantity and quality of his sources. Edward Gibbon would later refer alliteratively to 'the brutal bigotry of Baronius', but still found himself relying upon an updated version of this two-century-old work for his own classic *History of the Decline and Fall of the Roman Empire* (1776–89).[11]

One indication of Baronius's assiduous reliance on primary materials is the fact that he was one of the first to speak of the 'dark ages', referring to a period about which little could be said on account of the paucity of written sources. It was 'dark' for us: 'The new age [*saeculum*] which was beginning, for its harshness and barrenness of good could well be called iron, for its baseness and abounding evil leaden, and moreover for its lack of writers, dark.'[12] Protestant writers would begin to use this expression in a rather different sense, however, using it to characterise the spirit of medieval Catholicism. The inhabitants of Calvin's Geneva adopted the biblical phrase '*post tenebras lux*' (after darkness, light), implying that the Reformation represented the dawning of a new light after an age of medieval darkness.[13] This came

---

[10] Subsequent confessional histories on the Catholic side include Jacques Bénigne Bossuet's *Histoire des variations des églises protestantes* (Paris, 1688); Jaime Balmes, *El Protestantismo comparado con el Catolicismo en sus relaciones con la Civilización Europea*, 3 vols. (Barcelona, 1842–4). Earlier defences of the historical fidelity of English Catholicism include Thomas Stapleton, *A Fortresse of the Faith first planted amonge vs Englishmen* (Antwerp, 1565).

[11] Owen Chadwick, 'Gibbon and the Church Historians', *Daedalus* 105 (1976), 111–23.

[12] Caesar Baronius, *Annales Ecclesiastici*, 12 vols. (Rome, 1588–1607). vol. 10 (1602), p. 647. For Baronius the dark ages extended from the end of the Carolingian Empire in the late ninth century to the papacy of Clement II in the middle of the eleventh century. The expression is sometimes also associated with Petrarch who referred to men of brilliance who were surrounded by 'darkness' and 'gloom'. See Theodore E. Mommsen, 'Petrarch's Conception of the "Dark Ages"', *Speculum* 17 (1942), 226–42. For correctives to the 'dark ages' story see Peter S. Wells, *Barbarians to Angels: The Dark Ages Reconsidered* (New York: Norton, 2008); Chris Wickham, *The Inheritance of Rome: Illuminating the Dark Ages: 400–1000* (Harmondsworth: Penguin, 2010); Seb Falk, *The Light Ages: The Surprising Story of Medieval Science* (New York: Norton, 2020).

[13] Adapted from Job 17:12 (Vulgate): *post tenebras spero lucem* (after darkness I hope for light). John T. McNeill, *The History and Character of Calvinism* (Oxford: Oxford University Press, 1967), p. 157.

to be more broadly embraced as a motto of the Protestant Reformation and can still be seen inscribed on the 'Reformation Wall' in Geneva. In the seventeenth century, English writers would regularly use the descriptor 'dark ages' to depict various aspects of the defects of Catholicism, especially implicit faith, ignorance, and superstition.[14] The idea of successive ages of darkness and light represented a rough periodisation scheme that initially implied a restoration of what had been lost, although this image could also be imbued with a new idea of historical progress.

In the seventeenth century some thinkers took the further step of linking the Reformation of religion to other changes in the intellectual landscape of Europe, specifically, the advances in literary and scientific knowledge that we now refer to as the Renaissance and scientific revolution.[15] On the negative side, the argument was that the decay of learning and the corruption of true religion went hand in hand. Puritan divine and sometime Vice-Chancellor of the University of Cambridge, Thomas Hill, attributed the superstition of the 'darke ages' to neglect of truth and the slavish following of tradition: 'Hence it is observed that Learning and Religion have falne and risen together. When the light of Truth hath beene eclipsed, by the decay of learning.'[16] On the positive side, the dawning of light in the early modern period could be understood as a providentially ordained general reformation

---

[14] On the 'darkness' of implicit faith, see John Copely, *Doctrinal and Moral Observations concerning Religion* (London, 1612), p. 9; Anthony White, *Truth and Error Discovered* (Oxford, 1628), p. 9. More generally on the dark ages as periods of ignorance and superstition: George Abbot, *A Treatise of the Perpetuall Visibilitie and Succession of the True Church in All Ages* (London, 1624), sig. A3r; Richard Sibbs, *Beams of Divine Light* (London, 1639), p. 57; Edward Stillingfleet, *A relation of a conference held about religion at London* (London, 1687), p. 50; Daniel Whitby, *A Treatise of Traditions* (London, 1688), pp. vi, xxiv, xxxviii, lv, lxvi, 115, 116; Samuel Barton, *A Sermon Preached before the Honorable House of Commons* (London, 1696), p. 10; Matthew Hole, *Letters written to JM* (London, 1699), p. 90.

[15] While the labels 'Renaissance' and 'scientific revolution' date from the nineteenth and twentieth centuries, there was a sense at the time that tectonic changes in the spheres of letters and the sciences were taking place. It was Renaissance historian Leonardo Bruni who first gave us the division of history into ancient, medieval, and modern. *Historiae Florentini Populi* (c.1416–42). A similar schematisation is used by his contemporary Flavio Biodo, *Historiarum ab inclinatione Romanorum imperii* (c.1450). The French 'Renaissance' is attested from the early eighteenth century and was anglicised in 1832. Much earlier, from the sixteenth century, is the Italian *rinascita* (rebirth). 'Renaissance' was popularised by Jacob Burkhardt's *Die Cultur der Renaissance in Italien* (Basel, 1860). 'Scientific revolution' is a twentieth-century expression. A. R. Hall, *The Scientific Revolution* (London: Longmans, Green, and Co., 1954). For early modern perspectives on revolutionary change, see Peter Harrison, 'Was There a Scientific Revolution?', *European Review* 15 (2007), 445–57. For an excellent account of connections between the reformations of religion and learning see Brooke, *Science and Religion*, pp. 110–57.

[16] Thomas Hill, *The Trade of Truth Advanced* (London, 1642), p. 42.

that encompassed both religion and learning. Francis Bacon observed that 'in the age of ourselves and our fathers, when it pleased God to call the Church of Rome to account for their degenerate manners and ceremonies, and sundry doctrines obnoxious and framed to uphold the same abuses; at one and the same time it was ordained by the Divine Providence, that there should attend withal a renovation and a new spring of all other knowledges'.[17] This was as much a justification of the new sciences as the new religion, but both were argued to be different facets of a single, providentially intended, historical instauration. Later in the seventeenth century, in his defence of the aspirations of the fledgling Royal Society, Bishop Thomas Sprat would speak of 'the agreement that is between the present *Design* of the *Royal Society*, and that of our *Church* [of England] in its beginning'. This concord consisted in the fact that 'they both may lay equal claim to the word *Reformation*, the one having compass'd it in *Religion*, the other purposing it in *Philosophy*'.[18] In a similar deployment of the dark ages metaphor, Puritan Cotton Mather (1663–1728) spoke of the 'darkness' of medieval Europe, brought to an end by the Renaissance and Protestant Reformation: 'Incredible darkness was upon the Western parts of Europe two hundred years ago', he wrote. 'The revival of letters ... prepared the world for the Reformation of Religion and for the advancement of the sciences since.'[19] Less discriminating critics of religion in the following century would simply associate the rise of Christianity per se with the demise of learning and claim the label of the age of light for themselves.

Bacon's invocation of providence to lend legitimacy to the revolutionary changes taking place in both religion and the sciences drew upon a new trend in the interpretation of biblical prophecies. While Luther had observed a distinction between biblical and historical defences of Protestantism, he also held the two to be connected. The link was provided by the prophetical writings of scripture which foretold the end times and pointed to the signs

---

[17] Bacon, *Advancement of Learning*, *Works*, vol. 3, p. 300. Scientific innovators would accordingly be compared to Luther and Calvin. See, e.g., R. B., *The Difference between the aunciente Phisicke ... and the Latter Phisicke* (London, 1585), sigs. Cviii.v, Hvii.v; Charles Webster, *From Paracelsus to Newton* (Cambridge: Cambridge University Press, 1982), p. 4.

[18] Sprat, *History of the Royal Society*, p. 371. See also Thomas Culpeper, *Morall Discourses and Essayes* (London, 1655), p. 63; Samuel Hartlib, Sheffield University Library, Hartlib Papers XLVIII 17, reproduced in Charles Webster, *The Great Instauration: Science, Medicine, and Reform, 1626–1660* (London: Duckworth, 1975), Appendix 1, pp. 524–8; Biggs, *Mataetechnia Medicinae Praxeos*, 'To the Parliament'.

[19] Cotton Mather, *American Tears upon the Ruines of the Greek Churches* (Boston, 1701) pp. 42f. See also Gilbert Burnet, *History of the Reformation of the Church of England* (London, 1679), Epistle Dedicatory; *A Letter Writ by the Lord Bishop of Salisbury* (London, 1693), p. 15; *A Letter written upon the Discovery of the Late Plot* (London, 1678), pp. 9, 20.

that would accompany it. The case could be made that conflict between the true (Protestant) Churches and the false (Roman) Church, along with the rise of the Antichrist (the papacy) and the tribulations of the last days, had been foretold by the biblical prophets.[20] On this understanding, history had a hidden structure that could be partially revealed by correctly aligning biblical prophecies, in particular those of the books of Daniel and Revelation, with historical events.[21] Popular works of chronology, such as *Carion's Chronicles* (1532), did precisely this, setting out a universal history of the world from the creation to the present, identifying key historical junctures that revealed the hidden logic of history. The product of a number of hands, including the humanist astrologer Johan Carion, Philip Melanchthon, and his nephew Caspar Peucer, the *Chronicles* was translated from the original German into Latin and vernacular European languages, becoming a standard text in Protestant universities.[22] It partitions historical time into periods associated with four great kingdoms – Babylonian, Assyrian, Persian, and Roman. The Reformation took its place at the end of the Roman period and was understood to be a prelude to the last days.

Luther's take on the implications of biblical prophecy for the reading of contemporary historical events was a rather gloomy one: 'Now we see, that after this time in which the Pope has been revealed [as Antichrist], there is nothing to hope for or to anticipate, than the end of the world.'[23]

---

[20] For identifications of the papacy with the Antichrist see *Ecclesiastica Historia* [i.e., *Magdeburg Centuries*], *Duodecima Centuria*, cols. 846–7; Thomas Lanquet, *Coopers Chronicle* (London, 1560), p. 157.

[21] Luther, 'Epistle Dedicatory', in Barnes, *Vitae Romanorum Pontificum*, sig. a5r–v. Cf. Luther, 'Preface to the Revelation of St. John' [1545], *LW* 6, 481–9. Firth, *Apocalyptic Tradition*, p. 12.

[22] Latin trans. by Burchard of Ursberg, *Chronicvm Abbatis Vrspergensis* (Strasbourg: Mylius, 1537); English trans. by Lanquet, *Coopers Chronicle*. On its influence see Zakai, 'Reformation, History and Eschatology', 303; Mark A. Lotito, *The Reformation of Historical Thought* (Leiden: Brill, 2019), pp. 142–206. In England, Joseph Mede's immensely popular *Clavis Apocalyptica* (Cambridge, 1627) and *The Key to Revelation* (London, 1643) performed a similar role, mapping biblical prophecies to historical events. See Diarmaid MacCulloch, *The Reformation: A History* (New York: Viking, 2004), pp. 469–84. More generally on apocalypticism in England at this time: Patrick Curry, *Prophecy and Power: Astrology in Early Modern England* (Cambridge: Cambridge University Press, 1989); Christopher Hill, *Antichrist in Seventeenth-Century England* (Oxford: Oxford University Press, 1971); Kinch Hoekstra, 'Disarming the Prophets: Thomas Hobbes and Predictive Power', *Rivista di storia della filosofia* 1 (2004), 97–153.

[23] Luther, WA 11/2, 113. Quoted in Leigh T. I. Penman, *Hope and Heresy: The Problem of Chiliasm in Confessional Lutheranism, 1570–1630* (Dordrecht: Springer, 2019), p. xi. This is Augustine's view, that the present age is *saeculum senescens* – an age that grows old awaiting its end. See Eric Voegelin, *The New Science of Politics* [1952], *The Collected Works of Eric Voegelin*, vol. 5, ed. Manfred Henningsen (Columbia: University of Missouri Press, 1999), pp. 184f.

The Reformation, on this reading, was not a glorious ray of light that would usher in a new era of peace and harmony, but the final struggle against the forces of the Antichrist, conducted in the shadow of an impending eschaton. The object of Christian hope lay beyond time. The wars of religion lent some credence to Luther's melancholy prognostication. But the sixteenth and seventeenth centuries were home to a broad spectrum of apocalyptic interpretations of history, including those for whom the age of reformation signalled the dawn of a new golden age that would be realised within the span of historical time.[24] The inconvenient failure of the eschaton to materialise would eventually mute more exuberant expressions of optimistic apocalypticism. Arguably, however, the idea of an earthly, temporal realisation of eschatological hope was transmuted into the secular visions of material progress characteristic of dominant forms of Enlightenment thought.

An important medieval precedent for optimistic eschatological expectations can be found in the writings of the Cistercian monk Joachim of Fiore (c. 1135–1202). Joachim divided history into three epochs reflecting the three persons of the Trinity.[25] Joachim's third 'Age of the Spirit' represents the culmination of history that sees a new dispensation of universal love, the establishment of a contemplative utopia, and a new rule of 'the Just' that would replace the priesthood and ecclesiastical establishment. In a conspicuous instance of what political philosopher Eric Voegelin has referred to as 'immanentization of the Christian eschaton', the Age of the Spirit was to be realised within the span of historical time, rather than being postponed until the world to come.[26] Joachimite thought – especially that represented by his more enthusiastic disciples – largely remained on the fringes of official Christian theologies of history.[27] However, it had an unmistakable impact

---

[24] See esp. Penman, *Hope and Heresy*, which includes a survey of an extensive literature (pp. ix–xxii). For apocalyptic expectations among Calvinists, see Hotson, *Johann Heinrich Alsted*, and *Paradise Postponed: Johann Heinrich Alsted and the Birth of Calvinist Millenarianism* (Dordrecht: Kluwer, 2000).

[25] Brett E. Whalen, *Dominion of God: Christendom and Apocalypse in the Middle Ages* (Cambridge, MA: Harvard University Press, 2009), pp. 100–24.

[26] Voegelin, *The New Science of Politics*, pp. 184–5.

[27] The *Catechism of the Catholic Church* speaks of 'that messianic hope which can only be realized beyond history through the eschatological judgement' and condemns both religious 'millenarianism' and 'secular messianism' (§676), www.vatican.va/archive/ENG0015/__P1V.HTM, accessed 24 October 2021. Cf. 'Augsburg Confession', Art. VXII, 5, https://bookofconcord.org/augsburg-confession/article-xvii/, accessed 24 October 2021. Some of Joachim's ideas were censured at the Fourth Lateran Council, but these relate more to his Trinitarian teachings than his eschatology. www.papalencyclicals.net/councils/ecum12-2.htm#2, accessed 24 October 2021. Norman Cohn stressed the radical nature of medieval apocalyptic movements in his classic *The Pursuit of the Millennium: Revolutionary*

on more radical chiliast understandings of history during the Reformation period and beyond, extending (it has been argued) to the historical schemes of Hegel, Marx, and Engels.[28] The young Friedrich Engels would thus draw directly upon millenarian language to encourage those dreaming of a future socialist utopia: 'this is our vocation ... to gird our swords about our loins for its sake and cheerfully risk our lives in the last holy war, which will be followed by the millennium of freedom'.[29]

Elements of an apocalyptic understanding of time are especially evident in attempts to provide historical justifications for new scientific projects in seventeenth-century England. Francis Bacon drew upon the book of Daniel to explain that the voyages of discovery and expansion of the sciences had been pre-destined by God to take place in the last days:

> Nor should the prophecy of Daniel be forgotten, touching the last ages of the world: – "Many shall go to and fro, and knowledge shall be increased"; clearly intimating that the thorough passage of the world (which now by so many distant voyages seems to be accomplished, or in the course of accomplishment), and the advancement of the sciences, are destined by fate, that is, by Divine Providence, to meet in the same age.[30]

This eschatological vision was shared by the Puritan 'projectors' of the Interregnum period (1649–60). These individuals were enthusiastic

---

Millenarians and Mystical Anarchists in the Middle Ages (Oxford: Oxford University Press, 1957). Others have proposed that apocalypticism was more mainstream than the official doctrinal statements might suggest. See Bernard McGinn, *Visions of the End: Apocalyptic Traditions in the Middle Ages* (New York: Columbia University Press, 1979), pp. 28–36.

[28] Penman, *Hope and Heresy*, pp. 3–5; Marjorie Reeves, *Joachim of Fiore and the Prophetic Future* (Stroud: Sutton, 1999); Henri de Lubac, *La Postérité spirituelle de Joachim de Flore* (Paris: Lethielleux, 1979); Warwick Gould and Marjorie Reeves, *Joachim of Fiore and the Myth of the Eternal Evangel in the Nineteenth and Twentieth Centuries* (Oxford: Oxford University Press, 2002), pp. 15–19; Heiko A. Oberman, *The Impact of the Reformation* (Grand Rapids: Eerdmans, 1994), p. 135; Voegelin, *The New Science of Politics*, pp. 183–5; Matthias Riedel, 'Longing for the Third Age: Revolutionary Joachism, Communism and National Socialism', in *A Companion to Joachim of Fiore*, ed. Matthias Riedel (Leiden: Brill, 2018), pp. 267–318; Hans Jonas, *The Imperative of Responsibility: In Search of an Ethics for the Technological Age* (Chicago: University of Chicago Press, 1984), pp. 178–9; Jayne Svenungsson, *Divining History: Prophetism, Messianism and the Development of Spirit*, trans. Stephen Donovan (New York: Berghahn, 2016), esp. pp. 80–3. For Joachim's influence on early modern English apocalyptic writings, see Marjorie Reeves, 'History and Eschatology: Medieval and Early Protestant Thought in Some English and Scottish Writings', *Medievalia et Humanistica* 4 (1973), 106–10, and 'English Apocalyptic Thinkers, c.1540–1620', in *Storia e Figure dell'Apocalisse fra '500 e '600*, ed. R. Rusconi, Atti del 4ro congress internazionale di studi Gioachimiti (Rome, Italy, 1996), pp. 259–73.

[29] Quoted in Ernst Bloch, *The Principle of Hope*, 3 vols., trans. Neville Plaice, Stephen Plaice, and Paul Knight (Cambridge, MA: MIT Press, 1995), vol. 2, p. 515.

[30] Bacon, *Novum Organum*, bk. 1, §93, *Works*, vol. 4, p. 92.

advocates for a variety of social improvement schemes that encompassed education, science, medicine, and technology. With the encouragement and guidance of the central European émigrés Samuel Hartlib and Jan Amos Comenius, the projectors saw themselves as agents working to improve and reform society as a prelude to the end of history.[31] Communal human efforts to promote knowledge and learning were understood as divinely mandated duties that would be instrumental in bringing on the eschaton.[32] A biblical indicative – the instauration of learning before the end times – became an imperative. These eschatological aspirations were also important in motivating some of the founders of the Royal Society, although with the Restoration of the monarchy in 1660, fellows of that august body were disinclined to make too much of their indebtedness to a discredited Puritan millenarianism. For our purposes, what is significant in all of this is the use of 'external' historical arguments (Luther's a posteriori) to give legitimacy to the new forms of both Christianity and the sciences which might otherwise have been regarded as heretical deviations. With the muting of millenarian expectations, the means of hastening the much-anticipated eschaton would become an end in itself. Human hope would seek fulfilment not in the world to come but within the span of secular time.

Another relevant development came with the covenantal or 'federal' theology of the Dutch Calvinist Johannes Cocceius (1603–69), who also used prophecy to structure history. Like a number of his co-religionists, Cocceius envisaged the present historical moment as the final phase of an enduring struggle with the Antichrist. He did not, however, cherish millenarian hopes as such – for him the thousand-year period referenced in Revelation had already taken place. But he nonetheless anticipated 'a blessed state of the (Reformed) Church' that would come about before the last days.[33] More importantly, he understood scripture as offering an account of God's successive covenants with his people (hence 'covenantal' theology), with the kingdom of God being gradually revealed in the passage of history.[34]

---

[31] Webster, *Great Instauration*; Harrison, *Fall of Man*, pp. 186–91; Paul Slack, *The Invention of Improvement: Information and Material Progress in Seventeenth-Century England* (Oxford: Oxford University Press, 2015), pp. 91–128.

[32] Samuel Hartlib, *Macaria* (London, 1641), p. 4. Cf. Jan Comenius, *A Patterne of Universall Knowledge* (London, 1651), p. 65, and *Reformation of Schooles* (London, 1642), pp. 4, 26.

[33] Willem J. van Asselt, 'Amicitia Dei as Ultimate Reality: An Outline of the Covenant Theology of Johannes Cocceius (1603–1669)', *Ultimate Reality and Meaning: Interdisciplinary Studies in the Philosophy of Understanding* 21 (1998), 35–47 (41).

[34] Johannes Cocceius, *Summa doctrinae de foedere et testamento Dei* (Franeker, 1648). Lutheran theologian Georg Calixt set out a similar view in *De pactis quae Deus cum homninibus iniit* (Helmstedt, 1654). For a summary of their views see Arlis John Ehlen, 'Old Testament

6.1 HISTORY WARS

This implied a progressive divine revelation in historical time, with the content of revelation being matched to stages of the development of the human race.[35] The idea, which could also imply a corresponding historical development in the intellectual maturity of humanity, was later articulated in a different form by Gotthold Lessing and subsequently by nineteenth-century theologians who would speak directly of 'progressive revelation'.

These new readings of history represent a significant departure from previous Christian versions of the philosophy of history. The earlier historiography had typically observed a sharp distinction between the present world, with its trials and tribulations, and the hereafter, which was to bring relief from the many travails of earthly existence. Augustine's *City of God* spoke of an enduring tension between earthly and heavenly cities, but the ultimate end of the citizens of the heavenly city lay beyond historical time. The sphere of profane history, the *saeculum*, which lay between the coming of the Christ and the end of time, was essentially devoid of historical significance.[36]

Theology as *Heilsgeschichte*', *Concordia Theological Monthly* 35 (1964), 517–44 (523–5). The other relevant aspect of covenantal theology was the uptake of the notion of covenant in political theory, most notably in Hobbes. Both rely upon the notion of a 'representative person'. In the case of the covenantal theology it is successively Adam and Christ, who stand in for the whole human race. For Hobbes, it is the sovereign (or sovereign body). Hobbes, *Leviathan* 2.18, vol. 2, p. 264. Cf. Perkins, *Exposition of the Creed*, pp. 110f.; Samuel Pufendorf, *Divine Feudal Law* [1703] §§22–6 (Indianapolis: Liberty Fund, 2002), pp. 67–74, and *passim*. Thus, A. P. Martinich: 'Just as Adam and Jesus are representative persons in virtue of whom humans are either punished or saved, so the sovereign is a representative person in virtue of whom citizens are saved from the dangers of the state of nature.' *The Two Gods of Leviathan: Thomas Hobbes on Religion and Politics* (Cambridge: Cambridge University Press, 1992), pp. 149f. See also Ian Harris, 'The Politics of Christianity', in *Locke's Philosophy: Content and Context*, ed. G. A. J. Rogers (Oxford: Oxford University Press, 1994), pp. 197–216; Christopher Hill, 'Covenantal Theology and the Concept of a "Public Person"', in *Collected Essays*, vol. 3 (Brighton: Harvester Press, 1985), pp. 300–24 (pp. 304f.); Victoria Kahn, *Wayward Contracts: The Crisis of Political Obligation in England, 1640–1674* (Princeton: Princeton University Press, 2004), pp. 51, 55f.

[35] There is some debate about whether these phases should be read as stages of history, or stages in the religious life of the individual, or both. For the historical reading see G. Schrenk, *Gottesreich und Bund im älteren Protestantismus, vornehmlich bei Johannes Coccejus* (Basel: Brunnen-Verlag, 1985). For the debate, see Willem van Asselt, *The Federal Theology of Johannes Coccejus (1603–1669)* (Leiden: Brill, 2001).

[36] For Augustine's theory of history: R. A. Marcus, *Saeculum: History and Society in the Theology of Augustine* (Cambridge: Cambridge University Press, 1970), pp. 17–21; Löwith, *Meaning in History*, pp. 166–73; Theodor E. Mommsen, 'St. Augustine and the Christian Idea of Progress', *Journal of the History of Ideas* 12 (1951), 364–74. Augustine postulated stages of history, based on the days of creation. The age following the coming of Christ was the sixth and final stage. Augustine, *On the catechizing of the uninstructed* 22.39 (*NPNF* I, vol. 3, p. 307). Augustine also allowed for stages in the education of the human race. *City of God* 10.14. While Augustine might be taken as representing the 'official' position of the medieval Church, apocalyptic readings of history were not uncommon in the first

Earthly kingdoms might rise and fall, but there was no directional movement towards a more perfect or just society and scope for both good and evil to flourish. Aquinas would observe, along similar lines, that 'there is no sure order apparent in human events', explaining that this had led many to conclude that history was governed by fate.[37] It was only by faith that Christians could affirm that history was governed by divine providence. John Calvin would agree. Although historical events are in fact ordered by God, it can seem to us that they are fortuitous.[38] This view of things was reflected in the expression 'the invisible hand' which in its original early modern usages referred to God's unseen providential guidance of history.[39] In all this, there was little thought that the perfections of the world to come might be realised within the span of secular time.

In keeping with this conception of history, progress had commonly been understood by classical and Christian authors as something that took place at the level of the individual. Secular history might have had no end (*telos*) towards which it was striving, but human souls did. Progress consisted in the cultivation of the virtues, understood as those capacities that promoted the accomplishment of our natural (and for medieval Christian thinkers, supernatural) ends. Seneca, for example, explained that progress was to be understood not in terms of the sequential discovery of ingenious inventions, but as the movement of the soul towards wisdom, in which lies its natural perfection.[40] Medieval understandings of the development of the

three centuries and neither were they completely absent between the time of Augustine and Joachim. See, e.g., Richard Landes, 'Lest the Millennium be Fulfilled: Apocalyptic Expectations and the Pattern of Western Chronography, 100–800 CE', in *The Use and Abuse of Eschatology in the Middle Ages*, ed. W. Verbeke, D. Verhelst, and A. Welkenhuysen (Leuven: Leuven University Press, 1988), pp. 137–211.

[37] Aquinas, *Commentary on Job*, p. 7.

[38] Calvin, *Institutes* 1.16.9, vol. 1, p. 180. Protestant confessions of faith would uniformly condemn the 'Epicurean' view that history was governed by chance. See Joost Hengstmengel, 'Divine Oeconomy: The Role of Providence in Early Modern Economic Thought before Adam Smith', PhD thesis, Erasmus University Rotterdam, 2015, pp. 26f.

[39] Peter Harrison, 'Adam Smith and the History of the Invisible Hand', *Journal of the History of Ideas* 72 (2011), 29–49. Calvin's *Institutes* would refer to the secret stirring of the hand of God: '*ex secreta manus Dei agitatione prodire*'. John Calvin, *Institutio christianae religionis* (Londini, 1576), p. 85; Fr. the 'secret movement of the hand of God' [*mouvement secret de la main de Dieu*]. *Institution de la religion chrétienne par Jean Calvin* (Genève, 1888), p. 96. An eighteenth-century translation would use 'the invisible hand'. John Calvin, *The Institution of the Christian religion*, I.xvi.9, trans. Thomas Norton (Glasgow, 1762), bk. 1, p. 84.

[40] Seneca, *Epistles* 89.4; 90.24–9 (LCL 76, pp. 380–1, 412–19). Cf. Marcus Aurelius: 'That which is the purpose of each thing's construction and the destination of that construction is the destination of its progress; the destination of its progress is that in which its goal lies; where its goal lies is where each thing's advantage and good lie.' *Meditations* 5.16, trans. David Sedley, *Creationism and Its Critics*, p. 237. Cf. LCL 15, pp. 116f.

virtues – intellectual, moral, and theological habits that perfected different aspects of human nature – also exemplified this conception of personal progress. When Aquinas came to speak of progress in science, he had in mind individuals becoming more proficient in the performance of certain cognitive operations.[41] Because it was necessarily confined to the individual, this was not a progress that could be either cumulative or corporate. This conception was consistent, however, with the idea of the *saeculum* as the evanescent temporal frame within which individual souls would conduct their earthly pilgrimage, all the while oriented towards a world that was beyond time. This understanding of progress would inform John Bunyan's classic *The Pilgrim's Progress* (1678), an allegorical account of the progress of 'Christian' who is making his way from 'this world to that which is to come'.[42] In the next century the non-conformist clergyman Philip Doddridge could still write of *The Rise and Progress of Religion in the Soul* (1745). This best-selling work, to which William Wilberforce reported he owed his conversion, again exemplified the idea of progress as personal development.[43]

The modern projection of personal progress onto history was facilitated by a revision in how the virtues were understood.[44] This is evident in the way in which the Christian virtue of charity came to be linked with scientific practice and the promotion of human welfare. Reflecting on the Pauline maxim that 'knowledge puffs up while charity edifies' (I Cor. 8:1), Francis Bacon wrote that the true goal of scientific knowledge was not 'for pleasure of mind' but 'for the benefit and use of life; and that they perfect and govern it in charity'.[45] Contra Aquinas, the intellectual virtue of science (*scientia*), and the theological virtue of charity (*caritas*), were to be directed

---

[41] 'science can increase in itself by addition; thus when anyone learns several conclusions of geometry, the same specific habit of science increases in that man'. Aquinas, *ST* 1a2ae, 52, 2. Cf. *ST* 1a2ae, 54, 4; 2a2ae, 1, 7. The Latin for progress here is *profectus*, etymologically related to the English 'proficiency'. For similar usages see Aquinas, *ST* 1a, 43, 6; 1a2ae, 69, 2; 1a2ae, 87, 7; 1a2ae, 114, 8; 2a2ae, 24, 9. Also Peter Lombard, *Sententiarum*, bk. 2, dist. 24, pt. 1, chs. 1–3, *PL* 192: 701f. Lombard speaks of *proficere* (advance) and *profectus* (progress). See the discussion in Harrison, *Territories*, pp. 120–4.

[42] John Bunyan, *The Pilgrim's Progress* (London, 1678).

[43] Philip Doddridge, *The Rise and Progress of Religion in the Soul* (London, 1745). For earlier examples see John Smith, *Select Discourses*, p. 439; John Welles, *The Soules Progresse to the Celestiall Canaan* (London, 1639); Thomas Bromley, *The Way to the Sabbath of Rest, or The Souls Progress* (London, 1655); Anon., *Mundorum Explicatio ... shewing the True Progress of the Soul, from the Court of Babylon to the City of Jerusalem* (London, 1663).

[44] For a more extended argument to this effect see Harrison, *Territories*, pp. 117–36. More generally, on the modern eclipse of the virtues, see MacIntyre, *After Virtue*.

[45] Bacon, *Great Instauration*, *Works*, vol. 4, pp. 20f. Cf. Bacon, *Valerius Terminus*, *Works*, vol. 3, pp. 221f. See also Jerome B. Schneewind, 'Philosophical Ideas of Charity: Some Historical Reflections', in *Giving: Western Ideas of Philanthropy*, ed. Jerome B. Schneewind

towards the exterior goal of human welfare rather than just the perfection of the soul in preparation for the world to come. It is this revised understanding that makes it possible for an institution – *a* charity – to instantiate what had hitherto been regarded as a personal virtue. The same would be true of the new scientific institutions. Early modern experimental philosophers would argue that the practice of science, in theory at least, satisfied the two fundamental Christian commandments: love of God, because science uncovered the wisdom of God in nature; love of neighbour, because the practical benefits conferred by scientific study contributed to the relief of the human estate.[46] For their part, traditionalist critics of the new scientific approaches countered that the moral edification of the individual should be the primary goal of scientific activity.[47] These changes were related to the transformation of that other theological virtue, 'faith', by which it became possible to speak of *the* faith, understood in terms of an objective body of knowledge.[48] As already noted, the object of the third of the theological virtues, hope, became for some an idealised society that would be realised within historical time.[49] The precedent of inserting the eschaton into secular history provided the model for the progressivist histories of the Enlightenment *philosophes*, with Francis Bacon's eschatological reading of the significance of the rise of science representing an intermediate stage.[50]

(Bloomington: Indiana University Press, 1996), pp. 54–75; 'The Misfortunes of Virtue', in *Virtue Ethics*, ed. Roger Crisp and Michael Slote (Oxford: Oxford University Press, 1997), pp. 178–200.

[46] Joseph Glanvill, 'Usefulness of Real Philosophy to Religion', pp. 5, 25, in *Essays*; Robert Boyle, *Some Considerations*, Works, vol. 3, p. 192; Sprat, *History of the Royal Society*, pp. 322f.; John Edwards, *A Demonstration of the Existence and Providence of God* (London, 1696), pt. I, pp. 206–15, pt. II, p. 150.

[47] Casaubon, *Letter concerning Natural Experimental Philosophie*, pp. 5, 24, 31. Stubbe, *Campanella Revived*, p. 14; *Plus Ultra reduced to a Non-Plus*, p. 13. The two versions of improvement were not necessarily mutually exclusive, and Bacon and other advocates of experimental sciences were not uninterested in self-improvement, not least because the practice of science was thought to call for particular virtues on the part of the practitioner.

[48] Conceptions and the status of certain vices would also change. Curiosity thus became an intellectual virtue rather than a vice. See Harrison, 'Curiosity, Forbidden Knowledge'. More generally, the quest for material prosperity had been dissociated from the traditional vice of avarice. See Albert O. Hirschman, *The Passions and the Interests: Political Arguments for Capitalism before Its Triumph* (Princeton: Princeton University Press, 2013); Gregory, *Unintended Reformation*, pp. 285–91.

[49] A further linguistic marker of these changes was the invention of the English word 'improvement', which would eventually displace 'reformation' and 'revolution' which imply cataclysmic historical rather than gradual, cumulative, amelioration. See Slack, *Invention of Improvement*, esp. pp. 1–2.

[50] For Ernest Lee Tuveson, the 'almost sacred character of the dogma of unilinear progress was connected with a faith in progressive redemption through temporal history'.

In all of this, an incipient Protestant naturalism was also given a historical dimension. This arose out of the partitioning of historical time on the basis of the perceived legitimacy of miracles. A common feature of Protestant historiography, directly relevant to the history of modern naturalism, was a restriction of the performance of genuine miracles to the first few centuries of the Christian era. Catholic apologists, as already noted, had claimed that the ongoing performance of miracles in their tradition, unmatched by their Protestant counterparts, vindicated the truth of Catholicism.[51] Protestants responded that 'papist' miracles were necessarily fraudulent because the age of true miracles had long ended.[52] Miracles had been requisite in the apostolic era, it was conceded, but with the secure establishment of the Christian Church they became surplus to requirements. German reformer Zacharias Ursinus declared that the gifts of prophecy and miracle-working were bestowed upon 'certain men and certain times'. These were 'necessary for

Millennium and Utopia: A Study in the Background of the Idea of Progress (Berkeley: University of California Press, 1949), p. 201. On progress as secularised eschatology see also Löwith, *Meaning in History*, pp. 44, 188f., 200–3; Voegelin, *The New Science of Politics*, pp. 183–5.

[51] Robert Bellarmine thus asserted that miracles were one of the marks of the true Catholic Church. *De controversiis christianae, tom 1* (Lyon, 1596), ch. 14 (cols. 1006–13). Cf. Edmund Lechmere, *A Consultation about Religion, or What Religion is Best* (London, 1693), pp. 29–37; E. W., *A Discourse of Miracles wrought in the Roman Catholick Church* (Antwerp, 1676).

[52] On the cessation of miracles see Thomas Fuller, *The Holy State and the Profane State*, 3rd ed. (London, 1652), 39; James I, *Dæmonologie, in Forme of a Dialogue* (Edinburgh, 1597), pp. 65f.; John White, *The Way to the True Church*, 2nd ed. (London, 1610), pp. 301f.; Reginald Scot, *The Discoverie of Witchcraft* [1584] (Totowa: Rowman & Littlefield, 1973), pp. 125–34; Thomas Beverly, *A Discourse upon the Powers of the World to Come* (London, 1694), pp. 46–58; William Whiston, *Mr. W's Account of the Exact Time when Miraculous Gifts Ceas'd in the Church* (London, 1749), pp. 7, 9–11; Conyers Middleton, *A Free Enquiry into the Miraculous Powers which are supposed to have subsisted in the Christian Church* (London, 1749). Also D. P. Walker, 'The Cessation of Miracles', in *Hermeticism and the Renaissance: Intellectual History and the Occult in Early Modern Europe*, ed. Ingrid Merkel and Alan Debus (Washington, DC: Folger Shakespeare Library, 1988), pp. 110–24. The official position did not mean, however, that miracles were completely absent from the religious experiences of those living in Protestant territories. See especially Jane Shaw, *Miracles in Enlightenment England* (New Haven: Yale University Press, 2006). For discussions of the persistence of the miraculous see Keith Thomas, *Religion and the Decline of Magic* (New York: Scribner's, 1971), pp. 126–8; Rosemary Moore, 'Late Seventeenth-Century Quakerism and the Miraculous: A New Look at George Fox's "*Book of Miracles*"', in *Signs, Wonders, Miracles: Representations of Divine Power in the Life of the Church*, ed. Kate Cooper and Jeremy Gregory (Woodbridge: Boydell, 2005), pp. 335–44; Cameron, *Interpreting Christian History*, pp. 67–73; Alexandra Walsham, 'Invisible Helpers: Angelic Interventions in Post-Reformation England', *Past and Present* 208 (2010), 77–130. For the connection between the cessation of miracles and disenchantment more generally, see Robert A. Yelle, '"An Age of Miracles": Disenchantment as Secularized Theological Narrative', in *Narratives of Disenchantment*, ed. Yelle and Trein, pp. 129–48.

the Apostles and the primitive Church when the Gospel was first to be dispersed'.[53] The clear implication was that the era of miracle-working had now passed and that present-day miraculous performances should be treated with scepticism or even condemnation. John Calvin accordingly declared contemporary miracles to be 'mere delusions of Satan'.[54] The Puritan theologian William Perkins (1558–1602), agreed that the gift of performing miracles ceased about two hundred years after Christ, coinciding with the inception of 'popery': 'the true gift of miracles then ceased, and instead thereof came in delusions and lying wonders by the effectual working of Satan'.[55] The first systematic critiques of miracles in the West, and their identification with a discrete period of historical time, were thus pioneered by Protestant polemicists.

The large-scale confessional works of church history incorporated this perspective into their plotlines. On the Protestant side, the miracles of late antiquity and the Middle Ages correlated directly with a putative growth in superstition, credulity, and fraud. The monumental *Epitome of Church History* (1592–1604), compiled by the Lutheran theologian and composer Lucas Osiander the Elder (1534–1604), informs us that in the late sixth and early seventh century 'we enter the sea of superstitious cults .... There are many miracles ascribed to bishops, monks, and hermits ... which either never happened, but were invented by vain people and then taken up and spread abroad by foolish and credulous people as though they were true.'[56] In his apologetic account of 'the Protestant Religion', the English independent theologian John Owen (1616–83) agreed: 'Before the Reformation, possessions, apparitions, sprites, ghosts, fiends, with silly miracles about them, filled all places.'[57] These judgements were aligned with the timetable of events provided by the exegesis of biblical prophetic works. The book

---

[53] Zacharias Ursinus, *The Summe of Christian Religion* [1587–9] (London, 1645), p. 342.
[54] Calvin, *Institutes*, Prefatory Address, vol. 1, p. 10. Cf. John Calvin, *Tracts and Treatises on the Reformation of the Church*, 3 vols., trans. H. Beveridge (Edinburgh: Banner of Truth, 1844), vol. 1, p. 92; *Commentary on the Gospel According to John*, in *Calvin's Commentaries*, vol. 17, pp. 89f., 180f.; vol. 18, p. 281. See also Moshe Sluhovsky, 'Calvinist Miracles and the Concept of the Miraculous', *Reformation and Renaissance Review* 19 (1995), 5–21.
[55] William Perkins, *A Discourse of the Damned Art of Witchcraft* (Cambridge, 1610), pp. 238f. See also Thomas Beard, *Antichrist the Pope of Rome* (London, 1625), pp. 301–29; Fuller, *Church-History of Britain*, pp. 332–4.
[56] Lucas Osiander the Elder, *Epitomes Historiae Ecclesiasticae, Centuriae I.–XVI.*, 10 vols. (Tübingen, 1592–1604), Cent. 6 [vol. 5], pp. 3–4, trans. Euan Cameron, in *Interpreting Christian History*, p. 139. Osiander goes on to ascribe this to the work of Satan and the Antichrist.
[57] John Owen, *The State and Fate of the Protestant Religion* in *The Works of John Owen*, 16 vols., ed. William H. Gold (Edinburgh: Banner of Truth Trust, 1965), vol. 14, p. 539.

of Revelation had predicted that the Antichrist would perform 'great and miraculous signs' (13.13), seducing the people away from the true faith.[58] The use of biblical prophecy to structure historical time and secure the legitimacy of Protestant religion was thus closely tied to claims about the credibility of miracle reports associated with particular stages of history.

These theological judgements licensed scepticism about medieval and contemporary miracles in the philosophical literature. Thomas Hobbes, for example, appealed to the Protestant principle of the cessation of miracles as grounds for denying the 'pretended revelations' or 'inspirations' of private individuals.[59] Confessional disputes thus prompted a partition of history that allowed for the performance of genuine miracles in the distant past but offered a prima facie reason for denying them in the present. History could be divided into a period in which miracle reports were deemed credible, followed by another in which they were not. For Protestants, the challenge was to limit the temporal range of scepticism about miracles so that it did not impinge upon the credibility of the gospel accounts. However, to all appearances, miracles looked the same whenever performed: it was only the hypothesis of the hidden workings of providence, along with a conviction of the veracity of scripture, that gave the 'cessation of miracles' principle its explanatory force. In the absence of that commitment, we end up with Hume's version of history, in which Protestant scepticism about miracle-working is simply to be extended to *all* miracle reports.[60]

Hume, accordingly, signalled his indebtedness to Protestant critiques of Catholic miracles in the opening lines of his celebrated argument.[61] Huxley would also appeal to Protestant arguments and remark that 'the evidence for the later, is just as good as the evidence for the earlier wonders'.[62] Looking forward, the relevant division of history would be understood in terms of

---

[58] See, e.g., George Downame, *A Treatise concerning Antichrist* (London, 1603), pp. 106–25; Edmund Hall, Ἡ ἀπωστασία ὁ ἀντίχριστος: *Or, A Scriptural Discourse of the Apostasie and the Antichrist* (London, 1653), pp. 146–8; Henry Burton, *The seuen vials or a briefe and plaine exposition vpon the 15: and 16: chapters of the Revelation* (London, 1658), pp. 99–101; Beard, *Antichrist the Pope*, pp. 301–30.

[59] Hobbes, *Leviathan* 3.32, vol. 3, p. 584. Cf. Hobbes, *An Answer to Bishop Bramhall*, in *English Works*, ed. Molesworth, vol. 4, pp. 326–7.

[60] Conyers Middleton had identified the difficulty. We may grant the principle that miracles 'continued as long as they were necessary for the Church', but authors will 'extend that necessity to what length they please, or as far as they find it agreeable to the several systems, which they had previously entertained about them'. *Free Inquiry*, p. xi.

[61] Hume readily conceded that the argument of 'Of Miracles' was indebted to Anglican Archbishop John Tillotson's argument against the Catholic doctrine of transubstantiation. *Essay*, p. 109.

[62] Huxley, 'Agnosticism and Christianity', *CE*, vol. 5, p. 332.

the maturation of the human race from barbarism to civilisation, postulated as resulting from a process of natural development rather than a providential dispensation in the apostolic age. We might conclude, with the benefit of hindsight, that the arguments of Protestants and Romanists, considered together, gave rise to a kind of mutually assured destruction of the credibility of miracle reports, and that that was seized upon by more sceptical Enlightenment thinkers.

Doubts about miracle-working and the universalisation of the 'age of superstition' were destined to become central motifs of Enlightenment versions of history. The French *philosophes* would appropriate the darkness-to-light periodisation scheme of Protestant polemicists, ensuring that 'Enlightenment' came to be associated with their endeavours rather than those of the religious reformers. Their structuring of history would be shaped by the secularisation of eschatological hopes, originally essayed in various religiously inspired reform projects that had been associated with the new sciences. This gave rise to a new idea of progress and the embedding within secular history of the ideal of an amelioration of the human condition, now understood largely in terms of material welfare rather the spiritual salvation. The providential oversight of history was replaced by a conception of historical development governed by what were imagined to be natural laws.[63] These laws typically described stages of human progress, expressed in terms of inevitable displacement of 'primitive' metaphorical conceptions of nature by more accurate scientific ones. The advent of the new science (experimental natural philosophy) was also now written into the story, gradually assuming for itself the reforming role it had once shared with the Renaissance and Protestant Reformation. Science would come to represent the culminating stage of history, displacing earlier magic and religious stages. The coincidental development of a generic category 'religion' also facilitated the wider application of sceptical arguments originally developed in the context of confessional polemics. Protestant criticisms of Catholicism, especially those relating to miracles and the role of popes and priests, would now be applied indiscriminately to 'religion' in general. Similarly, the model of Catholicism as an unfortunate diversion from the natural course of history would be generalised into 'deviation' and 'blockage' plotlines that would identify a generic 'religion' as a historical handbrake on scientific progress. 'Superstitious' medieval Catholicism came to

---

[63] We might also think of this transition in terms of a move away from history grounded in philology and humanistic scholarship, to one informed by theological or philosophical reason. On this theme see J. G. A. Pocock, *Barbarism and Religion*, 6 vols. (Cambridge: Cambridge University Press, 1999–2015), vol. 5.

be understood as the religious rule rather than the exception. This led to the construction of narratives in which religion was posited as the prime inhibitor of the natural progression of the human race. In turn, this contributed to an increasingly common modernity story about an enduring historical struggle between faith and reason, or religion and science.

6.2 From Reform to Progress

One of the central motifs of Protestant histories that carried over into the writings of the eighteenth-century French *philosophes* was the idea of the Middle Ages as a period of superstition and incontinent miracle-working. Enlightenment thinkers were also given to writing themselves into history, with their own age of light conceptualised as humanity coming to its senses after a period of irrational darkness. Bernard Fontenelle (1657–1757) thus compared the history of Europe to a patient recovering from a long illness. For Charles Perrault (1628–1703), the arts and sciences were streams that had flowed underground for the period of the Middle Ages, eventually finding an opening to 'come forth again with the same abundance in which they had gone under'.[64] The theme of a subterranean survival, pioneered by the Protestant historians, was thus adapted by the *philosophes* to a rather different end. There was a new assumption of the inevitability of human progress, provided that inhibitory mechanisms to human advancement could be effectively nullified. These Enlightenment thinkers agreed with Protestant polemicists that the barrier to human progress was religious in nature but expanded arguments against Catholicism into a historical critique of religion in general. As for the motor of historical progress, this was no longer a divine providence occasionally made visible in the fulfilment of prophetic utterances, but 'laws' imagined to be inherent in historical processes.

The move to understand historical and social development in terms of such laws is already apparent in the Baron de Montesquieu's *The Spirit of Law* (1748). In his observations of the rise and fall of civilisations, Montesquieu contended that 'it is not chance that rules the world' but 'general causes, moral and physical, which act in every monarchy, elevating it, maintaining it, or hurling it to the ground'.[65] Montesquieu was no Panglossian advocate

---

[64] Fontenelle and Perrault both cited in Nathan Edelman, *Attitudes of Seventeenth-Century France toward the Middle Ages* (New York: King's Crown Press, 1946), pp. 14–18. Huxley employs a similar metaphor in 'The Progress of Science' [1887], *CE*, vol. 1, pp. 43, 44.

[65] Charles Louis Montesquieu, *Considerations on the Causes of the Greatness of the Romans and Their Decline*, trans. David Lowenthal (Indianapolis: Hackett, 1965), p. 120. The original

of historical progress. But his idea that laws of some kind might preside over the affairs of the human race became a feature of French Enlightenment historiography. One of the first prophets of progress, Anne Robert Jacques Turgot (1727–81), proposed that all the phenomena of nature, including the development of societies, are governed by 'constant laws'. Humanity, in his view, was destined to progress by means of revolutions that were of essentially the same type: 'The whole human race, through alternative periods of rest and unrest, of weal and woe, goes on advancing, although at a slow pace, towards greater perfection.'[66] For Turgot, revolutions in thought had taken place at two crucial historical junctures, giving rise to three distinct phases of human development. The earliest attempts to describe the phenomena of nature suffer from a failure of language, with primitive peoples resorting to 'allegories and fables to explain physical phenomena'. In the next phase, metaphysicians recognise 'the absurdity of these fables' and move to causal explanations of phenomena 'by way of abstract expressions like essences and faculties'. The final stage comes with the advent of mechanical and experimental philosophy, with a modern science based on observation offering a true account of the operations of nature.[67] Succession through these three stages, which clearly anticipate the later and better-known schema of Auguste Comte, owes little to the work of providence, being brought about instead by invariable laws.[68] Unlike most of the *philosophes*, Turgot allowed that Christianity had conferred significant benefits on the human race. But he shared with them the idea that the natural tendency of societies is to progress unless hindered by factors such as religiously motivated irrationality. The case Turgot had in mind was 'Mohammedanism', which 'opposes the wall of superstition to the natural march of improvement'.[69]

For many of his compatriots, Christianity had erected as many, if not more, walls of this nature: it was simply politic to direct censures of superstition in

---

speaks of 'Fortune' rather than 'chance'. *Considérations sur les causes de la grandeur des Romains et de leur décadence* (Amsterdam, 1734), p. 202. *De l'esprit des loix*, 2 vols., 1748, was originally published anonymously in Geneva.

[66] Anne Robert Jacques Turgot, *A Philosophical Review of the Successive Advances of the Human Mind* [1750], in *Turgot on Progress, Sociology, and Economics*, ed. and trans. Ronald L. Meek (Cambridge: Cambridge University Press, 1973), p. 41. See also Meek's introduction, p. 11.

[67] Turgot, *On Universal History*, in *Turgot on Progress*, pp. 92, 102.

[68] J. B. Bury points to the parallels between Turgot and Comte. *Idea of Progress: An Enquiry into Its Origin and Growth* (London: Macmillan, 1920), p. 157. See also Ronald Meek's introduction to *Turgot on Progress*.

[69] Turgot, *On Universal History*, in *Turgot on Progress*, p. 83. Ernest Renan would later contend that both Islam and Christianity had sought to impede scientific advance, the difference being that Islam succeeded whereas Christianity ultimately failed. *L'islamisme et la science* (Paris, 1883).

another direction. Abbé de Saint Pierre (1658–1743) had earlier produced a *Discourse against Mahometism*, focusing much of his criticism on its supposedly miraculous foundation. Voltaire astutely judged this work to be a thinly veiled attack on the supernatural elements of Christianity.[70] That the Abbé's target was miraculous relations in general is supported by his proposal that in order to diminish our 'tendency toward fanaticism' the Academy of Science offer an annual prize for the best naturalistic explanation of 'the prodigies that are related in the books of the Greeks and Romans, and the pretended miracles reported by the Protestants, schismatics, and Mahometans'.[71] The exclusion of Catholicism hardly mattered, given the genre of events in question. This attitude was accompanied by a formal understanding of the stages of progress of the human race. The Abbé's most celebrated publication, his *Project for Perpetual Peace in Europe* (1713), set out a novel division of historical periods, premised on the claim that the ancient poets had been mistaken about the legendary golden age and the succession of inferior ages that followed. Rather than an event in the distant past, the golden age was only now on the verge of being realised, as the last of a series beginning with the iron age. The 'savages' of Tartary, Africa, and America still languished at this infantile stage. It was followed, in succession, by the ages of bronze and silver.[72]

Diderot and d'Alembert's *Encyclopédie* filled out this revised version of this history with more details. In the Preliminary Discourse to the work, d'Alembert extended the dark ages to some twelve centuries. With the rise to power of the Church in the fourth century, ecclesiastical authorities 'forced reason to silence' almost to the point of 'forbidding the human race to think'. This phase would last until the Enlightenment – 'the light which gradually, by imperceptible degrees, would illuminate the world'. The Protestant originators of this motif were themselves now cast into the shadows. The true bearers of light, according to d'Alembert, were men of science: Bacon, Descartes, Newton, Locke, Galileo, Harvey, and Huygens.[73] In contrast to the Baconian periodisation, which coupled the Reformation and scientific revolution, Europe's epochal shift from benighted superstition to enlightenment was postponed and the religious reformations of

---

[70] Abbé de Saint Pierre, in *L'Abbé de Saint-Pierre, Sa Vie et ses Oeuvres*, ed. M. G. de Molinari (Paris, 1857), pp. 268–86. For Voltaire's assessment, see Molinari's comments, pp. 267f.
[71] Abbé de Saint Pierre, *Explication physique d'une apparition*, Oeuvres, pp. 286–302 (p. 302).
[72] Abbé de Saint Pierre, *Projet pour rendre la paix perpétuelle en Europe*, Oeuvres, pp. 139–41.
[73] Jean Le Rond d'Alembert, *Preliminary Discourse to the Encyclopedia of Diderot* [1751], trans. Richard N. Schwab (Chicago: University of Chicago Press, 1995), pp. 71, 73. Cf. Condorcet: 'Three great men have marked the transition from this stage of history to the

the sixteenth century nudged backwards in the direction of the barbarous Middle Ages. The idea of common ground between the reformations of religion and of science was surreptitiously replaced by a different story about an inevitable and long-standing conflict between science and religion. As evidence of this conflict, the Preliminary Discourse identified what would become two recurring tropes in subsequent repetitions of this new narrative: the flat earth myth and the Galileo affair.[74] The fact that the imagined scientific heroes of Enlightenment had, for the most part, urged the complementarity of science and religion was either silently ignored or countered with a rewritten history. Newton's piety and predilection for writing works of theology and biblical chronology was a particular problem, given his status as an icon of the Enlightenment. Accordingly, efforts were made to distance Newton's metaphysical and religious commitments from his science and to refashion Newtonian physics into a weapon that could be deployed against religion – directly contrary to what Newton himself had intended.[75]

Nicolas de Condorcet's *Sketch for a Historical Picture of the Progress of the Human Spirit* (1795), written in the immediate wake of the French Revolution (to which, ironically, he would eventually fall victim) brought together a number of key themes of French Enlightenment theories of history. At a general level, historical progress is governed by laws akin to those that are observed in the development of the human mind.[76] Applied to the specific case of European history, what we observe is that the fourth-century

---

next: Bacon, Galileo, Descartes.' Marquis de Condorcet, *Sketch for a Historical Picture of the Progress of the Human Spirit* [1795], in *Condorcet: Political Writings*, ed. Steven Lukes and Nadia Urbinati (Cambridge: Cambridge University Press, 2012), p. 87.

[74] d'Alembert, *Preliminary Discourse*, p. 73; Condorcet, *Sketch*, p. 87.

[75] 'When I wrote my treatise about our Systeme [the *Principia*] I had an eye upon such Principles as might work with considering men for the beleife of a Deity & nothing can rejoyce me more then to find it usefull for that purpose.' Newton to Bentley, 10 December 1692, www.newtonproject.ox.ac.uk/view/texts/normalized/THEM00254, accessed 4 April 2022. On Enlightenment reconstructions of Newton see J. B. Shank, *The Newton Wars and the Beginning of the French Enlightenment* (Chicago: University of Chicago Press, 2008) and 'Between Isaac Newton and Enlightenment Newtonianism', in *Science without God?*, ed. Harrison and Roberts, pp. 77–96; Rebekah Higgitt, 'Introduction', *Early Biographies of Isaac Newton 1660–1885*, 2 vols., ed. Rebekah Higgitt (London: Pickering & Chatto, 2006), vol. 2, pp. x–xiii. Consider, also, John Tyndall's mistaken assertion that Newton's 'best years' were devoted to his science, and his dotage to theology. 'Belfast Address', p. 453. Tyndall also found it necessary to discount Michael Faraday's conspicuous religiosity. 'Life and Letters of Faraday', *Fragments of Science*, pp. 303–20 (p. 381).

[76] Condorcet, *Sketch*, p. 2. Elsewhere Condorcet developed an elaborate mathematical model of social development. See Keith Michael Baker, *Condorcet: From Natural Philosophy to Social Mathematics* (Chicago: University of Chicago Press, 1975).

triumph of Christianity led to the complete stultification of philosophy and the sciences.[77] Condorcet argued that disdain for the sciences was a signal characteristic of Christianity because the sciences are 'very dangerous to the success of miracles'. The specific case of Christianity exemplified a broader theory of religion and its origins. Following Turgot, Condorcet proposed that it was the inadequacies of primitive language that had led to the rise of religious mythology and superstition: 'In the infancy of language, every word is a metaphor and every phrase an allegory.' As a consequence, when the priests sought to describe 'metaphysical notions' and 'scientific truths' they ended up laying the foundations of the most 'absurd beliefs'. This, according to Condorcet, accounted for 'the origin of almost all known religions'.[78] Religion was thus an erroneous way of looking at the world that arose out of the linguistic confusions of primitive peoples.[79] While religion had been cynically sustained by the interests of the priesthood, it was destined to be replaced by the more precise rational and philosophical languages of an enlightened Europe.

As already noted, part of what made this revised version of events possible was a new, generic category 'religion', of which both Protestantism and Catholicism could be regarded as specific forms. To these were added the newly imagined religions of the world. Not only was the religious disunity of Christendom projected onto the globe, but various elements of the Christian prototype – scripture, the priesthood, ecclesiastical institutions, rites and rituals, miracles – were presumed to have equivalents in these newly constructed religions. Rather than focusing on differences, as confessional histories had done, a nascent comparative science of religion stressed functional similarities. Paul-Henri Thiry, Baron d'Holbach, could thus explain that 'priest' was a universal type, characteristic of the religious institutions of 'the different peoples of the world'. Priests owed their existence to the superstitious proliferation of religious cults. Human sacrifices at the hands of the priesthood were thus functionally equivalent across religions – whether carried out by the Roman Inquisitors or by priests of

---

[77] Condorcet, *Sketch*, p. 51.   [78] Condorcet, *Sketch*, pp. 25f.
[79] In the background of Condorcet's speculations about the limitations of primitive language was a broader Enlightenment discussion about the possibility of a universal, scientific language that would unambiguously depict reality. The best-known project was John Wilkins, *Essay Towards a Real Character and a Philosophical Language* (London, 1668). See Lewis, *Language, Mind, and Nature*; Jaap Maat, *Philosophical Languages in the Seventeenth Century: Dalgarno, Wilkins, Leibniz* (Dordrecht: Kluwer, 2004). One of the goals of such language schemes was to moderate religious disputes, which were imagined to have arisen out of the ambiguity of religious language. See Wilkins, *Essay*, Epistle Dedicatory.

Aztec religion. Only in places enlightened 'by the light of reason and philosophy' were the excesses of priestcraft held in check.[80] This was the process by which miracles, too, came to be understood as much the same in every religion, with New Testament miracles susceptible to the same arguments that Protestants had once deployed against Catholics. These broad-brush treatments allowed for few shades of difference between the various historical manifestations of an essentialised 'religion'. For late modernity, the core of this generic religion would consist in *belief in the supernatural.*

In all of this, the connection of science to social progress, along with a thesis of the retrograde influence of all forms of Christianity, was central to the Enlightenment propagandists' sense of their own place in the story of human progress.[81] Arguably, their narrative, like Hume's identification of miracles with barbarism, also become integral to modern, secular self-understandings. As Dan Edelstein observed, this Enlightenment model of history is 'the story we tell ourselves about our values, our government, and our religions'. However, it was and remains a 'master narrative of modernity, even a myth'.[82] Because this myth is vital to the identity and self-understanding of those who originated it, and who continue to perpetuate it, it tends to be resistant to the demythologising efforts of historians.

6.3 The Science of Society

The Enlightenment assumption that society advanced in accordance with laws of progress provided a starting point for the development of the modern social sciences. Pioneer of sociology, Auguste Comte (1798–1857), famously proposed that human knowledge advances ineluctably through three successive stages: religious, metaphysical, and positive (or scientific).

---

[80] D'Holbach, 'Prêtres', in *Encyclopédie ou Dictionnaire raisonné des sciences, des arts et des métiers*, vol. 13, pp. 340f.

[81] See, e.g., Voltaire, 'Histoire', in *Encyclopédie ou Dictionnaire raisonné des sciences, des arts et des métiers*, vol. 8, pp. 220b–225b (p. 223a); *The Age of Louis XVI*, in *The Works of M. de Voltaire*, 35 vols. (London, 1761–81), vol. 6, p. 159. Dan Edelstein thus concludes that: 'The narrative of a "new science" progressively dismantling all remnants of superstition and Scholasticism in its way was central to the self-perception of the *philosophes*. Their very identity depended on it; the consciousness of their place in this historical trajectory, which crested in the present, endowed their worldly interventions with greater meaning.' Dan Edelstein, *The Enlightenment: A Genealogy* (Chicago: University of Chicago Press, 2010), p. 1.

[82] Edelstein, *The Enlightenment*, p. 116. 'The Enlightenment' has thus become a talisman for those seeking to endorse a brand of secular rationalism in the present. Stephen Pinker's *Enlightenment Now* (New York: Viking, 2018) represents an attempt to retell this foundational myth.

6.3 THE SCIENCE OF SOCIETY

The first stage is characterised by appeals to the supernatural to account for events in the natural world. In the second, transitory phase, supernatural agency is abstracted into causes. In the final, default stage, the quest for ultimate causal explanation is abandoned and is replaced by explanations in terms of laws. These laws extend to both natural and social worlds.[83]

If resort to supernatural agency was the mark of immature societies it was, for all that, a necessary stage. Possibly for this reason, Comte argued that the overly critical *philosophes* of the previous century had failed to appreciate the value of Christianity.[84] Comte also highlighted the role played by implicit faith in sustaining the authority of spiritual power and he rightly credited the Reformation with its demise. Luther had destroyed 'the principle of blind belief, replacing this principle with critical enquiry'. The latter 'would inevitably expand continuously and in the end embrace an unlimited field'.[85] But Comte also bought into the idea that Christianity (in concert with Platonism) had impeded scientific advance at key historical moments and he repeated what would become standard motifs in the science/religion conflict narrative. Augustine was supposed to have insisted upon a flat earth against the arguments of astronomers.[86] The discoveries

---

[83] Auguste Comte, 'Plan of the Scientific Work Necessary for the Reorganization of Society', and 'Philosophical Considerations on the Sciences and Scientists', both in *Early Political Writings*, ed. and trans. H. S. Jones (Cambridge: Cambridge University Press, 1988), pp. 47, 81f., 155. Comte appended the former work to the fourth volume of his mature *Système de politique positive* (Paris, 1854), Appendix, p. 77.

[84] Comte, 'Plan of Scientific Work', *Early Political Writings*, p. 70. Theological ideas are a way of explaining observed facts and constitute the necessary condition 'of any science at its cradle' (p. 81).

[85] Comte, 'Summary Appraisal of the General Character of Modern History', *Early Political Writings*, p. 10. Cf. pp. 17, 40. Comte also realised that his envisaged scientific society would require implicit faith in 'scientists' (*savants*). But he regarded this as different from 'totally blind submission' since it involved 'assent given to propositions about things that are capable of verification'. Scientists, he realised, also needed to have implicit faith in each other (pp. 41f.).

[86] Comte, 'The Sciences and Scientists', *Early Political Writings*, pp. 178f. No significant Christian thinkers held that the earth was flat. On the origins of the mistaken idea that the ancient and medieval thinkers believed in a flat earth see John Burton Russell, *Inventing the Flat Earth: Columbus and Modern Historians* (New York: Praeger, 1991); Lesley B. Cormack, 'That before Columbus, Geographers and Other Educated People Thought the Earth was Flat', in *Newton's Apple and Other Myths about Science,* ed. Ronald L. Numbers and Kostas Kampourakis (Cambridge, MA: Harvard University Press, 2015), pp. 16–22; James Hannam, *The Globe: How the Earth Became Round* (Chicago: University of Chicago Press, 2023). It has been argued that Isidore of Seville was a flat-earther, but the evidence is inconclusive. The relatively obscure sixth-century monk Cosmas Indicopleustes did propose a flat earth, but had few followers. See Cosmas Indicopleustes, *The Christian Topography of Cosmas, an Egyptian Monk*, ed. and trans. J. W. McCrindle (Cambridge: Cambridge University Press, 2010).

of Copernicus and Galileo were claimed to have been inimical to religion. This was on account of Comte's misplaced affirmation of the idea of a 'Copernican demotion', according to which the displacement of the earth from the centre of the universe precipitated 'the radical destruction of the theological system'. After Copernicus, Comte announced, 'all supernatural doctrines collapse'.[87] As for the Protestant Reformation, in spite of its advocacy of critical enquiry, it was regarded as having come about through a preceding growth in scientific knowledge, in accordance with Comte's understandings of the general laws of human progress.[88] All social advancement was thus ultimately reduced to scientific progress.

Comte sought not merely to describe the development of history, but to make an active contribution to its improvement, founding a 'science of society' that would apply laws to the social world in the manner of physics and by doing so assume the social functions of religion.[89] He called this science 'social physics' or 'sociology'.[90] In common with another of the founders of modern sociology, Émile Durkheim, Comte held that while religion is ostensibly concerned with the supernatural, its true sphere of operation is the ordering of society.[91] The anarchy that followed the French Revolution, for example, was plausibly attributed a loss of the social cohesion once provided by Christianity. For Comte, societies need an organising spirit akin to religion but ideally divested of supernatural elements.[92] Comte thus attempted to inject into the culminating, scientific stage of history a naturalised religion, replete with secular saints, holy days, and places of worship – 'Catholicism minus Christianity', as T. H. Huxley later

---

[87] Comte, 'Character of Modern History', *Early Political Writings*, p. 15. The Copernican demotion thesis is now widely held to be erroneous. See, e.g., Dennis Danielson, 'The Bones of Copernicus', *American Scientist* 97 (2009), 50–7; Michael N. Keas, 'That the Copernican Revolution Demoted the Status of the Earth', in *Newton's Apple*, ed. Numbers and Kampourakis, pp. 23–31.

[88] 'Luther's reformation was, in its turn, only the necessary result of the progress of the sciences of observation ....' Comte, 'Plan of Scientific Work', *Early Political Writings*, p. 52. Cf. p. 92.

[89] Comte thus held both that the development of civilisation is governed by a natural law, *and* that chance and human action play a role. 'Plan of Scientific Work', *Early Political Writings*, pp. 95–8. For a summary of his 'social physics', see 'The Sciences and Scientists', *Early Political Writings*, p. 159.

[90] The French *'sociologie'* was coined by Comte in 1839, but used earlier in an unpublished MS by E. J. Sieyès, in about 1780. See J. Guilhaumou, 'Sieyès et le non-dit de la sociologie: du mot à la chose', *Revue d'histoire des sciences humaines* 15 (2006), 117–34.

[91] Milbank, *Theology and Social Theory*, pp. 62–8.

[92] 'more advanced populations are vainly seeking for an universal religion ... no supernatural religion can satisfy this, the ultimate longing of humanity'. Auguste Comte, *The Catechism of Positivism*, trans. Richard Congreve (London: John Chapman, 1858), pp. 8–9.

6.3 THE SCIENCE OF SOCIETY

derisively described it.[93] A handful of positivist temples still stand in France and Brazil as forlorn relics of Comte's idiosyncratic religious vision. Yet the impulse that motivated this failed attempt to reconcile a secular faith with positive reason still haunts contemporary French social theory and arguably continues to inform modern sociology's 'sacred mission'.[94] Comte's project exemplifies other recurring features of modernity's own account of its origins: an indebtedness to preceding theological analyses (in the case of Comte, the social theology of Henri de Saint-Simon, Joseph de Maistre, and Louis de Bonald), the idea of a progression away from supernaturalism, and the beginnings of rudimentary naturalistic explanations for the prevalence of religion in the earliest stages of human development.[95]

The explicit theological indebtedness of the social sciences is more conspicuous in developments that took place across the channel. The Scottish historian-philosopher Adam Ferguson – another contender for the contested title of 'father of sociology' – made the celebrated observation that 'nations stumble upon establishments, which are indeed the result of human action, but not the execution of any human design'.[96] This establishes the concept of a social organisation that is more than the aggregate of the conscious actions and desires of its individual constituents. Ferguson is clear, however, that despite the absence of human design in the emergence of social order, there is nonetheless a purposeful agency involved – that of a providential Deity. Social organisation is thus the result of divine design, much as the intelligibility of the natural world is the result of divinely authored laws.[97] Ferguson would go on to develop, in typical Enlightenment fashion,

---

[93] T. R. Wright, *The Religion of Humanity: The Impact of Comtean Positivism on Victorian Britain* (Cambridge: Cambridge University Press, 1986); Huxley, 'On the Physical Basis of Life', *CE*, vol. 1, p. 156. These sentiments had strong affinities to earlier post-revolutionary attempts to replace Catholicism with a secular religion of reason. See, e.g., Alphonse Aulard, *Le Culte de la Raison et le Culte de l'Être Supreme* (Paris: Félix Alcan, 1892); Carlton J. H. Hayes, *Nationalism: A Religion* [1926] (London: Routledge, 2016).

[94] Andrew Wernick, *Auguste Comte and the Religion of Humanity: The Post-Theistic Program of French Social Theory* (Cambridge: Cambridge University Press, 2000), pp. 221–66; Christian Smith, *The Sacred Project of American Sociology* (Oxford: Oxford University Press, 2014).

[95] For Comte's theological forebears see Milbank, *Theology and Social Theory*, pp. 52–68.

[96] Adam Ferguson, *An Essay on the History of Civil Society* [1767], ed. Fania Oz-Salzberger (Cambridge: Cambridge University Press, 1995), p. 119, cf. pp. 173f.

[97] 'that physical powers, employed in succession, and combined to a salutary purpose, constitute those very proofs of design from which we infer the existence of God; and that this truth being once admitted, we are no longer to search for the source of existence; we can only collect the laws which the author of nature has established; and in our latest as well as our earliest discoveries, only come to perceive a mode of creation or providence before unknown'. Ferguson, *Essay*, p. 12. For Ferguson's laws of human nature see his *Institutes of Moral Philosophy*, pp. 3–6, 85–90.

a theory that referenced progressive transitions of humanity through three stages of social evolution, in his case 'savage, barbarous, and polished'. These unfold with a certain inevitability (although not irreversibly) as a dimension of the divine design that also permeated nature.[98]

The best-known of Scottish Enlightenment thinkers, Adam Smith (1723–90), had a similar, providentially informed, view of political economy in *The Wealth of Nations* (1776) – although some of his modern acolytes are reluctant to concede this. The expression which is indelibly fused with Smith's name – 'the invisible hand' – had long been understood as denoting the hand of the Deity. God's invisible hand was said to be at work in the course of history, determining the fortunes of earthly kingdoms. The fact that the elliptical descriptions of the fate of the four kingdoms set out in the prophetic book of Daniel were subsequently realised in history, for example, was attributed to the work of God's invisible hand.[99] The expression could also be used as a substitute for 'laws of nature' when speaking of the regularity and intelligibility of nature's operations. The Oxford divine Francis Atterbury (1663–1732), spoke of 'that invisible Hand, which wields the vast Machine, and directs all its Springs and Motions'.[100] Swiss naturalist Charles Bonnet (1720–93), who pioneered the use of the term 'evolution' in a scientific context, proposed that the goal-directed behaviours of animals were to be accounted for by the operation of an invisible hand.[101] It seems likely, given the history of

---

[98] Ferguson was less insistent on the inevitability of progress, however. See Lisa Hill, 'Adam Ferguson and the Paradox of Progress and Decline', *History of Political Thought* 18 (1997), 677–706.

[99] For uses of 'invisible hand' in this context see, e.g., Francis Atterbury, *Fourteen sermons preach'd on several occasions* (London, 1708), p. 252; Tillotson, *Works*, vol. 1, p. 154; Thomas Robinson, *Scripture characters*, 4th ed., 4 vols. (London, 1800), vol. 2, p. 408; Richard Graves, *A sermon on the deliverance of this kingdom*, 3rd ed. (Dublin, 1797), p. 10; Job Orton, *A short and plain exposition of the Old Testament*, 6 vols. (Shrewsbury, 1788–91), vol. 6, p. 247; Nathaniel Stephens, *A plain and easie calculation of the name, mark, and number of the name of the beast* (London, 1656), p. 146; Barrow, *Theological Works*, vol. 4, p. 485. Cf. Louis-Pierre Anquetil, *A summary of universal history*, 9 vols. (London, 1800), vol. 1, p. 212.

[100] Francis Atterbury, *Sermons and discourses on several subjects and occasions*, 2 vols. (London, 1723), vol. 1, p. 249. See also Law, *Call to a Devout and Holy Life*, pp. 444f.; Barker, *Natural Theology*, p. 29. See also Alexander Monro, *Sermons preached upon several occasions* (London, 1691), p. 6; Simon Berington, *Dissertations on the Mosaical creation* (London, 1750), p. 386; Charles Rollin, *The method of teaching and studying the belles lettres*, 4 vols. (London, 1734), vol. 4, p. 219.

[101] 'une main invisible'. Charles Bonnet, *The contemplation of nature*, 2 vols. (London, 1766), vol. 2, p. 208. Cf. *Contemplation de la nature* in *Oeuvres*, 18 vols. (Neuchâtel, 1779–83), vol. 4, p. 443.

6.3 THE SCIENCE OF SOCIETY

the expression, that Smith's use of the term was a deliberate reference to providence.[102] This would be entirely consistent with his earlier remarks in the *Theory of Moral Sentiments* (1759), where it is proposed that human beings act on the basis of particular passions with the unintended consequence of preserving and propagating the species. That end, however, is intended by 'the great Director of nature'.[103]

The cleric and political economist Thomas Malthus (1766–1834) can also be located within this trajectory. Like his French counterparts, Malthus sought to account for the emergence of social order by appealing to laws of nature. It is these laws, rather than 'the conduct and institutions of man', that govern human populations.[104] Accordingly, Malthus also drew upon the principle first articulated by Ferguson, that a certain level of order emerges in societies irrespective of the goals of the individual agents that comprise them: 'By this wise provision [of providence] the most ignorant are led to promote the general happiness, an end which they would have totally failed to attain if the moving principle of their conduct had been benevolence.' All of this he regarded as conformable 'to that system of general laws, according to which the Supreme Being appears with very few exceptions to act'.[105] This invocation of laws was an important aspect of Malthusian theodicy, with 'partial evils' being understood as the regrettable but inevitable by-product of the operation of general laws. These laws Malthus understood as 'calculated to promote the general good'.[106] Malthus and his God were thus utilitarians and this theological version of that ethical creed, shared with William Paley, preceded the better-known, secularised doctrine of Jeremy Bentham. Malthus's laws, with their rationalisation of evils that attended overpopulation, also provided an important precedent for Darwin's appeal

---

[102] See Harrison, 'Adam Smith and the History of the Invisible Hand'. For an alternative reading see Emma Rothschild, *Economic Sentiments: Adam Smith, Condorcet, and the Enlightenment* (Cambridge, MA: Harvard University Press, 2001), ch. 5.

[103] Adam Smith, *Theory of Moral Sentiments*, ed. D. D. Raphael and A. L. Macfie (Oxford: Clarendon Press, 1976), pp. 77f.

[104] Malthus, *A Summary View*, p. 41.

[105] Thomas Malthus, *An Essay on the Principle of Population*, ed. Donald Winch (Cambridge: Cambridge University Press, 1992), Appendix, p. 344. For further discussions of laws of nature see pp. 41, 42, 44, 68, 71. Malthus would thus insist that his principle of population, understood as a law of nature, 'instead of being inconsistent with revelation, must be considered as affording strong additional proofs of its truth'. Malthus, *A Summary View*, p. 77. On the theological background to Malthus's thought see J. M. Pullen, 'Malthus's Theological Ideas and Their Influence on His Principle of Population', *History of Political Economy* 13 (1981), 39–54; Ryan Walter, 'Malthus's Sacred History: Outflanking Civil History in the Late Enlightenment', *Re-thinking History* 24 (2020), 481–502.

[106] Malthus, *A Summary View*, p. 71.

to natural laws with its implicit theodicy.[107] Writing in the middle decades of the nineteenth century, Scottish lawyer and champion of phrenology George Combe perceptively drew out one of the common themes of these thinkers. Smith's *Wealth of Nations*, he opined, 'appeared to me to demonstrate that God actually governs in the relations of commerce; that He has established certain natural laws which regulate the interests of men'. So, too, Malthus 'appeared to me to prove that God reigns, through the medium of fixed natural laws, in another department of human affairs – namely, that of population'.[108]

The generalisation that British authors tended to more conscious of their indebtedness to providential understandings of history than their Francophone counterparts holds true only to a certain degree, however. The nineteenth century witnessed the influx into Britain of versions of French secularist thought, not least Comte's positivism. The Comtean impulse to impose a scientific structure on the study of human societies would strongly influence the development of the social sciences and also, to some extent, the discipline of history. English historian Henry Thomas Buckle (1821–62) thus sought to place history on a scientific basis, arguing that statistics revealed patterns of human behaviour that demonstrated how history is governed by principles as regular as those that operate in the physical world.[109] The main engine of civilisation, for Buckle, was the growth of human knowledge. The progressive version of history as set out by Comte was thus confirmed 'by everything we know of the barbarous nations; and … by the history of physical science'.[110] This distinction between

---

[107] Darwin wrote, on reading Malthus on laws of population, 'these operations of what we call nature, have been conducted almost ! invariably according to fixed laws: and since the world began, the causes of population & depopulation have been probably as constant as any of the laws of nature with which we are acquainted. – This applies to one species – I would apply it not only to population & depopulation, but extermination & production of new forms. – this number & correlations.' *Darwin's Notebooks on the Transmutation of Species*, ed. Gavin De Beer, part 4, 3, http://darwin-online.org.uk/content/frameset?pageseq=18&itemID=F1574d&viewtype=text, accessed 24 November 2023. This would become a form of theodicy in the *Origin*: 'From the war of nature, from famine and death, the most exalted object which we are capable of conceiving, namely the production of the higher animals, directly follows.' *On the Origin of Species by means of Natural Selection*, 1st ed. (London: James Murray, 1859), p. 490. On Darwin and Malthus see Dov Ospovat, 'Darwin after Malthus', *Journal of the History of Biology* 12 (1979), 211–30.

[108] Combe, *Science and Religion*, p. xii.

[109] See especially Ian Hesketh, *The Science of History in Victorian Britain* (Pittsburgh: University of Pittsburgh Press, 2020), ch. 1.

[110] Henry Thomas Buckle, *History of Civilization in England* [1857], new ed., 3 vols. (London: Longmans, Green, and Co., 1869), vol. 1, p. 374. Cf. John Lubbock: 'The true test of the

barbarous and scientific could be further reduced into a simple opposition between supernaturalistic and naturalistic approaches to nature: 'It is evident that a nation perfectly ignorant of physical laws will refer to supernatural causes all the phenomena by which it is surrounded. But so soon as natural science begins to do her work, there are introduced the elements of a great change.'[111] The corollary of this was that advocates of religion were 'the great obstructors of mankind' and that 'the antagonism between physical science and the theological spirit' was an enduring feature of history.[112]

Aspects of Comte's approach, and especially his 'stages' of human progress, also left a mark on nineteenth-century anthropology. Comte, especially in his earlier years, had been very much focused on Europe and the aftermath of the French Revolution – an event that had left unresolved the question of how to establish a legitimate political order on a secular basis. But there was a much wider, global picture and the prospect that non-European societies might conveniently serve as test cases for Western theories of social development. This was especially the case for cultures that were thought of as languishing on the first rung of the ladder of human development. The temporal development of the West might thus be mapped geographically through anthropological studies, more or less along the lines of sociology for the West, anthropology for the rest (notwithstanding the fact that Europe was thought by some to still have its own 'savages' – the Sami, Scottish highlanders, and the Irish). Spatially, as opposed to temporally, distanced societies were thus subjected to anthropological analyses that allotted them a place in the scale of evolutionary development.

E. B. Tylor (1832–1917), a seminal figure in the emerging discipline of anthropology, spoke in his classic *Primitive Culture* (1871) of the 'principle of development' that applied to all human cultures.

> By long experience of the course of human society, the principle of development in culture has become so ingrained in our philosophy that

---

civilization of a nation must be measured by its progress in science.' Presidential Address, in *Report of the Fifty-First Meeting of the British Association* (London: John Murray, 1882), pp. 1–51 (p. 51).

[111] Buckle, *History of Civilization*, pp. 373f.

[112] Buckle, *History of Civilization*, p. 372. An astute review of Buckle's work, in the 9th ed. of the *Encyclopaedia Britannica* observed that Buckle 'either could not define, or cared not to define, the general conceptions with which he worked, such as those denoted by the terms "civilization," "history," "science," "law," "scepticism," and "protective spirit"; the consequence is that his arguments are often fallacies'. And that he mistakenly thought that 'orderly historical development and providential government ... contradict and exclude each other' (s.v. 'Buckle', vol. 4, p. 422).

ethnologists, of whatever school, hardly doubt but that, whether by progress or degradation, savagery and civilization are connected as lower and higher stages of one formation.[113]

This principle amounted to a law that was directly analogous to laws of nature in the physical sciences.[114] Like Comte, Tylor specified three stages of social development: savagery, barbarism, and civilisation. The 'wild Australian' was his exemplar of savagery; the refined Englishman, of civilisation.[115] The stage of savagery was characterised by animism and belief in spiritual beings which, for Tylor, arose out of primitive man's attempt to answer what we would now regard as scientific questions. In time, the false answers to these questions were replaced with true 'scientific' ones. Contemporary belief in the supernatural was, for Tylor, a vestigial 'survival' from an earlier and more primitive age.[116] All of this was read from 'a science of history, that parallels the science of nature based on laws'.[117]

James George Frazer (1854–1941), author of *The Golden Bough* (1890, 1900, 1906–15) also plumped for a three-stage pattern of historical development for human societies, speaking of a necessary transition from magical to a religious phase of social development, and then on to a mature scientific stage. Frazer thus differs from Comte in distinguishing magic from religion, but the general direction of travel is more or less the same.[118] Frazer also shared something of Comte's desire to reform society along scientific

---

[113] Edward B. Tylor, *Primitive Culture: Researches into the Development of Mythology, Philosophy, Religion, Language, Art and Custom*, 2 vols. (London: John Murray, 1871), vol. 1, p. 33. Tylor opposed his view to a degeneration theory informed by theological dogma (p. 32). For an excellent account of Tylor and his views of religion see Timothy Larsen, 'E. B. Tylor, Religion and Anthropology', *British Journal for the History of Science* 46 (2013), 467–85. On the origins of anthropology see Marvin Harris, *The Rise of Anthropological Theory* (New York: Crowell, 1968). Margaret Hogden proposes an earlier starting point for anthropology in *Early Anthropology in the Sixteenth and Seventeenth Centuries* (Philadelphia: University of Pennsylvania Press, 1964).

[114] 'We need a science of history, that parallels the science of nature based on laws.' Tylor, *Primitive Culture*, vol. 1, pp. 1–5.

[115] Edward B. Tylor, *Anthropology: An Introduction to the Study of Man and Civilization* (London: Macmillan, 1881), pp. 23–4. In America, at around the same time, Lewis Henry Morgan also posited the three successive stages of savagery, barbarism, and civilisation, while differing from Tylor about how, precisely, they should be characterised. Lewis H. Morgan, *Ancient Society* (New York: Henry Holt, 1877), p. vi.

[116] E. B. Tylor, 'On the survival of savage thought in modern civilization', *Notices of the Proceedings at the Meetings of the Members of the Royal Institution of Great Britain* 5 (1869), 522–38.

[117] Tylor, *Primitive Culture*, vol. 1, pp. 1–5.

[118] James George Frazer, *The Golden Bough*, 3rd ed., 13 vols. (London: Macmillan, 1980), pt. 7, vol. 2, p. 304.

lines, regarding his endeavours as more than simply a matter of satisfying the 'enlightened curiosity … of the learned'. They were intended, in addition, to be 'a powerful instrument to expedite progress' by exposing 'weak spots in the foundations on which modern society is built'. New forms of society were to be built upon 'the rock of nature' rather than 'the sands of superstition'.[119]

It is clear that these early anthropologists and sociologists, while imagining themselves to be conducting a scientific exercise, were at the same time engaged in making normative judgements about what they were describing. The demise of supernatural religion was not just a fact of life: it was deemed requisite for human advancement. Some late nineteenth-century sociological works are unambiguous about this. Lester F. Ward, first president of the American Sociological Foundation, declared in one of the foundational texts of the new discipline that: 'All these phenomena are now satisfactorily explained on strictly natural principles. Among peoples acquainted with science, all such supernatural beings have been dispensed with, and the belief in them is declared to be false, and to always have been false.'[120] Added to this normative perspective was a predictive component. Given the lawful nature of the progress described there was assumed to be a certain inevitability to this progression. In a sinister turn, this did not necessarily mean that all societies were destined to progress through the relevant stages. One way of thinking about the disappearance of supernatural beliefs was to think in terms of the demise of the peoples who held them.[121] In *The Descent of Man* (1871) Darwin speaks for this trend with his sobering observation that: 'At some future period, not very distant as measured by centuries, the civilized races of man will almost certainly exterminate and replace throughout the world the savage races.'[122] Darwin was not advocating this as a course of

---

[119] Frazer, Preface to the second edition, *The Golden Bough*, vol. 1, pp. xxv–xxvi.
[120] Ward, *Dynamic Sociology*, vol. 2, pp. 266, 268–9. Cf. Guillaume de Greef: the only religious progress possible is 'the reduction of religion to an absurdity'. *Introduction à la Sociologie*, 2 vols. (Paris, Alcan, 1886), vol. 2, p. 208.
[121] Many early interpreters of Darwinism regarded evolution as directional and progressive. Because the genetic basis of natural selection was not understood, nor its importance in relation to other mechanisms, there was, arguably, a little room for such interpretations. The neo-Darwinian synthesis of the twentieth century seemed to foreclose on directional interpretations, although recent years have witnessed renewed discussions around convergent evolution and the 'extended evolutionary synthesis'. See, for example, Peter Harrison and Ian Hesketh (eds.), 'Replaying the Tape of Life: Evolution and Historical Explanation', special issue of *Studies in History and Philosophy of Science* 59 (2016), 1–122.
[122] Charles Darwin, *The Descent of Man*, 2 vols. (New York: Appleton, 1871), vol. 1, p. 193. This was certainly argued to be true for Australian aborigines and New Zealand Māori. A. K. Newman, 'A study of the causes leading to the extinction of the Maori', in *Transactions*

action but, like many of his contemporaries, believed that there was a tragic inevitability to this process. This assumption lay behind 'salvage anthropology' which sought to study 'vanishing' cultures and preserve their artefacts before they disappeared completely.[123]

Traces of these sentiments persist today in the disciplinary formation of social scientists. Introductory anthropology texts, for example, will often rehearse naïve historical narratives of social progress associated with secularisation. To be sure, there are no dismissive characterisations of non-European cultures as backward, barbarous, savage, or superstitious, and salvage anthropology has long gone. Yet the same cannot be said for the depiction of Europe's own past, to which only mildly nuanced versions of nineteenth-century progressivism are routinely applied. Anthropology undergraduates are often introduced to a view of Western history which, in its basic outline, could have been lifted directly from the pages of Comte. One standard introductory text thus speaks of the 'tremendous implications of heliocentrism' declaring that 'Copernicus revolutionized humankind's understanding of science and religion.' Thereafter, 'disagreements between science and religion would quickly become a persistent theme of history' with Newton and Darwin representing subsequent stages of conflict.[124] Another author tells us how 'the humanism of the Renaissance gave on to the Enlightenment, with its belief in rationality, as opposed to revelation'. This led, in turn, to liberalism, a belief in the inherent dignity of individuals, and social science, which applies scientific knowledge to human affairs with a view to the betterment of human life.[125] A recurring motif in these

and *Proceedings of the New Zealand Institute* 14 (1881), pp. 459–77; John Stenhouse, '"A disappearing race before we came here": Doctor Alfred Kingcome Newman, the Dying Maori, and Victorian Scientific Racism', *New Zealand Journal of History* 30 (1996), 124–40. See also Russell McGregor, *Imagined Destinies: Aboriginal Australians and the Doomed Race Theory, 1880–1939* (Melbourne: Melbourne University Press, 1997).

[123] For others, however, notions of cultural evolution were not simply theories, but projects. See, e.g., Reginald Horsman, *Race and Manifest Destiny* (Cambridge, MA: Harvard University Press, 1986); Patrick Brantlinger, *Dark Vanishings: Discourse on the Extinction of Primitive Races, 1800–1930* (Ithaca: Cornell University Press, 2003).

[124] James Bonanno, 'Enlightenment and Secularism', in *21st Century Anthropology: A Reference Handbook*, ed. H. James Birx (Los Angeles: Sage, 2010), pp. 463–72 (pp. 465, 468). For the sources in this paragraph I am indebted to Thomas Aechtner, who provides additional examples. Thomas H. Aechtner, 'Galileo Still Goes to Jail: Conflict Model Persistence within Introductory Anthropology Materials', *Zygon* 50 (2015), 209–26; 'Social Scientists', in *The Warfare between Science and Religion: The Idea That Would Not Die*, ed. Jeff Hardin, Ronald L. Numbers, and Ronald A. Binzley (Pittsburgh: University of Pittsburgh Press, 2018), pp. 302–23.

[125] Nigel Rapport and Joanna Overing, *Social and Cultural Anthropology: The Key Concepts* (London: Routledge, 2000), pp. 172f.

accounts is a version of secularisation in which 'aspects of the natural world that were formerly explained by religious ideology are now explained by means of science'.[126] It seems that induction into the discipline of anthropology still requires a catechetical repetition of its founding myths, even if the lessons are applied mostly to the West, rather than 'the rest'.

A common feature of the early social sciences is an assiduous appeal to laws of nature. This lent it a quasi-scientific character that gestured towards the possibility of offering predictions. As we have seen, in the natural sciences the notion of law and its accompanying assurance of the uniformity of nature had originally been directly linked to the idea of God as a divine lawgiver. This overtly theistic foundation was typically missing from social scientific accounts. It was as if in borrowing the concept from the natural sciences, the pioneers of social science, working at an extra degree of separation, found it unnecessary to probe more deeply into the origin or logic of social laws. Yet the connection between divine providence and putative laws of social progression is clearly visible in most Scottish Enlightenment constructions of social progress and is equally conspicuous in the contributions of Hegel and, more obscurely, in his Marxian progeny. In these thinkers we see more clearly the trail that leads back from social scientific approaches of the present to the providentialism of the past.

These scientifically inflected accounts of universal human history were bolstered by late nineteenth-century evolutionary theory, which was often read as lending scientific authority to notions of the historical progression of human societies. Darwin's evolutionary ideas meshed neatly with teleological theories of history and indeed were regarded by some as providing scientific justification for them. Ernst Haeckel, an energetic German promoter of evolutionary thought and social Darwinism, observed that 'the whole history of nations, or what is called "Universal History," must therefore by explicable by means of "natural selection," – must be a physico-chemical process, depending upon the interaction of Adaptation and Inheritance in the struggle for life'.[127] Herbert Spencer, who during

---

[126] Abraham Rosman, Paula G. Rubel, and Maxine Weisgrau, *The Tapestry of Culture: An Introduction to Cultural Anthropology* (Lanham: Alta Mira, 2009), p. 233. Cf. Bonanno: 'supernatural explanations diminished as humankind developed a greater understanding of the universe'. 'Enlightenment and Secularism', p. 469.

[127] Ernst Haeckel, *History of creation: Or the development of the earth and its inhabitants by the action of natural causes*, 2 vols., trans. G. R. Lankester (New York: Appleton, 1880), vol. 1, p. 170. Haeckel sets out the stages of history in *Monism as Connecting Religion and Science*. These begin with the 'animal' phase of prehistorical man, progressing through low stages of culture that 'still existing primitive peoples' enable us to imagine, and from these 'savages' via 'a long series of intermediate steps' to 'the more highly civilization nations'.

his lifetime had a larger profile as an advocate of evolutionary thinking than Darwin himself (it was he who coined the phrase 'survival of the fittest'), also sought to project the basic principle of organic evolution into an overarching historical thesis: 'the law of organic progress is the law of all progress'.[128]

The early psychological sciences bought into these accounts, with the jettisoning of religion understood in terms of societies' reaching full intellectual adulthood. Sigmund Freud's analysis of religion, set out in *The Future of an Illusion* (1927), explains that just as the religious impulse has its origins in the feelings of helplessness and dependence of the child, so religion as a phenomenon is associated with an infantile stage in the development of human civilisation:

> humanity as a whole, in its development through the ages, fell into states analogous to the neuroses, and for the same reasons .... Religion would thus be like the universal neurosis of humanity .... If this view is right it is to be supposed that a turning away from religion is bound to occur with the fatal inevitability of a process of growth, and that we find ourselves at this very juncture in the middle of this stage of development.[129]

Psychologically speaking, religious ideas arise 'from the infant's helplessness and longing for the father'; historically speaking, they are 'the mental products of primitive peoples and times'. All of religion, in Freud's judgement, is 'patently infantile'. Accordingly, it is destined to be replaced by science: 'religion no longer has the same influence on people that it used to' and this because of 'the increase of the scientific spirit in the upper strata of human society'. Freud confesses himself to be optimistic enough to believe that

---

In the familiar pattern, Haeckel describes how in earlier phases of human development explanations were couched in theological and teleological terms, but that these were, and would continue to be, replaced by naturalistic, scientific explanations (pp. 5–10). See Todd H. Weir (ed.), *Monism: Science, Philosophy, Religion, and the History of a Worldview* (New York: Palgrave Macmillan, 2012).

[128] Herbert Spencer, 'Progress: its Law and Cause', in *Essays, Scientific, Political and Speculative*, 3 vols. (London: Williams and Norgate, 1891), vol. 1, p. 10. Cf. *Social Statics* (London: Chapman, 1851), p. 451. On Spencer's broad influence on Victorian intellectual circles see Bernard Lightman, *Global Spencerism: The Communication and Appropriation of a British Evolutionist* (Leiden: Brill, 2015). Following in Spencer's wake, Walter Bagehot also thought that the principles of natural selection could be applied to societies. *Physics and Politics: Or, Thoughts on the Application of the Principles of 'Natural Selection' and Inheritance to Political Society* (London: Henry S. King, 1872).

[129] Sigmund Freud, *The Future of an Illusion*, in *The Standard Edition of the Complete Psychological Works of Sigmund Freud*, 24 vols., trans. James Strachey (London: Vintage, 2001), vol. 21, p. 43. This withering away of religion was not just Freud's dispassionate prediction, but his 'hope'. Cf. *New Introductory Lectures on Psychoanalysis*, *Complete Works*, vol. 22, p. 171.

eventually we will all grow up: 'mankind will surmount this neurotic phase, just as so many children grow out of their similar neurosis'.[130]

For all that these historical schemas present themselves as rational and dispassionate forms of social science, they are suffused with an unmistakably normative vision of the direction of travel. The apparent displacement of earlier forms of religious consciousness by Western science was regarded as inevitable and desirable, and whatever stood in the way of this progressive development was to be resisted and critiqued. J. G. Frazer well sums up the general mood in the closing paragraphs of *The Golden Bough*: 'the hope of progress – moral and intellectual as well as material – in the future is bound up with the fortunes of the sciences, and ... every obstacle placed in the way of scientific discovery is a wrong to humanity'.[131]

6.4 Providence Naturalised

Later editions of *The Golden Bough* end with some intriguing remarks about apparent similarities between Frazer's anthropology and philosopher G. W. F. Hegel's *Lectures on the Philosophy of Religion*. Prefacing his remarks with an understatement shared by many of Hegel's readers – 'so far as I understand the philosopher's exposition' – Frazer proposes that the similarity lies in a common view about the primacy of magic and the way that it gives rise to religion in a universal pattern of historical development.[132] Frazer thought that he shared with Hegel a general view about historical development and that they agreed on at least some of the details. That said, the trajectory of the most influential theories of history produced in Germany in the eighteenth and early nineteenth centuries went in interestingly different directions to patterns evident elsewhere and especially to the more religiously antagonistic offerings of many of the French *philosophes*. This reflects a greater influence of romanticism and idealism, as opposed to the more rationalist and materialist approaches characteristic of some French Enlightenment thinkers. The place of origin

---

[130] Sigmund Freud, *Civilization and its Discontents*, Complete Works, vol. 21, p. 72; *Future*, p. 38; *Civilization*, p. 74; *Future*, p. 53. Comte also relates individual development to cultural evolution, suggesting that: 'The human mind, by its nature, successively uses in each one of its researches three methods of philosophizing namely the theological, metaphysical and positive.' *Cours de philosophie positive* [1830–42], 6 vols. (Paris: Hermann, 1975), vol. 1, p. 21.

[131] Frazer, *Golden Bough*, pt. 7, vol. 2, p. 306.

[132] Frazer, 'Appendix: Hegel on Magic and Religion', *Golden Bough*, vol. 1, pp. 423–6; cf. vol. 1, p. x. Cf. G. W. F. Hegel, *Lectures on the Philosophy of Religion: One Volume Edition, The Lectures of 1827*, ed. Peter C. Hodgson (Oxford: Clarendon Press, 2006), pp. 229–35.

of the Protestant Reformation and Luther's ongoing status as a figure of national importance also meant that German thinkers tended to place a greater stress on the continuities between the Reformation and the Enlightenment. Hegel, for example, would excuse French Enlightenment thinkers for their harsh criticisms of religion because their attacks were not directed against 'the religion that Luther had purified, but the most wretched superstition, priestly domination, stupidity, degradation of mind [etc.]'.[133]

Hegel's contemporary, the Romantic poet and philosopher Novalis (1772–1801), made fewer concessions to French anti-clericalism than his compatriot, perceptively observing that in the works of the *philosophes* 'hatred against the Catholic faith gradually became a hatred of the Bible, of Christian belief, and finally of all religion'. In his estimation, the French Enlightenment had magnified and universalised the iconoclastic and desacralising forces incipient in Protestantism and these were now being applied indiscriminately to religion in general. According to Novalis, an unfortunate side-effect of this desacralising tendency was an extreme anthropocentrism. This had provided a justification for the exploitation of nature, now imagined to be an inert mechanism subject to the utilitarian purposes of human masters. The *philosophes* and their ilk had elevated humans 'above all other beings', turning 'the infinite creative music of the cosmos into the uniform clattering of a gigantic mill' and 'stripping the world of all bright ornament'.[134] We hear echoes of these sentiments in English Romanticism, with poet John Keats similarly lamenting the manner in which 'cold

---

[133] Hegel, *Lectures on the History of Philosophy*, p. 750. Condorcet, nonetheless, did have some positive things to say about Luther and the Reformation, although he concludes that 'the spirit that animated the reformers did not lead to true freedom'. *Sketch*, pp. 75–7, 79, 81f. Less ambivalent about the liberalising tendencies of the Reformation among Francophone authors were Charles de Villers and Benjamin Constant. De Villers, responsible for translating much of Kant's work into French, insisted that the system 'of liberality, or inquiry, and free criticism, established by the Reformation, became the aegis under which the Galileos of succeeding times, the Keplers, the Newtons, the Leibnizes, the Hevels, and finally the Laplaces, have been enabled with confidence to disclose their high speculations'. Charles de Villers, *An Essay on the Spirit and Influence of the Reformation of Luther*, trans. James Mill (London, 1805), p. 285. For Constant's views see Helena Rosenblatt, *Liberal Values: Benjamin Constant and the Politics of Religion* (Cambridge: Cambridge University Press, 2008), pp. 29–34, and *passim*. James Mill, who translated de Villers's essay, taught his son John Stuart Mill that the Reformation was 'the great and decisive contest against priestly tyranny for liberty of thought'. J. S. Mill, *Autobiography, Collected Works*, vol. 1, p. 45.

[134] Novalis, *Christendom or Europe: A Fragment*, in *The Early Political Writings of the German Romantics*, ed. Frederick C. Beiser (Cambridge: Cambridge University Press, 1996), pp. 69, 70.

philosophy' would 'Conquer all mysteries by rule and line, / Empty the haunted air, and gnomed mine'.[135]

Gotthold Lessing (1729–81) also took a more moderate line in his historical conjectures, speaking in terms of the maturation of religion rather than its displacement by a superior, rational philosophy or science. Lessing proposed that divine revelation was a means of educating the human race in its infancy. Revelation had been necessary in earlier ages since it was ideally matched to an 'uncouth' people, 'ill-equipped for abstract thoughts'.[136] This is again redolent of Turgot's characterisation of the primitive mentality in terms of its inability to form abstract conceptions. For Lessing, through a series of episodes that included the coming of Christ and the Protestant Reformation, humanity moved in the direction of an enlightened rational autonomy.[137] The first-century miracles were necessary to draw the attention of 'the mass of people', but in a more advanced epoch were unnecessary.[138] With the Reformation, a further stage was reached when Luther taught that knowledge of the truth was to be advanced by the autonomous judgement of the individual.[139] But in all of this, historical progression towards rational enlightenment, rather than being a purely 'natural' process guided by some imagined law, was understood as the work of divine providence. It was an 'inscrutable ... eternal providence' that drove 'the great

---

[135] John Keats, 'Lamia', lines 235–6, *The Poetical Works of John Keats* (London: Edward Moxon, 1823), p. 129.

[136] Gotthold Ephraim Lessing, *The Education of the Human Race*, §16 in *Philosophical and Theological Writings*, ed. H. B. Nisbet (Cambridge: Cambridge University Press, 2005), p. 221. Augustine, as far as I can tell, is the first to make reference to the 'true education of the human race' (*humani generis ... recta eruditio*), *City of God* 10.14 (LCL 14, 312) but Augustine is not referenced by Lessing. The latter does, however, seem to make a passing allusion to Joachim of Fiore's 'three stages', which is a possible source for subsequent tripartite division of history. *Education* §§87–90, p. 238. See Gould and Reeves, *Joachim of Fiore and the Myth of the Eternal Evangel*, p. 60. But cf. Yasakuta, *Lessing's Philosophy of Religion*, pp. 107f. Lessing's title is echoed in the first contribution to *Essays and Reviews* (1860) – Frederick Temple's 'The Education of the World'. Lessing's thesis, in a nutshell, is precisely that which Claude Lévi-Strauss would later contest: 'the supposed ineptitude of "primitive people" for abstract thought'. *The Savage Mind* (Chicago: University of Chicago Press, 1966), p. 1.

[137] Lessing, *Education*, §61, p. 232.

[138] Lessing, *The Spirit and the Power*, in *Philosophical and Theological Writings*, p. 87.

[139] Lessing, *Anti-Goetze, Sämmtliche Schriften*, p. 161. Lessing contrasted the 'spirit' of Luther with the 'letter' of his writings. Theologians and Church historian Johann Semler (1725–91), often identified as the father of German rationalism, had a similar view of Luther's significance. See Thomas Hahn-Bruckart, 'Luther in Protestant Historiography and Theology in the Nineteenth and Twentieth Centuries', in *Martin Luther: A Christian between Reforms and Modernity (1517–2017)*, 3 vols., ed. Alberto Melloni (Berlin: De Gruyter, 2017), vol. 1, pp. 1019–41 (pp. 1020f.).

slow-moving wheel which brings the [human] race closer to perfection'.[140] Similar views about progressive revelation would be articulated by a number of nineteenth-century theologians.[141]

Lessing is also well known for having articulated an apparent difficulty associated with arriving at necessary truths from the contingent facts of history. The principle associated with his name is that *'contingent truths of history can never become the proof of necessary truths of reason'*. Lessing confessed that this was an 'ugly, broad ditch which I cannot get across, however often and earnestly I have tried to make the leap'.[142] The conundrum assumes Leibniz's distinction between contingent and necessary truths, indirectly references Hume's questions about historical testimony to miracles, and raises the issue of the status of 'proofs' for Christian belief. Lessing's dictum is directed mostly against the assumption that historical facts can underpin certain forms of rational proof of the Christian faith. This was less of a problem for Lessing himself, since he proposed that factual truths revealed in history become rational for the individual when they are appropriated in the form of 'inner religion'.[143] But there is a general issue towards which Lessing's dictum gestures. The problem is how apparently contingent and inherently non-rational temporal processes might somehow yield rational outcomes – at the level of doctrines, concepts, and forms of social and economic order. More generally, this is a question of how a succession of contingent historical events might be understood normatively as 'progress'. Following the advent of the theory of evolution by natural selection, the related question of the

---

[140] Lessing, *Education*, §§91, 92 (p. 239).

[141] Frederick Temple's contribution to *Essays and Reviews*, entitled 'The Education of the World', was a conspicuous example. For Temple, 'the men of the earliest ages were, in many respects, still children as compared to ourselves, with all the blessings and all the disadvantages that belong to childhood'. *Essays and Reviews*, 9th ed. (London: Longman, Green, Longman, and Roberts, 1861), p. 4. Temple spoke of 'three stages' in the education of the world (p. 5). Princeton theologian Charles Hodge referred similarly to 'the progressive character of revelation' proposing that in scripture 'What at first is only obscurely intimated is gradually unfolded.' *Systematic Theology*, 2 vols. (New York: Charles Scribner's Sons, 1876), vol. 1, p. 446. For B. B. Warfield, revelation was 'not given all at once, but progressively ... in the form of a regular historical development'. 'Revelation', in *Johnson's Universal Encyclopedia*, 8 vols., ed. Charles Kendall Adams (New York: Appleton, 1895), vol. 7, p. 81a. See also Henry Cowles, *The Pentateuch, in its Progressive Revelations of God to Men* (New York: Appleton, 1884), pp. 5f.; and, more recently, Geerhardus Vos, *Biblical Theology: Old and New Testaments* [1934] (Eugene: Wipf and Stock, 2003), p. 5, and *passim*; J. Oliver Buswell, *Systematic Theology* (Grand Rapids: Zondervan, 1962), p. 383.

[142] Lessing, 'On the Proof of the Spirit and of Power', in *Philosophical and Theological Writings*, pp. 85, 87.

[143] On this point, see G. E. Michalson, Jr., 'Lessing, Kierkegaard, and the "Ugly Ditch"', *The Journal of Religion* 59 (1979), 324–34; Yasukata, *Lessing's Philosophy of Religion*, pp. 60–4.

capacity of human cognition to arrive at truth arises in the form of Darwin's 'horrid doubt': 'whether the convictions of man's mind, which has been developed from the mind of the lower animals, are of any value or at all trustworthy?'[144] The general question has not gone away and provides one of the thematic concerns of this book.

In the case of Christianity, the historical turn began with the Reformation history wars and was fine-tuned in the approaches of the Tübingen School of historical enquiry. What detailed historical investigations into the origins of Christianity revealed were the highly contingent factors involved in the constitution and deliberations of those church councils that had come to define the central dogmas of Christianity, especially the doctrines of Trinity and Incarnation. There was an apparent disjunction between the absolute and unchangeable status of the doctrines and the seemingly happenstance events that gave rise to their final formulation. The form of the solution in this case was a kind of *Deus ex machina* appeal to the hidden divine orchestration of historical events. God was thought to be at work in the actions of human agents who were to do his bidding (in some cases, unwittingly). In essence this is where Lessing ended up. This deference to providence was entirely consistent with Christian understandings of history. But it would hardly work to justify purely secular understandings of progress. Overall, Lessing's understanding of historical progression drew upon two precedents from Christian understandings of history: first, a restrained apocalypticism redolent of Joachim of Fiore; second, a 'Protestant' view of the age of miracles which consigned them to an earlier stage in the education of the human race.

Hegel was the next major figure to grapple with these issues, although it was also very much on the agenda of contemporary theologians.[145] Hegel shared the view of most theorists of history in believing that 'crude and barbarous peoples' exhibited no capacity for abstract thinking. He likewise followed Lessing in arguing for the gradual development of rational autonomy in the human race.[146] This was not so much the result of providence

---

[144] Darwin to William Graham, Darwin Correspondence Project, 'Letter no. 13230', www.darwinproject.ac.uk/letter/?docId=letters/DCP-LETT-13230.xml, accessed 12 November 2022.

[145] See Johannes Zachhuber, 'F. W. J. Schelling and the Rise of Historical Theology', *International Journal of Philosophy and Theology* 80 (2019), 23–38.

[146] Hegel, *Lectures on the Philosophy of Religion*, pp. 223–9, and *passim*. Further remarks along these lines are offered in 'The Natural Context or Geographical Basis of World History', appendix to *Lectures on the Philosophy of World History*, pp. 155–220. Hegel hints at the classical Greek/barbarian distinction by allotting the Greeks a special place in this trajectory: 'the consciousness of freedom first awoke among the Greeks'. *Lectures on the Philosophy of World History*, p. 54.

guiding historical developments from without, but was identified with the inner workings of an immanent Spirit (*Geist*). A simple religion of nature or 'immediate religion' was associated with the infancy of the human race. This was followed by the religion of spiritual individuality, manifested in three types: the religions of the sublime (Judaism), the beautiful (Greek), and the expedient (Roman). Finally, Christianity, 'the consummate religion', appears on the stage of history.[147] Christianity was itself then the object of further development in the direction of freedom and rational autonomy. Hegel wrote that history travelled 'from East to West' with Europe representing 'the absolute end of history, just as Asia is the beginning'.[148] Again, the German Reformation was accorded a special place in this development, having established 'an abiding right, the right in matters of religious opinion to follow one's own self-wrought or self-acquired conviction'.[149] Martin Luther received praise for having inaugurated a new age of freedom and autonomy. Hegel also imagined this to be a distinctively Teutonic achievement, suggesting that during a period when other European nations were looking outwards and busying themselves with colonial adventures, Germany, exemplified by Martin Luther, looked inwards.[150] Hegel even immodestly insinuated himself into this historical trajectory, hinting that his own proposed reforms of Germany's political, legal, and ethical systems amounted to a further realisation of Luther's original reforming effort.[151]

Given this account, it is not surprising that it was Hegel who identified the ancient Greek thinker, Thales of Miletus, as the founder of philosophy, firmly establishing the essentially European character of systematic, rational modes of thought.[152] But while Hegel's authority secured the wide acceptance of the Greek origins of philosophy, the idea did not originate with

---

[147] Hegel, *Lectures on the Philosophy of Religion*, pp. 199–209, 328–88, 389–416.
[148] Hegel, *Lectures on the Philosophy of World History*, p. 197.
[149] Hegel, *The Positivity of the Christian Religion*, in *Early Theological Writings*, p. 146.
[150] Hegel, *Lectures on the Philosophy of World History, Volume 1: Manuscripts of the Introduction and the Lectures of 1822–1823*, ed. and trans. Robert F. Brown and Peter C. Hodgson (Oxford: Oxford University Press, 2011), p. 503. For the special place of the 'Germanic world' in the evolution of the spirit of human freedom see *Lectures on the Philosophy of World History*, p. 206. Marx would later echo Hegel's judgement. 'Contribution to the Critique of Hegel's Philosophy of Right' [1844], in Karl Marx and Friedrich Engels, *On Religion* (Mineola: Dover, 2008), p. 51.
[151] Hegel, *On the Tercentenary of the Augsburg Confession*, in *Hegel: Political Writings*, pp. 186–96, esp. p. 189.
[152] E. F. Beall, 'Hegel and the Milesian "Origin of Philosophy"', *Classical and Modern Literature: A Quarterly* 13 (1993), 241–56; Maria Michela Sassi, *The Beginnings of Philosophy in Greece* (Princeton: Princeton University Press, 2018), pp. 2, 5; Alison Stone, 'Europe and Eurocentrism', *Aristotelian Society Supplementary Volume* 91 (2017), 83–104.

6.4 PROVIDENCE NATURALISED

him. Early modern thinkers had typically held that philosophical speculation began outside the West. Thomas Hobbes spoke for most of his contemporaries when he observed that 'The Gymnosophists of India, the Magi of Persia, and the Priests of Chaldea and Egypt, are counted the most ancient philosophers.' Philosophy, he concluded, 'was not risen to the Graecians, and other people of the West'.[153] The ancient Greeks themselves had thought much the same.[154] Claims for the unique philosophical acumen of Westerners is very much an eighteenth-century innovation. David Hume was one of the first to argue along these lines, proposing that 'the sciences arose in Greece, and Europe has been hitherto the most constant habitation of them'.[155] This view was taken up in the first detailed histories of philosophy produced by German scholars such as Christoph Meiners (1747–1810), Dietrich Tiedemann (1748–1803), and Wilhelm Gottlieb Tennemann (1761–1819) and remains the common view to this day.

Historian and philosopher Christoph Meiners has recently gained considerable notoriety on account of his status as one of the progenitors of scientific racism. Meiners coined the term 'Caucasian' to characterise one of two human lineages, the other being the inferior 'Mongols'.[156] These

---

[153] Hobbes, *Leviathan*, ch. 45, vol. 3, p. 1054. Thomas Stanley agreed, in the Preface to his *History of Philosophy*, 2 vols. (London, 1656), that 'Although some Grecians have challenged to their Nation the Original of Philosophy, yet the more learned of them have acknowledged it derived from the East' (vol. 1, sig. av). Greek philosophy was acknowledged to have begun with Thales. Ralph Cudworth set out a trajectory that went from Moses, through Solomon and the Egyptians, to the Greeks. *True Intellectual System*, p. 311. Early histories of philosophy in France tended to be more Eurocentric but were concerned with the more specific problems of the quarrel of the ancients and moderns. See G. Piaia, 'The Histories of Philosophy in France in the Age of Descartes', in *Models of the History of Philosophy*, ed. G. Santinello and G. Piaia (Dordrecht: Springer, 2010), pp. 3–91. For a more general survey of early modern views see Peter K. J. Park, *Africa, Asia, and the History of Philosophy: Racism and the Formation of the Philosophical Canon, 1780–1830* (Albany, NY: SUNY Press, 2013), pp. 70–6. For a recent critical assessment of the general claim see Tom Hercules Davies, 'Greek Cosmology and Its Bronze Age Background', PhD thesis, Princeton University, 2021.

[154] John A. Palmer, 'Aristotle on Ancient Theologians', *Apeiron* 33 (2000), 181–205; Cantor, 'Thales – the "First Philosopher"?'; Mor Segev, 'Aristotle on the Intellectual Achievements of Foreign Civilizations', in *Foreign Influences: The Circulation of Knowledge in Antiquity*, ed. Benoît Castelnérac, Luca Gili, and Laetitia Monteils-Laeng (Turnhout: Brepols, 2022). Hellenistic Jews and the Church Fathers typically assigned the origins of philosophy to the biblical patriarchs. Daniel Ridings, *The Attic Moses: The Dependency Theme in Some Early Christian Writers* (Göteborg: Acta Universitatis Gothoburgensis, 1995).

[155] David Hume, 'Of the Rise and Progress of the Arts and Sciences', in *Political Essays*, ed. Knud Haakonssen and Raymond Geuss (Cambridge: Cambridge University Press, 1994), p. 67. Europe, Hume maintained earlier in this essay, 'is at present a copy at large, of what Greece was formerly a pattern in miniature' (p. 65).

[156] Christoph Meiners, *Grundriß der Geschichte der Menschheit* (Lemgo, 1785), pp. 16–80.

groups would subsequently be characterised as the 'light and the beautiful' (Western Europeans or 'Celtic' people, along with less favoured 'Slavs' which also included Arabs, Jews, and Brahmins) and 'the dark-coloured and ugly' (everyone else).[157] This unfortunate view informed Meiners' history of philosophy. The 'dark and ugly' peoples, on account of their weakness in body and mind, were deemed constitutionally incapable of developing anything like systematic rational enquiry. This fell to the bright and the beautiful, and especially the Greeks, Britons, and Germans. The range of possible contenders for philosophical innovation in Meiners' history was thus predetermined by his anthropological prejudices. This necessitated the rejection of a long-standing consensus on the non-European origins of philosophy. Meiners accordingly spent the first sections of his history of philosophy successively dismissing traditional candidates for the founders of philosophy, gratuitously alluding along the way to the 'childishness and mediocrity of the knowledge of Asiatick and African peoples'.[158] This combination of racial theory and history is of a piece with Hume's assertions about the true origins of philosophy and the notorious footnote in his 'Of National Characters'.[159]

This version of the history of philosophy was subsequently taken up by Tiedemann, Tennemann, and, ultimately, Kant and Hegel.[160] Tiedemann did not explicitly adopt the racial basis of Meiners' exclusionary framing of philosophy, but nonetheless spoke of the 'semi-barbarous' thinking of the touted originators of philosophy – Chaldeans, Persians, Indians, and Egyptians. Their endeavours had failed to rise to the level of true philosophy on account of the admixture of 'fictions' and 'religious conceptions' along with a lack of any serious argument or conceptual sophistication.[161] Tiedemann's history thus included a naturalistic principle that not only determined the roster of genuine philosophers, but also shaped how their

---

[157] '*der hellen und schönen, und dem dunkelfarbigen und unhäßlichen*'. Meiners, *Grundriß der Geschichte der Menschheit*, pp. 29f. See the discussions in Park, *Africa, Asia, and the History of Philosophy*, pp. 77–82; Cantor, 'Thales – the "First Philosopher"?'.

[158] Christof Meiners, *Grundriß der Geschichte der Weltweisheit* (Lemgo, 1786), pp. 1–22, quoted from p. 7. The contenders in question were the Chaldeans, Phoenicians, Egyptians, Arabs and Ethiopians, Persians, Hindus, and Chinese.

[159] Hume clearly influenced the thinking of both Meiners and Kant on this issue. Whether, more specifically, the footnote played a role remains a matter of speculation. On this possibility see Dan Flory, 'Race: History, and Affect: Comments on Peter K. J. Park's "Africa, Asia, and the History of Philosophy"', *Journal of World Philosophies* 2 (2017), 48–59.

[160] For Kant, see Huaping Lu-Adler, *Kant and Racism: Views from Anywhere* (Oxford: Oxford University Press, 2023). For Hegel, see discussion below.

[161] Dietrich Tiedemann, *Geist der spekulativen Philosophie von Thales bis Sokrates*, 6 vols. (Marburg: Neue Akademische Buchhandlung, 1791–7), vol. 1, p. xix.

contributions were to be read and ranked. Necessarily, the doctrines of true philosophers would be read in ways that marginalised the mythic, the poetic, and the theological. Tennemann's later hellenocentric history would also exclude 'religion, poetry, and politics' from genuine philosophy.[162] Kant, too, would propose that the Greeks were distinguished by their capacity for theoretical abstraction and that this had enabled them to inaugurate both philosophy and natural science.[163] These proposals were part of a broader eighteenth- and nineteenth-century philhellenism that lauded the artistic and literary accomplishments of the ancient Greeks.[164]

These formative late eighteenth- and early nineteenth-century works on the history of philosophy overturned the unanimous verdict of thinkers going back to the ancient Greeks themselves about the extramural origins of European philosophy, replacing it with a model that identified systematic, rational thought with the cogitations of fair-skinned Europeans. At the same time, and in much the same way that the history of science was reconstructed in order to realign past 'science' with present naturalistic desiderata, historians of philosophy began to refashion their subject so that it was understood less along the lines of 'spiritual exercises', to use Pierre Hadot's apt characterisation of ancient philosophy, and more as theoretical activity that was concerned primarily with abstract questions in the newly defined realms of 'epistemology' and 'ontology'. It was against this background that Hegel developed his dynamic historical vision in which Western Europe becomes the site for the maturation of human freedom and rationality.

Part of what Hegel seems to be suggesting in *The Phenomenology of Spirit* (1807) is that the conceptual apparatus that we use to grasp the world is subject to historical development. Like Kant, Hegel proposes that we cannot but experience the world through a conceptual grid that is present in human consciousness and not the 'world'.[165] But unlike Kant, who takes these categories as given, Hegel sees them as resulting from historical developments.

---

[162] Wilhelm Gottlieb Tennemann, *Grundriß der Geschichte der Philosophie* [1812] (Leipzig, 1825), §20, p. 10.

[163] Immanuel Kant, *Lectures on Logic*, trans. J. Michael Young (Cambridge: Cambridge University Press, 1992), pp. 22, 261f., 340, 540.

[164] The seminal work in relation to Greek art was Johann Joachim Winckelmann, *Geschichte der Kunst des Altertums* (Dresden, 1764). Johann Wolfgang von Goethe (1749–1832), Friedrich von Schiller (1759–1805), and Friedrich Hölderlin (1770–1843) represent literary philhellenism. For secondary treatments, see, e.g., Alfred Noe (ed.), *Der Philhellenismus in der westeuropäischen Literatur 1780–1830* (Amsterdam: Rodopi, 1994).

[165] Kant calls these 'the pure objects of the understanding'. *Critique of Pure Reason*, B129–B169 (pp. 226f.).

This gives them a social dimension.[166] Hegel also stopped short of the unalloyed optimism of the Enlightenment. He envisaged the obligatory three stages of human development but held Western modernity to be an as-yet unfinished project that had reached only the threshold of the third stage.

Given his dialectical understanding of historical development, Hegel also acknowledged both losses and gains in the course of history. Premodern, traditional societies were characterised by 'ethical life' but lacked modern subjectivity. Modern European society had achieved a degree of self-conscious freedom and subjectivity but at the cost of becoming alienated from the ethical life characteristic of traditional societies. This situation presaged a third and final stage, characterised by 'absolute knowing', in which suitably transformed versions of both the ethical life and modern subjectivity could coexist.[167] To express it another way, traditional societies understood their ethical norms objectively, as given in nature. They tacitly identified with them or were 'at home' with them. Modern European society understood the role played by human agency in the construction of values and thus understood them subjectively. This gave rise to alienation because this subjective understanding was thought incompatible with those values having universal normative force. For Hegel, this provided the conditions for a further stage of development in which it would be possible to uphold the normative force of the ethical life while at the same time acknowledging the role played by social consciousness in its construction. This required understanding both that culture is constituted by free individuals and that free individuals are constituted by culture. As it relates to the specifics of an Enlightenment project to replace religion and faith with science and reason, Hegel took the view that 'Faith' and 'Enlightenment' each have deficiencies that can be rectified only by the other.[168]

Mystifying though it may be to his detractors, Hegel's ideas, variously interpreted, proved to be remarkably influential and continue to be so to this day.

F. C. Baur's own dialectic, noted earlier, consisted in his proposal that Christianity had emerged as a synthesis of Jewish Christianity (represented

---

[166] For this interpretation see Brandom, *A Spirit of Trust*, pp. 1–32. This reading also links Hegel to American pragmatism and the 'subjective naturalists' alluded to in the introduction (Brandom, *A Spirit of Trust*, p. 264). See also Willem A. deVries, 'Hegelian Spirits in Sellarsian Bottles', *Philosophical Studies* 174 (2017), 1643–54.

[167] G. W. F. Hegel, *Phenomenology of Spirit*, trans. A. V. Miller (Oxford: Oxford University Press, 1996), §§349–57, 476, 484 (pp. 212–17, 289f., 294). See Brandom, *A Spirit of Trust*, pp. 471–3.

[168] Hegel, *Phenomenology*, §566 (pp. 345f.).

6.4 PROVIDENCE NATURALISED

by Peter) and Gentile Christianity (represented by Paul).[169] More broadly, Jewish and Pagan religious impulses represented features of religion in general which culminated in the appearance of a universal Christianity. Baur's attention to the historical details, however, enabled critics to accuse him of providing a naturalistic account of the origins of Christianity, since the form that Christianity eventually assumed could be understood as the consequence not of the providential guidance of history, but of some ineluctable and dialectical historical process – this despite the fact that Baur shared with Hegel the view that history was a kind of outworking of the evolution of universal Spirit (or 'God').

As is well known, the 'Left Hegelians' developed Hegelian thought in an explicitly naturalistic direction. Ludwig Feuerbach (1804–72) offered a modified account of modern alienation, proposing that religion comes into existence through the projection of elements of human self-consciousness onto an illusory 'God'. Religion thus consists in a form of self-estrangement as humans now relate to their own essence as something exterior to themselves.[170] For Feuerbach, this alienation can be overcome through the recognition that theology is, in reality, just anthropology or psychology. Only through this naturalised understanding of the significance of theology, says Feuerbach, 'do we attain to a true, self-satisfying identity of the divine and human being, the identity of the human being with itself'.[171] To express it in

---

[169] F. C. Baur, *De Christliche Gnosis* (Tübingen, 1835), pp. 668–72. For Baur's Hegelianism see Martin Wendte, 'Ferdinand Christian Baur: A Historically Formed Idealist of a Distinctive Kind', in *Ferdinand Christian Baur and the History of Early Christianity*, ed. Martin Bauspiess, Christof Landmesser, and David Lincicum, trans. Peter C. Hodgson and Robert F. Brown (Oxford: Oxford University Press, 2017), pp. 67–79; Corneliu Simut, *F. C. Baur's Synthesis of Böhme and Hegel* (Leiden: Brill, 2014). Baur was not simply a Hegelian, however, and was arguably as much influenced by Schleiermacher and Schelling. See Eduard Zeller, 'Ferdinand Christian Baur', in *Vorträge und Abhandlungen geschichtlichen Inhalts* (Leipzig: Fues, 1865), pp. 354–434; Carl Hester, 'Gedanken zu Ferdinand Christian Baurs Entwicklung als Historiker anhand zweier unbekannter Briefe', *Zeitschrift für Kirchengeschichte* 84 (1973), 249–69.

[170] In Feuerbach's own construction (and here his affinity to Hegel's manner of expression becomes apparent): 'Man ... projects his being into objectivity, and then again makes himself an object to this projected image of himself thus converted into a subject; he thinks of himself, is an object to himself, but as the object of an object, of another being than himself.' *The Essence of Christianity* [1841], trans. [George Eliot] (London: John Chapman, 1854), p. 29.

[171] Feuerbach, *Essence of Christianity*, p. 228. Cf. Marx's reading of Feuerbach: 'Feuerbach starts out from the duplication of the world into a religious world and a secular one. His work consists in resolving the world into its secular basis.' 'Theses on Feuerbach', in Karl Marx and Friedrich Engels, *The German Ideology* (Moscow: Progress Publishers, 1976), p. 616.

terms of the categories that we have been tracing in this book, the positing of the supernatural was the source of human alienation. Naturalism thus offered both an escape from the condition of alienation and an explanation of how it came about by means of an illicit projection. This thesis, needless to say, rests upon the assumption of a sharp human/divine or natural/supernatural divide which Feuerbach assumes to be a kind of universal, anthropological constant.

The most celebrated of the Left Hegelians, Karl Marx, grasped the significance of Feuerbach's projection thesis, but offered a more comprehensive, materialist analysis of the sources of modern alienation. Human beings, as workers in the capitalist system, were not only alienated from their own essence, they were also alienated from the products of their labour, from the act of production, from the relations of production, and from their co-workers.[172] In this context, religion was not a primary source of human estrangement, but rather a palliative that masked the true origins of alienation and mitigated its demoralising impact. Marx argued that communism amounted to 'a fully developed naturalism' that would render such palliation unnecessary.[173] Friedrich Engels, too, relied on Feuerbach for his critique of religion, again stressing the importance of dispensing with the supernatural: 'We wish to get everything out of the way which offers itself as supernatural and superhuman, and thereby remove untruthfulness; for the pretence of the human and natural to desire to be superhuman, supernatural, is the root of all untruth and falsehood.'[174] Engels' essay on *The Origin of the Family, Private Property and the State* (1884) reinforced this message by demonstrating the natural, rather than divine, origins of these social institutions and linking their material history to, again, three stages of civilisation as set out in the writings of the American anthropologist Lewis Morgan.[175] In all of

---

[172] Karl Marx, 'Economic and Philosophic Manuscripts of 1844', in *Economic and Philosophic Manuscripts of 1844 and the Communist Manifesto* (New York: Prometheus Books, 1988), pp. 72, 74, 78. For commentary see Bertell Ollman, *Alienation* (Cambridge: Cambridge University Press, 1971), pp. 136–52; Marcello Musto, 'Alienation Redux: Marxian Perspectives', in *Karl Marx's Writings on Alienation*, ed. Marcello Musto (London: Palgrave Macmillan, 2021), pp. 3–48.

[173] 'This communism, as fully developed naturalism, equals humanism, and as fully developed humanism equals naturalism; it is the *genuine* resolution of the conflict between man and nature and between man and man …. Communism is the riddle of history solved, and it knows itself to be this solution.' Karl Marx, 'Private Property and Communism', in *The Marx-Engels Reader*, 2nd ed., ed. Robert C. Tucker (New York: Norton, 1978), p. 84.

[174] Friedrich Engels, 'Humanism versus Pantheism: On Thomas Carlyle', in *Reader in Marxist Philosophy*, ed. Howard Selsam and Harry Martel (New York: International Publishers, 1963), pp. 234–9 (p. 236).

[175] Friedrich Engels, *The Origin of the Family, Private Property and the State*, trans. Ernest Unterman (Chicago: Charles H. Kerr and Co., 1908). This work was based on Marx's

this we witness new accounts of the machinery of historical change. These are now naturalised and materialistic versions of a Hegelian dialectic that in its original form had been deeply reliant upon the immanent workings of absolute Spirit.[176] This leads to the question of how the wheels of the historical machine might turn without the *Geist* that had originally animated them.

6.5 Genealogies of Naturalism

The late nineteenth-century constructions of the history of scientific naturalism, along with the closely related science/religion conflict narratives, were heirs to common features of the various existing accounts of historical progress surveyed above. A number of the elements of these constructions had either a theological foundation or had arisen within the context of confessional controversy. For a start, and most generally, we see historical genealogy used as a method of legitimation. This follows the precedent of the history wars of the post-Reformation period. There was also a division of history into stages, with more advanced stages being associated with science or naturalism. Again, this partitioning of history had originally been informed by eschatological considerations or, as it pertains more directly to the history of naturalism, by Protestant claims about the temporal limits to the age of miracles. The periodisation of miracles would now take on a different complexion, however, with miracles being understood not as real events whose cessation was determined by a divine dispensation, but as artefacts of a primitive psychology characteristic of an earlier age. Lessing is located at a key moment of transition, with his notion of education allowing for both providential and primitive mindset readings of history. Progress was typically seen as ensuing from the operation of laws of nature. These laws had originally been understood as divine edicts or as the workings of providence, but their theological origins would increasingly be ignored or forgotten.

A number of naturalism narratives were on offer in the late nineteenth century. Those of John Tyndall and Thomas Henry Huxley were among the most influential. John Tyndall offered his most developed genealogy of scientific naturalism in the controversial 'Belfast Address', delivered to the

---

notes on Morgan's *Ancient Society*. Engels characterises the progression of stages more in terms of changes in the material conditions of production, rather than by changes in belief (pp. 22–34).

[176] Thus, F. W. J. von Schelling: 'History as a whole is the progressive, gradual self-disclosing revelation of the Absolute.' *System of Transcendental Idealism* [1800], trans. Peter Heath (Charlottesville: University of Virginia Press, 1978), p. 211. See the discussion in Zachhuber, 'Schelling and the Rise of Historical Theology'.

annual meeting of the British Association in 1874. Exercised by ecclesiastical interference in the business of science, and concerned to establish its intellectual and institutional independence, Tyndall sought to construct a vindicatory genealogy of scientific naturalism that traced its origins back to the first thinking beings. Tyndall explained that 'primeval man', driven by the same motives that now inform scientific investigation, sought to provide causal accounts of natural phenomena. These explanations, however, were contaminated by anthropomorphic bias and primitive races imagined events to be caused by agents similar in certain respects to themselves, but possessed of superhuman powers.[177] In time, 'more penetrating intellects' rejected these earlier explanations and sought to connect natural phenomena with 'their physical principles'. This called for the expulsion of all supernatural phenomena from true science: 'Now, as science demands the radical extirpation of caprice and the absolute reliance upon law in nature, there grew with the growth of scientific notions a desire and determination to sweep from the field of theory this mob of gods and demons.'[178] Laws of nature, understood by Tyndall as principles that were in direct competition with theistic explanation, were mistakenly assumed to have been characteristic of true science from its early beginnings.

This general thesis was fleshed out with people, places, and times. In keeping with the recently established thesis of the Greek origins of philosophical thought and the lamentable failure of non-Europeans to have developed anything that remotely resembled contemporary physics, the true progenitors of scientific reasoning were identified as Democritus and Epicurus (and, after them, Lucretius). These men were said to have proposed a doctrine of atoms and molecules similar in its basic details to modern physics. Tyndall went so far as to propose that 'the scientific method was rendered in a great measure complete' in ancient Greece. Between that time and the present, however, was a yawning gap of more than a thousand years during which 'the victorious advance' of science was halted and 'the scientific intellect compelled, like an exhausted soil, to lie fallow'. The cause of this regrettable lacuna was, in essence, Christianity.[179] Eventually, owing to the efforts of such luminaries as Copernicus, Bruno, Kepler, Bacon, Descartes, and Newton, science began afresh in Europe, although not without significant opposition from ecclesiastical censors. In what was beginning to look like an invariable pattern, Darwin's more recent theories also met with theological

---

[177] Tyndall, 'Belfast Address', pp. 443f. Tyndall cites Hume's *Natural History of Religion* on this point.
[178] Tyndall, 'Belfast Address', p. 444. [179] Tyndall, 'Belfast Address', pp. 444f.

opposition.[180] Given this history, Tyndall argued, it was high time for science to assert its authority once and for all:

> We claim, and we shall wrest from the theology, the entire domain of cosmological theory. All schemes and systems which thus infringe upon the domain of science must, in so far as they do this, submit to its control and relinquish all thought of controlling it. Acting otherwise always proved disastrous in the past, and it is simply fatuous to-day.[181]

The historical lesson was that scientific naturalism had a long pedigree and that its historical marginalisation by religion, for all that it lasted for almost two millennia, was a mere road bump on the highway of human progress. Theological thinking, for its part, had consistently been on the wrong side of history as an inhibitor of scientific advance. Religious dogmas were understood as offering false explanations of natural phenomena that competed directly with scientific ones. The religious impulses that gave rise to both the idea of laws of nature and the more recently asserted principle of the conservation of energy, were for the most part ignored.[182] Indeed, together these two principles were now taken to be inimical to religious readings of the world since they amounted to a version of the doctrine of what is now often referred to as 'causal closure'.[183] Like Huxley, Tyndall also imagined himself to be a reformer in the mould of Luther, taking the evolution of religion to its next stage. At times he could speak in terms not of the replacement of religion by science, but of its 'purification'. However, he also ominously declared that 'a final act of purification is needed'.[184]

---

[180] Tyndall, 'Belfast Address', pp. 457f., 470, 475. Elsewhere Tyndall gives further historical instances of science-religion conflict. See 'On Prayer as a Form of Physical Energy', in *Fragments of Science*, p. 372; 'Apology for the Belfast Address', in *Fragments of Science*, pp. 504f., 507f.

[181] Tyndall, 'Belfast Address', p. 491.

[182] Tyndall nonetheless acknowledged that God had been important for Descartes's cosmological speculations. 'Professor Virchow and Evolution', p. 627. He was also aware that the well-known piety of his mentor Michael Faraday constituted a difficulty for his thesis and took pains to argue on more than one occasion that Faraday's religious commitments had nothing to do with his scientific accomplishments. 'Life and Letters of Faraday', p. 381; 'Science and Man', pp. 621f.

[183] The principle of conservation of energy, according to Tyndall, '"binds nature fast in fate", to an extent not hitherto recognised, exacting from every antecedent its equivalent consequent, from every consequent its equivalent antecedent, and bringing vital as well as physical phenomena under the dominion of that law of causal connection which, so far as the human understanding has yet pierced, asserts itself everywhere in nature'. 'Belfast Address', p. 478.

[184] Tyndall, 'On Prayer as a Form of Physical Energy', p. 372. For Tyndall's references to Luther see Lightman, *Origins of Agnosticism*, pp. 124f.

Many of the general sentiments of Tyndall's history are characteristic of earlier Enlightenment narratives and of Protestant critiques of a repressive and superstitious Catholicism. The thesis of Christianity as a regressive and inhibitory force was advanced on the authority of the religiously respectable William Whewell, who in his authoritative three-volume *History of the Inductive Sciences* (1837) had indeed spoken of a 'stationary period of human knowledge' that coincided with the Middle Ages.[185] But for Whewell this was not a reproach to theology or Christianity as such, but to a corrupt Catholicism. Whewell, in other words, was endorsing the 'Protestant' version of history rather than a general thesis about the incompatibility of science and belief in the supernatural. Other Protestant writers of the period would agree that Catholic Christianity was inhospitable to the flourishing of science while maintaining at the same time that there was no fundamental dispute between science and religion.[186]

Tyndall also drew directly upon less religiously sympathetic sources. Foremost among them was Friedrich Albert Lange's *History of Materialism* (1866).[187] Lange was a German philosopher and social reformer who acknowledged the success of materialistic naturalism in the sciences, but harboured reservations about its capacity to serve as an overarching metaphysical system. His *History* was an extended defence, again by means of genealogy, of the gains achieved by materialistic naturalism operating in scientific contexts. Lange sought to demonstrate that materialism was neither a recent progressive innovation, nor was it a short-lived fad: rather, in the now familiar pattern, it had a long historical tradition that began with the Presocratic philosophers.[188] It was impeded by the Church, which had

---

[185] William Whewell, *History of the Inductive Sciences, from the Earliest to the Present Times*, 3 vols. (London: John Parker, 1837), vol. 1, pp. 23, 397–403. Whewell's stationary period was considerable shorter than Tyndall's. Neither did Whewell make Galileo out to be a martyr for science, suggesting that the Galileo affair tells us more about the Italian character than about science and religion. William Whewell, *Indications of the Creator*, 2nd ed. (London: John Parker, 1846), pp. 47f.

[186] Thomas Dick, *On the Improvement of Society by the Diffusion of Knowledge* (New York: J. & J. Harper, 1833), pp. 18, 20; Charles Shields, *Philosophia Ultim: or, Science of the Sciences*, 3 vols. (New York: Charles Scribner's Sons, 1888–1905), vol. 3, pp. 101f.; Samuel David Broughton, 'Scientific Letters to a Lady of Quality', *Metropolitan Magazine*, vol. 2, 1831, pp. 32–40, esp. pp. 36, 39.

[187] Friedrich Albert Lange, *Geschichte des Materialismus und Kritik seiner Bedeutung in der Gegenwart* (Iserlohn: J. Baedeker, 1866). A much expanded, two-volume edition appeared in 1873–5. Citations are from the (not entirely reliable) Thomas translation, *History of Materialism and criticism of its present importance*, 2nd ed., 3 vols., trans. Ernest Chester Thomas (Boston: James Osgood, 1877).

[188] Lange adopts a nuanced position on the question of the oriental origins of philosophy, speaking of 'the cruder view that the East taught philosophy to the Greeks', but noting

sanctioned rival Platonic and Aristotelian philosophies, and was eventually revived in the seventeenth century to provide the underpinnings for modern science.[189] Materialism was also proposed as having genuine emancipatory potential for the human race. Lange drew attention to its capacity to dispel superstition and reliance upon clerical authority and thus serve as an agent for the promotion of rational autonomy.[190] As for religion and theology, Lange offered the generalisation that 'every system of philosophy entered upon an inevitable struggle with the theology of its time'. Religious belief, for its part, was deemed to be childish and effeminate.[191] At the same time, not least on account of his Kantian commitments, Lange sought to retain a space for moral and aesthetic values that was resistant to the reductive tendencies of hard-core materialism. It is not difficult to see why this would prove attractive to Tyndall, who believed that materialism, when restricted to a scientific context, left space for the affective and aesthetic.[192] Tyndall would reference Lange as 'a non-materialist' while relying on critical, anti-supernaturalist aspects of his historical analysis.

Another of Tyndall's sources was the American chemist and part-time historian John William Draper (1811–82).[193] Draper is best known to historians of science as one of the architects of the 'conflict thesis' – the notion that Western history is characterised by a perennial battle between science and religion – set out in his seminal *History of the Conflict between Religion and Science* (1874). This notorious work draws upon the argument of Draper's earlier *History of the Intellectual Development of Europe* (1863) to which Tyndall refers in his 'Belfast Address'. In the earlier book Draper advanced the common view of the period that civilisation does not progress 'in an arbitrary

---

at the same time that it was in the more easterly Greek colonies that materialistic science began. *History of Materialism*, vol. 1, p. 9, n. 5.

[189] Frederick C. Beiser, *After Hegel: German Philosophy, 1840–1900* (Princeton: Princeton University Press, 2014), pp. 92–5.

[190] Beiser, *After Hegel*, p. 93.

[191] Lange, *History of Materialism*, vol. 1, p. 4. 'The great mass of the professors of all religions may indeed still be in a state of mind like that in which children listen to fairy-tales. The full masculine sense for reality and verifiable accuracy is simply yet undeveloped. Only with its appearance does the credibility of these stories disappear …' (vol. 3, p. 281).

[192] Tyndall's aesthetic sensibilities are on display in *Hours of Exercise in the Alps* (New York: Appleton 1896).

[193] For Draper's influence on Tyndall, see 'Belfast Address', pp. 451f., 456. In his 'Apology for the Belfast Address' (p. 509, n.), Tyndall recommends Draper's *History of the Conflict between Religion and Science*. For their correspondence, see James C. Ungureanu, 'Tyndall and Draper', *Notes and Queries* 64 (2017), 125–8. For Draper at the 1860 British Association, James C. Ungureanu, 'A Yankee at Oxford: John William Draper at the British Association for the Advancement of Science at Oxford, 30 June 1860', *Notes and Records of the Royal Society* 70 (2016), 135–50.

manner or by chance, but ... passes through a determinate succession of stages and is development according to law'.[194] In what was already becoming a tired analogy, Draper suggests that the stages of civilisation can be compared to the infancy, childhood, youth, and manhood of the individual. These stages also mapped onto cultures, with 'Australians' again being relegated to the lowermost rung of the human races while the uppermost was reserved for English scientists. The 'celestial genius of Newton' is thus contrasted with 'the Australian savage': 'This man lives in a hollow tree .... He is lost in filth and vermin. His life is like that of a beast; it is concerned only with to-day.'[195]

Draper's understanding of the history of intellectual development was thus tied to his dubious anthropological commitments. These were set out more explicitly in *Human Physiology, Statical and Dynamical* (1856), which drew, in turn, upon the racial theory of Johann Friedrich Blumenbach (1752–1840). In his book on the intellectual development of Europe, Draper sought to show that intellectual progress essentially equates to advancement in science and diminution in the powers of religion. Accordingly, Draper began to recount instances of an imagined science/religion conflict that would constitute the main subject of his subsequent and most successful work: the death of Hypatia at the hands of a religious mob, Pope Calixtus's anathematisation of Halley's comet, the flat earth enjoined by the Church but disproved by Columbus, and Galileo's fate at the hands of the Inquisition.[196] A good number of these were completely fictitious. At the same time, Draper also subscribed to a version of Protestant historiography, allowing that the Reformation 'made a great advance towards intellectual liberty' and 'put an end to the disgraceful miracles that for so many ages had been the scandal of Europe'.[197] He would subsequently declare that while Catholicism and sciences were 'absolutely incompatible ... a reconciliation of the Reformation with Science is not only possible, but would easily take place'.[198]

---

[194] Draper, *Intellectual Development of Europe*, vol. 2, p. 392.

[195] Draper, *Intellectual Development of Europe*, vol. 1, pp. 12f., 26f. Cf. John William Draper, *Human Physiology, Statical and Dynamical; or The Conditions and Course of the Life of Man*, 2nd ed. (New York: Harper and Brothers, 1858), pp. viii, 563f.

[196] Draper, *Intellectual Development of Europe*, vol. 1, p. 324; vol. 2, pp. 171f., 253, 294. To his credit, Draper did acknowledge the scientific contributions made by medieval Islamic scholars such as Alhazen but did not miss the opportunity to compare Islamic science 'with the contemporary monk miracles and monkish philosophy of Europe' (vol. 2, p. 47). Draper implies a preference for a strictly monotheistic Islam over an idolatrous and polytheistic Catholicism, with its 'adoration of the Virgin, the worship of images, the invocation of the saints, and devout attachments to relics and shrines' (vol. 2, p. 2).

[197] Draper, *Intellectual Development of Europe*, vol. 2, pp. 215f.

[198] John William Draper, *History of the Conflict between Religion and Science* [1874] (New York: Appleton, 1898), p. 363. Cf. p. 286. T. H. Huxley also regarded Catholicism as more

6.5 GENEALOGIES OF NATURALISM

Before turning to T. H. Huxley's historical reconstructions, it would be remiss not to advert briefly to Draper's co-accused as a perpetrator of crimes against the history of science, Andrew Dickson White, author of the influential *History of the Warfare of Science with Theology in Christendom* (1896). In fact, as we have seen, the science/religion conflict motif originates in the anti-Catholic rhetoric of the Protestant reformers and a good number of the historical set pieces of versions of the conflict thesis already appear in Enlightenment polemics.[199] But White's work, like that of Draper, was a powerful vector for the dissemination of the conflict story and some of its present-day advocates, curiously, still defer to its dubious authority. White eschewed the standard three-stage version of historical development, reducing it to two: 'More and more I saw [the struggle between Science and Dogmatic Theology] as the conflict between two epochs in the evolution of human thought – the theological and the scientific.'[200] The former was still evidenced among 'peoples of low culture' who represent the survival of 'childish modes of viewing nature, and childish ways of expressing the relations of man to nature'. Christianity represented a more organised form of these primitive impulses, but even in that form its establishment was alleged to have 'arrested the normal development of the physical sciences for over fifteen hundred years'.[201]

It is worth pointing out at this juncture that historical conflicts and tensions were not invariably viewed in a negative light. Hegelian histories had tended to stress creative tension as a driver of historical change and progress. In his seminal *History of Civilization in Europe* (1828), Huguenot statesman and historian François Guizot proposed that class conflict, along with a productive friction between Europe's Roman, Christian, and Germanic traditions, was a motor of historical progress (albeit under the superintendence of divine providence).[202] In England, J. S. Mill went so far as to propose

---

difficult to reconcile to science than Protestantism. See 'Mr Darwin's Critics', *CE*, vol. 2, pp. 146–8. Henry Thomas Buckle ran a similar line, *History of Civilization*, vol. 1, pp. 261–2. On Buckle's historiography see Hesketh, *The Science of History*.

[199] For a definitive account of the influence of Draper and White see James C. Ungureanu, *Science, Religion, and the Protestant Tradition: Retracing the Origins of Conflict* (Pittsburgh: University of Pittsburgh Press, 2018).

[200] Andrew Dickson White, *A History of the Warfare of Science with Theology in Christendom*, 2 vols. (London: Macmillan, 1897), vol. 1, p. ix.

[201] White, *History of the Warfare*, vol. 1, pp. 307, 375. White relied on Tylor's *Primitive Culture* for a number of his observations about social evolution.

[202] François Guizot, *Civilization in Europe*, 3 vols., trans. William Hazlitt (London: David Bogue, 1846), see esp., vol. 1, pp. 22–7. Guizot also held that the religious conflict of the Reformation led to 'the franchisement of the human mind, an insurrection of the

that 'the antagonism of influences ... is the only real security for continued progress'.[203] This principle could also be applied to tensions between science and religion. The popular lecturer and middling geologist Alexander Winchell maintained that 'this perpetual antagonism is not, nevertheless, an abnormal condition, but an example of the universal economy of God, who has ordained antagonism as the condition of progress in the natural and moral worlds'.[204] This comported with theistic interpretations of Darwin's 'struggle for existence' which, as already noted, also resonated with Thomas Malthus's unsavoury assertions about providentially guided population control. It is not surprising, then, that the chief architects of the new histories of naturalism were sympathetic to possible positive outcomes of historical conflict. Tyndall obliquely remarked, referring to the history of civilisation, that 'the plant is all the hardier for the bendings and buffetings it has undergone'.[205] Huxley, to whom we now turn, also thought that historical conflict could sometimes be fruitful, whether it be between the sciences and religion, or between 'the Semitic and Aryan race'.[206]

Thomas Henry Huxley's construction of the history of naturalism has much in common with Tyndall's genealogy and drew upon some of its sources, not least, Lange's *History of Materialism*.[207] In his 1887 essay 'The Progress of Science' Huxley sketched out the contours of the history of naturalism with a view to establishing that it was not a radical nineteenth-century novelty but the culmination of an intellectual movement that had begun with the Renaissance and Reformation. Variations on this genealogy would subsequently extend it back to the ancient Greeks. Science began 'in ancient Greece and, after being dammed up for a thousand years, once more began to flow three centuries ago'. The causes of the blockage were, predictably, the disruptions that ensued upon the decline of the Roman Empire and 'the diversion of men's thought from sublunary matters to the problems of the supernatural world suggested by Christian dogma in the

---

human mind against absolute power in the spiritual order' (vol. 1, p. 219). There are echoes of Guizot's general approach in Remi Brague's more recent *Eccentric Culture: A Theory of Western Civilization*, trans. Samuel Lester (South Bend: St Augustine's Press, 2002).

[203] J. S. Mill, *Considerations on Representative Government* (London: Parker, Son, and Bourn, 1861), pp. 42–3. I am grateful to Eric Schliesser for drawing my attention to this passage in Mill.

[204] Alexander Winchell, *Reconciliation of Science and Religion* (New York: Harper and Brothers, 1877), p. 41.

[205] Tyndall, 'Professor Virchow and Evolution', p. 625.

[206] Huxley, 'Genesis versus Nature', *CE*, vol. 4, p. 161.

[207] Huxley, 'Descartes' Discourse on Method', *CE*, vol. 1, p. 190, n.

Middle Ages'. This tributary of thought had its origins in the primitive speculations of the 'semi-barbarous Hebrew'.[208] The seventeenth century witnessed the realisation of the original inheritance of the Greeks and science has progressed at pace since then.[209] Against the background of this story of change and progress stood factors that were permanent features of human nature and society. On the one hand, science and its naturalistic methods 'are everywhere the same'. On the other, supernaturalism has 'deep roots in human nature'. Scientific progress, then, necessarily arises out of an ongoing contest between these opposed but perennial human tendencies.[210]

While Tyndall had followed Lange in attributing the origins of naturalism to Democritus and the Greek atomists, Huxley sought a more proximate origin – the scientific revolution and the age of Descartes. This was 'one of the great intellectual epochs of the intellectual life of mankind' – a period when science openly challenged philosophy and the Church.[211] Descartes's singular contribution was to have resolved all the phenomena of the universe 'into matter and motion or forces operating according to law'.[212] The invention of laws of nature is directly equated with 'the principle of scientific naturalism ... which was first clearly formulated by Descartes'. When adopted, this principle undercuts the evidence for any 'extant form of Supernaturalism'.[213] Descartes, of course, had attributed the authorship of laws of nature to God, with the divine will grounding their universality and immutability. And while he had espoused a kind of materialistic reductionism, he had also posited a non-material realm of mind completely distinct from that of matter. This was hardly thoroughgoing naturalism. In a sense, though, Huxley was correct to see that Descartes's innovations established

---

[208] Huxley, 'The Origin of Species', *CE*, vol. 2, p. 52.
[209] Huxley, 'The Progress of Science', *CE*, vol. 1, pp. 43, 44, 46. Cf. 'Controverted Questions', *CE*, vol. 5, pp. 38f. For a similar genealogy of agnosticism, see 'Agnosticism', *CE*, vol. 5, pp. 245f.; 'Controverted Questions', *CE*, vol. 5, p. 7. Ernst Haeckel set out a similar trajectory in his best-selling *Die Welträthsel* (1899). 'The triumph of Christianity and its mystic theories meant retrogression to anatomy, as it did to all other sciences.' Subsequently: 'With the Reformation begins the new birth of fettered reason, the reawakening of science, which the iron hand of the Christian Papacy had relentlessly crushed for 1200 years.' Ernst Haeckel, *The Riddle of the Universe*, trans. Joseph McCabe (London: Watts and Co., 1929), pp. 19, 261.
[210] Huxley, 'The Progress of Science', *CE*, vol. 1, p. 60; 'Controverted Questions', *CE*, vol. 5, p. 32.
[211] Huxley, 'On Descartes' *Discourse*', *CE*, vol. 1, pp. 179f. Huxley opposed the caricature of Descartes as an armchair speculator and pointed to his experimental work. 'On the Hypothesis that Animals are Automata', *CE*, vol. 1, p. 201.
[212] Huxley, 'On Descartes' *Discourse*', *CE*, vol. 1, p. 181.
[213] Huxley, 'Controverted Questions', *CE*, vol. 5, pp. 38f.

the conditions that made possible the emergence of a materialistic naturalism, once the theistic underpinning of laws of nature was repressed or ignored.

Huxley also drew upon the historical rhetoric of the early modern period, appropriating the language of religious reform and proposing that 'a new Reformation' was imminent.[214] This was not to be another phase in the evolution of Christianity, however, but rather a major intellectual shift in European culture that would finally see 'the foot of Science on the necks of her enemies'. Enemy number one was Christian theology.[215] There has been 'a historical evolution of humanity', Huxley contended, a progressive process that consists in the 'elimination of the supernatural from its originally large occupation of men's thoughts'.[216] His envisaged reformation would be the final step of this eliminative process. As we have seen, Tyndall had a similar idea about historical advance and the place of religion, speaking of its progressive historical 'purification', which would perhaps end with its elimination. It is true that Huxley sometimes observed a distinction between theology and religion, allowing for a more positive assessment of the latter.[217] But as William Gladstone astutely remarked, this was akin to advocating an admiration of trees and flowers while despising botany.[218]

With its newly constructed lineage, epitomised in the histories of Huxley, Tyndall, and others, naturalism was destined to become *the* distinguishing feature of science which, in turn, was increasingly understood as providing the only legitimate index of human advancement. As a rallying principle, naturalism proved to be more durable than any of the previously essayed alternatives – materialism, positivism, rationalism, agnosticism. At the close of the nineteenth century, the statesman and part-time philosopher Arthur James Balfour (of Balfour Declaration fame) observed that 'naturalism' had

---

[214] On Huxley's 'new Reformation' see B. G. Murphy, 'Thomas Huxley and His New Reformation', PhD thesis, Northern Illinois University, 1973, pp. 53–79; Bernard Lightman, 'Robert Elsmere and the Agnostic Crises of Faith', in *Victorian Faith in Crisis: Essays on Continuity and Change in Nineteenth-Century Belief*, ed. Richard J. Helmstadter and Bernard Lightman (Stanford: Stanford University Press, 1990), pp. 283–311, esp. 302–7; James C. Ungureanu, 'Science, Religion, and the New Reformation of the Nineteenth Century', *Science and Christian Belief* 31 (2019), 41–61. For Huxley's identification with Luther, see Huxley to Charles Kingsley, 23 September 1860, *Life and Letters of Thomas Henry Huxley*, vol. 1, p. 293.

[215] Huxley to Dyster, 30 January 1859, Huxley Papers 15.106, The Huxley File, http://alepho.clarku.edu/huxley/guide14.html, accessed 5 March 2022.

[216] Huxley, 'Controverted Questions', *CE*, vol. 5, p. 7.

[217] Huxley, 'Genesis versus Nature', *CE*, vol. 4, pp. 161f.

[218] William Ewart Gladstone, 'The Distinction between Religion and Theology', in *Thoughts from the Writings and Speeches of William Ewart Gladstone*, ed. G. Barnett Smith (London: Ward, Lock and Bowden, 1894), pp. 91–3 (p. 91).

now become the favoured label for advocates of scientific secularism. The attractions of this naturalism, moreover, he perceptively attributed to its questionable insinuation into the history and current practice of science: 'Who would pay the slightest attention to naturalism', wrote Balfour, 'if it did not force itself into the retinue of science, assume her livery, and claim, as a kind of poor relation, in some sort to represent her authority and to speak with her voice.'[219]

The thesis of a long-standing historical alliance of naturalism and science, along with their joint placement in the vanguard of human progress, was accompanied by retrospective realignments of historical figures. Science and philosophy were together placed on the side of naturalism and progress and there was a reordering of the lists of scientific heroes. The Presocratic 'naturalists' were one beneficiary of the new rankings, but there were far less congruous conscripts to the cause of science and progress – perhaps none more so than Giordano Bruno, whose negligible contributions were compensated for by the fact that he could be disingenuously depicted as a martyr for science at the hands of the Inquisition.

These dubious re-realignments did not go unchallenged. Henry Wentworth Acland, Oxford's Regius Professor of Medicine, felt it necessary to remined his colleagues in the Metaphysical Society – a venue where these issues were debated by some of the leading intellectuals of Victorian England – that in asserting his faith in 'an Infinite Being' he was sharing the commitments of a lineage of philosophical and scientific luminaries: 'Plato, Berkeley, Butler, Newton, Kant, and the Herschels'.[220] Friedrich Nietzsche, who it is safe to say did not share Acland's religious sympathies, nonetheless agreed that 'since Plato, all theologians and philosophers have been on the same track' heading in the direction of 'God' and 'the good'.[221] On the other side of the Atlantic, William James likewise claimed supernaturalism for the philosophical tradition: 'If one should make a division of all thinkers into naturalists and supernaturalists, I should undoubtedly go, *along with most philosophers*, into the supernaturalist branch.'[222] That we now find these alignments surprising is testimony to the remarkable success of

---

[219] Arthur James Balfour, *The Foundations of Belief* (New York: Longmans, Green, and Co., 1895), pp. 6, 135.
[220] Henry Wentworth Ackland, 'Faith and Knowledge', *Papers of the Metaphysical Society*, vol. 2, pp. 15–20.
[221] Friedrich Nietzsche, *Beyond Good and Evil*, 5, §191, trans. Adrian Del Caro, *Complete Works*, vol. 8 (Stanford: Stanford University Press, 2014), pp. 86f.
[222] William James, *The Varieties of Religious Experience* [1902] in *William James, Writings, 1902–1910* (New York: Library of America, 1987), p. 464 (my emphasis).

Tyndall, Huxley, and others in prosecuting the alternative, ahistorical view, which reversed long-standing alliances and rendered plausible the widespread post-nineteenth-century prejudice that science and philosophy had ever been united in their opposition to religion and 'supernaturalism'.

Just a few decades after the interventions of Tyndall and Huxley, philosopher Roy Wood Sellars could make the confident declaration that 'we are all naturalists now'.[223] While claiming for his version of naturalism a sophistication that he believed was lacking in earlier attempts of Huxley, Haeckel, and Spencer, Sellars was nonetheless singing from the same hymn-sheet: 'Naturalism has always arisen in opposition to what we may call "supernatural" propositions, whether these be the naïve mythological explanations of world phenomena found in the primitive religions, or supernatural popular metaphysics which usually accompanies the higher forms.' On the positive side of the ledger, naturalism was to be equated with the scientific perspective: a view of the world 'which flows by inner necessity from the accomplishments of science'. Sellars proposed that 'the spirit of naturalism would seem to be one with the spirit of science itself'.[224] Science, naturalism, and the rejection of supernatural entities, in short, are pretty much the same thing. All of this was reinforced with the same set of historical reconstructions that had informed the late nineteenth-century narratives: the progressive stages of history approach, the purported conflict between science and religion, and the identification of the same scientific heroes of human advancement.[225] In the century between Sellars and the present, naturalism in this basic sense has established itself as the default position in the Western intellectual tradition.

6.6 The Perfume of an Empty Vase

Recognition of the problematic nature of these stories about the origins and development of naturalism calls for more than just an acknowledgement that some familiar stories about the origins of secular modernity are untrue. These narratives also raise the general question of why we should think that historical processes, with all their messiness and contingency, should have uniquely delivered to our own moment in history and to our corner of

---

[223] Sellars, *Evolutionary Naturalism*, p. vii.
[224] Sellars, *Evolutionary Naturalism*, pp. 5, 18f. The reference on p. 5 originally comes from Rudolf Otto, *Naturalism and Religion*, trans. J. Arthur Thomson and Margaret R. Thomson (London: Williams and Norgate, 1907), p. 18.
[225] Roy Wood Sellars, *The Next Step in Religion: An Essay toward the Coming Renaissance* (New York: Macmillan, 1918), Foreword, pp. 4, 6, 29, 98, 117f.

the globe an approach to the world, a toolkit of scientific methods, and an ensemble of philosophical categories that are superior to anything that has come before – in Western culture or anywhere else. The obvious answer to this question, often explicitly articulated, is that scientific progress vindicates the naturalistic approach that characterises our present intellectual endeavours. However, this response rests upon two assumptions that have already been subjected to historical assessment and found wanting: first, that naturalism is intrinsic to science and hence to scientific progress; second, that the very terms in which the question is put – especially 'progress' and the 'naturalism/supernaturalism' distinction – are unproblematic and universal categories that can be applied without prejudice to the historical instances under consideration.[226]

Considering the first assumption, the relevant history suggests that naturalism is not intrinsic to science, unless we take the peculiarly narrow view that true science has existed only since the explicit adoption of naturalism in the late nineteenth century and that its rationality does not rely upon theological premises. Key figures in the history of science such as Kepler, Descartes, Boyle, Newton, Faraday, Maxwell, Planck, and Heisenberg hardly fit the mould of scientific naturalism. Moreover, their theistic commitment was often foundational to their views about the regularity of nature and the specific character of that regularity.[227] It looks very much as if advocacy of naturalism, understood as an appeal to invariant regularities in the physical world, is really just a version of deism under a different description. It was the task of late nineteenth-century champions of naturalism to overwrite inconvenient historical realities with their own version of history, introducing at the same time a modified conception of science that retrospectively constructed it as perennially naturalistic.

As for the second assumption, to do with uncritical acceptance of the conceptual framing of the arguments for naturalism, we have seen that these concepts have a past and that they were not even constants in the history of Western thought, far less further afield. It follows that the success of naturalistic science alone cannot vindicate naturalism, since naturalism need not be intrinsic to scientific endeavour. At the same time, the framing of the

---

[226] To these, we can add a third difficulty, which is that what is counted as 'scientific' success is often down to the achievements of engineering, technology, and public health measures. See Stephen Gaukroger, 'Does Science Get Credit for Too Much?', *Journal of the Proceedings of the Royal Society of New South Wales* 156 (2023), 195–200.

[227] On that general theme see Harrison and Roberts (eds.), *Science without God?*; Jordan, *Naturalism in the Christian Imagination*, pp. 6–10. On the attempt to vindicate naturalism on the basis of the 'success' of science, see Harrison, 'Naturalism and the Success of Science'.

argument in terms of 'success' combined with a naturalism/supernaturalism distinction begs the question, since there are uncritical assumptions buried in these notions that predetermine the outcome of an enquiry posed in these terms.

A related difficulty for progress stories that posit an inevitable historical movement away from religion to naturalistic science lies in the fact that the thesis of historical advancement in the direction of naturalism appears to be deeply indebted to providential and eschatological modes of thought. It has been repeatedly observed that Jewish and Christian views of history have been a key source of modern understandings of historical progress.[228] These generally take one of two forms. First, Judaeo-Christian eschatological hopes, which had traditionally been focused upon what was to take place at the end of history, are brought within the horizon of secular time. Alternatively, the idea of the providential guidance of history is taken over and given a secular or naturalistic gloss. At times, these two elements might be combined, and some of the commentary on the secularisation of historical directionality is not always clear about the distinction. In both cases, however, the idea is that secular prophets of progress have adopted an understanding of history that would make sense only within an overtly theological framework. The idea that history moves towards a particular end either draws on the unacknowledged motivating force of providence or amounts to an importation into secular time of a Christian conception of the eschaton.[229] Progressive philosophies of history, on this view, are essentially crypto-theologies of history. If this is true, it follows that our confidence in the superiority of naturalism as an approach to the world is, in fact, indebted to the religious assumptions upon which the idea of progress was original founded.

[228] See, e.g., Carl L. Becker, *The Heavenly City of the Eighteenth-Century Philosophers* (New Haven: Yale University Press, 1932); Bury, *Idea of Progress*, p. 73; Löwith, *Meaning in History*; John Baillie, *The Belief in Progress* (London: Oxford University Press, 1950); Christopher Dawson, *Progress and Religion: An Historical Enquiry* (London: Sheed and Ward, 1929). For further background, see Harrison, 'Normativity and the Critical Functions of Genealogy'.

[229] Walter Benjamin, for example, argued that Marxist conceptions of historical development made no sense without the assumption of a theological motor of history. 'On the Concept of History' [1930], in *Selected Writings, Vol. 4, 1938–1940* (Cambridge, MA: Harvard University Press, 2003), pp. 389–400. Eric Voegelin cautioned against attempts to make the eschaton immanent in historical time. *The New Science of Politics*, pp. 187–91, and *passim*. More recently, for Ernesto Laclau and Chantal Mouffe the eschatological animus of Marxism is a 'dangerous illusion'. *Hegemony and Social Strategy*, 2nd ed. (London: Verso, 2014), pp. 49, 127. Some nineteenth-century figures openly acknowledged this, linking scientific progress to eschatology, as Francis Bacon and others had done in the seventeenth century. See, e.g., Thomas Dick, *Improvement of Society* and *The Philosophy of a Future State* [1829] (Glasgow: William Collins, 1869), p. 47.

6.6 THE PERFUME OF AN EMPTY VASE

There has been no shortage of observers of history making this general point. In his classic *Meaning in History* (1949), Karl Löwith insisted that any philosophy of history must be 'entirely dependent on theology of history, in particular on the theological concept of history as a history of fulfilment and salvation'.[230] Lee Tuveson maintained similarly that the 'almost sacred character of the dogma of unilinear progress was connected with a faith in progressive redemption through temporal history'.[231] Russian philosopher and theologian Nikolai Berdyaev suggested that Christianity 'supplied the postulate of universal history without which a philosophy of history is altogether impossible'.[232] Twentieth-century political systems have often been presented as 'exhibit A' for this thesis. Sociologist Jacob Taubes would speak in similar terms of the 'philosophical eschatology' of Europe.[233] Carl Schmitt's celebrated (if not uncontested) observation about modern politics is yet another version of this thesis: 'All significant concepts of the theory of the state are secularized theological concepts.'[234]

Not only do these assessments seek to identify the true historical origins of various schemas of secular progress. They also raise the question of the

---

[230] Löwith, *Meaning in History*, p. 1, and *passim*. See also David Spadafora, *The Idea of Progress in Eighteenth-Century Britain* (New Haven: Yale University Press, 1990), pp. 105–33; Warren W. Wagar, *Terminal Visions: The Literature of Last Things* (Bloomington: Indiana University Press, 1982), pp. 18, 60; Abrams, *Natural Supernaturalism*, p. 63; Robin Barnes, 'Images of Hope and Despair: Western Apocalypticism ca. 1500–1800', in *The Continuum History of Apocalypticism*, ed. Bernard J. McGinn, John J. Collins, and Stephen J. Stein (New York: Continuum International Publishing, 2003), pp. 323–53. Hans Blumenberg criticised aspects of the Löwith's 'secularisation' thesis in his magisterial *The Legitimacy of the Modern Age*, trans. Robert M. Wallace (Cambridge, MA: MIT Press, 1985). For an account of the controversy see Peter E. Gordon, 'Secularization, Genealogy, and the Legitimacy of the Modern Age: Remarks on the Lowith-Blumenberg Debate', *Journal of the History of Ideas* 80 (2019), 147–70; Sjoerd Griffioen, *Contesting Modernity in the German Secularization Debate: Karl Löwith, Hans Blumenberg and Carl Schmitt in Polemical Contexts* (Leiden: Brill, 2022).

[231] Tuveson, *Millennium and Utopia*, p. 201.

[232] Nicolas Berdyaev, *The Meaning of History*, trans. George Reavey (London: Bles, 1949), p. 123, cf. p. 36.

[233] Jacob Taubes, *Occidental Eschatology*, trans. David Ratmoko (Stanford: Stanford University Press, 2009), pp. 125–90.

[234] Carl Schmitt, *Political Theology: Four Chapters on the Concept of Sovereignty* [1922/1934] (Chicago: University of Chicago Press, 2005), p. 41. William T. Cavanaugh offers a different version of the modern state as secularised Christian polity. *Theopolitical Imagination: Discovering the Liturgy as a Political Act in an Age of Global Consumerism* (London: T&T Clark, 2002). For an engaging critical take on the Schmittian idea, which incorporates the thought of Erik Peterson and Giorgio Agamben, see Nicholas Heron, *Liturgical Power: Between Economic and Political Theology* (New York: Fordham University Press, 2018). Part of Heron's argument is that because theology is already political, secular politics cannot be explained by a secularisation story.

internal coherence of these systems and of how they might actually 'work' when the animating impulse of a some 'non-natural' agency – whether transcendent or immanent – has been removed. These critiques, in other words, are not simply the naïve exemplifications of the genetic fallacy – assuming that revealing the origins of a form of thought will necessarily invalidate it. The issue is whether operative elements of the original theological premise have been illicitly carried over into their secularisation versions. In his comprehensive study of Western conceptions of perfectibility, historian of ideas John Passmore expressed it this way: 'Secular perfectibilism ... lacks that metaphysical underpinning which lends what plausibility it possesses, for all its vulnerability to philosophical criticism, to the idea of perfection by divine action.'[235] Others made the case for particular schemas. Comte's stages of history, understood as inexorable laws, were for Löwith merely 'a pale shadow of that eschatological expectation which constituted the core of early Christianity'. The historical determinism of Comte's system was 'hardly intelligible' outside the context of the Christian faith. A similar judgement was reserved for *The Communist Manifesto* of Marx and Engels. This was Christian eschatology 'perverted into secular prognostication' and exhibiting all 'the basic features of a messianic faith'.[236] Literary and social critic Walter Benjamin made the same point with his arresting image of 'the mechanical Turk'. (The mechanical Turk was a device constructed in the late eighteenth century which to all appearances was an ingenious chess-playing automaton. In reality, it was controlled by a concealed human operator.) Benjamin implied that Marxist theory, while ostensibly opposed to religion, continued to draw upon the hidden power of theological concepts now disguised beneath the veil of secularity. For the trick to work, the theological agency had to remain hidden. Yet, shattering this illusion and bringing this hidden agency to light becomes necessary at a certain point.[237] For Benjamin, theology had to be the motivating force for dialectical materialism if it were to

---

[235] John Passmore, *The Perfectibility of Man* (Indianapolis: Liberty Fund, 2000), p. 303.

[236] Löwith, *Meaning in History*, pp. 84, 44. For Marxism as secularised eschatology see also Alasdair MacIntyre, *Marxism and Christianity* (Notre Dame: University of Notre Dame Press, 1984), p. 27. MacIntyre points out that Marxism also inherits, via Hegel, Christian conceptions of fallenness or alienation, along with secularised notions of Christian virtue (pp. 62, 92, 142). For other aspects of Marxism potentially indebted to Protestant thought see Michael Sonenscher, *Capitalism: The Story behind the Word* (Princeton: Princeton University Press, 2022), pp. 87–90.

[237] Benjamin, 'On the Concept of History', p. 389. I am grateful to Nick Heron for discussions about the significance of this passage. This issue is not unrelated to other critiques of Marxism in relation to its own ungrounded normative commitments. See, e.g., Stefan Breuer, 'Die Depotenzierung der kritischen Theorie', *Leviathan* 10 (1982), 132–46.

6.6 THE PERFUME OF AN EMPTY VASE

retain its revolutionary potential.[238] This was equally true for the reforming aspirations of the early Frankfurt School with which Benjamin was affiliated.

Accounting for the hidden motive force of historical change was not the only difficulty for secular eschatologies. For many commentators writing in the aftermath of the Second World War, the rise of both Nazism and communism were understood as aberrant attempts to realise distorted versions of Judaeo-Christian hopes. Henri de Lubac suggested that modern conceptions as freedom, egality, and fraternity made sense only in their original Christian framework. As 'laicised' notions, extracted from their original context, they have a tendency to degenerate into dangerous ideologies and utopian fantasies.[239] For Eric Voegelin, both Bolshevism and Nazism were 'political religions' that resulted from the cardinal sin of attempting to 'immanentize' the Christian eschaton.[240] Again, these analyses parallel those of the Frankfurt School, with Max Horkheimer and Theodor Adorno also seeking to account for the abject failure of Europe to realise the high hopes of Enlightenment optimists, descending instead into barbarism and totalitarianism.[241]

Why all of this matters for our argument is that the legitimacy of the concepts and knowledge-yielding enterprises delivered to us by history requires the historical processes that generated them to be in some sense reliable, rational, or even truth-tracking. But if the lines of critique outlined above are on the right track, the reliability of what history delivers to our present moment is either accidental or turns out to be ultimately dependent upon some providential or teleological understanding of historical processes. On this reading, those who assume history to be leading inexorably towards a secular, naturalistic understanding of everything are unwittingly (and paradoxically) invoking a hidden theology of history.

The clearest indications of the theological underpinning of present-day progressive histories were provided by Hegel and some of the English and Scottish social theorists of the eighteenth century. If anything in Hegel is clear, it is the centrality of the operations of *Geist* in his historical vision. This

---

[238] Peter E. Gordon, *Migrants in the Profane: Critical Theory and the Question of Secularization* (New Haven: Yale University Press, 2020), pp. 20–63.

[239] Henri de Lubac, 'A Christian Explanation for our Times', in *Theology and History*, pp. 440–56. De Lubac also offered an alternative to Schmitt's version of the secularisation of Christian polity in his *Corpus Mysticum*, a thesis that influenced the secularisation theories of Ernst Kantorowicz, Georgio Agamben, and Marcel Gauchet. See Shortall, 'Theological Origins of Secularization'.

[240] Voegelin, *The New Science of Politics*, pp. 183–5.

[241] Max Horkheimer and Theodor W. Adorno, *Dialectic of Enlightenment* [1947], trans. E. Jephcott (Stanford: Stanford University Press, 2002).

would be carried over into the historical understandings of both Left and Right Hegelians, however much the former might have wished to ignore it. This Christian-Neoplatonic understanding of history is also explicit in the English idealist philosophers T. H. Green and R. G. Collingwood. For Green, progress in history implies an end 'which is not itself a series in time, but is both comprehended eternally in the eternal mind and intrinsically, or in itself eternal'.[242] In *The Idea of History*, R. G. Collingwood argued that Christianity had given rise to a new conception of history 'according to which the historical process is the working out not of man's purposes, but of God's'. It is this that enables the discernment of an 'intelligible pattern' in history.[243]

Many years before this, in a parallel argument, Ferguson, Malthus, and (arguably) Smith had straightforwardly attributed the emergence of social and economic order to providential superintendence. Only later was this overwritten with such causally vacuous notions as 'spontaneous order' – or 'design without a designer', as Austrian economist and political philosopher Friedrich Hayek expressed it.[244] As is well known, Hayek espoused the notion that the chief function of the state is to ensure the freedom of individuals and markets which, left to their own devices, will become self-regulating. Hayek was not unaware of the historical lineage of the key idea of spontaneous order, finding precedents in the Stoics, scholastics, early modern thinkers such as Bernard de Mandeville, and, especially, Scottish Enlightenment thinkers including Adam Ferguson.[245] But providence is conspicuously absent from the backstory that Hayek constructed for his own position. The great discovery of the eighteenth-century Scots, he

---

[242] T. H. Green, *Prolegomena to Ethics* (Oxford: Clarendon Press, 1883), §189, pp. 198f.
[243] R. G. Collingwood, *The Idea of History* (Oxford: Clarendon Press, 1948), pp. 48f.
[244] Friedrich A. Hayek, 'The Use of Knowledge in Society', in *Individualism and Economic Order* (Chicago: University of Chicago Press, 1948), pp. 77–91. For Hayek's adoption of the phrase see Louis Hunt, 'The Origin and Scope of Hayek's Idea of Spontaneous Order', in *Liberalism, Conservatism, and Hayek's Idea of Spontaneous Order*, ed. L. Hunt and P. McNamara (New York: Palgrave Macmillan, 2006), pp. 43–64. 'Spontaneous order' was coined by Michael Polanyi. See Straun Jacobs, 'Michael Polanyi's Theory of Spontaneous Orders', *Review of Austrian Economics* 11 (1999), 111–27. For the historical background of the expression see R. Hamowy, *The Scottish Enlightenment and the Theory of Spontaneous Order* (Carbondale: Southern Illinois University Press, 1987). For a comprehensive account of the appearance of notions of self-organisation in the eighteenth century see Jonathan Sheehan and Dror Wahrman, *Invisible Hands: Self-Organization and the Eighteenth Century* (Chicago: University of Chicago Press, 2015).
[245] Friedrich A. Hayek, 'The Results of Human Action but Not of Human Design', in *New Studies in Philosophy, Politics, Economics and the History of Ideas* (Chicago: University of Chicago Press, 1978), pp. 96–105.

contended, was that the emergence of social order 'need not therefore be ascribed to the design of a higher, supernatural intelligence', but was a matter of 'adaptive evolution'.[246] As we have seen, this flies in the face of what Ferguson actually says. Hayek's overwriting of history had the consequence of rendering invisible to his readers the true meaning of the 'invisible hand'. This sanitisation of the history of his own position was likely motivated by the desire to make his economic theory acceptable in an increasingly naturalistic intellectual environment. He was also understandably concerned to avoid the criticism that he had himself levelled against Marxist economists – that they were rehearsing a version of providential history in another guise. Whether 'spontaneous' is able to assume the explanatory burden originally borne by providence remains an open question. As Jessica Whyte has recently observed, 'Hayek's attempt to detach the idea of invisible order from its theological moorings therefore faced him with difficulties ... that only faith could resolve.'[247] In any event, the present-day notions of unintended benefits and self-regulating processes that still haunt some versions of modern economic theory can plausibly be seen as vestiges of earlier providential understandings of a divine economy.[248]

There is also a connection here to the history of scientific naturalism in relation to appeals to laws of nature. The theological origin of the concept

---

[246] Friedrich A. Hayek, *The Constitution of Liberty: The Definitive Edition*, ed. Ronald Hamowy (Chicago: University of Chicago Press, 2011), p. 115.

[247] Jessica Whyte, 'The Invisible Hand of Friedrich Hayek', *Political Theory* 47 (2019), 156–84. Hayek was not unaware of the difficulty of this conception: 'Much of the opposition to a system of freedom under general laws arises from the inability to conceive of an effective co-ordination of human activities without deliberate organization by a commanding intelligence.' 'Principles of a Liberal Social Order', in *Studies in Philosophy, Politics and Society* (London: Routledge & Kegan Paul, 1967), p. 167. Hayek's reference to 'adaptive evolution' may seem to be a nod in the direction of biological evolution. However, while biological evolution may seem to offer a parallel and supporting case, it is not teleological in the same sense, although a case might be mounted for instances of convergent evolution. For discussions of some of these parallels see Harrison and Hesketh, 'Replaying the Tape of Life'. An alternative evolutionary logic might suggest that stable social structures emerge and survive because of their utility. But on that account, the social structures of the oldest cultures in the world would rise to the top of our cultural hierarchies. This is somewhat at odds with the traditional rankings in which the most ancient surviving cultures, such as the Australian, fared poorly.

[248] See Jacob Viner, 'Fashion in Economic Thought', in *Essays on the Intellectual History of Economics*, ed. Douglas A. Irwin (Princeton: Princeton University Press, 1991), pp. 189–99; Robert H. Nelson, *Reaching for Heaven on Earth: The Theological Meaning of Economics* (Savage, MD: Rowman & Littlefield, 1991); Robin Klay and John Lunn, 'The Relationship of God's Providence to Market Economics and Economic Theory', *Journal of Markets and Morality* 6 (2003), 541–64. For the early modern background of these ideas, see Hengstmengel, 'Divine Oeconomy'.

of laws of nature in the scientific context is well established. As we have seen, that theological foundation remained in place for many scientific thinkers through the nineteenth century. To be sure, that original conception can be reframed so that laws are understood to have a different grounding – understood, for example, as generalisations constructed on the basis of cumulative observations.[249] This provides an escape clause for those wishing to avoid committing to the theistic logic of such laws. However, this weaker Humean formulation will not bestow upon laws of nature the kind of necessity that would make them exceptionless. More technically, we might say that it is not clear how laws of nature, understood in this attenuated sense, will support counterfactuals.[250] The bind for those seeking to deploy laws of nature against theistic interpretations of natural order is that for the argument to work they ideally need the stronger, exceptionless version of laws of nature. Historically, that version was theistically grounded. It does not follow that naturalism is untrue: it is just that a common assumption that it is supported by science is confused.[251]

The history of the use of 'laws' in the social sciences follows a similar course in some respects. While laws in this context lack the strictly deterministic character of the laws of physical world, they are nonetheless often thought to be sufficiently rigorous to have explanatory power and offer

---

[249] On the range of options for understanding laws of nature, which goes beyond this rather simple dichotomy, see David Armstrong, *What Is a Law of Nature?* (Cambridge: Cambridge University Press, 1983); John W. Carrol, *Laws of Nature* (Cambridge: Cambridge University Press, 1994); W. Ott and L. Patton (eds.), *Laws of Nature* (Oxford: Oxford University Press, 2018). For some of the theological issues see John Foster, *The Divine Lawmaker* (Oxford: Clarendon Press, 2004); Nancy Cartwright and Keith Ward (eds.), *Rethinking Order after the Laws of Nature* (London: Bloomsbury, 2016).

[250] On one common account, the criterion 'supporting counterfactuals' is what distinguishes genuine laws from simple (Humean) generalisations. See, e.g., Marc Lange, 'Laws, Counterfactuals, Stability, and Degrees of Lawhood', *Philosophy of Science* 66 (1999), 243–67; C. Swoyer, 'The Nature of Natural Laws', *Australasian Journal of Philosophy* 60 (1982), 203–23; Jim Woodward, 'What Is a Mechanism? A Counterfactual Account', *Philosophy of Science* 69 (2002), 366–77. For philosophical arguments pointing to the tension between naturalism and explanation in terms of natural regularities see Tomas Bogardus, 'If Naturalism is True, then Scientific Explanation is Impossible', *Religious Studies* 59 (2023), 115–38. Another alternative to account for natural regularities would be a return to something like Aristotelian substantial forms or causal powers. See, e.g., Nancy Cartwright, *The Dappled World: A Study of the Boundaries of Science* (Cambridge: Cambridge University Press, 1999); Rom Harré and E. H. Madden, *Causal Powers: A Theory of Natural Necessity* (Oxford: Blackwell, 1975).

[251] Philosopher Michael Ruse represents a common view that associates scientific naturalism with the appeal only to blind, unbroken, law. But there are no naturalistic grounds for asserting the immutability of laws of nature (whatever they might be in this account). Ruse, 'Removing God from Biology', in *Science without God?*, ed. Harrison and Roberts, pp. 130–46.

predictions about the future course of history.²⁵² The general assumption is that history will tend to follow a certain path, say, towards the classless society and the withering away of the state (Marx). Alternative versions would speak of the 'end of history' which sees secular liberal democracy as the likely destination of all modern nation-states (Fukuyama), or secularisation theories that posit the inevitable withering away of religion (Weber). The common 'three stages of human development' stories are earlier manifestations of the same kind of historical determinism, grounded in the notion of laws. One important difference in appeals to laws in the two domains, however, is that in the social scientific context there is often also a strong normative dimension. An assessment is rendered on the direction in which history is moving – typically a positive one. This is evident in the moral valence of the notion of progress and, harking back to the early schemas, the conviction that movement away from the magical and religious phases towards a scientific stage is generally a good thing.

These social scientific accounts, like standard secularisation stories, thus have descriptive, predictive, and normative components: history can be described as moving in a particular direction; the lawful nature of the historical development enables prediction of future developments; the course taken by history is judged to be progressive or positive. What the preceding analysis would suggest is that the purportedly descriptive elements have from the outset been contaminated by normative considerations. It is this that gives them their essentially mythical character.

The nineteenth century witnessed a remarkable realignment of laws of nature. From the time of their seventeenth-century inception, divinely instituted laws of nature had provided the primary lens for viewing the operations of the natural world, understood as the work of God. Analogous laws were also thought to be operative in the social world, guiding the evolution of human cultures. The scientific naturalists took over this conception, erased its original theological foundation, and forged it into a powerful weapon to be deployed against 'supernaturalists'. Believing scientists now found themselves forced to choose between a progressive but increasingly secular approach to science and what seemed to be backward-looking, obscurantist, supernaturalism. In effect, as Bernard Lightman has shown, they were wedged by the strategies of the scientific naturalists.²⁵³ The

---

²⁵² Thus Buckle: 'A discovery of the laws of European history is resolved, in the first instance, into a discovery of the laws of the human mind. These mental laws, when ascertained, will be the ultimate basis of the history of Europe.' *History of Civilization*, vol. 1, pp. 156–7.

²⁵³ Lightman, 'Naturalistic Metaphysics and the Dead Ends of Victorian Theology'.

compromise they eventually arrived at was 'methodological naturalism': in keeping the general secularising trend towards the privatisation of religion, religious commitment was no longer to have an acknowledged role in the public practice of science.

The recruitment of laws of nature to the services of the 'other side' was accomplished by means of the fabrication of a history of naturalism, narrated in terms of its purported struggles against the countervailing force of 'supernaturalism'. As we have seen from the previous chapter, this new story was made possible by the recent emergence of a naturalism/supernaturalism divide in the sphere of biblical criticism. This was imported into the self-image of the sciences and retrospectively applied to history. Naturalism was doubly indebted to religion, because its historical reconstruction drew upon an incipiently naturalistic Protestant model of history which posited a centuries-long conflict between genuine Christianity and superstitious Catholic miracle-mongering. The providential or eschatological structuring of history, which provided it with meaning and directionality, was similarly imported into the history of naturalism. Again, for obvious reasons, the theological motors of history were rendered invisible. Western ideas of progress and the uniformity of nature, which are central to the logic of naturalism and to its justification, thus have unmistakable theological roots.

7

WHAT THE GREEKS SAW

Language sets the limits and contours of all human knowledge.
    Herder, *Fragments on Recent German Literature*

The limits of my language are [*bedueten*] the limits of my world.
    Wittgenstein, *Tractatus*[1]

Hume's historical case against the credibility of supernatural relations began with the observation that taking such stories seriously would require the abandonment of our own understandings of how the world really operates. As we have seen, the logic of Hume's preference for a naturalistic outlook, in the face of a long standing and cross-cultural consensus, rested upon assumptions of Western exceptionalism and historical progress. Yet, even granting these assumptions, there remain puzzling questions about the nature of the experiences of those recounting stories of the supernatural. Hume seems not to have been overly curious about this, simply proposing that human beings are ruled by co-dependent propensities both to tell lies and to believe them.[2] However, that the ubiquity of supernatural relations is the result of people making things up and successfully persuading gullible contemporaries and a credulous posterity of their truth is a thesis that itself strains credibility. It was certainly resisted by Hume's contemporaries. Thomas Reid made the diametrically opposed claim that our natural

---

[1] Epigraphs: Johann Gottfried von Herder, *Fragmente zur deutschen Literatur* (Tübingen, 1805), pp. 14f.; Wittgenstein, *Tractatus* 5.6. Hilary Putnam characterised Wittgenstein's position in these terms: 'Wittgenstein thinks that secular Europeans see all other forms of life as "pre scientific" or "unscientific" and that this is a vulgar refusal to appreciate difference.' *Pragmatism: An Open Question* (Oxford: Wiley Blackwell, 1995), p. 51.

[2] 'the usual propensity of mankind towards the marvellous' combined with 'it is nothing strange, I hope, that men should lie in every age'. Hume, *Enquiries*, p. 119.

condition is, in fact, constituted by 'two reciprocal principles': the first, a propensity to tell the truth (veracity); the second, a tendency to believe what others tell us.[3] This stance is consistent with Reid's reliabilism and a pragmatic approach to knowledge that recognises its essentially social nature.

The empirical case against Hume's stance has not weakened significantly over time either. In the nineteenth century, Hume's dilemma was powerfully restated by the Quaker writer William Howitt. Confronting religious sceptics who professed allegiance to the principle that knowledge be grounded in cumulative experience, Howitt pointed to 'the statements of the most eminent historians and philosophers of all ages and nations on the manifestation of those spiritual agencies amongst them which we, for want of further knowledge, term supernatural.' He concluded that we must 'either to reject this universal evidence, by which we inevitably reduce all history to a giant fiction ... or accept it, in which case we find ourselves standing face to face with a principle of the most authoritative character for the solution of the spiritual enigmas stemming from the fatal progress of infidelity.'[4] Cataloguing of miracles and experiences of the supernatural continues to the present day, and not all of it is conducted by interested parties.[5] Consider, for example, Jacalyn Duffin, 'the atheist scientist who believes in miracles' as the headlines have it, who has examined numerous medical miracles used in canonisation proceedings of the Catholic Church.[6] Strictly speaking, she does not believe in miracles, but nonetheless describes numerous events that either run counter to current science, or defy explanation in terms of it.[7] None of this is suggestive of a long-running, cross-cultural conspiracy.

---

[3] Reid, *Inquiry* 6.24 (pp. 193–5). For Reid these principles were related to the fact that God made us social creatures.

[4] William Howitt, *The History of the Supernatural, in all ages and nations, and in all Churches, Christian and Pagan: Demonstrating a universal truth*, 2 vols. (London: Longman, Green, Longman, Roberts and Green, 1863), vol. 1, pp. v–vi.

[5] Among the interested parties, see Craig S. Keener, *Miracles: The Credibility of the New Testament Accounts* (Grand Rapids: Baker, 2011); *Miracles Today: The Supernatural Work of God in the Modern World* (Grand Rapids: Baker, 2021); Candy Gunther Brown, *Testing Prayer: Science and Healing* (Cambridge, MA: Harvard University Press, 2010). From a different perspective see also Ward, *Unbelievable*, pp. 1–20; Tanya Luhrmann, 'Metakinesis: How God Becomes Intimate in Contemporary US Christianity', *American Anthropologist* 106 (2004), 518–28.

[6] Marilyn Rodrigues, 'Meet the Atheist Scientist Who Believes in Miracles', *The Catholic Weekly*, 2 March 2017; Jacalyn Duffin, *Medical Miracles: Doctors, Saints, and Healing in the Modern World* (Oxford: Oxford University Press, 2008).

[7] More mundane encounters with the supernatural also continue unabated with a majority of Americans reporting religious or mystical experiences, and a good proportion telling of such occult experiences as communicating with the dead. Pew Survey, www.pewresearch.org/religion/2009/12/09/many-americans-mix-multiple-faiths/, accessed 28 February 2023.

Rather, it prompts questions about the sincerity of those reporting supernatural relations and how, from a naturalistic perspective, so many people have been systematically mistaken about what they encounter. How is it possible to have experiences of 'the supernatural' if there are no non-natural events or spiritual agents?

Before concluding the argument of this book and relating it to some other modernity stories, I want to offer some admittedly unsystematic observations on this residual question. Specifically: when confronted with stories of miracles, are our sole options *either* to dismiss them as falsehoods characteristic of primitive minds and backward societies, *or* to abandon our own scientific assumptions about nature's operations? I am not confident that any of possibilities set out below answer this in a definitive way, but I do not think that the question should be evaded. So even partial responses are worth exploring. What follows, then, is not so much an argument as an attempt to arrive at a partial understanding of the apparent gulf that lies between the commitments of the naturalist on the one hand and the religious experiences of the historical and cultural majority. These go to issues of salience; the theory dependence of observation; the effects of language, concepts, cultural conditioning; and what might be called cultural and scientific myths and liturgies.

7.1 The Wine-Dark Sea and the Invisible Gorilla

Modern readers of Homer might notice that there is something about his depictions of colour that in certain places seem odd. 'Rosy-fingered dawn' is fine, but 'wine-dark sea' makes you wonder what he was drinking.[8] Modern students of the classics were attuned to this issue and developed various theories to account for it. Remarking on Homer's vocabulary of colour, British statesman and part-time Hellenist William Gladstone pointed out that the Greek poet's colour vocabulary was some distance from the seven primary colours that he insisted had been 'determined for us by Nature'. Gladstone's hypothesis was that as we go backward in history the ability to discriminate colours is 'less and less mature'. Homer's 'immaturity' in this regard could be deduced from 'the paucity of his colours' and from the use of the same term to describe what for moderns are different colours. Gladstone concluded that 'the organ of colour and its impressions were but partially

---

[8] There are three references in the *Iliad* and twenty in the *Odyssey* to 'rosy-fingered dawn' (ῥοδοδάκτυλος Ἠώς), and twelve in the *Odyssey*, and five in the *Iliad* to 'wine-faced' or 'wine-eyed' (οἶνοψ πόντος).

developed among the Greeks of the heroic age'.[9] Goethe had earlier come to a similar conclusion (although he rejected the Newtonian analysis of the colour spectrum). The German polymath drew upon the recently described phenomenon of colour-blindness to suggest that the Greeks suffered from a kind of corporate defective vision.[10]

Friedrich Nietzsche, who began his career as a classical philologist, also puzzled over the apparently impoverished state of Homer's expressions for different colours and his idiosyncratic deployment of that limited vocabulary. He concludes that they must have seen a different world:

> How different nature must have appeared to the Greeks if, as we have to admit, their eyes were blind to blue and green, and instead of the former saw deep brown, instead of the latter yellow (so that they used the same word, for example, to describe the colour of dark hair, that of the cornflower, and that of the southern sea ...) how different and how much more like mankind nature must have appeared to them, since in their eyes the coloration of mankind also preponderated in nature and the latter as it were floated in the atmosphere of human coloration!

Nietzsche theorised that it was on account of this shortcoming that the Greeks of the heroic age were given to belief in anthropomorphic deities and the supernaturalising of nature: 'It is on this *deficiency* that there grew up in the Greeks the playful facility which distinguishes them for seeing natural events as gods and demi-gods, that is to say as human-like forms.' At the same time, to work our way out of this 'colourblindness' and discover new pleasures calls for a relinquishing of the old ones.[11]

While Gladstone's analysis is entirely predictable – a conflation of the natural and conventional along with a thesis of historical progress – Nietzsche's approach, in spite of reference to a 'deficiency', is more considered. He focuses on the difference in how the world is imagined and the fact that in spite of what seems to be the restricted colour palette of the Greeks, they were nonetheless able to see *more* in nature than we do. Admittedly, for Nietzsche, the 'more' that they saw may not really have been there, but it is at least theoretically possible to regard this as a difference rather than a deficiency, and this gets us close to what is perhaps a more convincing explanation of what is going on.

---

[9] William Gladstone, *Studies on Homer and the Homeric Age*, 3 vols. (Oxford: Oxford University Press, 1858), vol. 3, pp. 457, 488, 495f.

[10] J. W. von Goethe, 'Erste Abtheilung. Griechen', in *Zur Farbenlehre*, 2 vols. (Tübingen, 1810), vol. 2, pp. 1–59.

[11] Nietzsche, *Dawn*, §426.

7.1 THE WINE-DARK SEA AND THE INVISIBLE GORILLA   357

A more recent explanation of the Greeks' puzzling colour vocabulary, as Maria Michela Sassi has explained, is to do with saliency – subjective features of the appearance of objects that command our attention, and go beyond simple variables such as hue, brightness, and intensity. Salience, inevitably, will be culturally determined to some extent. As it pertains to the winey sea, it is not that the Greeks did not perceive the blue hues of the sea, but that they were more interested in describing another of its features which called to mind 'the shine of a liquid inside a cup'.[12] Here, again, then, it is a matter of what we attend to. It is not too big a stretch to think that differences between a religious and non-religious view of the world can be partly understood in terms of something like salience.

A related consideration comes from relatively recent discussions of the psychological phenomenon of 'predictive processing'. While there are several dimensions to this, the central idea is that the content of our perceptions is shaped less by raw sensory inputs than by 'top-down' mental constructs. The latter are based upon predictions of what is most likely to be the case in any observed scenario. As Jakob Hohwy expresses it:

> A standard conception is that the senses convey a rich signal that somehow represents worldly states of affairs, which the brain is passively soaking up in a bottom up manner …. On the prediction error minimization view, this picture is reversed. The rich representation of worldly states of affairs is signalled in the top down predictions of sensory input, maintained by the perceptual hierarchy of the brain. These predictions, as it were, *query* the world and dampen down predicted sensory input.[13]

There is a growing literature on this approach, characterised by its advocates as representing a 'profound reversal' in how we typically imagine the manner in which the senses depict the world. In short, our view of the world is to a large degree shaped by prior expectations of what we will perceive.[14]

---

[12] Maria Michela Sassi, 'The Sea was Never Blue', *Aeon Magazine*, 31 July 2017, https://aeon.co/essays/can-we-hope-to-understand-how-the-greeks-saw-their-world, accessed 30 November 2020. The Greeks' prioritising of lustre over hue was first proposed by Maurice Platnauer, who nonetheless still subscribed to the view of the Greeks' inferior colour terminology. 'Greek Colour-Perception', *Classical Quarterly* 15 (1921), 153–62. For further discussion see Melissa Funke, 'Colourblind: The Use of Greek Colour Terminology in Cultural Linguistics in the Late Nineteenth and Early Twentieth Centuries', in *Brill's Companion to Classics and Early Anthropology*, ed. Emily Varto (Leiden: Brill, 2018), pp. 255–76; Mark Bradley, 'Colour as a Synaesthetic Experience in Antiquity', in *Synaesthesia and the Ancient Senses*, ed. Shane Bulter and Alex Purves (London: Routledge, 2014), pp. 127–40.

[13] Jakob Hohwy, *The Predictive Mind* (Oxford: Oxford University Press, 2013), p. 47.

[14] In addition to Hohwy, *Predictive Mind*, see Karl Friston, 'Learning and Inference in the Brain', *Neural Networks* 16 (2013), 1325–52; 'A Theory of Cortical Responses', *Philosophical*

For readers of Kant this will have a very familiar ring to it and will not really call for a significant revision of how perception is understood. There are clear affinities between predictive processing and Kant's transcendental arguments to the effect that objects conform to our cognitions rather than the reverse. The Prussian philosopher has accordingly been recognised by some as an important precursor of cognitive science.[15]

Related to selective processing is the phenomenon of selective inattention. In a now classic experiment – the Gorilla Test – subjects who were asked to concentrate on a specific activity being undertaken in a video failed to register the presence of an individual decked out in a full gorilla suit wandering through the scene.[16] There is disagreement about whether stimuli fail to be processed at all, whether they are filtered out in later stages of perceptual processing, and/or whether inattention results from failures of perception and memory. In any event, the gorilla goes unnoticed. We might think, along these lines, that scientific naturalism serves to focus attention closely on certain features of the world – and for entirely good reason and with profitable outcomes. But that focus could potentially result in a failure to see features of the world that in other times and places have seemed obvious.

A comparable phenomenon is the well-known principle in the philosophy of science known as 'the theory-ladenness of observation'.[17] This principle (also referred to as the 'theory-*dependence* of observation') is associated with Norwood Hansen and subsequently became important in the accounts of science offered by Thomas Kuhn and Paul Feyerabend.[18] As the name

---

Transactions of the Royal Society of London, B: Biological Sciences 360 (2005), 815–36; A. Clark, 'Whatever Next? Predictive Brains, Situated Agents and the Future of Cognitive Science', *Behavioural and Brain Sciences* 36 (2013), 181–204.

[15] Link R. Swanson, 'The Predictive Processing Model has Its Roots in Kant', *Frontiers in Systems Neuroscience* 10 (2016), https://doi.org/10.3389/fnsys.2016.00079, accessed 23 November 2023. Cf. Hohwy, *Predictive Mind*, pp. 5f.; A. Brook, 'Kant and Cognitive Science', in *The Prehistory of Cognitive Science*, ed. A. Brook (New York: Palgrave Macmillan, 2007), pp. 117–36.

[16] Daniel J. Simons and Christopher F. Chabris, 'Gorillas in Our Midst: Sustained Inattentional Blindness for Dynamic Events', *Perception* 28 (1999), 1059–74. See also A. Mack and I. Rock, *Inattentional Blindness* (Cambridge, MA: MIT Press, 1998).

[17] For an overview see Alan Chalmers, *What Is This Thing Called Science?*, 4th ed. (Brisbane: University of Queensland Press, 2013), pp. 5–9, 244–51, and *passim*. For an extended discussion see James Bogen, 'Theory and Observation in Science', SEP, https://plato.stanford.edu/archives/sum2017/entries/science-theory-observation/.

[18] Norwood Hansen, *Patterns of Discovery: An Enquiry into the Conceptual Foundations of Science* (Cambridge: Cambridge University Press, 1958); Paul Feyerabend, *Against Method* (New York: Verso, 1975), and 'An Attempt at a Realistic Interpretation of Experience' [1959], in *Realism, Rationalism, and Scientific Method* (Cambridge: Cambridge University Press, 1985), pp. 17–36.

suggests, the idea is that there are no naked 'facts' in the sciences and that our observations are interpreted through a pre-existing grid of concepts and theories. What counts as a fact, and why we focus our attention on some things rather than others, are determined by what we are looking for and why we are looking for it. A weaker version of the principle operates at the semantic level and posits that the meaning of our observational language is at least partly determined by pre-existing theoretical commitments. A stronger, perceptual version holds that the investigator's perceptions are shaped by pre-observation theoretical commitments. Again, whatever the mode of operation of this principle, the history of science is replete with examples of it in operation and this generates obvious difficulties for naïve readings of science that assume a simple process of proceeding from given 'facts' to theories. For our purposes, the point is that investigators wedded to different theories will view the relevant features of the world in different ways according to pre-existing theoretical commitments. The same phenomenon can be spoken of as the sun's motion through the sky, or of the earth's rotation on its axis. What we 'see' is thus at least partly determined by what we already believe. This is not completely remote from Anselm's 'faith seeking understanding' and goes some way towards accounting for how the same event might be interpreted in ways that are consistent with both naturalism and non-naturalism.

7.2 Language and the Limits of Thought

If theorical commitments predetermine, to some extent, how we perceive the world, the same has been said for language. The focus of this book on the specific concepts of 'faith/belief' and 'the supernatural' raises questions about the role of language in shaping our experiences rather than simply reflecting them. These questions were already posed within the models of historical progress discussed in Chapter 6. Turgot, for example, contended that the stages of intellectual development of the human race correlated with the capacity of their languages to express abstract ideas. It was the 'poverty of languages and necessity of metaphor' that led to allegorical and fabulous accounts of physical phenomena. The first philosophers had seen the problem, but their application of categories such as 'essences' and 'faculties' was scarcely any better and explained nothing. Only with the advent of the modern sciences did there develop a language adequate for the true explanation of physical phenomena.[19] Analogous assumptions informed

---

[19] Turgot, *On Universal History*, in *Turgot on Progress, Sociology, and Economics*, ed. and trans. Meek, pp. 92, 102.

missionaries' assertions about a lack of a relevant theological vocabulary among indigenous peoples.

In accordance with the thesis of the Greek origins of philosophy, the classical philologist Bruno Snell (1896–1986) advanced the related thesis that the evolution of philosophical and scientific language was made possible in the West by features of the grammar of ancient Greek. The existence of the definite article, he contended, was the key to abstraction and generalisation, and its potential is evident in the transition from the mythical language of the poets Homer and Hesiod to the philosophical discourses of the Presocratic philosophers: 'from myth to logic', as he put it. Snell's focus was largely on what has been gained by such linguistic innovations – the emergence of 'concepts of man as an intellectual being which decisively influenced the subsequent evolution of European thought'. Greek language made possible 'the origin of scientific thought' which would have been inconceivable without a demarcation between the physical and non-physical.[20] Heidegger, who was given to intense reflection on the business of translation, also found a special place for Greek in shaping the possibilities of thought. For him the Greek language provided the source of the basic terminology of Western philosophy. German, too, occupied a privileged position since, according to Heidegger's reckoning at least, it was uncontaminated by Latin distortions of a pristine Greek philosophical lexicon.[21]

Snell and Heidegger, both German scholars, were likely drawing upon normative assumptions about the inherent superiority of European languages that can be found in some of their predecessors. Johann Gottfried Herder and Wilhelm von Humboldt proposed that language was the medium of thought and it followed for them that various languages were a reflection of the worldviews of ethnic groups. Herder wrote that 'each nation speaks in accordance with its thought, and thinks in accordance with its speech'.[22] For Humboldt, language was 'the formative organ of thought'.[23]

---

[20] Snell, *Discovery of the Mind*, pp. 1, 231 and esp. ch. 10, 'The Origins of Scientific Thought'. See also R. B. Onians, *The Origins of European Thought: About the Body, the Mind, the Soul, the World, Time and Fate* (Cambridge: Cambridge University Press, 1951).

[21] 'For along with German the Greek language is (in regard to its possibilities for thought) at once the most powerful and most spiritual of all languages.' Heidegger, *Introduction to Metaphysics*, p. 57. Along similar lines, Herder was unimpressed by the Roman suppression of Greek, and held that one of the most grievous offences of the Roman Church was to have inflicted Latin upon Europe as a common language. This deprived Germans of access to their native tongue. J. G. Herder, *Ideen zur Philosophie der Geschichte der Menschheit*, ed. Gerhart Schmidt (Wiesbaden: Löwit, 1971), pp. 508, 521.

[22] J. G. Herder, *Fragments on Recent German Literature* [1767–8], in *Philosophical Writings*, p. 50.

[23] '*Die Sprache ist das bildende Organ des Gedanken.*' Alexander von Humbolt, *Gesammelte Schriften*, 17 vols., ed. Albert Leitzmann et al. (Berlin: Behr, 1903–36), vol. 7, p. 53;

On Humboldt's analysis, the characteristic way in which words in the Indo-European languages are formed by inflection conferred upon those linguistic communities capabilities of expression that were lacking in what were imagined to be less advanced languages. Unsurprisingly, eighteenth- and nineteenth-century theories of language development tended to assume the inadequacies of 'primitive' languages, rather than reflect upon what capacities for expression, if any, might have been lost. As it relates to our topic, what these versions of history would suggest is that while the historical emergence of something like the natural/supernatural disjunction might be historically late and culturally exceptional, it nonetheless represents an advance on what came before.

Bruno Snell's more radical claim was that not merely had certain grammars enabled scientific thinking, but objective thought, rational deliberation, and human agency were capacities that had developed for the first time during the period of Greek antiquity. In his remarkable *The Discovery of the Mind* (1946) Snell points out that in Homer and the early lyric poets, 'human' thoughts are simply the voices of the gods. Thus: 'Homer does not know personal decisions; even when a hero is shown pondering two alternatives the intervention of the god plays the key role.'[24] The Irish classicist E. R. Dodds made similar observations about the peculiarities of the Greek sense of moral agency in relation to the activities of the gods, while psychologist Julian Jaynes went one further to suggest that consciousness itself was a historical product of this period.[25] Although Snell makes scant reference

---

Julia M. Penn, *Linguistic Relativity versus Innate Ideas: The Origins of the Sapir-Whorf Hypothesis in German Thought* (The Hague: Januae Linguarum, ser. minor 120, 1972), p. 102; R. H. Robins, *A Short History of Linguistics*, 4th ed. (London: Routledge, 1997), pp. 102, 155–70.

[24] Snell, *Discovery of the Mind*, p. 20.

[25] E. R. Dodds, *The Greeks and the Irrational* (Berkeley: University of California Press, 1951), pp. 1–27; Julian Jaynes, *The Origin of Consciousness in the Breakdown of the Bicameral Mind* (New York: Mariner, 2000); Martin Kuijsten (ed.), *Gods, Voices, and the Bicameral Mind: The Theories of Julian Jaynes* (Henderson, NY: Julian Jaynes Society, 2019). Iain McGilchrist has written more recently about the significance of the bicameral mind suggesting that since the Greek classical period, the left brain hemisphere (the emissary) has increasingly come to dominate the right (the master). This has given rise to an unfortunate dominance of an analytical, reductionistic, and word-based approach to reality at the cost of more holistic, metaphorical, and image-based understandings. This has implications for religious experience and modern disenchantment. McGilchrist suggests that Jaynes's hypothesis was in some sense on the right track, but got things the wrong way round in proposing that the relevant psychological transitions came about as a shift towards bicameral separation rather than integration. *The Master and His Emissary: The Divided Brain and the Making of the Western World* (New Haven: Yale University Press, 2009), p. 262, and *passim*.

to Hegel, his suggestions are entirely consistent with the latter's proposal that philosophy begins in the West and specifically among the Greeks with whom we see the consciousness of freedom first emerging.[26] As noted in the previous chapter, for Hegel, once freedom gets started in Greece, Europe takes the baton and develops it further by means of Christianity and especially Protestantism.

These suggestions amount to the proposal that the ancient Greeks did not have what we now call 'a theory of mind'. Such historical claims derive a measure of indirect support from anthropological studies which challenge the assumption that all cultures share a concept of mind analogous to ours.[27] This is not unrelated to similar suggestions made in Chapter 2 about the non-universality of concepts of belief. To revert to an example briefly mentioned in that chapter, for the Dinka people there seems to be no interior entity separate from the world that stores up experiences of the individual.[28] All of this calls to mind Charles Taylor's notion of 'porous selves', which he distinguishes from the 'buffered selves' of Western modernity. Porous selves, like the Homeric heroes, are ever open to influence by spirits, demons, and cosmic forces. For them, there is no theoretical question to be asked about the existence of these preternatural forces and beings: they are part and parcel of everyday experience.[29] The notion of a natural/supernatural divide is not part of this world and is instead a precondition for the emergence of modern buffered selves.

For Thomas Henry Huxley, modern accounts of religious experience were possible only because of survivals of a biblical language that retained in its grammar something like a notion of porous selves. Commenting on experiences recounted in the autobiography of seventeenth-century Quaker leader and miracle-worker George Fox, Huxley concedes that no one 'can doubt the man's utter truthfulness' (thus progressing beyond Hume's insouciance on this issue). But for Huxley, Fox's experiences can and should be *redescribed* in naturalistic language: 'When an ordinary person would say "I thought so and so," or "I made up my mind to do so and so," George Fox says, "It was opened up to me," or "at the command of God I did

---

[26] Hegel, *Lectures on the History of Philosophy*, p. 86. Cf. Snell: 'primitive man feels that he is bound to the gods; he has not yet roused himself to an awareness of his own freedom. The Greeks were the first to break through this barrier, and thus founded our western civilization.' *Discovery of the Mind*, pp. 31–2.

[27] T. M. Luhrmann, 'Mind and Spirit: A Comparative Theory about Representation of Mind and the Experience of Spirit', *Journal of the Royal Anthropological Institute*, new series, 26 (suppl. 13) (2020), 1–19.

[28] Lienhardt, *Divinity and Experience*, p. 149.   [29] Taylor, *A Secular Age*, pp. 37–42.

so and so.'" Predictably, Huxley points out that this language, 'steeped in supernaturalism and glorying in blind faith, is the mental antipodes of the philosopher, founded in naturalism and a fanatic for the evidence'.[30] But the general point is that executive functions of Huxley's mind and Fox's are likely to be the same, albeit susceptible to two different descriptions. In this case it is not that the supernatural is no longer directly experienced, but rather that what we experience is no longer labelled 'supernatural'. This also goes for the exceptional events that Jacalyn Duffin has catalogued which for her are simply inexplicable but for the Catholic Church are miraculous. It also calls to mind Aristotle's parable and the instances of 'seeing-as' discussed in earlier chapters.

I will not attempt to make the case for Fox's self-description but would suggest that arguably the putatively naturalistic locution 'I made up my mind' is attended with no fewer difficulties than Fox's preferred expression, or that of the Homeric heroes for that matter. The current options for a philosophy of mind run from a self-refuting eliminative materialism (conscious is not real), to the ontologically extravagant but currently fashionable panpsychism (everything is conscious), with positions such as Huxley's own epiphenomenalism (humans are conscious, but our conscious thoughts have no causal efficacy) sitting in the middle. These are all deeply counterintuitive, to say the least, and none of them, with the possible exception of panpsychism, is really consistent with the first-person statement 'I made up my mind' (which, in any case, runs up against the problem of recursion). Homeric heroes doing the bidding of the gods or medieval theories of divine illumination may require non-naturalist commitments, but when compared to the contortions of modern, naturalistic theories of mind they can seem relatively straightforward. Moreover, while Huxley may advert to 'evidence' in his dismissal of Fox's self-representation, it is not immediately obvious what kind of evidence, as opposed to a pre-existing preference, would count for one description over another.[31] In any event, Huxley nicely illustrates two related considerations for understanding the disparity between the world of modern naturalists and the world of everyone else: first, that the same

---

[30] Huxley, 'Witness to the Miraculous', CE, vol. 5, p. 189. Cf. Buno Snell on Homeric heroes: 'Whatever "strikes" him, whatever "thought comes" to him, is given from without, and if no visible external stimulus has affected him, he thinks that a god has stood by his side and given him counsel, either for his benefit or for his destruction.' Discovery of the Mind, p. 123.

[31] Huxley goes on to invoke the ethics of belief: the philosopher 'is compelled to ask for that rational ground of belief, without which, the man of science, assent is really a moral pretense'.

subjective phenomenon can be susceptible to divergent descriptions; second, that those divergent descriptions might be understood as instances of the theory-ladenness of data.

Simple redescription also offers another way of thinking about some of the historical transitions set out in this book. Laws of nature offer the most straightforward example. Initially understood as divine edicts, laws of nature were just redescribed in the nineteenth century in purely naturalistic terms even though they retained the same scientific content. Preference for one description over another might be determined on the basis that the historically more recent is also more 'advanced'. But as we have seen, that stance relies upon often unspoken commitments related to a hierarchy of cultures or an assumption of directionality that again makes sense only in the context of a theology of history. Not infrequently, naturalistic redescriptions also masquerade as explanations. Laws of nature are often presented as explaining regularities in a manner that competes with theistic accounts of nature. But arguably, as Wittgenstein has pointed out, the naturalistic version has less explanatory power than the theistic version.[32] 'Spontaneous order' offers another example of the redescription of what was once providential design. Again, however, the requirement for an actual explanation has quietly left the room.

Are there reasons for preferring one language of description over another? Are some conceptions a better fit for the world than others? To address these questions, we might consider not just the potential gains in the exclusive adoption of a naturalistic approach and its accompanying conceptual vocabulary, but also what might be lost in the process.

7.3 Lost in Translation

One of the great tragedies of the settlement of Australia has been the dispossession of its indigenous peoples, and the ensuing change in features of their language and culture. It is estimated that when Europeans first arrived in Australia more than 250 indigenous languages were spoken. Of these, now more than half are no longer heard, and all but a dozen or so are endangered. A remarkable feature of a number of these indigenous languages – including that of the Guugu Yimithirr people who live near Hopevale in my home state, Queensland – is a lack of equivalents for our directional descriptors 'left' and 'right'. Rather than expressing direction, place, and motion in our familiar observer-relative terms, the Guugu Yimithirr describe the position

---

[32] Wittgenstein, *Tractatus* 6.371–1.

of objects in terms of cardinal points, north, south, east, and west – not 'the object you are looking for is on your left', but rather, 'it is to your South'.

Speakers of these languages have an astonishing spatial memory and navigational capacity, almost as if they are aware of global geocentric coordinates that are independent of local terrains.[33] The inculcation of the language, then, seems to be related to the development of an internal compass that enables its speakers to naturally orientate themselves wherever they are. There is much more to it than this, but the general point would be that if we attempted to replace this language and its rich, navigational vocabulary with a simple left/right disjunction, not only would their language be significantly impoverished, but they would literally lose their sense of where they were in the world.[34] Linguists charting language loss among the Guugu Yimithirr have discovered that 'a transformation in the expression of spatial relations is underway'.[35] Loss of language brings with it a loss of ways of thinking about the world and, more than this, ways of being in the world.

The idea that the languages we speak shape the way in which we think about space and time is often referred to as 'Neo-Whorfian', after the Yale linguist Benjamin Whorf who, along with his mentor Edward Sapir, proposed that the structure of language determines the structure of thought.[36] Evidence for this perspective comes not only from those languages which specify direction in absolute rather than relative terms – this extends to

---

[33] John B. Haviland, 'Guugu Yimithirr Cardinal Directions', *Ethos* 26 (1998), 25–47. On the possibility that human brains can detect geomagnetic fields, and that this might provide a basis for navigation see Connie X. Wang, Isaac A. Hilburn, Daw-An Wu, et al., 'Transduction of the Geomagnetic Field as Evidenced from Alpha-Band Activity in the Human Brain', *eNeuro* 6 (2019), https://doi.org/10.1523/ENEURO.0483-18.2019, accessed 19 March 2019. The authors speculate that 'we and/or our nomadic hunter-gatherer ancestors could use a magnetic sense to navigate and survive'. The navigational abilities of indigenous peoples, and the implications of these abilities, have received increasing commentary in recent years. See, e.g., Harding, *Objectivity and Diversity*, pp. 80–104; Michael Bond, *Wayfinding: The Art and Science of How We Find and Lose Our Way* (London: Picador, 2020).

[34] For the case of the Gurindji people of the Northern Territory see Felicity Meakins, Caroline Jones, and Cassandra Algy, 'Bilingualism, Language Shift and the Corresponding Expansion of Spatial Cognitive Systems', *Language Sciences* 54 (2016), 1–13. I am grateful to Felicity Meakins for discussions of her remarkable research and its implications.

[35] Felicity Meakins and Cassandra Algy, 'Deadly Reckoning: Changes in Gurindji Children's Knowledge of Cardinals', *Australian Journal of Linguistics* 36 (2016), 479–501. Meakins and Algy conclude that 'a transformation in the expression of spatial relations is underway'.

[36] Edward Sapir, *Culture, Language and Personality: Selected Essays*, ed. David G. Mandelbaum (Berkeley: University of California Press, 1962); Benjamin Whorf, *Language, Thought, and Reality: Selected Writings of Benjamin Lee Whorf*, ed. John B. Carroll (Cambridge, MA: MIT Press, 1940).

almost one-third of the world's languages – but also from different vocabularies and grammars relating to colour, time, and even consciousness. These are correlated with what seem to be different ontologies, going beyond seeing the world in different colours or in terms of cardinal directions to understandings of consciousness, agency, and selfhood. We now understand that the loss of a language means the loss of a culture and even of certain 'natural' capacities. This is conspicuous in the legacies of colonisation and attempted assimilation. But we have been slow to realise that the same principle applies to Western culture itself. Perhaps this is because we can still trace etymological origins of the vocabulary of Western languages, even though the cultural contexts that bestowed the original meanings upon particular terms have long passed. Challenging the assumption of a linguistic and conceptual continuity of such basic analytic terms as 'faith/belief' and 'supernatural' has been one of the main aims of this book. This, in turn, raises the question of whether these transitions have effected an unambiguously positive refinement of our ways of understanding the world or whether something might have been forfeited in the process of their adoption and modification – something akin to the loss of orientation undergone by Anglophone Guugu Yimithirr.

According to Norse mythology, Odin sacrificed his eye to gain knowledge of the cosmos. For the philosopher and poet Owen Barfield, one of 'the Inklings', the one-eyed Odin stands in for modern Europeans whose technical proficiency and scientific knowledge has come at the cost of a unified vision of nature. The language of our ancient ancestors, according to Barfield, betrays no sharp division between the subjective and objective aspects of the world. In a move similar to that made by Snell, and at the same time redolent of Taylor's 'porous selves', Barfield proposed that the world was experienced in terms of a unity rather than a relation between observer and observed. On this account, our present scientific sophistication offers a limited perspective on the world that can be overcome through an embracing of the language of poets.[37]

The obvious response to all this, proposed by nineteenth-century scientific naturalists and virtually taken for granted today, is that science and technology are the fruits of these transitions and that together they vindicate

---

[37] Owen Barfield, *Poetic Diction* (Middletown: Wesleyan University Press, 1973), pp. 86–7. Thomas Macaulay expressed a similar sentiment, observing that it seems as though, 'as civilization advances, poetry almost necessarily declines'. 'Milton' [1825], in *Critical and Miscellaneous Essays*, 6 vols. (Philadelphia: Hart, Carey, and Hart, 1854), vol. 1, p. 12. For the context, see Thomas L. Jeffers, 'Nice Threads: Tennyson's Lady of Shalott as Artist', *Yale Review* 89 (2008), 54–68.

the relevant underlying conceptual changes. In any case (as in fact both Tyndall and Huxley argued) there remains a place for poetry and religion for those who still wish to so indulge themselves. But there are difficulties with this response. For a start, the success of naturalistic explanations, if the history recounted in this book is anything to go by, rests upon unexamined theistic assumptions. In a sense, naturalistic science is an ersatz theology, a disenchanting Protestantism pushed to the extreme. The natural sciences, as John Milbank has proposed for the social sciences, might be thought of as a Christian heresy.[38] Naturalism is thus a paradoxical amalgam of two contradictory impulses, a theistically grounded assumption of an intelligible world governed by imposed uniformity, combined with a denial of the supernatural. Once we understand it as a totalising crypto-theology, moreover, it becomes clear that it competes directly with alternative 'theological' approaches to nature and hence, in reality, leaves no conceptual space for the religious or the 'poetic'. This exclusionary consequence pertains as much to traditional cultures as to Western religion, the difference being that naturalism is the fratricidal offspring of the latter. It follows, for example, that a naturalistic outlook will be no less hostile to indigenous claims to a 'spiritual connection' to land than to Judaeo-Christian ideas of the world as God's creation.[39]

7.4 Contemporary Myths and Techno-Liturgies

There is a difference between the consciously adopted intellectual stance of naturalism and a more widespread tendency of modern individuals to perceive the world as disenchanted. The characteristics of the secular age, in other words, do not reside only in naturalism as an intellectual commitment or as a starting assumption for disciplinary enquiries in the natural and social sciences and the humanities. The secular outlook is part of a wider social imaginary, of which overt naturalism is one characteristic. That imaginary is not primarily a result of the conscious decisions of individual agents but is formed by practices and shaped by historically contingent conceptions that

---

[38] Milbank, *Theology and Social Theory*. Cf. Smith: 'American sociology's sacred project is a secular salvation story developed out of the modern traditions of Enlightenment, liberalism, Marxism ... and so on.' *Sacred Project of American Sociology*, p. 20.
[39] The 2017 'Uluru Statement from the Heart', produced by Australian Indigenous and Torres Strait Islander leaders, would be one such example, with its proposal of sovereignty as a 'spiritual notion' that has been in place 'from the Creation'. www.referendumcouncil.org.au/final-report.html#toc-anchor-ulurustatement-from-the-heart, accessed 18 June 2023.

are taken for granted. We can think about these formative factors in terms of modern myths and liturgies.

In the last century, biblical scholar Rudolf Bultmann controversially proposed a project for the demythologisation of Christianity, observing that: 'It is impossible to use electric light and the wireless and to avail ourselves of modern medical and surgical discoveries, and at the same time to believe in the New Testament world of spirits and miracles.'[40] It is important to understand that in spite of often being misunderstood on this point, Bultmann was not reverting to some progressive stages-of-history model according to which we have moved from a mythical world picture to a more secure, non-mythical, scientific one. It was rather a matter of our having exchanged one mythical worldview for another.[41] This is because for Bultmann, objectifying science is our modern mythology. Bultmann would say that 'all of our thinking is irrevocably formed [*geformt*] by science'.[42]

When Bultmann speaks of our being *formed* by science he makes reference to the electric light and the wireless, rather than the laws of physics. While he does not say this explicitly, the implication of his remark is that our habitual interactions with modern technologies involve rituals that link our habits and behaviours to an implicit faith in the scientific truths that we imagine lie behind them. In this sense it is our social practices, our continual engagement with ever-improving technologies, that serve to reinforce the legitimacy of the truth claims of the modern sciences. These practices involve 'the school, the press, the radio, the movies, and technology generally'.[43] Martin Heidegger, one of Bultmann's formative influences, would go further to propose that technology was not an innocent instrument derived from scientific discovery to be put to use for specific human purposes, but rather a distinctive and problematic way of 'revealing' the world. Technology, on this account, restricts our vision of nature and promotes a

---

[40] Rudolf Bultmann, 'The New Testament and Mythology', in *Kerygma and Myth*, ed. Hans Werner Bartsch (New York: Harper, 1961), pp. 1–44 (p. 5). For similar views among modern theologians see John Macquarrie, *Principles of Christian Theology*, rev. ed. (London: SCM, 1977), p. 248; Langdon Gilkey, 'Cosmology, Ontology, and the Travail of Biblical Language', in *God's Activity in the World: The Contemporary Problem*, ed. Owen C. Thomas (Chico: Scholars Press, 1983), pp. 29–44 (p. 31).

[41] 'Science has not replaced myth because science is itself mythical, in that both myth and science perpetuate a false understanding of God, the world, and ourselves – myth unreflectively and science reflectively.' David Congdon, *Mission of Demythologizing: Rudolf Bultmann's Dialectical Theology* (Philadelphia: Fortress Press, 2015), p. 608. See also Brent A. R. Hege, *Myth, History, and the Resurrection in German Protestant Theology* (Eugene: Pickwick, 2017), pp. 42–50.

[42] Bultmann, *New Testament Mythology*, p. 3.

[43] Bultmann, *New Testament Mythology*, p. 42.

disturbing tendency to see everything, including our fellow humans, as a resource to be exploited or manipulated.[44] More prosaically, we might say that technology has also blunted our capacity to attend to the miraculous. Proust remarked in this vein that the telephone was 'a supernatural instrument before whose miracles we used to stand amazed, and which we now employ without giving it a thought, to summon our tailor or to order an ice cream'.[45] Along similar lines, Wittgenstein suggested that science has damped down human wonder, and has 'put us to sleep'.[46]

There are obvious ways in which modern technologies contribute to a diminution of certain human capacities. Increased social media use, predictably, is correlated with shrinking attention spans.[47] More worryingly, it is associated with increased depression, loneliness, and social isolation.[48] A less loaded example would be the use of GPS technologies for the purposes of navigation. While the benefits of innovations in satellite navigation can hardly be overstated, it is now well established that their habitual use has a deleterious effect on spatial memory.[49] It could reasonably be argued that this does not really matter, since we now possess a much more efficient

---

[44] Martin Heidegger, *The Question Concerning Technology and Other Essays*, trans. William Lovitt (New York: Harper, 1977), pp. 3–35; *The Bremen and Frieberg Lectures*, trans. Andrew J. Mitchell (Bloomington: Indiana University Press, 2012), p. 63, and *passim*; Mark Blitz, 'Understanding Heidegger on Technology', *The New Atlantis* 41 (2014), 63–80.

[45] Marcel Proust, *Remembrance of Things Past*, trans. Charles Kenneth Scott-Moncrieff (New York: Vintage, 1981), vol. 3, p. 24.

[46] 'Man has to awaken to wonder – and so perhaps do peoples. Science is a way of sending him to sleep again.' Wittgenstein, *Culture and Value*, p. 5.

[47] P. Lorenz-Spreen, B. M. Mønsted, P. Hövel, and S. Lehmann, 'Accelerating Dynamics of Collection Attention', *Nature Communications* 10 (2019), https://doi.org/10.1038/s41467-019-09311-w, accessed 23 November 2023.

[48] Brian A. Primack, 'Social Media Use and Perceived Social Isolation among Young Adults in the U.S.', *American Journal of Preventative Medicine* 53 (2017), 1–8; E. Kross, P. Verduyn, E. Demiralp, J. Park, D. S. Lee, N. Lin, H. Shablack, J. Jonides, and O. Ybarra, 'Facebook Use Predicts Declines in Subjective Well-Being in Young Adults', *PLos One* 8 (2013), https://doi.org/10.1371/journal.pone.0069841, accessed 23 November 2023; L. Y. Lin, J. E. Sidani, A. Shensa, et al., 'Association between Social Media Use and Depression among U.S. Young Adults', *Depression and Anxiety* 33 (2016), 323–31.

[49] L. Dahmani and V. D. Bohbot, 'Habitual Use of GPS Negatively Impacts Spatial Memory during Self-Guided Navigation', *Scientific Reports* 10 (2020), 6310; A. L. Gardony, T. T. Brunyé, C. R. Mahoney, and H. A. Taylor, 'How Navigational Aids Impair Spatial Memory: Evidence for Divided Attention', *Spatial Cognition and Computation* 13 (2013), 319–50. Conversely, classic studies have shown changes to the brain structures of London cabbies who were required to have a detailed knowledge of London geography – 'the knowledge'. E. Maguire, K. Woollett, and H. Spiers, 'London Taxi Drivers and Bus Drivers: A Structural MRI and Neuropsychological Analysis', *Hippocampus* 16 (2006), 1091–101; L. K. Woollett and E. A. Maguire, 'Acquiring "The Knowledge" of London's Layout Drives Structural Brain Changes', *Current Biology* 21 (2011), 2109–14.

means of getting around. Thinking back to the example of the Guugu Yimithirr, it would seem that the prevalence of the rich spatial vocabulary that characterises the languages of traditional cultures is the long-term historical consequence of a lack of artificial means of getting around (the compass, typically touted as a tangible sign of civilisational advance, and the map). We have seen how the imposition of a modern language can lead to a literal loss of orientation. It now seems that new technologies can bring about similar losses in those same capacities.

A noteworthy feature of technologically assisted navigation is that an undeniable improvement in the practicalities of getting around seems to be accompanied by an atrophy of a once-useful instinctual capacity, along with a loss of topographical knowledge of the 'real' world. Generalising from this example to science and technology as such, we might ask whether the remarkable successes of science and technology might be accompanied by a similar process of atrophy and a distancing from reality. It is commonly assumed, to the contrary, that the predictive successes of the naturalistic sciences, along with the usefulness of related technological applications, is actually a measure of the *accuracy* of their representation of the world. Indeed, some have argued that scientific success vindicates the naturalistic approach of the modern sciences.[50] But there are numerous examples from the history of science that suggest otherwise. For a start, all past scientific theories must have had some element of predictive success if they were to gain acceptance in the first place. Yet theories that were successful in their time came to be replaced by other successful theories that have often posited radically different causal mechanisms and theoretical entities. This is not the occasion to discuss the full implications of this principle of 'pessimistic meta-induction' or put forward a case for scientific instrumentalism, not least because of the plurality of approaches undertaken in the natural sciences.[51] But another analogy, that invokes now familiar navigational and subterranean metaphors, is worth considering in this context.

Anyone who has attempted to find their way around London via the complex Underground rail network will appreciate the marvel of ingenuity and simplicity that is the Tube Map. Developed from the original 1933 design of electrical draftsman Harry Beck, the map was based on principles used in the circuit diagrams of the time. But while the map is a boon to underground travellers, it bears only a distant resemblance to the above-ground

---

[50] For examples and a counterargument see Harrison, 'Naturalism and the Success of Science'.
[51] The classic statement of the principle of pessimistic meta-induction is Larry Laudan, 'A Confutation of Convergent Realism', *Philosophy of Science* 48 (1981), 19–49.

topography (and indeed its representation even of the underground rail lines is highly stylised). It would be disorienting, to say the least, to attempt to navigate the streets of London armed with only a tube map intended for an entirely different purpose. Here again, the apparent subterranean reality does not quite square with what is manifest in the light of day. Scientific theories, based on the assumption of naturalism and often as elegant and simple as Beck's diagrammatic representation of the Underground, afford powerful ways of navigating certain aspects of the world. But it is at least possible that they achieve this not on account of directly mirroring reality but because they represent an abstraction or even a useful distortion of it.[52] Methodological naturalism might afford us the capacity to manipulate the natural world precisely because it offers a limited perspective.

Our habituation into such a naturalistic outlook comes not only from inherited concepts that shape our ways of thinking (such as a natural/supernatural distinction), nor simply from our technologically mediated interactions with the world, but also from what, following philosopher James K. A. Smith, we might call 'liturgies' through which we enact and reinforce a particular approach to the world. Smith speaks of the secular liturgies of the shopping mall and sports stadium. Liturgies, whether sacred or secular, 'prime us to approach the world in a certain way, to value certain things, to aim for certain goals, to pursue certain dreams, to work together on certain projects. In short, every liturgy constitutes a pedagogy that teaches us, in all sorts of precognitive ways, to be a certain kind of person.' Our institutions of education are also primary sites for the formation of secular, liberal subjects. Western educational routines, Smith tells us, inculcate 'a particular vision of the good life by inscribing or infusing that vision into the heart ... by means of material, embodied practices'.[53] William T. Cavanaugh has spoken in similar terms of the liturgies of nationhood. These communal acts – singing the national anthem, erecting the flag, voting, celebrating

---

[52] It is interesting in this context that for Aristotle abstraction did not involve drawing generalisations from an assortment of particulars, but rather removing certain things from consideration in order to create an object of enquiry: 'Abstraction involved eliminating something from consideration.' Ian Mueller, 'Aristotle on Geometrical Objects', *Archiv für Geschichte der Philosophie* 52 (1970), 156–71 (160). Thanks to Eric Schliesser for this point.

[53] James K. A. Smith, *Desiring the Kingdom*, pp. 25, 26; 'Secular Liturgies and the Prospect for a "Post-Secular" Sociology of Religion', in *The Post-Secular in Question: Religion in Contemporary Society*, ed. Philip S. Gorski, David Kyumam Kim, John Torpey, and Jonathan VanAntwerpen (New York: New York University Press, 2012), pp. 159–84. Smith's approach is not unrelated to Pierre Bourdieu's notion of 'habitus'. *Outline of a Theory of Practice*, trans. Richard Nice (Cambridge: Cambridge University Press, 1987), pp. 82f.

national holidays – help sustain the social imaginary necessary for the preservation of the secular state.[54]

Finally, we might consider the relevance of the other factors on Bultmann's list: 'the school, the press, the radio, the movies'. Here we move from the realm of liturgy back to mythology. Popular culture and our educational institutions continue to propagate the dubious historical narratives created by Enlightenment *philosophes* and nineteenth-century naturalists. Going back to the 1980s, the historical plotline of Carl Sagan's enormously popular book and television series *Cosmos* rehearsed the myths produced by Huxley, Tyndall, Draper, and White.[55] The 2014 follow-up to Sagan's television series – *Cosmos: A Spacetime Odyssey*, narrated by Neil deGrasse Tyson – revisited this well-worn territory with no indication of familiarity with the more nuanced accounts of the history of science produced by actual historians. The idea that religion and science are competing explanatory systems with one destined to replace the other was also a staple of the new atheist rhetoric from earlier this century, while the more recent *Enlightenment Now* (2018), by cognitive scientist Steven Pinker, uncritically repeats the ahistorical presumptions of some of the Enlightenment's more vociferous propagandists. Less excusably, as intimated in Chapter 6, the mythical backstories of naturalism and the conflict thesis also appear in undergraduate textbooks, especially in the social sciences where, presumably, they are intended to underscore the scientific nature of the enterprise understood in contradistinction to religious approaches to the world.[56]

---

[54] Cavanaugh, *Theopolitical Imagination*. See also Fredrik Portin, 'Liturgies in a Plural Age: The Concept of Liturgy in the Works of William T. Cavanaugh and James K. A. Smith', *Studia Liturgica* 49 (2019), 122–37.

[55] Carl Sagan, *Cosmos* (New York: Ballantine Books, 2013), pp. 180–2.

[56] Examples include: Bruce K. Alexander and Curtis P. Shelton, *A History of Psychology in Western Civilization* (Cambridge: Cambridge University Press, 2014), pp. 33–4; William Douglas Woody and Wayne Viney, *A History of Psychology*, 6th ed. (Abingdon: Routledge, 2017), pp. 47–54; Robert B. Lawson, Jean E. Graham, and Kristin M. Baker, *A History of Psychology* (New York: Routledge, 2016), pp. 66–7; Christer Sturmark and Douglas Hofstadter, *To Light the Flame of Reason* (Buffalo: Prometheus, 2022), pp. 245–7; Gregory J. Feist, *The Psychology of Science and the Origins of the Scientific Mind* (New Haven: Yale University Press, 2006), pp. 208–9; Donald K. Sharpes, *The Evolution of the Social Sciences* (Lanham: Lexington Books, 2009), pp. 67–9; R. P. Pathak, *Philosophical and Sociological Perspectives of Education* (New Delhi: Atlantic Books, 2007), pp. 54f.; Joseph Tangko, *The Way of Psychology* (Manila: Central Books, 2008), pp. 40–2; Jeanne H. Ballantine, Keith A. Roberts, and Kathleen Odell Korgen, *Our Social World: An Introduction to Sociology*, 7th ed. (Thousand Oaks: Sage, 2019), p. 40; Catherine Corrigall Brown, *Imagining Society: An Introduction to Sociology* (Thousand Oaks: Sage, 2019), ch. 10. For similar examples from anthropology texts, as noted in Chapter 6, see Aechtner, 'Galileo Still Goes to Jail' and 'Social Scientists'.

The success of these stories, given their variance with the evidence, may seem puzzling. But the fact is that few today are aware of the true histories. Moreover, in their favour, these narratives have the hallmarks of all good stories – heroes and villains, courageous individuals willing to stand up to repressive authorities, and a general plotline of the victory of reason over ignorance. These modern myths also have the advantage of reassuring us of our intellectual superiority. And, of course, the conceptual apparatus that these narratives bear along with them already does much of the work. Thus, while we persist with the idea that categories such as 'naturalism' and 'supernaturalism' genuinely divide up the world in a meaningful way, we are already half-way committed to the morals of these stories. Finally, these narratives were originally forged with a view to establishing the social legitimacy of the natural sciences and to secure their independence from undue external interference. And as science continues to be under threat today – from climate change deniers, anti-vaxxers, young earth creationists, and others – there is comfort in clinging to the myths that seem to reinforce its legitimacy.

7.5 Modernity Stories

The account of naturalism offered in this volume is another large-scale modernity story, and it is worth making brief reference to other examples of the genre, not only to indicate some points of convergence, but as a means of restating the central claims set out in the book. It should be clear that I am broadly sympathetic to the thesis of Charles Taylor's *A Secular Age*. Readers can draw their own conclusions about the parallels, but of prime importance is the way that Taylor characterises the secular age and his proposal that we think less about how the *content* of belief has changed over time and more about the underlying *conditions* that make certain beliefs possible. The new possibility of unbelief turns out to be a crucial way of understanding what is distinctive about the secular West, and it is this possibility that I have sought to account for in the present work. Related to this is the changing status of the *consensus gentium* 'argument', which exemplifies just how a theistic understanding of the world moved from being a taken-for-granted background assumption to a conscious propositional belief that was optional and needing to be justified. Taylor's notion of 'porous selves', adverted to in the examples above, also points to elements of the pre-modern and traditional experience of the transcendent and how they differ from those of the modern 'buffered' subject.

Brad Gregory's *Unintended Reformation* has rightly stressed the centrality of the Protestant Reformation in establishing, both directly and indirectly, the conditions for secular modernity. It should be obvious by now that my own view is that many aspects of modernity, including scientific naturalism, are indebted in complicated ways to the religious reformations of the early modern period. While the persistent attribution of features of modernity to changes in religious institutions and ideas may seem to err on the side of the mono-causal, perhaps this is only in comparison to the modern academy's failure to take religion seriously – the notable exception being 'bad' religion, understood as the cause of violence, a driver of political conservatism, a regressive historical force holding back the tide of reason and enlightenment, etc.[57] This failure amounts to a lack of intellectual curiosity and historical empathy, given the centrality of religion in the lives of past actors and those of other cultures. Related to this is the fact that, as Gregory himself expresses it, 'religious truth claims made by billions of people are excluded from consideration on their own terms in nearly all research universities'.[58] I am not sure that there is an easy way to deal with this. We might simply say that this is what universities do and accept it as a recognised limitation. But it should be acknowledged as such and not ignored. It is also worth noting that there are pressures on this stance coming from other directions, in relation to the status of indigenous knowledges and their place in the university curriculum. All of this takes us back to one aspect of 'Hume's dilemma' – how to manage the overwhelming burden of evidence of the experienced religion of others without resort to a thesis of historical progress and Western exceptionalism, or straightforward condescension, or both.

I have some reservations about decline narratives, of which I take the work of Gregory and John Milbank to be instances. Crudely put, these genealogies typically identify a historical juncture when things went awry. The force of the analysis is that we can rectify the present by means of a partial return to the conditions that obtained before the historical catastrophe that put things on the wrong course. The way forward, then, lies in the past. As a comparative, rhetorical exercise these decline narratives work well enough. But I wonder if they tend to discount positive features of the present and overemphasise the glories of the past. It may be that these accounts are insufficiently dialectical, in the sense of recognising that the historical developments in question are likely to bring both good and bad.[59]

---

[57] Gregory, *Unintended Reformation*, pp. 358–9.
[58] Gregory, *Unintended Reformation*, p. 299. See also Gregory, 'No Room for God'.
[59] Weber, for example, was ambivalent about secularisation, lamenting the fact that without religion, modern individuals would be constrained within the 'iron cage' of economically driven bureaucracy. Habermas, too, while an advocate of secularism, came to understand that his 'communicative rationality' had a normative deficit at its heart. Peter E. Gordon,

Emphasising the latter alone will produce a decline narrative and there is nothing wrong with focusing on the historical origins of what are regarded as undesirable elements of our modern world. But passing general assessments on historical eras is a fraught matter, not least because the relevant criteria are often internal to the period in question. Posing genealogical questions is actually a way of exposing the contingency of such judgements. By the same token, as has been consistently argued in this book, the assumption of historical progress is one such historical contingency and adopting it has ramifications that have not always been fully thought through. I should say that I have not sought to offer a decline narrative as such, but rather have tried to place in high relief the historically and culturally exceptional character of Western secularity and expose its implications. There is a relatively obvious (and I think unproblematic) normative thrust to this. If we are prepared to countenance the prospect that our religiously inclined forebears, the myriad adherents of religious traditions, and the vast bulk of past philosophers, are not our intellectual inferiors, we have grounds for questioning our present naturalistic commitments.

Turning to John Milbank, there are significant affinities between his treatment of 'secular reason' in *Theology and Social Theory*, and my own story about the birth of modern naturalism. Both accounts stress a hidden dependence of Western modernity on theological considerations. In Milbank's case this amounts to the suggestion that modern social scientific theories, while touting their scientific status, are actually theologies or anti-theologies in disguise. Thus, while much attention has been focused on a purported conflict between religion and the *natural* sciences, Milbank has rightly called attention to the way in which the ethos of secular modernity is perhaps better exemplified in the *social* sciences. That said, more recently, Milbank has also addressed the status of natural sciences, proposing that the dominant forms of present scientific thinking result from developments of certain aspects of what he calls 'disenchanted monotheism'.[60] Again this bears comparison to my own proposal that we think of modern naturalism as a kind of Protestantism-on-steroids.

Milbank is well known as an advocate of the 'Scotus story', suggesting that the late medieval Franciscan friar, John Duns Scotus, is 'the turning

---

'Contesting Secularization: The Idea of a Normative Deficit of Modernity after Max Weber', in *Formations of Belief: Historical Approaches to Religion and the Secular*, ed. Philip Nord, Katja Guenther, and Max Weiss (Princeton: Princeton University Press, 2019), pp. 184–201.

[60] John Milbank, 'Religion, Science, and Magic', in *After Science and Religion*, ed. Harrison and Milbank, pp. 75–143.

point in the destiny of the West'. This is said to be on account of Scotus's doctrine of the univocity of being. Brad Gregory, Catherine Pickstock, and others also subscribe to versions of this story.[61] It seems plausible to me that univocity – in simple terms, the view that God is a being just like other beings – could in principle lead to a posing of the question of the existence of God in new and unfavourable terms. Univocity could thus be understood as a form of theology that was ultimately complicit in its own secularisation. However, a number of Scotus scholars have challenged the idea that univocity of being in an ontological, as opposed to semantic sense, is actually a Scotist doctrine.[62] Others have pointed out that univocity of being, whether Scotist in origin or not, was not promoted by Protestants.[63] I am happy to leave these matters to the specialists. My own sense, nonetheless, is that late medieval theological developments were indeed significant factors in the emergence of secular modernity, especially voluntarism and nominalism. Undeniably, by the time of the early modern period we witness a flattening of causation, and God's activity in the world becomes one efficient cause among others. A key vector for this development was a modern science that rejected Aristotelian and scholastic understandings of causation, revived an atomic (strictly speaking, 'corpuscular') matter theory, and endorsed a voluntarist understanding of laws of nature. If there is a clear candidate for a late medieval Trojan horse it is a theological voluntarism that was operationalised in the modern scientific project. This laid the groundwork for the later nineteenth-century redescription of God's causal activity in a new and naturalistic reading of laws of nature.

The collapse of the causal order of the medieval world also led to the demise of teleological understandings of human nature. This left an indelible

---

[61] John Milbank, *The Word Made Strange* (Oxford: Blackwell, 1997), p. 44; Catherine Pickstock, 'Modernity and Scholasticism: A Critique of Recent Invocations of Univocity', *Antonianum* 78 (2003), 3–47; *After Writing: On the Liturgical Consummation of Philosophy* (London: Routledge, 1998), pp. 122–66; Gregory, *Unintended Reformation*, pp. 36f. See also Adrian Pabst, *Metaphysics: The Invention of Hierarchy* (Grand Rapids: Eerdmans, 2012); Gavin Hyman, *A Short History of Atheism* (London: I. B. Tauris, 2010), esp. pp. 47–81; Pfau, *Minding the Modern*, pp. 160f. The term 'Scotus story' seems to be the coinage of Daniel P. Horan, *Postmodernity and Univocity: A Critical Assessment of Radical Orthodoxy and John Duns Scotus* (Minneapolis: Fortress Press, 2014), p. vii.

[62] Richard Cross, 'Where the Angels Fear to Tread: Duns Scotus and Radical Orthodoxy', *Antonianum* 76 (2001), 7–41; 'Duns Scotus and Suárez at the Origins of Modernity', in *Deconstructing Radical Orthodoxy: Postmodern Theology, Rhetoric, and Truth*, ed. Wayne Hankey and Douglas Hedley (Burlington: Ashgate, 2005), pp. 65–80; Thomas Williams, 'The Doctrine of Univocity Is True and Salutary', *Modern Theology* 21 (2005), 575–85.

[63] Richard A. Muller, 'Not Scotist: Understandings of Being, Univocity, and Analogy in Early-Modern Reformed Thought', *Reformation and Renaissance Review* 14 (2012), 127–50.

mark on modern political thought, already evident in the thought of Hobbes and Pufendorf. Its effects were also profoundly felt in the moral sphere, as has been well established by Alasdair MacIntyre. In MacIntyre's narrative, the demise of Aristotelian Thomism, with its natural teleology and blurring of what would become for moderns a clear boundary between the realms of facts and values, led eventually to the incoherence of post-Enlightenment moral discourse. For MacIntyre, the ruling moral philosophy of modernity is now emotivism, which reduces all moral judgements to statements of preference. It follows that there is 'no rational way of securing moral agreement in our culture'. This seems to be even more true today than when he originally wrote those words some decades ago.[64] My suggestion has been that the decline of Aristotelian Thomism also led to the flattened understanding of natural causality referred to above, facilitating a new scientific understanding of natural order in terms of laws of nature. Because the original theological rationale of laws of nature has now simply been forgotten or suppressed, rather than explicitly erased, the natural sciences have not succumbed to the anomie that characterises present moral discourse.

Our present naturalistic versions of philosophy (in the most straightforward sense of 'naturalism') exhibit more self-awareness than the sciences. Accordingly, we now encounter in that enterprise a set of quandaries to do with justification that mirror the disorderly state of meta-ethical discourse. This is a downstream consequence of the 'invention' of epistemology which, as argued in Chapter 3, was summoned into being to resolve the new problem of the justification of religious belief. For a time, vestiges of a more robust theologically informed conception of reason made philosophical foundationalism internally coherent, as exemplified in the Cartesian project. But with the accession of secular reason the transcendental moorings of rational discourse were set adrift. Classic works of epistemology, such as those of Locke and Kant, thus turn their attention to the limits of what can be known. Scottish common sense philosophers, for their part, rejected the premise of evidentialism, returning to a reliabilism that was not too distant from the epistemological assumptions of the scholastics. An alternative response – or perhaps a capitulation – was proposed by Jakob Fries who, as we saw in Chapter 4, articulated the impossibility of a secular solution to the problem of rational justification, echoing a similar argument earlier proposed by the ancient sceptic Agrippa.[65] Most recently, honest souls in the philosophical community have done the same. Philosopher of religion

---

[64] MacIntyre, *After Virtue*, p. 6.
[65] Sextus Empiricus, *Outlines of Pyrrhonism* 1.15 (LCL 273, p. 95).

William Alston has maintained that pursuit of any robust justification is just a will-o'-the wisp.[66] Robert Fogelin, although approaching things from a rather different direction, also asserts that modern philosophers have no reason to think that they can progress beyond the ancient schools of philosophical scepticism.[67]

Here again, though, the history tells the story. The West *did* progress beyond ancient scepticism and did so by means of the marriage of theology and philosophy. This is refracted in Augustine's own biography, as he transitioned from philosophical sceptic to Christian theologian, writing critiques of philosophical scepticism along the way (and, arguably, providing ammunition later appropriated by Descartes). Medieval thinkers were not much exercised by epistemological concerns since they assumed that human beings are naturally oriented towards both knowledge and God, and this despite the disordering of human desires wrought by sin. This is the sense in which we can think of them as reliabilists or even 'subjective naturalists' since the reliability of our cognitive operations is gauged in terms of whether our natural propensities to acquire knowledge are operating as they should. This version of naturalism, however, is underpinned by the ongoing activity of God.

All this is by way of saying that the collapse of Aristotelian Thomism which MacIntyre identifies as the root cause of the disordered state of modern moral discourse also led to difficulties for the justification of any form of knowledge. This, combined with assaults on implicit faith and the appearance of a new conception of 'belief', fuelled the emergence of modern epistemology. With the Enlightenment naturalisation of reason we were left with new evidentiary demands for knowledge that could no longer be met with the meagre resources available. The alternatives to scepticism would seem to be a return to some version of Aristotelian teleology (which assumes that humans are naturally ordered to know and accordingly have the requisite cognitive apparatus) or perhaps something like the reliabilism that characterises 'reformed epistemology'. It is true that the modern sciences might offer some cause for optimism, and they are often held up as exemplars of justified knowledge. This accounts for attempts on the part of some social scientists and philosophers to mould their endeavours on the model of science. But the reputation of the natural sciences rests partly upon latent theological assumptions and partly on a suspect conflation of instrumentality with truth.

---

[66] William P. Alston, *Beyond 'Justification': Dimensions of Epistemic Evaluation* (Ithaca: Cornell University Press, 2005), pp. 22, 239.

[67] Robert J. Fogelin, *Pyrrhonian Reflections on Knowledge and Justification* (Oxford: Oxford University Press, 1994).

7.5 MODERNITY STORIES

Finally, what do we do with naturalism? There are good reasons to pursue naturalistic methods in the sciences if they yield useful results, the caveat being that naturalism is understood as a heuristic or methodological stance. What we might conclude about such 'success' is more along the lines of Paul Feyerabend's observation that in the pursuit of science 'anything goes' than a hard and fast metaphysical conclusion to the effect that the natural is all there is.[68] To put it another way, methodological naturalism is likely to generate difficulties only if accompanied by a strongly realist conception of science. An insistence on realism would highlight the paradox that 'naturalistic' assumptions about nature's intelligibility rest upon a hidden theology.

The difficulty is more keenly felt in history and the social sciences, which deal with human subjects.[69] Here it is less clear that naturalism is a helpful hermeneutical strategy. Leaving aside the question of whether it is true, one of the consequences of adopting naturalism is that it has become increasingly difficult to fully understand both our own history and other cultural traditions. The frame of naturalism leads to a systematic misrepresentation of the past ideas and commitments of the Latin West, while at the same time conspiring against the easy translation of other cultural traditions into a Western, secular idiom. This has practical implications, not only for a sensitive understanding of our own past, but for how we engage with other cultures. It is directly relevant to ambitions to understand and affirm the knowledges of indigenous cultures – an ambition that turns out to be incompatible with the ruling commitments of naturalism. Recent philosophical discussions in the field of social epistemology have accordingly labelled prejudice against testimony from particular sources as instances of epistemic injustice.[70] Dominant versions of naturalism have also fostered a

---

[68] Feyerabend, *Against Method*, p. vii. Feyerabend's notorious 'anything goes' is not a normative claim but an observation of what scientific practice can look like when viewed by someone with rigidly prescriptive assumptions about how science should work. See Peter Harrison, 'Science and Religion as Historical Traditions', in *After Science and Religion*, ed. Harrison and Milbank, pp. 15–34, esp. pp. 30f.

[69] It is now standard practice for historians simply to discount reports of supernatural agency made by indigenous populations. Thus Dipesh Chakrabarty: 'subaltern pasts ... cannot ever enter history as belonging to the historian's own position ... the historian as historian ... cannot invoke the supernatural in explaining/describing an event'. *Provincializing Europe: Postcolonial Thought and Historical Difference* (Princeton: Princeton University Press, 2000), pp. 105f. See also Luke Clossey, Kyle Jackson, Brandon Marriott, Andrew Redden, and Karin Vélez, 'The Unbelieved and Historians, Part I: A Challenge', *The History Compass* 14 (2016), 594–602.

[70] On epistemic injustice generally see Miranda Fricker, *Epistemic Injustice* (Oxford: Oxford University Press, 2007). For applications to religion and religious testimony see Pamela Sue Anderson, 'An Epistemological-Ethical Approach to Philosophy of Religion: Learning

view of the natural world as an ensemble of mechanically interacting particles that is intrinsically devoid of meaning and value. This aligned well with an 'objective' science but was also hospitable to industrial and commercial interests that fostered the unchecked exploitation of nature. This convenient partnership offers some explanation of how deeply religious understandings of the scientific enterprise that were characteristic of the seventeenth and eighteenth centuries gave way to the modern alliance of science and naturalism.[71] Naturalism, in short, seems to be implicated in two of the central concerns of our age: cross-cultural understanding and exploitative attitudes towards the natural world.

---

to Listen', in *Feminist Philosophy of Religion: Critical Readings*, ed. Pamela Sue Anderson and Beverley Clack (London: Routledge, 2004), pp. 87–102; Ian James Kidd, 'Epistemic Justice and Religion', in *The Routledge Handbook of Epistemic Injustice*, ed. Ian James Kidd, José Medina, and Gaile Pohlhaus (New York: Routledge, 2017), pp. 386–96. For postcolonial contexts, see Gayatri Chakravorty Spivak, 'Can the Subaltern Speak?', in *Marxism and the Interpretation of Culture*, ed. Cary Nelson and Lawrence Grossberg (London: Macmillan, 1988), pp. 271–313; Rajeev Bhargava, 'Overcoming the Epistemic Injustice of Colonialism', *Global Policy* 4 (2013), 413–17.

[71] See Akeel Bilgrami, 'The Wider Significance of Naturalism: A Genealogical Essay', in *Naturalism and Normativity*, ed. De Caro and Macarthur, pp. 23–54.

BIBLIOGRAPHY

Primary Sources

A. B. *The Mystery of Atheism* (London, 1699).
Abbé de Saint Pierre. *L' Abbé de Saint-Pierre, Sa Vie et ses Oeuvres*, ed. M. G. de Molinari (Paris, 1857).
Abbot, George. *A Treatise of the Perpetuall Visibilitie and Succession of the True Church in All Ages* (London, 1624).
Ackland, Henry Wentworth. 'Faith and Knowledge', *Papers of the Metaphysical Society*, vol. 2, pp. 15–20.
Adams, Rice. *Some Discourses: Wherein the Being of God, and of his Watchful Providence ... are Asserted* (London, 1736).
Adelard of Bath. *Conversations with His Nephew: 'On the Same and the Different', 'Questions on Natural Science', and 'On Birds'*, ed. and trans. Charles Burnett (Cambridge: Cambridge University Press, 1998).
Albertus Magnus. *B. Alberti Magni ... Opera omnia*, 38 vols., ed. Auguste Borgnet (Paris: Louis Vivès, 1890–5).
Alexander of Hales. *Summa theologica*, 4 vols. (Quaracchi: Collegium S. Bonaventurae, 1924–48).
Al-Ghazali, Muhammad-i. *Al-Ghazali's Path to Sufism: His Deliverance from Error (al-Munqidh min al-Dalal)*, trans. R. J. McCarthy (Louisville, KY: Fons Vitae, 2000).
Allix, Pierre. *Douze sermons sur divers textes*, 2nd ed. (Rotterdam, 1685).
Alsted, Johann Heinrich. *Theologia Naturalis* (Frankfurt, 1615).
Ames, William. *Medulla S.S. Theologiæ* (London, 1629).
Amyraut, Moïse. *De l'élévation de la foi et de l'abaissement de la raison* (Saumur, 1640).
Anderton, Thomas. *A soveraign remedy against atheism and heresy* (n.p., 1672).
Andrewes, Lancelot. *The pattern of catechistical doctrine at large* (London, 1650).
Anon. *A Catholic pill to purge Popery* (London, 1677).
Anon. *A Certain Way to Save England* (London, 1681).
Anon. *A Protestant's Resolution: shewing reasons why he will not be a Papist* (London, 1679).
Anon. *A Short Discourse concerning Miracles* (London, 1702).
Anon. 'Code Sacré', *L' ami de la religion: journal ecclésiastique, politique et littéraire* 89 (1836).
Anon. 'German Biblical Criticism', in *The New York Review*, 2nd ed. (New York: George Dearborn, 1838), pp. 133–45.

Anon. *Liberty of Conscience, Explicated and Vindicated* (London, 1689).
Anon. *Mundorum Explicatio ... shewing the True Progress of the Soul, from the Court of Babylon to the City of Jerusalem* (London, 1663).
Anon. 'Professor Lewis's Naturalism', *Literary World* 6 (1850), 559–61.
Anon. 'The Church and Modern Thought', *Irish Ecclesiastical Record* 10 (March 1874), 56–62, 102–9, 237–45.
Anon. 'Theology', in *The Christian Teacher*, new series, vol. 3, no. 12 (London: John Green, 1841), pp. 131–49.
Anquetil, Louis-Pierre. *A summary of universal history*, 9 vols. (London, 1800).
Anselm of Canterbury. *Anselmus Cantuariensis, Proslogion* 1, The Latin Library. www.thelatinlibrary.com/anselmproslogion.html#capi, accessed 2 February 2018.
Anselm of Canterbury. *Libri duo cur deus homo*, ed. Hugo Laemmer (Berlin, 1857).
Anselm of Canterbury. *The Major Works*, ed. Brian G. Davies and G. R. Evans (Oxford: Oxford University Press, 1998).
Anselm of Canterbury. *The Prayers and Meditations of Saint Anselm, with the Proslogion*, trans. Benedicta Ward (Harmondsworth: Penguin, 1953).
Aristotle. *The Complete Works of Aristotle*, 2 vols., ed. Jonathan Barnes (Princeton: Princeton University Press, 1984).
Arnauld, Antoine. *De le nécessité de la foi en Jésus-Christ pour être suavéi*, Oeuvres, vol. 10 (Paris, 1777).
Atterbury, Francis. *Fourteen sermons preach'd on several occasions* (London, 1708).
Atterbury, Francis. *Sermons and discourses on several subjects and occasions*, 2 vols. (London, 1723).
'Augsburg Confession', Art. VXII, 5. https://bookofconcord.org/augsburg-confession/article-xvii/, accessed 24 October 2021.
Augustine of Hippo, *De ordine*, trans. Silvano Borrusco (South Bend: St Augustine's Press, 2007).
Augustine of Hippo. *The Works of Saint Augustine*, 20 vols., ed. John Rotelle (New York, 1991–).
Aulard, Alphonse. *Le Culte de la Raison et le Culte de l'Être Supreme* (Paris: Félix Alcan, 1892).
Bacon, Roger. *The Opus Majus of Roger Bacon*, 2 vols., ed. Roger Bridges (Oxford: Clarendon Press, 1897).
Bacon, Francis. *The Works of Francis Bacon*, 14 vols., ed. James Spedding, Robert Ellis, and Douglas Heath (London: Longman, 1857–74).
Bagehot, Walter. *Physics and Politics: Or, Thoughts on the Application of the Principles of 'Natural Selection' and Inheritance to Political Society* (London: Henry S. King, 1872).
Baillet, Adrien. *La Vie de M. Des-Cartes*, 2 vols. (Paris, 1691).
Baker, John. *Lectures of I.B. vpon the xii. Articles of our Christian faith* (London, 1581).
Baker, Thomas. *Reflections upon Learning* (London, 1708).
Bale, John. *The Vocaycon of Iohan Bale* (Rome, 1553).
Balfour, Arthur James. *The Foundations of Belief* (New York: Longmans, Green, and Co., 1895).
Balmes, Jaime. *El Protestantismo comparado con el Catolicismo en sus relaciones con la Civilización Europea*, 3 vols. (Barcelona, 1842–4).
Balmes, Jaime. *Protestantism and Catholicism Compared, With Respect to European Civilization*, 2nd ed. (Baltimore: John Murphy, 1851).
Barker, Matthew. *Natural Theology* (London, 1674).

Barlow, Thomas. *Brutum fulmen* (London, 1681).
Baronius, Caesar. *Annales Ecclesiastici*, 12 vols. (Rome, 1588–1607).
Barrow, Isaac. *The Theological Works of Isaac Barrow*, 8 vols. (Oxford: Oxford University Press, 1830).
Barrow, Isaac. *The Usefulness of Mathematical Learning Explained and Demonstrated*, trans. John Kirby (London, 1734).
Barton, Samuel. *A Sermon Preached before the Honorable House of Commons* (London, 1696).
Baumgarten, Alexander G. *Metaphysics*, 4th ed. (Halle, 1757), ed. and trans. Courtney D. Fugate and John Hymers (London: Bloomsbury, 2014).
Baumgarten, Alexander G. *Sciagraphia encyclopaediae philosophicae* (Halle an der Saale, 1769).
Baur, F. C. *De Christliche Gnosis* (Tübingen, 1835).
Baxter, Richard. *A Moral Prognostication* (London, 1680).
Baxter, Richard. *The Safe Religion* (London, 1657).
Bayle, Pierre. *Historical and Critical Dictionary: Selections*, ed. Richard H. Popkin (Indianapolis: Bobbs Merrill, 1965).
Bayle, Pierre. *Oeuvres Diverses de M. Pierre Bayle*, 4 vols. (The Hague, 1727–31).
Bazán, B. and A. Zimmermann (eds.). *Siger de Brabant: Écrits de logique, de morale et de physique* (Louvain: Publications Universitaires, 1974).
Beard, Thomas. *A retractiue from the Romish Religion* (London, 1616).
Beard, Thomas. *Antichrist the Pope of Rome* (London, 1625).
Beattie, James. *An Essay on the Nature and Immutability of Truth* [1770] (London, 1778).
Bedford, Thomas. *A Treatise of the Sacraments* (London, 1638).
Bellarmine, Robert. *De controversiis christianae, tom 1* (Lyon, 1596).
Bellarmine, Robert. *Disputationes de Controversiis Christianae Fidei* (Ingolstadii, 1586).
Bellows, Henry Witney. *A Sequel to 'The Suspense of Faith'* (New York: D. Appleton, 1859).
Bentley, Richard. *The Folly and Unreasonableness of Atheism*, 4th ed. (London, 1699).
Bentley, Richard. *The Works of Richard Bentley, D.D.*, 3 vols., ed. Alexander Dyce (London: Macpherson, 1838).
Berington, Simon. *Dissertations on the Mosaical creation* (London, 1750).
Beverly, Thomas. *A Discourse upon the Powers of the World to Come* (London, 1694).
Biggs, Noah. *Mataetechnia Medicinae Praxeos* (London, 1651).
Binning, Hugh. *The Common Principles of Christian Religion* (Glasgow, 1667).
Blount, Charles. *A Just Vindication of Learning* (London, 1679).
Blount, Charles. *Miscellaneous Works* (London, 1695).
Blount, Charles. *Oracles of Reason* (London, 1693).
Bodin, Jean. *Colloquium heptaplomeres de rerum sublimium arcanis abditis* [1588], ed. L. Noack (Schwerin, 1857).
Boehme, Jacob. *Signatura Rerum, or the Signature of all Things* (London, 1651).
Bold, Samuel. *Some Passages in the Reasonableness of Christianity* (London, 1697).
Bonaventure. *Commentaria in Quatuor Libros Sententiarum*, 4 vols. (Quaracchi: Collegium S. Bonaventurae, 1882–1902).
Bonaventure. *Commentary on the Sentences: Philosophy of God*, ed. and trans. R. E. Houser and Timothy B. Noone (St. Bonaventure, NY: Franciscan Institute Publications, 2013).
Bonnet, Charles. *Oeuvres d'histoire naturelle et de philosophie*, 18 vols. (Neuchâtel, 1779–83).
Bonnet, Charles. *The contemplation of nature*, 2 vols. (London, 1766).
Bossuet, Jacques Bénigne. *Histoire des variations des églises protestantes* (Paris, 1688).

Boyer, Pierre. *Abrege de l'Histoire des Vaudois Ou On voit leur origine comme Dieu a conservé la Religion Chrêtienne en sa pureté parmi eux, dépuis le tems des Apôtres jusques à nos jours* (La Haye, 1691).
Boyle, Robert. *Boyle on Atheism*, ed. J. J. Macintosh (Toronto: University of Toronto Press, 2006).
Boyle, Robert. *The Works of Robert Boyle*, 14 vols., ed. Michael Hunter and Edward B. Davis (London: Routledge, 2016).
Boyle, Robert. *The Works of the Honourable Robert Boyle*, 6 vols., ed. T. Birch (London, 1772).
Bramston, William. *A Sermon preached at the opening of the Lecture at Maldon* (London, 1697).
Bridge, William. *The truth of the times vindicated* (London, 1643).
Broca, Paul. *Recherches sur l'hybridité animale en général et sur l'hybridité humaine* (Paris, 1860).
Bromley, Thomas. *The Way to the Sabbath of Rest, or The Souls Progress* (London, 1655).
Broughton, Samuel David. 'Scientific Letters to a Lady of Quality', *Metropolitan Magazine*, vol. 2, 1831, pp. 32–40.
Bruce, A. B. 'F. C. Baur and his Theory of the Origin of Christianity and of the New Testament Writings', *Present Day Tracts* 38 (1885).
Buckle, Henry Thomas. *History of Civilization in England* [1857], new ed., 3 vols. (London: Longmans, Green, and Co., 1869).
Buhle, Johann Gottlieb. *Lehrbuch der Geschichte der Philosophie* (Göttingen: Vandenhoeck & Ruprecht, 1796–1804).
Bunny, Francis. *A comparison betweene the auncient fayth of the Romans, and the new Romish religion* (n.p., 1595).
Bunyan, John. *The Pilgrim's Progress* (London, 1678).
Burchard of Ursberg. *Chronicvm Abbatis Vrspergensis* (Strasbourg: Mylius, 1537).
Burgess, Anthony. *A Treatise of original sin* (London, 1658).
Burgess, Anthony. *Expository Sermons upon the Whole 17th Chapter of the Gospel according to St. John* (London, 1656).
Burkhardt, Jacob. *Die Cultur der Renaissance in Italien* (Basel, 1860).
Burman, Franz. *Synopsis theologiae et speciatim oeconomiae foederum Dei*, 2 vols. (Geneva, 1678, The Hague, 1687).
Burnet, Gilbert. *A Letter Writ by the Lord Bishop of Salisbury* (London, 1693).
Burnet, Gilbert. *History of the Reformation of the Church of England* (London, 1679).
Burnet, Gilbert. *Letter written upon the Discovery of the Late Plot* (London, 1678).
Burton, Henry. *The seuen vials or a briefe and plaine exposition vpon the 15: and 16: chapters of the Revelation* (London, 1658).
Burton, Robert. *Anatomy of Melancholy* [1621], 3 vols., ed. Holbrook Jackson (London: Folio, 2005).
Bushnell, Horace. *Nature and the Supernatural, as Together Constituting the One System of God* [1858], 4th ed. (New York: Charles Scribner, 1859).
Butler, Joseph. *The Analogy of Religion*, ed. David McNaughton (Oxford: Oxford University Press, 2021).
Caldwell, John. *A Sermon preached before the right honorable Earle of Darbie* (London, 1577).
Calixt, Georg. *De pactis quae Deus cum hominibus iniit* (Helmstedt, 1654).
Calvin, John. *Calvin's Commentaries*, 22 vols. (Grand Rapids: Eerdmans, 2003).

Calvin, John. *Institutes of the Christian Religion*, 2 vols., trans. Henry Beveridge (Edinburgh: Calvin Translation Society, 1845).

Calvin, John. *Institutio christianae religionis* (Londini, 1576).

Calvin, John. *Institution de la religion chrétienne par Jean Calvin* (Genève, 1888).

Calvin, John. *Joannis Calvini Opera Selecta*, 5 vols., ed. P. Barth and W. Niesel (Munich: C. Kaiser, 1952–62).

Calvin, John. *The Institution of the Christian religion*, trans. Thomas Norton (Glasgow, 1762).

Calvin, John. *Tracts and Treatises on the Reformation of the Church*, 3 vols., trans. H. Beveridge (Edinburgh: Banner of Truth, 1844).

Campbell, George. *A Dissertation on Miracles* (Edinburgh, 1762).

Canaries, James. *A Discourse representing the Sufficient Manifestation of the Will of God* (Edinburgh, 1684).

Carlyle, Thomas. *On Heroes and Hero Worship* (London: Ward, Lock and Co., 1910).

Carpenter, William Benjamin. 'Of Mind and Will in Nature', *Papers of the Metaphysical Society*, vol. 1, pp. 47–66.

Carpenter, William Benjamin. 'On the mutual relations of the vital and physical forces', *Philosophical Transactions of the Royal Society* 140 (1850), 727–57.

Carpenter, William Benjamin. *Popular Cyclopaedia of Natural Science* (London, 1843).

Carpenter, William Benjamin. *Presidential Address, 1872, Report of the Forty-Second Meeting of the British Association* (London: John Murray, 1873).

Carpenter, William Benjamin. *Principles of General and Comparative Physiology* (London: John Churchill, 1839).

Cartwright, Christopher. *A Brief and Plain Exposition of the Creed* (London, 1649).

Cartwright, Christopher. *The Doctrine of Faith* (London, 1650).

Casal, Gaspar do. *De quadripertita iustitia, libri tres* (Venice, 1563).

Casaubon, Meric. *A Letter of Meric Casaubon, D.D. &c. to Peter du Moulin D.D., concerning Natural Experimental Philosophie* (Cambridge, 1669).

Casaubon, Meric. *A TREATISE PROVING Spirits, Witches, AND Supernatural Operations* (London, 1672).

Catechism of the Catholic Church. www.vatican.va/archive/ENG0015/__P1V.HTM, accessed 24 October 2021.

Cavendish, Margaret. 'Philosophical Letters' [1664], in *Essential Writings*, ed. David Cunning (Oxford: Oxford University Press, 2019), pp. 59–98.

Chalmers, Thomas. *Of the Adaptation of External Nature to the Moral and Intellectual Constitution of Man*, 2 vols. (London: William Pickering, 1833).

Chalmers, Thomas. *The Select Works of Thomas Chalmers, D.D., LL.D.*, 4 vols. (New York, 1850).

Chambers, Ephraim. *Cyclopaedia, or, An Universal Dictionary of Arts and Sciences*, 2 vols. (London, 1728).

Chambers, Ephraim. *Cyclopaedia: or an Universal Dictionary of Arts and Sciences*, 2nd ed., 2 vols. (London, 1738).

Chambers, Robert. *Vestiges of the Natural History of Creation* [1844], 8th ed. (London: John Chambers, 1850).

Charleton, Walter. *The Darknes of Atheism Dispelled by the Light of Nature. A Physico-theological Treatise* (London, 1652).

Charron, Pierre. *De la Sagesse livres trois* (Bourdeaux, 1601).

Chichon, Nicolas. *L'atheism e des pretendus reformes* (Poitiers, 1620).

Chillingworth, William. *The Religion of Protestants a Safe Way to Salvation* [1637], 6th ed. (London, 1687).
Chubb, Thomas. *The Comparative Excellence and Obligation of Moral and Positive Duties* (London, 1730).
Clarke, Samuel. *A Demonstration of the Being and Attributes of God, and Other Writings*, ed. Ezio Vailati (Cambridge: Cambridge University Press, 1998).
Clarke, Samuel. *The Works of Samuel Clarke, D.D.*, 2 vols. (London, 1738).
Clifford, Martin. *A Discourse of Humane Reason* (London, 1690).
Clifford, William Kingdon. *Lectures and Essays*, 2nd ed., ed. Leslie Stephen and Frederick Pollock (London: Macmillan, 1886).
Clodius, C. H. A. *Von Gott in der Natur, in der Menschengeschichte, und im Bewußtseyn*, 5 vols. (Leipzig, 1818).
Cocceius, Johannes. *Summa doctrinae de foedere et testamento Dei* (Franeker, 1648).
Collier, William. *Clavis Universalis, or A New Inquiry after Truth, being a Demonstration of the Non-Existence or Impossibility of an External World* [1713] (Edinburgh, 1836).
Combe, George. *On the Relation between Science and Religion*, 4th ed. (Edinburgh: MacLachlan and Stewart, 1857).
Comenius, Jan. *A Patterne of Universall Knowledge* (London, 1651).
Comenius, Jan. *Reformation of Schooles* (London, 1642).
Comte, Auguste. *Cours de philosophie positive* [1830–42], 6 vols. (Paris: Hermann, 1975).
Comte, Auguste. *Early Political Writings*, ed. and trans. H. S. Jones (Cambridge: Cambridge University Press, 1988).
Comte, Auguste. *Système de politique positive* (Paris, 1854).
Comte, Auguste. *The Catechism of Positivism*, trans. Richard Congreve (London: John Chapman, 1858).
Condorcet, Marquis de. *Condorcet: Political Writings*, ed. Steven Lukes and Nadia Urbinati (Cambridge: Cambridge University Press, 2012).
Cook, John. *What the Independents would Have* (London, 1647).
Copely, John. *Doctrinal and Moral Observations concerning Religion* (London, 1612).
Cosmas Indicopleustes. *The Christian Topography of Cosmas, an Egyptian Monk*, ed. and trans. J. W. McCrindle (Cambridge: Cambridge University Press, 2010).
Cowles, Henry. *The Pentateuch, in its Progressive Revelations of God to Men* (New York: Appleton, 1884).
Crawford, James. *Haereseo-Machea* (London, 1646).
Creide, Hartmann. *Querela medela cautela*, 2 vols. (Frankfurt, 1666).
Croll, Oswald. *A Treatise of Oswaldus Crollius of Signatures* (London, 1669).
Cromp, John. *Collections out of St Augustine* (London, 1638).
Crooks, George R. and John F. Hurst (eds.). *Theological Encyclopaedia and Methodology* (New York: Hunt and Eaton, 1894).
Cross, Walter. *The Instrumentality of Faith* (London, 1695).
Cudworth, Ralph. *The True Intellectual System of the Universe* (London, 1678).
Culpeper, Thomas. *Morall Discourses and Essayes* (London, 1655).
Culverwell, Nathaniel. *An Elegant and Learned Treatise of the Light of Nature* [1652], ed. Robert A. Greene and Hugh MacCallum (Indianapolis: Liberty Fund, 2001).
Cumberland, Richard. *De legibus naturae* (London, 1672).
d'Alembert, Jean Le Rond. *Preliminary Discourse to the Encyclopedia of Diderot* [1751], trans. Richard N. Schwab (Chicago: University of Chicago Press, 1995).

Daillé, Jean. *Sermons sur l'epître de l'apôtre saint Pauls aux Colossiens, seconde partie* (Paris, 1648).
Daneau, Lambert. *Christianae Isagoges ad Christianorum Theologorum Locos Communes* (Geneva, 1583).
Darwin, Charles. Darwin Correspondence Project. www.darwinproject.ac.uk/, accessed 12 November 2022.
Darwin, Charles. *Darwin's Notebooks on the Transmutation of Species*, ed. Gavin de Beer, part 4, 3. http://darwin-online.org.uk/content/frameset?pageseq=18&itemID=F157 4d&viewtype=text, accessed 23 November 2023.
Darwin, Charles. *On the Origin of Species by means of Natural Selection*, 1st ed. (London: James Murray, 1859).
Darwin, Charles. *On the Origin of Species by means of Natural Selection*, 2nd ed. (London: John Murray, 1860).
Darwin, Charles. *The Descent of Man*, 2 vols. (New York: Appleton, 1871).
de Balzac, Honoré. *La messe de l'athée* (Brussels, 1836).
de Bellingen, Fleury. *L'etymologie ou Explication des proverbes François* (La Haye, 1656).
de Bonald, Louis. *Oeuvres complètes*, 15 vols. (Geneva, 1982).
de Góis, Manuel. *Commentarii Collegii Conimbricensus ... in octo libros Physicorum Aristotelis stagiritae* (Coimbra, 1592).
de Greef, Guillaume. *Introduction à la Sociologie*, 2 vols. (Paris: Alcan, 1886).
de la Mettrie, Julien. *Man a Machine* [1747] (La Salle: Open Court, 1912).
de Lamennais, Félicité Robert. *Des progrès de la Révolution et de la guerre contre l'Eglise* (Brussels, 1829).
de Lamennais, Félicité Robert. *Du passe et de l'avenir du peuple* (Paris, 1841).
de Lamennais, Félicité Robert. *Essai sur l'indifférence en matière de religion*, 2 vols. (Paris, 1817, 1820).
de Léry, Jean. *Histoire d'un voyage faict en la terre du Brésil, autrement dite Amérique* (La Rochelle, 1578).
de Léry, Jean. *The History of a Voyage to the Land of Brazil* [1574], trans. Janet Whatley (Berkeley and Los Angeles: University of California Press, 1990).
de Maistre, Joseph. *Considerations on France* [1796], ed. and trans. R. Lebrun (Cambridge: Cambridge University Press, 2000).
de Silhon, Jean. *L'immortalité de l'âme* (Paris, 1634).
de Tocqueville, Alexis. *Democracy in America*, ed. and trans. Harvey C. Mansfield and Delba Winthrop (Chicago: University of Chicago Press, 2000).
de Villers, Charles. *An Essay on the Spirit and Influence of the Reformation of Luther*, trans. James Mill (London, 1805).
Denzinger, Heinrich (ed.). *Enchiridion Symbolorum*, 34th ed. (Freiburg: Herder, 1965).
Derham, William. *Astrotheology or, A Demonstration of the Being and Attributes of God, from a Survey of the Heavens*, 2nd ed. (London, 1715).
Derham, William. *Physico-Theology: or, A Demonstration of the Being and Attributes of God, from his Works of Creation*, 4th ed. (London, 1716).
Descartes, René. *Oeuvres de Descartes*, 12 vols., ed. Charles Adam and Paul Tannery (Paris: Cerf, 1897–1913).
Descartes, René. *The Method, Meditations and Philosophy of Descartes*, trans. John Veitch (Washington, DC: M. Walter Dunne, 1901).
Descartes, René. *The Philosophical Writings of Descartes*, 2 vols., trans. J. Cottingham, R. Stoothoff, and D. Murdoch (Cambridge: Cambridge University Press, 1985).

Descartes, René. *The Philosophical Writings of Descartes*, vol. 3: *The Correspondence*, trans. J. Cottingham, R. Stoothoff, D. Murdoch, and Anthony Kenny (Cambridge: Cambridge University Press, 1991).
Dick, Thomas. *On the Improvement of Society by the Diffusion of Knowledge* (New York: J. & J. Harper, 1833).
Dick, Thomas. *The Philosophy of a Future State* [1829] (Glasgow: William Collins, 1869).
Dictionnaire de la Langue Française, 5 vols. (Paris, 1883–4).
Diderot, Denis and Jean le Rond d'Alembert (eds.). *Encyclopédie ou Dictionnaire raisonné des sciences, des arts et des métiers*, 28 vols. (Paris, 1751–72).
Doddridge, Philip. *The Rise and Progress of Religion in the Soul* (London, 1745).
Doddridge, Philip. *The Works of the Rev. P. Doddridge, D.D.*, 10 vols. (Leeds, 1803).
Donne, John. *Essayes in Divinity*, ed. Evelyn Simpson (Oxford: Clarendon Press, 1952).
Donne, John. *LXXX Sermons* (London, 1640).
Downame, George. *A Treatise concerning Antichrist* (London, 1603).
Downame, John. *The Christian Warfare* (London, 1634).
Draper, John William. *A History of the Intellectual Development of Europe*, revised ed., 2 vols. (New York: Harper, 1875).
Draper, John William. *History of the Conflict between Religion and Science* [1874] (New York: Appleton, 1898).
Draper, John William. *Human Physiology, Statical and Dynamical; or The Conditions and Course of the Life of Man*, 2nd ed. (New York: Harper and Brothers, 1858).
Du Marnix, Philippe. *Le tableau des différens de la religion*, vol. 1 (Leiden, 1603).
Du Marnix, Philippe. *Traicte du Sacrement* (Saumur, 1601).
Du Perron, Jacques Davy. *Traitté du Sainct Sacrement de l'Eucharistie* (Paris, 1622).
Dupont, James. *Three Sermons* (London, 1676).
Durandus of St-Pourçain. *Super sententias theologiae Petri Lombardi commentariorum libri quatuor* (Venice, 1571).
Durham, William. *A Serious Exhortation to the Necessary Duties of Family and Person Instruction* (London, 1659).
Durkheim, Émile. *Les formes élémentaire de la vie religieuse, le système totémique en Australie* (Paris: Alcan, 1912).
Durkheim, Émile. *The Elementary Forms of the Religious Life*, trans. Carol Cosman (Oxford: Oxford University Press, 2008).
E. W. *A Discourse of Miracles wrought in the Roman Catholick Church* (Antwerp, 1676).
Eberhard, J. A. and I. Kant. *Preparation for Natural Theology: With Kant's Notes and the Danzig Rational Theology Transcript*, ed. and trans. Courtney D. Fugate and John Hymers (London: Bloomsbury, 2016).
Eckhart von Hochheim (Meister Eckhart). *The Complete Mystical Works of Meister Eckhart*, trans. Maurice O'C. Walshe (New York: Crossroad, 2009).
Edwards, John. *A Demonstration of the Existence and Providence of God* (London, 1696).
Edwards, John. *The Eternal and Intrinsick Reasons of Good and Evil* (Cambridge, 1699).
Edwards, Jonathan. *The Works of Jonathan Edwards*, 2 vols. (Peabody, MA: Hendrickson, 1998).
Eliot, John. *The Indian Grammar Begun* (Cambridge, MA, 1666).
Encyclopaedia Britannica, 5th ed., 20 vols. (Edinburgh, 1817).
Encyclopaedia Britannica, 9th ed., 24 vols. (New York: Charles Scribner's Sons, 1886).
Encyclopedia Americana, 14 vols. (Boston: B. B. Mussey & Co., 1851).

Engels, Friedrich. 'Humanism versus Pantheism: On Thomas Carlyle', in *Reader in Marxist Philosophy*, ed. Howard Selsam and Harry Martel (New York: International Publishers, 1963), pp. 234–9.
Engels, Friedrich. *The Origin of the Family, Private Property and the State*, trans. Ernest Unterman (Chicago: Charles H. Kerr and Co., 1908).
Estwick, Sampson. *A Sermon preached at the Cathedral-Church of St. Paul* (London, 1698).
Evagrius Ponticus. *Scholies aux Proverbes*, trans. Paul Géhin, Sources chrétiennes 340 (Paris: Cerf, 1987).
Evans, Edward. *Verba Dierum* (Oxford, 1615).
Fabisch, Peter and Erwin Iserloh (eds.). *Dokumente zur Causa Lutheri (1517–1521)*, 2 vols. (Münster: Aschendorff, 1988–91).
Farrar, F. W. 'On the Universality of Belief in God, and in a Future State', *The Anthropological Review* 2 (1864), ccxvii–ccxxii.
Fénelon, François. *Demonstration de l'Existence de Dieu*, 2nd ed. (Paris, 1713).
Féraud, Jean-François, *Dictionnaire critique de la langue Français*, 3 vols. (Marseille, 1787).
Ferguson, Adam. *An Essay on the History of Civil Society* [1767], ed. Fania Oz-Salzberger (Cambridge: Cambridge University Press, 1995).
Ferguson, Adam. *Institutes of Moral Philosophy*, 2nd ed. (Edinburgh, 1773).
Ferguson, Robert. *A Sober Enquiry into the Nature, Measure, and Principle of Moral Virtue* (London, 1673).
Ferguson, Robert. *The Interest of Reason in Religion* (London, 1675).
Ferrier, James F. *Institutes of Metaphysic* (Edinburgh: William Blackwood and Sons, 1854).
Feuerbach, Ludwig. *The Essence of Christianity* [1841], trans. [George Eliot] (London: John Chapman, 1854).
Ficino, Marsilio. *Platonic Theology*, 6 vols., ed. James Hankins, trans. Michael J. B Allen (Cambridge, MA: Harvard University Press, 2001–6).
Fieser, James (ed.). *Early Responses to Hume's Writings on Religion*, 2 vols. (London: Bloomsbury, 2005).
Filmer, Robert. *An Advertisement to the Jurymen of England touching Witches* (London, 1688).
Fischer, Kuno. *Descartes and his School*, ed. Noah Porter, trans. John P. Gordy (London: T. F. Unwin, 1890).
Fischer, Kuno. *Geschichte der neueren Philosophie*, 6 vols. (Berlin, 1852–77).
Flacius, M. et al. *Ecclesiastica Historia*, 14 vols. (Basel, 1560–74).
Fludd, Robert. *Mosaicall Philosophy* (London, 1659).
Forer, Laurenz. *Indifferentismus: Oder Allerley Gattung Kyrch* (Ingolstadt, 1656).
Franke, Walter. *An Epitome of Divinitie* (London, 1655).
Frazer, James George. *The Golden Bough*, 3rd ed., 13 vols. (London: Macmillan, 1980).
Freeman, Ireneus. *Logikē latreia the reasonablenesse of divine service* (London, 1661).
Freud, Sigmund. *The Standard Edition of the Complete Psychological Works of Sigmund Freud*, 24 vols., ed. James Strachey (London: Vintage, 2001).
Fries, Jakob. *Neue oder anthropologische Kritik der Vernunft* [1807], 10th ed., 3 vols. (Heidelberg, 1828–31).
Fries, Jakob. *Wissen, Glauben, und Ahndung* (Jena, 1805).
Fuller, Francis. *A Treatise of Faith and Repentance* (London, 1685).
Fuller, Thomas. *The Church-History of Britain* (London, 1655).
Fuller, Thomas. *The Holy State and the Profane State*, 3rd ed. (London, 1652).

Gale, Theophilus. *Christ's tears for Jerusalems unbelief and ruine* (London, 1679).
Gale, Theophilus. *The Anatomie of Infidelitie* (London, 1672).
Gale, Theophilus. *The Court of the Gentiles*, part IV (London, 1667).
Garasse, François. *La doctrine curieuse des beaux esprits de ce temps ou prétendus* (Paris, 1623).
Gassendi, Pierre. *Opera omnia*, 6 vols. (Lyon, 1658).
Gaule, John. *Select Cases of Conscience touching Witches* (London, 1646).
Gerhard, Johann. *Loci Theologici* [1610–25], 9 vols., ed. Eduard Preuss (Berlin, 1863–75).
Gersdorf, Ernst (ed.). *Repertorium der gesammten deutschen Literatur*, vol. 15 (Leipzig, 1838).
Gerson, Jean. *Early Works*, trans. Brian McGuire (New York: Paulist Press, 1998).
Gladstone, William Ewart. *Studies on Homer and the Homeric Age*, 3 vols. (Oxford: Oxford University Press, 1858).
Gladstone, William Ewart. *Thoughts from the Writings and Speeches of William Ewart Gladstone*, ed. G. Barnett Smith (London: Ward, Lock and Bowden, 1894).
Glanvill, Joseph. *Essays on Several Important Subjects* (London, 1676).
Glanvill, Joseph. *Logou thrēskeia, or, A Seasonable Recommendation and Defence of Reason in the Affairs of Religion* (London, 1670).
Glanvill, Joseph. *Saducismus triumphatus* (London, 1681).
Glanvill, Joseph. *Scepsis Scientifica: Or, Confest Ignorance, the Way to Science* (London, 1665).
Glanvill, Joseph. *The Vanity of Dogmatizing* (London, 1661).
Goclenius, Rudoph. *Lexicon philosophicum* (Frankfurt, 1613).
Goethe, J. W. von. *Zur Farbenlehre*, 2 vols. (Tübingen, 1810).
Goodman, Godfrey. *The Creatures Praysing God: Or, the Religion of Dumb Creatures* (London, 1622).
Goodman, John. *Seven Sermons Preach'd upon Several Occasions* (London, 1697).
Grantham, Thomas. *Christianismus Primitivus* (London, 1678).
Graves, Richard. *A sermon on the deliverance of this kingdom*, 3rd ed. (Dublin, 1797).
Green, T. H. *Prolegomena to Ethics* (Oxford: Clarendon Press, 1883).
Gregory the Great. *Moralia in Job*, 3 vols., trans. James Bliss (Jackson, MI: Ex Fontibus, 2015).
Graham, D. (ed. and trans.). *The Texts of Early Greek Philosophy*, 2 vols. (Cambridge: Cambridge University Press, 2010).
Gomarus, Franciscus. *Opera theologica*, 3 vols. (Amsterdam, 1644).
Grove, William Robert. *The Correlation of Physical Forces* [1846], 3rd ed. (London: Longman, Brown, Green and Longmans, 1855).
Guizot, François. *Civilization in Europe*, 3 vols., trans. William Hazlitt (London: David Bogue, 1846).
Guizot, François. *General History of Civilization in Europe*, ed. George Wells Knight (New York: Appleton, 1896).
Hackspan, Theodoricus. *Termini distinctiones et divisiones philosophico theologicae* (Altdorff, 1664).
Haeckel, Ernst. *History of creation: Or the development of the earth and its inhabitants by the action of natural causes*, 2 vols., trans. G. R. Lankester (New York: Appleton, 1880).
Haeckel, Ernst. *Monism as Connecting Religion and Science*, trans. J. Gilchrist (London: Adam and Charles Black, 1874).
Haeckel, Ernst. *The Riddle of the Universe*, trans. Joseph McCabe (London: Watts and Co., 1929).

Hagenbach, K. R. *Text-book of the History of Doctrine*, 2 vols., trans. Henry B. Smith (New York, 1869).
Hakewill, George. *King Dauids Vow for Reformation of Himselfe* (London, 1621).
Hall, Edmund. Ἡ απωστασία ὁ ἀντίχριστος: *Or, A Scriptural Discourse of the Apostasie and the Antichrist* (London, 1653).
Hallywell, Henry. *The Excellency of Moral Virtue* (London, 1692).
Hallywell, Henry. *The Sacred Method of Saving Humane Souls* (London, 1677).
Hamann, Johann Georg. *Writings on Philosophy and Language*, ed. Kenneth Haynes (Cambridge: Cambridge University Press, 2007).
Hamilton, John. *A Facile Traictise* (Leuven, 1600).
Hamilton, William. 'Philosophy of the Unconditioned' [1829], repr. in *Kant's Thought in Britain: The Early Impact*, ed. Robert Adamson (London: Routledge/Thoemmes Press, 1999).
Hancock, John. *Arguments to Prove the Being of God* (London, 1706).
Hardouin, Jean. *Opera varia* (Amsterdam, 1733).
Harrington, James. *The Prerogative of Popular Government* (London, 1658).
Harris, John. *The Atheistical objections against the being of God and his attributes fully considered and fully refuted* (London, 1698).
Harrison, Frederick. 'Neo-Christianity', *The Westminster Review*, vol. 74, no. 146 (1 October 1860), 293–332.
Harrison, Frederick. 'The Relativity of Knowledge', *Papers of the Metaphysical Society*, vol. 1, pp. 160–73.
Hartlib, Samuel. *Macaria* (London, 1641).
Harward, Philip. *German Anti-Supernaturalism* (London, 1841).
Hayes, Carlton J. H. *Nationalism: A Religion* [1926] (London: Routledge, 2016).
Hegel, G. W. F. *Die Positivität der christlichen Religion*, in *Hegels theologische Jugendschriften*, ed. Herman Nohl (Tübingen, 1907).
Hegel, G. W. F. *Early Theological Writings*, trans. Richard Kroner (Philadelphia: University of Pennsylvania Press, 1975).
Hegel, G. W. F. *Hegel: Political Writings*, ed. Lawrence Dickey and H. B. Nisbet (Cambridge: Cambridge University Press, 1999).
Hegel, G. W. F. *Hegel's Lectures on the History of Philosophy*, 3 vols. in 1, trans. E. S. Haldane and Frances H. Simpson (Delhi: Lector House, 2020).
Hegel, G. W. F. *Lectures on the Philosophy of History*, trans. Ruben Alvarado (Aalten: Wordbridge, 2011).
Hegel, G. W. F. *Lectures on the Philosophy of Religion: One Volume Edition, The Lectures of 1827*, ed. Peter C. Hodgson (Oxford: Clarendon Press, 2006).
Hegel, G. W. F. *Lectures on the Philosophy of World History*, trans. H. B. Nisbet (Cambridge: Cambridge University Press, 1975).
Hegel, G. W. F. *Lectures on the Philosophy of World History, Volume 1: Manuscripts of the Introduction and the Lectures of 1822–1823*, ed. and trans. Robert F. Brown and Peter C. Hodgson (Oxford: Oxford University Press, 2011).
Hegel, G. W. F. *Phenomenology of Spirit*, trans. A. V. Miller (Oxford: Oxford University Press, 1996).
Hegel, G. W. F. *The Encyclopaedia Logic* [1817], trans. T. F. Geraets, W. A. Suchting, and H. S. Harris (Indianapolis: Hackett, 1991).
Heidanus, Abraham. *Corpus theologiae Christianae*, 2 vols. (Leiden, 1654–9).

Helveys, Thomas. *Persecution for religion judg'd and condemned* (London, 1662).
Herbert of Cherbury, Edward, Lord. *De religione laici* [1645], ed. and trans. Harold R. Hutcheson (New Haven: Yale University Press, 1944).
Herbert of Cherbury, Edward, Lord. *De Veritate*, trans. Meyrick H. Carre (Bristol: J. W. Arrowsmith, 1937).
Herbert of Cherbury, Edward, Lord. *De veritate, prout distinguitur a Revelatione, a Verisimile, a Possibili, et a Falso* (Paris, 1624).
Herbert of Cherbury, Edward, Lord. *The Life of Edward, Lord Herbert of Cherbury*, ed. J. M. Shuttleworth (Oxford: Oxford University Press, 1976).
Herder, Johann Gottfried von. *Fragmente zur deutschen Literatur* (Tübingen, 1805).
Herder, Johann Gottfried von. *Ideen zur Philosophie der Geschichte der Menschheit*, ed. Gerhart Schmidt (Wiesbaden: Löwit, 1971).
Herder, Johann Gottfried von. *Philosophical Writings*, ed. Michael N. Forster (Cambridge: Cambridge University Press, 2008).
Herschel, John. *Preliminary Discourse on the Study of Natural Philosophy* [1830], new edition (London, 1851).
Hill, Thomas. *The Trade of Truth Advanced* (London, 1642).
Hinks, William. *Anti-Supernaturalism considered* (London: John Green, 1841).
Hitchcock, Edward. *Religion of Geology and its Connected Sciences* [1851] (London: James Blackwood, 1860).
Hobbes, Thomas. *Leviathan*, 3 vols., ed. Noel Malcolm (Oxford: Clarendon Press, 2012).
Hobbes, Thomas. *The English Works of Thomas Hobbes*, 11 vols., ed. William Molesworth (London: Bohn, 1851).
Hodge, Charles. *Systematic Theology*, 2 vols. (New York: Charles Scribner's Sons, 1876).
Hodson, F. M. *Encyclopedia Mancuniensis*, 2 vols. (Manchester, 1815).
Hole, Matthew. *Letters written to JM* (London, 1699).
Hooke, Robert. *Micrographia* (London, 1665).
Hooker, Richard. *The Works of that Learned and Judicious Divine Mr. Richard Hooker*, 3 vols. (Oxford: Clarendon Press, 1888).
Horn, John. *An Appeal to the Impartial & Judicious Reader* (London, 1660).
Hortius, Stanislaus. *Confutatio prolegomenon Brentii, quae primum scripsit adversus* (Antverpiae, 1561).
Howitt, William. *The History of the Supernatural, in all ages and nations, and in all Churches, Christian and Pagan: Demonstrating a universal truth*, 2 vols. (London: Longman, Green, Longman, Roberts and Green, 1863).
Huet, Pierre-Daniel. *Demonstratio Evangelica* [1673], 6th ed. (Frankfurt, 1722).
Hugh of St Victor. *Didascalicon*, trans. Jerome Taylor (New York: Columbia University Press, 1991).
Hugh of St Victor. *Hugh of St Victor on the Sacraments of the Christian Faith*, trans. Roy J. Deferrari (Eugene: Wipf and Stock, 1951).
Humbolt, Alexander von. *Gesammelte Schriften*, 17 vols., ed. Albert Leitzmann et al. (Berlin: Behr, 1903–36).
Hume, David. *Dialogues concerning Natural Religion* (London, 1779).
Hume, David. *Enquiries Concerning Human Understanding and Concerning the Principles of Morals*, 3rd ed., ed. L. A. Selby-Bigge and P. H. Nidditch (Oxford: Oxford University Press, 1975).
Hume, David. *Essays, Moral, Political, and Literary* [1758] (London, 1777).

Hume, David. *Natural History of Religion*, ed. H. E. Root (Stanford: Stanford University Press, 1957).
Hume, David. *Philosophical Essays: concerning human understanding* (London, 1748).
Hume, David. *Political Essays*, ed. Knud Haakonssen and Raymond Geuss (Cambridge: Cambridge University Press, 1994).
Huxley, Leonard. *The Life and Letters of Thomas Henry Huxley*, 3 vols. (Cambridge: Cambridge University Press, 2012).
Huxley, Thomas Henry. 'Agnosticism, a Symposium', *Agnostic Annual* 1 (1884), 5–20.
Huxley, Thomas Henry. *Collected Essays of Thomas Henry Huxley*, 9 vols. (Bristol: Thoemmes Press, 2001).
J. D. *Le tableau de la nouvelle Jérusalem* (Geneva, 1690).
James I. *Dæmonologie, in Forme of a Dialogue* (Edinburgh, 1597).
James, William. *The Varieties of Religious Experience* [1902] in *William James, Writings, 1902–1910* (New York: Library of America, 1987).
James, William. *The Will to Believe* [1897] *and other Essays in Popular Philosophy* (Cambridge: Cambridge University Press, 2014).
Jenisch, Daniel. *Sollte Religion den Menschen jemals entbehrlich werden?* (Berlin, 1797).
Jenkin, Robert. *The Reasonableness and Certainty of the Christian Religion* (London, 1698).
Jenny, John. *A Sermon Preached at the Funeral of Lady Frances Padget* (London, 1697).
Jevons, Frank B. *An Introduction to the History of Religion* (London: Methuen, 1896).
John Philoponus. *On Aristotle: Prior Analytics 1.1–8*, trans. Richard D. McKirahan (London: Duckworth, 2008).
John Scotus Eriugena. *On the Division of Nature*, trans. Myra L. Uhlfelder (Eugene: Wipf and Stock, 1976).
Johnson, Samuel. *A Sermon Preach'd before the Lord Mayor* (London, 1684).
Joule, James P. *The Scientific Papers of James Prescott Joule*, 2 vols. (London, 1887).
Jung, C. G. *Collected Works*, 20 vols., ed. Herbert Reid, Michael Fordham, and Gerhard Adler (Princeton: Princeton University Press, 1953–91).
Junius, Franciscus (the Elder). *A Treatise on True Theology* [1594], trans. David C. Noe (Grand Rapids: Reformation Heritage Books, 2014).
Junius, Franciscus (the Elder). *Opera theologica*, 2 vols. (Geneva, 1607).
Junius, Franciscus (the Elder). *Opuscula Theologia Selecta*, ed. Abraham Kuypers (Amsterdam, 1882).
Kant, Immanuel. *Critique of Practical Reason*, in *Practical Philosophy*, ed. and trans. Mary Gregor (Cambridge: Cambridge University Press, 1996).
Kant, Immanuel. *Critique of Pure Reason*, trans. Paul Guyer and Allen W. Wood (Cambridge: Cambridge University Press, 1998).
Kant, Immanuel. *Lectures on Logic*, trans. J. Michael Young (Cambridge: Cambridge University Press, 1992).
Kant, Immanuel. *Practical Philosophy*, ed. and trans. Mary Gregor (Cambridge: Cambridge University Press, 1996).
Kant, Immanuel. *Religion and Rational Theology*, ed. and trans. Allen W. Wood and George Di Giovanni (Cambridge: Cambridge University Press, 1996).
Keats, John. *The Poetical Works of John Keats* (London: Edward Moxon, 1823).
Keith, George. *Truth and innocency defended against calumny and defamation* (Philadelphia, 1692).
Kelly, J. N. D. *Early Christian Creeds*, 3rd ed. (London: Routledge, 1972).

Kepler, Johannes. *Mysterium Cosmographicum*, trans. A. M. Duncan (Norwalk, CT: Abaris, 1999).
Kesler, Andreas. *Pabsthumb. Gründlicher Bericht, von der Papisten Vrsprung, Lehre vnd Leben* (Coburg, 1630).
Kidder, Richard. *The Judgment of Private Discretion in Matters of Religion Defended* (London, 1687).
King, John H. *The Supernatural: Its Origin, Nature, and Evolution*, 2 vols. (London: Williams and Norgate, 1892).
King, Peter Lord (ed.). *The Life of John Locke, with extracts from his Correspondence, Journals and Common-Place Books* (London, 1829).
Kuchlinus, Johannes. *Ecclesiarum Hollandicarum* (Geneva, 1612).
La Mothe le Vayer, François de. *De la vertu des payens* (Paris, 1642).
Lafitau, François. *Moeurs des sauvages Américains*, 2 vols. (Paris, 1724).
Lamy, Dom François. *Le nouvel athéism renversé* (Paris, 1696).
Lange, Friedrich Albert. *Geschichte des Materialismus und Kritik seiner Bedeutung in der Gegenwart* (Iserlohn: J. Baedeker, 1866).
Lange, Friedrich Albert. *History of Materialism and criticism of its present importance*, 2nd ed., 3 vols., trans. Ernest Chester Thomas (Boston: James Osgood, 1877).
Lanquet, Thomas. *Coopers Chronicle* (London, 1560).
Law, William. *A Serious Call to a Devout and Holy Life* (London, 1729).
Law, William. *The Way to Divine Knowledge* (London, 1752).
Layton, Joseph. *A sermon preached at the anniversary meeting of the Eaton-scholars* (London, 1684).
Le Dictionnaire de l'Académie Française, 4th ed., 2 vols. (Paris, 1762).
Le Dictionnaire de l'Académie Française, 5th ed., 2 vols. (Paris, 1798).
Le Dictionnaire de l'Académie Française. 9th ed., 2 vols. (Paris, 1932). https://academie.atilf.fr/9/, accessed 1 February 2023.
le Faucheur, Michel. *Traitté de la Cène du Seigneur, où est monstré que c'est qu'il faut croire de la nature et de l'usage de ce saint sacrament* (Geneva, 1635).
Lechmere, Edmund. *A Consultation about Religion, or What Religion is Best* (London, 1693).
Lee, Henry. *Anti-Scepticism: or, Notes upon each Chapter of Mr. Lock's Essay concerning Humane Understanding* (London, 1702).
Leibniz, G. W. *Philosophical Essays*, trans. Roger Ariew and Daniel Garber (Indianapolis: Hackett, 1989).
Leibniz, G. W. *Philosophical Papers and Letters*, 2nd ed., ed. L. E. Loemker (Dordrecht: Kluwer, 1969).
Leibniz, G. W. *Philosophical Writings*, ed. G. H. R Parkinson (London: Dent, 1934).
Leibniz, G. W. *Theodicy* [1710], trans. E. M. Huggard (London: Routledge & Kegan Paul, 1952).
Leigh, Edward. *Annotations upon all the New Testament* (London, 1650).
Leland, John. *The Advantage and Necessity of the Christian Revelation*, 3rd ed., 2 vols. (Dublin, 1776).
Leslie, Charles. *The Case Stated between the Church of Rome and the Church of England in a Second Conversation* (n.p., 1721).
Lessing, Gotthold Ephraim. *Gotthold Ephraim Lessing's Sämmtliche Schriften*, vol. 10, ed. Karl Lachman (Leipzig, 1856).

Lessing, Gotthold Ephraim. *Philosophical and Theological Writings*, ed. H. B. Nisbet (Cambridge: Cambridge University Press, 2005).
Lessius, Leonardus. *De providentia numinis* (Antwerp, 1617).
Lessius, Leonardus. *Rawleigh his Ghost. Or a feigned apparition of Syr Walter Rawleigh to a friend of his ...*, trans. A. B. (Saint-Omer, 1631).
Lévi-Strauss, Claude. *The Savage Mind* (Chicago: University of Chicago Press, 1966).
Lewis, Tayler. 'Creation a Series of Supernatural Growths', *Methodist Quarterly Review* 47 (1865), 207–29.
Lewis, Tayler. 'Hickok's Rational Psychology', *Bibliotheca Sacra* 8 (1851), 169–217, 346–77.
Lewis, Tayler. 'Names for Soul', *The Biblical Repository and Classical Review* 21 (1850), 674–703.
Lewis, Tayler. *Nature, Progress, Ideas* (Schenectady, 1850).
Lewis, Tayler. *The Bible and Science; or, the World-Problem* (Schenectady, 1856).
Lewis, Tayler. *The Six Days of Creation* (Schenectady, 1855).
Lewis, Tayler. 'Two New Trinities', *Massachusetts Quarterly Review* 3 (1850), 191–200.
Locke, John. *A Second Letter concerning Toleration* (London, 1690).
Locke, John. *A Third Letter concerning Toleration* (London, 1692).
Locke, John. *An Essay Concerning Human Understanding*, ed. Peter H. Nidditch (Oxford: Clarendon Press, 1975).
Locke, John. *Of the Conduct of the Understanding*, new edition (London, 1801).
Locke, John. *Reasonableness of Christianity*, ed. John Higgins-Biddle (Oxford: Clarendon Press, 1999).
Locke, John. *The Works of John Locke*, 12th ed., 9 vols. (London, 1824).
Locke, John. *Two Treatises of Government*, ed. Peter Laslett (Cambridge: Cambridge University Press, 2003).
Locke, John. *Vindications of the Reasonableness of Christianity*, ed. Victor Nuovo (Oxford: Clarendon Press, 2012).
Lubbertus, Sibrandus. *Commentarius in Catechesin Palatino-Beligicam* (Franker, 1618).
Lubbertus, Sibrandus. *Thesis Prima* [1616] in L. Guedtman, *Illustrium exercitationum* (Leeuwarden, 1669).
Lubbock, John. *Prehistoric Times*, 4th ed. (London: Frederick Norgate, 1878).
Lubbock, John. 'Presidential Address', in *Report of the Fifty-First Meeting of the British Association* (London: John Murray, 1882), pp. 1–51.
Luther, Martin. *Complete Sermons*, 7 vols., ed. John Nicholas Lenker (Grand Rapids: Baker Books, 2000).
Luther, Martin. *D. Martin Luthers Werke: kritische Gesammtausgabe*, 72 vols. (Weimar, 1883–2009).
Luther, Martin. *De libertate christiana* (n.p., 1520).
Luther, Martin. 'Epistle Dedicatory' to Robert Barnes, *Vitae Romanorum Pontificum* [1536] (Basel, 1555).
Luther, Martin. *Exegetica opera Latina*, vol. 19 (Erlangen, 1847).
Luther, Martin. *Lectures on Romans*, trans. W. Pauck (Louisville: Westminster John Knox Press, 1961).
Luther, Martin. *Luther's Works*, 55 vols., ed. J. Pelikan and H. Lehman (St Louis: Concordia, 1955–75).
Luther, Martin. *Prefaces to the New Testament*, trans. Charles M. Jacobs (St Louis: Concordia, 2010).

Luther, Martin. *Table Talk*, ed. and trans. William Hazlitt (Fearn: Christian Heritage, 2003).
Lyell, Charles. 'State of the Universities', *The Quarterly Review*, 36/71 (June 1827), 216–68.
Macaulay, Thomas Babington. *Critical and Miscellaneous Essays*, 6 vols. (Philadelphia: Hart, Carey, and Hart, 1854).
Macaulay, Thomas Babington. *Speeches, with his Minute on Indian Education*, ed. G. M. Young (Oxford: Oxford University Press, 1935).
Mackenzie, George. *Reason: An Essay* (London, 1690).
Maignan, Emmanuel. *Philosophia sacra*, 2 pts. (Toulouse, 1661; Lyons, 1672).
Malebranche, Nicholas. *Dialogues on Metaphysics and Religion* [1688], ed. Nicholas Jolley, trans. David Scott (Cambridge: Cambridge University Press, 1997).
Malebranche, Nicholas. *Search after Truth*, ed. and trans. Thomas Lennon and Paul Olscamp (Cambridge: Cambridge University Press, 1997).
Malthus, Thomas. *A Summary View of the Principle of Population* (London: John Murray, 1830).
Malthus, Thomas. *An Essay on the Principle of Population*, ed. Donald Winch (Cambridge: Cambridge University Press, 1992).
Malthus, Thomas. *The Works of Thomas Robert Malthus*, vol. 4, ed. E. A. Wrigley and D. Souden (London: William Pickering, 1986).
Mandonnet, Pierre (ed.). *Siger de Brabant et l'averroïsme latin au XIIIme siècle, part 2, Textes inédits*, 2nd ed. (Louvain: Institut Supérieur de Philosophie de l'Université, 1908).
Mansel, Henry L. 'On Miracles as Evidences of Christianity', in *Aids to Faith: A Series of Theological Essays*, ed. William Thompson (London: John Murray, 1862), pp. 1–40.
Mansel, Henry L. *The Limits of Religious Thought*, 5th ed. (London: John Murray, 1867).
Mansel, Henry L. *The Philosophy of the Unconditioned* (London: Alexander Strahan, 1866).
Marshall, Catherine, Bernard Lightman, and Richard England (eds.). *The Papers of the Metaphysical Society, 1869–1880: A Critical Edition*, 3 vols. (Oxford: Oxford University Press, 2015).
Martineau, James. 'Is there any Axiom of Causality?', *Contemporary Review* 14 (April–July 1870), 636–44.
Marx, Karl. *Economic and Philosophic Manuscripts of 1844 and the Communist Manifesto* (New York: Prometheus Books, 1988).
Marx, Karl and Friedrich Engels. *On Religion* (Mineola: Dover, 2008).
Marx, Karl and Friedrich Engels. *The German Ideology* (Moscow: Progress Publishers, 1976).
Marx, Karl and Friedrich Engels. *The Marx-Engels Reader*, 2nd ed., ed. Robert C. Tucker (New York: Norton, 1978).
Mather, Cotton. *American Tears upon the Ruines of the Greek Churches* (Boston, 1701).
Maurice, F. D. 'On the Mode of Dealing with the Words which occur most Frequently in Treatises on Mental Philosophy', *The Contemporary Review* 19 (1871), 260–80.
Maurice, F. D. 'On the Words "Nature," "Natural," and "Supernatural"', in *The Papers of the Metaphysical Society*, 3 vols., ed. Catherine Marshall, Bernard Lightman, and Richard England (Oxford: Oxford University Press, 2015), vol. 1, pp. 296–309.
Maximus the Confessor. 'Various Texts', in *Philokalia*, vol. 2, trans. G. E. H. Palmer, Philip Sherrard, and Kallistos Ware (New York: Farrar, Straus & Giroux, 1990).
Maxwell, James Clerk. *Scientific Letters and Papers*, 3 vols., ed. P. M. Harman (Cambridge: Cambridge University Press, 2009).

Mede, Joseph. *Clavis Apocalyptica* (Cambridge, 1627).
Mede, Joseph. *The Key to Revelation* (London, 1643).
Meiners, Christoph. *Grundriß der Geschichte der Menschheit* (Lemgo, 1785).
Meiners, Christoph. *Grundriß der Geschichte der Weltweisheit* (Lemgo, 1786).
Melanchthon, Philip. *Commentarii Epistolam Pauli ad Romanos* (Wittenberg, 1532).
Melanchthon, Philip. *Loci communes* [1535 edition], in *Corpus Reformatorum* 21 (Braunschweig, 1854).
Melanchthon, Philip. *Loci Communes* [1543 edition], trans. J. A. O. Preus (St Louis: Concordia, 1992).
Melanchthon, Philip. *Orations on Philosophy and Education*, ed. Sachiko Kusukawa, trans. Christine F. Salazar (Cambridge: Cambridge University Press, 1999).
Mengering, Arnold. *Scrutinium conscientiae catecheticum* (Leipzig, 1687).
Mersenne, Marin. *L'impiete des deistes, athees et libertins de ce temps, combatue et renversee*, 2 vols. (Paris, 1624).
Mersenne, Marin. *L'usage de la raison* (Paris, 1623).
Mersenne, Marin. *Quaestiones Celeberrimae in Genesim* (Paris, 1623).
Meynard, Thierry (trans.). *Confucius Sinarum Philosophus* [1687] (Rome: Institutum Historicum Societatis Iesu, 2011).
Micraelius, Johannes. *Lexicon Philosophicum* (Stettin, 1662).
Middleton, Conyers. *A Free Enquiry into the Miraculous Powers which are supposed to have subsisted in the Christian Church* (London, 1749).
Mill, J. S. *Considerations on Representative Government* (London: Parker, Son, and Bourn, 1861).
Mill, J. S. *The Collected Works of John Stuart Mill*, 10 vols., ed. J. M. Robson (Indianapolis: Liberty Fund, 2006).
Milner, John. *An Account of Mr Lock's Religion* (London, 1703).
Milton, John. *Areopagitica*, in *Prose Works of John Milton*, 5 vols. (London: Henry Bohn, 1848), vol. 2.
Molière, Jean Baptiste. *The Plays of Molière*, 8 vols., trans. A. R. Waller (Edinburgh: John Grant, 1926).
Monro, Alexander. *Sermons preached upon several occasions* (London, 1691).
Montaigne, Michel de. 'Apology for Raymond Sebond' [1576], in *The Complete Essays*, ed. and trans. M. A. Screech (London: Penguin, 2003).
Montaigne, Michel de. *Complete Essays*, trans. Donald Frame (Stanford: Stanford University Press, 1958).
Montesquieu, Charles Louis. *Considerations on the Causes of the Greatness of the Romans and Their Decline*, trans. David Lowenthal (Indianapolis: Hackett, 1965).
Montesquieu, Charles Louis. *Considérations sur les causes de la grandeur des Romains et de leur décadence* (Amsterdam, 1734).
Montesquieu, Charles Louis. *De l'esprit des loix*, 2 vols. (Geneva, 1748).
More, Henry. *Ad V.C. epistola altera*, in *Opera Omnia*, vol. 1 (London, 1679).
More, Henry. *An Antidote against Atheisme: Or, an Appeal to the Natural Faculties of the Mind of Man whether there be not a God* (London, 1653).
More, Henry. *An Explanation of the Grand Mystery of Godliness* (London, 1660).
More, Henry. *Conjectura Cabbalistica* (London, 1653).
Morgan, Lewis H. *Ancient Society* (New York: Henry Holt, 1877).
Morgan, Thomas. *The Moral Philosopher*, vol. 1 (London, 1737).
Morton, Thomas. *A Catholike Appeale for Protestants* (London, 1609).

Nelson, Robert. *Transubstantiation contrary to Scripture* (London, 1688).
Ness, Christopher. *A Protestant antidote against the poyson of popery* (London, 1679).
Newman, A. K. 'A study of the causes leading to the extinction of the Maori', in *Transactions and Proceedings of the New Zealand Institute* 14 (1881), pp. 459–77.
Newman, John Henry. *An Essay in Aid of a Grammar of Assent* (London: Longmans, Green and Co., 1870).
Newman, John Henry. *Fifteen Sermons preached before the University of Oxford*, 3rd ed. London: Rivingtons, 1872).
Newman, John Henry. *Sermons, chiefly on the Theory of Religious Belief* (London: Rivingtons, 1843).
Newton, Isaac. 'A short Schem of true Religion', Keynes MS 7, 1r, King's College, Cambridge. www.newtonproject.ox.ac.uk/view/texts/normalized/THEM00007, accessed 4 April 2022.
Newton, Isaac. *Isaac Newton: The Principia*, trans. I. B. Cohen and A. Whitman (Berkeley: University of California Press, 1999).
Nicholas of Cusa. *Opera Omnia*, 20 vols. in 26, ed. Ernst Hoffmann, Raymond Klibansky, et al. (Hamburg: Felix Meiner, 1932–2014).
Nicholas of Cusa. *Selected Spiritual Writings*, trans. H. Lawrence Bond (New York: Paulist Press, 1997).
Nicols, Daniel. *A Sermon Preached in the Cathedral of Lincoln* (London, 1681).
Nietzsche, Friedrich. *Beyond Good and Evil*, trans. Adrian Del Caro, *Complete Works*, vol. 8 (Stanford: Stanford University Press, 2014).
Nietzsche, Friedrich. *Dawn*, trans. Brittain Smith, *Complete Works*, vol. 5 (Stanford: Stanford University Press, 2011).
Norris, John. *An Account of Reason and Faith: in Relation to the Mysteries of Christianity* [1697], 12th ed. (London, 1724).
Norris, John. *An Essay Towards the Theory of the Ideal or Intelligible World, Part 1* (London, 1701).
Norris, John. *Cursory Reflections upon a Book called An Essay concerning Human Understanding* [1690] (London, 1713).
Novalis [Georg Philipp Friedrich Freiherr von Hardenberg]. *Christendom or Europe: A Fragment*, in *The Early Political Writings of the German Romantics*, ed. Frederick C. Beiser (Cambridge: Cambridge University Press, 1996).
Oersted, Hans Christian. *Soul in Nature* (London: Bohn, 1852).
Oresme, Nicole. *Le Livre du ciel et du monde*, ed. and trans. A. D. Menut and A. J. Denomy (Madison: University of Wisconsin Press, 1968).
Origen of Alexandria. *Contra Celsum*, trans. Henry Chadwick (Cambridge: Cambridge University Press, 1980).
Orton, Job. *A short and plain exposition of the Old Testament*, 6 vols. (Shrewsbury, 1788–91).
Osiander, Lucas, the Elder. *Epitomes Historiae Ecclesiasticae, Centuriae I.–XVI.*, 10 vols. (Tübingen, 1592–1604).
Otto, Rudolf. *Mysticism East and West: A Comparative Analysis of the Nature of Mysticism*, trans. Bertha L. Bracey and Richenda C. Payne (Eugene: Wipf and Stock, 2016).
Otto, Rudolf. *Naturalism and Religion*, trans. J. Arthur Thomson and Margaret R. Thomson (London: Williams and Norgate, 1907).
Otto, Rudolf. *The Idea of the Holy* [1917], 2nd ed., trans. John W. Harvey (Oxford: Oxford University Press, 1958).

Otto, Rudolf. *The Philosophy of Religion Based on Kant and Fries*, trans. E. B. Dicker (London: Williams and Norgate, 1931).
Owen, John. *The Works of John Owen*, 16 vols., ed. William H. Gold (Edinburgh: Banner of Truth Trust, 1965).
Paley, William. *The Works of William Paley, D.D.*, 7 vols. (London, 1875).
Papal Encyclicals Online. www.papalencyclicals.net/pius09/p9quanta.htm, accessed 19 July 2022.
Parker, Matthew. *De antiquitate Britannicae ecclesiae et privilegiis ecclesiae Cantuariensis* (London, 1572).
Parker, Samuel. *Tentamina physico-theologica de Deo* (Oxford, 1665).
Parker, Theodore. *A Discourse pertaining to Matters of Religion* (Boston, 1842).
Pascal, Blaise. *Great Shorter Works of Pascal*, trans. Emile Cailliet and John C. Blankenagel (Eugene: Wipf and Stock, 2018).
Pascal, Blaise. *Pensées*, trans. A. J. Krailsheimer (London: Penguin, 1966).
Pearson, Karl. *The Grammar of Science* (London: Walter Scott, 1892).
Pelling, Edward. *A Discourse concerning the Existence of God* (London 1696).
Penington, Isaac. *The ancient principle of truth, or, The light within asserted* (London, 1672).
Penn, William. *England's great interest in the choice of this new Parliament* (London, 1669).
Pennyman, Joseph. *A Looking Glass for the Quakers* (London, 1689).
Pepys, Samuel. *The Diary of Samuel Pepys*, 8 vols., ed. R. Latham and W. Matthews (London: Bell, 1971).
Perkins, William. *A commentarie or exposition, vpon the fiue first chapters of the Epistle to the Galatians* (London, 1617).
Perkins, William. *A Discourse of the Damned Art of Witchcraft* (Cambridge, 1610).
Perkins, William. *An Exposition of the Symbole or Creed of the Apostles* (Cambridge, 1595).
Persons, Robert. *The Warn-word to Sir Francis Hastinges Wast-word* (n.p., 1602).
Peter Lombard. *Sentences*, 4 vols., trans. Giulio Silano (Toronto: Pontifical Institute of Medieval Studies, 2007–10).
Philo of Alexandria. *The Works of Philo*, trans. C. D. Yonge (Peabody, MA: Hendrickson, 1993).
Philologus. *A seasonable discourse of the right use and abuse of reason in matters of religion* (London, 1676).
Pintard, René. *Le libertinage érudit dans la première moitié du XVIIe siècle* [1943] (Geneva and Paris: Slatkine, 1983).
Pirie, W. R. *Natural Theology* (London: Blackwood, 1867).
Plato. *The Collected Dialogues*, ed. Edith Hamilton and Huntington Cairns (Princeton: Princeton University Press, 1961).
Plotinus. *Enneads*, trans. Stephen MacKenna and B. S. Page (Chicago: William Benton, 1953).
Pluche, Noël Antoine. *Le spectacle de la nature, ou Entretiens sur les particularités de l'histoire naturelle, qui ont paru les plus propres à rendre les jeunes gens curieux, et à leur former l'esprit*, 9 vols. (Paris, 1732–42).
Pluche, Noël Antoine. *Spectacle de la Nature or Nature Display'd. Being Discourses on such Particulars of Natural History*, 8th ed., 4 vols. (London, 1757).
Powell, Baden. 'The Uniformity of Nature', in *Essays on the Spirit of Inductive Philosophy, the Unity of Worlds, and the Philosophy of Creation* (London: Longman, Brown, Green and Longmans, 1855).

Proust, Marcel. *Remembrance of Things Past*, trans. Charles Kenneth Scott-Moncrieff (New York: Vintage, 1981).
Pseudo-Dionysius. *On the Divine Names and the Mystical Theology*, trans. C. E. Rold (London: SPCK, 1920).
Ptolemy. *Ptolemy's Almagest*, trans. R. Catesby Taliaferro (Chicago: Encyclopedia Britannica, 1952).
Pufendorf, Samuel. *De jure naturae et gentium* (Francofurti & Lipsiae, 1759).
Pufendorf, Samuel. *Divine Feudal Law* [1703] (Indianapolis: Liberty Fund, 2002).
Pupin, Michael. *The New Reformation: From Physical to Spiritual Realities* (New York: Charles Scribner's Sons, 1927).
R. B. *The Difference between the auncient Phisicke ... and the Latter Phisicke* (London, 1585).
Ray, John. *The Wisdom of God Manifested in the Works of Creation* (London, 1691).
Raymon Sibiuda [Raymond Sebunde]. *Theologia naturalis, sive, liber creaturarum*, ed. F. Stegmüller (Stuttgart-Bad Canstatt: Frommann, 1966).
Raynaud, Théophile. *Theologia naturalis* (Lyon, 1622).
Reid, Thomas. *An Inquiry into the Human Mind on the Principles of Common Sense*, ed. Derek R. Brookes (Edinburgh: Edinburgh University Press, 1997).
Reid, Thomas. *Essays on the Intellectual Powers of Man*, ed. Derek R. Brookes (Edinburgh: Edinburgh University Press, 2002).
Reid, Thomas. *Thomas Reid on Religion*, ed. James J. S. Foster, introduction by Nicholas Wolterstorff (Edinburgh: Library of Scottish Philosophy, 2017).
Renan, Ernest. *Disours de réception de M. V. Cherbuliez, Response de M. Ernest Renan* (Paris, 1882).
Renan, Ernest. *L'islamisme et la science* (Paris, 1883).
Renan, Ernest. *The Future of Science* [1848] (Boston: Roberts Brothers, 1893).
Renan, Ernest. *Vie de Jésus*, 13th ed. (Paris, 1867).
Reynolds, Edward. *A Treatise of the Passions* (London, 1647).
Reynolds, Edward. *The Lord's Property in his Redeemed People* (London, 1660).
Rich, Barnaby. *The Irish Hubbub* (London, 1618).
Richard of Middleton. *Super Quatuor Libros Sententiarum* (Brescia, 1591).
Ritschl, Albrecht. *Fides implicita: Eine Untersuchung über Köhlerglauben, Wissen und Glauben, Glauben und Kirche* (Bonn: Adolph Marcus, 1890).
Rituale Romanum (Baltimore: Murphy, 1873).
Roberts, Francis. *A Communicant Instructed* (London, 1659).
Robinson, Ralph. *Panoplia. Universa arma. Hieron* (London, 1656).
Robinson, Thomas. *Scripture characters*, 4th ed., 4 vols. (London, 1800).
Röhr, Johann Friedrich. *Briefe über den Rationalismus* (Aachen, 1813).
Rollin, Charles. *The method of teaching and studying the belles lettres*, 4 vols. (London, 1734).
Rust, George. *A Discourse of the Use of Reason in Matters of Religion* (London, 1683).
Rust, George. *A Discourse on Truth* (London, 1677).
Rust, George. *The remains of that reverend and learned prelate, Dr. George Rust* (London, 1686).
Saintes, Amand. *A Critical History of Rationalism in Germany* (London, 1849).
Sanderson, Robert. *Logicae Artis Compendium* (Oxford, 1614).
Saunders, Richard. *Saunders Physiognomie and Chiromancie, Metoposcopie*, 2nd ed. (London, 1671).

Schelling, F. W. J. von. *System of Transcendental Idealism* [1800], trans. Peter Heath (Charlottesville: University of Virginia Press, 1978).
Schoock, Maarten. *Admiranda Methodus novæ philosophiæ Renati Des Cartes* (Utrecht, 1643).
Schroeder, H. J. (ed. and trans.). *Canons and Decrees of the Council of Trent* (London: Herder, 1941).
Schürmann, Clamor. *A Vocabulary of the Parnkalla Language, Spoken by the Natives inhabiting the Western Shores of Spencer's Gulf* [1844], facsimile ed. (Adelaide: Public Library of Australia, 1962).
Schwarz, Carol. *Zur Geschichte der neuesten Theologie*, 3rd ed. (Leipzig, 1864).
Scot, Reginald. *The Discoverie of Witchcraft* [1584] (Totowa: Rowman & Littlefield, 1973).
Scott, William. *The Course of Conformity* (Amsterdam, 1622).
Sellars, Roy Wood. *Evolutionary Naturalism* (Chicago: Open Court, 1922).
Sellars, Roy Wood. *The Next Step in Religion: An Essay toward the Coming Renaissance* (New York: Macmillan, 1918).
Selsam, Howard and Harry Martel (eds.). *Reader in Marxist Philosophy* (New York: International Publishers, 1963).
Shadwell, Thomas. *The Virtuoso* (London, 1676).
Shaftesbury, Anthony Earl of. *Characteristics of Men, Manners, Opinions, Times*, 3 vols. (Basel, 1790).
Sherlock, William. *A Vindication of both parts of the Preservative against popery* (London, 1688).
Shields, Charles. *Philosophia Ultim: or, Science of the Sciences*, 3 vols. (New York: Charles Scribner's Sons, 1888–1905).
Sibbs, Richard. *Beams of Divine Light* (London, 1639).
Smith, Adam. *Theory of Moral Sentiments*, ed. D. D. Raphael and A. L. Macfie (Oxford: Clarendon Press, 1976).
Smith, John. *Select Discourses* (London, 1660).
Sommier, Jean-Claude. *Histoire dogmatique de la religion ou La religion prouvée par l'autorité divine & humaine, & par les lumières de la raison*, 3 vols. (Paris, 1708–11).
Sorabji, Richard (ed.). *The Philosophy of the Commentators 200–600 AD*, vol. 2: *Physics* (London: Duckworth, 2003).
South, Robert. *Sermons preached upon Several Occasions*, 5 vols. (New York: Hurd and Houghton, 1872).
Spencer, Herbert. *Essays, Scientific, Political and Speculative*, 3 vols. (London: Williams and Norgate, 1891).
Spencer, Herbert. *Social Statics* (London: Chapman, 1851).
Spinoza, Baruch. *Spinoza: Complete Works*, ed. Michael L. Morgan, trans. Samuel Shirley (Indianapolis: Hackett, 2002).
Spitzel, Theophil. *Scrutinium atheismi historico-ætiologicum* (Augsburg, 1663).
Sprat, Thomas. *History of the Royal Society* (London, 1667).
Stanley, Thomas. *History of Philosophy*, 2 vols. (London, 1656).
Stapleton, Thomas. *A Fortresse of the Faith first planted amonge vs Englishmen* (Antwerp, 1565).
Starkey, George. *Alchemical Laboratory Notebooks and Correspondence*, ed. William R. Newman and Lawrence M. Principe (Chicago: University of Chicago Press, 2004).

Stäudlin, Karl Friedrich. *Geschichte des Rationalismus und Supernaturalismus* (Göttingen, 1826).
Stephens, Nathaniel. *A plain and easie calculation of the name, mark, and number of the name of the beast* (London, 1656).
Sterry, Peter. *The spirit convincing of sinne* (London, 1645).
Stillingfleet, Edward. *A Rational account of the grounds of Protestant Religion* (London, 1665).
Stillingfleet, Edward. *A relation of a conference held about religion at London* (London, 1687).
Stillingfleet, Edward. *Origines Sacrae*, 1st ed. (London, 1662).
Stillingfleet, Edward. *Origines Sacrae*, 4th ed. (London, 1675).
Stillingfleet, Edward. *The Bishop of Worcester's Answer to Mr. Locke's Second Letter* (London, 1698).
Strauss, David. *Das Leben Jesu, kritisch bearbeitet* (Tübingen, 1835–6).
Strauss, David. *Die Christliche Glaubenslehre in ihrer geschichtlichen Entwicklung und in ihrem Kampf mit der modernen Wissenschaft*, 2 vols. (Tübingen, 1840–1).
Strauss, David. *The Life of Jesus, critically examined*, 4th ed., trans. George Eliot (London: George Allen & Unwin, 1913).
Strauss, David. *The Old Faith and the New: A Confession*, 2nd ed., trans. Mathilde Blind (London: Asher and Co., 1873).
Stuart, William. *Presbyteries Triall* (Paris, 1657).
Stubbe, Henry. *A Censure upon certaine passages contained in the history of the Royal Society* (Oxford, 1670).
Stubbe, Henry. *Campanella Revived* (London, 1670).
Stubbe, Henry. *Legends no Histories: or a Specimen of some Animadversions upon the History of the Royal Society ... together with the Plus Ultra reduced to a Non-Plus* (London, 1670).
Swift, Jonathan. *The Works of Dr Jonathan Swift*, 8 vols. (Edinburgh, 1761).
Swift, Jonathan. *Travels into Several Remote Regions of the World* (London, 1726).
T. A. *Religio Clerici* (London, 1681).
Tappert, Theodore G. (ed. and trans.). *The Book of Concord* (Philadelphia: Fortress Press, 1959).
Taylor, Jeremy. *The Righteousness Evangelicall Describ'd* (Dublin, 1663).
Taylor, Jeremy. Θεολογία ἐκλεκτική. *A discourse on freedom of thinking in matters of Religion* [1647] (Oxford, 1763).
Te Velde, R. T. and Riemer Faber (eds.). *Synopsis Purioris Theologia* [1625], 3 vols. (Leiden: Brill, 2014–19).
Teichelmann, Christian and Clamor Schürmann, *Outlines of a Grammar: Vocabulary and Phraseology of the Aboriginal Language of South Australia* (Adelaide, 1840).
Temple, Frederick. *The Relations between Religion and Science* (New York: Macmillan, 1884).
Temple, Frederick, et al. *Essays and Reviews*, 9th ed. (London: Longman, Green, Longman, and Roberts, 1861).
Tenison, Thomas. *A friendly debate between a Roman Catholick and a Protestant* (London, 1688).
Tennemann, Wilhelm Gottlieb. *A Manual of the History of Philosophy*, trans. Arthur Johnson (Oxford: Talboys, 1832), rev. J. R. Morell (London: Bohn, 1852).
Tennemann, Wilhelm Gottlieb. *Grundriß der Geschichte der Philosophie* [1812] (Leipzig, 1825).
Tennemann, Wilhelm Gottlieb. *Grundriß der Geschichte der Philosophie*, 2nd ed. (Leipzig: Barth, 1816).
The Popular Encyclopedia, 7 vols. (Glasgow: Blackie and Son, 1830–41).

Thomas Aquinas. *Commentary on Metaphysics*, trans. John P. Rowan, *Latin/English Edition of the Works of Thomas Aquinas*, vols. 50–1 (Lander, WY: Aquinas Institute, 2020).
Thomas Aquinas. *Commentary on the Book of Job*, trans. Brian Mullady, *Latin/English Edition of the Works of Thomas Aquinas*, vol. 32 (Lander, WY: Aquinas Institute, 2016).
Thomas Aquinas. *Commentary on the Gospel of Saint John*, trans. James A. Weisheipl and Fabien R. Larcher (Toronto: Pontifical Institute of Medieval Studies, 1980).
Thomas Aquinas. *Commentary on the Posterior Analytics of Aristotle*, trans. F. R. Larcher (Albany, NY: Magi Books, 1970).
Thomas Aquinas. *Opera omnia. Editio Leonina* (Rome: Typographia Vaticana, 1882).
Thomas Aquinas. *Summa contra gentiles*, trans. Laurence Shapcote, *Latin/English Edition of the Works of Thomas Aquinas*, vols. 11–12 (Green Bay, WI: Aquinas Institute, 2018).
Thomas Aquinas. *Summa theologiae*, trans. Laurence Shapcote, *Latin/English Edition of the Works of Thomas Aquinas*, vols. 13–20 (Lander, WY: Aquinas Institute, 2012).
Thomas Aquinas. *Super Epistolas S. Pauli lectura*, 8th ed., 2 vols., ed. Raphael Cai (Turin: Marietti, 1953).
Thomas Aquinas. *Super Libros Sententiarum*, 2 vols., ed. R. P. Mandonnet (Paris, 1929).
Thomas Aquinas. *Truth*, 3 vols., trans. James V. McGlynn et al. (Indianapolis: Hackett, 1964).
Thomasius, Christian. *Vollständige Erläuterung Der Kirchen-Rechts-Gelahrtheit*, 2 vols. (Frankfurt and Leipzig, 1738).
Thwaites, Reuben Gold (ed.). *The Jesuit Relations and Allied Documents*, 73 vols. (Cleveland: Burrows Bros, 1896–1901).
Tiedemann, Dietrich. *Geist der spekulativen Philosophie von Thales bis Sokrates*, 6 vols. (Marburg: Neue Akademische Buchhandlung, 1791–97).
Tillotson, John. *Several discourses upon the attributes of God* (London, 1699).
Tillotson, John. *The Works of the Most Reverend Dr John Tillotson*, 3rd ed., 2 vols. (London, 1722).
Tittmann, Johann. *Über Supranaturalismus, Rationalismus und Atheismus* (Leipzig, 1816).
Toland, John. *Christianity not Mysterious* (London, 1696).
Toland, John. *Letters to Serena* (London, 1704).
Toleti, Francisci. *Summa casuum conscientiæ absolutissima* (Duaci, 1622).
Tournemine, René Joseph. *Réflexions sur l'athéisme attribué à quelques peuples par les premiers missionnaires qui leur ont annoncé l'Evangile* in *Mémoires de Trévoux* (n.p. 1717).
Toussain, Daniel. *Warhaffter Bericht von der vorgenommenen Verbesserung in Kirchen* (Utrecht, 1584).
Troeltsch, Ernst. *Die Bedeutung des Protestantismus für die Entstehung der modernen Welt* [1911] (Aalen: Otto Zeller, 1963).
Troeltsch, Ernst. *Protestantism and Progress: The Significance of Protestantism for the Rise of the Modern World* (Philadelphia: Fortress Press, 1986).
Turgot, Anne Robert Jacques. *A Philosophical Review of the Successive Advances of the Human Mind* [1750], in *Turgot on Progress, Sociology, and Economics*, ed. and trans. Ronald L. Meek (Cambridge: Cambridge University Press, 1973).
Turner, William. *The history of all religions in the world, from the creation down to this present* (London, 1695).
Turretin, Franciscus. *Institutio Theologiae Elencticae*, 3 vols. (Geneva, 1679–85).
Turretin, Jean-Alphonse. *Cogitationes et dissertationes theologicae* (Geneva, 1737).

Tylor, Edward B. *Anthropology: An Introduction to the Study of Man and Civilization* (London: Macmillan, 1881).
Tylor, Edward B. 'On the survival of savage thought in modern civilization', *Notices of the Proceedings at the Meetings of the Members of the Royal Institution of Great Britain* 5 (1869), 522–38.
Tylor, Edward B. *Primitive Culture: Researches into the Development of Mythology, Philosophy, Religion, Language, Art and Custom*, 2 vols. (London: John Murray, 1871).
Tyndall, John. *Fragments of Science*, 6th ed. (New York: A. L. Burtt, n.d.).
Tyndall, John. *Hours of Exercise in the Alps* (New York: Appleton, 1896).
Tzschirner, Heinrich. *Memorabilien für das Studium und die Amtsführung des Predigers*, 8 vols. (Leipzig, 1810–23).
Ueberweg, Friedrich. *A History of Philosophy*, trans. G. S. Morris (London: Hodder & Stoughton, 1872–3).
'Uluru Statement from the Heart'. www.referendumcouncil.org.au/final-report.html#toc-anchor-ulurustatement-from-the-heart, accessed 18 June 2023.
Ursinus, Zacharias. *Corpus doctrinae Christianae* (Heidelberg, 1621).
Ursinus, Zacharias. *The Summe of Christian Religion* [1587–9] (London, 1645).
Valleton, Jean. *Le Réveille-matin des apostats sur la révolte de Jaques Illaire, ou la reutation des escrits publiez au nom d'icelui sous le faux et fantastique titre de conversion des Huguenots à la Foy Catholique* (Geneva, 1608).
Vico, Giambattista. *The New Science* [1725], trans. T. G. Bergin and M. H. Frisch (Ithaca: Cornell University Press, 1948).
Vignier, Nicholas. *Theatre de l'Antichrist*, vol. 1 (Geneva, 1613).
Vincent of Lérins. *Vincentius Lerinensis, Commonitorium*, ed. Reginald Stewart Moxon (Cambridge: Cambridge University Press, 1915).
Voetius, Gisbertus. *Selectae Disputationes Theologicae*, 5 vols. (Utrecht, 1648–69).
Vogt, Carl. *Köhlerglaube und Wissenschaft* (Giessen, 1855).
Volney, Constantin-François. *La Loi Naturelle*, in *Les Ruins, ou Méditation sur les Révolutions les Empires*, 11th ed. (Paris, 1822).
Voltaire [François-Marie Arouet]. *The Works of M. de Voltaire*, 35 vols. (London, 1761–81).
von Arnim, Hans (ed.). *Stoicorum Veterum Fragmenta*, 4 vols. (Stuttgart: Teubner, 1903–5).
Wagner, Rudolph. *Menschenschöpfung und Seelensubstanz* (Göttingen, 1854).
Walker, Clement. *The Mystery of the two ivntos, Presbyterian and Independent* (n.p., 1647).
Wallace, Alfred Russel. *Contributions to the Theory of Natural Selection: A Series of Essays*, 2nd ed. (London: Macmillan, 1871).
Wallace, Alfred Russel. 'Geological Climates and the Origin of Species', *The Quarterly Review* 126, no. 252 (1869), 359–94.
Wallace, Alfred Russel. *The Organic Law of Change*, ed. James T. Costa (Cambridge, MA: Harvard University Press, 2013).
Warburton, William. *A View of Lord Bolingbroke's Philosophy* (London, 1754).
Warburton, William. *The Doctrine of Grace*, 2 vols. (London, 1763).
Warburton, William. *The Principles of Natural and Revealed Religion* (Dublin, 1753).
Warburton, William and David Hurd. *Remarks on David Hume's Essay on the Natural History of Religion* (London, 1757).
Ward, James. *Naturalism and Agnosticism*, 2nd ed., 2 vols. (London: Adam and Charles Black, 1903).
Ward, Lester F. *Dynamic Sociology*, 2 vols. (New York: Appleton, 1883).

Warfield, B. B. 'Revelation', in *Johnson's Universal Encyclopedia*, 8 vols., ed. Charles Kendall Adams (New York: Appleton, 1895), vol. 7.
Warly, John. *The Natural Fanatick* (London, 1676).
Warner, John. *Dr. Stillingfleet's principles of Protestancy cleared, confuted, and retorted* (London, 1673).
Warren, Albert. *An Apology for the Discourse of Humane Reason* (London, 1680).
Washburn, Edward E. 'Parallel between the Philosophical Relations of Early and Modern Christianity', *Bibliotheca Sacra* 8 (1851), 34–57.
Weber, Max. *The Protestant Ethic and the Spirit of Capitalism*, trans. Stephen Kalberg (London: Routledge, 2012).
Weber, Max. *Theory of Social and Economic Organization*, trans. A. R. Anderson and Talcott Parsons (New York: Free Press, 1947).
Welles, John. *The Soules Progresse to the Celestiall Canaan* (London, 1639).
Welte, Benedikt and Heinrich Joseph Wetzer (eds.). *Kirchen-Lexikon oder Encyklopädie der katholischen Theologie und ihrer Hilfswissenschaften*, 12 vols. (Freiburg im Bresgau, 1853).
Wesley, John. *The Works of the Rev. John Wesley*, 3rd ed., 7 vols., ed. John Emory (New York: Carlton and Porter, 1856).
Whewell, William. *Astronomy and General Physics considered with reference to Natural Theology*, 2nd ed. (London: William Pickering, 1833).
Whewell, William. *History of the Inductive Sciences, from the Earliest to the Present Times*, 3 vols. (London: John Parker, 1837).
Whewell, William. *Indications of the Creator*, 2nd ed. (London: John Parker, 1846).
Whichcote, Benjamin. *Moral and Religious Aphorisms* (London: Matthews and Morrot, 1930).
Whichcote, Benjamin. *Select Sermons of Dr. Whichcot [sic] in two parts* (London, 1698).
Whichcote, Benjamin. *The Works of the Learned Benjamin Whichcote, D.D.*, 4 vols. (Aberdeen, 1751).
Whiston, William. *A New Theory of the Earth* (London, 1696).
Whiston, William. *Mr. W's Account of the Exact Time when Miraculous Gifts Ceas'd in the Church* (London, 1749).
Whitby, Daniel. *A Treatise of Traditions* (London, 1688).
White, Andrew Dickson. *A History of the Warfare of Science with Theology in Christendom*, 2 vols. (London: Macmillan, 1896).
White, Anthony. *Truth and Error Discovered* (Oxford, 1628).
White, John. *A Defence of the Way to the True Church* (London, 1614).
White, John. *The Way to the True Church*, 2nd ed. (London, 1610).
Wilkins, John. *Essay Towards a Real Character and a Philosophical Language* (London, 1668).
Wilkins, John. *Of the Principles and Duties of Natural Religion* (London, 1675).
Willet, Andrew. *Hexapla* (London, 1611).
Williams, Roger. *A Key into the Languages of America* (London, 1643).
Williams, Roger. *Christenings Make Not Christians* [1645], ed. Henry Martyn Dexter (Providence, 1881).
Winchell, Alexander. *Reconciliation of Science and Religion* (New York: Harper and Brothers, 1877).
Winckelmann, Johann Joachim. *Geschichte der Kunst des Altertums* (Dresden, 1764).
Wiseman, Nicolas. *Twelve Lectures on the Connexion between Science and Revealed Religion*, 2nd ed. (London: Joseph Booker, 1836).

Wolff, Christian. *De differentia nexus rerum sapientis et fatalis necessitatis* [1724], 2nd ed. (Halle, 1734).
Wolff, Christian. *Philosophia prima sive ontologia* (Frankfurt and Leipzig, 1730).
Wolff, Christian. *Theologia naturalis scientifica pertractata*, 2 vols. (Frankfurt, 1736–7).
Wollebius, Johannes. *Christianae theologiae compendium* (Basel, 1626).
Wolseley, Charles. *The Reasonableness of Scripture-Beleif* [sic] (London, 1672).
Wolseley, Charles. *The Unreasonablenesse of Atheism Made Manifest*, 2nd ed. (London, 1669).
Wright, Thomas. *Passions of the Mind* (London, 1601).
Wylie, James. *The Papacy: Its History, Dogmas, Genius, and Prospects* (Edinburgh, 1851).
Wyttenbach, Daniel. *Tentamen theologiæ dogmaticæ methodo scientifica pertractatæ* (Frankfurt am Main, 1747–9).
Yves de Paris. *Demonstration de l'Existence de Dieu*, 2nd ed. (Paris, 1713).
Yves de Paris. *La Théologie Naturelle*[1633–8], 4 vols. (Paris, 1640).
Zöckler, Otto. *Theologia naturalis. Entwurf einer systematischen naturtheologie vom offenbarungsgläubigen standpunkte aus*, vol. 1 (Frankfurt am Main: Heyder & Zimmer, 1860).
Zöllich, Christian Ferdinand. *Briefe über den Supernaturalismus* (Sondershausen und Nordhausen, 1821).

Secondary Sources

Abrams, M. H. *Natural Supernaturalism: Tradition and Revolution in Romantic Literature* (New York: Norton, 1971).
Abulafia, David. *Frederick II: A Medieval Emperor* (Oxford: Oxford University Press, 1988).
Adams, Edward. 'Calvin's View of Natural Knowledge of God', *International Journal of Systematic Theology* 3 (2001), 280–92.
Adams, Marilyn McCord. *William Ockham*, 2 vols. (Notre Dame: University of Notre Dame Press, 1987).
Adamson, Peter. *Classical Philosophy: A History of Philosophy Without Any Gaps*, vol. 1 (Oxford: Oxford University Press, 2014).
Aechtner, Thomas H. 'Galileo Still Goes to Jail: Conflict Model Persistence within Introductory Anthropology Materials', *Zygon* 50 (2015), 209–26.
Aechtner, Thomas H. 'Social Scientists', in *The Warfare between Science and Religion: The Idea That Would Not Die*, ed. Jeff Hardin, Ronald L. Numbers, and Ronald A. Binzley (Pittsburgh: University of Pittsburgh Press, 2018), pp. 302–23.
Agostini, Igor. 'Descartes' Proofs of God and the Crisis of Thomas Aquinas's Five Ways in Early Modern Thomism', *Harvard Theological Review* 108 (2015), 235–62.
Ahmepp, Arif. 'Belief and Religious "Belief"', *Religious Studies* 56 (2020), 80–94.
Albertini, Tamara. 'Crisis and Certainty of Knowledge in Al-Ghazali and Descartes', *Philosophy East and West* 55 (2005), 1–14.
Alexander, Bruce K. and Curtis P. Shelton. *A History of Psychology in Western Civilization* (Cambridge: Cambridge University Press, 2014).
Alexander, Nathan G. 'Defining and Redefining Atheism: Dictionary and Encyclopedia Entries for "Atheism" and their Critics in the Anglophone World from the Early Modern Period to the Present', *Intellectual History Review* 30 (2020), 253–71.

Alexandre, Jr., Manuel. 'Twofold Human Logos in Philo of Alexandria', in *Pouvoir et puissances chez Philon d'Alexandrie*, ed. Francesca Calabi, Olivier Munnich, Gretchen Reydams-Schils, and Emmanuele Vimercati (Turnhout: Brepols, 2016), pp. 37–59.

Algra, K. 'The Beginnings of Cosmology', in *The Cambridge Companion to Early Greek Philosophy*, ed. A. A. Long (Cambridge: Cambridge University Press, 1999), pp. 45–65.

Almond, Philip C. *Rudolf Otto: An Introduction to his Philosophical Theology* (Chapel Hill: University of North Carolina Press, 1984).

Almond, Philip C. *The Buddha from East to West* (Cambridge: Cambridge University Press, 2024).

Alston, William P. *Beyond 'Justification': Dimensions of Epistemic Evaluation* (Ithaca: Cornell University Press, 2005).

Alston, William P. *Perceiving God: The Epistemology of Religious Experience* (Ithaca: Cornell University Press, 1991).

Althaus, Paul. *The Theology of Martin Luther*, trans. Robert C. Schultz (Philadelphia: Fortress Press, 1966).

Amery, Rob. 'Beyond their Expectations: Teichelmann and Schürmann's Efforts to Preserve the Kaurna Language Continue to Bear Fruit', in *The Struggle for Souls and Science – Constructing the Fifth Continent: German Missionaries and Scientists in Australia*, ed. Walter Veit (Alice Springs: Strehlow Research Centre Occasional Paper, 2004), pp. 9–28.

Andersen, David. *Martin Luther: The Problem of Faith and Reason* (Bonn: Verlag für Kultur und Wissenschaft, 2009).

Anderson, Greg. *The Realness of Things Past: Ancient Greece and Ontological History* (Oxford: Oxford University Press, 2018).

Anderson, Pamela Sue. 'An Epistemological-Ethical Approach to Philosophy of Religion: Learning to Listen', in *Feminist Philosophy of Religion: Critical Readings*, ed. Pamela Sue Anderson and Beverley Clack (London: Routledge, 2004), pp. 87–102.

Annas, Julia. 'Becoming Like God: Ethics, Human Nature, and the Divine', in *Platonic Ethics, Old and New* (Ithaca: Cornell University Press, 1999), pp. 52–71.

Anstey, Peter. 'Experimental Versus Speculative Natural Philosophy', in *The Science of Nature in the Seventeenth Century*, ed. Peter Anstey and J. A. Schuster (Dordrecht: Springer, 2005), pp. 215–42.

Anstey, Peter (ed.). *The Idea of Principles in Early Modern Thought* (London: Routledge, 2017).

Anstey, Peter and Alberto Vanza. 'The Origins of Early Modern Experimental Philosophy', *Intellectual History Review* 22 (2012), 499–518.

Arkes, H. 'Cost and Benefits of Judgement Errors: Implications for Debiasing', *Psychological Bulletin* 110 (1992), 486–98.

Armogathe, Jean-Robert. '"*An sit deus*". Les preuves de Dieu chez Marin Mersenne', *Les études philosophiques* 1 (1994), 161–70.

Armstrong, David. *What Is a Law of Nature?* (Cambridge: Cambridge University Press, 1983).

Arnett, J. 'The Neglected 95%: Why American Psychology Needs to Become Less American', *American Psychologist* 63 (2008), 602–14.

Arnold, John H. 'Voicing Dissent: Heresy Trials in Later Medieval England', *Past and Present* 245 (2019), 3–37.

Asad, Talal. *Genealogies of Religion: Discipline and Reasons of Power in Christianity and Islam* (Baltimore: Johns Hopkins University Press, 1993).

Atran, Scott. *In Gods We Trust: The Evolutionary Landscape of Religion* (New York: Oxford University Press, 2002).
Austin, J. L. *How to Do Things with Words*, 2nd ed. (Cambridge, MA: Harvard University Press, 1975).
Baggett, David and Jerry L. Walls. *Good God: The Theistic Foundations of Morality* (Oxford: Oxford University Press, 2012).
Baghdassarian, Fabienne. *La question du divin chez Aristote: Discours sur les dieux et science du principe* (Leuven: Peeters, 2016).
Baillie, John. *The Belief in Progress* (London: Oxford University Press, 1950).
Baker, Keith Michael. *Condorcet: From Natural Philosophy to Social Mathematics* (Chicago: University of Chicago Press, 1975).
Ballantine, Jeanne H., Keith A. Roberts, and Kathleen Odell Korgen. *Our Social World: An Introduction to Sociology*, 7th ed. (Thousand Oaks: Sage, 2019).
Ban, N. C., A. Frid, M. Reid, B. Edgar, D. Shaw, and P. Siwallace. 'Incorporate Indigenous Perspectives for Impactful Research and Effective Management', *Nature Ecology & Evolution* 2 (2018), 1680–3.
Barfield, Owen. *Poetic Diction* (Middletown: Wesleyan University Press, 1973).
Barnes, Robin. 'Images of Hope and Despair: Western Apocalypticism ca. 1500–1800', in *The Continuum History of Apocalypticism*, ed. Bernard J. McGinn, John J. Collins, and Stephen J. Stein (New York: Continuum International Publishing, 2003), pp. 323–53.
Barnett, S. J. 'Where Was Your Church before Luther? Claims for the Antiquity of Protestantism Examined', *Church History* 68 (1999), 14–41.
Barrett, Justin L. 'Exploring the Natural Foundations of Religion', *Trends in Cognitive Sciences* 4 (2000), 29–34.
Barrett, Justin L. and R. A. Richert. 'Anthropomorphism or Preparedness? Exploring Children's God Concepts', *Review of Religious Research* 44 (2003), 300–12.
Barth, Hans-Martin. *Atheismus und Orthodoxie: Analysen und Modelle christlicher Apologetik im 17. Jahrhundert* (Göttingen: Vandenhoeck & Ruprecht, 1971).
Barth, Karl. *Church Dogmatics*, 13 vols., ed. Thomas F. Torrance and Geoffrey Bromiley (Edinburgh: T&T Clark, 1979).
Bartlett, Robert. *The Natural and the Supernatural in the Middle Ages* (Cambridge: Cambridge University Press, 2008).
Barton, Carlin A. and Daniel Boyarin. *Imagine No Religion: How Modern Abstractions Hide Ancient Realities* (New York: Fordham University Press, 2016).
Barton, Ruth. 'John Tyndall, Pantheist: A Re-Reading of the Belfast Address', *Osiris* 3 (1987), 111–34.
Barton, Ruth. *The X Club: Power and Authority in Victorian Science* (Chicago: University of Chicago Press, 2018).
Bates, Matthew W. 'The External-Relational Shift in Faith (*Pistis*) in New Testament Research: Romans 1 as Gospel-Allegiance Test Case', *Currents in Biblical Research* 18 (2020), 176–202.
Bauckham, Richard. *Tudor Apocalypse: Sixteenth Century Apocalypticism, Millenarianism and the English Reformation, from John Bale to John Foxe and Thomas Brightman* (Oxford: Oxford University Press, 1978).
Beale, Walter H. 'Rhetorical Performative Discourse: A New Theory of Epideictic', *Philosophy and Rhetoric* 11 (1978), 221–46.

Beall, E. F. 'Hegel and the Milesian "Origin of Philosophy"', *Classical and Modern Literature: A Quarterly* 13 (1993), 241–56.
Beck, Andreas J. 'Melanchthonian Thought in Gisbertus Voetius' Scholastic Doctrine of God', in *Scholasticism Reformed*, ed. Maarten Wisse, Marcel Sarot, and Willemien Otten (Leiden: Brill, 2010), pp. 107–26.
Beck, L. J. *The Metaphysics of Descartes: A Study of the Meditations* (Oxford: Oxford University Press, 1965).
Becker, Carl L. *The Heavenly City of the Eighteenth-Century Philosophers* (New Haven: Yale University Press, 1932).
Beckwith, C. A. 'Rationalism and Supernaturalism', in *The New Schaff-Herzog Encyclopedia of Religious Knowledge*, 15 vols. (Grand Rapids: Baker, 1977), vol. 9, pp. 393a–402a.
Beiser, Frederick C. *After Hegel: German Philosophy, 1840–1900* (Princeton: Princeton University Press, 2014).
Bell, Catherine. '"The Chinese believe in spirits": Belief and Believing in the Study of Religion', in *Radical Interpretation in Religion*, ed. N. Frankenberry (Cambridge: Cambridge University Press, 2002), pp. 100–28.
Bell, M. 'Hume and Causal Power: The Influences of Malebranche and Newton', *British Journal for the History of Philosophy* 5 (1997), 68–86.
Benedict, Barbara M. *Curiosity: A Cultural History of Early Modern Inquiry* (Chicago: University of Chicago Press, 2001).
Benjamin, Walter. 'On the Concept of History', in *Selected Writings, Vol. 4, 1938–1940* (Cambridge, MA: Harvard University Press, 2003), pp. 389–400.
Berdyaev, Nicolas. *The Beginning and the End* (New York: Harper, 1957).
Berdyaev, Nicolas. *The Meaning of History*, trans. George Reavey (London: Bles, 1949).
Berger, Peter L. (ed.). *The Desecularization of the World: Resurgent Religion and World Politics* (Grand Rapids: Eerdmans, 1999).
Berkes, Fikret. *Sacred Ecology*, 4th ed. (Abingdon: Routledge, 2018).
Bermon, Emmanuel. *Le Cogito dans la Pensées de Saint Augustin* (Paris: Vrin, 2001).
Berti, Enrico. 'Aristotle's Concept of Nature: Traditional Interpretation and Results of Recent Studies', Evolving Concepts of Nature, Pontifical Academy of Sciences, Acta 23, Vatican City 2016. www.accademiascienze.va/content/dam/accademia/pdf/acta23/acta23-berti.pdf, accessed 10 March 2020.
Bethell, S. L. *The Cultural Revolution of the Seventeenth Century* (London: D. Dobson, 1951).
Beversluis, John. *C. S. Lewis and the Search for Rational Religion*, rev. ed. (Amherst: Prometheus, 2007).
Beyer, Oswald. 'Philosophical Modes of Thought of Luther's Theology as an Object of Inquiry', in *The Devil's Whore: Reason and Philosophy in the Lutheran Tradition*, ed. Jennifer Hockenbery Dragseth (Philadelphia: Augsburg Fortress, 2011), pp. 13–21.
Bhargava, Rajeev. 'Overcoming the Epistemic Injustice of Colonialism', *Global Policy* 4 (2013), 413–17.
Bhogal, Harjit. 'Humeanism about Laws of Nature', *Philosophy Compass* 15 (2020), 1–10.
Bickerman, Elias J. 'The Name of Christians', *Harvard Theological Review* 42 (1949), 109–24.
Bilgrami, Akeel. 'The Wider Significance of Naturalism: A Genealogical Essay', in *Naturalism and Normativity*, ed. Mario De Caro and David Macarthur (New York: Columbia University Press, 2010), pp. 23–54.
Biller, Peter. Review of *The War on Heresy: Faith and Power in Medieval Europe* (review no. 1546). https://reviews.history.ac.uk/review/1546, accessed 28 August 2019.

Bishop, John. *Believing by Faith: An Essay in the Epistemology and Ethics of Religious Belief* (New York: Oxford University Press, 2007).
Bishop, John. 'Faith', in *The Stanford Encyclopedia of Philosophy* (Winter 2016 Edition), Edward N. Zalta (ed.). https://plato.stanford.edu/archives/win2016/entries/faith/.
Black, Deborah L. 'Knowledge (*'Ilm*) and Certainty (*Yaqīn*) in al-Fārābī's Epistemology', *Arabic Sciences and Philosophy* 14 (2006), 11–45.
Blair, Ann. 'Noël Antoine Pluche as a Jansenist Natural Theologian', *Intellectual History Review* 26 (2016), 91–9.
Blair, Ann and Kaspar von Greyerz (eds.). *Physico-Theology: Religion and Science in Europe 1650–1750* (Baltimore: Johns Hopkins University Press, 2020).
Blanck, Andreas and Dana Jalobeanu. 'Common Notions: An Overview', *Journal of Early Modern Studies* 8 (2019), 9–24.
Blanshard, Brand. *Reason and Belief* (London: George Allen & Unwin, 1974).
Blitz, Mark. 'Understanding Heidegger on Technology', *The New Atlantis* 41 (2014), 63–80.
Bloch, Ernst. *The Principle of Hope*, 3 vols., trans. Neville Plaice, Stephen Plaice, and Paul Knight (Cambridge MA: MIT Press, 1995).
Bloom, Paul. 'Religion Is Natural', *Developmental Science* 10 (2007), 147–51.
Bloom, Paul. 'Religious Belief as an Evolutionary Accident', in *The Believing Primate: Scientific, Philosophical, and Theological Reflections on the Origin of Religion*, ed. Jeffrey Schloss and Michael Murray (Oxford: Oxford University Press, 2009), pp. 118–27.
Bloor, Joshua. 'New Directions in Western Soteriology', *Theology* 118 (2015), 179–87.
Blowers, Paul M. '"Entering This Sublime and Blessed Amphitheatre": Contemplation of Nature and Interpretation of the Bible in the Patristic Period', in *Nature and Scripture in the Abrahamic Traditions,* vol. 1: *To 1700*, ed. Scott Mandelbrote and Jitse van de Meer (Leiden: Brill, 2008), pp. 147–77.
Blumenberg, Hans. *Höhlenausgänge* (Frankfurt: Suhrkamp, 1989).
Blumenberg, Hans. *Modernity and the Hegemony of Vision*, ed. David Michael Levin (Berkeley: University of California Press, 1993).
Blumenberg, Hans. *Paradigms for a Metaphorology*, trans. Robert Savage (Ithaca: Cornell University Press, 2010).
Blumenberg, Hans. *The Legitimacy of the Modern Age*, trans. Robert M. Wallace (Cambridge, MA: MIT Press, 1985).
Boespflug, Mark. 'Thomistic Faith Naturalized? The Epistemic Significance of Aquinas's Appeal to Doxastic Instinct', *Faith and Philosophy* 38 (2021), 245–61.
Bogardus, Tomas. 'If Naturalism is True, then Scientific Explanation is Impossible', *Religious Studies* 59 (2023), 115–38.
Bogen, James. 'Theory and Observation in Science', *The Stanford Encyclopedia of Philosophy* (Summer 2017 Edition), Edward N. Zalta (ed.). https://plato.stanford.edu/archives/sum2017/entries/science-theory-observation/
Bonanno, James. 'Enlightenment and Secularism', in *21st Century Anthropology: A Reference Handbook*, ed. H. James Birx (Los Angeles: Sage, 2010), pp. 463–72.
Bond, Michael. *Wayfinding: The Art and Science of How We Find and Lose Our Way* (London: Picador, 2020).
Bonin, Thérèse. *Creation as Emanation: The Origin of Diversity in Albert the Great's On the Causes and the Procession of the Universe* (Notre Dame: University of Notre Dame Press, 2001).

Bonino, Serge-Thomas (ed.). *Surnaturel: A Controversy at the Heart of Twentieth-Century Thomistic Thought*, trans. Robert Williams, trans. rev. Matthew Levering (Ave Maria, FL: Sapientia Press of Ave Maria University, 2009).
Bonk, Thomas. *Underdetermination: An Essay on Evidence and the Limits of Natural Knowledge* (Dordrecht: Springer, 2008).
Bos, A. P. *Cosmic and Metacosmic Theology in Aristotle's Lost Dialogues* (Leiden: Brill, 1989).
Bossy, John. *Christianity in the West 1400–1700* (Oxford: Oxford University Press, 1985).
Bourdieu, Pierre. *Outline of a Theory of Practice*, trans. Richard Nice (Cambridge: Cambridge University Press, 1987).
Bourget, B. and D. J. Chalmers. 'What Do Philosophers Believe?', *Philosophical Studies* 170 (2014), 465–500.
Boyarin, Daniel. 'The Concept of Cultural Translation in American Religious Studies', *Critical Inquiry* 44 (2017), 17–39.
Boyer, Pascal. *Religion Explained: The Evolutionary Origins of Religious Thought* (New York: Basic Books, 2001).
Braaten, Carl E. and Robert W. Jenson (eds.). *Union with Christ: The New Finnish Interpretation of Luther* (Grand Rapids: Eerdmans, 1998).
Bradley, Denis J. M. *Aquinas on the Twofold Human Good: Reason and Human Happiness in Aquinas's Moral Science* (Washington, DC: The Catholic University of America Press, 1997).
Bradley, Mark. 'Colour as a Synaesthetic Experience in Antiquity', in *Synaesthesia and the Ancient Senses*, ed. Shane Bulter and Alex Purves (London: Routledge, 2014), pp. 127–40.
Brague, Rémi. *Eccentric Culture: A Theory of Western Civilization*, trans. Samuel Lester (South Bend: St Augustine's Press, 2002).
Brague, Rémi. *The Wisdom of the World: The Human Experience of the Universe in Western Thought*, trans. Teresa Fagan (Chicago: University of Chicago Press, 2003).
Brandom, Robert. *A Spirit of Trust: A Reading of Hegel's Phenomenology* (Cambridge, MA: Harvard University Press, 2019).
Brantlinger, Patrick. *Dark Vanishings: Discourse on the Extinction of Primitive Races, 1800–1930* (Ithaca: Cornell University Press, 2003).
Breuer, Stefan. 'Die Depotenzierung der kritischen Theorie', *Leviathan* 10 (1982), 132–46.
Briggs, Richard S. 'Getting Involved: Speech Acts and Biblical Interpretation', *Anvil* 20 (2003), 25–34.
Briggs, Richard S. *Words and Actions: Speech-Act Theory and Biblical Interpretation* (Edinburgh: T&T Clark, 2001).
Brightman, Edgar S. 'An Empirical Approach to God', *The Philosophical Review* 46 (1937), 157–8.
Broadie, Sarah. 'Rational Theology', in *The Cambridge Companion to Early Greek Philosophy*, ed. A. A. Long (Cambridge: Cambridge University Press, 1999), pp. 205–24.
Brook, A. 'Kant and Cognitive Science', in *The Prehistory of Cognitive Science*, ed. A. Brook (New York: Palgrave Macmillan, 2007), pp. 117–36.
Brooke, John Hedley. *Science and Religion: Some Historical Perspectives* (Cambridge: Cambridge University Press, 1991).
Brooke, John Hedley and Geoffrey Cantor. *Reconstructing Nature: The Engagement of Science and Religion* (Edinburgh: T&T Clark, 1998).

Brown, Candy Gunther. *Testing Prayer: Science and Healing* (Cambridge, MA: Harvard University Press, 2010).
Brown, Catherine Corigall. *Imagining Society: An Introduction to Sociology* (Thousand Oaks: Sage, 2019).
Brown, Stephen. 'Key Terms in Medieval Theological Vocabulary', in *Méthodes et instruments du travail intellectuel au moyen âge*, ed. Olga Weijers (Turnhout: Brepols, 1990), pp. 82–97.
Browne, Janet. 'Charles Darwin as a Celebrity', *Science in Context* 16 (2003), 175–94.
Bruce, Steve. *God Is Dead: Secularization in the West* (Oxford: Blackwell, 2002).
Brucker, Nicolas. 'What Abbé Pluche Owed to Early Modern Physico-Theologians', in *Physico-Theology: Religion and Science in Europe 1650–1750*, ed. Ann Blair and Kaspar von Greyerz (Baltimore: Johns Hopkins University Press, 2020), pp. 183–93.
Brundell, Barry. *Pierre Gassendi: From Aristotelianism to a New Natural Philosophy* (Dordrecht: Reidel, 1987).
Brunn, Uwe. *Des contestataires aux 'Cathares'* (Paris: Collection des Études Augustiniennes, Série Moyen Âge et Temps Modernes, 41, 2006).
Bruns, Gerald L. *Hermeneutics Ancient and Modern* (New Haven: Yale University Press, 1992).
Buc, Philippe. *The Dangers of Ritual: Between Early Medieval Texts and Social Scientific Theory* (Princeton: Princeton University Press, 2001).
Buckser, Andrew. 'Cultural Change and the Meanings of Being Jewish in Copenhagen', *Social Analysis* 52 (2008), 39–55.
Bucur, Bogdan G. 'The Other Clement of Alexandria: Cosmic Hierarchy and Interiorized Apocalypticism', *Vigiliae Christianae* 60 (2006), 251–68.
Buell, Denise Kimber. *Why This New Race? Ethnic Reasoning within Early Christianity* (New York: Columbia University Press, 2005).
Bueno, Irene. *Defining Heresy: Inquisition, Theology, and Papal Policy in the Time of Jacques Fournier* (Leiden: Brill, 2015).
Bullivant, Stephen. *The Salvation of Atheists and Catholic Dogmatic Theology* (Oxford: Oxford University Press, 2012).
Bullivant, Stephen and Michael Ruse (eds.). *The Cambridge History of Atheism*, 2 vols. (Cambridge: Cambridge University Press, 2021).
Bultmann, Rudolf. *New Testament Mythology and Other Basic Writings*, ed. Schubert M. Ogden (Philadelphia: Fortress Press, 1984).
Bultmann, Rudolf. 'The New Testament and Mythology', in *Kerygma and Myth*, ed. Hans Werner Bartsch (New York: Harper, 1961), pp. 1–44.
Bultmann, Rudolf and Artur Weiser. 'πιστεύω, πίστις, etc.', in *Theological Dictionary of the New Testament*, 10 vols., ed. Gerhard Kittel and Gerhard Friedrich (Grand Rapids: Eerdmans, 1977), vol. 6, pp. 174–228.
Bunch, Bryan and Alexander Hellemans. *The History of Science and Technology* (Boston: Houghton Mifflin, 2004).
Burns, Robert M. *The Great Debate on Miracles from Joseph Glanvill to David Hume* (Lewisburg: Bucknell University Press, 1981).
Bury, J. B. *The Idea of Progress: An Enquiry into Its Origin and Growth* (London: Macmillan, 1920).
Bush, Douglas. 'Two Roads to Truth: Science and Religion in the Early Seventeenth Century', *ELH* 8 (1941), 81–102.

Bussanich, John. 'Socrates and Religious Experience', in *A Companion to Socrates*, ed. Sara Ahbel-Rappe and Rachana Kamtekar (New York: Wiley, 2009), pp. 200–13.
Buswell, J. Oliver. *Systematic Theology* (Grand Rapids: Zondervan, 1962).
Buswell, Robert E. and Donald Lopez Jr. *Princeton Dictionary of Buddhism* (Princeton: Princeton University Press, 2013).
Camelot, Th. '*Credere deo, credere deum, credere in deum* pour l'histoire d'une formule traditionnelle', *Revue des Sciences philosophiques et théologique* 30 (1940–1), 149–55.
Cameron, Euan. *Interpreting Christian History: The Challenge of the Churches' Past* (Oxford: Oxford University Press, 2005).
Cantor, Geoffrey. *Michael Faraday: Sandemanian and Scientist* (London: Macmillan, 1993).
Cantor, Lea. 'Thales – the "First Philosopher"? A Troubled Chapter in the Historiography of Philosophy', *British Journal for the History of Philosophy* 30 (2022), 727–50.
Carlisle, Clare. *Spinoza's Religion: A New Reading of the Ethics* (Princeton: Princeton University Press, 2021).
Carraud, Vincent. *Causa sive Ratio. La raison de la cause de Suárez à Leibniz* (Paris: Presses Universitaires de France, 2002).
Carrol, John W. *Laws of Nature* (Cambridge: Cambridge University Press, 1994).
Carroll, Sean M. *The Big Picture: On the Origins of Life, Meaning, and the Universe Itself* (Harmondsworth: Penguin, 2017).
Carter, J. Adam, Andy Clark, Jesper Kallestrup, S. Orestis Palermos, and Duncan Pritchard (eds.). *Socially Extended Epistemology* (Oxford: Oxford University Press, 2018).
Cartwright, Nancy. *The Dappled World: A Study of the Boundaries of Science* (Cambridge: Cambridge University Press, 1999).
Cartwright, Nancy and Keith Ward (eds.). *Rethinking Order after the Laws of Nature* (London: Bloomsbury, 2016).
Caston, Victor. 'Aristotle's Two Intellects: A Modest Proposal', *Phronesis* 44 (1999), 199–227.
Cavaillé, Jean-Pierre. 'L'histoire des "libertins" reste à faire', *Les Dossiers du Grihl*, 18 October 2010. http://journals.openedition.org/dossiersgrihl/4498, accessed 26 February 2021.
Cavanaugh, William T. *The Myth of Religious Violence: Secular Ideology and the Roots of Modern Conflict* (New York: Oxford University Press, 2009).
Cavanaugh, William T. *Theopolitical Imagination: Discovering the Liturgy as a Political Act in an Age of Global Consumerism* (London: T&T Clark, 2002).
Chadwick, Owen. *From Bossuet to Newman*, 2nd ed. (Cambridge: Cambridge University Press, 1987).
Chadwick, Owen. 'Gibbon and the Church Historians', *Daedalus* 105 (1976), 111–23.
Chakrabarty, Dipesh. *Provincializing Europe: Postcolonial Thought and Historical Difference* (Princeton: Princeton University Press, 2000).
Chalmers, Alan. *The Scientist's Atom and the Philosopher's Stone: How Science Succeeded and Philosophy Failed to Gain Knowledge of Atoms* (Dordrecht: Springer, 2009).
Chalmers, Alan. *What Is This Thing Called Science?* 4th ed. (Brisbane: University of Queensland Press, 2013).
Champion, Justin. *The Pillars of Priestcraft Shaken: The Church of England and Its Enemies, 1660–1730* (Cambridge: Cambridge University Press, 1992).
Charbonnier, Pierre, Gildas Salmon, and Peter Skafish (eds.). *Comparative Metaphysics* (Lanham: Rowman & Littlefield, 2016).

Châtellier, Louis. *Tradition chrétienne et renouveau catholique dans le cadre de l'ancien diocèse de Strasbourg (1650–1724)* (Paris: S.E.V.P.E.N., 1964).
Chiu, Hilbert. 'The Intellectual Origins of Medieval Dualism', MPhil thesis, University of Sydney, 2009.
Cizewski, Wanda. 'Reading the World as Scripture: Hugh of St. Victor's *De tribus diebus*', *Florilegium* 9 (1987), 65–88.
Clanton, J. Caleb. 'John Calvin and John Locke on the *Sensus Divinitatis* and Innatism', *Religions* 8 (2017), 1–14.
Clark, A. 'Whatever Next? Predictive Brains, Situated Agents and the Future of Cognitive Science', *Behavioural and Brain Sciences* 36 (2013), 181–204.
Clark, Kelly James and Justin L. Barrett. 'Reidian Religious Epistemology and the Cognitive Science of Religion', *Journal of the American Academy of Religion* 79 (2011), 639–75.
Clark, Stuart. *Thinking with Demons* (Oxford: Oxford University Press, 1997).
Clarke, Desmond M. *Descartes: A Biography* (Cambridge: Cambridge University Press, 2006).
Clossey, Luke, Kyle Jackson, Brandon Marriott, Andrew Redden, and Karin Vélez. 'The Unbelieved and Historians, Part I: A Challenge', *The History Compass* 14 (2016), 594–602.
Cohn, Norman. *The Pursuit of the Millennium: Revolutionary Millenarians and Mystical Anarchists in the Middle Ages* (Oxford: Oxford University Press, 1957).
Colish, Marcia. 'St. Thomas Aquinas in Historical Perspective: The Modern Period', *Church History* 44 (1975), 433–49.
Colledge, Richard J. 'Rethinking Disagreement: Philosophical Incommensurability and Meta-Philosophy', *Symposium* 18 (2014), 33–55.
Collingwood, R. G. *The Idea of History* (Oxford: Clarendon Press, 1948).
Congdon, David. *Mission of Demythologizing: Rudolf Bultmann's Dialectical Theology* (Philadelphia: Fortress Press, 2015).
Connell, D. *The Vision in God: Malebranche's Scholastic Sources* (Louvain: Nauwelaerts, 1967).
Cooper, John M. *Pursuits of Wisdom: Six Ways of Life in Ancient Philosophy, from Socrates to Plotinus* (Princeton: Princeton University Press, 2012).
Cormack, Lesley B. 'That before Columbus, Geographers and Other Educated People Thought the Earth was Flat', in *Newton's Apple and Other Myths about Science*, ed. Ronald L. Numbers and Kostas Kampourakis (Cambridge, MA: Harvard University Press, 2015), pp. 16–22.
Cornford, F. M. *From Philosophy to Religion* [1912] (Princeton: Princeton University Press, 1991).
Corr, Charles Anthony. 'The Existence of God, Natural Theology and Christian Wolff', *International Journal for Philosophy of Religion* 4 (1973), 105–18.
Coyne, Jerry. *Faith versus Fact: Why Science and Religion Are Incompatible* (London: Penguin, 2015).
Crawford, John R. 'Calvin and the Priesthood of all Believers', *Scottish Journal of Theology* 21 (1968), 145–56.
Cross, Richard. 'Duns Scotus and Suárez at the Origins of Modernity', in *Deconstructing Radical Orthodoxy: Postmodern Theology, Rhetoric, and Truth*, ed. Wayne Hankey and Douglas Hedley (Burlington: Ashgate, 2005), pp. 65–80.

Cross, Richard. 'Where the Angels Fear to Tread: Duns Scotus and Radical Orthodoxy', *Antonianum* 76 (2001), 7–41.
Cullen, Christopher M. *Bonaventure* (Oxford: Oxford University Press, 2006).
Curry, Patrick. *Prophecy and Power: Astrology in Early Modern England* (Cambridge: Cambridge University Press, 1989).
d'Aquili, Eugene and Charles Laughlin. 'The Biopsychological Determinants of Religious Ritual Behavior', *Zygon* 10 (1975), 32–58.
Dahmani, L. and V. D. Bohbot. 'Habitual Use of GPS Negatively Impacts Spatial Memory during Self-Guided Navigation', *Scientific Reports* 10 (2020), 6310.
Dakin, A. *Calvinism* (London: Duckworth, 1940).
Daniel, Dafydd Mills. *Ethical Rationalism and Secularization in the British Enlightenment* (London: Palgrave Macmillan, 2020).
Daniélou, Jean. *Platonisme et théologie mystique*, 2nd ed. (Paris: Éditions Montaigne, 1953).
Danielson, Dennis. 'The Bones of Copernicus', *American Scientist* 97 (2009), 50–7.
Daston, Lorraine. 'Marvellous Facts and Miraculous Evidence in Early Modern Europe', *Critical Inquiry* 18 (1991), 93–124.
Daston, Lorraine and Katherine Park. *Wonders and the Order of Nature* (New York: Zone Books, 1998).
Daston, Lorraine and Michael Stolleis (eds.). *Natural Law and Laws of Nature in Early Modern Europe* (Aldershot: Ashgate, 2005).
Dauben, Joseph. *Georg Cantor* (Princeton: Princeton University Press, 1990).
Davie, Grace. 'Believing without Belonging: Is This the Future of Religion in Britain?', *Social Compass* 37 (1990), 455–69.
Davies, Brian. 'Is "Sacra Doctrina" Theology?', *New Blackfriars* 71 (1990), 141–7.
Davies, Tom Hercules. 'Greek Cosmology and Its Bronze Age Background', PhD thesis, Princeton University, 2021.
Davison, Andrew. *Participation in God* (Cambridge: Cambridge University Press, 2019).
Dawkins, Richard. *The God Delusion* (London: Transworld, 2016).
Dawson, Christopher. *Progress and Religion: An Historical Enquiry* (London: Sheed and Ward, 1929).
Dawson, Gowan. '"The Cross-Examination of the Physiologist": T. H. Huxley and the Resurrection', in *The Metaphysical Society (1869–1880): Intellectual Life in Mid-Victorian England*, ed. Catherine Marshall, Bernard Lightman, and Richard England (Oxford: Oxford University Press, 2019), pp. 91–118.
Dawson, Gowan and Bernard Lightman (eds.). *Victorian Scientific Naturalism: Community, Identity, Continuity* (Chicago: University of Chicago Press, 2014).
Day, Matthew. 'Reading the Fossils of Faith: Thomas Henry Huxley and the Evolutionary Subtext of the Synoptic Problem', *Church History* 74 (2005), 534–56.
De Bary, Philip. *Thomas Reid and Scepticism: His Reliabilist Response* (London: Routledge, 2002).
De Caro, Mario and David Macarthur (eds.). *Naturalism and Normativity* (New York: Columbia University Press, 2010).
De Castro, Eduardo Viveiros. 'The Relative Native', *Hau: Journal of Ethnographic Theory* 3 (2013), 473–502.
De Cruz, Helen. *Religious Disagreement* (Cambridge: Cambridge University Press, 2019).
De Cruz, Helen and Johan De Smedt. *Natural History of Natural Theology: A Cognitive Science of Theology and Philosophy of Religion* (Cambridge, MA: MIT Press, 2014).

De Haas, Frans A. J. 'Deduction and Common Notions in Alexander's Commentary on Aristotle's *Metaphysics* A 1–2', *History of Philosophy and Logical Analysis* 74 (2021), 71–102.
De Lubac, Henri. *Corpus Mysticum: The Eucharist and the Church in the Middle Ages*, trans. Gemma Simmonds with Richard Price and Christopher Stephens (Notre Dame: University of Notre Dame Press, 2007).
De Lubac, Henri. *La Postérité spirituelle de Joachim de Flore* (Paris: Lethielleux, 1979).
De Lubac, Henri. *Medieval Exegesis: The Four Senses of Scripture*, 3 vols., trans. Mark Sebanc and E. M. Macierowski (Grand Rapids: Eerdmans, 1998–2009).
De Lubac, Henri. 'Remarques sur l'histoire du mot *surnaturel*', *Nouvelle revue théologique* 61 (1934), 225–49.
De Lubac, Henri. *Surnaturel: Études historiques* (Paris: Aubier, 1946).
De Lubac, Henri. *The Mystery of the Supernatural*, trans. Rosemary Sheed, introduction by David L. Schindler (New Yok: Herder and Herder, 1998).
De Lubac, Henri. *The Splendor of the Church* (San Francisco: Ignatius Press, 1999).
De Lubac, Henri. *Theology in History* (San Franscisco: St Ignatius Press, 1996).
Dear, Peter. 'Divine Illumination, Mechanical Calculators, and the Roots of Modern Reason', *Science in Context* 23 (2010), 351–66.
Deferrari, Roy J. and M. Inviolata Barry. *A Lexicon of St. Thomas Aquinas* (Washington, DC: Catholic University of America Press, 1948–9).
Dein, S. 'The Category of the Supernatural: A Valid Anthropological Term?', *Religion Compass* 10 (2016), 35–44.
Delumeau, Jean. *Catholicism between Luther and Voltaire* (London: Burns and Oates, 1977).
Delumeau, Jean. 'The Journey of a Historian', *Catholic Historical Review* 96 (2010), 435–48.
Deming, David. *Science and Technology in World History*, 2 vols. (Jefferson, NC: McFarland, 2010).
Deneffe, August. 'Geschichte des Wortes "supernaturalis"', *Zeitschrift für katholische Theologie* 46 (1922), 337–60.
Dennett, Daniel. *Breaking the Spell: Religion as a Natural Phenomenon* (New York: Viking Penguin, 2006).
Desmond, Adrian and James Moore. *Darwin* (London: Michael Joseph, 1991).
Devaux, Michaël and Marco Lamanna. 'The Rise and Early History of the Term Ontology (1606–1730)', *Quaestio* 9 (2009), 173–208.
deVries, Willem A. 'Hegelian Spirits in Sellarsian Bottles', *Philosophical Studies* 174 (2017), 1643–54.
DeYoung, Ursula. *A Vision of Modern Science: John Tyndall and the Role of the Scientist in Victorian Culture* (Basingstoke: Palgrave Macmillan, 2011).
Dhanani, A. *The Physical Theory of Kalam: Atoms, Space, and Void in Basrian Mu'tazili Cosmology* (Leiden: Brill, 1994).
di Risi, Vincenzo. 'Euclid's Common Notions and the Theory of Equivalency', *Foundations of Science* (2020). https://doi.org/10.1007/s10699-020-09694-w, accessed 23 November 2023.
Dodds, E. R. *The Greeks and the Irrational* (Berkeley: University of California Press, 1951).
Dole, Andrew. 'Schleiermacher and Otto on Religion', *Religious Studies* 40 (2004), 389–413.

Donís, Marcelino Rodríguez. '*Consensus Gentium* et *prolepsis* dans la philosophie de Gassendi', in *Gassendi et la Modernité*, ed. S. Taussig (Turnhout: Brepols, 2008), pp. 261–78.

Doolan, Gregory T. *Aquinas on the Divine Ideas as Exemplary Causes* (Washington, DC: Catholic University of America Press, 2008).

Doty, Ralph. 'Ennoēmata, Prolēpseis, and Common Notions', *Southwestern Journal of Philosophy* 7 (1976), 143–8.

Dragos, Andrei Giulea. 'Apprehending "Demonstrations" from the First Principle: Clement of Alexandria's Phenomenology of Faith', *The Journal of Religion* 89 (2009), 187–213.

Dragseth, Jennifer Hockenbery (ed.). *The Devil's Whore: Reason and Philosophy in the Lutheran Tradition* (Philadelphia: Augsburg Fortress, 2011).

Drozdek, Adam. *Greek Philosophers as Theologians: The Divine Arche* (Aldershot: Ashgate, 2007).

Duffin, Jacalyn. *Medical Miracles: Doctors, Saints, and Healing in the Modern World* (Oxford: Oxford University Press, 2008).

Duffy, Eamon. *The Stripping of the Altars: Traditional Religion in England, 1400–1580* (New Haven: Yale University Press, 1992).

Duhem, Pierre. *Le système du monde*, vol. 1 (Paris: A. Hermann and Sons, 1913).

Duhem, Pierre. *The Aim and Structure of Physical Theory*, trans. P. W. Wiener (Princeton: Princeton University Press, 1954).

Dupré, Louis. *Passage to Modernity* (New Haven: Yale University Press, 1993).

Durant, Will and Ariel Durant. *The Age of Reason Begins* (New York: Simon & Schuster, 1961).

Durkin, Philip. 'Linguistic History of the Terms "Atheism" and "Atheist"', in *The Cambridge History of Atheism*, 2 vols., ed. Stephen Bullivant and Michael Ruse (Cambridge: Cambridge University Press, 2021), vol. 1, pp. 11–13.

Dutant, Julien. 'The Legend of the Justified True Belief Analysis', *Philosophical Perspectives* 29 (2015), 95–145.

Dyson, Henry. *Prolepsis and Ennoia in the Early Stoa* (Berlin: De Gruyter, 2009).

Earman, John. *Hume's Abject Failure: The Argument against Miracles* (Oxford: Oxford University Press, 2000).

Ecklund, Elaine Howard and Christopher P. Scheitl. 'Religion among Academic Scientists: Distinctions, Disciplines, and Demographics', *Social Problems* 54 (2007), 289–307.

Ede, Andrew and Lesley B. Cormack. *A History of Science in Society*, 2nd ed. (Toronto: University of Toronto Press, 2012).

Edelman, Nathan. *Attitudes of Seventeenth-Century France toward the Middle Ages* (New York: King's Crown Press, 1946).

Edelstein, Dan. *The Enlightenment: A Genealogy* (Chicago: University of Chicago Press, 2010).

Edwards, Paul. 'Common Consent Arguments for the Existence of God', in *The Encyclopedia of Philosophy*, 8 vols., ed. Paul Edwards (New York: Macmillan, 1967), vol. 2, pp. 147–55.

Ehlen, Arlis John. 'Old Testament Theology as *Heilsgeschichte*', *Concordia Theological Monthly* 35 (1964), 517–44.

Elders, Leo. 'Justification des "cinq voies"', *Revue Thomiste* 61 (1961), 207–25.

Elders, Leo. *Philosophical Theology of Aquinas* (Leiden: Brill, 1990).
Engberg-Pedersen, Troels. 'Philo's *De vita contemplativa* as a Philosopher's Dream', *Journal for the Study of Judaism in the Persian, Hellenistic, and Roman Period* 30 (1999), 40–64.
Engelmann, Edward. 'Aristotelian Teleology, Presocratic Hylozoism, and 20th Century Interpretations', *American Catholic Philosophical Quarterly* 64 (1990), 297–312.
Erdozain, Dominic. *The Soul of Doubt* (Oxford: Oxford University Press, 2016).
Ernst, Cornelius. 'Metaphor and Ontology in *Sacra Doctrina*', *The Thomist* 38 (1974), 403–25.
Evans, Donald D. *The Logic of Self Involvement: A Philosophical Study of Everyday Language with Special Reference to the Christian Use of Language about God as Creator* (London: SCM, 1963).
Evans, G. R. *Old Arts and New Theology: The Beginning of Theology as an Academic Discipline* (Oxford: Clarendon Press, 1980).
Evans-Pritchard, Edward E. *Witchcraft, Oracles, and Magic among the Azande* (Oxford: Clarendon Press, 1976).
Falk, Seb. *The Light Ages: The Surprising Story of Medieval Science* (New York: Norton, 2020).
Farr, Jason. 'Point: Westphalia Legacy and the Modern Nation-State', *International Social Science Review* 80 (2005), 156–9.
Farrington, B. *The Philosophy of Francis Bacon* (Liverpool: Liverpool University Press, 1964).
Fawcett, W. W. Nicolas. 'Aristotle's Concept of Nature: Three Tensions', PhD thesis, University of Western Ontario, 2011.
Febvre, Lucien. *The Problem of Unbelief in the Sixteenth Century: The Religion of Rabelais*, trans. Beatrice Gottlieb (Cambridge, MA: Harvard University Press, 1982).
Feingold, Lawrence. *The Natural Desire to See God according to Thomas Aquinas and His Interpreters*, 2nd ed. (Ave Maria, FL: Sapientia Press, 2010).
Feist, Gregory J. *The Psychology of Science and the Origins of the Scientific Mind* (New Haven: Yale University Press, 2006).
Ferreira, M. Jamie. *Scepticism and Reasonable Doubt: The British Naturalist Tradition in Wilkins, Hume, Reid, and Newman* (Oxford: Clarendon Press, 1986).
Feser, Edward. *Aristotle's Revenge: The Metaphysical Foundations of Physical and Biological Science* (Neunkirchen-Seelscheid: Editiones Scholasticae, 2019).
Feyerabend, Paul. *Against Method* (New York: Verso, 1975).
Feyerabend, Paul. *Realism, Rationalism, and Scientific Method* (Cambridge: Cambridge University Press, 1985).
Figura, Michael. 'Übernatürlich, I. Begriffsgeschichte', in *Lexikon für Theologie und Kirche*, 3. Auflage (Freiburg, 1993–2001), vol. 10, pp. 336–8.
Fine, Gail. 'Aristotle's Two Worlds: Knowledge and Belief in "Posterior Analytics" 1.33', *Proceedings of the Aristotelian Society*, new series, 110 (2010), 323–46.
Firth, Katharine R. *The Apocalyptic Tradition in Reformation Britain: 1530–1645* (Oxford: Oxford University Press, 1979).
Fisch, H. 'The Scientist as Priest: A Note on Robert Boyle's Natural Theology', *Isis* 44 (1953), 252–65.
Fitzmeyer, J. 'The Designations of Christians in Acts and their Significance', in *Unité et Diversité dans l'eglise* (Vatican City: Editrice Vaticana, 1989), pp. 223–36.
Flanagan, Owen. *The Science of Mind* (Cambridge, MA: MIT Press, 1991).
Fletcher, Richard. *The Barbarian Conversion: From Paganism to Christianity* (Berkeley: University of California Press, 1999).

Flory, Dan. 'Race: History, and Affect: Comments on Peter K. J. Park's "Africa, Asia, and the History of Philosophy"', *Journal of World Philosophies* 2 (2017), 48–59.
Fogelin, Robert J. *Pyrrhonian Reflections on Knowledge and Justification* (Oxford: Oxford University Press, 1994).
Force, James E. and Richard H. Popkin. *Essays on the Context, Nature, and Influence of Isaac Newton's Theology* (Dordrecht: Kluwer, 1990).
Force, Pierre. 'Innovation as Spiritual Exercise: Montaigne and Pascal', *Journal of the History of Ideas* 66 (2005), 17–35.
Foster, John. *The Divine Lawmaker* (Oxford: Clarendon Press, 2004).
Foster, M. B. 'The Christian Doctrine of Creation and the Rise of Modern Natural Science', *Mind*, new series, 18 (1934), 446–68.
Foucault, Michel. *Discipline and Punish*, trans. Alan Sheridan (New York: Vintage, 1979).
Foucault, Michel. *The History of Sexuality, Vol. 3: The Care of the Self*, trans. Robert Hurley (New York: Vintage, 1986).
Frances, Bryan. *Disagreement* (Cambridge: Polity Press, 2014).
Frankfurt, Harry. 'Freedom of the Will and the Concept of a Person', *The Journal of Philosophy* 68 (1971), 5–20.
Fransen, Piet. 'A Short History of the Expression "Fides et Mores"', in *Hermeneutics of the Councils and Other Studies*, ed. H. E. Mertens and F. De Graeve (Leuven: Leuven University Press, 1985), pp. 287–318.
Freddoso, Alfred. 'God's General Concurrence with Secondary Causes: Why Conservation Is Not Enough', *Philosophical Perspectives* 5 (1991), 553–85.
Frede, Michael and David Charles (eds.). *Aristotle's Metaphysics Lambda* (Oxford: Oxford University Press, 2000).
Freeman, Charles. *The Closing of the Western Mind* (New York: Vintage, 2005).
Freyberger, G. *Fides: étude sémantique et religieuse depuis les origines jusqu'à l'époque Augustéenne*, 2nd ed. (Paris: Société d'Édition Les Belles Lettres, 2009).
Fricker, Miranda. *Epistemic Injustice* (Oxford: Oxford University Press, 2007).
Friston, Karl. 'A Theory of Cortical Responses', *Philosophical Transactions of the Royal Society of London, B: Biological Sciences* 360 (2005), 815–36.
Friston, Karl. 'Learning and Inference in the Brain', *Neural Networks* 16 (2013), 1325–52.
Fritsche, Johannes. 'Meaning and Function of Aristotle's Two Definitions of Nature (*Physics* B, 192b8–193a9), *Physics* B, and his Biology', *Revue de philosophie ancienne* 36 (2018), 215–87.
Funke, Melissa. 'Colourblind: The Use of Greek Colour Terminology in Cultural Linguistics in the Late Nineteenth and Early Twentieth Centuries', in *Brill's Companion to Classics and Early Anthropology*, ed. Emily Varto (Leiden: Brill, 2018), pp. 255–76.
Funkenstein, Amos. *Theology and the Scientific Imagination* (Princeton: Princeton University Press, 1986).
Gadamer, Hans-Georg. *Truth and Method*, rev. 2nd ed. (London: Bloomsbury, 2004).
Gale, Mary-Anne. *Dhangum Djorra'wuy Dhäwu: A History of Writing in Aboriginal Languages* (Adelaide: Aboriginal Research Institute, University of South Australia, 1997).
Ganss, Karein. 'Affectivity and Knowledge Lead to Devotion to God', in *A Companion to the Abbey of Saint Victor in Paris*, ed. Hugh Feiss and Juliet Mousseau (Leiden: Brill, 2017), pp. 422–68.
Garber, Daniel. 'Descartes among the Novatores', *Res Philosophica* 92 (2015), 1–19.

Garber, Daniel. 'Telesio among the Novatores: Telesio's Reception in the Seventeenth Century', in *Early Modern Philosophers and the Renaissance Legacy*, ed. C. Muratori and G. Paganini (Dordrecht: Springer, 2016), pp. 119–33.

Gardony, A. L., T. T. Brunyé, C. R. Mahoney, and H. A. Taylor. 'How Navigational Aids Impair Spatial Memory: Evidence for Divided Attention', *Spatial Cognition and Computation* 13 (2013), 319–50.

Gaukroger, Stephen. *Descartes: An Intellectual Biography* (Oxford: Oxford University Press, 2005).

Gaukroger, Stephen. *Descartes' System of Natural Philosophy* (Cambridge: Cambridge University Press, 2002).

Gaukroger, Stephen. 'Does Science Get Credit for Too Much?', *Journal of the Proceedings of the Royal Society of New South Wales* 156 (2023), 195–200.

Gaukroger, Stephen. 'Science, Religion and Modernity', *Critical Quarterly* 47 (2005), 1–31.

Gaukroger, Stephen. *The Emergence of a Scientific Culture* (Oxford: Oxford University Press, 2006).

Gaukroger, Stephen. *The Failures of Philosophy: A Historical Essay* (Princeton: Princeton University Press, 2020).

Gaukroger, Stephen (ed.). *The Soft Underbelly of Reason: The Passions in the Seventeenth Century* (London: Routledge, 1998).

George, Marie. 'Aquinas on the Nature of Trust', *Thomist: A Speculative Quarterly Review* 70 (2006), 103–23.

Gerrish, Brian. *Grace and Reason: A Study in the Theology of Luther* (Oxford: Clarendon Press, 1962).

Gersh, Stephen. *From Iamblichus to Eriugena: An Investigation of the Prehistory and Evolution of the Pseudo-Dionysian Tradition* (Leiden: Brill, 1978).

Gerson, Lloyd P. *Ancient Epistemology* (Cambridge: Cambridge University Press, 2012).

Gettier, Edmund. 'Is Justified True Belief Knowledge?', *Analysis* 23 (1963), 121–3.

Gilbert, Margaret. 'Modelling Collective Beliefs', *Synthese* 73 (1987), 185–204.

Gilkey, Langdon. 'Cosmology, Ontology, and the Travail of Biblical Language', in *God's Activity in the World: The Contemporary Problem*, ed. Owen C. Thomas (Chico: Scholars Press, 1983), pp. 29–44.

Gillespie, Michael Allen. *The Theological Origins of Modernity* (Chicago: University of Chicago Press, 2008).

Gilson, Étienne. *Christian Philosophy: An Introduction*, trans. Armand Maurer (Toronto: Pontifical Institute of Medieval Studies, 1993).

Gilson, Étienne. 'Pourquoi Saint Thomas a critiqué Saint Augustin', *Archives d'Histoire Doctrinale et Littéraire du Moyen Âge* 1 (1927), 5–127.

Gilson, Étienne. 'Roger Marston: Un cas d'Augustinisme Avicennisant', *Archives d'Histoire Doctrinale et Littéraire du Moyen Âge* 8 (1933), 37–42.

Goldin, Owen. 'Two Traditions in the Ancient Posterior Analytics Commentaries', in *Interpreting Aristotle's Posterior Analytics in Late Antiquity and Beyond*, ed. Mariska Leunissen and Marije Martijn (Leiden: Brill, 2011), pp. 155–82.

Goldman, Alvin I. *Epistemology and Cognition* (Cambridge, MA: Harvard University Press, 1986).

Gooch, Todd A. *The Numinous and Modernity: An Interpretation of Rudolf Otto's Philosophy of Religion* (Berlin: De Gruyter, 2000).

Goodich, Michael E. *Miracles and Wonders: The Development of the Concept of Miracle, 1150–1350* (London: Routledge, 2007).
Gordon, Peter E. 'Contesting Secularization: The Idea of a Normative Deficit of Modernity after Max Weber', in *Formations of Belief: Historical Approaches to Religion and the Secular*, ed. Philip Nord, Katja Guenther, and Max Weiss (Princeton: Princeton University Press, 2019), pp. 184–201.
Gordon, Peter E. *Migrants in the Profane: Critical Theory and the Question of Secularization* (New Haven: Yale University Press, 2020).
Gordon, Peter E. 'Secularization, Genealogy, and the Legitimacy of the Modern Age: Remarks on the Löwith-Blumenberg Debate', *Journal of the History of Ideas* 80 (2019), 147–70.
Gorski, Philip S. *The Disciplinary Revolution: Calvinism and the Rise of the State in Early Modern Europe* (Chicago: University of Chicago Press, 2003).
Gould, Warwick and Marjorie Reeves. *Joachim of Fiore and the Myth of the Eternal Evangel in the Nineteenth and Twentieth Centuries* (Oxford: Oxford University Press, 2002).
Gow, Peter. 'Forgetting Conversion: The Summer Institute of Linguistics Mission in the Piro Lived World', in *The Anthropology of Christianity*, ed. Fenella Cannell (Durham, NC: Duke University Press, 2006), pp. 211–39.
Grafton, Anthony. 'Where Was Salomon's House? Ecclesiastical History and the Intellectual Origins of Bacon's *New Atlantis*', in *Die Europäische Gelehrtenrepublik im Zeitalter des Konfessionalismus*, ed. Herbert Jaumann (Wiesbaden: Harrassowitz, 2001), pp. 21–38.
Grant, Edward. *Foundations of Modern Science in the Middle Ages* (Cambridge: Cambridge University Press, 1996).
Grant, Edward. *The Nature of Natural Philosophy in the Late Middle Ages* (Washington, DC: The Catholic University of America Press, 2010).
Greene, Robert A. 'Thomas Hobbes and the Term "Right Reason": Participation to Calculation', *History of European Ideas* 41 (2015), 997–1028.
Gregory, Brad S. 'No Room for God: History, Science, Metaphysics and the Study of Religion', *History and Theory* 47 (2008), 495–519.
Gregory, Brad S. *The Unintended Reformation: How a Religious Revolution Secularized Society* (Cambridge, MA: Harvard University Press, 2012).
Griffioen, Sjoerd. *Contesting Modernity in the German Secularization Debate: Karl Löwith, Hans Blumenberg and Carl Schmitt in Polemical Contexts* (Leiden: Brill, 2022).
Gross, Neil and Solon Simmons. 'The Religiosity of American College and University Professors', *Sociology of Religion* 70 (2009), 101–29.
Gruen, E. 'Greek *pistis* and Roman *fides*', *Athenaeum*, new series 60 (1982), 50–68.
Guerlac, Henry. 'Theological Voluntarism and Biological Analogies in Newton's Physical Thought', *Journal of the History of Ideas* 44 (1983), 219–29.
Guilhaumou, J. 'Sieyès et le non-dit de la sociologie: du mot à la chose', *Revue d'histoire des sciences humaines* 15 (2006), 117–34.
Hadot, Pierre. *Philosophy as a Way of Life: Spiritual Exercises from Socrates to Foucault*, trans. Arnold I. Davidson (Oxford: Blackwell, 1995).
Hadot, Pierre. *What Is Ancient Philosophy?*, trans. Michael Chase (Cambridge, MA: Harvard University Press, 2002).
Hadot, Pierre. *Wittgenstein et les limites du langage* (Paris: Vrin, 2004).
Hahn-Bruckart, Thomas. 'Luther in Protestant Historiography and Theology in the Nineteenth and Twentieth Centuries', in *Martin Luther: A Christian between Reforms*

and Modernity (1517–2017), 3 vols., ed. Alberto Melloni (Berlin: De Gruyter, 2017), vol. 1, pp. 1019–41.

Hale, Piers. 'Between Intuition and Empiricism: William Benjamin Carpenter on Man, Mind, and Moral Responsibility', in *The Metaphysical Society (1869–1880): Intellectual Life in Mid-Victorian England*, ed. Catherine Marshall, Bernard Lightman, and Richard England (Oxford: Oxford University Press, 2019), pp. 204–27.

Hall, A. R. *The Scientific Revolution* (London: Longmans, Green, and Co., 1954).

Hall, Vance M. D. 'The Contribution of the Physiologist, William Benjamin Carpenter (1813–1885), to the Development of the Principles of the Correlation of Forces and the Conservation of Energy', *Medical History* 23 (1979), 129–55.

Halvorson, Hans. 'What Is Methodological Naturalism?', in *The Blackwell Companion to Naturalism*, ed. Kelly James Clark (Oxford: Blackwell, 2016), pp. 136–49.

Hamelin, Octave. *La théorie de l'intellect d'après Aristote et ses commentateurs* (Paris: Vrin, 1948).

Hamowy, R. *The Scottish Enlightenment and the Theory of Spontaneous Order* (Carbondale: Southern Illinois University Press, 1987).

Hanks, William F. *Converting Words: Maya in the Age of the Cross* (Berkeley: University of California Press, 2010).

Hannam, James. *The Globe: How the Earth Became Round* (Chicago: University of Chicago Press, 2023).

Hansen, Bert. *Nicole Oresme and the Marvels of Nature: A Study of His De Causis Mirabilium with Critical Edition* (Toronto: Pontifical Institute of Medieval Studies, 1985).

Hansen, Norwood. *Patterns of Discovery: An Enquiry into the Conceptual Foundations of Science* (Cambridge: Cambridge University Press, 1958).

Hardin, Jeff, Ronald L. Numbers, and Ronald A. Binzley (eds.). *The Warfare between Science and Religion: The Idea That Would Not Die* (Pittsburgh: University of Pittsburgh Press, 2018).

Harding, Sandra. *Objectivity and Diversity* (Chicago: University of Chicago Press, 2015).

Harland, Philip. *Dynamics of Identity in the World of the Early Christians* (London: T&T Clark, 2009).

Harré, Rom and E. H. Madden. *Causal Powers: A Theory of Natural Necessity* (Oxford: Blackwell, 1975).

Harris, Ian. 'The Politics of Christianity', in *Locke's Philosophy: Content and Context*, ed. G. A. J. Rogers (Oxford: Oxford University Press, 1994), pp. 197–216.

Harris, Marvin. *The Rise of Anthropological Theory* (New York: Crowell, 1968).

Harrison, Peter. 'Adam Smith and the History of the Invisible Hand', *Journal of the History of Ideas* 72 (2011), 29–49.

Harrison, Peter. 'Angels on Pinheads and Needles' Points', *Notes and Queries* 63 (2016), 45–7.

Harrison, Peter. 'Curiosity, Forbidden Knowledge, and the Reformation of Natural Philosophy in Early-Modern England', *Isis* 92 (2001), 257–78.

Harrison, Peter. 'Experimental Religion and Experimental Science in Early Modern England', *Intellectual History Review* 21 (2011), 413–33.

Harrison, Peter. 'Laws of God or Laws of Nature: Natural Order in the Early Modern Period', in *Science without God? Historical Perspectives on Scientific Naturalism*, ed. Peter Harrison and Jon H. Roberts (Oxford: Oxford University Press, 2019), pp. 58–76.

Harrison, Peter. 'Laws of Nature in Seventeenth-Century England: From Cambridge Platonism to Newtonianism', in *The Divine Order, the Human Order, and the Order of*

Nature: Historical Perspectives, ed. Eric Watkins (New York: Oxford University Press, 2013), pp. 127–48.
Harrison, Peter. 'Miracles, Early Modern Science, and Rational Religion', *Church History* 75 (2006), 493–511.
Harrison, Peter (ed.). *Narratives of Secularization* (London: Routledge, 2017).
Harrison, Peter. 'Naturalism and the Success of Science', *Religious Studies* 56 (2020), 274–91.
Harrison, Peter. 'Newtonian Science, Miracles, and the Laws of Nature', *Journal of the History of Ideas* 56 (1995), 531–53.
Harrison, Peter. 'Normativity and the Critical Functions of Genealogy: The Case of Modern Science', *Modern Theology* 39 (2023), 682–707.
Harrison, Peter. 'Original Sin and the Problem of Knowledge in Early Modern Europe', *Journal of the History of Ideas* 63 (2002), 239–59.
Harrison, Peter. 'Physico-Theology and the Mixed Sciences: The Role of Theology in Early Modern Natural Philosophy', in *The Science of Nature in the Seventeenth Century*, ed. Peter Anstey and John Schuster (Dordrecht: Springer, 2005), pp. 165–83.
Harrison, Peter. 'Reading the Passions: The Fall, the Passions, and Dominion over Nature', in *The Soft Underbelly of Reason: The Passions in the Seventeenth Century*, ed. Stephen Gaukroger (London: Routledge, 1998), pp. 49–78.
Harrison, Peter. *'Religion' and the Religions in the English Enlightenment* (Cambridge: Cambridge University Press, 1990).
Harrison, Peter. 'Science and Religion as Historical Traditions', in *After Science and Religion: Fresh Perspectives from Philosophy and Theology*, ed. Peter Harrison and John Milbank (Cambridge: Cambridge University Press, 2022), pp. 15–34.
Harrison, Peter. 'Sentiments of Devotion and Experimental Philosophy in Seventeenth-Century England', *Journal of Medieval and Early Modern Studies* 44 (2014), 113–33.
Harrison, Peter. *The Bible, Protestantism and the Rise of Natural Science* (Cambridge: Cambridge University Press, 1998).
Harrison, Peter. *The Fall of Man and the Foundations of Science* (Cambridge: Cambridge University Press, 2007).
Harrison, Peter. '"The Fashioned Image of Poetry or the Regular Instruction of Philosophy?" Truth, Utility, and the Natural Sciences in Early Modern England', in *Science, Literature, and Rhetoric in Early Modern England*, ed. D. Burchill and J. Cummins (Aldershot: Ashgate, 2008), pp. 15–36.
Harrison, Peter. 'The Forgotten Proof: The Existence of God and Universal Consent', *The Journal of Religion* 104 (2024), 1–34.
Harrison, Peter. *The Territories of Science and Religion* (Chicago: University of Chicago Press, 2015).
Harrison, Peter. 'Voluntarism and Early Modern Science', *History of Science* 40 (2002), 63–89.
Harrison, Peter. 'Voluntarism and the Origins of Modern Science: A Reply to John Henry', *History of Science* 47 (2009), 223–31.
Harrison, Peter. 'Was Newton a Voluntarist?', in *Newton and Newtonianism: New Studies*, ed. James E. Force and Sarah Hutton (Dordrecht: Kluwer, 2004), pp. 39–64.
Harrison, Peter. 'Was There a Scientific Revolution?', *European Review* 15 (2007), 445–57.
Harrison, Peter. 'What Is Natural Theology? And Should We Dispense with It?', *Zygon* 57 (2022), 114–40.

Harrison, Peter. 'What Was Historical about Natural History? Contingency and Explanation in the Science of Living Things', *Studies in History and Philosophy of Science* 58 (2015), 8–16.

Harrison, Peter. 'What's in a Name? Physico-Theology in Seventeenth-Century England', in *Physico-Theology: Religion and Science in Europe 1650–1750*, ed. Ann Blair and Kaspar von Greyerz (Baltimore: Johns Hopkins University Press, 2020), pp. 39–51.

Harrison, Peter and Ian Hesketh (eds.). 'Replaying the Tape of Life: Evolution and Historical Explanation', special issue of *Studies in History and Philosophy of Science* 59 (2016), 1–122.

Harrison, Peter and John Milbank (eds.). *After Science and Religion: Fresh Perspectives from Philosophy and Theology* (Cambridge: Cambridge University Press, 2022).

Harrison, Peter, Ronald L. Numbers, and Michael H. Shank (eds.). *Wrestling with Nature: From Omens to Science* (Chicago: University of Chicago Press, 2011).

Harrison, Peter and Jon H. Roberts (eds.). *Science without God? Historical Perspectives on Scientific Naturalism* (Oxford: Oxford University Press, 2019).

Harrison, Thomas. 'Beyond the Polis? New Approaches to Greek Religion', *Journal of Hellenic Studies* 135 (2015), 165–80.

Hart, David Bentley. *The Experience of God* (New Haven: Yale University Press, 2013).

Hart, David Bentley. *You Are Gods: On Nature and Supernature* (Notre Dame: University of Notre Dame Press, 2022).

Hatfield, Gary. 'The Senses and the Fleshless Eye: The Meditations as Cognitive Exercises', in *Essays on Descartes' Meditations*, ed. Amélie O. Rorty (Berkeley: University of California Press, 1986), pp. 45–79.

Haviland, John B. 'Guugu Yimithirr Cardinal Directions', *Ethos* 26 (1998), 25–47.

Hayek, Friedrich A. *Individualism and Economic Order* (Chicago: University of Chicago Press, 1948).

Hayek, Friedrich A. *New Studies in Philosophy, Politics, Economics and the History of Ideas* (Chicago: University of Chicago Press, 1978).

Hayek, Friedrich A. *Studies in Philosophy, Politics and Society* (London: Routledge & Kegan Paul, 1967).

Hayek, Friedrich A. *The Constitution of Liberty: The Definitive Edition*, ed. Ronald Hamowy (Chicago: University of Chicago Press, 2011).

Heckel, Martin. 'Luthers Traktat "Von der Freiheit eines Christenmenschen" als Markstein des Kirchen- und Staatskirchenrechts', *Zeitschrift für Theologie und Kirche* 109 (2012), 122–52.

Heckel, Martin. *Vom Religionskonflikt zur Ausgleichsordnung: Der Sonderweg des deutschen Staatskirchenrechts vom Augsburger Religionsfrieden 1555 bis zur Gegenwart* (Munich: C. H. Beck, 2007).

Hedrick, Lisa Landoe. 'The Ontological Turn's New Animists and the Concept of Belief', *The Journal of Religion* 103 (2023), 257–82.

Hefner, R. W. 'World-Building and the Rationality of Conversion', in *Conversion to Christianity*, ed. R. W. Hefner (Berkeley: University of California Press, 1993), pp. 3–46.

Hege, Brent A. R. *Myth, History, and the Resurrection in German Protestant Theology* (Eugene: Pickwick, 2017).

Heidegger, Martin. *An Introduction to Metaphysics*, trans. Ralph Manheim (New Haven: Yale University Press, 1959).

Heidegger, Martin. *Being and Time*, trans. John Macquarrie and Edward Robinson (New York: HarperCollins, 2008).
Heidegger, Martin. *Essays in Metaphysics* (New York: Philosophical Library, 2015).
Heidegger, Martin. *The Bremen and Frieberg Lectures*, trans. Andrew J. Mitchell (Bloomington: Indiana University Press, 2012).
Heidegger, Martin. *The Question Concerning Technology and Other Essays*, trans. William Lovitt (New York: Harper, 1977).
Heimann, P. M. 'Conversion of Forces and the Conservation of Energy', *Centaurus* 18 (1973–4), 147–61.
Heimann, P. M. 'Voluntarism and Immanence: Conceptions of Nature in Eighteenth-Century Thought', *Journal of the History of Ideas* 39 (1978), 271–83.
Helleman, W. E. 'Philo of Alexandria on Deification and Assimilation to God', *Studia Philonica Annual* 2 (1990), 51–71.
Helm, Paul. 'John Calvin, the *Sensus Divinitatis*, and the Noetic Effects of Sin', *International Journal for Philosophy of Religion* 43 (1998), 87–107.
Hemming, Lawrence Paul and Susan Frank Parsons. *Restoring Faith in Reason* (Notre Dame: University of Notre Dame Press, 2003).
Hempton, David. *Methodism: Empire of the Spirit* (New Haven: Yale University Press, 2005).
Hendrix, Scott H. *Ecclesia in Via* (Leiden: Brill, 1974).
Hendrix, Scott H. *Recultivating the Vineyard: The Reformation Agendas of Christianization* (Louisville: Westminster John Knox Press, 2004).
Hengstmengel, Joost. 'Divine Oeconomy: The Role of Providence in Early Modern Economic Thought before Adam Smith', PhD thesis, Erasmus University Rotterdam, 2015.
Henrich, Joseph. *The WEIRDest People in the World: How the West Became Psychologically Peculiar and Particularly Prosperous* (New York: Farrar, Straus & Giroux, 2020).
Henrich, Joseph, Steven J. Heine, and Ara Norenzayan. 'The Weirdest People in the World?', *Behavioral and Brain Sciences* 33 (2010), 1–75.
Henry, John. 'Henry More versus Robert Boyle', in *Henry More (1614–87): Tercentenary Essays*, ed. Sarah Hutton (Dordrecht: Kluwer, 1990), pp. 55–76.
Henry, John. 'Metaphysics and the Origins of Modern Science: Descartes and the Importance of Laws of Nature', *Early Science and Medicine* 9 (2004), 73–114.
Henry, John. 'Voluntarist Theology at the Origins of Modern Science: A Response to Peter Harrison', *History of Science* 47 (2009), 79–113.
Herdt, Jennifer A. 'Artificial Lives, Providential History, and the Apparent Limits of Sympathetic Understanding', in *David Hume: Historical Thinker, Historical Writer*, ed. Mark Spencer (University Park, PA: Pennsylvania State University Press, 2013), pp. 37–59.
Heron, Nicholas. *Liturgical Power: Between Economic and Political Theology* (New York: Fordham University Press, 2018).
Hesketh, Ian. 'Technologies of the Scientific Self: John Tyndall and His Journal', *Isis* 110 (2019), 466–9.
Hesketh, Ian. *The Science of History in Victorian Britain* (Pittsburgh: University of Pittsburgh Press, 2020).
Hester, Carol. 'Gedanken zu Ferdinand Christian Baurs Entwicklung als Historiker anhand zweier unbekannter Briefe', *Zeitschrift für Kirchengeschichte* 84 (1973), 249–69.
Hetche, Matt. 'Descartes and the Augustinian Tradition of Devotional Meditation: Tracing a Minim Connection', *Journal of the History of Philosophy* 48 (2010), 283–311.

Hick, John. 'Seeing-as and Religious Experience', in *Problems of Religious Pluralism* (New York: St. Martin's Press, 1985), pp. 16–27.
Higgitt, Rebekah. 'Introduction', in *Early Biographies of Isaac Newton 1660–1885*, 2 vols., ed. Rebekah Higgitt (London: Pickering & Chatto, 2006), vol. 2, pp. x–xiii.
Hill, Christopher. *Antichrist in Seventeenth-Century England* (Oxford: Oxford University Press, 1971).
Hill, Christopher. 'Covenantal Theology and the Concept of a "Public Person"', in *Collected Essays*, vol. 3 (Brighton: Harvester Press, 1985), pp. 300–24.
Hill, Lisa. 'Adam Ferguson and the Paradox of Progress and Decline', *History of Political Thought* 18 (1997), 677–706.
Hirsch, Emanuel. *Geschichte der neuern evangelischen Theologie*, 5 vols. (Gütersloh: Gerd Mohn, 1964).
Hirschman, Albert O. *The Passions and the Interests: Political Arguments for Capitalism before Its Triumph* (Princeton: Princeton University Press, 2013).
Hödl, L. '"*Opus naturae est opus intelligentia*": Ein neuplatonisches Axiom im aristotelischen Verständnis des Albertus Magnus Averroismus im Mittelalter', in *Averroismus im Mittelalter und in der Renaissance*, ed. Friedrich Niewöhner and Loris Sturlese (Zürich: Spur, 1994), pp. 132–48.
Hoekstra, Kinch. 'Disarming the Prophets: Thomas Hobbes and Predictive Power', *Rivista di storia della filosofia* 1 (2004), 97–153.
Hoffman, Paul. 'Final Causation in Spinoza', in *Final Causes and Teleological Explanation*, ed. Dominik Perler and Stephan Schmid (Leiden: Brill, 2011), pp. 40–50.
Hoffmann, Georg. *Die Lehre von der Fides implicita* (Leipzig: Hinrichs, 1906).
Hogden, Margaret. *Early Anthropology in the Sixteenth and Seventeenth Centuries* (Philadelphia: University of Pennsylvania Press, 1964).
Hohwy, Jakob. *The Predictive Mind* (Oxford: Oxford University Press, 2013).
Holbraad, Martin. 'The Contingency of Concepts', in *Comparative Metaphysics*, ed. Pierre Charbonnier, Gildas Salmon, and Peter Skafish (Lanham: Rowman & Littlefield, 2016), pp. 133–58.
Hoopes, Robert. *Right Reason in the English Renaissance* (Cambridge, MA: Harvard University Press, 1961).
Höpfl, H. M. 'Isms', *British Journal of Political Science* 13 (1983), 1–17.
Horan, Daniel P. *Postmodernity and Univocity: A Critical Assessment of Radical Orthodoxy and John Duns Scotus* (Minneapolis: Fortress Press, 2014).
Horkheimer, Max. *Critique of Instrumental Reason*, trans. Matthew J. O'Connell (London: Verso, 2014).
Horkheimer, Max and Theodor W. Adorno. *Dialectic of Enlightenment*, trans. E. Jephcott (Stanford: Stanford University Press, 2002).
Horsman, Reginald. *Race and Manifest Destiny* (Cambridge, MA: Harvard University Press, 1986).
Hotson, Howard. *Johann Heinrich Alsted 1588–1638: Between Renaissance, Reformation, and Universal Reform* (Oxford: Oxford University Press, 2000).
Hotson, Howard. *Paradise Postponed: Johann Heinrich Alsted and the Birth of Calvinist Millenarianism* (Dordrecht: Kluwer, 2000).
Hunt, Louis. 'The Origin and Scope of Hayek's Idea of Spontaneous Order', in *Liberalism, Conservatism, and Hayek's Idea of Spontaneous Order*, ed. L. Hunt and P. McNamara (New York: Palgrave Macmillan, 2006), pp. 43–64.

Hunter, David G. 'The Virgin, the Bride, and the Church: Reading Psalm 45 in Ambrose, Jerome, and Augustine', *Church History* 69 (2000), 281–303.
Hunter, Ian. 'Human Nature, the State of Nature, and Natural Law', in *The Cambridge Companion to Pufendorf*, ed. Knud Haakonssen and Ian Hunter (Cambridge: Cambridge University Press, 2023), pp. 109–39.
Hunter, Michael. *Science and Society in Restoration England* (Cambridge: Cambridge University Press, 1981).
Hunter, Michael. *Science and the Shape of Orthodoxy* (Woodbridge: Boydell, 1995).
Hunter, Michael. 'The Problem of "Atheism" in Early Modern England', *Transactions of the Royal Historical Society* 35 (1985), 135–57.
Hurtado, Larry. *Destroyer of the Gods: Early Christian Distinctiveness in the Roman World* (Waco: Baylor University Press, 2016).
Hutchison, Keith. 'Dormitive Virtues, Scholastic Qualities, and the New Philosophies', *History of Science* 29 (1991), 245–78.
Hyman, Gavin. *A Short History of Atheism* (London: I. B. Tauris, 2010).
Ingold, Tim. 'Dreaming of Dragons: On the Imagination of Real Life', *Journal of the Royal Anthropological Institute* 19 (2013), 734–52.
Inwood, Brad. *Reading Seneca* (Oxford: Oxford University Press, 2005).
Ip, Pui Him. 'Physics as Spiritual Exercise', in *After Science and Religion: Fresh Perspectives from Philosophy and Theology*, ed. Peter Harrison and John Milbank (Cambridge: Cambridge University Press, 2022), pp. 282–98.
Jackson-McCabe, Matt. 'The Stoic Theory of Implanted Conceptions', *Phronesis* 49 (2004), 323–47.
Jacobs, N. 'On "Not Three Gods"—Again: Can a Primary-Secondary Substance Reading of *ousia* and *hypostasis* Avoid Tritheism?', *Modern Theology* 24 (2008), 331–58.
Jacobs, Straun. 'Michael Polanyi's Theory of Spontaneous Orders', *Review of Austrian Economics* 11 (1999), 111–27.
Jaeger, Werner. *The Theology of the Early Greek Philosophers* (Oxford: Clarendon Press 1948).
Janowski, B. 'Das Licht des Lebens: Zur Lichtmetaphorik in den Psalmen', in *Metaphors in the Psalms*, ed. Pierre Van Hecke and Antje Labahn (Leuven: Peeters, 2010), pp. 87–113.
Janz, Denis R. 'Whore or Handmaid? Luther and Aquinas on the Function of Reason in Theology', in *The Devil's Whore: Reason and Philosophy in the Lutheran Tradition*, ed. Jennifer Hockenbery Dragseth (Philadelphia: Augsburg Fortress, 2011), pp. 47–52.
Jay, Martin. *Reason after Its Eclipse: On Late Critical Theory* (Madison: University of Wisconsin Press, 2016).
Jaynes, Julian. *The Origin of Consciousness in the Breakdown of the Bicameral Mind* (New York: Mariner, 2000).
Jeffers, Thomas L. 'Nice Threads: Tennyson's Lady of Shalott as Artist', *Yale Review* 89 (2008), 54–68.
Jenkins, Michelle. 'Plato's Godlike Philosopher', *Classical Philology* 111 (2016), 330–52.
Jessen, Tyler D., Natalie C. Ban, Nicholas XEMȾOLTW Claxton, and Chris T. Darimont. 'Contributions of Indigenous Knowledge to Ecological and Evolutionary Understanding', *Frontiers in Ecology and the Environment* 20 (2022), 93–101.
Jiri, O., P. L. Mafongoya, and P. Chivenge. 'Indigenous Knowledge Systems, Seasonal "Quality" and Climate Change Adaptation in Zimbabwe', *Climate Research* 66 (2015), 103–11.

Johnson, A. P. *Ethnicity and Argument in Eusebius' "Praeparatio Evangelica"* (Oxford: Oxford University Press, 2006).
Johnson, Ann Marie and John A. Maxfield (eds.). *The Reformation as Christianization* (Tübingen: Mohr Siebeck, 2012).
Johnson, M. R. 'Nature, Spontaneity, and Voluntary Action in Lucretius', in *Lucretius: Poetry, Philosophy, Science*, ed. D. Lehoux, A. D. Morrison, and A. Sharrock (Oxford: Oxford University Press, 2013), pp. 99–130.
Jolley, Nicholas. *Locke: His Philosophical Thought* (New York: Oxford University Press, 1999).
Jonas, Hans. *The Imperative of Responsibility: In Search of an Ethics for the Technological Age* (Chicago: University of Chicago Press, 1984).
Jones, Matthew. 'Descartes's Geometry as Spiritual Exercise', *Critical Inquiry* 28 (2001), 40–72.
Jordan, Peter N. *Naturalism in the Christian Imagination: Providence and Causality in Early Modern England* (Cambridge: Cambridge University Press, 2022).
Judge, Edwin. 'Was Christianity a Religion?', in *The First Christians in the Roman World*, ed. James R. Harrison (Tübingen: Mohr Siebeck, 2008), pp. 404–9.
Jungkuntz, R. 'Fathers, Heretics and Epicureans', *Journal of Ecclesiastical History* 17 (1966), 3–10.
Kahn, Victoria. *Wayward Contracts: The Crisis of Political Obligation in England, 1640–1674* (Princeton: Princeton University Press, 2004).
Kahneman, D. *Thinking, Fast and Slow* (New York: Farrar, Straus & Giroux, 2011).
Kail, Peter. 'On Hume's Appropriation of Malebranche: Causation and Self', *European Journal of Philosophy* 16 (2007), 55–80.
Kainz, Howard P. *The Existence of God and the Faith-Instinct* (Cranbury, NJ: Susquehanna University Press, 2010).
Kaplan, Mark. 'It's Not What You Know that Counts', *The Journal of Philosophy* 82 (1985), 350–63.
Katajala-Peltomaa, Sari. *Gender, Miracles, and Daily Life: The Evidence of Fourteenth-Century Canonization Processes* (Turnhout: Brepols, 2009).
Kavka, Gregory S. 'Right Reason and Natural Law in Hobbes's Ethics', *The Monist* 66 (1983), 120–33.
Keas, Michael N. 'That the Copernican Revolution Demoted the Status of the Earth', in *Newton's Apple and Other Myths about Science*, ed. Ronald L. Numbers and Kostas Kampourakis (Cambridge, MA: Harvard University Press, 2015), pp. 23–31.
Keener, Craig S. *Miracles: The Credibility of the New Testament Accounts* (Grand Rapids: Baker, 2011).
Keener, Craig S. *Miracles Today: The Supernatural Work of God in the Modern World* (Grand Rapids: Baker, 2021).
Keitt, Andrew W. *Inventing the Sacred: Imposture, Inquisition, and the Boundaries of the Supernatural in Golden Age Spain* (Leiden: Brill, 2005).
Kelemen, Deborah. 'Are Children "Intuitive Theists"? Reasoning about Purpose and Design in Nature', *Psychological Science* 15 (2004), 295–301.
Kelemen, Deborah. 'British and American Children's Preferences for Teleo-Functional Explanations of the Natural World', *Cognition* 88 (2003), 201–21.
Kellenberger, J. '"Seeing-as" in Religion: Discovery and Community', *Religious Studies* 38 (2002), 101–8.

Kelley, Donald R. *Foundations of Modern Historical Scholarship* (New York: Columbia University Press, 1970).
Kelly, Geffrey B. '"Unconscious Christianity" and the "Anonymous Christian" in the Theology of Dietrich Bonhoeffer and Karl Rahner', *Philosophy and Theology* 9 (1995), 117–49.
Kelly, Thomas. '*Consensus Gentium*: Reflections on the "Common Consent" Argument for the Existence of God', in *Evidence and Religious Belief*, ed. Kelly James Clark and Raymond J. VanArragon (Oxford: Oxford University Press, 2011), pp. 135–56.
Kelly, Thomas and Sarah McGrath. 'Are There Any Successful Philosophical Arguments?', in *Being, Freedom, and Method: Themes from the Philosophy of Peter van Inwagen*, ed. John A. Keller (Oxford: Oxford University Press, 2017), pp. 324–42.
Kenney, John Peter. '"None Come Closer to Us than These": Augustine and the Platonists', *Religions* 7 (2016), 1–16.
Kennington, Richard. 'Descartes' *Olympia*', in *On Modern Origins: Essays on Early Modern Philosophy*, ed. P. Kraus and F. Hunt (New York: Lexington Books, 2004), pp. 79–100.
Kenny, J. P. *The Supernatural: Medieval Theological Concepts to Modern* (New York: Alba House, 1972).
Kerr, Fergus. *After Aquinas: Versions of Thomism* (Oxford: Blackwell, 2002).
Kerschensteiner, Julia. *Kosmos: Quellenkritische Untersuchungen zu den Vorsokratikern* (München: C. H. Beck, 1962).
Keyser, Ariela and Juhem Navarro-Rivera. 'A World of Atheism: Global Demographics', in *The Oxford Handbook of Atheism*, ed. Stephen Bullivant and Michael Ruse (Oxford: Oxford University Press, 2013), pp. 553–86.
Kidd, Ian James. 'Epistemic Justice and Religion', in *The Routledge Handbook of Epistemic Injustice*, ed. Ian James Kidd, José Medina, and Gaile Pohlhaus (New York: Routledge, 2017), pp. 386–96.
King, Peter and Nathan Ballantyne. 'Augustine on Testimony', *Canadian Journal of Philosophy* 39 (2009), 195–214.
Kinneavy, James L. *Greek Rhetorical Origins of Christian Faith: An Inquiry* (New York: Oxford University Press, 1987).
Kinzig, Wolfram. 'The Creed in Liturgy: Prayer or Hymn?', in *Jewish and Christian Liturgy and Worship*, ed. Albert Gerhards and Clemens Leonard (Leiden: Brill, 2007), pp. 229–46.
Kitcher, Philip. 'A Priori Knowledge', *The Philosophical Review* 86 (1980), 3–23.
Kittel, Gerhard and Gerhard Friedrich (eds.). *Theological Dictionary of the New Testament*, 10 vols. (Grand Rapids: Eerdmans, 1977).
Klay, Robin and John Lunn. 'The Relationship of God's Providence to Market Economics and Economic Theory', *Journal of Markets and Morality* 6 (2003), 541–64.
Kleeberg, Bernhard. 'Vestiges of the Book of Nature: Religious Experience and Hermeneutic Practices in Protestant German Theology, ca. 1900', in *Historical Perspectives on Erklären and Verstehen*, ed. Uljana Feest (Dordrecht: Springer, 2010), pp. 37–60.
Klinck, Denis R. '*Vestigia Trinitatis* in Man and His Works in the English Renaissance', *Journal of the History of Ideas* 42 (1981), 13–27.
Kochiras, Hylarie. 'The Mechanical Philosophy and Newton's Mechanical Force', *Philosophy of Science* 80 (2013), 557–78.

Kolbet, Paul R. *Augustine and the Cure of Souls: Revising a Classical Ideal* (Notre Dame: University of Notre Dame Press, 2010).
Kors, Alan Charles. *Atheism in France, 1650–1729, Volume 1: The Orthodox Sources of Disbelief* (Princeton: Princeton University Press, 1990).
Kors, Alan Charles. 'Scepticism and the Problem of Atheism', in *Scepticism and Irreligion in the Seventeenth and Eighteenth Centuries*, ed. Richard Popkin and Arjo Vanderjagt (Leiden: Brill, 1993), pp. 185–215.
Krafft, Fritz. 'Kunst und Natur. Die Heronische Frage und die Technik in der klassischen Antike', *Antike und Abendland* 19 (1973), 1–19.
Krasner, Stephen D. 'Westphalia and All That', in *Ideas and Foreign Policy: Beliefs, Institutions, and Political Change*, ed. Judith Goldstein and Robert O. Keohane (Ithaca: Cornell University Press, 1993), pp. 235–64.
Krause, Katja. 'Source Mining: Arabic Natural Philosophy and *experientia* in Albert the Great's Scientific Practices', in *Albert the Great and His Arabic Sources: Medieval Science between Inheritance and Emergence*, ed. Katja Krause and Richard C. Taylor (Turnhout: Brepols, in press).
Krause, Katja and Richard C. Taylor (eds.). *Albert the Great and His Arabic Sources: Medieval Science between Inheritance and Emergence* (Turnhout: Brepols, in press).
Krause, Katja and Richard C. Taylor. 'Albert's Philosophical *scientia*: Origins, Geneses, Emergences', in *Albert the Great and His Arabic Sources: Medieval Science between Inheritance and Emergence*, ed. Katja Krause and Richard C. Taylor (Turnhout: Brepols, in press).
Kretzmann, Norman. *The Metaphysics of Creation: Aquinas's Natural Theology in Summa Contra Gentiles* (Oxford: Oxford University Press, 1998).
Krop, Henri. 'Spinoza and the Low Countries', in *The Cambridge History of Atheism*, 2 vols., ed. Stephen Bullivant and Michael Ruse (Cambridge: Cambridge University Press, 2021), vol. 1, pp. 223–41.
Kross, E., P. Verduyn, E. Demiralp, J. Park, D. S. Lee, N. Lin, H. Shablack, J. Jonides, and O. Ybarra. 'Facebook Use Predicts Declines in Subjective Well-Being in Young Adults', *PLos One* 8 (2013). https://doi.org/10.1371/journal.pone.0069841, accessed 23 November 2023.
Krumenacker, Yves. 'The Use of History by French Protestants and its Impact on Protestant Historiography', in *History and Religion: Narrating a Religious Past*, ed. Bernd-Christian Otto, Susanne Rau, and Jörg Rüpke (Berlin: De Gruyter, 2015), pp. 189–201.
Kuehn, Manfred. *Scottish Common Sense in Germany* (Montreal: McGill-Queen's University Press, 1987).
Kuhn, Thomas. *The Structure of Scientific Revolutions*, 4th ed. (Chicago: University of Chicago Press, 2012).
Kuijsten, Martin (ed.). *Gods, Voices, and the Bicameral Mind: The Theories of Julian Jaynes* (Henderson, NY: Julian Jaynes Society, 2019).
Kurunmäki, Jussi and Jani Marjanen. 'A Rhetorical View of Isms: An Introduction', *Journal of Political Ideologies* 23 (2018), 241–55.
Kvanvig, J. L. 'The Idea of Faith as Trust: Lessons in Noncognitivist Approaches to Faith', in *Reason and Faith: Themes from Richard Swinburne*, ed. M. Bergmann and J. Brower (Oxford: Oxford University Press, 2016), pp. 4–26.
Lackey, Jennifer. 'Socially Extended Knowledge', *Philosophical Issues* 24 (2014), 282–98.

Laclau, Ernesto and Chantal Mouffe. *Hegemony and Social Strategy*, 2nd ed. (London: Verso, 2014).
Lacoste, Jean-Yves. 'Homoousios et homoousios: La substance entre théologie et philosophie', *Recherches de Science Religieuse* 98 (2010), 85–100.
LaCugna, Catherine Mowry. 'Philosophers and Theologians on the Trinity', *Modern Theology* 2 (1986), 169–81.
Lagerlund, Henrik. 'The Unity of Efficient and Final Causality: The Mind/Body Problem Reconsidered', *British Journal for the History of Philosophy* 19 (2011), 587–603.
Lagrée, Jacqueline. 'Mersenne traducteur d'Herbert de Cherbury', *Les Études philosophiques* 1/2 (1994), 25–40.
Lancaster, James A. T. and Andrew McKenzie-McHarg. 'Priestcraft: Early Modern Variations on the Theme of Sacerdotal Imposture', themed issue of *Intellectual History Review* 28/1 (2018).
Lancaster, Raelee. 'Decolonisation to Indigenisation: How Can Institutions Centre Indigenous Knowledge?', *Times Higher Education Supplement*, 20 June 2023. www.timeshighereducation.com/campus/decolonisation-indigenisation-how-can-institutions-centre-indigenous-knowledge, accessed 18 July 2023.
Landes, Richard. 'Lest the Millennium Be Fulfilled: Apocalyptic Expectations and the Pattern of Western Chronography, 100–800 CE', in *The Use and Abuse of Eschatology in the Middle Ages*, ed. W. Verbeke, D. Verhelst, and A. Welkenhuysen (Leuven: Leuven University Press, 1988), pp. 137–211.
Lange, Marc. 'Laws, Counterfactuals, Stability, and Degrees of Lawhood', *Philosophy of Science* 66 (1999), 243–67.
Lännström, Anna. 'Trusting the Divine Voice: Socrates and His Daimonion', *Apeiron* 45 (2012), 32–49.
Lanzillotta, Lautaro Roig. 'A Way of Salvation: Becoming Like God in Nag Hammadi', *Numen* 60 (2013), 71–102.
Laplanche, François. *Le Bible en France entre mythe et critique, XVIe–XIXe siècle* (Paris: Albin Michel, 1994).
Larsen, Timothy. 'E. B. Tylor, Religion and Anthropology', *British Journal for the History of Science* 46 (2013), 467–85.
Larson, Jens Kristian. 'Measuring Humans against Gods: On the Digression of Plato's *Theaetetus*', *Archiv für Geschichte der Philosophie* 101 (2019). https://doi-org.ezproxy.library.uq.edu.au/10.1515/agph-2019-1001, accessed 23 November 2023.
Latour, Bruno. *Down to Earth: Politics in the New Climatic Regime*, trans. Catherine Porter (Cambridge: Polity Press, 2018).
Laudan, Larry. 'A Confutation of Convergent Realism', *Philosophy of Science* 48 (1981), 19–49.
Launonen, Lari. 'Natural Religion in Science and Theology', PhD thesis, University of Helsinki, 2022.
Lawson, Robert B., Jean E. Graham, and Kristin M. Baker, *A History of Psychology* (New York: Routledge, 2016).
Leclercq, Jean. *The Love of Learning and the Desire for God*, trans. Catherine Misrahi (New York: Fordham University Press, 2008).
Leech, David. 'Some Reflections on the Category "Cambridge Platonism"', *The Cambridge Platonist Research Group*. https://cprg.hypotheses.org/517, accessed 5 March 2020.

Leff, Gordon. 'Gregory of Rimini', *Revue d'Études Augustiniennes et Patristiques* 7 (1961), 153–70.
Lehoux, Daryn. '"All Things are Full of Gods": Naturalism in the Classical World', in *Science without God? Historical Perspectives on Scientific Naturalism*, ed. Peter Harrison and Jon Roberts (Oxford: Oxford University Press, 2019), pp. 19–36.
Lehoux, Daryn. 'Laws of Nature and Natural Laws', *Studies in History and Philosophy of Science, Part A* 37 (2006), 527–49.
Lehoux, Daryn. 'Why Does Aristotle Think Bees Are Divine?', *British Journal for the History of Science* 52 (2019), 383–403.
Lehrer, Keith and Bradley Warner. 'Reid, God and Epistemology', *American Catholic Philosophical Quarterly* 74 (2000), 357–72.
Leiter, Brian. *The Future for Philosophy* (New York: Oxford University Press, 2004).
Leunissen, Mariska and Marije Martijn (eds.). *Interpreting Aristotle's Posterior Analytics in Late Antiquity and Beyond* (Leiden: Brill, 2011).
Levitin, Dmitri. *Ancient Wisdom in the Age of the New Science* (Cambridge: Cambridge University Press, 2015).
Lewis, C. S. *Mere Christianity* (London: HarperCollins, 2002).
Lewis, C. S. *Studies in Words*, 2nd ed. (Cambridge: Cambridge University Press, 1967).
Lewis, Charleton T. and Charles Short. *A Latin Dictionary* (Oxford: Clarendon Press, 1962).
Lewis, Rhodri. *Language, Mind, and Nature: Artificial Languages in England from Bacon to Locke* (Cambridge: Cambridge University Press, 2007).
Lienhardt, Godfrey. *Divinity and Experience: The Religion of the Dinka* (Oxford: Clarendon Press, 1961).
Lienhardt, Godfrey. 'Modes of Thought', in *The Institutions of Primitive Society, a Series of Broadcast Talks*, ed. E. E. Evans-Pritchard et al. (Glencoe: Free Press, 1954), pp. 96–7.
Lienhardt, Godfrey. *Social Anthropology* (Oxford: Oxford University Press, 1964).
Lieu, Judith. *Christian Identity in the Jewish and Graeco-Roman World* (Oxford: Oxford University Press, 2004).
Lightman, Bernard. *Global Spencerism: The Communication and Appropriation of a British Evolutionist* (Leiden: Brill, 2015).
Lightman, Bernard. 'Henry Longueville Mansel and the Genesis of Victorian Agnosticism', PhD thesis, Brandeis University, 1978.
Lightman, Bernard. 'Robert Elsmere and the Agnostic Crises of Faith', in *Victorian Faith in Crisis: Essays on Continuity and Change in Nineteenth-Century Belief*, ed. Richard J. Helmstadter and Bernard Lightman (Stanford: Stanford University Press, 1990), pp. 283–311.
Lightman, Bernard. 'Science at the Metaphysical Society', in *The Age of Scientific Naturalism: Tyndall and His Contemporaries*, ed. Bernard Lightman and Michael S. Reidy (Abingdon: Routledge, 2016), pp. 187–206.
Lightman, Bernard. 'The Many Lives of Charles Darwin: Early Biographies and the Definitive Evolutionist', *Notes and Records of the Royal Society of London* 64 (2010), 339–58.
Lightman, Bernard. 'The Nineteenth-Century Origins of the Problem: Naturalistic Metaphysics and the Dead Ends of Victorian Theology', in *After Science and Religion: Fresh Perspectives from Philosophy and Theology*, ed. Peter Harrison and John Milbank (Cambridge: Cambridge University Press, 2022), pp. 35–58.

Lightman, Bernard. *The Origins of Agnosticism: Victorian Unbelief and the Limits of Knowledge* (Baltimore: Johns Hopkins University Press, 2019).
Lightman, Bernard. 'The Theology of Victorian Scientific Naturalists', in *Science without God? Historical Perspectives on Scientific Naturalism*, ed. Peter Harrison and Jon H. Roberts (Oxford: Oxford University Press, 2019), pp. 235–53.
Lin, L. Y., J. E. Sidani, A. Shensa, et al. 'Association between Social Media Use and Depression among U.S. Young Adults', *Depression and Anxiety* 33 (2016), 323–31.
Lin, Martin. 'Spinoza's Arguments for the Existence of God', *Philosophy and Phenomenological Research* 75 (2007), 269–97.
Lindberg, David C. (ed.). *Science in the Middle Ages* (Chicago: University of Chicago Press, 1978).
Lindberg, David C. *The Beginnings of Western Science*, 2nd ed. (Chicago: University of Chicago Press, 2007).
Lindquist, Galina and Simon Coleman. 'Introduction: Against Belief?' *Social Analysis* 52 (2008), 1–18.
Lisska, Anthony J. 'Right Reason in Natural Law Moral Theory', in *Reason, Religion, and Natural Law from Plato to Spinoza*, ed. Jonathan A. Jacobs (Oxford: Oxford University Press, 2012), pp. 155–74.
Livingstone, David N. *Darwin's Forgotten Defenders: The Encounter between Evangelical Theology and Evolutionary Theory* (Grand Rapids: Eerdmans, 1987).
Lohr, C. H. 'The Medieval Interpretation of Aristotle', in *The Cambridge History of Later Medieval Philosophy*, ed. Norman Kretzmann, Anthony Kenny, and Jan Pinborg (Cambridge: Cambridge University Press, 1982), pp. 80–98.
LoLordo, Antonia. *Pierre Gassendi and the Birth of Early Modern Philosophy* (Cambridge: Cambridge University Press, 2007).
Long, Steven A. *Natura Pura: On the Recovery of Nature in the Doctrine of Grace* (New York: Fordham University Press, 2010).
Lorenz-Spreen, P., B. M. Mønsted, P. Hövel, and S. Lehmann. 'Accelerating Dynamics of Collection Attention', *Nature Communications* 10 (2019). https://doi.org/10.1038/s41467-019-09311-w, accessed 23 November 2023.
Lorini, Gualtiero. '"Diversa Theologiae naturalis systemata": Christian Wolff's Ways to God', *Revista de Storia della Filosophia* 76 (2021), 760–81.
Lotito, Mark A. *The Reformation of Historical Thought* (Leiden: Brill, 2019).
Louth, Andrew. *Discerning the Mystery: An Essay on the Nature of Theology* (Oxford: Clarendon Press, 1983).
Löwith, Karl. *Meaning in History* (Chicago: University of Chicago Press, 1949).
Lu-Adler, Huaping. *Kant and Racism: Views from Anywhere* (Oxford: Oxford University Press, 2023).
Lucas, Lamadrid. 'Anonymous or Analogous Christians? Rahner and Von Balthasar on Naming the Non-Christian', *Modern Theology* 11 (1995), 363–84.
Luhrmann, Tanya. 'Metakinesis: How God Becomes Intimate in Contemporary US Christianity', *American Anthropologist* 106 (2004), 518–28.
Luhrmann, Tanya. 'Mind and Spirit: A Comparative Theory about Representation of Mind and the Experience of Spirit', *Journal of the Royal Anthropological Institute*, new series 26 (suppl. 13) (2020), 1–19.
Lüthy, C., J. E. Murdoch, and William R. Newman (eds.). *Late Medieval and Early Modern Corpuscular Matter Theories* (Leiden: Brill, 2001).

Lyman, J. Rebecca. 'Heresiology: The Invention of "Heresy" and Schism"', in *The Cambridge History of the Christian Church*, vol. 2, ed. Augustin Casiday and Frederick W. Norris (Cambridge: Cambridge University Press, 2014), pp. 296–313.

Lyon, Greg B. 'Baudouin, Flacius, and the Plan for the Magdeburg Centuries', *Journal of the History of Ideas* 64 (2003), 253–72.

Lyons, Henry. *The Royal Society, 1660–1940: A History of Its Administration under Its Charters* (Cambridge: Cambridge University Press, 1944).

Maat, Jaap. *Philosophical Languages in the Seventeenth Century: Dalgarno, Wilkins, Leibniz* (Dordrecht: Kluwer, 2004).

MacCulloch, Diarmaid. *The Reformation: A History* (New York: Viking, 2004).

MacDonald, Scott (ed.). *Being and Goodness* (Ithaca: Cornell University Press, 1999).

MacGaffey, Wyatt. *Religion and Society in Central Africa: The BaKongo of Lower Zaire* (Chicago: University of Chicago Press, 1986).

Machamer, Peter, J. E. McGuire, and Hylarie Kochiras. 'Newton and the Mechanical Philosophy: Gravitation as the Balance of the Heavens', *Southern Journal of Philosophy* 50 (2012), 370–88.

MacIntyre, Alasdair. *After Virtue*, 2nd ed. (Notre Dame: University of Notre Dame Press, 1984).

MacIntyre, Alasdair. *Marxism and Christianity* (Notre Dame: University of Notre Dame Press, 1984).

Mack, A. and I. Rock. *Inattentional Blindness* (Cambridge, MA: MIT Press, 1998).

Mack, Phyllis. *Heart Religion in the British Enlightenment* (Cambridge: Cambridge University Press, 2008).

Macquarrie, John. *Principles of Christian Theology*, rev. ed. (London: SCM, 1977).

Maguire, E., K. Woollett, and H. Spiers. 'London Taxi Drivers and Bus Drivers: A Structural MRI and Neuropsychological Analysis', *Hippocampus* 16 (2006), 1091–101.

Mahoney, Paul. 'Christian Inspiration in Descartes' Olympic Dreams', *Heythrop Journal* 54 (2013), 371–84.

Maier, Anneliese. 'Finalkausalität und Naturgesetz', in *Metaphysische Hintergründe der spätscholastischen Naturphilosophie* (Rome: Edizioni di Storia et Letteratura, 1955), pp. 273–335.

Maioli, Roger. 'The First Avowed British Atheist: Lord Hervey?', *Eighteenth Century Studies* 54 (2021), 357–79.

Mair, Jonathan. 'Cultures of Belief', *Anthropological Theory* 12 (2012), 448–66.

Malcolm, Norman. 'Anselm's Ontological Arguments', *The Philosophical Review* 69 (1960), 41–62.

Malcolm, Norman. *Wittgenstein: A Religious Point of View?* (London: Routledge, 1993).

Malet, Antoni. 'Isaac Barrow on the Mathematization of Nature: Theological Voluntarism and the Rise of Geometrical Optics', *Journal of the History of Ideas* 58 (1997), 265–87.

Mander, William J. *The Philosophy of John Norris* (Oxford: Oxford University Press, 2008).

Mander, William J. *The Unknowable: A Study in Nineteenth-Century British Metaphysics* (Oxford: Oxford University Press, 2020).

Mantovani, Mattia. 'Herbert of Cherbury, Descartes and Locke on Innate Ideas and Universal Consent', *Journal of Early Modern Studies* 8 (2019), 83–115.

Marcus, R. A. *Saeculum: History and Society in the Theology of Augustine* (Cambridge: Cambridge University Press, 1970).

Marenbon, John. *Pagans and Philosophers: The Problem of Paganism from Augustine to Leibniz* (Princeton: Princeton University Press, 2015).
Marion, Jean-Luc. *In the Self's Place: The Approach of St Augustine*, trans. Jeffrey L. Kosky (Stanford: Stanford University Press, 2012).
Marion, Jean-Luc. *On the Ego and on God: Further Cartesian Questions*, trans. Christina Gschwandtner (New York: Fordham University Press, 2007).
Maritain, Jacques, *Three Reformers: Luther, Descartes, Rousseau* (New York: Charles Scribner, 1950).
Markschies, Christoph. *Kaiserzeitliche Christliche Theologie und ihre Insitutionen: Prolegomena zur einer Geschichte der antiken christlichen Theologie* (Tübingen: Mohr Siebeck, 2007).
Marmura, Michael. 'Al-Ghazālī', in *The Cambridge Companion to Arabic Philosophy*, ed. Peter Adamson and Richard C. Taylor (Cambridge: Cambridge University Press, 2005), pp. 137–54.
Marmura, Michael. 'The *Fortuna* of the *Posterior Analytics* in the Arabic Middle Ages', in *Knowledge and the Sciences in Medieval Philosophy*, 3 vols., ed. M. Asztalos, J. E. Murdoch, and I. Niiniluoto (Helsinki: Acta Philosophica Fennica, 1990), vol. 1, pp. 85–103.
Marrone, Steven. *The Light of Thy Countenance: Science and Knowledge of God in the Thirteenth Century* (Leiden: Brill, 2001).
Marshall, Catherine, Bernard Lightman, and Richard England (eds.). *The Metaphysical Society (1869–1880): Intellectual Life in Mid-Victorian England* (Oxford: Oxford University Press, 2019).
Martinich, A. P. *The Two Gods of Leviathan: Thomas Hobbes on Religion and Politics* (Cambridge: Cambridge University Press, 1992).
Marty, Martin E. 'Luther's Living Legacy', *Christian History* 39 (1993), 51–3.
Matheson, Jonathan. *The Epistemic Significance of Disagreement* (London: Palgrave Macmillan, 2015).
Matthews, Gareth B. *Thought's Ego in Augustine and Descartes* (Ithaca: Cornell University Press, 1992).
Mayer, Johannes. 'Man Is Inclined to His Last End by Nature, though He Cannot Reach It by Nature but Only by Grace: The Principle of the Debate about Nature and Grace in Thomas Aquinas, Thomism and Henri de Lubac', *Angelicum* 88 (2011), 887–939.
McCalla, Arthur. 'The Mennaisian "Catholic Science of Religion": Epistemology and History in Early Nineteenth-Century French Study of Religion', *Method and Theory in the Study of Religion* 21(2009), 285–309.
McCauley, Robert N. and Emma Cohen. 'Cognitive Science and the Naturalness of Religion', *Philosophy Compass* 5 (2020), 779–92.
McCoy, Marina Berzins. 'Eros, Woundedness, and Creativity in Plato's Symposium', in *Wounded Heroes: Vulnerability as a Virtue in Ancient Greek Philosophy and Literature* (Oxford: Oxford University Press, 2013), pp. 115–39.
McGilchrist, Iain. *The Master and His Emissary: The Divided Brain and the Making of the Western World* (New Haven: Yale University Press, 2009).
McGinn, Bernard. *Visions of the End: Apocalyptic Traditions in the Middle Ages* (New York: Columbia University Press, 1979).
McGinn, Colin. 'Can We Solve the Mind-Body Problem?', *Mind* 98 (1989), 349–66.
McGinnis, Jon. 'Avicenna's Naturalised Epistemology and Scientific Method', in *The Unity of Science in the Arabic Tradition*, ed. Shahid Rahman, Tony Street, and Hassan Tahiri (Dordrecht: Springer, 2008), pp. 129–52.

McGinnis, Jon. 'Natural Knowledge in the Arabic Middle Ages', in *Wrestling with Nature: From Omens to Science*, ed. Peter Harrison, Ronald L. Numbers, and Michael H. Shank (Chicago: University of Chicago Press, 2011), pp. 59–82.
McGrath, Alister. *Reformation Thought* (Oxford: Blackwell, 1993).
McGrath, Alister. *Re-Imagining Nature: The Promise of Christian Natural Theology* (Oxford: Wiley Blackwell, 2016).
McGregor, Russell. *Imagined Destinies: Aboriginal Australians and the Doomed Race Theory, 1880–1939* (Melbourne: Melbourne University Press, 1997).
McInerny, Ralph. *Praeambula Fidei: Thomism and the God of the Philosophers* (Washington, DC: Catholic University of America Press, 2006).
McKirahan, Jr., Richard D. 'Aristotle's Subordinate Sciences', *British Journal for the History of Science* 11 (1978), 197–200.
McNeill, John T. *The History and Character of Calvinism* (Oxford: Oxford University Press, 1967).
McPherran, Mark L. 'Socratic Religion', in *The Cambridge Companion to Socrates*, ed. Donald R. Morrison (Cambridge: Cambridge University Press, 2011), pp. 111–37.
Meakins, Felicity and Cassandra Algy, 'Deadly Reckoning: Changes in Gurindji Children's Knowledge of Cardinals', *Australian Journal of Linguistics* 36 (2016), 479–501.
Meakins, Felicity, Caroline Jones, and Cassandra Algy. 'Bilingualism, Language Shift and the Corresponding Expansion of Spatial Cognitive Systems', *Language Sciences* 54 (2016), 1–13.
Menn, Stephen. 'Aristotle's Theology', in *The Oxford Handbook of Aristotle*, ed. Christopher Shields (Oxford: Oxford University Press, 2012), pp. 422–64.
Menn, Stephen. *Descartes and Augustine* (Cambridge: Cambridge University Press, 1998).
Mentzer, Raymond A. 'The Persistence of "Superstition and Idolatry" among Rural French Calvinists', *Church History* 65 (1996), 220–33.
Mesnard, Pierre. 'L'Arbre de la sagesse', *Descartes, Cahiers de Royaumont, Philosophy* II (Paris, 1957), 336–49.
Methuen, Charlotte. 'History and Heresy in the Lutheran Reformation', *Renaissance and Reformation Review* 24 (2022), 3–22.
Mews, Constant J. 'Faith as *Existimatio rerum non apparentium*: Intellect, Imagination and Faith in the Philosophy of Peter Abelard', in *Intellect and Imagination in Medieval Philosophy*, ed. M. C. Pacheco and J. Meirinhos (Turnhout: Brepols, 2006), pp. 915–26.
Michalson, Jr., G. E. 'Lessing, Kierkegaard, and the "Ugly Ditch"', *The Journal of Religion* 59 (1979), 324–34.
Midena, Daniel. 'Wine into Wineskins: The Neuendettelsau Missionaries' Encounter with Language and Myth in New Guinea', in *Savage Worlds: German Encounters Abroad, 1798–1914*, ed. Matthew Fitzpatrick and Peter Monteath (Manchester: Manchester University Press, 2018), pp. 86–104.
Milbank, Alison. *God and the Gothic: Religion, Romance, and Reality in the English Literary Tradition* (Oxford: Oxford University Press, 2018).
Milbank, John. 'Religion, Science, and Magic', in *After Science and Religion: Fresh Perspectives from Philosophy and Theology*, ed. Peter Harrison and John Milbank (Cambridge: Cambridge University Press, 2022), pp. 75–143.
Milbank, John. *The Suspended Middle* (London: SCM, 2005).
Milbank, John. *The Word Made Strange* (Oxford: Blackwell, 1997).

Milbank, John. *Theology and Social Theory: Beyond Secular Reason*, 2nd ed. (Oxford: Blackwell, 2006).
Miller, Fred D. 'Aristotle on Belief and Knowledge', in *Reason and Analysis in Ancient Greek Philosophy*, ed. Georgios Anagnostopoulos and Fred D. Miller (Dordrecht: Springer, 2013), pp. 285–307.
Milton, J. R. 'Laws of Nature', in *The Cambridge History of Seventeenth-Century Philosophy*, 2 vols., ed. Daniel Garber and Michael Ayers (Cambridge: Cambridge University Press, 1998), vol. 1, pp. 680–701.
Mimouni, Simon C. 'Qu'est-ce qu'un "chrétien" aux Ier et IIe siècles? Identité ou conscience?', *Annali di storia dell' esegesi* 267 (2010), 11–34.
Mistry, J. 'Indigenous Knowledges', in *International Encyclopedia of Human Geography*, ed. Rob Kitchin and Nigel Thrift (Amsterdam: Elsevier, 2009), pp. 371–6.
Mjaaland, Marius Timmann (ed.). *The Reformation of Philosophy* (Berlin: Mohr Siebeck, 2020).
Mommsen, Theodore E., 'Petrarch's Conception of the "Dark Ages"', *Speculum* 17 (1942), 226–42.
Mommsen, Theodore E. 'St. Augustine and the Christian Idea of Progress', *Journal of the History of Ideas* 12 (1951), 364–74.
Montner, William. 'Popular Piety in Late Medieval Europe', in *Ritual, Myth and Magic in Early Modern Europe* (Athens: Ohio University Press, 1983), pp. 6–22.
Moon, Paul. 'Missionaries and Māori Language in Nineteenth-Century New Zealand: A Mixed Inheritance', *Journal of Religious History* 43 (2019), 495–510.
Moore, James R. *The Post-Darwinian Controversies* (Cambridge: Cambridge University Press, 1981).
Moore, R. I. 'The Cathar Middle Ages as an Historiographical Problem', in *Christianity and Culture in the Middle Ages: Essays to Honor John Van Engen*, ed. D. C. Mengel and L. Wolverton (Notre Dame: University of Notre Dame Press, 2015), pp. 58–86.
Moore, R. I. 'The Debate of April 2013 in Retrospect', in *Cathars in Question*, ed. A. Sennis (York: York Medieval Press, 2016), pp. 257–73.
Moore, R. I. *The Formation of a Persecuting Society: Authority and Deviance in Western Europe, 950–1250* (Oxford: Blackwell, 2007).
Moore, R. I. *The War on Heresy: Faith and Power in Medieval Europe* (London: Profile Books, 2012).
Moore, Rosemary. 'Late Seventeenth-Century Quakerism and the Miraculous: A New Look at George Fox's "*Book of Miracles*"', in *Signs, Wonders, Miracles: Representations of Divine Power in the Life of the Church*, ed. Kate Cooper and Jeremy Gregory (Woodbridge: Boydell, 2005), pp. 335–44.
Morgan, Theresa. *Roman Faith and Christian Faith: Pistis and Fides in the Early Roman Empire and Early Churches* (Oxford: Oxford University Press, 2015).
Mori, Gianluca. *Bayle philosophe* (Paris: Champion, 1999).
Mori, Gianluca. *Early Modern Atheism from Spinoza to D'Holbach* (Liverpool: Liverpool University Press, 2021).
Mori, Gianluca. 'Pierre Bayle on Scepticism and "Common Notions"', in *The Return of Scepticism: From Hobbes and Descartes to Bayle*, ed. Gianni Paganini (Dordrecht: Kluwer, 2003), pp. 393–413.
Moriarty, Michael. *Disguised Vices: Theories of Virtue in Early Modern French Thought* (Oxford: Oxford University Press, 2011).

Morris, William Edward and Charlotte R. Brown, 'David Hume', in *The Stanford Encyclopedia of Philosophy* (Spring 2021 Edition), ed. Edward N. Zalta. https://plato.stanford.edu/archives/spr2021/entries/hume/
Morrison, Kenneth, et al. 'Native American Religions', *Religion* 22, no. 3 (1992), 201–86.
Mosser, Carl. 'The Greatest Possible Blessing: Calvin and Deification', *Scottish Journal of Theology* 55 (2002), 36–57.
Moulin, Isabelle and David Twetten, 'Causality and Emanation in Albert', in *A Companion to Albert the Great*, ed. Irven M. Resnick (Leiden: Brill 2013), pp. 694–721.
Muchembled, Robert. *Popular Culture and Elite Culture in France: 1400–1750*, trans. Lydia Cochcrane (Baton Rouge: Louisiana State University Press, 1985).
Mueller, Ian. 'Aristotle on Geometrical Objects', *Archiv für Geschichte der Philosophie* 52 (1970), 156–71.
Mulcahy, Bernard. *Aquinas's Notion of Pure Nature and the Christian Integralism of Henri de Lubac* (New York: Peter Lang, 2011).
Mulhall, Stephen. *On Being in the World: Wittgenstein and Heidegger on Seeing Aspects* (London: Routledge, 1993).
Muller, Richard A. *Dictionary of Latin and Greek Theological Terms*, 2nd ed. (Grand Rapids: Baker Books, 2017).
Muller, Richard A. '*Fides* and *Cognitio* in Relation to the Problem of Intellect and Will in the Theology of John Calvin', *Calvin Theological Journal* 25 (1990), 207–24.
Muller, Richard A. 'Not Scotist: Understandings of Being, Univocity, and Analogy in Early-Modern Reformed Thought', *Reformation and Renaissance Review* 14 (2012), 127–50.
Muller, Richard A. *Post-Reformation Reformed Dogmatics*, 4 vols. (Grand Rapids: Baker, 2005).
Mulligan, Lotte. '"Reason," "Right Reason," and "Revelation" in Mid-Seventeenth-Century England', in *Occult and Scientific Mentalities in the Renaissance*, ed. Brian Vickers (Cambridge: Cambridge University Press, 1984), pp. 375–401.
Muramoto, Osamu and Walter G. Englert, 'Socrates and Temporal Lobe Epilepsy', *Epilepsia* 47 (2006), 652–4.
Murphy, B. G. 'Thomas Huxley and His New Reformation', PhD thesis, Northern Illinois University, 1973.
Murphy, J. H. *The Preternatural Gifts of our First Parents in the Fathers of the First Four Centuries* (Maynooth: St Patrick's College, 1947).
Murray, Andrew. 'The Spiritual and Supernatural according to Thomas Aquinas'. www.cis.catholic.edu.au/Files/Murray-SpiritualSupernatural.pdf, accessed 21 February 2018.
Murray, Michael J. 'Scientific Explanations of Religion and the Justification of Religious Belief', in *The Believing Primate: Scientific, Philosophical, and Theological Reflections on the Origin of Religion*, ed. Jeffrey Schloss and Michael Murray (Oxford: Oxford University Press, 2009), pp. 168–79.
Musto, Marcello. 'Alienation Redux: Marxian Perspectives', in *Karl Marx's Writings on Alienation* ed. Marcello Musto (London: Palgrave Macmillan, 2021), pp. 3–48.
Naddaf, Gerard. *The Greek Concept of Nature* (Albany, NY: SUNY Press, 2005).
Needham, Rodney. *Belief, Language and Experience* (Oxford: Blackwell, 1972).
Needham, Rodney. *Circumstantial Deliveries* (Berkeley: University of California Press, 1982).

Nehamas, Alexander. *The Art of Living: Socratic Reflections from Plato to Foucault* (Berkeley: University of California Press, 1998).
Nelson, Leonard. 'The Impossibility of the "Theory of Knowledge"', in *Socratic Method and Critical Philosophy, Selected Essays*, trans. T. Brown, III (New York: Dover, 1965).
Nelson, Robert H. *Reaching for Heaven on Earth: The Theological Meaning of Economics* (Savage, MD: Rowman & Littlefield, 1991).
Neufeld, Dietmar. *Reconceiving Texts as Speech Acts: An Analysis of John 1* (Leiden: Brill, 1994).
Newman, William R. 'Art, Nature and Experiment among Some Aristotelian Alchemists', in *Texts and Contexts in Ancient and Medieval Science: Studies on the Occasion of John E. Murdoch's Seventieth Birthday*, ed. E. Sylla and M. McVaugh (Leiden: Brill, 1997), pp. 305–17.
Newman, William R. *Atoms and Alchemy: Chymistry and the Experimental Origins of the Scientific Revolution* (Chicago: University of Chicago Press, 2006).
Newman, William R. 'Spirits in the Laboratory: Some Helmontian Collaborators of Robert Boyle', in *For the Sake of Learning: Essays in Honor of Anthony Grafton*, ed. Ann Blair and Anja-Silvia Goeing (Leiden: Brill, 2016), pp. 621–40.
Newman, William R. and Lawrence M. Principe. *Alchemy Tried in the Fire* (Chicago: University of Chicago Press, 2002).
Nichols, Ryan and Robert Callergård. 'Thomas Reid on Reidian Belief Forming Faculties', *The Modern Schoolman* 88 (2011), 329–47.
Noe, Alfred (ed.). *Der Philhellenismus in der westeuropäischen Literatur 1780–1830* (Amsterdam: Rodopi, 1994).
Nolan, Lawrence. 'The Ontological Argument as an Exercise in Cartesian Therapy', *Canadian Journal of Philosophy* 35 (2005), 521–62.
Nongbri, Brent. *Before Religion: A History of a Modern Concept* (New Haven: Yale University Press, 2013).
Norton, David Fate. 'The Myth of British Empiricism', *History of European Ideas* 1 (1981), 331–44.
Numbers, Ronald L. and Kostas Kampourakis (eds.). *Newton's Apple and Other Myths about Science* (Cambridge, MA: Harvard University Press, 2015).
Nuovo, Victor. *John Locke: The Philosopher as Christian Virtuoso* (Oxford: Oxford University Press, 2017).
O'Briant, Walter H. 'Is There an Argument "Consensus Gentium"?', *International Journal for Philosophy of Religion* 18 (1985), 73–9.
O'Connell, Robert J. 'The Plotinian Fall of the Soul in St. Augustine', *Traditio* 19 (1963), 1–35.
O'Day, Rosemary. 'The Clergy of the Church of England', in *The Professions in Early Modern England*, ed. Wilfred Prest (London: Routledge, 1987), pp. 25–63.
O'Madagain, Cathal. 'Outsourcing Concepts: Social Externalism, the Extended Mind, and the Expansion of Our Epistemic Capacity', in *Socially Extended Epistemology*, ed. J. Adam Carter, Andy Clark, Jesper Kallestrup, S. Orestis Palermos, and Duncan Pritchard (Oxford: Oxford University Press, 2018), pp. 24–35.
O'Rourke, Fran. 'The Triplex Via of Naming God', *The Review of Metaphysics* 69 (2016), 519–54.
Oakes, Peter. '*Pistis* as Relational Way of Life in Galatians', *Journal for the Study of the New Testament* 40 (2018), 255–75.

Oakley, Francis. 'Christian Theology and the Newtonian Science: The Rise of the Concept of Laws of Nature', *Church History* 30 (1961), 433–57.
Oakley, Francis. 'Voluntarist Theology and Early-Modern Science: The Matter of the Divine Power, Absolute and Ordained', *History of Science* 56 (2018), 72–96.
Obbink, Dirk. 'What All Men Believe – Must Be True: Common Conceptions and *consensio omnium* in Aristotle and Hellenistic Philosophy', *Oxford Studies in Ancient Philosophy* 10 (1992), 193–231.
Oberman, Heiko A. 'Headwaters of the Reformation', in *The Dawn of the Reformation* (Edinburgh: T&T Clark, 1986), pp. 39–83.
Oberman, Heiko A. *The Impact of the Reformation* (Grand Rapids: Eerdmans, 1994).
Olivo, Giles. 'L'efficience en cause: Suárez, Descartes et la question de la causalité', in *Descartes et le Moyen Âge*, ed. Joël Biard and Roshdi Rashed (Paris: Vrin, 1997), pp. 94–102.
Ollman, Bertell. *Alienation* (Cambridge: Cambridge University Press, 1971).
Onians, R. B. *The Origins of European Thought: About the Body, the Mind, the Soul, the World, Time and Fate* (Cambridge: Cambridge University Press, 1951).
Osborn, Eric. 'Arguments for Faith in Clement of Alexandria', *Vigiliae Christianae* 48 (1994), 1–24.
Osiander, Andreas. 'Sovereignty, International Relations, and the Westphalian Myth', *International Organization* 55 (2001), 251–87.
Osler, Margaret J. *Divine Will and the Mechanical Philosophy: Gassendi and Descartes on Contingency and Necessity in the Created World* (Cambridge: Cambridge University Press, 1994).
Osler, Margaret J. 'Fortune, Fate, and Divination: Gassendi's Voluntarist Theology and the Baptism of Epicureanism', in *Atoms, Pneuma, and Tranquillity: Epicurean and Stoic Themes in European Thought*, ed. Margaret Osler (Cambridge: Cambridge University Press, 1991), pp. 155–74.
Ospovat, Dov. 'Darwin after Malthus', *Journal of the History of Biology* 12 (1979), 211–30.
Ott, W. and L. Patton (eds.). *Laws of Nature* (Oxford: Oxford University Press, 2018).
Otten, Willemien. 'Religion as *Excitatio Mentis*: A Case for Theology as a Humanist Discipline', in *Essays Offered to Arjo Vanderjagt on the Occasion of His Sixtieth Birthday*, ed. Z. R. W. M. von Martels and A. MacDonald (Leiden: Brill, 2009), pp. 60–73.
Pabst, Adrian. *Metaphysics: The Invention of Hierarchy* (Grand Rapids: Eerdmans, 2012).
Pace, Michael and Daniel J. McLaughlin. 'Judaeo-Christian Faith as Trust and Loyalty', *Religious Studies* 58 (2022), 30–60.
Pacho, Julián, 'The Universe as Cosmos: On the Ontology of the Greek World Image', in *Concepts of Nature*, ed. Hans Ulrich Vogel and Günter Dux (Leiden: Brill, 2010), pp. 136–59.
Palmer, John A. 'Aristotle on Ancient Theologians', *Apeiron* 33 (2000), 181–205.
Papineau, David. 'Naturalism', in *The Stanford Encyclopedia of Philosophy* (Summer 2020 Edition), ed. Edward N. Zalta. https://plato.stanford.edu/archives/sum2020/entries/naturalism/
Park, Peter K. J. 'Africa, Asia, and the History of Philosophy', *Journal of World Philosophies* 2 (2017), 48–59.
Park, Peter K. J. *Africa, Asia, and the History of Philosophy: Racism and the Formation of the Philosophical Canon, 1780–1830* (Albany, NY: SUNY Press, 2013).
Pasnau, Robert. *After Certainty: A History of Our Epistemic Ideals and Illusions* (Oxford: Oxford University Press, 2017).

Pasnau, Robert. 'Divine Illumination', in *The Stanford Encyclopedia of Philosophy* (Spring 2020 Edition), Edward N. Zalta (ed.). https://plato.stanford.edu/archives/spr2020/entries/illumination/
Pasnau, Robert. 'Henry of Ghent and the Twilight of Divine Illumination', *Review of Metaphysics* 49 (1995), 49–75.
Pasnau, Robert. 'The Latin Aristotle', in *The Oxford Handbook of Aristotle*, ed. Christopher Shields (Oxford: Oxford University Press, 2012), pp. 665–89.
Passmore, John. *The Perfectibility of Man* (Indianapolis: Liberty Fund, 2000).
Pásztori-Kupán, István. *Theodoret of Cyrus* (London: Routledge, 2006).
Pathak, R. P. *Philosophical and Sociological Perspectives of Education* (New Delhi: Atlantic Books, 2007).
Pécharman, Martine. 'Pascal's Rejection of Natural Theology', in *Physico-Theology: Religion and Science in Europe 1650–1750*, ed. Ann Blair and Kaspar von Greyerz (Baltimore: Johns Hopkins University Press, 2020), pp. 141–53.
Pegg, Mark Gregory. *The Corruption of Angels: The Great Inquisition of 1245–1246* (Princeton: Princeton University Press, 2001).
Pegg, Mark Gregory. 'The Paradigm of Catharism: or, the Historians' Illusion', in *Cathars in Question*, ed. Antonio Sennis (York: York Medieval Press, 2016), pp. 21–54.
Pelikan, Jaroslav. *The Spirit of Medieval Theology* (Toronto: Pontifical Institute of Medieval Studies, 1985).
Penman, Leigh T. I. *Hope and Heresy: The Problem of Chiliasm in Confessional Lutheranism, 1570–1630* (Dordrecht: Springer, 2019).
Penn, Julia M. *Linguistic Relativity versus Innate Ideas: The Origins of the Sapir-Whorf Hypothesis in German Thought* (The Hague: Januae Linguarum, ser. minor 120, 1972).
Perälä, Mika. 'Affirmation and Denial in Aristotle's *De interpretatione*', *Topoi* 39 (2020), 645–56.
Perler, D. and U. Rudolph, *Occasionalismus: Theorien der Kausalität in arabisch-islamischen und im europäischen Denken* (Göttingen: Vandenhoeck & Ruprecht, 2000).
Pfau, Thomas. *Minding the Modern: Human Agency, Intellectual Traditions, and Responsible Knowledge* (Notre Dame: University of Notre Dame Press, 2013).
Phillips, J. 'Stoic "Common Notions" in Plotinus', *Dionysius* 11 (1987), 40–1.
Piaia, G. 'The Histories of Philosophy in France in the Age of Descartes', in *Models of the History of Philosophy*, ed. G. Santinello and G. Piaia (Dordrecht: Springer, 2010), pp. 3–91.
Pickstock, Catherine. *After Writing: On the Liturgical Consummation of Philosophy* (London: Routledge, 1998).
Pickstock, Catherine. 'Modernity and Scholasticism: A Critique of Recent Invocations of Univocity', *Antonianum* 78 (2003), 3–47.
Pinker, Steven. *Enlightenment Now* (New York: Viking, 2018).
Pinot, Virgile. *La Chine et la formation de l'esprit philosophique en France (1640–1740)* (Geneva: Slatkine Reprints, 1971).
Plantinga, Alvin. 'Reason and Belief in God', in *Faith and Rationality*, ed. Alvin Plantinga and Nicholas Wolterstorff (Notre Dame: University of Notre Dame Press, 1983), pp. 16–93.
Plantinga, Alvin. *Warrant and Proper Function* (Oxford: Oxford University Press, 1993).
Plantinga, Alvin. *Warrant: The Current Debate* (Oxford: Oxford University Press, 1993).
Plantinga, Alvin. *Warranted Christian Belief* (New York: Oxford University Press, 2000).

Plantinga, Alvin. *Where the Conflict Really Lies: Science, Religion, and Naturalism* (Oxford: Oxford University Press, 2011).
Plantinga, Alvin and Michael Tooley. *Knowledge of God* (Oxford: Blackwell, 2008).
Plantinga, Alvin and Nicholas Wolterstorff (eds.). *Faith and Rationality* (Notre Dame: University of Notre Dame Press, 1983).
Platnauer, Maurice. 'Greek Colour-Perception', *Classical Quarterly* 15 (1921), 153–62.
Platt, John. *Reformed Thought and Scholasticism* (Leiden: Brill, 1982).
Pocock, J. G. A. *Barbarism and Religion*, 6 vols. (Cambridge: Cambridge University Press, 1999–2015).
Pohlig, Matthias. *Zwischen Gelehrsamkeit und konfessioneller Identitätsstiftung: Lutherische Kirchen- und Universalgeschichtsschreibung 1546–1617* (Tübingen: Mohr Siebeck, 2007).
Popper, Karl. *Conjectures and Refutations* (London: Routledge & Kegan Paul, 1963).
Popper, Karl. *The Logic of Scientific Discovery* (London: Routledge, 2002).
Portin, Fredrik. 'Liturgies in a Plural Age: The Concept of Liturgy in the Works of William T. Cavanaugh and James K. A. Smith', *Studia Liturgica* 49 (2019), 122–37.
Pouillon, Jean. *Le Cru et le Su* (Paris: Éditions du Seuil, 1993).
Preller, Victor. *Divine Science and the Science of God: A Reformulation of Thomas Aquinas* (Princeton: Princeton University Press, 1967).
Price, H. H. *Belief* (London: George Allen & Unwin, 1969).
Price, Huw. 'Naturalism without Representationalism', in *Naturalism in Question*, ed. Mario De Caro and David Macarthur (Cambridge, MA: Harvard University Press, 2004), pp. 71–88.
Price, Simon. *Religions of the Ancient Greeks* (Cambridge: Cambridge University Press, 1999).
Price, Simon. *Rituals and Power: The Roman Imperial Cult in Asia Minor* (Cambridge: Cambridge University Press, 1984).
Primack, Brian A. 'Social Media Use and Perceived Social Isolation among Young Adults in the U.S.', *American Journal of Preventative Medicine* 53 (2017), 1–8.
Principe, W. H. 'Preternatural', *New Catholic Encyclopedia*, 2nd ed. (Detroit: Gale, 2003), vol. 11, pp. 686–7.
Pullen, J. M. 'Malthus's Theological Ideas and Their Influence on His Principle of Population', *History of Political Economy* 13 (1981), 39–54.
Putnam, Hilary. 'Meaning and Reference', *The Journal of Philosophy* 70 (1973), 699–711.
Putnam, Hilary. *Pragmatism: An Open Question* (Oxford: Wiley Blackwell, 1995).
Quine, W. V. *Theories and Things* (Cambridge, MA: Harvard University Press, 1981).
Quine, W. V. *Word and Object* (Cambridge, MA: MIT Press, 1960).
Radde-Gallwitz, Andrew. *Basil of Caesarea, Gregory of Nyssa, and the Transformation of Divine Simplicity* (Oxford: Oxford University Press, 2009).
Rapport, Nigel and Joanna Overing. *Social and Cultural Anthropology: The Key Concepts* (London: Routledge, 2000).
Rea, Michael. 'Naturalism and Material Objects', in *Naturalism: A Critical Analysis*, ed. William L. Craig and J. P. Moreland (London: Routledge, 2016), pp. 110–32.
Reddoch, M. J. 'Enigmatic Dreams and Onirocritical Skill in De somniis 2', *The Studia Philonica Annual* 25 (2013), 1–16.
Reese, Bryan C. 'Aristotle on Divine and Human Contemplation', *Ergo* 7/4 (2020). https://doi.org/10.3998/ergo.12405314.0007.004, accessed 27 April 2023.

Reeves, Marjorie. 'English Apocalyptic Thinkers, c.1540–1620', in *Storia e Figure dell'Apocalisse fra '500 e '600*, ed. R. Rusconi. Atti del 4rò congress internazionale di studi Gioachimiti (Rome, Italy, 1996), pp. 259–73.

Reeves, Marjorie. 'History and Eschatology: Medieval and Early Protestant Thought in Some English and Scottish Writings', *Medievalia et Humanistica* 4 (1973), 106–10.

Reeves, Marjorie. *Joachim of Fiore and the Prophetic Future* (Stroud: Sutton, 1999).

Reid, Jasper. 'The Common Consent Argument from Herbert to Hume', *Journal of the History of Philosophy* 53 (2015), 401–33.

Reinhardt, Tobias. 'On Endoxa in Aristotle's Topics', in *Rheinisches Museum für Philologie*, Neue Folge, 158. Bd., H. 3/4 (2015), pp. 225–46.

Reydams-Schils, Gretchen. '"Becoming like God" in Platonism and Stoicism', in *From Stoicism to Platonism: The Development of Philosophy, 100 BCE–100 CE*, ed. T. Engberg-Pedersen (Cambridge: Cambridge University Press, 2017), pp. 142–58.

Riaudel, Olivier. '*Fides qua creditur et Fides quae creditur*: Retour sur une distinction qui n'est pas chez Augustin', *Revue théologique de Louvain* 43 (2012), 169–94.

Ridings, Daniel. *The Attic Moses: The Dependency Theme in Some Early Christian Writers* (Göteborg: Acta Universitatis Gothoburgensis, 1995).

Riedel, Matthias. 'Longing for the Third Age: Revolutionary Joachism, Communism and National Socialism', in *A Companion to Joachim of Fiore*, ed. Matthias Riedel (Leiden: Brill, 2018), pp. 267–318.

Rist, John M. *Augustine: Ancient Thought Baptized* (Cambridge: Cambridge University Press, 1994).

Rist, John M. 'Plotinus and the *Daimonion* of Socrates', *Phoenix* 17 (1963), 13–24.

Ristuccia, Nathan. *Christianization and Commonwealth in Early Medieval Europe: A Ritual Interpretation* (Oxford: Oxford University Press, 2018).

Ristuccia, Nathan. '*Lex*: A Study on Medieval Terminology for Religion', *Journal of Religious History* 43 (2019), 532–48.

Ritchie, Sarah Lane. 'Integrated Physicality and the Absence of God: Spiritual Technologies in Theological Context', *Modern Theology* 37 (2021), 296–315.

Rivett, Sarah. *Unscripted America: Indigenous Languages and the Origins of a Literary Nature* (Oxford: Oxford University Press, 2017).

Robins, R. H. *A Short History of Linguistics*, 4th ed. (London: Routledge, 1997).

Rocke, Alan J. *Image and Reality: Kekulé, Kopp, and the Scientific Imagination* (Chicago: University of Chicago Press, 2010).

Rodrigues, Marilyn. 'Meet the Atheist Scientist Who Believes in Miracles', *The Catholic Weekly*, 2 March 2017.

Roger, Jacques. *The Life Sciences in Eighteenth-Century French Thought*, ed. Keith R. Benson, trans. Robert Ellrich (Stanford: Stanford University Press, 1998).

Rohrmoser, Günter. *Emanzipation und Freiheit* (Munich: Wilhelm Goldmann Verlag, 1970).

Roover, Jakob. 'Incurably Religious? Consensus Gentium and the Cultural Universality of Religion', *Numen* 61 (2014), 5–32.

Rorty, Amélie O. 'The Structure of Descartes' *Meditations*', in *Essays on Descartes' Meditations*, ed. Amélie O. Rorty (Berkeley: University of California Press, 1986), pp. 1–20.

Rorty, Richard. 'Naturalism and Quietism', in *Naturalism and Normativity*, ed. Mario De Caro and David Macarthur (New York: Columbia University Press, 2010), pp. 55–68.

Rorty, Richard. *Philosophy and the Mirror of Nature* (Princeton: Princeton University Press, 1981).
Rosenberg, Randall S. *The Givenness of Desire: Concrete Subjectivity and the Natural Desire to See God* (Toronto: University of Toronto Press, 2017).
Rosenblatt, Helena. *Liberal Values: Benjamin Constant and the Politics of Religion* (Cambridge: Cambridge University Press, 2008).
Rosman, Abraham, Paula G. Rubel, and Maxine Weisgrau, *The Tapestry of Culture: An Introduction to Cultural Anthropology* (Lanham: Alta Mira, 2009).
Ross, Anne. 'Challenging Metanarratives: The Past Lives in the Present', *Archaeology in Oceania* 55 (2020), 65–71.
Rothschild, Emma. *Economic Sentiments: Adam Smith, Condorcet, and the Enlightenment* (Cambridge, MA: Harvard University Press, 2001).
Rovelli, Carlo. *Anaximander and the Nature of Science* (London: Penguin, 2023).
Rowe, C. Kavin. *One True Life: The Stoics and Early Christians as Rival Traditions* (New Haven: Yale University Press, 2015).
Rubidge, Bradley. 'Descartes's *Meditations* and Devotional Meditations', *Journal of the History of Ideas* 51 (1990), 27–49.
Rue, Rachel. 'The Philosopher in Flight: The Digression in Plato's *Theaetetus*', *Oxford Studies in Ancient Philosophy* 11 (1993), 71–100.
Ruel, Malcolm. 'Christians as Believers', in *Religious Organization and Religious Experience*, ed. J. Davis (London: Academic Press, 1982), pp. 9–31.
Ruse, Michael. 'Removing God from Biology', in *Science without God? Historical Perspectives on Scientific Naturalism*, ed. Peter Harrison and Jon H. Roberts (Oxford: Oxford University Press, 2019), pp. 130–46.
Russell, Daniel C. 'Virtue as "Likeness to God" in Plato and Seneca', *Journal of the History of Philosophy* 44 (2004), 241–60.
Russell, John Burton. *Inventing the Flat Earth: Columbus and Modern Historians* (New York: Praeger, 1991).
Russell, Norman. *The Doctrine of Deification in the Greek Patristic Tradition* (New York: Oxford University Press, 2004).
Russell, Paul. *The Riddle of Hume's Treatise: Skepticism, Naturalism, and Irreligion* (Oxford: Oxford University Press, 2008).
Ryrie, Alec. *Unbelievers: An Emotional History of Doubt* (Cambridge, MA: Belknap Press, 2019).
Saarinen, Risto. 'Nature and Supernature', *Religion Past and Present* 9 (2010), 68–9.
Saastamoinen, Kari. *The Morality of Fallen Man: Samuel Pufendorf on Natural Law* (Helsinki: Societas Historica Finlandiae, 1995).
Sabra, A. I. '*Kalam* Atomism as an Alternative Philosophy to Hellenizing *Falsafa*', in *Arabic Theology, Arabic Philosophy: From the Many to the One – Essays in Celebration of Richard M. Frank*, ed. J. E. Montgomery (Leuven: Peeters, 2006), pp. 199–272.
Sagan, Carl. *Cosmos* (New York: Ballantine Books, 2013).
Sahlins, Marshall. *The New Science of the Enchanted Universe: An Anthropology of Most of Humanity* (Princeton: Princeton University Press, 2022).
Sapir, Edward. *Culture, Language and Personality: Selected Essays*, ed. David G. Mandelbaum (Berkeley: University of California Press, 1962).
Sassi, Maria Michela. *The Beginnings of Philosophy in Greece* (Princeton: Princeton University Press, 2018).

Sassi, Maria Michela. 'The Sea was Never Blue', *Aeon Magazine*, 31 July 2017. https://aeon.co/essays/can-we-hope-to-understand-how-the-greeks-saw-their-world, accessed 30 November 2020.

Sayre, Gordon. *Les Sauvages Américains: Representations of Native Americans in French and English Colonial Literature* (Chapel Hill: University of North Carolina Press, 1997).

Schaller, J. J. 'Performative Language Theory: An Exercise in the Analysis of Ritual', *Worship* 62 (1988), 415–32.

Schibli, Hermann S. *Hierocles of Alexandria* (Oxford: Oxford University Press, 2002).

Schiefsky, Mark J. 'Art and Nature in Ancient Mechanics', in *The Artificial and the Natural: An Evolving Polarity*, ed. B. Bensaude-Vincent and W. R. Newman (Cambridge, MA: MIT Press, 2007), pp. 67–108.

Schilson, Arno. *Geschichte im Horizont der Vorsehung: G. E. Lessings Beitrag zu einer Theologie der Geschichte* (Mainz: Matthias-Grünewald-Verlag, 1974).

Schliesser, Eric. 'On Aristotle's Cave', *Digressions&Impressions*, 18 January 2019. https://digressionsnimpressions.typepad.com/digressionsimpressions/2019/01/on-aristotles-cave-on-platos-cave-via-ahh-yes-cicero.html, accessed 19 January 2019.

Schloss, Jeffrey and Michael Murray (eds.). *The Believing Primate: Scientific, Philosophical, and Theological Reflections on the Origin of Religion* (Oxford: Oxford University Press, 2009).

Schluchter, Wolfgang. *The Rise of Western Rationalism: Max Weber's Developmental History*, trans. Guenther Roth (Berkeley: University of California Press, 1981).

Schmaltz, Tad. *Early Modern Cartesianisms* (Oxford: Oxford University Press, 2017).

Schmid, Stephan. 'Finality without Final Causes? – Suárez's Account of Natural Teleology', *Ergo* 2 (2016). https://doi.org/10.3998/ergo.12405314.0002.016, accessed 23 November 2023.

Schmidt, Mario. 'Godfrey Lienhardt as a Skeptic; or, Anthropology as Conceptual Puzzle-Solving', *HAU: Journal of Ethnographic Theory* 7 (2017), 351–75.

Schmidt-Hofner, Sebastian. 'Plato and the Theodosian Code', *Early Medieval Europe* 7 (2019), 35–60.

Schmitt, Carl. *Political Theology: Four Chapters on the Concept of Sovereignty* (Chicago: University of Chicago Press, 2005).

Schmutz, Jacob. 'The Medieval Doctrine of Causality and the Theology of Pure Nature (13th to 17th Centuries)', in *Surnaturel: A Controversy at the Heart of Twentieth-Century Thomistic Thought*, ed. Serge-Thomas Bonino, O.P., trans. Robert Williams, trans. rev. Matthew Levering (Ave Maria, FL: Sapientia Press of Ave Maria University, 2009), pp. 203–50.

Schneewind, Jerome B. 'Philosophical Ideas of Charity: Some Historical Reflections', in *Giving: Western Ideas of Philanthropy*, ed. Jerome B. Schneewind (Bloomington: Indiana University Press, 1996), pp. 54–75.

Schneewind, Jerome B. 'The Misfortunes of Virtue', in *Virtue Ethics*, ed. Roger Crisp and Michael Slote (Oxford: Oxford University Press, 1997), pp. 178–200.

Scholten, C. *Antike Naturphilosophie und christliche Kosmologie in der Schrift "De opificio mundi" des Johannes Philoponos* (Berlin: De Gruyter, 1996).

Schott, J. M. 'Founding Platonopolis: The Platonic πολιτεία in Eusebius, Porphyry, and Iamblichus', *Journal of Early Christian Studies* 11 (2003), 501–31.

Schrenk, G. *Gottesreich und Bund im älteren Protestantismus, vornehmlich bei Johannes Coccejus* (Basel: Brunnen-Verlag, 1985).

Schulz, Michael. 'Natural Knowledge of God in Early American Protestant and Catholic Theology', in *Philosophy of Religion in Latin America and Europe*, ed. Michael Schulz and Roberto Hofmeister Pich (Göttingen: Bonn University Press, 2020), pp. 51–74.

Schumacher, Lydia. *Divine Illumination: The History and Future of Augustine's Theory of Knowledge* (Oxford: Wiley Blackwell, 2011).

Schumacher, Lydia. 'The Lost Legacy of Anselm's Argument: Re-thinking the Purpose for the Proofs of the Existence of God', *Modern Theology* 27 (2011), 87–101.

Schwartz, Seth. 'How Many Judaisms Were There? A Critique of Neusner and Smith on Definition and Mason and Boyarin on Categorization', *Journal of Ancient Judaism* 2 (2011), 208–38.

Schwarz, Reinhard. 'Die Wahrheit der Geschichte im Verständnis der Wittenberger Reformation', *Zeitschrift für Theologie und Kirche* 76 (1979), 159–90.

Scott, Allan. *Origen and the Life of the Stars* (Oxford: Clarendon Press, 1994).

Scott, Michael W. 'The Anthropology of Ontology (Religious Science?)', *Journal of the Royal Anthropological Institute* 19 (2013), 859–72.

Searle, John. 'Contemporary Philosophy in the United States', in *The Blackwell Companion to Philosophy*, ed. N. Bunnin and E. P. Tsui-James (Oxford: Blackwell, 1996), pp. 1–24.

Seckler, Max. *Instinkt und Glaubenswille nach Thomas von Aquin* (Mainz: Matthias-Grünewald, 1961).

Secord, James A. *Victorian Sensation: The Extraordinary Publication, Reception, and Secret Authorship of Vestiges of the Natural History of Creation* (Chicago: University of Chicago Press, 2001).

Sedley, David. *Creationism and Its Critics in Antiquity* (Berkeley: University of California Press, 2007).

Sedley, David. 'The Ideal of Godlikeness', in *Plato 2: Ethics, Politics, Religion, and the Soul*, ed. Gail Fine (Oxford: Oxford University Press, 1999), pp. 309–28.

Segev, Mor. 'Aristotle on the Intellectual Achievements of Foreign Civilizations', in *Foreign Influences: The Circulation of Knowledge in Antiquity*, ed. Benoît Castelnérac, Luca Gili, and Laetitia Monteils-Laeng (Turnhout: Brepols, 2022).

Seidentop, Larry. *Inventing the Individual* (Cambridge, MA: Belknap Press, 2014).

Sellars, Wilfrid. *Empiricism and the Philosophy of Mind* (Cambridge, MA: Harvard University Press, 1997).

Sellars, John. *The Art of Living: The Stoics on the Nature and Function of Philosophy* (Aldershot: Ashgate, 2003).

Sellier, Anne-Laure, Irene Scopelliti, and Carey K. Morewedge. 'Debiasing Training Improves Decision Making in the Field', *Psychological Science* 30 (2019), 1371–9.

Sepper, Dennis. 'The Texture of Thought: Why Descartes' *Meditationes* Is Meditational, and Why It Matters', in *Descartes' Natural Philosophy*, ed. Stephen Gaukroger, John Schuster, and John Sutton (London: Routledge, 2000), pp. 736–50.

Serjeantson, Richard. 'Herbert of Cherbury before Deism: The Early Reception of the *De veritate*', *The Seventeenth Century* 16 (2001), 217–38.

Sessions, William Lad. *The Concept of Faith: A Philosophical Investigation* (Ithaca: Cornell University Press, 1994).

Shagan, Ethan H. *The Birth of Modern Belief: Faith and Judgment from the Middle Ages to the Enlightenment* (Princeton: Princeton University Press, 2018).

Shank, J. B. 'Between Isaac Newton and Enlightenment Newtonianism', in *Science without God? Historical Perspectives on Scientific Naturalism*, ed. Peter Harrison and Jon H. Roberts (Oxford: Oxford University Press, 2019), pp. 77–96.

Shank, J. B. *The Newton Wars and the Beginning of the French Enlightenment* (Chicago: University of Chicago Press, 2008).

Shank, Michael J. 'Naturalist Tendencies in Medieval Science', in *Science without God? Historical Perspectives on Scientific Naturalism*, ed. Peter Harrison and Jon H. Roberts (Oxford: Oxford University Press, 2019), pp. 37–57.

Shapin, Steven. *A Social History of Truth: Science and Civility in Seventeenth-Century England* (Chicago: University of Chicago Press, 1994).

Shapin, Steven. 'The Invisible Technician', *American Scientist* 77 (1989), 554–63.

Shapiro, Barbara J. *Probability and Certainty in Seventeenth-Century England* (Princeton: Princeton University Press, 1983).

Sharpes, Donald K. *The Evolution of the Social Sciences* (Lanham: Lexington Books, 2009).

Shaw, David Gary. 'Modernity between Us and Them: The Place of Religion within History', *History and Theory* 45 (2006), 1–9.

Shaw, Jane. *Miracles in Enlightenment England* (New Haven: Yale University Press, 2006).

Sheehan, Jonathan. 'When Was Disenchantment? History and the Secular Age', in *Varieties of Secularism in a Secular Age*, ed. Jonathan VanAntwerpen, Craig Calhoun, and Michael Warner (Cambridge, MA: Harvard University Press, 2010), pp. 217–42.

Sheehan, Jonathan and Dror Wahrman. *Invisible Hands: Self-Organization and the Eighteenth Century* (Chicago: University of Chicago Press, 2015).

Sheppard, Kenneth. *Anti-Atheism in Early Modern England 1580–1720* (Leiden: Brill, 2015).

Shogimen, Takashi. 'Re-thinking Heresy as a Category of Analysis', *Journal of the American Academy of Religion* 88 (2020), 726–48.

Shook, John R. 'Are People Born to Be Believers, or Are Gods Born to Be Believed?', *Method & Theory in the Study of Religion* 29 (2017), 353–73.

Shook, John R. and Paul Kurtz (eds.). *The Future of Naturalism* (Buffalo: Prometheus Books, 2009).

Shortall, Sarah. 'From the Three Bodies of Christ to the King's Two Bodies: The Theological Origins of Secularization', *Modern Intellectual History* 20 (2023), 785–807.

Shorter, David. 'Binary Thinking and the Study of Yoeme Indian Lutu'uria/Truth', *Anthropological Forum* 13 (2003), 195–203.

Shriner, Susan E. *The Theatre of His Glory: Nature and the Natural Order in the Thought of John Calvin* (Grand Rapids: Baker, 1991).

Shulevitz, Deborah. 'Historiography of Heresy: The Debate over "Catharism" in Medieval Languedoc', *History Compass* 17 (2019), e12513. https://doi.org/10.1111/hic3.12513, accessed 23 November 2023.

Simons, Daniel J. and Christopher F. Chabris. 'Gorillas in Our Midst: Sustained Inattentional Blindness for Dynamic Events', *Perception* 28 (1999), 1059–74.

Simpson, A. D. 'Epicureans, Christians, Atheists in the Second Century', *Transactions and Proceedings of the American Philological Association* 72 (1941), 372–81.

Simpson, William M. R., Robert C. Koons, and Nicholas J. Teh (eds.). *Neo-Aristotelian Perspectives on Contemporary Science* (London: Routledge, 2018).

Simut, Corneliu. *F. C. Baur's Synthesis of Böhme and Hegel* (Leiden: Brill, 2014).

Slack, Paul. *The Invention of Improvement: Information and Material Progress in Seventeenth-Century England* (Oxford: Oxford University Press, 2015).

Sluhovsky, Moshe. *Believe Not Every Spirit: Possession, Mysticism, & Discernment in Early Modern Catholicism* (Chicago: University of Chicago Press, 2007).
Sluhovsky, Moshe. 'Calvinist Miracles and the Concept of the Miraculous', *Reformation and Renaissance Review* 19 (1995), 5–21.
Smith, A. D. *Anselm's Other Argument* (Cambridge, MA: Harvard University Press, 2014).
Smith, Christian. *The Sacred Project of American Sociology* (Oxford: Oxford University Press, 2014).
Smith, Courtney Weiss. *Empiricist Devotions: Science, Religion, and Poetry in Early Eighteenth-Century England* (Charlottesville: University of Virginia Press, 2016).
Smith, Crosbie. *The Science of Energy* (Chicago: University of Chicago Press, 1998).
Smith, Crosbie and M. Norton Wise. *Energy and Empire: A Biographical Study of Lord Kelvin* (Cambridge: Cambridge University Press, 1989).
Smith, James K. A. *Desiring the Kingdom: Worship, Worldview, and Cultural Formation* (Grand Rapids: Baker, 2009).
Smith, James K. A. 'Secular Liturgies and the Prospect for a "Post-Secular" Sociology of Religion', in *The Post-Secular in Question: Religion in Contemporary Society*, ed. Philip S. Gorski, David Kyumam Kim, John Torpey, and Jonathan VanAntwerpen (New York: New York University Press, 2012), pp. 159–84.
Smith, Justin E. H. (ed.). *The Problem of Animal Generation in Early Modern Philosophy* (Cambridge: Cambridge University Press, 2006).
Smith, Quentin. 'The Metaphilosophy of Naturalism', *Philo* 4 (2001), 195–215.
Smith, Wilfred Cantwell. *Belief and History* (Charlottesville: University Press of Virginia, 1977).
Smith, Wilfred Cantwell. *Faith and Belief* (Princeton: Princeton University Press, 1979).
Smith, Wilfred Cantwell. *The Meaning and End of Religion* (London: SPCK, 1978).
Smolarz, Sebastian. *Covenant and the Metaphor of Divine Marriage* (Eugene: Wipf and Stock, 2010).
Smoller, Laura. 'Defining the Boundaries of the Natural in Fifteenth Century Brittany: The Inquest into the Miracles of Saint Vincent Ferrer (d. 1419)', *Viator* 28 (1997), 333–59.
Snell, Bruno. *The Discovery of the Mind* [1946], trans. T. G. Rosenmeyer (New York: Dover, 1982).
Somma, Emilio Di. *Fides and Secularity: Beyond Charles Taylor's Open Faith* (Eugene: Pickwick, 2018).
Sommerville, James. *The Enigmatic Parting Shot: What was Hume's "Compleat Answer to Dr Reid and to that Bigotted Silly Fellow, Beattie"* (Aldershot: Avery Press, 1987).
Sonenscher, Michael. *Capitalism: The Story behind the Word* (Princeton: Princeton University Press, 2022).
Sorabji, Richard (ed.). *Philoponus and the Rejection of Aristotelian Science* (Ithaca: Cornell University Press, 1987).
Sorabji, Richard. *Self: Ancient and Modern Insights about Individuality, Life, and Death* (Oxford: Oxford University Press, 2008).
Sorensen, Rob. *Martin Luther and the German Reformation* (London: Anthem Press, 2016).
Sosa, E. and J. Kim (eds.). *Epistemology: An Anthology* (Oxford: Blackwell, 2004).
Spadafora, David. *The Idea of Progress in Eighteenth-Century Britain* (New Haven: Yale University Press, 1990).
Spannent, M. *Le Stoïcisme des Pères de l'Église* (Paris, 1957).
Spellman, W. M. *John Locke and the Problem of Depravity* (Oxford: Clarendon Press, 1988).

Spencer, Mark G. (ed.). *David Hume: Historical Thinker, Historical Writer* (University Park, PA: Pennsylvania State University Press, 2013).
Spencer, Nick. *Atheists: The Origin of the Species* (London: Bloomsbury, 2014).
Spivak, Gayatri Chakravorty. 'Can the Subaltern Speak?', in *Marxism and the Interpretation of Culture*, ed. Cary Nelson and Lawrence Grossberg (London: Macmillan, 1988), pp. 271–313.
Spruit, Leen. *Species Intelligibilis: From Perception to Knowledge*, vol. 2 (Leiden: Brill, 1995).
Spurr, John. 'Rational Religion in Restoration England', *Journal of the History of Ideas* 49 (1988), 563–85.
Stagman, David. 'Piet Fransen's Research on *Fides et Mores*', *Theological Studies* 64 (2003), 69–77.
Stanford, P. Kyle. *Exceeding Our Grasp: Science, History, and the Problem of Unconceived Alternatives* (New York: Oxford University Press, 2006).
Stanley, Matthew. 'By Design: James Clerk Maxwell and the Evangelical Unification of Science', *The British Journal for the History of Science* 45 (2012), 57–73.
Stanley, Matthew. 'God and the Uniformity of Nature: The Case of Nineteenth-Century Physics', in *Science without God? Historical Perspectives on Scientific Naturalism*, ed. Peter Harrison and Jon H. Roberts (Oxford: Oxford University Press, 2019), pp. 97–109.
Stanley, Matthew. *Huxley's Church and Maxwell's Demon: From Theistic Science to Naturalistic Science* (Chicago: University of Chicago Press, 2015).
Steinle, Friedrich. 'From Principles to Regularities: Tracing "Laws of Nature" in Early Modern Europe', in *Natural Law and Laws of Nature in Early Modern Europe*, ed. Lorraine Daston and Michael Stolleis (Aldershot: Ashgate, 2005), pp. 213–32.
Steinmetz, David C. *Calvin in Context* (Oxford: Oxford University Press, 1995).
Stenhouse, John. '"A disappearing race before we came here": Doctor Alfred Kingcome Newman, the Dying Maori, and Victorian Scientific Racism', *New Zealand Journal of History* 30 (1996), 124–40.
Stenhouse, John. 'Reading Darwin during the New Zealand Wars: Science, Religion, Politics and Race, 1835–1900', *Studies in History & Philosophy of Science* 96 (2022), 87–99.
Stewart, Alastair C. 'The Early Alexandrian Baptismal Creed: Interrogative or Declaratory ... or Both?', *Questions liturgiques* 95 (2014), 237–53.
Stich, S. *Deconstructing the Mind* (Oxford: Oxford University Press, 1996).
Stock, Brian. *After Augustine: The Meditative Reader and the Text* (Philadelphia: University of Pennsylvania Press, 2001).
Stock, Brian. 'Science, Technology, and Economic Progress in the Early Middle Ages', in *Science in the Middle Ages*, ed. David C. Lindberg (Chicago: University of Chicago Press, 1978), pp. 1–51.
Stohrer, Walter. 'Descartes and Ignatius Loyola: La Flèche and Manresa Revisited', *Journal of the History of Philosophy* 17 (1979), 11–27.
Stone, Alison. 'Europe and Eurocentrism', *Aristotelian Society Supplementary Volume* 91 (2017), 83–104.
Storm, Jason Josephson. *The Myth of Disenchantment* (Chicago: University of Chicago Press, 2017).
Strauss, Gerald. *Luther's House of Learning: Indoctrination of the Young in the German Reformation* (Baltimore: Johns Hopkins University Press, 1978).

Stroud, Barry. 'The Charm of Naturalism', *Proceedings and Addresses of the American Philosophical Association* 70 (1996), 43–55.
Stroumsa, Guy. *A New Science: The Discovery of Religion in the Age of Reason* (Cambridge, MA: Harvard University Press, 2010).
Stump, Eleonore. *Aquinas* (London: Routledge, 2003).
Sturmark, Christer and Douglas Hofstadter. *To Light the Flame of Reason* (Buffalo: Prometheus, 2022).
Svenungsson, Jayne. *Divining History: Prophetism, Messianism and the Development of Spirit*, trans. Stephen Donovan (New York: Berghahn, 2016).
Swanson, Link R. 'The Predictive Processing Model Has Its Roots in Kant', *Frontiers in Systems Neuroscience* 10 (2016). https://doi.org/10.3389/fnsys.2016.00079, accessed 23 November 2023.
Swoyer, C. 'The Nature of Natural Laws', *Australasian Journal of Philosophy* 60 (1982), 203–23.
Syfret, R. H. 'Some Early Critics of the Royal Society', *Notes and Records of the Royal Society of London* 8 (1950), 20–64.
Tangko, Joseph. *The Way of Psychology* (Manila: Central Books, 2008).
Tarrant, Neil. *Defining Nature's Limits: The Roman Inquisition and the Boundaries of Science* (Chicago: University of Chicago Press, 2022).
Taubes, Jacob. *Occidental Eschatology*, trans. David Ratmoko (Stanford: Stanford University Press, 2009).
Taylor, Charles. *A Secular Age* (Cambridge, MA: Harvard University Press, 2007).
Taylor, Charles. *Sources of the Self: The Making of the Modern Identity* (Cambridge, MA: Harvard University Press, 1992).
Thaidigsmann, Edgar. '"Sapere aude": Auflärung und Theologie bei Melanchthon und Kant', *Zeitschrift für Theologie und Kirche* 111 (2014), 389–415.
Thayer, H. S. 'Aristotle on the Meaning of Science', *Philosophical Inquiry* 1 (1979), 87–104.
Thiessen, Matthew. *Contesting Conversion: Genealogy, Circumcision, and Identity in Ancient Judaism and Christianity* (Oxford: Oxford University Press, 2011).
Thiselton, Anthony C. *New Horizons in Hermeneutics* (Grand Rapids: Zondervan, 1992).
Thiselton, Anthony C. 'Speech-Act Theory and the Claim that God Speaks', *Scottish Journal of Theology* 50 (1997), 97–110.
Thomas, Keith. *Religion and the Decline of Magic* (New York: Scribner's, 1971).
Thomassen, Beroald. *Metaphysik als Lebensform: Untersuchungen zur Grundlegung der Metaphysik im Metaphysikkommentar Alberts des Grossen* (Münster: Aschendorff, 1985).
Thompson, James T. *A History of Historical Writing*, 2 vols. (New York: Macmillan, 1942).
Thomson, Arthur. 'Ignace de Loyola et Descartes: L'influence des exercises spirituels sur les oeuvres philosophiques de Descartes', *Archivs de philosophie* 35 (1972), 61–85.
Thurow, Joshua. 'Does Religious Disagreement Actually Aid the Case for Theism?', in *Probability in the Philosophy of Religion*, ed. Jake Chandler and Victoria Harrison (Oxford: Oxford University Press, 2012), pp. 209–24.
Tibiletti, Carlo. 'Tertulliano e la dottrina dell'anima "naturaliter christiana"', *Atti della Accademia delle scienze di Torino, tom. 2: Classe di scienze morali storiche e filologiche* 88 (1953-4), 84–117.
Todd, Robert B. 'The Stoic Common Notions: A Re-examination and Reinterpretation', *Symbolae Osloenses* 48 (1993), 47–75.

Tolonen, Pekka. 'Medieval Memories of the Origins of the Waldensian Movement', in *History and Religion: Narrating a Religious Past*, ed. Bernd-Christian Otto, Susanne Rau, and Jörg Rüpke (Berlin: De Gruyter, 2015), pp. 165–87.

Topham, Jonathan R. *Reading the Book of Nature* (Chicago: University of Chicago Press, 2023).

Tornay, Stephen. *Ockham: Studies and Selections* (LaSalle: Open Court, 1938).

Torrance, Eugenia. 'God of the Gaps, or the "God of Design and Dominion": Revisiting Newton's Theology', *Zygon* 58 (2023), 64–79.

Turner, Frank M. *Contesting Cultural Authority: Essays in Victorian Intellectual Life* (Cambridge: Cambridge University Press, 1993).

Turner, Frank M. 'Lucretius among the Victorians', *Victorian Studies* 16 (1973), 329–49.

Turner, Frank M. 'Victorian Scientific Naturalism and Thomas Carlyle', *Victorian Studies* 18 (1975), 325–43.

Turner, Geoffrey. 'Aquinas on the "Scientific" Status of Theology', *New Blackfriars* 78 (1997), 464–76.

Tuveson, Ernest Lee. *Millennium and Utopia: A Study in the Background of the Idea of Progress* (Berkeley: University of California Press, 1949).

Twetten, David. 'The Emanation Scheme of Albert the Great and the Questions of Divine Free Will and Mediated Creation', in *Albert the Great and His Arabic Sources: Medieval Science between Inheritance and Emergence*, ed. Katja Krause and Richard C. Taylor (Turnhout: Brepols), in press.

Tyson, Paul. *Faith's Knowledge* (Eugene: Pickwick, 2013).

Uehlein, Friedrich A. 'Whichcote, Shaftesbury and Locke: Shaftesbury's Critique of Locke's Epistemology and Moral Philosophy', *British Journal for the History of Philosophy* 25 (2017), 1031–48.

Ungureanu, James C. 'A Yankee at Oxford: John William Draper at the British Association for the Advancement of Science at Oxford, 30 June 1860', *Notes and Records of the Royal Society* 70 (2016), 135–50.

Ungureanu, James C. 'Science, Religion, and the New Reformation of the Nineteenth Century', *Science and Christian Belief* 31 (2019), 41–61.

Ungureanu, James C. *Science, Religion, and the Protestant Tradition: Retracing the Origins of Conflict* (Pittsburgh: University of Pittsburgh Press, 2018).

Ungureanu, James C. 'Tyndall and Draper', *Notes and Queries* 64 (2017), 125–8.

van Asselt, Willem J. 'Amicitia Dei as Ultimate Reality: An Outline of the Covenant Theology of Johannes Cocceius (1603–1669)', *Ultimate Reality and Meaning: Interdisciplinary Studies in the Philosophy of Understanding* 21 (1998), 35–47.

van Asselt, Willem J. *The Federal Theology of Johannes Cocceius (1603–1669)* (Leiden: Brill, 2001).

van Asselt, Willem J. 'The Fundamental Meaning of Theology: Archetypal and Ectypal Theology in Seventeenth-Century Reformed Thought', *Westminster Theological Journal* 64 (2002/3), 319–35.

van Berkel, Klaus and Arjo Vanderjagt (eds.). *The Book of Nature in Early Modern and Modern History* (Leuven: Peeters, 2006).

van den Berg, Robert M. 'As we are always speaking of them and using their names on every occasion. Plotinus, *Enn.* III.7 [45]: Language, Experience and the Philosophy of Time in Neoplatonism', in *Physics and Philosophy of Nature in Greek Neoplatonism*, ed. Riccardo Chiaradonna and Franco Trabattoni (Leiden: Brill, 2009), pp. 101–20.

van den Brink, Gijsbert. 'How Theology Stopped Being *Regina Scientiarum*—and How Its Story Continues', *Studies in Christian Ethics* 34 (2019), 442–54.
Van Engen, John. *Religion in the History of the Medieval West* (London: Routledge, 2004).
Van Engen, John. 'The Christian Middle Ages as an Historiographical Problem', *American Historical Review* 91 (1986), 519–52.
van Fraassen, Bas. 'Belief and the Will', *Journal of Philosophy* 81 (1984), 235–56.
van Fraassen, Bas. *The Empirical Stance* (New Haven: Yale University Press, 2002).
van Inwagen, Peter. 'It Is Wrong, Always, Everywhere, and for Anyone, to Believe Anything, Upon Insufficient Evidence', in *Faith, Freedom, and Rationality*, ed. J. Jordan and D. Howard-Snyder (Lanham: Rowman & Littlefield, 1996), pp. 137–54.
Van Liere, Katherine, Simon Ditchfield, and Howard Louthan (eds.). *Sacred History: Uses of the Christian Past in the Renaissance World* (Oxford: Oxford University Press, 2012).
Vander Schel, Kevin M. *Embedded Grace: Christ, History, and the Reign of God in Schleiermacher's Dogmatics* (Minneapolis: Fortress Press, 2013).
Vanza, Alberto. 'Empiricism and Rationalism in Nineteenth-Century Histories of Philosophy', *Journal of the History of Ideas* 77 (2016), 253–82.
Vanza, Alberto. 'Kant on Empiricism and Rationalism', *History of Philosophy Quarterly* 30 (2013), 53–74.
Vendler, Z. 'Descartes' Exercises', *Canadian Journal of Philosophy* 19 (1989), 193–224
Venturi, Franco. 'Sapere Aude!', *Revista storica italiana* 71 (1959), 119–28.
Verbeek, Theo. 'Descartes and the Problem of Atheism: The Utrecht Crisis', *Nederlands archief voor kerkgeschiedenis / Dutch Review of Church History* 71 (1991), 211–23.
Verbeek, Theo. 'The Invention of Nature: Descartes and Regius', in *Descartes' Natural Philosophy*, ed. Stephen Gaukroger, John Schuster, and John Sutton (London: Routledge, 2000), pp. 149–67.
Verbeke, G. 'Pensée et discernement chez saint Augustin: Quelques réflexions sur le sens du terme "cogitare"', *Recherche Augustiniennes* 2 (1962), 59–80.
Verbin, N. K. 'Religious Beliefs and Aspect Seeing', *Religious Studies* 36 (2000), 1–23.
Verhaegh, Sander. *The Nature and Development of Quine's Naturalism* (Oxford: Oxford University Press, 2010).
Versnel, Henk. *Coping with the Gods: Wayward Readings in Greek Theology* (Leiden: Brill, 2011).
Vilaça, Aparecida. 'Christians without Faith: Some Aspects of the Conversion of the Wari' (Pakaa Nova)', *Ethnos* 62 (1997), 91–115.
Villepelet, Denis. *L'avenir de la Catéchèse* (Paris: Éditions de l'Atelier, 2003).
Viner, Jacob. 'Fashion in Economic Thought', in *Essays on the Intellectual History of Economics*, ed. Douglas A. Irwin (Princeton: Princeton University Press, 1991), pp. 189–99.
Vlastos, Gregory. 'The Individual as an Object of Love in Plato', in *Platonic Studies*, 2nd ed. (Princeton: Princeton University Press, 1981), pp. 3–42.
Voegelin, Eric. *The New Science of Politics* [1952]. *The Collected Works of Eric Voegelin*, vol. 5, ed. Manfred Henningsen (Columbia: University of Missouri Press, 1999).
Vogt, Katja, 'Ancient Skepticism', in *The Stanford Encyclopedia of Philosophy* (Winter 2022 Edition), ed. Edward N. Zalta and Uri Nodelman. https://plato.stanford.edu/archives/fall2018/entries/skepticism-ancient/
von Staaden, Heinrich. 'The Rule and the Exception: Celsus on a Scientific Conundrum', in *Maladie et maladies dans les textes latins antiques et médiévaux*, ed. C. Deroux (Brussels: Latomus, 1998), pp. 105–28.

Vos, Antonie. *The Philosophy of John Duns Scotus* (Edinburgh: Edinburgh University Press, 2012).
Vos, Geerhardus. *Biblical Theology: Old and New Testaments* (Eugene: Wipf and Stock, 2003).
Vuillemin, Jean-Claude. *Épistémè baroque. Le mot et la chose* (Paris: Hermann, 2013).
Wagar, Wareen W. *Terminal Visions: The Literature of Last Things* (Bloomington: Indiana University Press, 1982).
Wainwright, G. 'The Language of Worship', in *The Study of Liturgy*, 2nd ed., ed. C. Jones, G. Wainwright, and E. Yarnold (London: SPCK, 1992), pp. 519–28.
Walbridge, John. *The Science of Mystic Lights: Qutb al-Din Shirazi and the Illuminationist Tradition in Islamic Philosophy* (Cambridge: Cambridge University Press, 1992).
Walker, D. P. *The Ancient Theology* (Ithaca: Cornell University Press, 1972).
Walker, D. P. 'The Cessation of Miracles', in *Hermeticism and the Renaissance: Intellectual History and the Occult in Early Modern Europe*, ed. Ingrid Merkel and Alan Debus (Washington, DC: Folger Shakespeare Library, 1988), pp. 110–24.
Wallace, William A. 'Is Finality Included in Aristotle's Definition of Nature?', in *Final Causality in Nature and Human Affairs*, ed. Richard F. Hassing (Washington, DC: Catholic University of America Press, 1997), pp. 52–70.
Walsh, J. J. 'On Christian Atheism', *Vigiliae Christianae* 45 (1991), 255–77.
Walsh, K. and A. Currie. 'Caricatures, Myths and White Lies', *Metaphilosophy* 46 (2015), 414–35.
Walsham, Alexandra. 'Invisible Helpers: Angelic Interventions in Post-Reformation England', *Past and Present* 208 (2010), 77–130.
Walter, Ryan. 'Malthus's Sacred History: Outflanking Civil History in the Late Enlightenment', *Re-thinking History* 24 (2020), 481–502.
Walzer, Richard. *Galen on Jews and Christians* (London: Oxford University Press, 1949).
Wang, Connie X., Isaac A. Hilburn, Daw-An Wu, et al. 'Transduction of the Geomagnetic Field as Evidenced from Alpha-Band Activity in the Human Brain', *eNeuro* 6 (2019). https://doi.org/10.1523/ENEURO.0483-18.2019, accessed 19 March 2019.
Ward, Graham. *How the Light Gets In: Ethical Life 1* (Oxford: Oxford University Press, 2016).
Ward, Graham. 'Supernaturalism', in *Encyclopedia of Science and Religion*, ed. Wentzel van Huyssteen (New York: Macmillan, 2003), pp. 846–8.
Ward, Graham. *Unbelievable: Why We Believe and Why We Don't* (London: I. B. Tauris, 2014).
Ward, James. *Naturalism and Agnosticism*, 2nd ed., 2 vols. (London: Adam and Charles Black, 1903).
Warren, J. *Presocratics* (Berkeley: University of California Press, 2007).
Wasserman, Daniel. *Truth in Many Tongues: Religious Conversion and the Languages of the Early Spanish Empire* (University Park: Pennsylvania State University Press, 2020).
Waterfield, Robin. *The First Philosophers* (Oxford: Oxford University Press, 2000).
Watkins, C. J. *History and the Supernatural in Medieval England* (Cambridge: Cambridge University Press, 2007).
Webster, Charles. *From Paracelsus to Newton* (Cambridge: Cambridge University Press, 1982).
Webster, Charles. *The Great Instauration: Science, Medicine, and Reform, 1626–1660* (London: Duckworth, 1975).

Weijers, Olga. 'Some Notes on *Fides* and Related Words in Medieval Latin', *Archivum Latinitatis Medii Aevi* 40 (1977), 77–192.
Weinhardt, J. 'Supranaturalismus', in *Theologische Realenzyklopädie*, ed. Gerhard Krause and Gerhard Muller (New York: De Gruyter, 2001), vol. 32, 467–77.
Weintraub, Karl. *The Value of the Individual: Self and Circumstance in Autobiography* (Chicago: University of Chicago Press, 1978).
Weir, Todd H. (ed.). *Monism: Science, Philosophy, Religion, and the History of a Worldview* (New York: Palgrave Macmillan, 2012).
Weisheipl, James A. 'The Axiom "*Opus naturae est opus intelligentia*" and Its Origins', in *Albertus Magnus—Doctor Universalis 1280/1980*, ed. Gerbert Meyer and Albert Zimmermann (Mainz: Matthias-Grünewald-Verlag, 1980), pp. 441–63.
Wells, Peter S. *Barbarians to Angels: The Dark Ages Reconsidered* (New York: Norton, 2008).
Wendte, Martin. 'Ferdinand Christian Baur: A Historically Formed Idealist of a Distinctive Kind', in *Ferdinand Christian Baur and the History of Early Christianity*, ed. Martin Bauspiess, Christof Landmesser, and David Lincicum, trans. Peter C. Hodgson and Robert F. Brown (Oxford: Oxford University Press, 2017), pp. 67–79.
Wernick, Andrew. *Auguste Comte and the Religion of Humanity: The Post-Theistic Program of French Social Theory* (Cambridge: Cambridge University Press, 2000).
Weststeijn, Thijs. '*Spinoza sinicus*: An Asian Paragraph in the History of the Radical Enlightenment', *Journal of the History of Ideas* 68 (2007), 537–61.
Whalen, Brett E. *Dominion of God: Christendom and Apocalypse in the Middle Ages* (Cambridge, MA: Harvard University Press, 2009).
White, Paul. 'The Conduct of Belief', in *Victorian Scientific Naturalism: Community, Identity, Continuity*, ed. Gowan Dawson and Bernard Lightman (Chicago: University of Chicago Press, 2014), pp. 220–42.
Whitmarsh, Tim. *Battling the Gods: Atheism in the Ancient World* (New York: Alfred A. Knopf, 2015).
Whorf, Benjamin. *Language, Thought, and Reality: Selected Writings of Benjamin Lee Whorf*, ed. John B. Carroll (Cambridge, MA: MIT Press, 1940).
Whyte, Jessica. 'The Invisible Hand of Friedrich Hayek', *Political Theory* 47 (2019), 156–84.
Wickham, Chris. *The Inheritance of Rome: Illuminating the Dark Ages: 400–1000* (Harmondsworth: Penguin, 2010).
Wildberg, C. 'Impetus Theory and the Hermeneutics of Science in Simplicius and Philoponus', *Hyperboreus* 5 (1999), 107–24.
Wilkins, John S. and Paul E. Griffiths. 'Evolutionary Debunking Arguments in Three Domains: Fact, Value, and Religion', in *A New Science of Religion*, ed. James McLaurin and Greg Dawes (London: Routledge, 2012), pp. 133–46.
Williams, Rowan. *On Christian Theology* (Oxford: Wiley Blackwell, 2000).
Williams, Rowan. *The Edge of Words* (London: Continuum, 2015).
Williams, Thomas. 'The Doctrine of Univocity Is True and Salutary', *Modern Theology* 21 (2005), 575–85.
Wilson, Derek. *Out of the Storm: The Life and Legacy of Martin Luther* (New York: Macmillan, 2008).
Wilson, E. O. *Consilience: The Unity of Knowledge* (New York: Random House, 1998).
Wilson, Robert. *Astronomy through the Ages* (Princeton: Princeton University Press, 1997).

Wittgenstein, Ludwig. *Culture and Value*, trans. Peter Winch (Chicago: University of Chicago Press, 1984).
Wittgenstein, Ludwig. *Philosophical Investigations*, 2nd ed., trans. G. E. M. Anscombe (Oxford: Blackwell, 1963).
Wittgenstein, Ludwig. *Tractatus Logico-Philosophicus*, trans. D. F. Pears and B. F. McGuiness (London: Routledge & Kegan Paul, 1961).
Woleński, Jan. 'History of Epistemology', in *Handbook of Epistemology*, ed. I. Niiniluoto, M. Sintonen, and J. Woleński (Berlin: Springer, 2004), pp. 3–54.
Wolff, Hans. *Hosea*, trans. G. Stanswell (Philadelphia: Fortress Press, 1974).
Wolterstorff, Nicholas. 'Can Belief in God Be Rational if It Has No Foundations?', in *Faith and Rationality*, ed. Alvin Plantinga and Nicholas Wolterstorff (Notre Dame: University of Notre Dame Press, 1983), pp. 135–86.
Wolterstorff, Nicholas. *Divine Discourse* (Cambridge: Cambridge University Press, 1995).
Wolterstorff, Nicholas. *John Locke and the Ethics of Belief* (Cambridge: Cambridge University Press, 1996).
Wood, William. 'Thomas Aquinas on the Claim that God is Truth', *Journal of the History of Philosophy* 51 (2013), 21–47.
Woods, Michael J. 'Aristotle on Sleep and Dreams', *Apeiron* 25 (1992), 179–88.
Woodward, Jim. 'What Is a Mechanism? A Counterfactual Account', *Philosophy of Science* 69 (2002), 366–77.
Woody, William Douglas and Wayne Viney. *A History of Psychology*, 6th ed. (Abingdon: Routledge, 2017).
Woollett, L. K. and E. A. Maguire. 'Acquiring "The Knowledge" of London's Layout Drives Structural Brain Changes', *Current Biology* 21 (2011), 2109–14.
Wray, W. Brad. 'Collective Belief and Acceptance', *Synthese* 129 (2001), 319–33.
Wright, John P. 'Kemp Smith and the Two Kinds of Naturalism in David Hume's Philosophy', *Rivista di Storia della Filosofia* 62/3, Supplemento (2007), 17–36.
Wright, T. R. *The Religion of Humanity: The Impact of Comtean Positivism on Victorian Britain* (Cambridge: Cambridge University Press, 1986).
Wüstenberg, Ralph K. '*Fides implicita* "revisited": Versuch eines evangelischen Zugangs', *Neue Zeitschrift für Systematiche Theologie* 49 (2007), 71–85.
Yasakuta, Toshimasa. *Lessing's Philosophy of Religion and the German Enlightenment* (Oxford: Oxford University Press, 2003).
Yelle, Robert A. '"An Age of Miracles": Disenchantment as Secularized Theological Narrative', in *Narratives of Disenchantment and Secularization: Critiquing Max Weber's Idea of Modernity*, ed. Robert A. Yelle and Lorenz Trein (London: Bloomsbury, 2021), pp. 129–48.
Yelle, Robert A. and Lorenz Trein (eds.). *Narratives of Disenchantment and Secularization: Critiquing Max Weber's Idea of Modernity* (London: Bloomsbury, 2021).
Yengoyan, A. A. 'Religion, Morality, and Prophetic Traditions: Conversion among the Pitjantjara of Central Australia', in *Conversion to Christianity*, ed. R. W. Hefner (Berkeley: University of California Press, 1993), pp. 233–57.
Yolton, John. *John Locke and the Way of Ideas* (New York: Oxford University Press, 1956).
Zachhuber, Johannes. 'F. W. J. Schelling and the Rise of Historical Theology', *International Journal of Philosophy and Theology* 80 (2019), 23–38.
Zachhuber, Johannes. 'Nature', in *The Routledge Companion to Early Christian Philosophy*, ed. Mark Edwards (Abingdon: Routledge, 2021), pp. 27–40.

Zagzebski, Linda. 'Epistemic Self-Trust and the Consensus Gentium Argument', in *Evidence and Religious Belief*, ed. Kelly James Clark and Raymond J. VanArragon (Oxford: Oxford University Press, 2011), pp. 22–36.

Zakai, Avihu. 'Reformation, History, and Eschatology in English Protestantism', *History and Theory* 26 (1987), 300–18.

Zakzouk, Mahmoud. *Al-Ghazālīs philosophie im vergleich mit Descartes* (Frankfurt: Peter Lang, 1992).

Zeller, Eduard. 'Ferdinand Christian Baur', in *Vorträge und Abhandlungen geschichtlichen Inhalts* (Leipzig: Fues, 1865), pp. 354–434.

Zerner, Monique (ed.). *Inventer l'hérésie?* (Nice: Presses Universitaires de Nice, 1998).

INDEX

Acland, Henry Wentworth, 341
Adam, 25, 154
    Fall of, 101–2, 109
Adelard of Bath, 230
Adorno, Theodor W., 347
agnosticism, 279–80, 340
Albert the Great, 231, 233
    incipient naturalism of, 230, 237
Al-Ghazali, 237
Alston, William, 378
Ambrose of Milan, 130
Anaxagoras, 221
Anaximander, 222
Anselm of Canterbury, 47, 61, 183
    'faith seeking understanding', 47, 174, 184, 359
    ontological argument, 144, 171, 178
Antichrist, the, 286, 289–90
    as miracle-worker, 299
Aquinas, Thomas. *See* Thomas Aquinas
Aristotelianism, 39, 66, 89, 198, 223, 234, 335
    Aristotelian logic, 62
    causal explanations in, 197, 202, 234, 260, 376
    and Christianity, 65
    conceptions of science in, 39, 60, 66
    criticisms of, 66, 101, 124, 197, 229, 376
    scholastic, 79, 124, 197, 377–8
    teleological aspects of, 95, 145–6, 378
Aristotle, 36, 40, 55, 65, 87, 89, 92, 101, 103, 153, 169, 175, 178, 222
    on belief, 37
    on causation, 191, 222, 234
    on the divinity of the heavens, 223
    on eternity of the world, 224
    on existence of gods, 141, 167, 172

logic of, 37, 141, 157
medieval translations of, 229
on natural/accidental distinction, 224
on natural/violent distinction, 224
on 'nature', 254
on origins of philosophy, 220
Posterior Analytics, 59
on 'science', 37, 59–60
Ash'arite philosophy, 94
atheism, 131, 133, 191, 196, 216, 265
    early modern definitions of, 134–8
Atterbury, Francis, 310
Augustine of Hippo, 47, 86, 93, 143, 145, 169, 177, 235, 307
    on authority, 55–7, 120
    on baptism, 69–70
    on belief without understanding, 57
    on divine illumination, 146, 242–50
    on faith, 44–5
    on literal and allegorical interpretation, 196
    on miracles, 20
    theology of history, 293
    on 'true religion', 52
    vestigia trinitatis, 174
Austin, J. L., 46
Averroes, 233
Avicenna, 233
    naturalism of, 237

Bacon, Francis, 109, 157, 197–201, 288, 303, 332
    on biblical prophecy, 291, 296
    criticism of final causes, 200
    on science as charitable activity, 295
Bacon, Roger, 178–9
Baius, Michael, 261

457

Bale, John, 284
Balfour, Arthur James, 340
Bampton Lectures, 276
Barfield, Owen, 366
Baronius, Caesar, 286
Barrow, Isaac, 81, 97, 112
Baumgarten, Alexander
    on natural theology, 208, 264
Baur, F. C., 272, 328
Bayle, Pierre, 93, 162
    on nations of atheists, 26, 161
Beattie, James, 153
Belfast Address. *See* Tyndall, John
belief, 21, 25, 32, 43–4, 49, 55, 65, 68, 77,
    111–12, 160, 182, 251, 260, 359, 373.
    See also ethics of belief; faith; implicit faith
    articles of, 43
    as assent, 30, 43, 47, 50, 63, 113
    belief in and belief that, 40, 51, 112
    changing conceptions of, 2–3, 8–9, 18–19,
        21, 23, 32, 43, 65, 77, 129–30, 139, 210,
        217, 263, 378
    as constitutive of 'religion', 21–2, 26,
        35, 125
    distinguished from practice, 73, 75, 79
    heterodox, 48
    justification of, 8–9, 22, 39, 52, 67, 80, 82,
        85, 127, 131, 138, 158, 165–6, 186, 196,
        213, 258, 265, 280, 377
    naturalness of, 64, 136, 196
    propositional, 21, 34, 42, 48, 63, 65, 67, 127,
        130, 133, 196, 373
    relation to knowledge, 37, 39, 52, 67
    relation to liturgy, 71, 73
    in the supernatural, 2, 9, 17–18, 30, 141,
        143, 252, 306, 314, 334
    terminology of, 8, 24–33
    as trust, 51, 57, 112, 130
    and unbelief, 3, 17, 64, 79, 112, 131, 133,
        183, 373
    a Western conception, 2–3, 28–30,
        128, 362
Bellarmine, Robert, 75
Benjamin, Walter, 346
Bentham, Jeremy, 311
Bentley, Richard, 136, 147, 203
    on laws of nature, 236
Berdyaev, Nikolai, 283, 345
Berkeley, George, 94, 341
Bernard of Clairvaux, 63
Beza, Theodore, 284

Biard, Pierre, 24, 26, 68–9, 71–2
biblical criticism, 253, 270–4.
    See also Tübingen School
    as a science, 271, 278
    T. H. Huxley's interest in, 275
Blake, William, 284
Blumenbach, Johann Friedrich, 336
Boethius, 144, 177–8
Bolshevism, 347
Bonaventure, 91, 144, 146, 175, 195, 229
    on causation, 192, 194
Bonnet, Charles, 310
book of nature metaphor, 189, 194–6, 198
Boyle, Robert, 122, 131, 134, 139, 169, 179,
    189, 234, 237, 264, 343
    on final causes, 201
    on implicit faith, 120
    on knowledge without understanding, 122
    on laws of nature, 236
    on miracles, 264
    on natural theology, 207
    on scientific priesthood, 123
Boyle Lectures, 131, 135–6, 139, 190, 203,
    208, 216, 237
Bridgewater Treatises, 190, 248
Bruno, Giordano, 332, 341
Buckle, Henry Thomas, 312
    on laws of history, 312
Buddhism, 162
Bultmann, Rudolf, 368, 372
Bunyan, John, 295
Buridan, John, 229
Bushnell, Horace, 269
Butler, Joseph, 248, 341

Cajetan, Thomas, 261
Calvin, John, 71–2, 74, 169, 261
    on Catholic miracles, 298
    on history, 294
    on natural theology, 207
    on reason, 101–3
    sensus divinitatis, 147–9, 213, 215
Calvinism, 156, 205
Cambridge Platonists, 94, 109–11, 149
Carion's Chronicles, 289
Carlyle, Thomas, 125
Carpenter, William Benjamin, 247–8, 250
Casaubon, Meric, 112
Cavanaugh, William T., 371
Cavendish, Margaret, 216
Chalcedon, Symbol of, 41

Chambers, Robert, 247, 269–70
Charleton, Walter, 97
Chillingworth, William, 78
Christianisation, 70–1
Chrysippus, 142
Cicero, 99, 143, 168
  on the *consensus gentium*, 19, 141, 165
Clarke, Samuel, 135
  cosmological argument, 208
  on laws of nature, 237
  on natural/supernatural distinction, 237, 265
Clement of Alexandria, 37, 143, 227
  on faith as a first principle, 38
Clifford, William Kingdon, 82–3, 270, 279–80
Cocceius, Johannes, 292
cognitive science of religion, 213
Collier's Catechism, the, 68, 79
Collingwood, R. G., 348
Collins, Anthony, 216
Columbus, Christopher, 336
Combe, George, 312
Comenius, Jan Amos, 292
common notions, 37, 115, 142–3, 148–9, 152–8, 163, 188, 212. *See also* Herbert of Cherbury, on common notions; innate ideas; Stoicism, common notions
common sense philosophy, 152–3
Comte, Auguste, 306–9, 312, 314, 316
  law of three stages, 302, 306, 313, 346
  religion of humanity, 308
Condorcet, Nicolas de, 304, 320n133
  on historical progress, 304
  on origin of religion, 305
conflict thesis, 252, 304, 307, 313, 316, 335, 337, 342, 372
Constantine the Great, 42–3, 47, 50
Copernican demotion, 308
Copernicus, Nicolaus, 308, 316, 332
corpuscular matter theory, 197, 200, 236, 376
Council of Trent, 72
Counter-Reformation, 69, 72
creation, 198, 228, 246
  Creator/creation distinction, 198, 227, 255
  doctrine of, 193, 195, 198, 225, 227, 230, 234, 367
  ex nihilo, 227
creeds, Christian, 42–50. *See also* Chalcedon, Symbol of; Nicene Creed
Cudworth, Ralph, 97, 150, 162, 240
Cyril of Alexandria, 255

d'Alembert, Jean le Rond, 114, 303
Dante Alighieri, 168
dark ages, 286–7
Darwin, Charles, 238, 248, 250, 270, 280, 316, 338
  The Descent of Man, 315
  'horrid doubt', 323
  Origin of Species, 248, 276–7
Darwinism
  religious critics of, 250, 332
  religious supporters of, 250
  social, 317
Dawson, Gowan, 268
de la Mettrie, Julien, 216
de Lamennais, Félicité Robert, 268
de Lubac, Henri, 64n138, 262, 347
  on natural and supernatural ends, 261
  on 'pure nature', 260
de Tocqueville, Alexis, 120
deification, 88–90, 171
deism, 111, 149, 163, 343
Democritus, 163, 240, 332, 339
Derham, William, 188, 190
Descartes, René, 22, 86, 152, 154, 157–8, 181, 183, 188, 197, 204, 238, 303, 332, 339, 343
  and Augustine, 58
  criticism of final causes, 201
  doctrine of vortices, 240
  innate ideas, 151, 158
  on laws of nature, 234–5, 339
  on light of nature, 87, 90
  Meditations, 181, 185, 197
  night of dreams, 180
  ontological argument, 181
  proofs for God's existence, 156–7, 204–5, 216, 239
  and the way of ideas, 158–9
d'Holbach, Paul-Henri, 305
Diderot, Denis, 114
Diet of Worms, 76, 100, 125
Dinka tribe, 29, 362
disagreement, philosophy of, 22
divine illumination, 242–50
Dodds, E. R., 361
Donne, John, 99
Draper, John William, 335
Duffin, Jacalyn, 354, 363
Duhem, Pierre, 229
Duns Scotus, John, 375–6
Durkheim, Émile, 214, 218, 308

Eberhard, Johannes, 164
Eckhart, Meister, 195
Edelstein, Dan, 306
Edwards, Jonathan, 118
Elders, Leo, 185
Encyclopédie, the, 114–15, 303
Engels, Friedrich, 330, 346
    secular millenarianism of, 291
    stages of civilisation, 330
Enlightenment, the, 10, 85, 115, 124–5, 162, 290, 300, 303–4, 328, 337, 372, 378. *See also philosophes*
    Scottish, 152, 310, 317
Epictetus, 87
Epicureanism, 124, 134, 169, 197, 202, 225, 233, 237
    as atheistic, 228
    and chance, 233–4, 249
    doctrine of *prolepsis*, 142
    doctrine of 'the swerve', 225
Epicurus, 332
epiphenomenalism, 363
epistemic injustice, 11, 379
epistemology, 86, 91, 127, 280, 377. *See also* ethics of belief; evidentialism; foundationalism; reformed epistemology; reliabilism
    and belief, 39
    inception of, 39, 67, 127, 327, 377
    John Locke's, 83, 107
Eriugena, John Scotus, 256
eschatology, 331, 344, 352
    and early modern science, 291, 296
    immanentization of, 347
    secularisation of, 4, 300, 344, 347
Essays and Reviews, 277
ethics of belief, 8, 18, 76–85, 111, 116, 127, 129, 133, 135, 137, 160, 165, 216, 263, 279. *See also* belief; Clifford, William Kingdon; faith; Locke, John; Wolterstorff, Nicholas
Euclid, 142
evidentialism, 151, 196, 217, 271, 377
evolution, 215, 225, 238, 249–50, 310, 317
    based on laws, 247, 250, 318
    social, 3, 166, 273
evolutionary debunking arguments, 215
experimental religion. *See* religion, experimental
experimental science, 66, 109, 116
    and experimental religion, 117–18
    religious legitimation of, 203

faith, 43–5, 47, 51–3, 60, 62–3, 65–6, 143, 153, 172, 183, 204–6, 349, 359, 363. *See also* Anselm of Canterbury, 'faith seeking understanding'; belief; implicit faith
    articles of, 54, 72, 184, 198
    as assent, 59, 67, 84, 113
    changing conceptions of, 19, 23, 32, 40, 43, 65, 72, 80, 111–12, 128, 139, 263
    a divine gift, 34, 41, 64, 114, 258
    early Christian conceptions of, 32–42
    a first principle, 37
    justification of, 3, 128
    a natural instinct, 64
    privatisation of, 66, 72
    and reason, 84–5, 99, 101, 108, 115–16, 130, 184, 208, 264, 301, 328
    reification of, 40–1
    relation to opinion, 60
    relation to *scientia*, 37, 39, 60, 66
    rule of, 268
    a supernatural gift, 263
    terminology of, 2, 8, 32–3
    a theological virtue, 257, 296
    as trust, 34–6, 43, 51, 55, 65, 72, 111, 127–8
falsafa, 229, 233
falsification, 121n197
Faraday, Michael, 246, 333n182, 343
    on laws of nature, 243
fear theory, 163
federal theology, 292–3
Fénelon, François, 97, 136
Ferguson, Adam, 153, 309, 348–9
Fermat's last theorem, 186
Feuerbach, Ludwig, 329–30
Feyerabend, Paul, 358, 379
Ficino, Marsilio, 91, 146
Flacius, Matthias, 285
flat earth myth, 304, 307, 336
Fontenelle, Bernard, 301
foundationalism, 158, 377
Fox, George, 362–3
Frankfurt School, 347
Frazer, J. G., 314, 319
French Revolution, 308, 313
Freud, Sigmund, 318–19
Fries, Jakob Friedrich, 210–11, 377
    direct intuition of God, 210
Fukuyama, Francis, 351

Galileo Galilei, 120, 229, 303, 308
    condemnation of, 204, 304, 336

Gassendi, Pierre, 124, 201
  and Epicureanism, 234
  on existence of God, 151
Gibbon, Edward, 286
Gladstone, William, 340, 355–6
Goethe, Johann Wolfgang von, 356
Gorilla Test, 358
Green, T. H., 348
Gregory, Brad, 10, 72, 373–4, 376
Grove, William Robert, 246
Guizot, François, 125, 337
Guugu Yimithirr people, 364–6, 370

Hadot, Pierre, 175, 327
Haeckel, Ernst, 317, 342
Hakewill, George, 99
Hamilton, Sir William, 276
Hansen, Norwood, 358
Harrison, Frederick, 277
  on laws of nature, 251
Hart, David Bentley, 24
Hartlib, Samuel, 157, 292
Harvey, William, 303
Hayek, Friedrich, 348
hedonistic calculus, 106
Hegel, G. W. F., 1, 130, 165, 272, 291, 317, 319–20, 323–4, 326–9, 347, 362
  on alienation, 328
  on Christianity as agent of secularisation, 232
  dialectical understanding of history, 328
  and J. G. Frazer, 319
  on origins of philosophy, 324
  on the Protestant Reformation, 76, 125
Heidegger, Martin, 223, 360, 368
Heisenberg, Werner, 343
Henry of Ghent, 91
Heraclitus, 87
Herbert of Cherbury, 125, 149, 154, 157–8, 179, 188
  on common notions, 107, 148
Herder, Johann Gottfried, 353, 360
heresy, 43
  medieval, 48–50
  and social order, 47
Herschel, Caroline, 341
Herschel, John, 248, 341
  on laws of nature, 243
Herschel, William, 341
Hesiod, 222, 360
Hierocles of Alexandria, 88
history
  laws of, 302

  of philosophy, 86, 93, 209, 324–7
  Protestant versions of, 281, 283–8, 297, 334, 336, 352
  providential understandings of, 4, 288, 291, 294, 299, 301, 321, 323, 337, 344, 347, 349, 352
  of science, 9, 224, 250, 253, 281, 327, 337–8, 343, 359, 370, 372
  teleological theories of, 317, 347
  theology of, 283, 294, 345, 347–8, 352
Hobbes, Thomas, 106–7, 135–6, 163, 241, 299, 377
  on implicit faith, 112
  on origins of philosophy, 325
Homer, 222, 360–1
  colour vocabulary of, 355
Hooke, Robert, 109
Hooker, Richard, 99
Horace, 119
Horkheimer, Max, 347
Howitt, William, 354
Hugh of St Victor, 53, 61, 195
Humboldt, Wilhelm von, 360
Hume, David, 1, 163, 269, 275
  on 'barbarous nations', 16
  on causation, 192, 202
  criticism of design argument, 198
  on Greek origins of philosophy, 325
  as a historian, 13
  indebtedness to Protestant critiques of miracles, 299
  on laws of nature, 15, 242, 251
  on miracles, 3, 10, 14–23, 65, 271–2, 322, 353
  Natural History of Religion, 26
  naturalism of, 10, 14, 18, 266, 353
Huxley, Thomas Henry, 218–20, 227, 232, 265, 267, 270, 274–9, 308, 333, 338–40, 342, 362–3, 367
  on the history of naturalism, 253
  on laws of nature, 251
  on miracles, 299
  on naturalism and supernaturalism, 218, 270, 274
Huygens, Christiaan, 303
Hypatia, 336

Ignatius of Antioch, 40–1
implicit faith, 8, 69, 112, 117, 121, 127, 131, 149, 287, 307, 368. *See also* belief; ethics of belief; faith
  criticisms of, 66, 71, 75–85, 110–11, 118–19, 155, 216, 263, 378

implicit faith (cont.)
    demise of, 114, 125, 127, 129, 196
    medieval conception of, 53–5
    in the sciences, 120, 123–4
imposture theory, 163
innate ideas, 37, 84, 93, 100, 104, 107, 114,
    149, 152, 155, 158, 187. *See also* common
    notions; Descartes, René, innate ideas
    criticism of, 160
    of God, 139–41, 143, 145–6, 156–8, 166,
        169, 212, 215. *See also* Calvin, John,
        sensus divinitatis
Inquisition, Roman, 305, 336, 341
invisible hand, the, 294, 310

James, William, 18, 341
    'The Will to Believe', 59
Jansenism, 103, 156, 205
Jaynes, Julian, 361
Jevons, Frank, 214
Joachim of Fiore, 290–1, 323
Joseph of Arimathea, legend of, 284
Joule, James, 246
Justin Martyr, 143

kalām, 229, 237
Kant, Immanuel, 18, 116, 165, 208, 242, 272,
    276, 326, 341
    classification of proofs, 164–5, 209–10, 216
    on the Enlightenment, 124
    on Greek origins of philosophy, 327
    as precursor of cognitive science, 358
    a priori intuitions, 148, 165, 202, 327
Keats, John, 320
Kelvin, Lord, 246
Kepler, Johannes, 245, 332, 343
Kierkegaard, Søren, 18
Kuhn, Thomas S., 358

Lactantius, 145, 227
Lange, Friedrich Albert, 334–5, 338–9
Latour, Bruno, 119
laws of nature, 10, 197, 252, 310, 351,
    364, 377
    as divine injunctions, 4, 20, 235–6, 238,
        242–50, 317, 350–1
    as human conventions, 251, 350
    Hume on, 15, 350
    John Tyndall on, 332
    and naturalism, 5, 352, 376
    secularisation of, 250–2
    a seventeenth-century concept, 19

Left Hegelians, 329
Lehoux, Daryn, 222
Leibniz, G. W., 97, 106, 133, 322
    criticisms of Newton, 237, 241
    principle of sufficient reason, 159, 208
Lessing, Gotthold, 125, 293, 321–3, 331
    The Education of the Human Race, 321
    on historical progress, 323
    Lessing's dictum, 322
    on miracles, 321
Lessius, Leonardus, 139, 151, 156, 163
Leucippus, 240
Lewis, C. S., 253, 255
Lewis, Tayler, 269
Lightman, Bernard, 268, 276, 351
Lindberg, David, 230
liturgies, secular, 371
Locke, John, 78, 104, 111, 157, 215, 303
    on belief as assent, 113–14
    critique of innate ideas, 160
    ethics of belief, 82–4, 160
    on nations of atheists, 26, 160
    on reason, 107–8
    and the way of ideas, 159
Löwith, Karl, 345–6
Lucretius, 225, 233, 238, 332
Luther, Martin, 71–2, 74, 86, 100–2, 125, 261,
    283, 307, 320–1, 324
    on biblical prophecy, 288–9
    on experimental religion, 117
    on reason, 100–2

Macaulay, Thomas Babbington, 233
Machiavelli, Niccolò, 163
MacIntyre, Alasdair, 10, 261n153, 346n236,
    377–8
Magdeburg Centuries, 285
magic, 179, 259
    demonic, 259
    distinguished from religion, 314
    natural, 259
    as stage of social development, 4, 300, 314,
        319, 351
Malebranche, Nicholas, 93–4, 96, 136
    Search after Truth, 103
Malthus, Thomas, 311–12, 338, 348
    influence on Darwin, 311
    utilitarianism of, 311
Mandeville, Bernard de, 348
Mansel, Henry L., 276–7
Marx, Karl, 291, 330, 346
    on alienation, 330

Marxism, 346, 349, 351
  hidden eschatology of, 346
materialism, 334–5, 339–40
  dialectical, 346
  eliminative, 363
Mather, Cotton, 288
Maximus the Confessor, 89
Maxwell, James Clerk, 343
  on laws of nature, 245
McGilchrist, Iain, 361n25
mechanical philosophy, 234
Meiners, Christoph, 325–6
  on European origins of philosophy, 326
  scientific racism of, 325
Melanchthon, Philip, 124, 187, 289
  on natural theology, 206–7
Mersenne, Marin, 132, 135, 139, 157
  on atheism, 132
Metaphysical Society, the, 341
Middle Platonism, 176
Milbank, John, 10, 367, 374–6
Mill, J. S., 140, 165–6, 276, 337
  on laws of nature, 243
miracles, 251, 262, 271, 275, 282, 306, 354, 363. *See also* Hume, David, on miracles
  Aquinas on, 257–8
  cessation of, 10, 297–8, 331
  compatibility with laws of nature, 251
  denial of, 270
  distinguished from wonders, 259
  as evidence, 21, 258, 263
  medieval criteria for, 231
  not contrary to nature, 258
  Protestant critiques of, 298–300, 306
  as Satanic delusions, 298
Montaigne, Michel de, 75, 163
Montesquieu, Baron de, 301
More, Henry, 131–2, 149, 216, 240
Morgan, Lewis, 330
Morgan, Teresa, 33–4, 40
Moses, 155, 240

natural selection, 238, 249–50
natural theology, 116, 133, 138, 197, 209, 264
  changing conceptions of, 202–10, 264
  changing status of, 9
naturalism, 2, 265, 281, 375, 379
  associated with science, 4, 9, 219, 274, 278, 327, 332, 340–3, 380
  conflict with supernaturalism, 219, 250
  contrasted with supernaturalism, 2, 217–18, 250, 281, 373

definitions of, 4, 266–70
  as an ethical stance, 278, 280
  histories of, 253, 331–43, 352
  in humanities and social sciences, 5, 377
  indebtedness to religion, 3–4, 352, 379
  legitimized by history, 331
  metaphysical, 5
  methodological, 5, 201, 217, 352, 371, 379
  objective, 7
  in philosophy, 5, 326, 341–2, 377
  and progress, 10
  scientific, 201, 267–70, 274, 278, 281, 331, 343, 351, 374
  subjective, 7–8
  and the success of science, 4, 238, 344
naturalism/supernaturalism distinction, 352
  history of, 253–65
natural/supernatural distinction, 2, 9, 20, 23, 64–5, 67, 86, 92–3, 226, 252, 361
  and buffered selves, 362
  and naturalised epistemology, 65
  not biblical or patristic, 256
nature. *See also* laws of nature
  book of, 189, 194–6, 198
  contemplation of, 189, 201
  definitions of, 8, 229, 253–5
  as divine, 221–4, 226–7
  does nothing in vain, 145
  dominion over, 198
  inherently miraculous, 169
  intelligibility of, 252
  light of, 66, 85–100, 149
  scholastic views of, 231, 233
  source of innate truths, 151, 153
  source of moral norms, 143, 189–91, 193
  wonders of, 170, 187
Nazism, 347
Needham, Rodney, 29
Neoplatonism, 87, 92, 169, 171, 173, 191, 259, 348
Newman, John Henry, 130, 153
  on the creeds, 45
Newton, Isaac, 155, 197, 234, 237, 245, 303–4, 316, 332, 341, 343
  on gravity, 122
  law of gravitation, 241
  voluntarism of, 242
Nicaea, Council of, 42–3, 47, 52
Nicene Creed, 41–2
Nicholas of Autrecourt, 94
Nicholas of Cusa, 145
Nietzsche, Friedrich, 341, 356

Noah, 25, 155
nominalism, 104–6, 376
Norris, John, 94
Novalis, 320

occasionalism, 94, 265
Ockham, William of, 104
Odin, 366
Oresme, Nicole, 229–30, 233
  naturalism of, 231
Origen, 193
Osiander the Elder, Lucas, 298
Otto, Rudolf, 211–12
Owen, John, 298

Paley, William, 190, 193, 248
  utilitarianism of, 311
panpsychism, 363
Pascal, Blaise, 18, 164
  criticism of Descartes, 240
  on limits of reason, 103
  on proofs for God's existence, 206
  the wager, 182–3
Passmore, John, 346
Perkins, William, 298
Perrault, Charles, 301
pessimistic meta-induction, 370
Peter Abelard, 60
  on 'theology', 62
Peter Lombard, 54
  on implicit faith, 54
Philoponus, John, 228, 245
  criticisms of Aristotle, 229
  incipient naturalism of, 228
  inertial theory of, 228
philosophes, 124, 162, 300–7, 319–20, 372
  self-image of, 301, 306
  view of history, 301
physico-theology, 138, 188–91, 203–5, 208, 217, 264, 280
  distinguished from metaphysical proofs, 208
  distinguished from natural theology, 209
Pickstock, Catherine, 376
Pinker, Steven, 372
Planck, Max, 343
Plantinga, Alvin, 153, 213
Plato, 36, 40, 45, 87–8, 90, 92, 98, 103, 141, 169, 175, 341
  allegory of the cave, 168–9, 173, 178
  on belief, 36–7
  theory of forms, 104

Platonism, 85, 88, 145, 234, 307, 335
Plotinus, 87–8, 143, 173
Pluche, Noël Antoine, 190, 208
positivism, 312, 340
predictive processing, 357
Presocratic philosophy, 220–2, 233, 341
preternatural, the, 257, 259
Price, Huw, 7
priestcraft, 74, 305
primitive monotheism, 26, 154
principle of sufficient reason, 138, 159, 165, 208
progress
  an assumption of naturalism, 3
  as cultivation of virtues, 294
  ideas of, 294–5, 351
  laws of, 300–2, 306, 314–15, 331, 351
  linked to science, 308, 341
  linked to secularisation, 340
  narratives of, 253
  of science, 339
  as secularised eschatology, 344–5
prolepsis, 37, 143, 150
proofs for the existence of God, 9, 23, 129–217, 264. *See also* natural theology
  consensus gentium argument, 9, 139–67, 373
  cosmological argument, 138, 191, 204, 209, 217
  design argument, 168, 176, 187
  Kant's classification of, 138
  ontological argument, 93, 138, 144, 171, 174, 176, 181, 191, 204, 208–9, 217
  physico-theological argument, 138, 189, 209
  teleological argument, 138, 191, 208, 217
Prosper of Aquitaine, 71
Proust, Marcel, 369
providence, 205, 239, 262, 302, 311, 323, 347–9
  denial of, 134, 201, 233, 270
  and eschatology, 4
  hidden, 294, 299
  and laws of nature, 331
  and progress, 317, 321, 323, 331, 337, 344
  and rise of science, 288, 291
  secularisation of, 319–31
  Thomas Malthus on, 311
Pseudo-Dionysius, 185, 193
  use of 'supernaturalis', 256
Ptolemy, Claudius, 176
Pufendorf, Samuel, 241–2, 377
  on natural state of human beings, 241

pure nature, 260–1
Puritan 'projectors', 291

Quine, W. V. O., 6

rationalism, 85, 93, 236, 267, 340
  contrasted with supernaturalism, 270–4
Ray, John, 189
Raymond of Sebunde, 195
reason, 57, 66–7, 76, 85, 105, 107, 124,
    132, 135, 137, 144, 146, 153, 181–2,
    184, 193, 195, 205–6, 209, 212, 268,
    306, 373, 377
  a criterion for belief, 77, 84–5, 93, 96–7, 99,
    102, 108, 111–12, 115, 128, 139
  as divine image, 89, 110
  divine origin of, 67, 85, 87–90, 93–4, 96,
    102, 107, 178, 223
  fallen, 101–2, 104, 109, 173, 206
  instrumental, 52, 85, 93, 106, 110,
    115–16, 208
  a 'natural light', 66–7, 85–100, 134, 188
  practical, 116, 165
  reliability of, 97–8
  right, 98, 153
  scope of, 85, 101–4, 108, 170, 201, 272
  secularisation of, 85, 100–10, 375, 378
Reformation, 65–6, 99, 116, 124, 131, 135,
    253, 260, 268, 281, 283, 288–9, 298, 300,
    303, 320, 338, 373
  as age of light, 10, 124, 286
  generated religious pluralism, 52
  led to new conception of religion, 21,
    73, 128
  precipitated epistemic crisis, 117, 128,
    149, 152
  and privatisation of faith, 66, 72
  as stage in human emancipation, 76, 125,
    279, 307, 321, 324, 336
reformed epistemology, 153, 213, 216, 378
Reid, Thomas, 152, 353
  on *principles of common sense*, 212
reliabilism, 147, 151–4, 213, 354, 377–8
religion, 74, 85, 107, 110, 116, 123, 125–6,
    131, 133, 148, 160, 211, 264, 267–8,
    271–2, 287–8, 320, 324, 328, 330,
    351, 374
  as belief in the supernatural, 2–3, 306
  cognitive science of, 213
  concept of, 18, 21–2, 26, 35, 74, 127–8, 266,
    300, 305

critics of, 115, 288, 301, 320, 330, 342
  experimental, 117–18
  of humanity, 308
  natural, 266
  naturalistic explanations of, 163, 215, 305,
    309, 318, 329
  an obstacle to progress, 301, 305, 307, 313,
    315, 335
  philosophy of, 19, 133, 138, 178, 191, 203,
    216, 377
  and reason, 84, 90, 96, 99, 110, 115
  revealed, 207
  a stage of social development, 306, 314, 318,
    333, 344
  true, 53, 90, 204, 263, 285, 287
  wars of, 290
Renan, Ernest, 283
right reason, 99, 106
rituals, modern, 368
Rowe, C. Kavin, 227
Royal Society, the, 109, 119, 203, 288, 292
  motto of, 119

saeculum, the, 286, 293
Sagan, Carl, 372
Sahlins, Marshall, 1, 29, 31
Saint Pierre, Abbé de, 303
  on historical progress, 303
  on pretended miracles, 303
Saint-Simon, Henri de, 309
Sapere aude, 124
Sapir, Edward, 365
Sapir-Whorf Hypothesis, 365
scepticism, 22, 58, 378
Schmitt, Carl, 345
Schumacher, Lydia, 185
scientific method, 119, 121, 201, 278, 332
scientific revolution, 116, 124, 233–42, 303
  as mark of progress, 281, 287, 339
secularisation, 1–2, 4, 67, 126, 316–17, 351
Sedley, David, 88, 222
Sellars, Roy Wood, 5, 342
Sellars, Wilfrid, 6
Seneca, 87, 141, 226
  on progress, 294
sensus divinitatis. See Calvin, John, *sensus
    divinitatis*
Shagan, Ethan H., 25n2
Shapin, Steven, 120
Siger of Brabant, 145
Simplicius, 176

Smith, Adam, 310, 312, 348
Smith, James K. A., 371
Snell, Bruno, 360–1, 366
social sciences, 126, 367, 375, 379
　appeal to laws, 317, 350
　normative element of, 315, 319, 351
　as replacement for religion, 308
Socrates, 177, 279
Spencer, Herbert, 276, 317, 342
Spinoza, Baruch, 132, 135–6, 162, 241
　on final causes, 202
　God *or* Nature, 238
　on miracles, 272
　principle of sufficient reason, 159, 208
spontaneous order, 348, 364
Sprat, Thomas, 68, 110, 288
Stanley, Matthew, 252
Starkey, George, 179
Stillingfleet, Edward, 113
Stoicism, 38, 153, 169, 176, 234, 348
　common notions, 142
　divinised nature, 226
　seminal principles, 143
Strauss, David Friedrich, 218, 269, 272–3, 275
　on miracles, 273
Suárez, Francisco, 261
supernatural, the, 31, 65. *See also* naturalism; natural/supernatural distinction; supernaturalism
　belief in, 2–3, 9, 17–19, 30, 143, 306
　concept of, 18
　disbelief in, 9
　experience of, 179
　and historical explanation, 14
　history of the concept, 2, 64, 253–65
　Hume on, 10–11, 14–17
　not a biblical conception, 255
　not opposed to the natural, 86, 92, 131, 152, 197
　supernatural entities, 5–6, 8
　supernatural events, 15, 20
　testimony to, 14–16, 354–5
　a Western conception, 28, 30–1
supernaturalism, 373
　and biblical criticism, 9, 253, 270–4
　contrasted with rationalism, 271
　not a medieval category, 232
　opposed to science, 278, 342
supranaturalism, 272. *See also* supernaturalism
Swift, Jonathan, 123
　criticism of Royal Society, 203

Taubes, Jacob, 345
Taylor, Charles, 3, 10, 133, 218, 373
　buffered selves, 262, 362, 373
　porous selves, 362, 373
technology, 368–70
Temple, Frederick, 322n141
Tennemann, Wilhelm Gottlieb, 325–6
Tertullian, 143
Thales of Miletus, 220
　as originator of philosophy, 324
theory-ladenness of observation, 358, 364
thermodynamics, laws of, 246
Thomas Aquinas, 145, 198, 206, 262, 294
　on allegorical interpretation, 196
　on causation, 192, 194, 199
　on divine illumination, 91
　on faith, 61, 63–4
　five ways, 144, 183–6, 191
　on implicit faith, 54
　on miracles, 257–8
　on progress, 295
　on right reason, 99
　on *scientia*, 295
　on theology as science, 61
　uses of 'supernatural', 64, 256–9
Tiedemann, Dietrich, 325–6
Tillotson, John, 97, 113, 154
Toland, John, 111
Topham, Jonathan, 190
Trent, Council of, 52
Troeltsch, Ernst, 125
Tübingen School, 272, 323
Turgot, Anne Robert Jacques, 302, 305, 321, 359
Tuveson, Lee, 345
Tylor, E. B., 313
Tyndall, John, 249, 270, 276, 279–80, 331–5, 340, 342, 367
　Belfast Address, 331, 335
　history of naturalism, 331
Tyson, Neil deGrasse, 372

University of Paris, 53, 91, 231
univocity, 376
Ursinus, Zacharias, 297
utilitarianism, 106

Van Helmont, Jan Baptista, 179
Vanini, Lucilio, 136
Vico, Giambattista, 163
Vincent of Lérins, 155

Voegelin, Eric, 290, 347
Voetius, Gisbertus, 134–7
voluntarism, 105–6, 226, 376
    and science, 105n139, 265, 376

Waldensians, 284
Wallace, Alfred Russel, 248
Ward, Lester F., 315
Weber, Max, 351
    on charisma, 41
Wesley, John, 128
Whewell, William, 190, 244, 248, 250, 334
    on laws of nature, 243
Whichcote, Benjamin, 94–6, 151
Whiston, William, 236

White, Andrew Dickson, 337
Whorf, Benjamin, 365
Whyte, Jessica, 349
Wilberforce, William, 295
Williams, Roger, 25–6
Winchell, Alexander, 338
Wittgenstein, Ludwig, 24, 119, 238, 353, 369
    on laws of nature, 238, 364
Wolff, Christian
    on natural theology, 207–8
    principle of sufficient reason, 159
Wolterstorff, Nicholas, 153, 213

young earth creationism, 249
Yves of Paris, 150–1, 188

For EU product safety concerns, contact us at Calle de José Abascal, 56–1º, 28003 Madrid, Spain or eugpsr@cambridge.org.

www.ingramcontent.com/pod-product-compliance
Lightning Source LLC
LaVergne TN
LVHW041206250326
834689LV00002BA/31